Civil Litigation

Civil Litigation

Eighth Edition

John O'Hare, LLB

of Lincoln's Inn, Barrister
Taxing Master of the Supreme Court of England and Wales

Robert N Hill

Solicitor (John Mackrell Prizeman)
District Judge of the Kingston upon Hull District Registry of
the High Court of Justice and of the Kingston upon Hull
County Court

LAW & TAX

© Pearson Professional Limited 1997

The authors have asserted their right under the Copyright, Designs and Patents Act 1988
to be identified as the authors of this work

ISBN 0752 000152

Published by
FT Law & Tax
21–27 Lamb's Conduit Street,
London WC1N 3NJ

A Division of Pearson Professional Limited

Associated offices
Australia, Belgium, Canada, Hong Kong, India, Japan, Luxembourg, Singapore,
Spain, USA

First published 1980
Eighth edition (edited by John O'Hare) 1997

A CIP catalogue record for this book is available from the British Library

Printed in Great Britain by Bell & Bain Ltd, Glasgow

Contents

Preface

The usual time gap between editions of this book is 24 months. This edition is being published a little over 18 months after the last one. The most important event in civil litigation during the last 18 months was the publication of Lord Woolf's Final Report together with the first draft of the new Civil Proceedings Rules. Lord Woolf's recommendations are dealt with in this edition but only very briefly, and only in Chapter 7.

Why then is this edition being published so early? My answer is twofold. First there have in fact been many other changes during the last 18 months including in particular the Civil Evidence Act 1995 and the new rules of court thereunder, the Damages Act 1996 and the Civil Procedure Act 1997, ss 7 and 8. There have also been many law reports to include and comment upon.

Secondly, the main bulk of the recommendations made by Lord Woolf are not likely to be implemented before October 1998 and many current, ie pre-Woolf, cases are likely to continue moving through the civil courts for at least a couple of years after that. I want to update the text of this book one final time in relation to those cases. Future editions of this book will concentrate on the new rules and will include no more than an updating supplement (to this edition) for pre-Woolf cases.

Many people fear the new style rules proposed by Lord Woolf and hope they will not be brought in. Personally, as an author, I long for them. The current sets of rules have become vastly over-complex and therefore expensive. Current civil practice spends far too much time, effort and therefore money on peripheral issues, procedural skirmishing and brinkmanship. I hope that the new rules will bring with them a return to a simpler practice when courts decided cases according to general principle and a broad sense of justice, when fewer cases were reported and when those reports were brief and to the point.

There are, I accept, serious dangers inherent in any programme of reform. Changes brought in to remedy one set of problems can sometimes cause or aggravate other problems. This is true of two reforms recently made. The automatic strike out rule in county court cases (see p 363) has, without doubt, been a disaster. This edition covers all the important new case-law thereon. The other reform I have in mind is the computerisation of county court record cards and orders, the CASEMAN project. Previously, county court orders were often printed on forms which set out a list of possible orders. The court staff completed and deleted these forms as appropriate. For examples see the forms illustrated on pp 246 and 333 of this edition. Once a county court has been computerised (all will be by December 1997) its computer automatically produces forms for each of its cases including all relevant details (names of parties, addresses for service etc) and excluding irrelevant details. A problem arises when the circumstances of a particular case do not coincide with the options available for the draft order in the computer's memory. Given that the court staff cannot override the computer there is a natural tendency for them to edit orders to fit the computer rather than edit forms to fit the case. A different view is taken by the judiciary who insist that orders should be accurate. However, this involves completely retyping the document in question and, as you might expect, once the computer system is installed the number of secretarial staff is usually reduced. In his lectures, published in 1909, Professor Maitland said 'The forms of action we have buried, but they still rule us from their graves.' Now it seems new forms to rule us have been created by computer.

My information about CASEMAN comes from Robert Hill, formerly my co-author, now my consulting editor. A full-time district judge in Kingston upon Hull district registry and county court, he also sits in the Crown Court as an assistant recorder. In 1996 he became the first county court district judge to be appointed an editor of the *White Book*.

My own lifestyle has changed significantly since the last edition of this book. Indeed in one week in December 1995 three things happened to me: the previous edition of this book was published, I became a full-time taxing master and my son Alexander Thomas was born. The new job and new baby were, and still are, a delight. Nevertheless I am hoping for a quieter publication day on this edition.

I would like to acknowledge in print the sincere gratitude I have already expressed to the following people who have given so generously and freely of their time to help me produce this edition; Mr Registrar Simmonds who has greatly improved Chapter 26 (Insolvency), Mr John Hocking of NWL (Law Costs) who has updated the bill of costs and legal aid schedule and my wife, Alison, and son, Alexander, for tolerating the lifestyle of a single parent family for the last six months.

The law in this edition is generally stated as at 1 July 1997 but I have also included the new law on recoupment of state benefits which comes into force in October 1997.

John O'Hare
20 July 1997

List of Figures

List of Tables

Table of Cases

Table of Statutes

liv

Table of Rules and Regulations

European Legislation

Abbreviations

AJA	Administration of Justice Act
CCA	County Courts Act 1984
CCR	County Court Rules 1981
CJJA	Civil Jurisdiction and Judgments Act 1982
CLSA	Courts and Legal Services Act 1990
IA	Insolvency Act 1986
IR	Insolvency Rules 1986
RSC	Rules of the Supreme Court 1965
SCA	Supreme Court Act 1981
MIB	Motor Insurers' Bureau

Copyright Acknowledgments

The following forms are Crown Copyright and are reproduced with the kind permission of the Controller of Her Majesty's Stationery Office: County Court N244, N1, N2, N205A, N216, N234, N9, N206, N15, N243, N349, N337.

We gratefully acknowledge the permission of the Solicitors' Law Stationery Society Ltd to reproduce the following forms: County Court N265; HCA1, B37, D2, S3, B34, E22, E33, B5, B90, B89, S30(PR), B70A, Insolvency Bankruptcy forms 6.1, 6.4, 6.5, 6.7 and Insolvency Company form 4.1.

The Legal Aid Green Form and Application for Legal Aid Form are reproduced with the kind permission of the Legal Aid Board.

Chapter 1

Introduction

Rules and rule-books

The major sources of the law of procedure in the High Court and county courts are the rules of court, a form of delegated legislation, made by rule committees under powers conferred by the Supreme Court Act 1981 and the County Courts Act 1984. The High Court rules currently in force are the Rules of the Supreme Court 1965, as amended, which are set out in a publication officially entitled *The Supreme Court Practice* but usually known as the *'White Book'*. This is undoubtedly the most comprehensive and authoritative treatise on procedure available, and one cannot study the subject in any depth without it.

The current edition of the *White Book* comprises three hardback volumes, three paperbacks and a series of newsletters published ten times a year. Volume 1 contains the full text of the rules. These are grouped in Orders (at present 115) which are subdivided into numbered rules and sub-rules or paragraphs. Beneath the text of most rules a full commentary is set out, in smaller type. A mistake frequently made by beginners is to assume that the commentary forms part of the rule; it does not. In the margin beside each passage the appropriate reference number is given, in bold type. For example, 14/2 refers to the second rule of Order 14: 14/2/1 refers to the first paragraph of commentary to that rule.

Volume 2 contains the prescribed forms, the practice directions issued by the masters (see below) and a miscellany of special rules, statutes and other information relating to procedure. The current numbering system in Volume 2 sets a heavy test of endurance for most beginners. The text is divided into Parts, the first one being Part 2, Forms. Most of the paragraphs are given reference numbers from 1 to 1419 and from 3600 to 6218. For example, see 3600 which begins Part 11, Solicitors. Unhappily, substantial expansion of material in Parts 7 to 10 of the volume has entirely overpowered this simple numbering system; in between paras 1419 and 3600 the paragraphs are numbered from 7–001 to 10–176. Expect jams also in the House of Lords Appeals area: paras 16–001 to 16–268 have been squeezed in between paras 4808 and 5100. Experienced practitioners save themselves a lot of futile searching by placing four flags in the volume, labelled *Pts 7 to 10, 3600 to 4808, Pt 16* and *5100 onwards*.

The third hardback volume to the *White Book* contains the index to Volumes 1 and 2 plus tables of statutes, statutory instruments and cases (a duplicate index is printed at the back of Volume 1). The three *White Book* paperbacks are: the Annual Practice, a selection of key rules with short commentaries thereon; the full text of the County Court Rules and a supplement showing recent alterations and additions to the text and commentaries. Cumulative supplements are issued at half-yearly intervals until a new *White Book* is published (about every two or three years). Make it a habit always to cross check references in the most up-to-date supplement. For example, 14/2/4 in the 1997 *White Book* should now be read in the light of the further information given in the current supplement to it.

The rules of the county court currently in force are known as the County Court Rules 1981 as amended and the full text and short commentaries on them are set out in *The County Court Practice*, popularly known as the '*Green Book*', a single volume work published annually. The *Green Book* also has separate sections containing the text (with commentaries) of the CCA 1984, the county court forms and lastly (about half the book) various statutes which give the county court jurisdiction. References in the text of this book are to the 1997 *Green Book*.

The RSC and the CCR are drafted by rule committees appointed by the Lord Chancellor. Their statutory authority is limited to matters of procedure only. Any rule which purports to alter the substantive law is *ultra vires* and void to that extent (*Ward v James* [1966] 1 QB 273). Many new rules are made after the substantive law has been changed by statute (eg RSC Ord 24, r 7A and CCR Ord 13, r 7; pre-action and non-party discovery in personal injury cases made under the SCA 1981, ss 33–35 and CCA 1984, ss 52–54; see p 407). Some very important changes can be made simply by changing the rules of procedure (eg RSC Ord 38, r 2A and CCR Ord 20, r 12A; exchange of witness statements; see p 426 (these rules were subsequently confirmed by statute, CLSA 1990, s 5)). In the past, county court practice has usually followed rather than led High Court practice; see eg CCA 1984, s 76 which states:

> In any case not expressly provided for by or in pursuance of this Act, the general principles of practice in the High Court may be adopted and applied to proceedings in a county court.

Effect of non-compliance with rules of court

Failure to comply with any requirement of the rules is treated as an irregularity only and does not nullify any step, document, judgment or order (RSC Ord 2, r 1; CCR Ord 37, r 5). If some irregularity occurs the court may set aside the proceedings or part of them or make any other order it thinks just. For example, in *Barclays Bank plc v Piper* (1995) *White Book*, 14/2/6, the Court of Appeal set aside an order for summary judgment (see p 221) which had been obtained on the basis of an affidavit which was defective. However, the courts have never insisted upon compliance with the rules merely for the sake of it. Therefore if the irregularity causes no prejudice to the other side, the court might simply ignore it and allow the proceedings to continue (*Tsai v Woodworth* (1984) *White Book* 12/1/3 noted on p 204 below). In addition to the question of prejudice, the court can also have regard to other factors including the gravity of the irregularity and the conduct of the parties and their advisers (*Oyston v Blaker* [1996] 1 WLR 1326 at 1336).

The High Court cannot wholly set aside proceedings merely because the wrong method of commencing an action was used (RSC Ord 2, r 1(3); county court practice is similar—see *Green Book* commentary to CCR Ord 3, r 4).

A party can apply for an order setting aside for irregularity only if he does so within a reasonable time and before taking any step in the action (other than acknowledging service) with knowledge of the irregularity. In other words, he must act promptly and without waiving his right to object. However, given the court's willingness to forgive merely technical breaches, he might just as well consent to, or not bother to challenge, any departure from the normal procedure which the court is likely to allow.

Practice directions

Practice directions are issued from time to time by the judges and other officers of the High Court and county courts. Although most of them are rules of practice rather than rules of law (ie they lack statutory authority, see *Re Langton* [1960] 1 WLR 246) compliance with them may be enforced by means of costs penalties and other penalties. Every court has an inherent jurisdiction to regulate its own procedures. Even a county court, which is entirely a creature of statute, has inherent jurisdiction to enforce its local practice directions so long as they are not inconsistent with the rules of court and other statutory provisions (*Langley v North West Water Authority* [1991] 1 WLR 697; for a definition of inherent jurisdiction in this context see *per* Lord Diplock in *Bremer Vulkan Schiffbau und Mashinenfabrik v South India Shipping Corp Ltd* [1981] AC 909, at p 977 'acts which [the court] must have power to do in order to maintain its character as a court of justice').

The High Court

The High Court is one of three constituent courts going to make up the Supreme Court of England and Wales (the other two courts are the Crown Court and the Court of Appeal). The High Court itself comprises three divisions:

(1) the Chancery Division (which includes the Companies Court and the Patents Court);

(2) the Queen's Bench Division (which includes the Admiralty Court and the Commercial Court); and

(3) the Family Division.

Business is allocated between the divisions as prescribed principally by the SCA 1981, s 61, for which see *White Book* 5260. Despite this allocation of business all three divisions have equal jurisdiction. Each has wide powers to transfer any case to any other division or indeed to retain a case, even though it was started in the wrong division. There is a large overlap of business between the Queen's Bench and Chancery Divisions, especially in contract cases.

There are four types of *originating process*: writs, originating summonses, originating notices of motion and petitions. In starting an action the plaintiff chooses which form of process to use (see further p 110) and chooses which division to assign it to, by marking the process with the name of that division and taking it to the appropriate court office for issue. Originating process can be issued either at the office of the Supreme Court at the Royal Courts of Justice (Central Office for Queen's Bench cases, Chancery Chambers for Chancery cases) or at any district registry (the 130 or so provincial offices of the High Court throughout England and Wales).

The issue of the originating process begins the *interlocutory stage* of the action. This is the preparatory stage through which every case passes until trial or compromise is reached.

The court

Interlocutory matters are dealt with by 'the court' which is defined by RSC Ord 1, r 4(2), as follows:

> In these rules, unless the context otherwise requires, 'the court' means the High Court or any one or more judges thereof, whether sitting in court or in chambers or any master ... or a [district judge] of a district registry.

Each of these judicial officers is described below.

Queen's Bench masters

These are appointed by the Lord Chancellor from persons who have 'a 7 year general qualification' within the meaning of CLSA 1990, s 71, ie currently only barristers or solicitors. Every Queen's Bench action proceeding in the Central Office is assigned to a particular master when the first summons in the action is issued and thereafter that master deals with virtually all the interlocutory matters in that action. Certain matters, however, are reserved for the judge in chambers (see below). Each day one Queen's Bench master sits as 'Practice Master' to deal with many *ex parte* applications, to grant consent orders in certain cases (see p 370) and generally to superintend the business of the Central Office and to give directions on points of practice to any litigants or lawyers seeking his help (RSC Ord 63, r 2). There is a right of appeal from every decision of a Queen's Bench master: in most cases the appeal lies to the judge in chambers (see further p 645). Although the title 'master' is an ancient one the office of master of the Queen's Bench Division is comparatively recent (Superior Courts (Officers) Act 1837) and of course is a title from a bygone age when all judges were men. In this book, unless the context otherwise requires, the term 'district judge' (see below) includes a master.

Chancery masters

Although their qualification for appointment is the same as that for a Queen's Bench master, Chancery masters' duties are more administrative than judicial. Chancery cases require less procedural preparation but more post-trial tasks such as the taking of accounts, the arranging of sales, the making of inquiries, investigations to determine classes of beneficiaries or next of kin, and the instruction and supervision of receivers, trustees and the like. It is sometimes said that Chancery cases do not properly begin until after the judgment is entered. The jurisdiction of Chancery masters is derived from the judges who from time to time issue practice directions (see *White Book* 854). As in the case of Queen's Bench masters, there is a right of appeal from a Chancery master to a judge in chambers.

District judges

These are appointed by the Lord Chancellor from barristers or solicitors of at least seven years' standing. They also serve as district judges of the county court in the same district (see p 12). *Inter alia* district judges are the 'out of London' equivalent of High Court masters and deal with both Queen's Bench and Chancery cases. However, only eight district registries have full Chancery jurisdiction: Birmingham, Bristol, Cardiff, Leeds, Liverpool, Manchester, Newcastle upon Tyne and Preston. In practice, most Chancery cases are either commenced in London or a Chancery district registry or, if commenced elsewhere later transferred to London or to a Chancery district registry (see generally *White Book* 824).

RSC Ord 63, r 11 provides that the practice of the Central Office shall be followed in the district registries. In this book, the term 'judge' is used to refer to a High Court or Circuit judge but not to a district judge. The term 'district judge' is always used in full.

Judges in chambers

These officers hear the following interlocutory applications: appeals from orders made by a district judge; matters which in the opinion of the district judge should properly be decided by a judge (RSC Ord 32, r 12) and certain applications for which district judges have no jurisdiction. Examples of this last category are:

(1) applications relating to the liberty of the subject such as committal for contempt or bail applications;
(2) applications under certain statutes such as SCA 1981, s 42 (see p 94);
(3) applications for injunctions: in the High Court, district judges can grant an injunction only if all parties consent both to the making of the order and to its terms or if it is ancillary to certain methods of enforcement of judgments (see further p 602)

Although interlocutory applications to a judge are normally 'in chambers', there is power to adjourn the hearing into court. This is commonly done where an application involves a point of principle and the judge or parties wish it to be reported (see for example *Brookes v Harris* [1995] 1 WLR 918).

Taxing masters

These are appointed by the Lord Chancellor from barristers or solicitors of at least seven years' standing. They do not come within the definition of 'the court' for the purpose of interlocutory applications. Their primary function is to tax, ie allow, disallow or alter items in bills of costs in most Queen's Bench and Chancery cases: for cases outside London the taxation is usually done by the district judge. The process of taxation is inevitably a painful one for the loser but can sometimes be so even for the party in whose favour costs are awarded. A successful litigant can enforce against an opponent only the taxed bill which may be less than the sum which the solicitor for the successful litigant is entitled to charge (see Chapter 23).

An appeal from the taxing master follows a two-stage process. First, the taxing master must be asked to review the decision. Only thereafter does an appeal lie to the judge in chambers (see p 531).

Interlocutory applications in writ actions

Although evidence at the trial is normally given orally, evidence on interlocutory applications is normally given by *affidavit*, ie a written statement of facts made under oath. An affidavit sworn for the purpose of being used in interlocutory proceedings may contain statements of information or belief, provided that the sources and grounds thereof are stated (RSC Ord 41, r 5(2); contrast affidavits for use at the trial).

Despite the fact that every solicitor with a current practising certificate has power to administer oaths and take affidavits (Solicitors Act 1974, s 81), 'no affidavit shall be sufficient if sworn before the solicitor of the party on whose behalf the affidavit is to be used or before any agent, partner or clerk of that solicitor' (RSC Ord 41, r 8; CCR Ord 20, r 10). Thus the person swearing the affidavit is put to the trouble of going to another firm of solicitors to do so, or must swear the affidavit at the court office before one of the senior clerks there, or before a licensed conveyancer or any other person authorised by CLSA 1990, s 113.

There are four ways of applying to the court during the interlocutory stage:

Ex parte

Applying *ex parte* means applying without giving notice to the other side. *Ex parte* applications to district judges usually concern merely administrative or preliminary matters (eg leave to extend the validity of a writ, see p 205). A hearing is not always necessary. Initially the party applying leaves the affidavit at the court office on one day and collects it on the following day by which time the order will have been made or an appointment to attend for a hearing will have been arranged. (In Queen's Bench cases, all *ex parte* applications to district judges may be made by post: see below.) If the applicant is dissatisfied with the district judge's decision he can appeal to the judge in chambers. On the other hand, if an *ex parte* order is made and the other parties wish to challenge it, they can apply to the district judge to have it set aside (RSC Ord 32, r 6).

Ex parte applications can also be made to a judge, eg for an urgent interlocutory injunction (see further p 290).

By summons

Most interlocutory applications are made by serving on the other parties a summons to attend a hearing. The summons is completed by the applicant and must state the grounds of each application (the same summons can be used for more than one application). The summons is 'issued' when it is stamped with the court seal by an officer at the appropriate court office. At the time of issue the applicant should be ready to file any affidavit intended to be used. (On most masters' summonses in London affidavits are not in fact filed until later.) The office will fix the 'return day', ie the day upon which the summons will be heard, which is then written on the summons. The applicant must serve the summons and a copy of the affidavit on the other party to the action not more than fourteen days after the issue of the summons and not less than two clear days before the return day (RSC Ord 32, r 3). For some applications the summons must be served more than two clear days before the return day (see RSC Ords 14, 25 and 29, rr 11 and 19). If the other party also wishes to make an application that party normally has to use a separate summons (then called a 'cross-summons'). A party issuing a 'cross-summons' should ask the court to give it the same return day as the first summons. On most masters' summonses in London the affidavits relied on are filed (ie handed to the Master) on the return day.

It used to be said that every writ action going to trial had at least one interlocutory summons, the summons for directions. This is no longer true. In many Queen's Bench personal injury cases the summons for directions is replaced by 'automatic directions'. In all Chancery cases 'standard directions' are available if the parties consent (see further pp 472 and 474).

By notice under the summons for directions
In those cases in which a summons for directions is used, it is normally issued by the plaintiff. A defendant who seeks additional directions does so by giving notice under the summons for directions. This is the only occasion when a party can make an application on the opponent's summons.

By motion
This is the method of applying to a judge sitting in open court. Motions are rare in the Queen's Bench Division but fairly common in the Chancery Division. In order to apply by motion, a notice of motion must be prepared and served by the applicant. The most common example of a motion in the Chancery Division is an application for an interlocutory injunction, whether or not preceded by an *ex parte* application. (In the Queen's Bench Division a summons to the judge in chambers, rather than a motion, is used.) During term-time the applicant can apply to the judge having given at least two clear days' notice to his opponent. The applicant should pay the appropriate fee and file certain documentation including a completed 'Motions Information Form' (see *White Book* 879). The motion will then be listed in the Daily Cause List for the day on which it is to be heard (see generally *White Book* 850.) Since the application is made in open court only litigants in person, barristers and solicitors granted appropriate Higher Courts Advocacy Qualifications have rights of audience.

We have already commented on the overlap of jurisdiction between the Chancery and Queen's Bench Divisions. One reason for choosing the Chancery Division could be to attract publicity on an injunction application (the judge sits in an open court). Conversely one might choose the Queen's Bench Division if it were desirable to avoid publicity (the judge sits in chambers).

Drawing up interlocutory orders

In Queen's Bench cases where an order is made in chambers, the district judge or judge indexes a note of his decision on the original summons or (on an *ex parte* hearing) the affidavit. The applicant must then 'draw up the order', ie lodge the document in the appropriate office with two completed forms. The forms are stamped; one of them is filed and the other is returned. If the applicant fails to draw up the order within seven days after it is made the opponent may draw it up. (See generally RSC Ord 42, r 5 and *White Book* 743.) In the Chancery Division, orders are usually drawn up by the court office (see RSC Ord 42, r 6 and *White Book* 857). The following types of order need not be drawn up unless they contain special terms or unless the court otherwise directs (RSC Ord 42, r 4):

(1) an order which extends any time period fixed by the rules or by any order of the court (overleaf);

(2) an order which grants leave to issue a writ, other than a writ for service out of the jurisdiction (see Chapters 8 and 11);

(3) an order which grants leave to amend a writ or other originating process or a pleading (see Chapter 10).

Sittings, vacations and office hours (RSC Ord 64)

The High Court year is divided into four terms: Michaelmas, Hilary, Easter and Trinity. The intervals between these terms are vacations: Christmas, Easter, Whitsun and the Long Vacation. Each year vacation judges are appointed to deal with urgent cases which cannot be delayed until the following term. Although the Long Vacation comprises August and September in fact much work is done during September. There are no restrictions on district judges' hearings during September and the Court of Appeal now sits in September. Although a summons returnable before a district judge can be issued at any time of the year, some restrictions are imposed on certain Queen's Bench cases during the month of August (see *White Book* 64/3/2). The High Court offices in London remain open every day except Saturdays, Sundays, two days at Christmas, three days at Easter, bank holidays and such other days as the Lord Chancellor may in certain circumstances direct. The hours when the offices are open to the public are from 10 am to 4.30 pm except during the month of August when the hours are from 10 am to 2.30 pm.

The days and hours during which any district registry is open usually coincide with the days and hours of the county court offices for the same district.

All parties to an action are entitled without leave to inspect and take copies of any documents filed in the court office in respect of that action (eg the writ, orders and affidavits). Other persons (eg journalists) have only limited rights of inspection and copying (see generally RSC Ord 63, rr 4 and 4A).

Computation of time (RSC Ord 3)

Periods of time fixed by the rules or by an order of the court are usually *exclusive*, eg so many days *after* a specific date, or so many *clear* days before a return day (see the example given overleaf). There are two important exceptions where the time periods are *inclusive*; the duration of a writ for the purpose of service and the time for acknowledgment of service (see Chapter 11).

Two provisions concern computation of time with regard to days when the court office is closed:

(1) Where a time period for doing an act *at the court office* expires on a day on which that office is closed 'the act shall be in time if done on the next day on which that office is open' (RSC Ord 3, r 4).

(2) In computing time periods of seven days or less, Saturdays, Sundays, bank holidays, Christmas Day and Good Friday are not counted (RSC Ord 3, r 2(5): note that this rule does not list every day the court office is closed).

Example

If a party issues an interlocutory summons on a Friday intending to serve it on that day, the earliest possible return day would be the following Wednesday. The two *clear* days' notice necessary would be the Monday and Tuesday.

In any action the court may, on such terms as it thinks just, make an order extending or abridging any time period fixed by the rules (RSC Ord 3, r 5). An application for such an order is usually made to the district judge on a 'time summons'. In Queen's Bench cases proceeding in London the summons will be returnable before a deputy master and need be served only one day before the return day (*White Book* 736). In most cases 'time orders' do not have to be drawn up (see p 8).

Conduct of business in person or by post

Many steps during the interlocutory stage of an action can be taken 'without leave', ie simply by producing the right papers to the clerk at the appropriate court office. Most of the routine matters can also be effected by post; eg issuing writs and summonses, lodging acknowledgments of service (see p 207), drawing up orders and applying *ex parte* to district judges. Some business can also be transacted by telephone (see generally RSC Ord 1, r 10, and *White Book* 705, 810 and 811).

Save for one exception (issue of writ out of Admiralty and Commercial Registry when that Registry is closed, see p 274) the rules of court make no provision for the conduct of business with the court by fax. However, most court offices now have fax machines and these are regularly used to solve minor queries, supply duplicate copies of missing documents and supply advance information about urgent matters likely to be placed before the court within twenty-four hours. However, it is often unwise to make use of the court fax machine without first telephoning the court office and discussing the matter with a senior clerk.

The county courts

There are about 250 county courts throughout England and Wales. The system was created in 1846 to provide a cheap and simple system for the recovery of small debts which were disproportionately expensive or uneconomic to recover in the then Court of Queen's Bench. The jurisdiction in 1846 was limited in contract and tort cases to claims not exceeding £20. The figure was increased from time to time until the High Court and County Courts Jurisdiction Order 1991 came into force in July 1991. *Inter alia* the order provides that the county court has unlimited jurisdiction in contract and tort cases. Thus, instead of limiting smaller cases to the county courts, the 1991 Order limits important and/or specialist cases to the High Court.

A county court's jurisdiction is not unlimited for all purposes and it is necessary to have regard to art 2 of the High Court and County Courts Jurisdiction Order 1991 (set out in full in the *Green Book* commentary to CCA 1984, s 15 and in the *White Book* 5513). For example the county court's equity jurisdiction has largely remained at the £30,000 level set in 1981 (see further p 108). It is also important to note that county courts are also given special jurisdiction in a variety of matters which are important in practice but which are outside the scope of this book, eg adoption, family provision, undefended divorce cases.

Because an action is commenced in a county court it does not follow that it will be tried there and likewise with the High Court as there are detailed provisions for the transfer of cases between courts; see further p 373.

The county court's original function as a court for the collection of small debts has not been abandoned. Many special rules apply to claims under £3,000 (usually referred to as 'small claims' although that expression is not used in the rules). Such cases are dealt with by way of arbitration rather than trial by the district judge (see further p 279).

An important reform in the county court has been the establishment of seventy trial centres throughout England and Wales. By operating a running list of cases a trial centre enables a trial to proceed to conclusion without the need for adjournment to a later date. The County Court Directory, set out as an Appendix in the *Green Book*, indicates the appropriate trial centre for each county court.

The court office and officers

The court office

Every county court office is open to the public from 10 am to 4 pm every day except Saturdays, Sundays and public holidays (CCR Ord 2, r 2: the list of public holidays is similar to that given for the High Court offices in London). There are no vacation periods as such.

As to the inspection of documents filed in court by, eg, parties and journalists, CCR Ord 50, r 10 is more restrictive than the High Court rule, RSC Ord 63, r 4 (noted on p 9).

Circuit judges

These are the judges appointed by the Lord Chancellor to serve in both the Crown Court and the county courts. So far as civil interlocutory applications are concerned, they are the county court equivalent of the High Court judge in chambers (as to which, see p 5).

District judges

All county court district judges outside London are also appointed district judges of the High Court and so many handle both Queen's Bench and Chancery cases in addition to their county court work. The interlocutory jurisdiction of the county court district judge is more similar to that of a Queen's Bench master than that of a Chancery master: he deals with most interlocutory applications (except applications for committal to prison but including the granting of injunctions, both interlocutory and final, in matters which fall within the district judge's trial jurisdiction). He has power to refer matters to the judge without himself making any order (CCR Ord 13, r 1, compare RSC Ord 32, r 12 above). Unlike the Queen's Bench master, the district judge is also the taxing officer of his court (see Chapter 23). The district judge also has a significant trial jurisdiction and sits as arbitrator in 'small claims' (see pp 279 and 479). Every judgment or order made by the district judge can be taken, by way of appeal or review, to the judge (see Chapter 27). The district judge also has extensive jurisdiction in insolvency (see Chapter 26) and in matters outside the scope of this book, eg divorce and admiralty.

Administrative staff

Most tasks of a formal or administrative character, such as issuing summonses and other originating documents, arranging service of all process to be served by that court office, the listing of appointments, the drawing up of orders and the supervision of their execution, are carried out by the administrative staff responsible to a *chief clerk* (CCR Ord 1, r 3). When parties write to the court, they should address all forms and letters to the Chief Clerk and quote the case number.

Each court office also employs full-time *bailiffs* whose primary functions are to effect service of summonses etc where the plaintiff so requires (see p 133) and, in certain cases to execute judgments and orders (see Chapters 24 and 25). (The High Court has no direct equivalent to the county court bailiffs.)

Conduct of business in the county courts

On the whole county court procedure is simpler and less technical than High Court procedure. This is attributable to several matters:
  (1) Some steps in an action are arranged by the court thereby reducing the costs and inconvenience to the parties: note, for example, the

service of process and pleadings, the drawing up of most judgments and orders (CCR Ord 22, r 1), and the convening and arranging of the pre-trial review in fixed date actions.

(2) The wider use of automatic directions (see p 465).

(3) Interlocutory applications are made either *ex parte* (usually only for consent orders) or on notice. There is no prescribed form of notice, but applicants normally use or copy out Form N244 which is obtainable from the court (see fig 1 overleaf). The applicant must deliver at least two forms of notice to the court. One is filed; the other is marked with a return day and is given back to the applicant to serve on the respondent at least two clear days before the return day. The district judge will usually hear the application in chambers on affidavit evidence (CCR Ord 13, r 1 and Ord 20, r 5).

(4) The parties or their solicitors have to attend the court only on the return days fixed on a summons or notice. All other business such as the issue of process or the filing of notices can be done by post (CCR Ord 2, r 5).

In theory, county court procedure should be faster than High Court procedure. In practice, this is not so. The huge pressure of work in the county courts is such that there can be delays before the court staff can attend to papers submitted by litigants or their solicitors.

Computation of time (CCR Ord 1, r 9)

As in the High Court, periods of time fixed by the rules or by an order of the court are usually exclusive. Generally speaking the time periods fixed by the County Court Rules are shorter than their High Court equivalents. In computing periods of time of three days or less, Saturdays, Sundays and other days on which the court office is closed are not counted; compare and contrast the High Court rule which makes similar provision for periods of seven days or less (RSC Ord 3, r 2(5), above). As in the High Court application may be made to the district judge on notice to extend any time period fixed by the rules (CCR Ord 13, r 4).

Court fees

In both courts prescribed fees are payable at the following stages: commencement, setting down or requesting a date for trial, taxation of costs and execution of judgment. Fees are also payable on taking an appointment before a master, district judge, official referee, or judge in chambers; on lodging a motion for hearing before a judge in the Chancery Division and on an application to review a taxation. Provided one has the current fees orders available in the office (see *White Book* 1001 and *Green Book* 1714), it is not necessary to memorise them and in view of the frequent changes made, no purpose is served by trying to do

[*continued on p 15*]

Fig 1: County court notice of application

Notice of Application

Plaintiff / defendant's address

In the
KINGSTON UPON HULL
County Court

Case no.
Warrant no. *(if applicable)*
Plaintiff *(include Ref. no.)*
Defendant

State nature and grounds of application I wish to apply for

SPECIMEN

Signed .... Plaintiff / Defendant   Dated ....

Address for ....

service...

This section to be completed by the court

To the plaintiff / defendant

Take notice that this application will be heard by the District judge / Judge

at   COMBINED COURT CENTRE, LOWGATE, KINGSTON UPON HULL HU1 2EZ

on   at   o'clock

If you do not attend the Court will make such order that it thinks fit

The court office at
KINGSTON UPON HULL COMBINED COURT CENTRE, LOWGATE, KINGSTON UPON HULL HU1 2EZ   Telephone 01482 586161
is open from 10 am to 4 pm Monday to Friday. When corresponding with the courts please address forms or letters to the Chief Clerk
and quote the case number.

N244 *Notice of application   Order 13 Rule 1 (2) (12.94)*   N244 239   *Printed by Satellite Press Limited* so. The brief moment it takes to check the fee is well spent, as it causes a considerable amount of inconvenience to the court if the wrong fee is sent through the post and they have to write back with a refund or asking for the balance. A solicitor who always gets the fees wrong will soon acquire a bad reputation with the court clerks and this can do no good for either solicitor or client.

Interest on debts, damages and judgments

This is a topic which has become of increasing importance and complexity in recent years. For convenience the whole of the topic is outlined here, detailed provisions being left to subsequent chapters which are cross-referenced.

Interest payable as of right

The most important example of interest payable as of right is contractual interest. Any contract under which sums of money are payable may include a suitably worded provision for the payment of interest in the event of delayed payment or non-payment. (In drafting such a provision account should be taken of the Consumer Credit Act 1974, s 139 concerning extortionate credit agreements.) In both the High Court and the county court a creditor under such a contract who properly pleaded and pursued a claim would have a right to that interest, at the rate and for the period specified in the contract, up until judgment or sooner payment. In theory a contractual rate of interest may even continue to be payable until execution of the judgment or sooner payment (see *White Book* 6/2/13).

Various statutes provide for what might otherwise be called 'contractual interest'; see for example the Bills of Exchange Act 1882, interest (described as damages) recoverable in an action upon a dishonoured cheque (*White Book* 6/2/15) and the Solicitors' (Non-Contentious Business) Remuneration Order 1994, interest payable on a solicitor's bill of costs in certain, limited, circumstances (*White Book* 3861).

The points made below, under the headings 'Pleading interest' and 'Default judgments' also apply to interest payable as of right.

Interest payable in the court's discretion

The most important examples of interest payable in the court's discretion stem from SCA 1981, s 35A and CCA 1984, s 69 (for other examples see *White Book* 6/2/9). Under these sections the courts have power to award interest in all debt or damages actions.

Discretionary nature of the courts' powers

Whether interest should be awarded, and if so, at what rate, and for what period, are all in the discretion of the court. Nowadays one normally expects the court to award interest in any debt or damages case. The rate payable on judgment debts (hereinafter called 'the judgment debt rate', see further, below) has been adopted in rules of court relating to default judgments (see below). For the sake of uniformity and simplicity this is the rate which the court most frequently adopts except in, eg large commercial cases (see p 274), cases concerning personal injuries (see p 75) and of course except in cases in which a different rate has been contractually agreed (see further, *White Book* 6/2/12 and *Watts v Morrow* [1991] 1 WLR 1421, at pp 1443 and 1446). The court's discretion to withhold interest, or to stipulate a lower or higher rate is now reserved for exceptional cases.

Pleading interest

A party claiming interest (whether under the statutory powers or otherwise) must say so in his pleadings (RSC Ord 18, r 8; CCR Ord 6, r 1A). If no claim for interest is pleaded, no interest will be awarded unless an amendment is made (which is not always possible: see p 182). The details as to how interest should be pleaded are set out in Chapter 9 (see p 155). It is sufficient to note here that in most debt claims it is advisable to specify the rate at which interest is claimed (ie the contractually agreed rate, if any, otherwise the judgment debt rate) and then calculate in pounds and pence the sum of interest which has accrued before commencement of action and also the daily rate at which it accrues; this facilitates the entry of a default judgment (see below: there are some additional points to note concerning interest on claims in a foreign currency as to which see *White Book* 42/1/13 supplement). In all damages claims, the claim for interest is pleaded in more general terms: the precise amount of the damages is unknown until the court assesses it and therefore it is not possible to make a precise calculation of the interest.

Default judgments

If a money claim ends by default, ie the defendant does not bother to contest the claim, a default judgment can be entered for the debt or damages claimed and also for interest thereon. In a damages claim there has to be a hearing at which the damages are assessed and, at that hearing, the court will also assess the interest payable. In a debt claim no hearing is necessary to assess the amount of the debt. If interest thereon was pleaded in the detailed way described above, judgment can also be entered for interest calculated up to the date of the judgment. The advantage of pleading interest precisely is that, in a debt claim, the final judgment can be obtained more speedily and the plaintiff can proceed directly to enforcement.

Personal injuries claims

In the case of a claim for damages for personal injuries or death the court must award interest if the damages exceed £200 unless there are special reasons to the contrary (ss 35A(2), 69(2)). One special reason for not awarding interest would be that no claim for it had been pleaded. Other examples and also an account of the detailed principles concerning the rate of interest and the period for which it is allowed are given in Chapter 4 (p 75).

Interest where part of the claim is paid before judgment

It frequently happens that defendants pay plaintiffs part of the debt or damages claimed before the plaintiff obtains judgment thereon. Such payments may be made voluntarily, eg by a debtor wishing to reduce his indebtedness. Alternatively the court may have ordered the defendant to make an interim payment before trial (see p 308). In these cases, when judgment is later entered for the balance of the claim, two calculations of interest may have to be made. One, in respect of the sums previously paid, for interest up to the date of payment. Another, in respect of the balance of the claim, for interest up to the date of judgment.

Debt claim: interest where whole debt paid before judgment

Under the old law the court had no power to order interest to be paid on sums which had already been paid and which had not been the subject of its judgment. We have seen that the law is now altered in the case of part payment in debt or damages cases. It is also altered, in debt cases, where the whole debt is paid (s 35A(3), s 69(3): for an exceptional case concerning damages expressed as a fixed sum, see *Edmunds v Lloyds Italico SpA* [1986] 1 WLR 492). But for this change debtors not obliged to pay contractually agreed interest would in effect obtain interest-free credit if they withheld payment until sued but then paid up (debt and costs) before the plaintiff could enter judgment. Such debtors can in fact still obtain some interest-free credit if they withhold payment of their debts until the moment before the plaintiff commences proceedings: see the House of Lords' decision in *President of India v La Pintada Compania Navigacion SA* [1985] AC 104.

The law works perfectly well in a case in which the payment of the whole debt is made at a late stage in the proceedings. The plaintiff would be entitled to go on, to trial if necessary, and obtain a full award for interest up to the date of payment and an order for costs. However there are some doubts and difficulties in respect of post-commencement interest in cases in which the defendant pays the whole debt within fourteen days after the service of court proceedings. Details are given in Chapters 11 (p 202) and 16 (p 335). It is fair to say that the amount of interest in question in these cases is likely to be comparatively small. Plaintiffs who receive prompt payment of the whole debt, interest up to commencement

and their costs may not think it worthwhile pursuing post-commencement
interest as well even if it is possible to do so.

Interest on judgments

Topics covered so far in this chapter have considered what interest may
be awarded *in* a judgment. Such interest runs only to the date of judgment
or sooner payment. Interest *on* the judgment is entirely different. It is not
discretionary or subject to the parties' prior agreement. No pleading or
application to the court is necessary to obtain it. It is payable also on
judgments for interest and costs.

In the High Court judgment interest is payable under the Judgments
Act 1838, s 17, the rate being that prescribed by statutory instrument
(currently 8 per cent; see *White Book* 6/2/12) unless the judgment
provides for payment at a different rate (eg a contractually agreed rate or,
in the case of a foreign currency claim, the rate appropriate to that
currency, see *White Book* 42/1/13 supplement). Although statutory
instruments alter the rate from time to time (for previous statutory
instruments see *White Book* 42/1/12), the rate applicable to any particular
judgment is that rate in force when the judgment was made (*Rocco
Giuseppe & Figli v Tradax Export SA* [1984] 1 WLR 742).

In a damages case, the judgment creditor's right to judgment interest
runs from the date the damages are assessed, ie the date upon which the
amount of damages (and interest) is quantified. For periods before that
date the court may, in its discretion, award interest *in* the judgment under
SCA 1981, s 35A. A different rule applies in the case of an order for
costs. With costs, the judgment creditor is entitled to interest *on* the
judgment from the first date the costs in question were awarded even
though the amount of costs (and interest) may not be quantified until
taxation which could be several months or even years later. This
retrospectivity in the case of costs seems strange at first until one recalls
that the court has no discretion to award interest *in* the judgment so far as
costs are concerned (see generally, *Thomas v Bunn* [1991] 1 AC 362).

What seems at first sight to be the strangest rule of all applies to orders
for costs made by appeal courts in respect of work done in lower courts,
eg where an appellant succeeds in persuading the Court of Appeal to
reverse a judgment and order for costs which was made by a trial judge.
So as to protect the appellant's entitlement to interest calculated
retrospectively, the appeal court may back-date its order for costs below
to the date of the order now being reversed (*Kuwait Airways Corp v Iraqi
Airways Co (No 2)* [1994] 1 WLR 985 in which the Court of Appeal in
fact back-dated its costs order to an intermediate date, the relevant rates
of interest having changed between the date of trial and the date of
appeal).

Judgment interest is also obtainable on county court judgments of
£5,000 and more (currently 8 per cent, see generally, *Green Book*

commentary to CCA 1984, s 74). Unlike the High Court, county court judgments frequently provide for payment by instalments. Accordingly where under the terms of the relevant judgment payment of a judgment debt is not required to be made until a specified date or is to be made by instalments, interest does not accrue until that date or until the amount of any instalment falls due as the case may be. Thereafter any money paid by the debtor in respect of that judgment debt is first to be appropriated to discharge or reduce the principal and then towards the interest. Where a judgment creditor takes proceedings in a county court to enforce payment under a judgment (other than proceedings under the Charging Orders Act 1979, see p 600) the judgment debt ceases to carry interest thereafter unless the enforcement proceedings fail to produce any payment from the debtor. If the enforcement proceedings are wholly unsuccessful interest continues to accrue as if those enforcement proceedings had never been taken.

County court judgments under £5,000 do not carry interest and for this reason some creditors prefer to sue in the High Court even in matters which are clearly suitable for trial in the county court. Obviously the case would be transferred if defended but many will be terminated by default judgments.

Chapter 2

Preliminary Stages of Litigation

The first interview

The client may well be nervous and tense, especially if he has not consulted a lawyer before. The client does not expect ten minutes small talk, but a brief exchange of pleasantries is not just courteous, it helps to put the client at ease and to achieve this is the first task.

Ask the client why he has consulted you and what he wants you to do for him. Then let him tell his own story in his own way. Clients are not always very clear about what is relevant to their problem. They will tell you much that is wholly irrelevant. Do not try to interrupt the flow of the story too much. The client will not be satisfied that a topic is unimportant unless you allow him to tell you of it in the first place. Nevertheless it is obviously necessary to strike a balance: given the opportunity some clients will talk incessantly and the interview needs to be kept within reasonable limits.

After the client has had his say there are four main tasks for the solicitor to perform:

Giving general advice on the law

Find simple language by which to explain to the client the general law relevant to the case. In road accident cases there are two matters which must always be considered: the question of contributory negligence; and the client's rights against insurers. If a client intending to bring a claim also has an insurance policy covering his loss explain his rights under that policy. If the claim is against a motorist the client may also be able to seek compensation from the motorist's insurer or from the Motor Insurers' Bureau. Insurance topics are considered separately on pp 37–40.

Taking the client's statement

This will of course form the basis of the case file. It is dealt with on p 24.

Answering the client's questions

'How much will I get if I win?' Every client with a personal injuries claim will ask this question. Similarly every defendant wants to know what it will cost him if he has to pay. These topics are considered in Chapter 4. 'How long will the case take?' Tell the client the steps which will have to be taken. Reassure him that many cases are settled without any court proceedings being commenced and that only a tiny proportion of cases actually go to trial.

In answering either of these questions it would be unwise to give the client too precise an estimate since much will depend on whether liability is accepted and what attitude the opponents take to negotiations. Give the client broad estimates only and promise that you will keep him informed as the case progresses. (Make sure you keep that promise.)

'Will I receive/have to pay interest?' This topic is considered separately on pp 15–19.

Dealing with the topic of costs

The main points to cover here are the availability of legal aid, billing arrangements in non-legal aid cases and the risk of being ordered to pay the opponent's costs if the case is lost.

Unless the circumstances clearly indicate otherwise, the client must be advised of the existence of the legal aid and legal advice schemes: this is so whether or not the solicitor undertakes legal aid work (see *The Guide to the Professional Conduct of Solicitors 1996*, p 128).

The Law Society has published written professional standards on costs information to be given to clients. Every solicitor should, at the outset of instructions:

(1) Explain the firm's basis of charging, eg who is going to do the work, their respective hourly rates, and what, if any, sums will be payable on account. In non-legal aid cases it is a common practice to ask the client to pay a sum such as £2,000 on account, on the basis that the firm will from time to time submit bills for immediate payment as and when costs and disbursements totalling approximately £2,000 have been incurred.

(2) Give clients the best information possible about the likely costs of the matter, eg the likely number of hours of work which will be incurred and the effect of orders likely to be made by the court dealing with costs between the parties. In most types of litigation it is not possible to estimate the costs in advance. However, the client can of course set a limit on what you will incur on their behalf, eg as a further refinement of the interim billing arrangement described above.

(3) Consider whether the client's liability for costs may be covered by insurance.

(4) Give clients written confirmation of items (1) and (2) above.

(See, generally, *The Guide to the Professional Conduct of Solicitors 1996*, pp 226–232: there are proposals to incorporate these standards into a separate code on costs in order to give them greater prominence.)

There is a double aspect to costs which most clients find totally baffling until it is clearly explained to them. It is necessary to distinguish between the sums they must pay to their own solicitors (solicitor-and-own-client costs) and the additional sums which a court may order them to pay in respect of their opponent's costs if the litigation fails (costs between litigants or *inter partes* costs). Consider the position of a client who does not obtain legal aid:

(1) if the client loses he will have two sets of bills to pay, ie his own solicitor-and-own-client bills and the opponent's *inter partes* bill;

(2) if the client wins he will still have to pay his own solicitor-and-own-client bills and will receive from the opponent *inter partes* taxed costs. Any difference between the solicitor-and-own-client bills and the taxed costs received will have to be found out of the client's own pocket or any money recovered in the action;

(3) if the client wins but the opponent goes bankrupt or simply disappears the client still has to pay the solicitor-and-own-client bills.

Costs are considered more fully in Chapter 23.

For a client who does obtain legal aid the position is not quite so bad. Consider the position of a client suing for damages:

(1) the client may have a contribution to pay towards legal aid depending upon earnings, savings and other assets;

(2) if the client loses the action normally there is no other bill for costs to be paid. It is possible however that the court will order them to pay their opponent's costs;

(3) if the client wins the action the Legal Aid Board will pay the solicitor and will collect *inter partes* taxed costs. It is possible that a sum will be deducted from the client's damages to cover any difference between taxed costs received and the amount paid to the solicitor.

Legal aid is considered fully in Chapter 3.

The letter before action

The so-called 'letter before action' is the first letter written by the prospective plaintiff's solicitor to the prospective defendant stating the claim that is being made. The letter should set out the general nature of the allegations and a summary of the damage that has been sustained. It is important to make the letter as comprehensive as possible. Usually it will be necessary to do some preliminary work before writing it. Preparing the client's statement and having it checked (see p 25) is the very minimum that must be done.

Since it initiates the plaintiff's claim, the letter before action will usually have to be addressed to the defendant in person. If the defendant is likely to be insured in respect of the claim, take the opportunity to

[*continued on p 24*]

Figs 2a and b: Specimen letters before action

Fig 2a: Damages claim [Date]

Dear Sirs

We have been consulted by John Smith in connection with the unfortunate accident which occurred on 21 June 1995 at your Westgate Road factory. As you will be aware, our client's left arm was caught in the circular saw used to make quarters. He has suffered a severe injury including the loss of two fingers, part of the palm of his hand and part of his arm up to the elbow. It is, of course, too early to give a firm prognosis: our client is likely to require hospital treatment for some considerable time.

From our instructions it is clear that:

(1) the machine in question was unsafe; and
(2) you failed to provide a safe system of work; and
(3) our client was given no, or no adequate, training in how to use the machine.

In these circumstances, our client holds you entirely to blame for the accident and looks to you to pay substantial damages.

No doubt you are insured against accidents of this sort and will pass this letter to your insurers to conduct the case on your behalf.

Although we have taken a full statement from Mr Smith we would obviously like to see the particular machine in question. We would be quite happy for you to have your insurers or solicitors present at the same time. When would it be convenient for our representative to call? No doubt you will put this suggestion to your insurers.

We look forward to receiving your reply to this letter by return:

(1) stating the name and address of your insurers and the insurers' reference identifying the policy in question; and
(2) confirming that no modifications will be carried out to the machine until we have seen and photographed it.

Yours faithfully

Fig 2b: Debt claim 10 November 1997

Dear Sir

<u>Northern Emporium Ltd and Yourself</u>

We act for Northern Emporium Ltd whose retail premises are in the Shopping Precinct in Weyford. We have received instructions to collect a debt of £5,401 from you, that sum being the balance outstanding in respect of a stereo system which has been sold to you.

We are instructed that the goods were supplied some time ago, and that despite repeated demands for payment, the stated balance remains outstanding.

Payment of the full amount outstanding should be made to this office within the next ten days, ie to arrive here on or before 20 November 1997, failing which we have instructions to commence court proceedings against you without further notice.

If proceedings are commenced against you, our clients will also claim interest and legal costs, so increasing the total amount claimed against you.

Yours faithfully

inquire about this and ask that the letter be passed on to the insurers. In practice they are the persons who will conduct negotiations on behalf of the defendant. If you know who the insurers are, send a copy of the letter to them direct. Where it is known that the defendant already has a solicitor acting in the matter the letter before action should be addressed to that solicitor. It is improper for one solicitor to contact the opposing solicitor's client directly.

The form the letter before action should take is largely a matter of style. Normally there is no point in making it aggressive: in fact this is likely to be counter-productive. The plaintiff's claim should be stated firmly but courteously. A typical letter might be as illustrated in fig 2a (p 23). Obviously a certain amount of work had to be done before this letter was written including taking the client's statement on which it was in part based.

Turning now to a debt action, the letter before action is usually short and aggressive. The debtor has no doubt been given one or more reminders to pay. What is needed now is a brief letter making clear your instructions that, unless payment is made, court proceedings will be commenced. A typical letter might be as illustrated in fig 2b (p 23). The solicitor should make clear to his client the importance of informing the solicitor immediately if in fact payment is made directly to the client.

Where a debt exceeds the minimum bankruptcy level (currently £750) there is the option of not writing a letter before action to be followed if necessary by proceedings but instead serving a statutory demand to be followed if necessary by a bankruptcy or winding-up petition: this is discussed in Chapter 26 (see pp 613 and 628).

First steps in preparation of evidence

Unless otherwise stated the following notes relate to the conduct of a *claim* in a personal injury case.

The client's statement

As the client is telling the story the solicitor will jot down the main points and later will pose a few questions to elicit any further information required. From these notes the solicitor can then compose the statement. Although it has to be comprehensive it need not necessarily run to any considerable length.

When a statement has been prepared a copy of it should be sent to the client for approval. The client should be asked to add to or amend it as and where necessary and to date and sign it. Having it signed is not essential but is certainly a desirable and most advisable practice. Cases take some time to get to trial and the client might well say some time later that the statement you have prepared was not accurate. This sort of misunderstanding can be avoided by careful preparation and checking.

Despite this careful preparation and checking, the client's initial statement will no doubt have to be amended and updated during the course of the action. The final statement, the one likely to be ordered to stand as evidence at the trial (see p 429), will focus much more sharply on the matters upon which the client's testimony is relied upon. Because it is prepared later, it will also be much more up to date and comprehensive on those matters than the initial statement is. For example, in due course the client will be able to say rather more about the injuries and loss of earnings. It is often best to omit from the client's initial statement much of the detail as to the client's amount of earnings or statutory sick pay. Such matters are invariably dealt with, and agreed, separately (see further, p 66).

Preparing for discovery of documents

Discovery is considered fully in Chapter 18. It occurs in virtually all cases including, as far as the plaintiff is concerned, road accident cases. Usually each litigant is required to prepare a list detailing all documents which are or have been in his possession, custody or power which are relevant to the matters being litigated. The list must disclose all documents, even those for which privilege from inspection may be claimed (indeed the claim for privilege is made in the list itself). Although in practice discovery does not usually occur until after the pleadings are closed, the client must be made to appreciate at the outset the nature of and obligation to make discovery. Ideally the client should bring all documents to the first interview. If this is done the solicitor can ensure that there will be no panic or surprise later on caused by some long-forgotten document which throws a completely different light on the story.

Preparing for discovery is particularly important in contract cases where the correspondence between the parties, both before and after the making of the contract, may well be voluminous.

Obtaining official records

Police accident report

If, in a road accident case, it is likely that the police would have attended at the scene, write to the chief superintendent of the area where the accident occurred asking for a copy of the accident report and describing the accident in as much detail as possible; the date, the time and place, the registration numbers of the vehicles involved, the names of the parties, and so on. A fee is payable for a copy of the police accident report (as to guidelines issued by the Association of Chief Police Officers, see (1997) *Law Society Gazette* 16 April, p 30). It will contain statements taken from the parties concerned, the names and addresses of witnesses and probably also measurements, a sketch plan, and perhaps even photographs. As a general rule the more serious the accident, the more detailed is the investigation the police will have carried out. It may be necessary to interview the police officer. This can be done by further arrangement and on the payment of an additional fee. Police officers can, of course, give evidence in civil cases but they will insist on being served with a *subpoena* (in the High Court) or witness summons (in the county court).

Criminal proceedings

The police will not release the report until any criminal proceedings which they have decided to bring have been concluded. If proceedings are proposed, ask the police to inform you of the court and the date of the hearing. It may then be prudent to attend that hearing and make a note of the evidence and of the findings. If the defendant in the criminal proceedings is to be the defendant in the civil proceedings in which you have been instructed, then, by virtue of the Civil Evidence Act 1968, s 11, a criminal conviction is admissible as evidence in the civil proceedings. Even if the defendant in the criminal proceedings is acquitted it does not follow that the civil proceedings are hopeless. The prosecution may have been lost on a technicality. Further, the prosecutor in a criminal case is required to prove the case beyond all reasonable doubt. In the civil proceedings the plaintiff need only prove the case on a balance of probabilities.

Inquests

In a fatal accident case you should attend any inquest held. Your object in attending is not merely to take notes. If you represent a relative of the deceased you are entitled to put questions to the witnesses if those questions are likely to assist the coroner in reaching a verdict as to the cause of death.

Employer's accident report book

In respect of injuries suffered at work employers are required to keep an accident report book. This book must of course be inspected (see further, opposite). Also, the factories inspector (part of the Health and Safety Executive) may have been notified of the accident and may be preparing a report. If so, you should obtain a copy.

Inspecting and photographing property

It is frequently necessary for the solicitor to carry out some form of inspection after the client's initial instructions. Often, it will help to have a look at the *locus in quo* so as to obtain a firm mental picture of what occurred. The scene of a motor accident should usually be photographed. For example, photographs showing the degree of visibility from a junction; the position which the car had to take to negotiate a bend; the width left for the other vehicle, and so on. It is much easier to present a case or to obtain statements from witnesses with the aid of a photograph or plan to describe or explain the event.

If vehicles were involved, find out where they now are and inspect and photograph them if this has not already been done (sometimes the police will have taken photographs and copies can be obtained from them). The police report may merely state 'front offside wing—dented'. The size and depth of the dent is not revealed by this and a photograph may well be vital evidence if, say, a dispute subsequently emerges over the speed of the vehicle. It may be possible to prove by expert evidence that a dent of such size could not have occurred if the driver was proceeding at the speed which he alleges. A vital piece of evidence has been missed if no photograph has been taken.

In the case of an accident at work, any machine concerned should be inspected as soon as possible and certainly before any alterations are carried out to it. The accident may have brought to the attention of the employers a danger of which they were not previously aware. Now aware of it, they will want to take steps to ensure that no similar accident occurs again and it is likely that they will want to modify their machine as quickly as possible. You must get in first and photograph the machine before this happens. Most employers will agree to a request for facilities to do so and often an inspection can be arranged in the presence of a representative from the employer's insurance company (which reassures the employer). The insurers too will be carrying out their investigation and will want to inspect. Though certainly the insurers will wish to interview their insured when you are not there, there is no harm in purely background information being obtained together so that an agreed bundle of photographs can be prepared. It will frequently be helpful if a brochure describing the machine can be obtained. The employer may have some and be willing to let you have one. If not, write to the manufacturers. While you are at the employer's premises remember to inspect their accident report book. In the event of employers being unco-operative, an order from the court can be obtained both for pre-action discovery of documents (see p 408) and for pre-action inspection of property (see p 305). If your initial inquiry is refused make it clear that these procedures will be used unless they have a change of heart.

Incidentally, it may be helpful to photograph the client himself in order to show the full extent of the injuries. This will often have to be arranged in co-operation with medical advisers so that dressings can be removed.

Interviewing witnesses

Witnesses often say 'But I have already given a statement to the police' or 'the man from the insurance company' or whoever. There is no 'property' in a witness. Any person is entitled to interview them and sometimes witnesses have to be reassured on this point.

The solicitor needs to use tact and persuasion when taking a statement. The witness should not be led but should merely be asked to state in his own words what he knows of the event which has occurred. The statement, however, may not be reliable. For example, the witness may say 'The sports car came through the lights on red at one hell of a speed and knocked down the pedestrian.' This should be tested by polite cross-examination. The truth of the matter may well be that the witness saw nothing at all. Perhaps he was walking along the road at the time of the accident when he heard the sound of a collision behind him. He turned round and saw that there had been an accident and that the traffic lights were now on red for the defendant's car. In his mind he has reconstructed what he genuinely believes to be the cause of the accident. Nevertheless, the fact is that he saw nothing of the accident itself. He will not be able to say at what speed the car was going (though maybe he heard the screech of brakes before the impact and can say that) and he will not know at what point the lights changed. Unfortunately this often happens with witnesses. Very few of them deliberately lie: but they may try too hard to be helpful.

How should one arrange the appointment to take a statement from a witness? It is not only discourteous but pointless writing to him in terms such as 'Please call in at our office at 10 am on Monday next in order to be interviewed by the writer.' It is best simply to call round one evening without any appointment. (The client may be able to tell you when the witness will be at home.) If the time you choose to call is inconvenient for the witness ask him to suggest a couple of other dates which will suit him. The fact that you have taken the trouble to call will at least make him appreciate the importance of the matter. A possibly cheaper method is to write first to potential witnesses enclosing a questionnaire. If this is completed and returned you can then decide whether it is necessary to arrange a personal interview.

Some solicitors employ inquiry agents for the purpose of taking statements. There is nothing inherently wrong with this practice provided the inquiry agent is a good one (ex-policemen may be particularly good, although they are often better at criminal rather than civil work). Inquiry agents are also useful, of course, in tracing witnesses who have moved or in establishing the identity of unknown witnesses.

There is little that can be done if a witness absolutely refuses to give a statement. The witness may not wish to say anything against his employer: he may simply not wish to 'get involved'. Of course, if the case comes on for trial, a *subpoena* or witness summons can be served and the witness will be put in the box and can be asked questions. Leave can be obtained, where appropriate, for him to be treated as a hostile witness. However, the disadvantage is clear. You have no idea what the witness is going to say. This emphasises how important it is to get the witness to volunteer the statement by using tact and persuasion.

Obtaining medical evidence

This is one type of evidence that does not have to be sought immediately. On the contrary it is usually better to wait. There is little point in sending the client to a medical expert for a report on a broken leg when the leg is still in plaster from thigh to ankle. The solicitor will get his report—and the medical expert will have to be paid for it—but the report will be virtually useless.

In the case of fractures, wait until the client has been attending physiotherapy for four to six weeks. In the case of plastic surgery, it is usually essential to wait at least six months for a report on how the surgery has progressed. In the case of arthritic change, wait until the client has finished treatment or gone back to work. These are only general guides which will need to be varied depending on particular circumstances.

Whom does one instruct in order to obtain medical evidence? When acting for a plaintiff, it is the custom to instruct the consultant who has charge of the client's case. This is, of course, a private matter: such reports are not available under the NHS and the consultant has to be instructed privately and paid. A report from a general practitioner can be useful by way of background information (eg if the other side suggests that your client is a malingerer) but generally speaking he will not be familiar with the task of writing medico-legal reports. In the light of experience each solicitor conducting personal injury cases builds up a file of local experts suitable for each type of injury. Sometimes, if the client has sustained more than one type of injury, reports from different medical experts will be required.

It is generally agreed that the plaintiff enjoys an advantage in being able to instruct the consultant in charge of his case. A defendant could not instruct that consultant without the plaintiff's prior permission (which is unlikely to be forthcoming). If there is a genuine medical dispute (which is rare) it is highly unlikely that a trial judge will find against a plaintiff's own doctor. A consultant, by the time of the trial, may well have had the care of the client for several years and it is very difficult for a judge to be able to say that throughout that period the consultant was wrong or the client has been receiving the wrong treatment.

A possible disadvantage in obtaining medical evidence from the client's own doctors is that they sometimes have a tendency to be over-optimistic. Naturally, a doctor likes to think that, because of the treatment he has been giving, the client has made excellent progress and this may make the doctor subconsciously exaggerate the extent of the client's recovery. This is a danger the solicitor needs to be aware of.

On receipt of the medical report it is necessary to study it and make sure that it is understood. A good medical dictionary is a useful aid. Every report on a bone injury will contain references to flexion, extension, abduction or adduction, and the meaning of these and any other technical

terms used must be known. For example, it is not uncommon for a client
in a road accident to suffer a 'peri-orbital haematoma'—this being the
medical term for a black eye. If necessary, however, do not be afraid to
go back to the doctor for a less technical explanation of the injuries.

Should the medical report be shown to the client? (Surprisingly, clients
rarely ask to see it.) Generally speaking, one should keep confidential any
report which contains a statement the doctor would not have made had he
known it was to be shown to the client. But otherwise it is often
convenient to fix an appointment with the client, show the report, explain
it, and ask the client to comment especially on anything it contains which
may limit the amount of damages obtainable. If it is possible that the
prognosis is somewhat over-optimistic or if the client feels that the
injuries are more serious than described it may be worthwhile instructing
another doctor to give a second opinion. It is courteous to inform the
original doctor and to ask him to recommend someone suitable to provide
the second opinion. Obviously you must go to a more senior doctor. If
you instruct someone junior to your original doctor the junior may well
be influenced by the senior's opinion.

Medical reports often end up by stating that another examination will
be required in, say, six months' time. The solicitor must therefore make
an appropriate diary entry to ensure that this is done.

Whenever instructing a doctor you have not previously instructed it is
always advisable to inquire what the fee will be. In a legal aid case get
authority to pay that fee. In a non-legal aid case, make sure that the client
appreciates the cost of obtaining the evidence. A medical report will cost
at least £50 and often costs substantially more. Psychiatrists, for example,
may need to see the client for several hours over a period of time before
they are in a position to provide a report. Plaintiffs in personal injury
cases are required to serve a copy of a medical report with their first
pleading (see further, p 155).

It is convenient to consider here the question of agreeing medical
evidence with the other side. It is of course necessary to distinguish
between a plaintiff (someone who has commenced proceedings and is
therefore subject to rules of court) and a claimant (someone who is no
more than a potential plaintiff and who is not yet subject to rules of
court). Let us consider first the position of a plaintiff. Unless the injuries
are trivial the defendant's advisers will wish to obtain their own medical
report, and indeed the plaintiff will normally insist upon this. The plaintiff
is required to assist the defendant by submitting to medical examination.
The court has no power to order a plaintiff to be medically examined, but
unless he agrees to it the court will stay his action (*Edmeades v Thames
Board Mills* [1969] 2 QB 69). A plaintiff can impose reasonable
conditions as to the terms upon which facilities will be provided. Make
sure that there is definite agreement as to these. Do not simply consent to
an examination 'on the usual terms'. What is usual in one case may be
unusual in another. Suitable terms to agree are as follows:

(1) that the defence will pay the cost of the plaintiff attending the examination and any loss of earnings involved;

(2) that the defendant's doctor will consider only the injuries and not the accident and will not discuss the accident with the plaintiff, more than as is necessary for the purpose of preparing a medical report; and

(3) that no other person will be present, apart from the client and the doctor carrying out the examination (see *Hall v Avon Area Medical Authority* [1980] 1 WLR 481).

It is not considered reasonable to require the defendant to give a copy of his medical report to the plaintiff. The plaintiff's interests are sufficiently protected by the rules of court, under which each party is usually obliged to disclose to his opponent the reports of the medical witnesses he intends to call at the trial (see *Megarity v DJ Ryan & Sons Ltd* [1980] 1 WLR 1237 and p 422).

Whatever conditions have been imposed it is of course necessary to explain them to the client. The reason why we suggest condition (2) above is to protect the plaintiff against the risk (admittedly rare) of partiality on the part of the doctor instructed by the defence. Most medical witnesses are scrupulously fair and will prepare an objective report regardless of whether they are instructed by the plaintiff's solicitors or the defendant's solicitors. Unfortunately there is a minority who will exceed their function as independent expert and subject the plaintiff to a needless and irrelevant cross-examination. There needs to be some discussion between the witness and the plaintiff but this should be limited to a discussion necessary for the purpose of obtaining a report, and the length and type of this discussion will therefore vary according to the injuries concerned.

Can a plaintiff control who the defence wish to instruct as their medical witness? In *Starr v National Coal Board* [1977] 1 WLR 63 the Court of Appeal upheld a stay of the plaintiff's action where the plaintiff had refused to submit to an examination by a named doctor but had agreed to submit to an examination by anyone else. *Prima facie* it is the defendant's right to nominate the doctor he wishes to use and only in exceptional cases will the court interfere. The plaintiff's advisers should, however, consider the tactics involved if such a situation were to arise, because medical evidence can be attacked in the same way as other evidence. Consequently, if the defendant wishes to obtain evidence which is likely to be lacking in credibility and easily discredited, why should the plaintiff wish to prevent this?

It has been noted that if a plaintiff refuses to submit to a medical examination the court can stay the action. In the case of a claimant there is no action to stay, and accordingly there are no steps that a potential defendant can take to force the claimant to submit to an examination. It follows that a claimant is freer to impose conditions which might be regarded as unreasonable if imposed by a plaintiff, eg conditions as to who will conduct the examination, what discussion can take place, and whether a copy of the report will be sent to the plaintiff.

Insurers are often anxious to carry out a medical examination of a claimant. Some solicitors misinterpret this as a willingness by insurers to compromise the claim. In fact, insurers wish to know their potential liability for their own reasons, and not necessarily with a view to a quick settlement of the claim. Solicitors specialising in personal injury litigation sometimes refuse to allow a claimant to be medically examined by the other side unless an admission of liability has first been obtained. Of course, if the other side are denied facilities for a pre-action medical examination, or are unwilling to agree to the claimant's conditions, the parties will not be able to agree an early compromise of the claim. It is, therefore, a matter of tactics for those advising claimants whether or not to agree to pre-action medical examinations.

Is the defendant entitled to a stay if the plaintiff refuses to submit to a medical examination which is unpleasant, painful or even risky? The answer to this will have to await clarification from the Court of Appeal. For differing approaches at first instance, see *Aspinall v Sterling Mansell* [1981] 3 All ER 866 and *Prescott v Bulldog Tools* [1981] 3 All ER 869 (and see *White Book* 25/6/2).

In practice most medical reports are exchanged either voluntarily or in accordance with rules of court with a view to agreeing medical evidence. A real dispute between medical experts is rare. Sometimes there may be apparent discrepancies in medical evidence on the face of the reports. If this happens show a copy of the other side's report to your own expert and invite comments. This may resolve the apparent discrepancies but if not, then it may be worthwhile considering with the other side a joint examination of the plaintiff in order to reach agreement. If this fails to produce agreement, the medical evidence will have to be fought out at the trial.

It has long been good practice to arrange joint examinations or joint meetings where there is a disagreement between experts. Rules of court enable the court to direct the parties to convene a 'without prejudice' meeting of experts 'for the purpose of identifying those parts of their evidence which are in issue'. The experts can then prepare a joint statement indicating those parts of their evidence on which they are, and those on which they are not, in agreement. These rules are not of course confined to medical experts (see further, p 422, 423).

There are many other matters upon which an expert's report may be necessary. Reports from consulting engineers, handwriting experts and scientific and technical experts are just some examples. Sometimes it will be necessary to have scale plans drawn or a scale model made. Such demonstrative evidence can be expensive but, while its function is mainly illustrative, it can also be persuasive.

Negotiations with a view to settlement

There is no negotiations stage in an action. Negotiations are conducted throughout the whole case, from the reply to the letter before action until compromise or the trial is reached. The conduct of negotiations is included in this chapter for these reasons: many cases are compromised before a writ or summons is issued; of actions which are commenced, not more than one per cent reaches a trial. It is not difficult to understand why this should be so. In civil cases, unlike criminal cases, there is no obligation to seek a court-room decision if the parties can come to terms before then. It appears therefore that the solicitor conducting civil litigation needs to be as skilled a negotiator as he is a lawyer. Indeed it could be said that skill as a negotiator is more important: solicitors handle more negotiations than proceedings. The proceedings themselves can be looked upon as just another stage of negotiation.

Successful negotiations are more desirable than successful litigation. A reasonable compromise saves the client the expense and the worry of a trial and yet he has still 'won'. The psychological pressure of litigation on a client must never be underestimated. If the case proceeds to trial usually one party wins and this necessarily means that the other loses. How much better if they can both win!

What makes a good negotiator? First and foremost, you need to be a good lawyer—to know all the relevant law applicable to the case—so as to be able to assess the strengths and weaknesses not only of the client's case but also of the opponent's. A knowledge of court procedure is important here. The lawyer needs to know all the steps available to be used if necessary, eg pre-action discovery; preservation and inspection of property; the *ex parte* injunction; interrogatories. In short you will know how to use the rules of court to your client's best advantage. Secondly, you need to know thoroughly the facts of the case in hand and to have done the relevant preparation and groundwork. Often there will be disputes of fact: the likely areas of dispute will have to be identified in advance and an opinion will have to be formed as to which version of events is nearer the truth. Finally, you need to be able to estimate what negotiations can achieve. Enter negotiations with a realistic assessment of what you can hope to gain by them and judge your success by how far you achieved these aims.

Compromise

As a matter of strict law a solicitor has no implied or ostensible authority to compromise a claim before the issue of proceedings. After issue the solicitor does have ostensible authority if acting *bona fide* and not contrary to the express instructions of the client of which the other party is aware (*White Book* 3879; and see *Waugh v HB Clifford & Sons Ltd* [1982] Ch 374). However, compromise is not a matter which should be left to the construction of fine points of law. Unless given express authority, the solicitor should conduct negotiations making it clear that any agreement reached will be provisional only and subject to the client's decision.

Without prejudice

Negotiations should normally be conducted 'without prejudice'. Nothing said or done will then be admissible in evidence should the matter come to trial unless the parties consent. This is an important protection for litigants. Neither side could negotiate freely if to do so risked damaging the presentation of its case. The fact that a party made, or replied to, or indeed ignored, a 'without prejudice' offer of compromise, cannot be used as an admission prejudicial to his case.

The protection can apply only to negotiations made in an attempt to settle a dispute. Thus it is the purpose of the statement that determines whether it is 'without prejudice' and not the mere addition or omission of the words themselves. For example, merely adding the words to a defamatory letter would not prevent its admissibility in a libel action. Omitting words from an offer of compromise might not be fatal if, eg the letter was written in response to the opponent's letter which was clearly marked 'without prejudice'. (In practice, a solicitor should always mark a letter 'without prejudice' if this is the intention. The court may infer that the addition or omission of the words was deliberate.) As the words 'without prejudice' will cover the whole contents of a letter, one should not include in such a letter statements one will wish to adduce in evidence. Solicitors often include in the same envelope two letters, only one of which is marked 'without prejudice'.

In three circumstances 'without prejudice' statements are admissible in evidence:

(1) If both parties consent, or, expressly or by implication, waive their right to object: for an example of an implied waiver see *Turner v Fenton* [1982] 1 WLR 52.

(2) If, as a result of 'without prejudice' negotiations, the parties reach a concluded contract of compromise. In *Tomlin v Standard Telephones & Cables Ltd* [1969] 1 WLR 1378 'without prejudice' correspondence was held admissible to prove an agreement between the parties to a personal injuries action on the basis of 50 per cent liability.

(3) Solely upon the issue of costs, after the other issues have been resolved *if* the 'without prejudice' statement expressly reserved the right to refer to it on the issue of costs, ie a Calderbank offer, as to which see further p 329.

Negotiations with insurers

Many claims are initially handled by insurance companies themselves and not by their solicitors. Although their representative is not a lawyer, he or she will still be an expert in the relevant areas of law and will have considerable experience of similar claims or be able to consult others who have such experience. One should prepare for negotiations with an insurer's representative just as thoroughly as one would prepare for negotiations with a solicitor. There are however three special points to note:

(1) Insurance representatives are sometimes keen to fix an appointment to discuss the case before the solicitor has completed investigations as to *quantum*. Do not let your client be stampeded into an ill-considered compromise.

(2) The representative's first offer of compromise is usually unreasonably low, the purpose being to sort out the false claims from the genuine claims. If you think the claim is genuine, indicate that by threatening to commence proceedings promptly unless a reasonable offer of compromise is made.

(3) Insurers have a vested interest in delaying payment. If you think the claim is strong tell them that you will commence proceedings promptly, and press for an interim payment (see p 308).

Wherever a claim can be compromised by payment without proceedings it is important to agree terms as to costs. The defendant or his insurers should agree two sets of figures: one relating to the claimant's compensation and the other relating to the claimant's solicitor's costs. If negotiations with the insurance company do not end in a compromise and proceedings have to be commenced, the insurance company will then nominate solicitors to act for the defendant. Thus the defence solicitors come onto the scene at a much later stage and are presented with a fairly full file where virtually all of the initial investigative work has been done. Once solicitors have been instructed all further correspondence and negotiations must be conducted through them.

Payment into court

Payment into court is one of the most valuable weapons in the defendant's armoury. If negotiations falter, the defendants may pay the money they offered into court. If the plaintiff accepts within the stipulated time he is entitled to his costs up to the time of giving notice of acceptance. If he does not accept, the payment is not an admission of liability; the case will proceed to trial, and the judge will not be told of it until the end. It will make no difference if at the trial the plaintiff recovers more than the amount paid in. If however the plaintiff recovers the same amount or less, the court, in exercising its discretion as to costs, is obliged to take into account the payment into court and its amount. This usually means that the plaintiff will receive no costs as from the date of the payment into court.

Suppose that the client is advised that if successful the claim is worth £20,000 but that the chance of success is 75 per cent. Faced with such advice should a payment into court of £10,000 be accepted? Probably it should be, but there is no simple answer. Regrettably, it may depend on the extent to which the client can afford to lose. Defendants are very quick to take advantage of this unhappy state of affairs. An insurance company, defending many cases, can afford to risk losing some of them. For the injured plaintiff this is not one of many cases; it is the only case. The burden of losing will not merely be a set-back—it will be a disaster. The solicitor bears a heavy burden in advising such a client. The actual decision to accept a payment must be left to the client but must be based on sound advice from his solicitor. In difficult cases counsel's opinion might be sought. Sometimes a conference with counsel is desirable.

Clients sometimes complain that they have been pressurised into making a settlement against their better judgment. Such pressure should never come from their own advisers. Give the client the appropriate advice—strong advice where necessary—but then leave the client to make the decision. A good practice is to give the client the advice orally so that you can be certain he understands the position fully. Then, in addition to making the usual attendance note on the file, write to him summarising the advice given and asking for his instructions when he has decided what to do.

'Doorstep' settlements

The practice of settling claims literally on the court doorstep before the hearing is not one to be encouraged. Settlements should be reached away from the courtroom where the psychological pressures are somewhat less. When the client has finally got as far as the door of the court many will regard the time for negotiation as having passed and will prefer a judge imposed solution. Yet it is surprising how 'the door of the court' does focus the mind. The strong case seems not quite so strong and the intransigent party suddenly becomes reasonable. Settlements at the door of the court are remarkably common.

Defendants or their insurers may try to take unfair advantage of a plaintiff's inexperience of litigation. The psychological pressure of an action on a plaintiff can be immense, and if he turns up at court ready for trial (probably having not slept all night through worrying about it) it may be devastating to be confronted by solicitor and counsel both now saying that the case must be settled. It is essential to prepare the ground for a 'doorstep' offer by discussing the possibility with the client beforehand. Suppose, for example, a plaintiff decides not to accept a payment in of £16,000 but on taking advice decides to accept £20,000 if it is offered. If on the morning of the court hearing the defendant now increases the offer to £20,000 the plaintiff can accept with confidence.

Motor insurers

The plaintiff's policy

If a client's car, properly parked on the highway, is damaged by another driver (whether or not known and/or insured) but the client has prudently obtained comprehensive insurance for the car, then, of course, the client is able to claim on that policy. However, there may be three disadvantages of doing this:

(1) the client may lose a 'no-claims bonus' (or one or more 'steps' of the bonus);
(2) the client will have to pay the 'excess' (if any) under the policy, ie the uninsured element such as the first £100 of the damage; and
(3) the client will not get any compensation for loss of or damage to property in the car not covered by insurance.

For these, smaller, sums the client may consider suing a known defendant. If the claim is for £3,000 or less it can be brought in the county court and be determined informally by arbitration as a 'small claim' (see p 279). In such a case it may be that the plaintiff's insurers are also intending to sue the defendant in order to get back what they can of the sums they have paid to the plaintiff. Under their so-called rights of subrogation the insurers can require the plaintiff to lend his name to such an action. The insurers should not start proceedings without first notifying the plaintiff, at which time, he may tell them to sue also in respect of the uninsured losses numbered (2) and (3) above. Similarly a plaintiff should not sue for any uninsured losses without first notifying his insurers in case they wish to bring the action (see *Buckland v Palmer* [1984] 1 WLR 1109).

The defendant's policy

Consider now a claim against an insured motorist by any person, including a pedestrian or passenger injured in an accident. The claimant has no rights under the defendant's policy directly except where the defendant is made bankrupt and the Third Parties (Rights against Insurers) Act 1930 applies, as fortified by the Road Traffic Act 1988, Pt VI. The rights conferred by these statutory provisions are very limited and are subject to many restrictions. They will not be considered further here (see 25 *Halsbury's Laws* (4th ed) paras 768 *et seq* and see *Motor and General Insurance Co Ltd v Pavey* [1994] 1 WLR 462).

A plaintiff may have statutory rights *outside* the policy under the Road Traffic Act 1988, s 151. Where the plaintiff obtains judgment against a driver he can, subject to two limitations, enforce it against any insurer who issued a certificate of insurance in respect of the insured vehicle. The plaintiff can enforce the judgment in this way 'notwithstanding that the insurer may be entitled to avoid or cancel, or may have avoided or cancelled, the policy'. (For what it may be worth, the insurers have the right to recoup from the defendant any sums they have paid for which they were not liable under the policy.) Sometimes the insurers who have to satisfy the plaintiff's judgment will not even be the defendant's insurers.

Example

Jean has insured her car but only for herself and her spouse to drive. She lends her car to John who has no car and consequently no insurance. John negligently runs down Justin. Justin can sue John and, subject to notice having been given (see below), Jean's insurers will have to satisfy the judgment (s 151(2)(b)).

The two limitations on the plaintiff's right to enforce under s 151 are as follows:

(1) The section applies only to a judgment 'in respect of any such liability as is required to be covered by a policy of insurance under section 145', ie liability for (*a*) the personal injury or death of any other person; (*b*) the cost of emergency hospital treatment; and (*c*) damage to property other than the insured vehicle itself and goods carried in it for hire or reward. Insurance in respect of (*c*), liability for property damage, is compulsory only up to the value of £250,000.

(2) No sum is payable in respect of any judgment unless before or within seven days after the commencement of proceedings the insurer had notice of the bringing of proceedings (s 152). There is no prescribed form of notice. The better practice is to write to the insurers giving them notice, immediately before a writ or summons is issued specifying the court in which proceedings are to be commenced and the approximate date of commencement (*Harrington v Pinkey* [1989] RTR 345). Make this a habit in every road accident case. In case that first letter is delayed in the post, also send a follow-up letter enclosing a copy of the writ of summons. In a case where it is not yet clear whether an insurance company or the MIB (see below) will meet the claim it is sensible to give notice to both.

The Motor Insurers' Bureau

The Motor Insurers' Bureau (MIB) is an independent body voluntarily set up and financed by the motor insurance companies to settle claims brought by injured persons in cases in which the driver is uninsured or untraced. The Bureau has made two main agreements with the Minister of Transport (now succeeded for this purpose by the Secretary of State for the Environment). Strictly speaking the agreements are enforceable only by the Secretary of State but in cases merely turning on construction of the agreements, claimants often sue the Bureau direct. The privity of contract point would never be taken against them (see *Albert v MIB* [1972] AC 301 and *Cooper v MIB* [1985] 2 WLR 248, rejecting a claim made *by* the driver where both he and the owner were uninsured).

Copies of the agreements are obtainable from HMSO. The full text (and the very helpful notes) must be studied whenever a particular case arises. What follows is only the basic outline.

MIB (Compensation of Victims of Uninsured Drivers) Agreement
  (1) The agreement applies only to compulsory risks (see above). However, the MIB will not meet the first £175 in respect of any property damage claimed.
  (2) The claimant must sue the driver in the usual way.
  (3) Within seven days after commencement, written notice of the proceedings must be given to the MIB or to the defendant's insurer. (NB Whether or not notice is given before commencement is irrelevant; contrast the Road Traffic Act 1988, s 152, above.) As to documentation which must accompany the notice, see *Cambridge v Callaghan* (1997) *The Times*, 21 March. In *O'Neill v O'Brien* (1997) *The Times*, 21 March a plaintiff who failed to give proper notice to the MIB but did not realise his mistake until after obtaining a default judgment successfully applied to set aside that default judgment in order to start again.
  (4) The plaintiff must obtain judgment against the driver. If it remains unpaid for seven days the MIB will pay it (including costs).
  (5) The judgment must be assigned to or to the order of the MIB.

MIB (Compensation of Victims of Untraced Drivers) Agreement
  (1) The agreement applies only to personal injury or death claims.
  (2) An application to the MIB must be made within three years of the road accident.
  (3) There must be proof that the untraced driver was negligent. The MIB will carry out a full investigation, the applicant giving all such assistance as may reasonably be required.
  (4) The death or injury must not have been caused deliberately by the untraced driver (contrast the first-mentioned agreement, as to which see *Gardner v Moore* [1984] AC 548).
  (5) If appropriate, the MIB makes an award assessed in the same way as a court would have assessed damages (with minor differences: see clause 4).
  (6) There is an appeal procedure, by way of arbitration by a Queen's Counsel.
  (7) The MIB is under no obligation to pay any costs or expenses incurred by the claimant or his solicitor. In practice the MIB pays to solicitors a 'standard fee' plus certain disbursements such as for a medical report and a police accident report.

For cases up to £50,000 there is also an accelerated procedure which, in effect, allows the claimant and the MIB to compromise the application without a full investigation and without any right of appeal.

The Criminal Injuries Compensation Authority

The Criminal Injuries Compensation Authority (CICA) is a statutory body (Criminal Injuries Compensation Authority Act 1995) which replaces the Criminal Injuries Compensation Board first set up under the Royal Prerogative in 1964. Like its predecessor, the CICA provides *ex gratia* compensation to victims of violence (or, if the victim dies, his dependants). The authority administers the Criminal Injuries Compensation Scheme made by the Home Secretary in the exercise of powers conferred by the 1995 Act which applies to all applications received by the CICA on or after 1 April 1996. Under the scheme compensation is assessed in manner similar to that used by courts when assessing damages for personal injuries. However there are important differences:

    (i) The 'general award' is set according to a detailed tariff running from level 1 (£1,000, eg chipped front tooth requiring crown) to level 25 (£250,000, eg quadriplegia).

   (ii) Claims in respect of loss of earnings are subject to certain limits (eg no claim for first 28 weeks; all claims capped at earnings equal to one-and-a-half times the gross national average).

  (iii) The compensation is subject to set minimum and maximum figures. No compensation is payable for injuries which, according to the tariff, do not merit a general award at level 1. The maximum payable on any single claim is £500,000.

The scheme itself, a detailed guide thereto plus tariff and a claim form are obtainable free of charge from the Criminal Injuries Compensation Authority, Tay House, 300 Bath Street, Glasgow G2 4JR (telephone 0141-331 2726; fax 0141-331 2287).

Chapter 3

Legal Aid

The Legal Aid Act 1988 contains two schemes under which persons of limited means can obtain financial help from the state in bringing or defending a civil action in the High Court or county court. First, *legal advice and assistance* which for present purposes can be regarded as providing the first two hours worth of work by a solicitor at the start of the action. Secondly, *legal aid* which entitles the applicant to retain at the state's expense (possibly subject to certain contributions) a solicitor both to represent him in proceedings and to take the preliminary steps in investigation and negotiation in just the same way as a privately instructed solicitor would.

Both schemes apply to any person regardless of nationality, domicile or residence. However, the word 'person' in this context is defined to exclude companies and other artificial persons unless they are acting in 'a representative, fiduciary or official capacity' (s 2(10) of the 1988 Act). Thus, companies, however impecunious, cannot apply except in the case of, eg, a trust corporation such as Barclays Bank Trust Company plc when it is acting for a modest trust or estate.

Both schemes are arranged and administered by the Legal Aid Board on behalf of the Lord Chancellor. From time to time the Board prepares a *Handbook* setting out all the relevant statutory materials, notes for guidance thereon and other reference materials. The current edition is the *Legal Aid Handbook 1996/97*.

Advice and assistance

The legal advice and assistance scheme is generally referred to as the 'Green Form Scheme'. Under this scheme, any person who is over school-leaving age and who is financially eligible can obtain the following services from a solicitor (and, if necessary in an exceptional case, from counsel):

(1) Oral or written *advice* on any question of English law concerning the client.

(2) Oral or written *advice* as to the steps the client may take in relation to that question.

(3) *Assistance* in taking those steps, including for example writing letters on the client's behalf, but excluding speaking for the client in court.

(4) *Assistance by way of representation* (ABWOR) ie advising and assisting a client and speaking in court on his behalf. See generally, 1988 Act, s 2.

In the context of this book, the conduct of High Court and county court cases, ABWOR is virtually non-existent. It is limited to county court cases in which it is not reasonably possible to obtain *emergency legal aid* (see below), the client has not already been refused state help in connection with these proceedings and is financially eligible and the court authorises the representation of the client at a hearing which has begun or is about to begin, by a solicitor who happens to be within the precincts of the court in connection with some other business (Legal Advice and Assistance (Scope) Regulations 1989, reg 8).

A typical example of ABWOR in the context of this book would be a defendant to a possession action who turns up at the trial without having previously consulted a solicitor but whose defence or circumstances appear to be complex. The judge might invite a solicitor at court for another matter to advise this defendant and may grant ABWOR for the purpose of the possession hearing.

The application for Green Form help requires brief details of the case, and of the client's financial eligibility (pp 2 and 3 of a proposed new draft form are illustrated at fig 3). There is no question of merits at this stage. It should be completed by the solicitor and by the client in person. However, it may be completed by another person authorised by the client if the client cannot attend for good reason (Legal Advice and Assistance Regulations 1989 (LAA Regs 1989), reg 10). The usual reason would be that the client was ill or temporarily disabled by the accident on which advice is now sought. If a child or patient under the Mental Health Act 1983 asks for advice and assistance, Green Form is not normally available. It is available to a parent, guardian, receiver or next friend on the child's behalf (LAA Regs 1989, reg 14). One form should be completed for each separate matter on which the solicitor is consulted (LAA Regs 1989, reg 17). Financial eligibility is calculated by the solicitor and in this as in all other forms of legal aid, the means of cohabitees (defined as a man and a woman living together in the same household as husband and wife (LAA Regs 1989, reg 13 and Sched 2(2)) are now aggregated in the same way as husband and wife unless they have a contrary interest in the matter in question.

In order to qualify, the applicant's net disposable income and capital must be within the limit prescribed by regulation. It is worth noting that allowances against income are fewer in Green Form and ABWOR than in civil legal aid and the capital allowance is less for Green Form than ABWOR, and less in both than in the calculation for eligibility for civil

[*continued on p 45*]

Fig 3: Green Form (extract)

Type of advice

Matrimonial and family: ☐ Divorce   ☐ Judicial separation   ☐ Nullity

☐ Injunctions and committal   ☐ Financial and property   ☐ Actions involving children

Non-matrimonial:

☐ Negligence (includes personal injury)   ☐ Employment   ☐ Malicious falsehood

☐ Nuisance   ☐ Debt   ☐ Immigration

☐ Trespass   ☐ Company Law   ☐ Administrative Law

☐ Interference with goods   ☐ Contract   ☐ Probate and inheritance

☐ Wrongful arrest, false imprisonment or malicious prosecution   ☐ Housing   ☐ Intellectual property

☐ Land law (includes s14 Trusts of Land and Appointment of Trustees Act 1996)   ☐ Data protection

☐ Partnership   ☐ Advice and assistance for wills

☐ Criminal   ☐ Trusts

Main alleged offence: _____   Date of alleged offence: ____/____/____

Case details

Give a brief description of the case and the issues involved:

Date of any incident: ____/____/____

If the client is the petitioner in a matrimonial case, has the petition been drafted?

☐ Yes   ☐ No

Can the claim be assessed in monetary terms?   ☐ Yes   ☐ No

If yes, give an estimate of the value £____:____

Is property at issue?   ☐ Yes   ☐ No

If yes, is it: ☐ Land - value £____:____   ☐ Money - value £____:____

☐ Other - value £____:____   Details:_____

Your client's involvement

Is your client: ☐ bringing the case?   ☐ defending the case?   ☐ involved in another way?

If involved in another way, say how:

Fig 3: contd

Capital details

How many dependants does your client have?
(partner, children or other dependent relatives in the client's household)

_____

Give the total savings and other capital which
your cleint has (and their partner, if relevant):

The client: £ _____ : _____

Partner (if living with the client as man and wife): £ _____ : _____

Total: £ _____ : _____

Income details

Does your client get Income Support, Income Based Job Seeker's Allowance, Family Credit or Disability Working Allowance?

☐ Yes. Ignore the rest of this section   ☐ No. Give the total weekly income of:

The client: £ _____ : _____

The client's partner (if living with the client as man and wife): £ _____ : _____

Total: £ _____ : _____

Calculate the total allowable deductions:

Income tax: £ _____ : _____

National Insurance contributions: £ _____ : _____

Partner (if living with the client as man and wife): £ _____ : _____

Attendance allowance, disability living allowance, constant
attendance allowance and any payment made out of the
Social Fund: £ _____ : _____

Dependent children and other dependants:

	Age	Number	
Up to 11	_____	£ _____ : _____	
11 to 16	_____	£ _____ : _____	
16 to 18	_____	£ _____ : _____	
18 and over	_____	£ _____ : _____	

Less total deductions: £ _____ : _____

Total weekly disposable income: £ _____ : _____

legal aid. It does not therefore follow that the client who is ineligible for Green Form will be refused either ABWOR or a civil legal aid certificate on financial grounds.

The Green Form scheme provides remuneration for up to two hours work (three hours in divorce and judicial separation cases) and thus a solicitor can claim up to two times the prescribed hourly rate. As at April 1997 the rates were £44 per hour and £46.50 in London *Legal Aid Handbook 1996/97*, p 530 and [1997] *Gazette* 26 March, p 4 reporting a legal aid pay freeze for 1997: firms awarded a franchise by the Legal Aid Board are paid higher rates).

As the Green Form itself indicates, any money or property recovered or preserved by the client is subject to a lien known as the 'statutory charge'. This charge is explained in greater detail in the context of a full certificate. However it is important to note at this stage certain practical differences in its application between Green Form and ABWOR on one hand and civil legal aid on the other. In Green Form and ABWOR the solicitor does not account to the Board for property recovered or preserved. The statutory charge arises in favour of the solicitor (s 11(2)) and not in favour of the Board as it does in civil legal aid (s 16(6)). The solicitor therefore recoups costs directly from the property and accounts for any balance to the client. It may be therefore that the solicitor will not need to complete a claim for costs as there is no 'assessed deficiency' to claim. Where the property recovered or preserved is other than money, the solicitor may have difficulty in enforcing the charge. In that case, or where the solicitor thinks it would cause 'grave hardship or distress' to enforce the charge, the solicitor can apply to the Board to waive it (LAA Regs 1989, reg 33). If the Board agrees, the solicitor claims against the fund a sum which would otherwise have been recovered through the statutory charge.

In cases where civil litigation is contemplated, the Green Form is used merely to set the wheels in motion, to initiate the investigations and negotiations and to finance the completion of the forms of application for a full certificate.

Civil legal aid

Civil legal aid covers non-criminal litigation including personal injury, contract disputes, negligence, matrimonial, consumer and debt matters. If the client is financially eligible and the case has merit, the client will be granted a legal aid certificate. The solicitor will pursue the action under the terms of that certificate, and at the end claim payment from the legal aid fund.

Part IV (ss 14–18) of the 1988 Act provides the framework and there are a large number of regulations governing this apparently simple transaction. Civil legal aid is available *inter alia* for the following matters:

(1) all civil actions before any county court, the High Court, Court of Appeal and House of Lords. References by an English court to the European Court of Justice are covered where the matter is one for which civil legal aid is available. No other 'European' applications are covered;

(2) matrimonial matters except most undefended petitions for divorce or judicial separation; and

(3) family matters in the magistrates' court (however, these matters are normally covered by a grant of ABWOR).

Civil legal aid is not available *inter alia* for:

(1) defamation;

(2) county court proceedings connected with a judgment summons, or solely relating to how a defendant pays a debt or costs;

(3) small claims (see p 279).

New forms of application are to be introduced in 1997. They are designed so as to enable most clients to complete them without the help of a solicitor. However the Green Form can be used to pay for help given (if the client is financially eligible for Green Form assistance). Because the application is more likely to be granted if the proper information is provided, it is worth the solicitor making the application. In any case there are certain parts of the form which must be completed by the solicitor: p 2, which specifies the need for the solicitor to have a valid practising certificate and p 11 in which the solicitor certifies that certain matters have been explained to the client, namely:

(1) the effect of the statutory charge;

(2) the duty on the client to inform the Board of changes in the client's financial circumstances; and

(3) the solicitor's estimates as to the prospects of success in the proceedings and as to the likely costs thereof.

Pages 7 and 11 of a proposed new draft form are illustrated at fig 4. It is very important to explain these matters to the client, especially the statutory charge which may have a fundamental effect on the outcome of the case, and therefore on its conduct. It is good practice to follow up the oral explanation with a letter to the client. The client will also receive a second notice about the statutory charge and about the possibility of an order for costs against the client, when the Legal Aid Board sends an offer of legal aid. A legal aid application can be made to any area office, but in practice it is made to the area in which the solicitor practises.

Generally speaking an applicant can expect to wait at least two weeks after submitting his application form before he is notified of the result. In urgent cases, eg just before expiry of a limitation period, or when the client is a defendant against whom proceedings have already begun, it is

[*continued on p 49*]

Fig 4: Application for legal aid (extract)

Costs and merits

➤ *Your solicitor must fill in this section*

Which of the following best describes the prospects of achieving the outcome your client wants?

☐ A Very good
     (80%+)

☐ B Good
     (60–80%)

☐ C Average
     (50–60%)

☐ D Below
     average

☐ E Impossible to say.
     Seeking a limited certificate.

If you have ticked boxes C, D or E please say what factors lead you to make this assessment and why legal aid should be granted:

Estimate your likely final costs, assuming the case goes to trial, including disbursements. Your estimate will need to take account of your view of likely settlement.

☐ Less than £1,500

☐ £1,500–£2,500

☐ £2,500–£5,000

☐ £5,000–£7,500

☐ £7,500–£10,000

☐ Over £10,000

If over £10,000 please give an approximate amount £_____:_____

Give an estimate of the likely value of any claim   £_____:_____

If you have selected box E, or are seeking a limited certificate for other reasons, tell us what work needs to be done under a limited certificate and at what cost.

at an estimated cost of: £_____:_____

Give details of any properties which are in dispute, e.g. shares, insurance policies, a boat, a house, business, money.

Address
of property in dispute _____
(if relevant)

Town: _____

County: _____ Postcode: _____

Fig 4: contd

Declaration to be signed by the applicant

➤ *This page must be completed.*

I promise to tell the Legal Aid Board straight away if:

➤ my financial position changes;
➤ I stop living with my spouse or partner;
➤ I get married or start living with somebody as husband and wife;
➤ I change my address.

I also promise to provide information promptly if the Legal Aid Board asks me for it.

I understand that:

➤ if I do not keep these promises, my legal aid may be stopped or cancelled;
➤ if my legal aid is cancelled, I will have to pay for all my case as if I never had legal aid and, if the court orders me to pay my opponent's solicitor's charges, I will be liable for them as if I never had legal aid;
➤ the Legal Aid Board may use any information about my case to carry out any of its functions under the Legal Aid Act 1988, but my name and other personal details which could identify me will be kept confidential;
➤ I may have to pay for some or all of my case, out of any money or property I recover or protect;
➤ unless my legal aid contribution is NIL, I will be sent an offer of legal aid which sets out the contribution I will have to pay if I accept the offer;
➤ if my financial position changes my legal aid contribution could be changed;
➤ if I no longer qualify financially, my legal aid will be stopped;
➤ If I get emergency legal aid, this will only cover urgent action and will be cancelled if I do not qualify financially or if I do not accept an offer of full legal aid.

My solicitors have given me to keep:

➤ The Legal Aid Board's leaflet explaining what happens next;
➤ The Legal Aid Board's leaflet explaining the statutory charge.

My solicitors have explained the legal aid statutory charge to me.

I authorise the Legal Aid Board to give information about my case to:

_____

As far as I know, all the information I have given is true and I have not withheld any relevant information. I undrstand that if I knowingly give false information or withhold relevant information my legal aid may be stopped or cancelled and criminal proceedings may be taken against me.

Signed: _____   Date:___/___/_____

Solicitor's certificate

I certify that:

➤ We have explained to the applicant their obligations and the meaning of their declaration.
➤ We have given the applicant to keep the Legal Aid Board's leaflets referred to in their declaration and have explained the statutory charge to them.
➤ We have provided as accurately as possible the information requested on page 7 of this form.

Signed: _____   Date:___/___/_____
(A Solicitor)

Name: _____

possible to obtain an emergency certificate within twenty-four hours. If it later turns out that the client is not financially eligible for legal aid, this emergency certificate will later be revoked rather than discharged (as to the difference between revocation and discharge, see p 58).

Financial eligibility

Assessment of means is carried out by the DSS Benefits Agency. It is intended that ultimately the Board will have this responsibility (s 3(4)).

Eligibility depends on the level of the applicant's disposable income and capital. This is assessed in accordance with the Civil Legal Aid (Assessment of Resources) Regulations 1989 as amended. 'Disposable' has the special meaning given to it by the regulations (CLA(R) Regs 1989, reg 4, Scheds 2 and 3). An applicant in receipt of income support is deemed to have disposable income and capital below the 'free' level and therefore makes no contribution. In outline, disposable income is calculated by taking a weekly income figure for the applicant and spouse or cohabitee, net of tax and national insurance, deducting permitted allowances including the cost of travel to work, housing costs and fixed sums in respect of dependants. Disposable capital comprises any capital asset which belongs to the applicant, their spouse or cohabitee at the date of the application. The DSS can also take into account any assets which the applicant has disposed of or converted in order to make himself eligible for legal aid or in order to reduce any contribution payable (CLA(R) Regs 1989, reg 9). Excluded from the assessment are the applicant's home (save to the extent that its net value exceeds £100,000), tools of trade and the subject matter of the dispute.

It is worth stressing that resources now include not only those of the applicant's spouse, provided they are living together and do not have a contrary interest but also any other person in the same household with whom the applicant is living as husband or wife. It is also worth noting that, although the subject matter of the dispute (eg the damages claimed or the share of the house being fought over) is excluded from the financial eligibility test, it may later become subject to the statutory charge (see p 53).

There are special regulations governing the treatment of applications by those acting in a representative fiduciary or official capacity (eg their personal resources are not normally taken into account; CLA(R) Regs 1989, regs 6 and 8). Since 1990 parents' income and capital are no longer taken into consideration in a child's application.

Once the certificate is granted, the assisted person is under a duty to inform the Area Director of any changes in means throughout the life of the certificate, if he believes the changes may affect the terms of the certificate or its continuation. A reassessment will be made by the DSS if the assisted person's resources have increased or decreased by more than the amounts specified in the assessment regulations, or there is new evidence which would affect the assessment made.

Merits of the application

The main question which the Area Director must ask in deciding on the merits of the application is whether the client has satisfied the Board that he has reasonable grounds for taking, defending or being party to the proceedings in question (s 15(2) and (3)). The Civil Legal Aid (General) Regulations 1989 (CLA Regs 1989), regs 29 and 30 also list other considerations which the Area Director must take into account when considering the application:

(1) the applicant would gain only trivial advantage from the proceedings, eg a boundary dispute over a narrow and valueless strip of land;

(2) it is not a matter where a solicitor would normally be employed, eg a small claim (see p 279);

(3) the applicant could finance the proceedings from another source, eg he has legal insurance; or

(4) the applicant is a member of a body which might help him, eg a trade union or motoring organisation.

It is not the job of the Area Director to try the case, and indeed often both sides are in receipt of legal aid.

Grant or refusal of certificate

If a certificate is to be granted on terms that the client will pay a contribution towards the cost, an offer of legal aid is sent out direct to the client, with a copy to the solicitor. The contribution specified may be from income or capital or both. A contribution payable from capital is normally required in full immediately whereas contributions required from income are normally payable on a monthly basis during the currency of the certificate. If no contribution is payable the offer stage is omitted and a certificate sent out immediately.

The application may of course be refused. If it is, the applicant will be sent a notice of refusal. Grounds for refusal are:

(1) financial ineligibility—no appeal;

(2) proceedings for which legal aid may not be given;

(3) reasonable grounds for being party to the proceedings not shown; or

(4) it is unreasonable in all the circumstances of the case.

If the ground for refusal is (3) or (4) the notice of refusal must give brief reasons. There is no right of appeal from the refusal of an application for an emergency certificate or from a refusal of any certificate on financial eligibility grounds (or as to the amount of contributions required). The applicant can appeal against a refusal under (2), (3) and (4) to the area committee, which considers the application afresh. The procedure is contained in CLA Regs 1989, regs 36–38. The committee can grant the application on such terms as it thinks fit, or refuse it, or refer it back to the Area Director. The committee's decision is final. An unsuccessful applicant can apply for legal aid again in the same matter in the event of a relevant change, eg a new witness comes forward. However, beware of pestering the area office with any particular application as this can lead to a prohibitive direction against the applicant. This can bar the applicant from applying for legal aid on a particular matter, or on any matter at all, for up to five years.

Scope of the certificate

Each certificate covers only one matter and one client. If the client has more than one problem a certificate is required for each matter. Two or more clients involved in the same action each need their own certificate. The certificate when issued may be either limited in its scope or conditional. It is always advisable to keep a copy of the certificate and any subsequent amendments on top of the file or in some other clearly visible place, so as to be reminded of the cover available, as the solicitor will not be paid by the Board for work done outside the scope of the certificate, and may not claim payment from the client.

Common examples of limitations are:

(1) to counsel's opinion only;
(2) to all steps up to close of pleadings, and counsel's opinion thereafter.

Once the limit is reached, application must be made to the Area Director for the certificate to be amended before any further action can be taken.

A further limiting factor on all certificates is the requirement that authority be obtained for expenditure on counsel's fees in certain circumstances. Two or more counsel or a Queen's Counsel may not be used without express prior authority (CLA Regs 1989, reg 59(1)). The regulations also permit application for prior authority in several other cases. The advantage to the solicitor of applying is that provided the expenditure is still relevant and necessary when incurred and the solicitor does not go beyond the authority given, no question can be raised on taxation about the sums spent. If costs are incurred for which prior authority could have been but was not obtained the costs are not necessarily disallowed, but are not guaranteed in the same way. The expenditure contemplated is experts' reports, transcriptions, and other acts either unusual in themselves or unusually expensive. As well as obtaining the authority of the Area Director, the solicitor should also obtain his own client's authority for all non-routine expenses. This authority should be in writing for particularly large ones. It may be the fund's money that is being spent whilst the certificate is current, but at the end of the case the client may be paying as a result of a contribution or the statutory charge (in *Re Solicitor: Taxation of Costs* [1982] 1 WLR 745).

Effect on the conduct of litigation

Duty to notify court and other parties

Immediately upon receipt of the certificate or, if proceedings have not yet commenced, when they do, the solicitor must file the original certificate at the appropriate court office and must inform all other parties of the fact that the client has legal aid by giving notice of issue in the prescribed form (CLA Regs 1989, reg 50); as to penalties for non-compliance see *wasted costs orders*, p 537.

Similar obligations to file and give notice also arise whenever a certificate is revoked, discharged or amended (on these topics, see further, p 58). There is one exception. Although copies of amendment must be filed with the court, no notice of amendment need be given to other parties if the amendment merely relates to the amount of contribution payable.

When giving other parties notice of issue or notice of amendment, should the notice reveal the contents of any condition or limitation on the certificate? Many years ago the Legal Aid Regulations imposed a rule of secrecy but this was not repeated in the 1989 Regulations (see further, a 1956 Practice Direction, reference to which still lingers on in the *White Book* 4055). This is no prescribed form of notice. The relevant regulations were amended in 1994 to refer to 'a form approved by the Board' but, as yet, no general approval of any form has been published.

Arguments in favour of secrecy include:

(1) Compliance with the guidance set out in the *Legal Aid Handbook 1996/97*, at p 87.
(2) The desirability of keeping all confidential information secret unless and until one is clearly instructed or required not to.

Arguments agains secrecy include:

(1) Case law: *Scarth v Jacobs-Paton* (1978) *The Times*, 1 November (but see how this case is explained in the *Legal Aid Handbook 1996/97*, at p 98).
(2) The apparent futility of a notice which states, eg 'an amendment has been made to the conditions and limitations on the certificate' if the recipient knows neither the original conditions and limitations (if any) nor the new ones.
(3) The fact that rules of court give all parties an unfettered right to inspect any document filed in the action (RSC Ord 63, rr 4 and 4A; CCR Ord 50, r 10).
(4) The fact that copies of any amendment are included in the *setting down bundle* in the High Court and in the *trial bundle* in the

county court (CLA Regs 1989, reg 54(2), RSC Ord 34, r 3 and CCR Ord 17, r 12; as to the bundles mentioned, see further, p 492).

When instructing counsel, a copy of the certificate and any amendments must always be enclosed with each set of instructions. This puts counsel on notice to check that the certificate covers what he is instructed to do (see *Legal Aid Handbook 1996/97*, p 88).

Relationship between solicitor and client

The normal duties in a solicitor/client relationship apply when a legal aid certificate has been issued. In addition certain extra duties arise once the client becomes legally aided. The regulations impose a duty on the solicitor named on the certificate to report matters affecting the certificate to the Board (CLA Regs 1989, regs 66–72). The regulations override the solicitor's usual duty of confidentiality to his client. The solicitor must breach this when required by the regulations, whether the client agrees or not.

The essence of the regulations is that if the client acts unreasonably in any way or provides false information, or if the solicitor feels that for any reason it is not reasonable for the client to continue to be assisted under a certificate the solicitor must report this fact to the Area Director. Virtually all certificates are now issued with a condition requiring the solicitor to report to the area office if and when the profit costs, disbursements and counsel's fees reach a stated figure. The Legal Aid Board treat this as akin to the restriction which a fee-paying client may place upon his/her solicitor authorising expenditure only up to a stated amount (see further, the *Legal Aid Handbook 1996/97*, pp 94, 95).

The sanctions against the solicitor for breach of these duties are that he may not be paid all or any of his costs, and if the fund has lost money, he may have to make up the deficit. The sanctions against the client are that his certificate may be discharged or revoked and he may be sued for any loss to the fund and also prosecuted (s 39). The solicitor is also under duties at the end of the proceedings in respect of property which may be the subject of the statutory charge.

The statutory charge

The Legal Aid Board has a statutory charge over all money or other property 'recovered or preserved' for the assisted party 'in the proceedings' whether by judgment or compromise (s 16(6)).

The meaning of the section is very wide. *'Property'* includes all financial compensation, and real or personal property, wherever situated, including all rights under any compromise or settlement and any costs recovered. *'Recovered'* means that the client has successfully claimed or asserted rights to property or to part of it. *'Preserved'* means that the client has warded off another's claim or assertion of rights to property or to part of it.

> The underlying principle of the charge is to put the legally assisted person as far as possible in the same position in relation to proceedings as an unassisted person, whose first responsibility at the end of the proceedings is to pay whatever legal costs are not being paid by the other side. It prevents an assisted person from making a profit at the expense of legal aid and is a deterrent to running up costs unreasonably. (*Legal Aid Handbook 1996/97*, p 132)

Before property can be touched by the charge it must have been recovered or preserved 'in the proceedings'. It is a question of fact whether or not property has been the subject of the proceedings. It is not necessary for court action to have been taken. The statutory charge potentially arises in respect of costs incurred during the certificate when a matter is settled by negotiation without actual court proceedings. Property which has been challenged in correspondence only and for reasons of tactics alone can be the subject of the charge. One *caveat* to this is that by deliberately excluding property from the contest the client's means are thereby increased, as it is no longer property in dispute.

In an ideal world the victorious client would not only come away from a case with the compensation he sought but with all his costs met by the losing party. However, in reality the client often does have to pay some costs even when he wins if the whole amount could not be justified on taxation, or he did not get a full order for costs. Where the client is legally aided the statutory charge comes into play at this point. Any claim for costs which the solicitor has against the Board for whatever reason is met by the Board first out of the client's contribution, then out of 'any property which is recovered or preserved for him in the proceedings' (s 16(6)), even if this should happen to consume all the client's winnings.

Whatever the circumstances in which the charge arises, the solicitor must follow the procedure of reporting the matter to the Board, and paying over moneys, eg damages recovered, in full to the Board pending the outcome of taxation/assessment of the solicitor's costs (CLA Regs 1989, Pt XI). This is not the complete story, however as the position is mitigated in practice in several ways, most notably by the powers of postponement of the charge in certain cases, the exceptions to the charge and the right of the solicitor to ask the Board to take only that sum which will protect its interests and release the balance to the assisted person.

Rules on the postponement of the charge are contained in CLA Regs 1989, regs 96 and 97. These permit the Board in certain cases to postpone the enforcement of the charge not only where a home is recovered or preserved, but also where money is awarded for the purchase of a home for the assisted person and/or dependants. Simple interest will be added to the charge.

The exceptions to the charge are listed in CLA Regs 1989, reg 94 for the full certificate and LAA Regs 1989, reg 32 and Sched 4 for the solicitor's charge under the Green Form scheme. In non-matrimonial cases the only notable exceptions are interim payments of debts or damages (see p 308) and in the case of Green Form any enforcement which would cause grave hardship or distress to the client or where enforcement itself would be unreasonably difficult.

The statutory charge bites, in favour of the legal aid fund, upon any property (including money) recovered or preserved by the assisted person. In some cases, the opposing party is also allowed to bite upon that property. In these cases the general rule is that the opposing party is allowed the first bite. Consider the following three cases.

In *Cooke v Head (No 2)* [1974] 1 WLR 972 both parties had legal aid. In their dispute as to the ownership of a bungalow which had been bought in the defendant's name, the Court of Appeal held that the plaintiff was entitled to a one-third share and that the defendant should pay the costs of the action and appeal. Each party had therefore 'recovered or preserved property' and therefore each party's share was subject to a statutory charge. It was held that the defendant's share should first be used to pay the plaintiff's order for costs (so minimising statutory charge problems for the plaintiff) and would then be available to discharge his own costs of the litigation. In the result, the one-third owner ended up with £704 and the two-thirds owner £98.

> This shows that when the sole asset is the proceeds of a house, it is much better for the disputing parties to settle at the outset: because, if they go to law, much of these proceeds will be eaten up in costs, even though the parties are both legally aided with a nil contribution (*per* Lord Denning MR, *Cooke v Head (No 2)*).

In *Cook v Swinfen* [1967] 1 WLR 457 a legally aided plaintiff recovered damages against the defendant but, because she failed to beat a payment into court, was ordered to pay a large part of the costs (see p 334). The defendant was held entitled to set off the damages he was obliged to pay against the costs he was entitled to receive. The statutory charge would operate against the net award of damages thus payable.

In *Lockley v National Blood Transfusion Service* [1992] 1 WLR 492 the plaintiff, an assisted person, lost an interlocutory battle against the defendant. The Court of Appeal allowed orders for costs against the plaintiff, including the costs of appeal, with directions that the sums payable under these orders should be set off against any damages and costs which the assisted person might *in future* recover in the action.

Costs against the assisted party

Generally speaking 'costs follow the event'. If the assisted person loses the action, an order requiring him to pay his opponent's costs may be made against him. However, the amount of costs which will be awarded to a winner where the opponent was legally aided is restricted (Legal Aid

Act 1988, s 17; for ABWOR cases, see s 12). Legally aided losers can be required to pay only an amount 'which is a reasonable one for him to pay, having regard to all the circumstances, including the financial resources of all the parties and their conduct in connection with the dispute' (s 17(1)). The court must examine both means and conduct of all involved before reaching a decision on what costs to order.

The assisted party is protected by s 17 only for the duration of the certificate and in respect of those matters covered by it. In all other circumstances, for example where the Board refuses to lift a limitation on a certificate, or after the certificate has been discharged but the proceedings continue, he is treated like an unassisted litigant. The client then has no special protection against a full order for the costs incurred outside the period he was legally aided. Moreover, s 17 gives no protection from orders setting off costs against any money or property recovered or preserved in the action (eg a *Lockley* order; see *Lockley v National Blood Transfusion Service* [1992] 1 WLR 492, above).

The question of costs can be decided either immediately, eg at the trial or at a determination hearing convened subsequently perhaps after an inquiry has been held into the assisted party's means. At the determination hearing the court fixes the maximum amount which the assisted person might be liable to pay in accordance with s 17. The court then decides the extent of the assisted person's liability, if any, within that maximum amount and when that liability should be met. The Area Director may attend the determination and/or submit written representations. In practice a determination hearing is likely to be held only in a case where the successful party wishes to apply for costs against the fund under s 13 or s 18 (see below). All this means further delay and expense for the successful unassisted party. After having succeeded at the trial there may be argument about costs following which there could be an adjournment to another occasion for the consideration of the means and liability of the unsuccessful legally aided party, to be followed by a formal application under s 18 (see below) which in turn is followed by a formal taxation of costs. Small wonder that this often proves all too much and that a practice rejected by the Court of Appeal thirty years ago (*Gooday v Gooday* [1969] P 1) still persists. This practice is for the court of trial to order the legally aided loser to pay the unassisted winner's costs limited to a sum equal to the amount which the legally aided party had to pay by way of contribution towards his own costs. This order has more simplistic symmetry to it than it has logic. Nonetheless it does have the merit of being simple and this no doubt explains why the practice persists.

Other possible orders (including the now quaintly named 'football pools order') are explained in and illustrated by *Parr v Smith* [1995] 2 All ER 1031 and *Wraith v Wraith* [1997] 2 All ER 536.

Costs against the fund

A successful unassisted party deprived of his costs by the workings of s 17 of the Act may turn for help to s 18 (s 13 in ABWOR cases). This allows the court in certain circumstances to order payment of all or part of those costs from the legal aid fund. The purpose of the section is to 'mitigate the hardship to a successful unassisted party of modest means' (*Megarity and others v The Law Society; Gayway Linings Ltd v The Law Society* [1981] 1 All ER 641).

There are several preconditions to the making of an order under s 18:

(1) the proceedings were instituted by the assisted party;

(2) they were finally decided in favour of the unassisted party;

(3) no order or only a partial order has been made because of s 17;

(4) it is just and equitable for the court to order all or part of the costs against the Board;

(5) the unassisted party would otherwise suffer severe financial hardship; and

(6) an order for costs would be made in the proceedings if it were not for the Legal Aid Act.

As to (1) *Proceedings instituted by the assisted party*: If the unassisted party commenced the proceedings, s 18 is not available to him. However where the unassisted party commenced the proceedings but is also the defendant to a counterclaim, he can apply for the costs of successfully defending the counterclaim. This is because a counterclaim is treated as separate proceedings and the unassisted party did not institute the counterclaim. Preconditions (1) and (5) apply to costs incurred at first instance only. They do not apply to costs of appeals.

As to (2) *Finally decided*: Proceedings are to be treated as finally decided in favour of the unassisted party if either there is no right to appeal, or the assisted party does not avail himself of his rights. A House of Lords decision on an interlocutory appeal is a final decision for the purposes of s 18 (*Herd v Clyde Helicopters Ltd* [1997] 2 WLR 380).

In favour of the unassisted party: This has been taken to mean 'wholly or substantially' in favour of the unassisted party. This re-definition offered by the Court of Appeal in *Kelly v London Transport Executive* [1982] 2 All ER 842, allows the court to look at the whole of the case and not just the final outcome. The principle seems to be that where the assisted party is defeated, or where the assisted party succeeds but only in a very limited way, such as to amount to a defeat, then for the purposes of an order under s 18 the unassisted party will be treated as successful.

As to (4) *Just and equitable in all the circumstances*: These words have been interpreted very broadly. Unless the unassisted party did a great deal to bring the litigation on himself, it generally follows that the 'just and equitable' requirement will be satisfied (*Hanning v Maitland (No 2)* [1970] 1 All ER 812).

As to (5) *Severe financial hardship*: After earlier restrictive intepreta-tions of these words, the Court of Appeal in *Hanning v Maitland (No 2)* (see above) interpreted them as applying to persons of 'modest income or modest capital who would find it hard to bear their own costs'. Precondition (5), like precondition (1), does not apply to costs of appeals. Multi-million pound organisations such as banks and local authorities frequently recover their costs in respect of successful appeals.

Where the unsuccessful assisted party was assisted for only part of the proceedings or for one issue among several or for one particular step, the rules under s 18 apply only to that part of the total costs incurred under the certificate. The basic procedure is that the unassisted party prepares an affidavit of costs and resources in prescribed form (CLA Regs 1989, reg 137 and Sched 2), and thereafter there is a determination at which a provisional order is made. The Area Director may appear or submit representations. Applications for costs by unassisted parties are usually referred to the district judge (regs 138 and 143).

Amendment, discharge and revocation of certificate

The Area Director has power to amend the certificate, as often as he thinks fit. Amendments are available:
(1) where there is a mistake in the certificate;
(2) to extend it to further proceedings or steps;
(3) to add or substitute parties;
(4) to cover cross-actions, cross-appeals or replies; or
(5) to change the named solicitor.
If the amendment in (2) above involves the lifting of a limitation on the certificate, and the Area Director is not minded to grant it, then before refusing he must give the assisted person opportunity to show cause why the application should not be refused and the certificate therefore discharged. Once the amendment has been granted notice of amendment must be given in the same way as when the certificate was originally issued (see p 52).

A client ceases to be an assisted party when his certificate is discharged or revoked. The effects of discharge and revocation are quite different. Discharge simply makes the client no longer an assisted party. He retains all the benefits of assistance in respect of matters which arose in the life of the certificate, in particular costs. The statutory charge will apply in respect of any costs under the certificate. Revocation means that the person is treated as if he never was assisted. He receives no help from the fund for any of his costs, and has none of the protection from an order for costs that a certificate otherwise gives. The Board can also recover from him all costs paid to the solicitor. The solicitor is not prejudiced by the revocation and is still paid for work done under the certificate.

A certificate may be discharged if the assisted party has become financially ineligible, or has required the case to be conducted unreason-ably or has fallen behind on his contributions.

Since revocation is a very serious penalty for the client there is only one situation where it is compulsory: if a client with an emergency certificate proves on assessment to be financially ineligible for a full certificate, the emergency certificate must be revoked. A solicitor applying for emergency legal aid should therefore attempt to assess the client's eligibility before applying and warn the client of the consequences if his position is borderline.

Revocation is an option available to the Area Director if the assisted party has lied to the Board in respect of his finances or the facts of the case. If revocation or discharge is being considered, the assisted party often has the opportunity to show cause why it should not be discharged/revoked before a decision is taken. Note that the Area Director's decision is appealable in the same way as is the refusal of a certificate.

Assessment of costs

At the conclusion of an action and before payment is made by the Board all costs must be taxed (see p 527), except:
(1) where there have been no court proceedings;
(2) where the costs and disbursements, excluding VAT, do not exceed £1,000 and there are no *inter partes* costs;
(3) where a matter is settled by consent with no direction as to costs on terms that include an agreed amount for all the solicitor's and counsel's costs of the assisted person;
(4) where a matter is brought to an end by judgment, decree or final order and there is agreement as to solicitor's and counsel's costs;
(5) where, by reason of special circumstances, taxation would be contrary to the interests of the assisted party or would increase the cost to the Board, eg the case has died and taxation will awaken the other side or the certificate is unclear due to the Board's error;
(6) where further costs are incurred after taxation, eg enforcing a costs order for the benefit of the Board (CLA Regs 1989, regs 105 and 106).

In (1) above, the simpler procedure of assessment *must* be used. Similarly assessment must be used where costs and disbursements excluding, VAT, do not exceed £500 and there are no *inter partes* costs. In (2)–(6) it is available as an alternative.

Assessment is a method of getting paid which is both simpler and quicker than taxation. It is obtained by completing the appropriate form. This has to be sent in duplicate to the area office together with the documents listed on the form. These include: vouchers, correspondence, pleadings, judgment or order, instructions to counsel and counsel's fee notes.

The Area Director then assesses the costs on the assumption that they are being taxed on the standard basis. An appeal against the assessment is made by written representations sent within twenty-one days to the area committee, setting out reasons in full and justifying the costs originally sought. If still dissatisfied after the result of that review, the solicitor may within twenty-one days of the result ask the committee to certify a point of principle of general importance. If this certificate is given he may appeal to a committee appointed by the Board. At each stage of the appeal the decision appealed may be confirmed, or amended by increasing or decreasing the assessment.

The solicitor must notify counsel of the result of the assessment if counsel's fees are reduced or disallowed (CLA Regs 1989, reg 105(8)). If counsel is dissatisfied he may ask in writing that the area committee review the assessment, before using the formal appeal procedure as above.

Payment on account of costs and disbursements

The private client is normally expected to pay the solicitor money on account of costs and to defray disbursements (see p 21). The Board does the same thing, though perhaps, on occasion, less flexibly or generously.

There are four possibilities, namely disbursements paid on account (CLA Regs 1989, reg 101), hardship to solicitor or counsel in a long running matter (CLA Regs 1989, reg 101(1)), counsel's fees unpaid six months after the end of the case (CLA Regs 1989, reg 101(2)) and most significantly the permanent payment on account system (CLA Regs 1989, reg 100).

The permanent payment on account system provides a means of regular payments on account of costs incurred during the life of the certificate. Claims can be made annually in a period not more than two months before or four months after the anniversary date of a certificate.

The amount to be claimed on each occasion is the total of all costs, disbursements and VAT to the date of the claim, including any amounts previously paid on account. The Board pays a prescribed percentage of the total amount claimed on account less any previous payment on account. These sums must be brought into account after the final taxation/assessment.

If at the conclusion of the case there is no claim on the fund, all costs and disbursements received on account are recouped by the Board. The Board will deduct the amount of a returnable payment on account from the next composite payment it makes to the solicitor which will of course be on totally different matters from the one where the payment on account was made.

Chapter 4

Personal Injury Damages

This chapter is intended to provide an introduction to the general principles applicable to the classification and calculation of damages in the largest category of compensation claims, personal injury claims. The first classification to be made is between *special damages* and *general damages*. Special damages in this context are items of pecuniary loss which can be quantified precisely, eg the cost of repairs, medical expenses, travelling expenses and loss of earnings from date of accident to trial. Each of these items claimed has to be specifically pleaded (see Chapter 9).

General damages are not capable of precise calculation. They have to be assessed by the trial judge (unless the case is tried by jury—rare in civil cases: see p 463—when the assessment is made by the jury). The judge will be guided, though not of course bound, by earlier cases. General damages include compensation for pain and suffering, loss of amenity, loss of future earnings and earning capacity and compensation for the cost of future expenses such as nursing or medical care. They do not have to be specifically pleaded as such, but particulars of the injuries suffered must be given. The plaintiff must also plead any special factors (eg the loss of exceptional career prospects: *Domsalla v Barr* [1969] 1 WLR 630) which the court would not normally infer.

Personal injury damages, both general and special, usually carry interest and this must also be pleaded. The detailed principles as to calculation of interest are described on p 75, and the method of pleading interest is described in Chapter 9.

Special damages

Loss of earnings to trial

Obviously the plaintiff's pleading will be able to state the plaintiff's losses only up to the date at which it is drafted. If it is the case that they will continue after the trial this must be pleaded (*Ilkiw v Samuels* [1963] 1 WLR 991).

The general measure of damages is *restitutio in integrum*, that is to put the plaintiff in the position he was in immediately before the accident. Thus the plaintiff can claim no more than he has lost. Damages for loss of earnings in this context are not taxable. Therefore, to prevent the plaintiff being over-compensated, the court takes into account the tax and national insurance he would have paid (*BTC v Gourley* [1956] AC 185; *Cooper v Firth Brown Ltd* [1963] 1 WLR 418) and any compulsory private pension contributions where his pension rights have been left unaffected (*Dews v NCB* [1986] 3 WLR 227). Thus he is allowed only the net loss and not the gross loss. By this method of assessment the plaintiff neither gains or loses. It is the defendant who gains and the Inland Revenue which loses.

The award may be increased to take into account the likelihood of overtime, promotion, bonuses etc. A common method of estimating the effect of these factors is to examine the earnings of a comparable employee or employees for a similar period.

The court also takes into account the benefit of any income tax rebate the plaintiff obtains (*Hartley v Sandholme Iron Co* [1975] QB 600). Since the personal allowances for income tax are calculated on an annual basis a plaintiff who returns to work after a tax year has started often pays no tax for the first few weeks. This 'income tax holiday' also has to be taken into account (*Brayson v Wilmot-Breedon* (1976) Kemp & Kemp 9–010).

The effect of these rules is that it is often simpler to calculate damages for past loss of earnings by working on an annual basis. It is necessary to know the plaintiff's tax position. One then calculates what his earnings would have been if he had worked throughout the tax year (6 April–5 April) and then calculates what his earnings actually were for the period in question. The difference is the net amount attributable to loss of past earnings. Doing the calculation in this way automatically takes into account the tax implications.

Contractual sick pay

If the plaintiff has been paid whilst off work as of right under the contract, then of course there is no loss of earnings and none can be claimed. The plaintiff's right to contractual sick pay thus benefits the defendant rather than the plaintiff. To meet this, many contracts of employment now guarantee employees a right to sick pay but, in return, the employee is required to pursue a claim for loss of earnings and to reimburse the employer appropriately. This gives the employee a legal entitlement to sick pay and also enables the employee to recover such payments from the defendant. Whether or not the employer is in fact reimbursed is a private matter between the employer and the plaintiff (as to employer's liability cases, ie injuries at work where the employer is the defendant, see *B R B v Franklin* [1993] *Gazette*, 23 June, at p 8).

Social security benefits

The state provides a variety of benefits which may be payable to an injured person. How do such benefits affect the calculation of damages?

The relevant legislation is now the Social Security Administration Act 1992 (the main provisions of which are set out in the *Green Book* 1279–1289). It contains a scheme the primary aim of which is to require defendants to reimburse the state for the benefits that the plaintiff has received. Therefore (to use the terms of the legislation) 'compensators' are required to deduct from 'compensation payments' sums equivalent to 'relevant benefits' paid to the victim over the 'relevant period' and pay such sums to the DSS.

As a general principle the legislation catches all compensation payments whether paid voluntarily or under order of the court and whether general or special damages. However, the original scheme operated unfairly in some cases, especially where the compensation agreed or ordered was heavily reduced because of contributory negligence. The full burden of state benefits was still recoupable by the state and was therefore deducted from the compensation. In some cases this could wipe out the compensation award. If it was likely to do so some plaintiffs accepted instead a 'small payment' not exceeding £2,500 which, at that time, meant that the State made no recoupment at all. Thus, because of the recoupment scheme the defendant gained and both the plaintiff and the State lost out.

For further details of the original scheme reference may be made to the previous edition of this book. As from 1 October 1997 a revised scheme applies to all cases not by then settled or determined. The new law is set out in the Social Security (Recovery of Benefits) Act 1997 the full text of which will no doubt appear in future editions of the *Green Book*. Under the new scheme a compensator must make a full refund to the State of certain benefits ('the listed benefits') and the exemption which used to apply to small payments is abolished. In order to protect the plaintiff the compensator is limited as to the heads of damage (see below) from which he can make deductions. For example, employment related state benefits paid to the plaintiff are deductible only from certain loss of earnings claims. Attendance allowances paid to the plaintiff and therefore recoupable by the state are deductible only from compensation claimed for the cost of care incurred during the relevant period. Mobility allowances paid to the plaintiff and therefore recoupable by the state are deductible only from compensation claimed for loss of mobility during the relevant period. In particular, no deductions can be made from the head of damages known as the 'pain and suffering' award (see below). Thus, under the new scheme, if the degree of contributory negligence is high the State still gains full recoupment, the plaintiff gets reduced damages but full state benefits and it is the defendant who 'loses out'.

The relevant period over which a benefit is paid begins in the case of an accident or injury on the day following the occurrence and in the case of a disease on the day of the first claim for benefit. The period ends five years later or when the final compensation is paid (whichever is sooner). There is, therefore, a definite cut-off point. There is no need to speculate as to what the victim's future entitlement to state benefit will be. Obviously, this cut-off point strongly encourages plaintiffs to reach an early compromise of their claims.

Within fourteen days of being notified of the claim, the alleged compensator must send a completed Form CRU1 to the Compensation Recovery Unit of the DSS at Reyrolle Building, Hebburn, Tyne and Wear NE31 1XB. This will give personal details of the victim; the accident; the victim's employer etc. Clearly, it is envisaged that the victim on making a claim must notify the alleged compensator of these details. Thereafter no compensation payment is to be paid until the CRU has furnished the compensator with a certificate of total benefit.

The certificate is obtained by the compensator by the means of Form CRU4. The CRU will acknowledge the application and a certificate will be issued to the compensator stating the amount of the benefit paid or to be paid by a specified date. As the case progresses, clearly more than one certificate may be necessary.

Having now received the certificate the compensator will deduct what he can from the compensation payment and on paying compensation to the victim will provide a certificate of deduction and pay to the CRU an amount equal to the full 'listed benefits' within fourteen days.

Other receipts

Redundancy payments are not to be deducted unless they relate to incapacity to work (*Colledge v Bass Mitchells and Butlers* [1988] 1 All ER 536). 'Charitable payments' such as moneys and gifts from friends are not taken into account as a matter of public policy (*Parry v Cleaver* [1970] AC 1). Similarly the plaintiff is not required to give credit for moneys received under a policy of insurance where he has paid the premiums (*Bradburn v Great Western Railway Co* [1874–80] All ER Rep 195).

Maintenance at the public expense

Section 5 of the AJA 1982 provides that any saving to an injured person which is attributable to his maintenance wholly or partly at the public expense in a hospital, nursing home or other institution is to be calculated and set off against any income lost as a result of the injuries. The saving may be made on food, drink and, in the rare case, rent and rates. However in practice the calculation is apparently frequently ignored as in the majority of cases the saving would be *de minimis*. In certain cases where the plaintiff is subject to lengthy detention in hospital the saving may be of significance.

Medical expenses

Section 2(4) of the Law Reform (Personal Injuries) Act 1948 provides that the plaintiff can claim the cost of private medical treatment. The plaintiff does not have to show that there were exceptional circumstances to justify private treatment, and the fact that the same treatment may have been available free under the National Health Service is ignored. Defendants' insurers may be willing to finance private medical treatment pre-trial since, if treatment is thereby obtained more quickly, the plaintiff's claim for damages for pain and suffering (see below) will then be diminished.

A plaintiff whose need for medical or nursing care is likely to continue after the trial is also entitled to general damages for future medical expenses. The calculation to be made is similar to the calculation made for damages for loss of future earnings (see below).

There must be deducted from any claim in respect of past or future medical expenses any maintenance element those expenses contain (*Lim Poh Choo v Camden & Islington Area Health Authority* [1980] AC 174 and compare AJA 1982, s 5, above, where deductions are made from lost earnings).

In the more catastrophic cases it may be that the plaintiff's home has to be adapted in order to cope with his disability or even new accommodation may have to be found. All or part of the outlay may be recoverable where necessary based on the multiplier and multiplicand system (for the method of calculation see *Roberts v Johnstone* [1988] 3 WLR 1247).

Services rendered by third persons

The plaintiff may claim the value of services provided by third persons (often, in practice, relatives) where those services have been rendered reasonably necessary by the accident. Thus, a plaintiff may add to a claim for special damages, eg reasonable expenses incurred and the value of wages reasonably foregone by a relative who visited him in hospital or who nursed him back to health (*Hunt v Severs* [1994] 2 AC 350 where in fact the sums claimed were disallowed on appeal; see further, below). It is unnecessary to show that the plaintiff is obliged to reimburse the third person or even that the third person actually incurred loss, eg loss of wages (*Cunningham v Harrison* [1973] QB 942). Similarly general damages may be awarded to cover any future losses and expenses likely to be incurred by third persons.

The question of quantum of compensation was considered by the Court of Appeal in *Housecroft v Burnett* [1986] 1 All ER 332. The court expressly rejected two extreme solutions:

(1) to assess the full commercial rate for supplying the needs by employing someone to do what the relative does;

(2) to assess the cost at nil just as it is assessed at nil where the plaintiff is cared for under the NHS.

The plaintiff's needs in each case must be considered on its own facts, as this element of the award is to provide a capital sum to the plaintiff to provide for reasonable and proper care including the ability to make reasonable recompense to a relative. Where the relative has given up gainful employment to look after the plaintiff the court should award sufficient to enable the plaintiff to ensure that the relative does not lose out, but the ceiling would be the commercial rate for providing the services which the relative now provides. The Court of Appeal declined to interfere with the judge's award of £39,000 in respect of the care provided by the plaintiff's mother (based on £3,000 *per annum*) where a twenty-two year old plaintiff would require such care and attention for the rest of her life.

In *Hunt v Severs* [1994] 2 AC 350 a young couple were injured in a motor cycle accident. The plaintiff, who had been riding pillion on her boyfriend's bike, was very severely injured. It was held that the accident was caused by his negligence. The trial judge awarded her damages against him exceeding £500,000 which included the following items:

> *Special damages*: £4,429, reasonable travel costs incurred by the defendant visiting the plaintiff in hospital and £17,000, the value of nursing care rendered by him up to the date of the trial.

> *General damages*: £60,000, the value of nursing care to be rendered by him in the future.

In the appeal to the House of Lords, all of these sums were disallowed. It was held that the defendant could not be ordered to pay the plaintiff extra damages simply to enable her to reward him for his generosity. It was said that to award such compensation would be wrong in principle, even though of course, in reality, this principle was protecting the defendant's insurers only and was financially disadvantageous to the defendant himself.

Agreeing special damages

In practice special damages are normally agreed. The plaintiff now has to provide a calculation of special damages annexed to the statement of claim (High Court) or particulars of claim (county court) (see further p 155). Consequently special damages can usually be agreed at an early stage of the action. It is merely a matter of calculation, and the rules are clear. If for some reason the parties cannot agree on the method of calculation, prepare a statement showing the alternative methods and agree their arithmetic. Then the judge only has to decide the method to adopt and not the actual *quantum*.

General damages

Pain and suffering

Damages may be awarded for past and future pain and suffering attributable to the injury and to any consequential operations etc. Such damages are assessed subjectively. The plaintiff must actually experience pain and suffering for any damages to be awarded under this head. Thus in *Wise v Kaye* [1962] AC 326 the House of Lords held that damages for pain and suffering were not recoverable for a period during which the plaintiff was unconscious and incapable of experiencing pain and suffering. Similarly, in *Deeley v McCarthy and Leeds Area Health Authority* [1977] CLY 764 where a boy aged three was seriously injured, the court included nothing for pain and suffering as the boy was totally unable to appreciate his condition. The award did, however, include a very large sum for loss of amenities.

Damages under this head include compensation for any mental anguish suffered and may take into account any additional, subjective, factors which increase the suffering. Thus in *Rourke v Barton* (1982) *The Times*, 23 June the injuries suffered by the plaintiff prevented her looking after her invalid husband; the additional distress this caused the plaintiff was taken into account. If, because of his injuries, the plaintiff's life expectancy has been reduced, the award for pain and suffering should take into account any suffering caused or likely to be caused by his awareness of that reduction. There is no separate head of damages for loss of expectation of life.

Loss of amenities

If the injuries deprive the plaintiff of some enjoyment he is entitled to damages under this head. The plaintiff is entitled to compensation for the deprivation of bodily capacity *per se* (*H West & Son Ltd v Shephard* [1964] AC 326). Thus an objective element is involved in the assessment. In addition the plaintiff must also be compensated for being deprived of any recreation or hobbies previously enjoyed. Thus, there is also a subjective element in the assessment. It is therefore necessary to inquire of the plaintiff what amenities have been lost. For example, a young man who has lost part of his right hand will obviously have suffered some loss of amenity in any case. The damages can be increased where appropriate to take account of the particular circumstances of the case. Thus, the loss of a right arm by a right-handed man whose hobbies included bowling at cricket and playing darts and skittles will be compensated by a greater award than would have been the case had his sole hobby been watching television. Age is, of course, always a factor, as the younger the plaintiff, the longer he has to live with the disability.

Damages for pain and suffering and for loss of amenity are generally assessed together and given as one lump sum. Awards of damages under these heads are also available for mental as well as physical impairment including, in particular, damages for nervous shock.

Loss of future earnings

The court will first assess the net annual loss as at the date of trial. It then applies the appropriate 'multiplier', and thereby calculates the appropriate lump sum award. What figure should be taken as the multiplier? If the plaintiff has a life expectancy of, say, twenty years and the net annual loss at the date of trial is, say, £10,000, then simply to multiply these two figures together would result in gross over-compensation. The plaintiff would receive a sum of £200,000 as a lump sum which could then be invested. The interest alone would compensate for actual loss, yet on eventual death of the plaintiff the capital would still be intact. Thus the multiplier is far less than the actual expectation of life. The aim is to provide a sum that could purchase an annuity yielding the appropriate annual loss for the relevant period. In calculating damages in this way the court assumes a nominal interest rate of four or five per cent. Thus the lump sum received by the plaintiff is, it is assumed, to be invested at this nominal rate of interest, and the income thus produced, plus an appropriate amount from the capital itself, will provide each year the amount of the loss. Gradually, the capital will be eaten into and the interest will diminish so that on the plaintiff's death there will be a nil balance. That is the theory behind calculating compensation for future loss of earnings. Of course, once he has received a lump sum the plaintiff can please himself what he does with it.

The discount to the multiplier also takes account of contingencies: eg early death or periods of unemployment. This means that in practice multipliers rarely exceed sixteen or seventeen, even if the plaintiff is young and has a normal life expectancy.

For some years now the Government has published certain actuarial tables for use in personal injury and fatal accident cases ('the Ogden Tables', see below) which strongly advocate the adoption of a lower nominal interest rate (two to three per cent). The difference is not significant in the case of short periods (eg the working life expectancy of a 58-year-old) but would substantially increase the compensation payable in larger cases. As a result of recommendations made by the Law Commission in a report published in 1994 Parliament has made two enactments which relate to this topic. However neither enactment is yet in force and there is some doubt as to whether they will ever be brought into force.

Under the Damages Act 1996, s 1 (not yet in force) the Lord Chancellor has power to prescribe the rate of interest which the courts should use. Under the Civil Evidence Act 1995, s 10 (when in force) the Ogden Tables will be admissible in evidence on production of an HMSO copy thereof. Controversy arises because, in *Wells v Wells* [1997] 1 WLR 652 the Court of Appeal heard full argument as to the rate of interest to adopt the Ogden Tables and the Law Commission recommendations but was not persuaded to change from the present conventional rate. That case is now on appeal to the House of Lords. It seems unlikely that s 1 of the Damages Act 1996 will be brought into force before proceedings in that case have been concluded. As to s 10 of the Civil Evidence Act 1995 Hirst LJ (giving the judgment of the court in *Wells v Wells*) stated as follows

> Clearly the Ogden Tables are very useful as a check and we therefore favour the sanction of their admissibility as proposed in section 10 of the Act of 1995,

together with those parts of the explanatory notes which are truly explanatory. This recommendation does not however apply to those parts of the explanatory notes which espouse [a nominal rate of interest] as the appropriate guideline.

Loss of earnings and loss of marriage prospects

For most women who marry there is a possibility that, for at least part of their married life, they will cease paid work for a number of years in order to bring up children. This must be taken into account in any compensation for loss of future earnings. But what of the case of a woman or girl who, because of her injuries, is now unlikely ever to work and unlikely ever to marry? She has lost the opportunity to earn, and the chance of happiness which marriage can bring, and the economic support of a husband which would have been important during the child-rearing years. The principles to be applied were considered in *Hughes v McKeown* [1985] 1 WLR 963. Where the prospects of earnings and the prospects of marriage are both nil, a full loss of future earnings award should be made (ie without a notional deduction in respect of child-rearing years since there will be none) and an additional sum should be allowed in the pain and suffering and loss of amenity award to cover the loss of comfort and companionship which marriage might have brought. This latter sum should not include any element of economic loss relevant to the loss of prospects of marriage since that has already been allowed for in the loss of earnings award. (In the end, the multiplier to be used and the compensation for loss of marriage prospects to be awarded are the same whether the plaintiff is male or female.) In *Housecroft v Burnett* [1986] 1 All ER 332 these principles were approved, subject to the qualification that some reduction should be made in the case of a woman who would have received very high earnings.

Loss of earnings and loss of life expectancy

When a plaintiff's life expectancy has been shortened by the accident the loss of earnings claim is to be calculated as follows. The relevant multiplier is the *pre-accident* life expectancy but this is subdivided into two parts: his *actual* life expectancy (as shortened by the accident) and the remaining balance which is known as *the lost years*. Each part of the multiplier is subject to its own multiplicand. For the actual life expectancy the multiplicand is the usual one, the net annual loss as at the date of the trial. For the lost years the usual multiplicand is reduced by an estimated sum which is intended to represent what would have been the plaintiff's living expenses during the lost years (*Pickett v British Rail Engineering Ltd* [1980] AC 134). The estimation of living expenses here differs substantially from a superficially similar calculation in Fatal Accidents Act cases (*Harris v Empress Motors Ltd* [1984] 1 WLR 212; *Phipps v Brooks Dry Cleaning Services Ltd* (1996) *The Times*, 18 July).

Where a victim of negligence dies (whether instantly, at the time of the accident, or before litigation is completed) his estate may bring proceedings under the Law Reform (Miscellaneous Provisions) Act 1934. The estate is entitled to recover reasonable funeral expenses and any special damages the deceased could have claimed including loss of earnings for the period (if any) between the date of the accident and the date of his death. A claim can also be made for general damages for pain and suffering and loss of amenity, unless, at the time of the accident, the deceased was killed instantly (*Hicks v Chief Constable of South Yorkshire Police* [1992] 2 All ER 65). 'Lost years' compensation is now restricted to living plaintiffs only. Where the victim of negligence dies instantly, or before litigation is completed, the 1934 Act claim should not include a claim for lost years' compensation. Instead, his dependants will have a claim under the Fatal Accidents Act 1976 (see below).

For over ten years now, the government has published *Actuarial Tables with Explanatory Notes for Use in Personal Injury and Fatal Accident Cases* (the 'Ogden Tables'). The full text of the 1994 revision of the tables is set out in Pritchard and Solomon, *Personal Injury Litigation*, 8th ed (FT Law & Tax, 1995) pp 476–493 and, as to use of actuarial evidence generally, see further, pp 72–74. In the past, many judges expressed a reluctance to rely upon actuarial tables.

> ... the courts have been traditionally mistrustful of reliance on actuarial tables as the primary basis of calculation, approving their use only as a check on assessments arrived at by the familiar conventional methods (*per* Lord Bridge in *Hunt v Severs* [1994] 2 AC 350).

Nevertheless they must accept evidence which is admissible and appears to be credible unless it is contradicted by other evidence. Once s 10 of the Civil Evidence Act 1995 is brought into force the Ogden Tables together with their explanatory notes will be admissible in evidence upon production of an HMSO copy thereof (see further p 68).

Loss of earning capacity

The plaintiff may be entitled to compensation for loss of earning capacity even though there is no loss of future earnings. This is to compensate the plaintiff if he is now at a disadvantage in the labour market were he, for any reason, to lose his job (*Smith v Manchester Corporation* (1974) 17 KIR 1; *Moeliker v Reyrolle* [1977] 1 WLR 132). In *Foster v Tyne and Wear CC* [1986] 1 All ER 567 Lloyd LJ said:

> ... when it comes to estimating loss of earning capacity there is no such thing as a conventional approach; there is no rule of thumb which can be applied. It would be so much easier if there were. But there is not. In each case the trial judge has to do his best to assess the plaintiff's handicap, as an existing disability, by reference to what may happen in the future. As has been said so often, that is necessarily a matter of speculation; it is necessarily a matter of weighing up risks and chances in all the circumstances of a particular case.

Awards of provisional damages for personal injuries

The basic rule is that the damages to which a plaintiff is entitled from the defendant in respect of a wrongful act must be recovered once and for all. A plaintiff cannot bring a second action upon the same facts simply because the injury subsequently proves to be more serious than was thought when judgment was given (*Fitter v Veal* (1701) 12 Mod 542). Accordingly it is crucial to ensure that the evidence before the court is sufficient for the judge to make an appropriate assessment of damages once and for all.

Provisional damages are appropriate in cases which might be described as 'chance' cases. These are cases where there is a chance, ie a possibility which is less than a probability, that the plaintiff will at some future date suffer very serious additional damage. For example, a plaintiff who has lost one eye can sometimes suffer later from sympathetic ophthalmia whereby sight is lost in the good eye leading to total blindness. There is a vast difference between the loss of one eye and total blindness. Other examples would be the onset of traumatic epilepsy or certain kinds of mental illness.

Previously, if the medical evidence assessed the risk of, say, sympathetic ophthalmia at five per cent the plaintiff would be compensated for that five per cent risk. A five per cent risk means that for every hundred persons who suffered the injury, ninety-five would not develop the deterioration that was feared, but five would. Each plaintiff would be compensated for the five per cent risk, thus leading to over-compensation for 95 per cent of claimants, but gross under-compensation for the unfortunate five per cent.

This difficulty can be avoided if the court makes an award of provisional damages under SCA 1981, s 32A. The section applies to an action for damages for personal injuries in which there is proved or admitted to be a chance that at some definite or indefinite time in the future the injured person will, as a result of the act or omission which gave rise to the cause of action, develop some serious disease or suffer some serious deterioration of his physical or mental condition. The court can award damages on the assumption that the injured person will not develop the disease or suffer the deterioration. These are known as provisional damages. For the majority of plaintiffs the award will also in practice turn out to be final. The unfortunate minority of plaintiffs who do then develop the disease or suffer the deterioration can come back to court for further damages at a future date. If such plaintiffs die before the further damages have been agreed or ordered their dependants may commence proceedings under the Fatal Accidents Act 1976 (see Damages Act 1996, s 3).

It is not necessary for the court to make an award of provisional damages in those cases where, although a forecast of future disease or deterioration is given, the court has before it sufficient evidence on which to assess damages once and for all. For example, the medical evidence might forecast that the plaintiff who has suffered a leg injury will now suffer osteo-arthritis in the injured joint so that by the age of fifty-five he would not be able to run for a bus, by the age of sixty he would have to walk with a stick, and by the age of sixty-five he would be in a wheelchair. Although this could be viewed as 'a serious deterioration of his physical condition' and there is a 'chance' of it occurring, nonetheless this forecast of the plaintiff's deterioration is a sufficient basis on which damages can be assessed once and for all. This distinguishes a 'forecast' case from a 'chance' case. In the latter, any assessment (without the ability to award provisional damages) is bound to be wrong.

Provisional damages are, therefore, appropriate only in a minority of cases. They are available in both the High Court (RSC Ord 37, rr 7–10) and county court (CCR Ord 22, r 6A) and the procedures are essentially the same. Claims for provisional damages must be pleaded (for a precedent, see Pyke and Oldham, *Practical County Court Precedents* (FT Law & Tax) vol 1, para 9.58). Pleadings are more often than not settled and served before the plaintiff's medical condition has stabilised. In all but the most clear-cut cases (where it is obvious that provisional damages are or are not appropriate) practitioners may prefer to include a claim for provisional damages (with a view to not proceeding with it if it turns out to be inappropriate) rather than not plead such a claim and then have to seek leave to amend later (see p 182).

Pleading a claim for provisional damages has certain consequences. The plaintiff cannot later obtain judgment in default either with or without leave. Instead the case must go to trial (or compromise). A 1988 *Practice Direction* (*White Book* 37/7–10/1) recommends that, if no defence is served, the plaintiff should obtain from the court a direction which in effect debars the defendant from contesting the issue of liability. Under RSC Ord 37, r 9 (which also applies in the county court), a defendant may at any time (whether or not he makes a payment into court) make a written offer to the plaintiff to submit to an award of provisional damages and to tender a sum of money in satisfaction of those provisional damages. The offer must identify the disease or deterioration (see below) in question. Any such offer must *not* be brought to the attention of the judge until the court has determined the claim for provisional damages. As with a payment into court, the plaintiff has twenty-one days to accept such an offer. (The principles underlying written offers and payments into court are set out in Chapter 16.)

An order for provisional damages will specify the disease or deterioration which may occur in the future and will normally specify a period within which the plaintiff may come back to the court to seek a further award of damages. An application for a further award is governed by RSC Ord 37, r 10. It will of course be necessary at that subsequent hearing for the plaintiff to show that the later disease or deterioration in health is attributable to the tort of the defendant.

SCA 1981, s 32A requires that an award of provisional damages must be the subject of an order by the court. Accordingly, where the case has been settled by agreement, application must be made to the district judge by summons for leave to enter judgment by consent in the terms of a draft order which must be annexed to the summons. If the plaintiff is under disability, the approval of the court should be sought at the same time (see further p 371).

The procedure to be followed where there has been an award of provisional damages both after trial and after settlement is fully explained in *Practice Direction (Provisional Damages: Procedure)* [1985] 1 WLR 961. *Inter alia* the practice direction specifies the documents to be placed on the 'case file' which is preserved after an award of provisional damages for use at any subsequent application.

Structured settlements

In cases of very severe injuries, the plaintiff may be entitled to compensation sufficient to cover the costs of future earnings loss and future medical and other expenses for the rest of his life. The sums involved, if capitalised, could be huge. The plaintiff and/or his family may prefer to avoid the immense worry and stress which the investment and management of large sums of money often involves.

Practitioners should always consider advising as to the possibilities of a structured settlement in cases in which the total value of the claim exceeds £500,000. In a structured settlement plaintiffs normally agree a lump sum of damages in respect of past pain and suffering and past expenses and, for the future, a series of payments of damages which, from the plaintiff's point of view, are similar to an annuity guaranteeing a stream of payments for the rest of the plaintiff's life.

The courts now have power to order the payment of damages in this way if the parties consent (Damages Act 1996, s 2). Therefore, structures are arrived at only by settlement, ie agreement between the plaintiff and either the defendant or the defendant's insurers. The structure may well in fact involve the purchase of an annuity, but, for reasons relating to tax avoidance, the annuity will be bought (or sometimes directly financed) by the defendant or his insurers and not by the plaintiff. Personal injury compensation by way of periodic payments does not give rise to a liability to income tax in the hands of the recipient plaintiff provided that the agreement is properly drawn up.

The form which is most commonly used provides 'indexed terms for life' whereby the plaintiff will receive until death periodic payments (inflation-proofed by reference to the retail price index) with the option of a pre-set minimum number of payments. This was the form used in the first structured settlement agreement in this country. In *Kelly v Dawes* (1990) *The Times*, 27 September the plaintiff was left permanently brain damaged. Damages worth £410,000 were awarded paid as a lump sum of

£110,000, the balance producing an index-linked annuity of £2,130 per month with guaranteed payments for at least ten years.

As to the procedure for seeking the court's approval to a structure on behalf of a minor or mental patient see *Practice Note (Structured Settlements: Courts Approval)* [1992] 1 WLR 328 (*White Book* 80/10–11/ 5).

Fatal Accidents Act cases

Under the Fatal Accidents Act 1976, where by any wrongful act a defendant causes the death of a person, an action for damages can be brought against him 'for the benefit of the dependants' of the deceased. Although this is a personal action for the dependants and quite separate from any claim made for the benefit of the deceased's estate, the Fatal Accidents claim should be brought by the personal representatives of the deceased. However, if there is no personal representative, or if he fails to sue within six months of the death the action may be brought by all, or any, of the dependants.

The term 'dependants' includes a spouse or former spouse of the deceased; a person who was living with the deceased as a 'husband' or 'wife' for at least two years immediately before the deceased's death; any parent or other ascendant of the deceased including a person who was treated as a parent; any child or other descendant of the deceased including a child treated as a child of the family by the deceased; and any person who is, or is the issue of, a brother, sister, uncle or aunt of the deceased.

The Fatal Accidents Act allows a claim for 'damages for bereavement'. This claim is only for the benefit of a husband or a wife of the deceased or, where the deceased was a minor who never married, for the benefit of his parents. The court awards as damages such sum as may be specified by statutory instrument whether or not the recipient was a dependant of the deceased. Since 1991 the amount specified has been £7,500.

Apart from damages for bereavement, where applicable, the dependants' claim is for the loss of their dependency on the deceased. There must be evidence that the deceased contributed to their financial support. This is, of course, usually very simple to prove in the case of a claim by the widow and children, and in such a case the value of their dependency is usually calculated as a proportion of the deceased's earnings. Any benefits which have accrued or will or may accrue to any dependant from the deceased's estate are disregarded. (Consider for example the value of any claim under the Law Reform (Miscellaneous Provisions) Act 1934; see pp 69, 70.)

Compensation for loss of dependency is assessed in two stages: (1) the actual loss to the date of trial and (2) the estimated future loss, for which a multiplier is used based on the probable length of earning period the deceased would have had. The two assessments are thus similar to the assessment of past and future loss of earnings in personal injury claims. There is one important difference, however. In personal injury claims the multiplier is a figure selected as at the date of the trial. In Fatal Accidents Act cases it is a figure selected as at the date of death minus the number of pre-trial years (*Graham v Dodds* [1983] 1 WLR 808).

In the case of the death of a non-wage earning wife and mother the court may value the husband's loss by reference to the cost of employing a housekeeper plus the value of 'unreplaceable services' (*Regan v Williamson* [1976] 1 WLR 305) or where the husband has reasonably given up work to look after the family, by reference to his lost earnings (*Mehmet v Perry* [1977] 2 All ER 529). The loss to any children on the death of the mother must also be quantified. In *Spittle v Bunney* [1988] 1 WLR 847 Croom-Johnson LJ stated that 'where a very young child is orphaned and no substitute is provided, there is a practice of valuing the services of the mother by having regard to the cost of hiring a nanny [but] ... one cannot value [a mother's services] at a constant figure for the whole of the child's dependency'. The Court of Appeal in this case substituted an award of £25,000 for the original 'nanny formula' award of £47,500.

Interest on damages

In personal injury actions the court *must* award interest if the damages exceed £200 unless there are special reasons to the contrary (see p 17). Any sums paid by the defendant in respect of interest on personal injury damages are, like the damages themselves, exempt from income tax, whether or not the sums were paid under an order of the court.

Guidelines as to the calculation of interest

Guidelines, as to the periods for which interest should be allowed and as to the rates of interest which should be used, have been laid down in a series of Court of Appeal and House of Lords cases; notably, *Jefford v Gee* [1970] 2 QB 130, *Cookson v Knowles* [1979] AC 556, *Birkett v Hayes* [1982] 1 WLR 816 and *Wright v British Railways Board* [1983] 2 AC 773. In the last case cited it was said that, in the interests of certainty, these guidelines will not in future be subject to frequent change. The guidelines are not rules of law; the trial judge has a discretion (to be exercised judicially) as to whether to follow them. However, in the interest of simplicity, they are expressed as broad principles to be applied to the generality of cases. The courts are reluctant to depart from them in any particular case unless it is apparent that their application would result in substantial injustice (see *Dexter v Courtaulds Ltd* [1984] 1 WLR 372).

Fatal Accidents Act cases
The damages awarded have to be divided into three categories.

(1) Damages from the date of death to the date of trial carry interest annually for that period at half the average of the special account rates which were in force during that period (see below).

(2) Damages for bereavement carry interest at full special account rate (see *Sharman v Sheppard*, p 77).

(3) Damages for future loss from the date of trial carry no interest.

Personal injury cases

The damages awarded have to be divided into three categories.

(1) Special damages carry interest annually for the period from the date of accident to the date of trial at half the average of the special account rates which were in force during that period.

(2) Damages for pain and suffering and loss of amenities carry interest at the rate of two per cent *per annum* from the date of service of court proceedings to the date of trial.

(3) Damages for future loss of earnings (and *a fortiori* damages for loss of earnings capacity and for future expenses) carry no interest.

Explanation of the guidelines

The 'special account rate' is a rate of interest payable in certain, limited, circumstances on money paid into court and invested, eg on behalf of trustees or persons under disability (see p 371). The current rate as from February 1993 is eight per cent (for a full list see *White Book* 6/2/12). In order to calculate what was the *average* rate for any period it is convenient to consult conversion tables (such as those prepared by R M Nelson-Jones BA, Solicitor, and published from time to time in *The Law Society's Gazette*).

The reason for awarding interest on certain sums at only half the special account rate is as follows. Most of the sums will have been mounting up at a steady rate over the relevant period but interest is assessed on the total sum for the whole of the period. To simplify the task of calculation the 'half rate' guideline should normally be applied even to sums which were not mounting up over the period (eg cost of car repairs) or which were not mounting up at a steady rate (eg medical bills). However, in a very exceptional case, for example a claim including a medical bill for an expensive operation which was paid some years before the trial, interest at the full rate may be allowed on that item from the date it was paid (see generally *Dexter v Courtaulds Ltd* [1984] 1 WLR 372 and see p 155; for a case of equal authority to *Dexter* which suggests a greater readiness to allow the full rate for large items of special damages, see *Prokop v DHSS* [1985] CLY 1037).

The reasons for allowing interest on pain and suffering and loss of amenity awards at only two per cent *per annum* and from the service of court proceedings (rather than eg the date of the accident) are as follows. A nominal rate of interest is appropriate because the damages in question are assessed by reference to the level of awards as at the date of trial, not as at the date of the accident. Thus the plaintiff has already been compensated for any depreciation in the value of money which has occurred since the accident: to allow a full rate of interest as well would cause unjustifiable over-compensation. Interest from the date of the accident is said to be inappropriate because *inter alia* at that time the amount of damages to be awarded is not capable of being quantified. The defendant should not normally be required to pay interest in respect of an item, the value of which it is not possible to estimate. Accordingly, a convenient start point for the award of interest is usually the date of service of court proceedings (see further *Wright v British Railways Board* [1983] AC 773 *per* Lord Diplock).

Into which category should one place *bereavement damages* (see p 74)? They would appear to be a head of general damages but allowing a nominal rate of two per cent *per annum* seems inappropriate for an item which does not frequently fluctuate in value. If they are to be treated as special damages, the 'half rate' guideline seems inappropriate for so large and fixed an item. There is county court authority for allowing interest at the full rate (*Sharman v Sheppard* [1989] CLY 1190 and see *Green Book* 1279).

Special reasons for not awarding interest

There are no guidelines as to what amounts to a 'special reason' for not awarding interest. In each case the matter lies in the discretion of the trial judge with, as yet, very little by way of assistance from the appellate courts. Decisions to withhold or reduce interest in personal injury cases are very rare. We suggest two possible examples:

(1) the plaintiff failed to plead a claim for interest and no leave to amend should be given (see pp 155 and 183);

(2) the plaintiff was guilty of unreasonable delay in bringing the action to trial (see the various case examples cited in the *White Book* 6/2/16, the *Green Book* 1279 and see *Cresswell v Eaton* [1991] 1 WLR 1113, at p 1125).

Advising on *quantum*

How does the solicitor calculate the likely award of general damages? One way is to instruct counsel. This can be a useful practice provided proper use is made of it. Usually it is better if counsel is asked to give a second opinion or to comment on a specific difficulty that has arisen. As a general rule counsel should not be asked to advise on *quantum* until the solicitor has first formed a view on the case. The instructions to counsel preferably should not reveal that view. Counsel's opinion can then be compared with the solicitor's own assessment. It is not essential, however, to instruct counsel in every case. A solicitor doing a large volume of personal injury work will handle far more cases, particularly small ones,

than counsel and can often accurately assess damages without the need
for a second opinion.

There are several excellent sources for cases on *quantum*. A useful
starting point is provided by the *Guidelines for the Assessment of General
Damages in Personal Injury Cases*, 2nd ed (Blackstone Press, 1994)
which is prepared by the Judicial Studies Board and circulated to all
judges, recorders and district judges. The main textbook is Kemp &
Kemp, *The Quantum of Damages*, which is published in looseleaf format
and is regularly updated. There are the monthly publications, *Current Law*
and *Halsbury's Monthly Review*. Also some computer services designed
for solicitors are programmed to supply summaries of recent *quantum*
cases.

All lawyers specialising in personal injury work develop a 'feel' for the
case and can instinctively assess the appropriate sum to be awarded as
damages for pain and suffering and loss of amenities. Nonetheless, this
'feel' is best verified by checking in one of the sources mentioned.

Chapter 5

Limitation of Actions

It is of the utmost importance at the first interview to ascertain when the relevant limitation period will expire. The relevant law is set out in the Limitation Act 1980, although this consolidating statute has itself been amended several times. There are two important preliminary points to note:

(1) A plaintiff is required only to commence the action within the relevant limitation period. Thus in High Court cases the plaintiff need only *issue* a writ (or other process) and in county court cases need only *issue* a summons (or other process) within the appropriate limitation period. The plaintiff does not have to serve the writ within the limitation period so long as it is served within the period of its validity (usually four months, see p 204).

(2) Despite the phrase 'an action . . . shall not be brought' the Limitation Act does not prevent a plaintiff starting an action out of time. However, unless the case can be brought within one of the extensions of the basic period (see p 83) the defendant will have an impregnable defence. Strictly speaking a defendant must plead the Limitation Act in order to rely on it; the Limitation Act is unusual in that the court does not draw it to the attention of the parties (see p 161). In practice, however, as the defence is impregnable, it is invariably taken.

Ordinary time limits

Actions founded on simple contract or on tort (ss 2 and 5)

Save for those cases to which some other section applies (see below) the basic period is six years from the date when the cause of action accrued, ie six years from the date of breach of contract or from the date of commission of the tort. In contract, the cause of action accrues as soon as the contractual duty is broken. However, since negligence is actionable only on proof of damage, the action in negligence accrues only when some damage occurs. This may be a considerably later starting point than the date when the breach of duty occurred: see eg *Dove v Banhams*

Patent Locks Ltd [1983] 1 WLR 1436. However, personal injury cases apart, most negligence actions are now subject to a long-stop limitation period of fifteen years from the date of the defendant's breach of duty (see s 14B of the Act, discussed on p 82.

The ordinary time limits do not apply to a claim for specific performance of a contract or for an injunction or other equitable relief unless the court, in exercising its equitable discretion applies them by analogy (see s 36 and see further *Nelson v Rye* [1996] 1 WLR 1378).

Defamation cases (s 4A)

For actions for libel or slander the basic period (as amended by the Defamation Act 1996) is reduced to twelve months from the date on which the cause of action accrued. In certain circumstances leave can be granted extending this time limit (see s 32A, below).

Limitation in case of certain loans (s 6)

This section applies to any contract of loan which does not make any effective provision as to the time of repayment. In such a case the basic period is six years from the date the lender makes a demand in writing for repayment (instead of six years from the date the loan was made). Section 6 is intended to apply to loans between members of a family or between friends. The section makes good the assumption which is often made in such cases that the time limit applicable to the loan continues indefinitely until a formal demand for repayment is made. As to the operation of the section in cases in which the borrower delivers a promissory note as security for the loan see *Boot v Boot* [1996] *The Times*, 9 May.

Actions upon a specialty (s 8)

For actions on a bond or on a contract under seal the basic period is twelve years unless a shorter period is prescribed by some other section. Under ss 19 and 20 a six-year period is specified for arrears of rent and arrears of mortgage interest.

Claims for contribution (s 10)

Where two or more persons are liable in respect of the same damage (eg joint tortfeasors, joint covenantors) but only one of them pays or is ordered to pay compensation to the person injured, he is entitled to recover contribution from the other persons liable (Civil Liability (Contribution) Act 1978, s 1). Normally a claim for contribution is raised in the same action in which the person injured seeks compensation (see

Chapter 15). However, where separate proceedings are contemplated the limitation period is two years from either:
(1) the date on which judgment for the compensation was given, or on which an award was made on an arbitration; or
(2) if there was no judgment or award, the earliest date on which the amount of compensation was agreed between the person being compensated and the person now claiming contribution.

Personal injury litigation (s 11)

Where in any action (whether for negligence, nuisance or breach of duty, statutory, contractual or otherwise) the plaintiff claims damages which 'consist of or include damages in respect of personal injuries to the plaintiff or any other person' the basic period of limitation is only three years. However this reduced period runs from:
(1) the date on which the cause of action accrued; or
(2) the date (if later) of the plaintiff's knowledge.
The expression 'date of knowledge' is defined in s 14. Basically it is the first date when the plaintiff knew or might reasonably be expected to have known certain specified facts, including the seriousness of his injury, its cause, and the identity of the defendant. Knowledge or ignorance of the law is irrelevant. To cover the exceptional hard case, eg where a plaintiff knew the facts but did not know his legal rights, s 33 of the Act provides a discretionary power for the courts to override the time limit where it would be equitable to do so. This power is considered on p 85.

Knowledge of injury and its cause, topics which are usually straight-forward in road accident cases, can be immensely difficult in medical negligence cases; the leading authorities are *Dobbie v Medway Health Authority* [1994] 1 WLR 1234, *Forbes v Wandsworth Health Authority* [1996] 3 WLR 1108 and the cases cited therein. *Dobbie* and *Forbes* are both noted on p 87, below. The two most recent Court of Appeal cases on this topic are *Spargo v North Essex Health Authority* (1997) *The Times*, 21 March and *Saxby v Morgan* (1997) *The Times*, 2 May.

Does the s 11 time limit apply to a professional negligence action against a solicitor who, it is alleged, failed to commence a personal injury action in time? There is no direct authority at present but there are *dicta* either way; see further on this at p 407.

Fatal Accidents Act claims (s 12)

The basic period is three years from the date of death or the date of knowledge of the person for whose benefit the action is brought whichever is the later. The s 14 definition of 'date of knowledge' applies (see above). Where there is more than one person for whose benefit the action is brought their respective dates of knowledge have to be calculated separately to determine whether any of them should be excluded from the benefit of the action (s 13).

Negligence actions in respect of latent damage (s 14A)

This section applies 'to any action for damages for negligence other than one to which section 11 . . . applies' (see above) where facts relevant to the cause of action are not known at the date of accrual; in other words, non-personal injury cases in negligence where, at the time the cause of action accrued, the damage in question was still latent rather than patent. The section provides an alternative limitation period of three years from the date of knowledge of certain material facts (defined in a manner similar to the 'date of knowledge' in s 14; see above). For the position of subsequent owners of property at a time when damage in respect of that property is still latent, see Latent Damage Act 1986, s 3.

To protect defendants from what would otherwise be a perpetual risk of liability, s 14B provides a long-stop limitation period of fifteen years from the date of the alleged breach of duty. Like s 14A, s 14B applies to actions 'for damages for negligence, other than one to which section 11 . . . applies'. However s 14B is wider in ambit than s 14A: the long stop can bar a cause of action at a date earlier than the date of the claimant's knowledge. Indeed s 14B can bar a cause of action before it has accrued (see s 14B(2)).

It is now settled that s 14A applies only to actions for negligence and does not apply to actions in which the claims arise solely in contract (*Société Commerciale de Réassurance v ERAS (International) Ltd* [1992] 2 All ER 82 and the cases cited therein). However, it is also now settled that tortious duties and contractual duties with the same content can co-exist. Thus, in a negligence claim against professional advisers the plaintiff may frame his case in tort simply to obtain the advantageous limitation period it enjoys (see *Henderson v Merrett Syndicates Ltd* [1994] 3 WLR 761, HL, especially at p 781A and p 789B and *Nelson v Rye* [1996] 1 WLR 1378 at p 1389A–C).

New claims in pending actions (s 35)

To ascertain whether a claim is statute-barred one must measure the time period between the date the cause of action arose and the date of commencement of proceedings. As far as the original action is concerned commencement means the date of *issue* of the writ (or other originating process) (see p 79). But some claims can be raised as part of an existing case and thus without the issue of a separate writ (or other originating process), *viz* by the plaintiff, claims raised by amending the original action; by the defendant, set-offs and counterclaims (claims for remedies against the plaintiff, see p 163) and third party proceedings (claims for eg contribution or indemnity against a person who is not already a party to the action, see p 320). Section 35 defines when, for limitation purposes, these claims are deemed to be commenced. Plaintiffs' claims raised by amendment and all set-offs and counterclaims are deemed to have been commenced on the same date as the original action. All claims made in third party proceedings are deemed to have been commenced on the date the third party notice was issued.

As far as third party proceedings are concerned the deeming provision of s 35 may not seem very important. The date specified (issue of notice) is a date which usually occurs well before the relevant limitation period even begins. The limitation period for claims for contribution (two years) does not begin to run until the main action is determined (see s 10 noted above). The limitation period for claims for indemnity (six years) does not begin to run until the extent of the liability to be indemnified is known (see s 5 and *R & H Green & Silley Weir v British Railways Board* [1985] 1 WLR 570). Thus at first sight s 35 appears to be saying 'claims which are made today must be made before tomorrow'. In fact the importance of the provision, and indeed the main purpose of s 35, concerns the making of amendments after the expiry of a limitation period. When is it fair to allow parties to an existing action to raise by way of amendment matters which would be statute-barred if they attempted to raise them in a new action? This aspect of s 35 is dealt with on p 184.

Extension or exclusion of ordinary time limits

The Limitation Act 1980 provides for several exceptional cases in which the basic periods can be extended.

Disability (ss 28 and 28A)

Limitation periods do not begin to run against a minor until the minor dies or comes of age: limitation periods do not begin to run against a mental patient until the patient dies or recovers. Thus a child born in 1990 who suffered personal injuries in 1995 could commence a valid action at any time until the year 2011 (ie three years after attaining the age of eighteen; see the facts of *Tolley v Morris* [1979] 1 WLR 592, HL).

Section 28A applies to cases governed by ss 14A and 14B. It provides an extension to the special three-year limit for plaintiffs who are not under a disability when the cause of action accrues, but are when the special limit starts to run. Thus the period will run from the date of cessation of disability or death but subject to the fifteen-year long-stop period (see p 82).

Debts: acknowledgment or part payment (s 29(5))

Where a debtor acknowledges his indebtedness or makes a part payment in respect of the debt the creditor's right of action 'shall be deemed to have accrued on and not before the date of the acknowledgment or payment'. To be effective for the purposes of s 29 an acknowledgment must be 'in writing and signed by the person making the acknowledgment' (s 30). For the effect of an acknowledgment or part payment on persons other than the maker or recipient, see s 31.

Section 29(7) provides that a current limitation period may be repeatedly extended by further acknowledgments or payments but a right of action once barred cannot be revived by any subsequent acknowledgment or payment.

Fraud, concealment or mistake (s 32)

In each of the following cases, namely:
(1) where the action is based upon the fraud of the defendant or his agent;
(2) where any fact relevant to the plaintiff's right of action was deliberately concealed from him by any such person;
(3) where the action is for relief from the consequences of a mistake (eg an action in quasi-contract for the return of money paid under a mistake of fact);

the relevant limitation period is six years from the date the plaintiff discovered the fraud, concealment or mistake or could with reasonable diligence have discovered it. The words 'reasonable diligence' require only the taking of such steps (if any) as an ordinarily prudent plaintiff would take (*Peco Arts Inc v Hazlitt Gallery Ltd* [1983] 1 WLR 1315).

For the effect of this section on persons who are innocent third parties see subss (3) and (4).

In (2) above it matters not whether the deliberate concealment is made initially (ie at the time the cause of action accrued) or subsequently; see *Sheldon v RHM Outhwaite (Underwriting Agencies) Ltd* [1995] 2 WLR 570, HL. Moreover, negligence actions involving deliberate concealment are not subject to any long-stop period of fifteen years which might otherwise apply (s 32(5)).

Defamation cases (s 32A)

As already noted, the basic limitation period for actions for libel or slander is only twelve months from the date on which the cause of action accrued (see s 4A, above). In this instance, knowledge (or ignorance) of the accrual is irrelevant: contrast ss 11, 12 and 14A. However s 32A does give the court a discretion to allow commencement at a later time. The intending claimant must apply for the exercise of that discretion within one year of the earliest date on which he or she knew 'all the facts relevant to' the cause of action. The section does not say which facts are the relevant facts for this purpose, but see further as to this, *C v Mirror Group Newspapers* [1996] 4 All ER 511. The application for leave should be made by originating summons, proper notice being given to the potential defendant to the defamation action (*Oyston v Blaker* [1996] 1 WLR 1326).

Consumer Protection Act 1987

This Act came into force on 1 March 1988 and applies to products supplied on or after that date. Part I renders producers and (in defined circumstances) suppliers strictly liable for personal injury, death or damage to 'consumer' property (other than the defective product itself) caused by defective products. There is no claim for property damage alone unless the property was for private use and consumption and the damages exceed £275. Schedule 1 introduces s 11A into the Limitation Act 1980. The section imposes a ten-year long stop on actions for breach of the statutory duty. Time runs from the time when the defendant supplied the defective product to another. Contrary to the normal rule that a plaintiff's rights are merely barred and not extinguished, after the ten-year period the right of action is extinguished. For actions for personal injury (including actions which survive for the benefit of the estate under the Law Reform (Miscellaneous Provisions) Act 1934) the basic time limit is otherwise the same as under s 11, ie three years from the date when the cause of action accrued (or death) or the date of the injured person's knowledge, whichever is the later. This same basic limit also applies to an action for loss of or damage to property. For actions under the Fatal Accidents Act 1976 for death caused by a defective product, the basic limit remains that laid down in s 12 of the Limitation Act 1980 (see p 81) subject to the ten-year long stop. The s 33 discretion to disapply the basic time limits (see below) applies to all actions under Pt 1 of the 1987 Act with the important proviso that there is no discretion to disapply the ten-year long stop period.

Section 28(7) of the Limitation Act deals with the extension of the limitation period in cases of disability: the ten-year long stop overrides the normal disability provisions in s 28 (see p 83) which otherwise apply.

Section 32(4A) provides that the ten-year long stop also overrides the normal provisions concerning deliberate concealment of facts relating to a cause of action under the 1987 Act.

Personal injury and death claims (s 33)

In personal injury and death claims the ordinary time limit is three years from the date the claimant knew he had a cause of action (see ss 11, 12 and 14 noted above). The ordinary time limit does not cover cases where plaintiffs know all the facts but, until too late, do not know the law. Thus ignorance of the law does not give a right to bring an action late, but in such cases s 33 of the Act gives the court a discretion to disapply the time limit where it thinks it is equitable to do so after taking into account two matters: first the degree to which the plaintiff is prejudiced by the provisions of s 11 or s 12, and secondly the degree to which the defendant would be prejudiced if an order disapplying that time limit were made. In acting under this section the court must have regard to all the circumstances of the case and in particular to six specified matters including '(*a*) the length of and the reasons for the delay on the part of the plaintiff' and '(*f*) the steps if any taken by the plaintiff to obtain medical, legal or other expert advice and the nature of any such advice he may have received'.

In the High Court, applications under s 33 may be dealt with pre-trial by the district judge (RSC Ord 32, r 9A). In most cases however it is preferable to go straight to the judge. In strongly contested cases which are borderline the application could be very lengthy involving a close examination of all the conduct of the parties since the accident occurred. Even if you start such an application with the district judge it is likely to be taken to the judge anyway. The district judge has power so to refer it (see p 5). Alternatively, the losing party could go to the judge by way of appeal. In order to go straight to the judge the application could be delayed until the trial, or, if liability or *quantum* are also being strongly contested, set down as a preliminary point after discovery has taken place.

In the county court there is at present no rule equivalent to RSC Ord 32, r 9A. In *Hughes v Jones* (1996) *The Times*, 18 July it was held that the county court district judge has jurisdiction under s 33 only if the case otherwise falls within his final jurisdiction (as to which, see p 479).

Appeals to the Court of Appeal are seldom appropriate. Section 33 confers a discretion on the courts and in such cases the Court of Appeal will not normally substitute its own opinion for that of the judge (see p 666).

Section 33 gives the court a general discretion to inquire into the merits of many personal injury cases begun outside the limitation period to see whether justice would be better served by denying the defendants the opportunity to take what may well be an arbitrary and unmeritorious defence. Of the six factors specified in s 33 the first two factors, length of and reasons for delay and the effect which the delay has had on the evidence available to the defendant, are often the decisive ones. (The other four factors deal with the conduct of the parties and the duration of any period of supervening mental incapacity suffered by the plaintiff. *NB* the court is not limited to considering only these factors. It is also relevant to consider the strength of the plaintiff's case, ie the plaintiff's chances of success even if the limitation defence is defeated.)

> In *Thompson v Brown* [1981] 1 WLR 744, HL, P notified D of his claim within weeks of the accident. Because of an oversight by P's solicitors, the writ was issued thirty-seven days late. P's application under s 33 was successful even though he had conceded that he had a cast iron case against his solicitors.

In *Hartley v Birmingham City District Council* [1992] 1 WLR 968, P notified D of her claim within weeks of the accident. The writ was issued one day late. Both parties accepted that, but for the limitation point, P had a cast iron case on liability against D and that, but for this application, P also had an unanswerable claim against her solicitors. P's application under s 33 was successful.

In *Donovan v Gwentoys Ltd* [1990] 1 WLR 472, HL, P, a minor, was injured in an accident in December 1979. She first consulted the solicitors in April 1981, a few days before her eighteenth birthday. The solicitors first contacted D about the claim in September 1984, some five months after the limitation period had expired, and the writ was issued in October 1984. The House of Lords refused P's application under s 33.

In *Dobbie v Medway Health Authority* [1994] 1 WLR 1234, in April 1973 P underwent an operation for the removal of a lump from her breast with a view to its being analysed to check whether it was malignant. In fact, the surgeon also removed the breast entirely. Shortly afterwards she was told that the lump had not in fact been malignant. In May 1988 P found out from radio and newspaper reports about another case similar to hers in which compensation had been sought. P then contacted solicitors who promptly contacted D and a writ was issued in May 1989. In 1990, an expert appointed by P's solicitors prepared a report stating that the surgeon who conducted P's operation had not followed correct procedure. The Court of Appeal held that, for the purposes of s 14 (see p 81) the three-year limitation period began in 1973, on the date, shortly after the date of the operation, when she had been told that the lump was not in fact malignant. Her application under s 33 failed.

In *Forbes v Wandsworth Health Authority* [1996] 3 WLR 1108 P (who died before this appeal was heard) had first had by-pass operations on his legs in 1975 and 1978. In 1982 he had a further by-pass operation which was unsuccessful. Within seventeen hours after that operation another by-pass operation was performed but that also was unsuccessful. Shortly thereafter it was necessary to have one leg amputated and this was done. In 1982 P believed that the amputation was attributable to the medical condition in respect of which the by-pass operations had been performed. The plaintiff now wished to allege that the amputation was in fact attributable to negligent delay by D in the seventeen hour period between the two by-pass operations in 1982. P first took legal advice on this matter in 1991 as a result of which he received medical advice raising the negligent delay point and the writ was issued in 1992. The Court of Appeal held that, for the purposes of s 14 (see p 81 the three-year limitation period must have begun before 1985. The test to be applied was mainly objective: a reasonable man in the position of P, knowing of the amputation, would have sought further medical advice as to its cause within the following two years. Therefore, P had constructive knowledge of the facts now relied on as constituting negligence. The plaintiff's application under s 33 failed, particular emphasis being placed upon the overall weakness of the case.

In *Coad v Cornwall Health Authority* [1997] 1 WLR 189 P was a hospital nurse who, in 1983, suffered a significant back injury while at work. Although the injury caused her severe health problems thereafter she continued at work until, in 1990, after yet another relapse, she accepted that her career as a nurse was over. She then sought legal advice and, in 1991, gave notice of her claim to D and, in 1993, commenced proceedings against D. P did not dispute that the three-year limitation period had begun in 1983: the length of her delay therefore exceeded seven years. However throughout that time she had had an honest and genuine belief that she had no cause of action so long as her employment as a nurse continued. Her application under s 33 was successful. The Court of Appeal held that, under s 33(3)(a) the 'reasons for the delay' should be considered subjectively (contrast other parts of s 33(3) and s 14). Therefore, in an application under s 33 ignorance of the law, even a foolish or unreasonable ignorance, can provide a good excuse.

'Second action cases'

The purpose of s 33 is to enable courts to alleviate the prejudice suffered by plaintiffs who do not start proceedings within the relevant limitation period. Thus, if a plaintiff starts an action within time but for any reason fails to proceed with it, it is not thereafter open to him to seek to take advantage of s 33 (see *Walkley v Precision Forgings Ltd* [1979] 1 WLR 606, HL and *Thompson v Brown* [1981] 1 WLR 744). In *Walkley v Precision Forgings Ltd* [1979] 1 WLR 606, HL, the plaintiff had issued a writ in 1971, just within the limitation period, but that action was liable to be dismissed for want of prosecution (see p 364). In 1976 he issued a second writ and asked the court to disapply the time limit. In the House of Lords the point was taken that, under (what is now) s 33, the court has power to disapply the time limits only having regard to the prejudice they caused the plaintiff. The House reasoned that since the plaintiff had previously started an action within the three-year period the time limit plainly caused him no prejudice. The only cause of prejudice was the reason why this first action had faltered.

> The only exception I have been able to think of where it might be proper to give a direction ... despite the fact that the plaintiff had previously started an action within the primary limitation period but had subsequently discontinued it, would be a case in which the plaintiff had been induced to discontinue by a misrepresentation or other improper conduct by the defendant: but there is no suggestion of this in the instant case (*per* Lord Diplock in *Walkley*).
>
> It may seem anomalous that a defendant should be better off where, unknown to him, a writ has been issued but not served than he would be if the writ had not been issued at all; but this is a consequence of the greater anomaly ... that, for the purposes of a limitation period, an action is brought when a

writ or other originating process is issued (*per* Lord Diplock in *Thompson*; see further as to this *dictum*, *Forward v Hendricks* [1997] 2 All ER 395 (CA)).

As a general rule the words of the statute must be applied however harsh or anomalous the result. The fact that a defendant voluntarily made an interim payment does not allow an exception. The *dictum* from *Walkley* quoted above does not give 'a Judge carte blanche to disregard [the] general rule in any case in which he thought the circumstances were exceptional' (*per* Lord Diplock, in *Deerness v Keeble & Son* [1983] 2 Lloyd's Rep 260).

As to the separate question of whether a plaintiff can avoid the difficulty of a second action by applying in the first action to renew, ie extend the validity of the writ or county court summons for service, see p 205.

Foreign limitation periods

The Foreign Limitation Periods Act 1984 affects cases in which an English court has to apply foreign law (eg a contract action in which the contract validly adopts French law). The limitation period is that provided by the foreign law. English law continues to govern questions as to whether and when proceedings have been commenced. The Act creates exceptions on grounds of public policy and for cases involving undue hardship.

Chapter 6

Parties to Actions

Solicitors are entitled to act for any person able to instruct them to bring or defend proceedings in court. But does their client have authority to give them instructions? Is the client the best person to take or defend proceedings? And with whom or against whom should proceedings be taken? This chapter summarises the rules of court relating to particular types of litigant and relating to the joinder of causes of action and joinder of parties.

Types of litigants

Minors (RSC Ord 80; CCR Ord 10)

A minor is a person under the age of eighteen, whether married or unmarried. The former description of such a person 'infant' is still used in the RSC. A minor sues by a 'next friend' and defends by a 'guardian *ad litem*'. (In the county court there are two exceptions: (1) claims by a minor for wages, etc (CCA 1984, s 47); (2) claims against a minor for a liquidated sum, if the court so directs (CCR Ord 10, r 8).) The court prefers a relative (often a parent) to be appointed to this office except where, eg he or she is already a party on the other side (see further *White Book* 80/3/1). Normally no hearing is necessary for the appointment. A next friend simply delivers to the court certain papers (see RSC Ord 80, r 3(8); CCR Ord 10, r 2) before the issue of a writ or other originating process. A guardian *ad litem* can be appointed when the necessary papers are filed (in the High Court, on acknowledgment of service; in the county court, on delivering the admission or defence). In Queen's Bench cases and county court cases the name of the person appointed will be added to the title of the action. For example:

BETWEEN   SARAH LAWSON (minor)
by ANN LAWSON (her mother and next friend)

Plaintiff

AND

STUART MOOR (minor)
by DENNIS MOOR (his guardian *ad litem*)

Defendant

The next friend or guardian *ad litem* is an officer of the court appointed to take all measures for the benefit of the person he represents (*Rhodes v Swithinbank* (1889) 22 QBD 577). Thus he has the conduct of the litigation on behalf of the minor and may agree with the other side, eg as to the extension of time for pleadings or as to the manner in which evidence will be produced at the trial. These agreements will bind the minor only if they can fairly be said to be for his benefit. There is one agreement a next friend or guardian has no power to make by himself. Where money is claimed on behalf of a minor, no settlement, compromise or acceptance of money paid into court is valid unless approved by the court (see further p 371). In the High Court (but not the county court) a next friend or guardian *ad litem* must act by a solicitor.

Both a next friend and a guardian will be liable to give discovery, etc (RSC Ord 80, r 9; CCR Ord 10, r 12, and see Chapter 18). They differ in their liability for costs. A next friend is always personally liable for costs, usually with an indemnity (for what it is worth) against the minor. In the county court, the next friend has to give an undertaking to this effect (CCR Ord 10, r 2). A guardian *ad litem* is liable for costs only if they are caused by his personal negligence or misconduct (*White Book* 62/B/123; CCR Ord 10, r 12). A solicitor may be penalised in costs if he improperly commences proceedings by a minor suing without a next friend (*White Book* 80/2/1).

A minor who comes of age during proceedings may adopt or repudiate them simply by serving notice to that effect (*White Book 759; Green Book* commentary to CCR Ord 10, r 2).

There are other special rules relating to minors: as to service, see p 128; as to default procedures, see p 218; and as to the High Court rule of implied admissions in pleadings, see p 159.

For a collection of useful precedents concerning minors and concerning other topics covered in this chapter, see Pyke and Oldham, *Practical County Court Precedents* (FT Law & Tax) Precedents 7–53.

Patients or mental patients (RSC Ord 80; CCR Ord 10)

In High Court rules 'patient' means a person who, by reason of mental disorder within the meaning of the Mental Health Act 1983, is incapable of managing or administering his property and affairs (RSC Ord 80, r 1). Hereafter we shall use the county court designation which is 'mental patient' (CCR Ord 1, r 3). In the rules of both courts minors and mental patients are referred to collectively as 'persons under disability'. Virtually all the rules relating to minors also apply to mental patients. Note however two important qualifications. First, if a person has been authorised by the Court of Protection to bring or defend proceedings on behalf of a mental patient that person should normally be appointed next friend or guardian *ad litem*. Secondly, a mental patient who has recovered and wishes to adopt the proceedings must make an application to the court supported by credible medical evidence (*White Book* 759; the practice is the same in the county court, see CCA 1984, s 76).

Companies and other corporate bodies

Companies and other corporate bodies are legal persons and therefore can sue and be sued in their own names. In the case of a public company with a nominal share capital of £50,000 or more the name will end with the description 'public limited company' or 'plc' or the Welsh equivalents 'cwmni cyfyngedig cyhoeddus' or 'ccc'. Other companies' names usually end with the word 'Limited'. In the High Court companies have no right to begin or carry on proceedings, or, as defendants, take any step therein, except by a solicitor (RSC Ord 5, r 6; for an important exception, see p 207 and see also p 507). This is not true of the county court, where they may act through any agent duly appointed (*Green Book* commentary to CCR Ord 3, r 1). A solicitor can be made personally liable for costs if he commences proceedings in the name of a company without the authority of, eg its directors or officers capable of giving instructions, or if he commences proceedings in the name of a dissolved company even though he acts *bona fide*, having been deceived by his client (*White Book* 3874).

There are special rules for the service of writs and summonses on companies (see Chapter 8).

Partnerships (RSC Ord 18; CCR Ord 5, r 9)

Partnerships are not legal persons. However, if partners carry on business in England or Wales, they may sue or be sued in the name of their firm, which is treated as their collective description. Under the rules of the High Court and the county court other parties can compel persons joined in a firm name to disclose the names and addresses of all the members constituting the firm. The better practice, however, where a plaintiff wishes to *sue* a firm, is to make inquiries before proceedings are commenced. Especially in debt claims it is better to know in advance whether the members of the firm are worth the powder and shot. The Business Names Act 1985 provides that a person or persons carrying on business in another name must, *inter alia*, give an address for service on all business letters, written orders for goods or services to be supplied to the business, invoices and receipts issued in the course of the business and written demands for payment of debts. Slightly different rules may apply in the case of documents issued by professional partnerships of more than twenty persons (a trading partnership of more than twenty persons is not permitted). Breach of the disclosure rules may prevent enforcement of a claim against persons suffering financial loss as a result of the breach (1985 Act, s 5 and see generally, *Green Book* commentary to CCR Ord 5, r 9).

There are both advantages and disadvantages in suing partners in their firm name. The advantages are: the easier service rules (see Chapter 8) and the ability to enforce the judgment against partnership property (Partnership Act 1890, s 23). The disadvantages are the need to seek leave to enforce a judgment against persons not identified in the proceedings as partners (RSC Ord 81, r 5; CCR Ord 25, r 9), and in actions between a firm and one of its members, or between firms with members in common (RSC Ord 81, r 6; CCR Ord 25, r 10).

Sole traders carrying on business in a name or style other than their own *can be sued* in that name or style as if it were a firm name. However, unlike partners, they are not allowed to *sue* in their business name.

Estates of deceased persons (RSC Ord 15, rr 6A, 7, 14, 15; CCR Ord 5, rr 7, 8, 11)

Both the High Court and the county court rules contain four provisions dealing with litigation concerning the estates of deceased persons.

(1) *The basic rule.* The estate should be represented by the deceased's personal representatives (ie executors or administrators) joined in their capacity as such.

(2) *Where a litigant dies during the action.* An action solely for damages for bereavement automatically determines on the death of the plaintiff (see p 74). The death of the applicant determines an application under the Inheritance (Provision for Family and Dependants) Act 1975 (see *Green Book* commentary to s 1 of the 1975 Act). A defamation action automatically determines on the death of either the plaintiff or the defendant. In other cases the action will not abate and the court may order the personal representatives to be joined and order the action to be carried on as if they had been substituted for the deceased. (Similar rules apply where a litigant becomes bankrupt or where an action is brought by or against a person as the holder of an office and, during the action, that person goes out of office.)

(3) *Where a party to an action dies and no personal representatives are appointed.* The court may require notice to be given to any person having an interest in the deceased's estate: for example in an action against a motorist now deceased, notice might be given to an insurer or to the MIB (see p 38). The court may then order that the action should proceed in the absence of any person representing the estate or may appoint a person to represent the estate *for the purpose of those proceedings.* In either event any judgment given in the action will bind the estate as if a personal representative had been joined.

An order under this provision would be futile in debt claims against a litigant who dies because, for all practical purposes, the judgment would be unenforceable. In such cases the creditor himself should take out letters of administration to the deceased's estate (assuming he thinks the estate large enough to cover his debt and expenses).

(4) *Where a prospective defendant dies before proceedings are commenced and no personal representatives are appointed.* The plaintiff can issue a writ or other originating process naming as defendant *either* 'The Personal Representatives of AB deceased' even though none exist, *or* simply the deceased's name, even though he knows that person is dead. Instead of attempting to serve the process the plaintiff must then apply for an order appointing some person to represent the estate under (3) above. The application must be made during the first four months after issue otherwise the action will be lost. If personal representatives are appointed (whether before or after the action commences) the court will simply substitute them as the defendants (see *White Book* 15/6A/5).

The provisions just described do not permit the commencement of a defamation action, or any action in the name of a plaintiff who is already dead.

Vexatious litigants (SCA 1981, s 42)

We use the expression 'vexatious litigant' here to describe any person who has habitually and persistently and without any reasonable ground *instituted vexatious legal proceedings,* whether in the High Court or county courts, or *made vexatious applications* in any such proceedings, whether they were instituted by him or by someone else. In respect of such a litigant the High Court may make an order requiring him to obtain the leave of the High Court before instituting or making applications in any civil action. (Query whether the litigant needs leave to appeal against the order under s 42 itself.) Application is made by the Attorney-General to a Divisional Court by originating motion (RSC Ord 94, r 15). A copy of the order is printed in the *London Gazette* and will be noted in the Central Office and in every district registry and county court office.

Thereafter if the person does wish to institute or make applications in any civil proceedings the leave of a High Court judge is required and there is no appeal from a refusal to grant leave. If leave is granted the intended opponent cannot challenge the grant of leave itself (*Jones v Vans Colina* [1996] 1 WLR 1580) but may of course resist the permitted application itself (perhaps by means of an application under RSC Ord 18, r 19 as to which see p 190).

Similar orders can also be obtained in respect of criminal proceedings (see, generally, *White Book* 5181 and 94/15/2).

Joinder

Many people find the rules relating to joinder somewhat difficult to understand in theory but usually plain and straightforward to apply in practice. Would anyone doubt that the two passengers in a car, injured in a road accident, can bring one action together to sue the driver? Or that a landlord suing his ex-tenant for possession can also claim arrears of rent? Or that a person injured by drinking bad ginger-ale can sue in the same action both the shopkeeper who sold it and the manufacturer who made it? The rules provide for joinder of causes of action and joinder of parties in all these cases. In our view these rules can be summarised as follows: the court desires as few actions as possible with as few parties as possible. Having as few actions as possible means allowing much joinder of *causes*. Having as few parties as possible means allowing joinder of *parties* only where the claims by or against them are interrelated.

Joinder by plaintiff

'As few actions as possible'

The plaintiff can join in one action any number of causes of action against the same defendant (RSC Ord 15, r 1; CCR Ord 5, r 1). In the vast majority of actions, joinder of causes can be made without leave. Leave is required only where the plaintiff sues or the defendant is being sued in more than one capacity, eg in his personal capacity and in his capacity as trustee in bankruptcy or personal representative. Even here an exception is made. No leave is necessary to join causes where some of them relate to a party's capacity as a personal representative and the rest relate to his personal capacity but 'with reference to' the deceased's estate.

> *Example*
>
> Alan, a wholesale trader, dies and John is appointed his executor. Whilst winding up the estate John continues Alan's business. A manufacturer could sue John joining without leave claims for the price of goods delivered to the business during Alan's lifetime *and* since his death. Similarly John could sue a customer joining without leave claims for the price of goods sold to him by Alan during his lifetime *and* by John since Alan's death.

In cases where leave is necessary it should be sought *ex parte* before the issue of the writ or other originating process. Consider what might happen if leave were not sought.

> *Example*
>
> H and W are both injured in a road accident. H dies from his injuries. W is appointed his executrix and, without obtaining leave, issues a writ claiming damages under the Law Reform (Miscellaneous Provisions)

Act 1934 on behalf of H's estate, damages for loss of dependency under the Fatal Accidents Act 1976 and damages for her own personal injuries. The third claim is not 'with reference to' H's estate and therefore the writ is irregular. But surely the court would not set it aside under RSC Ord 2, r 1 since, had W sought leave to join the cause, leave would have been granted.

'As few parties as possible'

An action may be commenced without leave even though it joins two or more persons together, as plaintiffs or defendants, if:

(a) the claims by or against them involve some common question of law or fact; and

(b) all rights to relief claimed in the action (whether they are joint, several or alternative) are in respect of, or arise out of, the same transaction or series of transactions.

(See RSC Ord 15, r 4; CCR Ord 5, r 2.) If the conditions (a) and (b) are not both satisfied, there can be a joinder of parties only with leave, and such leave is seldom granted.

Example

David, a car driver, knocks down Peter, a pedestrian, on a pelican crossing. Peter is not badly hurt. In the ensuing argument Derek, David's passenger, punches Peter on the nose. The next day, on a different crossing, Peter is knocked down again, this time by Donald. In one action Peter could sue both David and Derek since both conditions (a) and (b) are satisfied. As to his claim against Donald condition (a) is satisfied but not condition (b). Consider whether leave to add Donald as a defendant would be granted.

Suppose further that David owes Peter a debt in respect of some entirely different matter. If Peter sued David alone he could claim both the personal injury damages and the debt. But what if Peter sued both David and Derek in one action? It seems that leave would be necessary to claim the debt: see condition (b) which begins 'if *all* rights to relief . . . .'.

Similarity of case (condition (a)) is the basic precondition to joinder of parties. By itself it does not justify joinder *without leave,* but a plaintiff might successfully apply for leave to join. Joinder of parties without leave is allowed only where the similar cases are 'causally related' (condition (b)).

Co-plaintiffs

The joinder of parties as plaintiffs has one very important consequence. Generally speaking co-plaintiffs have to be represented by the same solicitor and counsel, and cannot make allegations inconsistent with their colleagues' allegations. The court will allow them to 'sever' only in the most exceptional circumstances (*Lewis v Daily Telegraph (No 2)* [1964] 2

QB 601). If co-plaintiffs fall out with each other the court will not usually order separate trials. Instead one or other of them will be struck out from the action and then will either be added as a defendant or will be left to bring his own proceedings (see *White Book* 15/4/3 and 15/6/5).

Costs orders where defendants are sued in the alternative

Who will be ordered to pay the costs of the successful defendant? Normally one would expect the plaintiff to pay the costs of parties joined unnecessarily. But what if it was reasonable for the plaintiff to add parties as alternative defendants? And when is it reasonable to do so? Both these points are dealt with in two important cases from which the names of the relevant costs orders have been taken.

In *Bullock v London General Omnibus Co* [1907] 1 KB 264 the plaintiff was injured when a bus collided with a cart. The bus company and the cart owner each blamed the other for the accident. At the trial it was proved that only the bus company was at fault. The plaintiff was ordered to pay the cart owner's costs but was allowed to add them to her own costs and to recover both from the bus company.

In *Sanderson v Blyth Theatre Co* [1903] 2 KB 533 the plaintiff sued the defendant for the price of certain building works he had carried out on the instructions of the theatre architect. On the defendant's denial that the architect was their agent the plaintiff joined him as second defendant. At the trial it was proved that the theatre was liable. It was held that the court had power to order the theatre company to pay the architect's costs directly. (In fact a '*Bullock* order' was made.)

Note that if a '*Bullock* order' is made the plaintiff still has to pay the successful defendant's costs whether or not the losing defendant has the means to reimburse him. In choosing which order to make, the court's desire is to protect the successful defendant first (*Mayer v Harte* [1960] 1 WLR 770) and accordingly the court usually considers a '*Bullock* order' first. However, a '*Sanderson* order' is more appropriate if the plaintiff is legally aided or insolvent and the losing defendant is insured in respect of the claim or wealthy enough to pay.

Choosing whom to sue

Retailer and manufacturer? Wherever possible proceedings may be taken against both. There are three causes of action to consider. A claim in negligence against any person who puts defective goods in circulation, if it is proved that that person knew or ought to have known of the defect and if loss was suffered which was foreseeable: on this cause of action a plaintiff cannot normally recover damages if the only losses suffered are purely economic. Secondly, under the Consumer Protection Act 1987 against a 'producer' (as defined therein) of goods which were defective and cause loss; although it is largely based on strict liability principles, this cause of action is limited in a variety of ways. In particular, it applies only to goods manufactured after February 1988 which cause loss to a 'consumer' (as defined in the Act). There is no compensation for loss or damage to the goods themselves, or for pure economic loss, or for loss not exceeding £275, or where the development risks defence applies (ie that the defect was one which, at the time of production, no producer of such goods could have avoided). Thirdly, as between the injured buyer and the immediate seller, a claim in contract. Subject to the terms of their contract, this claim may well impose strict liability on the seller and avoid the other limitations placed on the other two causes of action mentioned. It is, however, limited by the doctrine of privity of contract: it does not apply unless the person injured was the buyer and the person sued is the seller from whom he bought the goods.

Employer and employee? Where a tort is committed by an employee (or agent) acting in the course of his employment it is usual to sue *both* the employee and his employer: the latter will be vicariously liable for the former.

Motorist and insurer? When a tort is committed by an insured person the victim has no right at common law to sue the insurer directly since he is not privy to the contract of insurance (*Post Office v Norwich Union* [1967] 2 QB 363). Note however that:

(1) the insurer usually has the contractual right, as against the defendant, to conduct the defence on his behalf;

(2) in an action against a motorist the plaintiff usually has a statutory right to enforce against the insurer any *judgment* he obtains against the defendant (see p 37); and

(3) in an action against a bankrupt see the restricted rights given by the Third Parties (Rights against Insurers) Act 1930.

Tenant and spouse? Where a tenant's lease has expired or has been determined by a notice to quit the landlord should bring an action for possession against the tenant only and not against the tenant's spouse or children. The landlord will be able to enforce any order for possession he obtains against all occupiers of the land (see p 608). On the other hand, a spouse, or any other person who is in possession of the land (whether in actual possession or by a tenant) may apply to be added as a party (RSC Ord 15, r 10; CCR Ord 15, r 3).

Trustee and beneficiaries? Suppose a stranger to a trust wishes to sue the trustees to enforce a contract for the sale of land or an executor sues the trustees of an *inter vivos* trust to determine the validity of a legacy in favour of their trust. In both these cases it would be unnecessary to join the beneficiaries as additional defendants. A judgment given in any action involving trustees is binding on all the beneficiaries (unless the court otherwise orders) (RSC Ord 15, r 14; CCA 1984, s 76).

Joinder by defendant

'As few actions as possible'
A defendant can add causes of action by raising a counterclaim against a plaintiff for any relief or remedy in respect of any matter whenever and

however arising (RSC Ord 15, r 2; CCA 1984, s 38). Counterclaims against the plaintiff are not limited to money claims and are not limited to matters related to the plaintiff's claim (contrast set-offs, p 161). For virtually all purposes a claim and a counterclaim are treated as two independent actions (compare third party proceedings, p 320). Thus:

(1) The rules governing joinder of causes of action by a plaintiff apply to counterclaims, *mutatis mutandis*.

(2) The rules of pleading apply to counterclaims and defences to counterclaims as though they were, respectively, claims and defences (see Chapter 9).

(3) In respect of a counterclaim the plaintiff can make payments into court and/or take third party proceedings and/or raise a counterclaim to the counterclaim. (The third course mentioned would be highly unusual: for an example, see p 197.)

(4) The defendant may proceed with his counterclaim 'notwithstanding the fact that judgment has been given for the plaintiff in the action or that the action is stayed, discontinued or dismissed' (RSC Ord 15, r 2(3): compare CCR Ord 21, r 4).

(5) The defendant may obtain summary judgment (see p 221).

(6) In the High Court it is possible to obtain judgment in default of defence to counterclaim (see p 237).

For some purposes, of course, counterclaims differ from independent actions:

(1) For the purposes of the Limitation Act 1980 (see p 82).

(2) For the purposes of costs and execution where both claim and counterclaim are successful (see p 566).

(3) In the county court the default procedure does not apply to a counterclaim.

The court's preference for 'as few actions as possible' is not absolute and unlimited. RSC Ord 15, r 5(2) empowers the court to strike out a counterclaim or order it to be tried separately if it appears that the subject matter of the counterclaim ought to be disposed of by way of separate proceedings. In *Ernst & Young v Butte Mining plc* (No 2) [1997] 2 All ER 471 the court struck out a counterclaim under this rule even though it was, for limitation purposes, too late for the counterclaimant to begin again any fresh action. It is important to note that this counterclaim was not initiated until after the relevant limitation period had expired; see further p 194.

'As few parties as possible'

The ordinary method by which the defendant adds parties to an action is by issuing third party proceedings: these are described separately in Chapter 15.

In both the High Court and the county court the rules make some limited provisions enabling a defendant to add 'co-defendants to counterclaim'. This is possible only if the plaintiff is also made a defendant to the counterclaim and the counterclaim is for relief or remedies related to or connected with the plaintiff's claim (contrast joinder of parties by a plaintiff: RSC Ord 15, r 4, conditions (*a*) and (*b*)).

Example

P, D and Q are three drivers involved in a road accident. They each have different opinions as to who was at fault. P sues D. D denies liability and counterclaims against P and Q for damages for his own injuries. (Q could counterclaim to the counterclaim by taking proceedings against P and D: *White Book* 15/3/5.)

In the High Court D could join Q as a co-defendant to counterclaim without leave (RSC Ord 15, r 3). The counterclaim would have to be sealed by the court and served on Q as if it were a writ. The copy served on him should contain certain prescribed notices and be accompanied by a form of acknowledgment of service, a copy of the writ and all pleadings served so far in the action (see *White Book* 15/3/3). Q would have to acknowledge service within fourteen days or suffer judgment in default. In order to show the relationship of the parties the title of the action would have to be severed, as shown below.

BETWEEN	P	Plaintiff
	and	
	D	Defendant
	(by original action)	
AND BETWEEN	D	Plaintiff
	and	
	P and Q	Defendants
	(by counterclaim)	

In the county court D would have to apply to the district judge for an order joining Q (CCR Ord 9, r 15). If the district judge makes the order he will give all such directions as may be necessary to deal with the matter. As to the title of the action the practice differs in different county courts. Sometimes the High Court model is used (which, in our view, is the better practice). Sometimes, however, the co-defendant's name is just added after the defendant's with the description 'defendant to counterclaim only'.

Neither the High Court rules nor the county court rules make special provision for a defendant who wishes to add a 'co-counterclaimant', ie a person *with whom* he would counterclaim against the plaintiff. In an appropriate case the defendant could apply under the general power of the court to add or substitute parties (see below). Normally however such joinder would only embarrass or inconvenience the trial. In *Montgomery v Foy* [1895] 2 QB 321 it was held that a co-counterclaimant should be joined only if his presence is *necessary* to determine the issues raised by the *plaintiff*.

Example

X employed P to ship goods to London. D, who was X's selling agent, received the goods by depositing the freight charge with the warehouseman. P sought a declaration against D that the freight charge belonged to P. D wished to rely on the contract between X and P to complain of short delivery and damage to cargo. The court ordered that X should be added as a party in order to raise these claims. This was appropriate because X was the person ultimately responsible to pay the freight charge P was claiming: *Montgomery v Foy* [1895] 2 QB 321 (and see *White Book* 15/6/6).

Power to order separate trials etc

In any action, what the parties have joined together the court may put asunder (RSC Ord 15, r 5; CCR Ord 5, r 3; CCA 1984, s 76). The court will exercise this power wherever it thinks any joinder of causes or parties may embarrass or delay the trial or is otherwise inconvenient. The court can make any of the following orders:
(1) order for separate trials of the plaintiff's claims;
(2) order for separate trial of a counterclaim;
(3) order that some claims or counterclaims be struck out;
(4) order that some parties be struck out;
(5) order entitling a party not to attend parts of the proceedings with which he is not concerned.
Order (1) is not normally used to sever the joint representation of co-plaintiffs. If co-plaintiffs disagree with each other, order (4) might be made allowing them to elect which plaintiff should proceed and which should be struck out (see further, p 96).

Misjoinder or non-joinder

Both courts have wide powers to cure any irregularity in the joinder or non-joinder of parties by removing, adding or substituting parties (RSC Ord 15, r 6; CCR Ord 15, r 1). Alternatively the court may allow an action to proceed regardless of any misjoinder or non-joinder (RSC Ord 15, r 6; CCR Ord 5, r 4). However, proceedings commenced in the name of a non-existent corporation are a nullity which cannot be cured (*White Book* 15/6/1).

No one can be added as a plaintiff unless he gives consent in writing. However, anyone can be made a defendant even against his wishes and against the wishes of the plaintiff. A person can even be joined on his own application and for this purpose he is called an 'intervener'.

Examples

In *Gurtner v Circuit* [1968] 2 QB 587 the Court of Appeal held that an intervener could be added if he could show that any order in the action would directly affect him *either* legally *or* financially. P was injured in a road crash with D. D gave his name, address and details of his insurance policy to the police but later emigrated. P could not trace either D or D's insurer. Some years after issuing a writ (see p 204) P eventually obtained an order for substituted service on D and was about to enter judgment in default. Because of their agreement with the Minister of Transport, the Motor Insurers' Bureau (MIB) would have been liable to pay the amount of any judgment P obtained. MIB successfully applied to be added as defendants in order to prevent judgment in default, raise the defence of plaintiff's negligence and take part in any assessment of P's damages.

In *The Mardina Merchant* [1975] WLR 147 it was held that the High Court has inherent jurisdiction to add an intervener as a party where the action causes that party serious hardship, difficulty or danger. P brought an Admiralty action *in rem* against a ship which was then 'arrested' at its mooring at Newhaven. The harbour authority complained that the presence of the ship was harmful to the commerce of the port and successfully intervened to obtain an order for the ship's removal.

As to interveners in *Mareva* proceedings, see p 300. See also the addition of persons as defendants in actions for possession of land and actions for wrongful interference with goods (RSC Ord 15, rr 10, 10A; CCR Ord 15, rr 3, 4). The complex topic of joinder of parties after the expiry of a limitation period is dealt with on p 184.

Joinder by consolidation

Any party may apply for the consolidation of two or more actions into one action if two conditions are fulfilled (RSC Ord 4, r 9; CCR Ord 13, r 9):

(1) The cases to be consolidated are all pending in the same division of the High Court, or in the same county court. Cases can be transferred to a particular division or to a particular county court simply to enable their consolidation; and

(2) Either (*a*) there is some common question of law or fact in each of them or (*b*) the rights to relief claimed in each arose out of the same transaction or series of transactions or (*c*) consolidation is desirable for some other reason. Compare and contrast (*a*) and (*b*) with conditions (*a*) and (*b*) in RSC Ord 15, r 4 and CCR Ord 5, r 2. For the purpose of consolidation they are given as alternatives. Under the rules last mentioned both must be satisfied if a plaintiff wishes to join parties *without leave*.

The advantage of consolidation is that it saves costs by avoiding the duplication of interlocutory stages such as pleadings and discovery. It cannot be allowed if a plaintiff in one action is a defendant in another, or if one plaintiff will not agree to joint representation, unless, in either case, that plaintiff can be turned into a counterclaiming defendant or third party.

There are three orders the district judge can make as alternatives to consolidation:

(1) Order that the actions be tried at the same time. This is quite commonly done with appeals: see for example *Ridehalgh v Horsefield* [1994] Ch 205. In *Aiden Shipping Co Ltd v Interbulk Ltd* [1986] AC 965, it was held that orders for costs in these circumstances can be made as between any of the persons before the court, ie the costs of one action may be ordered to be paid by someone who is not a party to that action.

(2) Order that the actions be tried consecutively by the same judge. This may at least reduce the duplication of counsel's fees and witnesses' expenses.

(3) Order that some actions be stayed until after the determination of one of them. The case which then proceeds will be a 'test case' for the others. The other parties will not be bound by the test case unless they agree to be bound, which they frequently will.

In multi-party litigation, eg hundreds of separate actions all arising out of a major disaster, such as an aircraft or railway accident in which many people are injured, or all concerning the effect of a drug which has been widely prescribed, orders providing for common pleadings, standardised expert reports and discovery etc may be made, common issues identified and lead actions selected to litigate them subject to costs sharing orders binding all plaintiffs (see further p 525 and see the 'Guide for Use in Group Actions' referred to in *White Book* 15/12/6).

Representative actions

Sometimes there are so many potential plaintiffs or defendants to an action, say twenty or more, that it would be inconvenient to join them all. The general rule is that only the persons joined as parties to an action will be bound by any judgment obtained. However where the parties are numerous the courts relax the general rule and permit one or more members of the group to *represent* the whole group (RSC Ord 15, r 12; CCR Ord 5, r 5; and see also the special rules for equity cases: RSC Ord 15, r 13; CCR Ord 5, r 6; and RSC Ord 15, r 13A concerning proceedings under AJA 1985, ss 47, 48 construing a will or trust where the funds in question are too small to justify full representation).

A plaintiff wishing to bring proceedings by or against a group can do so without leave, but should always seek the court's approval as soon as possible thereafter. A defendant wishing to defend on behalf of a group always needs the leave of the court. The description of the group being represented will appear in the title of the action.

The full title of *Moon v Atherton* [1972] 2 QB 435 (see below) was as follows:

BETWEEN

GLENNYS MOON (spinster) suing on behalf of
herself and the tenants of a block of flats known as
Petherton Court Harrow (except Catherine Eluned
Roberts)   Plaintiff

AND

ERIC ATHERTON   Defendant

(The description 'spinster' is no longer necessary (*White Book* 6/1/4).)

When allowed

The rules allow representative actions where numerous persons have the 'same interest'. Although this is not now regarded as a rigid limitation (*John v Rees* [1970] Ch 345), representation would not be allowed where the interests or liabilities of the group were too diverse. The remedy sought *in favour of* a group is usually a declaration or injunction. So far as money remedies are concerned, the court might allow liquidated claims or even damages, eg where they relate to damage to property collectively owned by the group (see *per* Lord Denning MR in *Moon v Atherton* [1972] 2 QB 435, below) or to infringements of copyrights collectively owned by the group (*EMI Records Ltd v Riley* [1981] 1 WLR 923). But damages could not be ordered if they would require separate assessment for each member of the group (*Markt v SS Knight* [1910] 2 KB 1021). Damages can be awarded *against* a group, in favour of an individual (*Campbell v Thompson* [1953] 1 QB 445, below; *Irish Shipping Ltd v Commercial Union Assurance Co plc* [1990] 2 WLR 117, in which a representative action against a group of seventy-seven insurers in respect of twelve insurance contracts was permitted even though some of those represented were overseas and could not have been served as defendants without leave). The court can also grant an injunction against a group (see for example *EMI Records Ltd v Kudhail* (1983) *The Times*, 28 June noted in *White Book* 15/12/1).

The Supreme Court Procedure Committee has provided a 'Guide for Use in Group Actions' which the *White Book* describes as 'essential reading' (*White Book* 15/12/6).

Status of persons represented

The members of a group being represented are regarded as parties but not *full* parties. This has four consequences:
  (1) They are not primarily liable for costs or subject to discovery, etc (see *Ventouris v Mountain* [1990] 1 WLR 1370).
  (2) If some of them object to being represented they can apply to be excepted from the representation and join as parties separately, either in their own names, or by their own representative if they are numerous (*John v Rees*, above).

(3) If the representative wishes to discontinue the action one or more of the group can apply to be added as full parties as if they had been substituted for the representative.

Example

In *Moon v Atherton*, above, a group of tenants wished to sue the architect. After starting the action most of them changed their minds. One tenant (who obtained legal aid) wished to continue the action. Because the relevant limitation period had expired it was too late for her to start a new action. She successfully applied to be added as a full party in substitution for the named plaintiff.

(4) The judgment will be binding on all persons represented. The courts avoid any injustice this might cause in two ways. First, by allowing representative actions only where the court is sure that the proceedings are for the benefit of the group represented and that the proceedings are being fully and properly argued (*Prudential Assurance v Newman Industries Ltd* [1981] Ch 229, 257, varied on appeal on other grounds). Secondly, where the plaintiff seeks to enforce a judgment against a represented person, by allowing that person to dispute liability on the grounds of his own special circumstances. This is done by requiring the plaintiff to seek leave before enforcing the judgment.

Example

On 18 January 1995 P, an employee at a gentlemen's club, fell down some stairs at the club and was injured. P brings an action against D and E, the treasurer and secretary of the club 'on their own behalf and on behalf of all other members of the Blue's Club on 18 January 1995'. P obtains judgment. On a summons to enforce the judgment against F, F might argue (1) that he was not a member of the club at the time P was injured and/or (2) that P owes him a debt in respect of some entirely different matter. F is not entitled to deny the judgment or allege contributory negligence by P.

In this example the facts before judgment are based on *Campbell v Thompson*, above. As to the position if P had been another member of the club and not an employee, see *Robertson v Ridley* [1989] 1 WLR 872 and *Jones v Northampton Borough Council* (1990) *The Times*, 21 May; being appointed an officer of the club does not by itself create a duty of care towards other members (*Robertson*) but taking on a task to be performed for other members of the club (making arrangements to hire a sports hall) may (*Jones*).

Although the plaintiff can enforce the judgment against a person represented, the representative himself cannot. If eg the representative is not insured in respect of a claim and wishes to claim a contribution from other members of the group he represents he should commence third party proceedings (*Choudhury v Hussain* (1989) *The Times*, 10 October; and see p 320).

Derivative actions

A derivative action is an action commenced by a minority shareholder in a company in order to prosecute causes of action vested in the company, eg misfeasance claims against the directors of the company. In the past attempts were made to adapt the rules relating to representative actions to cover such cases but this led to many procedural complexities. RSC Ord 15, r 12A now provides a workable procedure. As in a representative action, a person wishing to sue on behalf of the company must obtain the court's leave to do so before the defendants are put to the expense of serving a defence. If the court is persuaded to grant such leave, it may also make orders entitling the parties to an indemnity as to the costs of the action out of the assets of the company.

Chapter 7

Outline of the Civil Process

The purpose of this chapter is to describe in simple outline the jurisdiction of the High Court and county courts and to summarise the consequences of using the different forms of originating process available in each court. Both of these topics are of course dealt with at greater length in the subsequent chapters of this book. It is also convenient to add at the end of this chapter some basic points about the role of the solicitor in litigation and about alternatives to litigation.

High Court or county court?

In the past, one assumed that most civil cases would go to the High Court. Today the reverse is true; 90 per cent of all civil cases start and finish in the county courts (source: *Court of Appeal Review Consultation Paper 1997*). This is because the High Court and County Courts Jurisdiction Order 1991 entirely re-wrote the system which allocates business between the civil courts. The county courts are now the courts of general jurisdiction. The High Court is now a specialist court suitable for the weightiest and most complex cases only.

The text of the High Court and County Courts Jurisdiction Order 1991 deals mainly with transfers between the two courts and is therefore covered in Chapter 17 (see p 373). What follows is the briefest of summaries needed in order to explain the diagram set out overleaf (table 1).

Initially of course, it is up to the plaintiff to choose where to commence the proceedings. However, the defendant will subsequently receive full opportunity to apply for a transfer if he wishes to do so. As a general rule, cases should be commenced in the court in which they are likely to be tried (should they get that far) if only to avoid the cost and inconvenience of transfer later.

If an application for transfer is made, the rules to be applied (set out in the 1991 Order) are tilted in favour of proceeding in the county court. They specify four criteria which may be considered: financial substance, importance, complexity and speed of trial. The greater the financial substance, importance and complexity, the more suitable the case is for trial in the High Court. The lower the financial substance, importance and

[*continued on p 109*]

Table 1: Commencement in High Court or county court?*

Basic contract and tort cases		Specialist areas		
Personal injury cases	*Non-personal injury cases*	*Landlord and tenant*	*Equity*	*Insolvency*
Up to £1,000 County court summons (small claims procedure if defended)	*Up to £3,000* County court summons (small claims procedure if defended)	*Possession action in respect of a dwelling* County court for district in which the dwelling is situate (fixed date summons in most cases) *Business tenant's application for a new tenancy* County court originating application or High Court originating summons depending upon the 'value' to the plaintiff and the presumptions and other factors relevant in basic non-personal injury cases (NB 'Value' here may depend upon, eg, the tenant's likely relocation costs if the application is unsuccessful)	*Specific performance of contract for the sale of land* County court for the district in which D resides or in which the contract was made (fixed date summons), but only if the purchase price does not exceed £30,000 or if P and D agree to confer greater jurisdiction on the county court (see CCA 1984, ss 23 and 24). Otherwise, High Court writ *Inheritance (Provision for Family and Dependants) Act 1975* County court originating application or High Court originating summons depending upon the 'value' to the plaintiff and the presumptions and other factors relevant in basic non-personal injury cases	*Bankruptcy* The nominated county court or, in London, the High Court, depending upon the debtor's place of residence or business during the six months prior to commencement; see further, p 629 *Corporate insolvency (winding up)* The High Court in London in almost all cases; see further, p 640
£1,001 to £49,999 County court summons (seek transfer later if, eg, importance and complexity make High Court proceedings more suitable)	*£3,001 to £24,999* County court summons (unless the presumptions as to value can be rebutted)			
£50,000 or more High Court writ (or county court summons if plaintiff prefers)	*£25,000 or more* High Court writ (or county court summons if plaintiff prefers)			

*   General guidance only

complexity, the more suitable the case is for trial in the county court. The fourth factor, speed of trial, may go either way, depending upon how busy the courts are. Unlike the other factors, speed of trial can never be a conclusive factor. It is no more than a make-weight which can be used to strengthen a case based on other factors.

The four factors just mentioned are of course relevant to transfer rather than to commencement. It would often be unfair to put upon the plaintiff the burden of calculating their relative weight at the outset of the case when of course little might be known at that stage as to, eg the nature of the defendant's defence or the size and nature of any counterclaim which may be raised. In order to guide the plaintiff at commencement, and to guide the court on any subsequent application for transfer, the 1991 Order provides certain presumptions which turn upon 'value'. Value and financial substance are defined in the 1991 Order to mean two very different things. Put simply, 'value' means the plaintiff's reasonable estimate of the *gross value* of his claim, ignoring most matters of defence and counterclaim. 'Financial substance' is more precise. It looks at what the case is really worth, all things considered.

Those cases in which the plaintiff's reasonable estimate of gross value is below £25,000 are presumed to be suitable for the county court unless one or other party can show, eg, that they are in fact complex and/or important. Cases in which the plaintiff's reasonable estimate of gross value exceeds £50,000 are presumed suitable for the High Court unless, eg, the 'financial substance' (net value) is much lower.

What of cases in the £25,000 to £50,000 band? No presumptions apply to guide the plaintiff on commencement as to these. There are however two other points which should be borne in mind. Article 5 of the 1991 Order states that personal injury cases not exceeding £50,000 (ie most personal injury cases) *must* be commenced in the county court. As to non-personal injury cases, a 1991 *Practice Direction* (noted on p 379) gives guidance as to what types of cases may be considered important and therefore suitable for the High Court. The first example in the list is professional negligence cases.

Although the 1991 Order's factors and presumptions govern most civil cases (ie most cases concerning the basic law of contract and tort) they do not govern all cases. In some specialist areas, the jurisdiction of the county court is still subject to fixed pecuniary or geographical limits. Table 1 gives examples.

Proceedings commenced in the wrong court

Taking 'wrong court' to mean 'less appropriate court', mistakes or differences of opinion as to this may result in a transfer to the other court (see further p 373).

Taking 'wrong court' to mean 'inappropriate level of court', it is never wrong to start basic contract or tort cases in the county court. It is wrong to start a personal injury action in the High Court if it is clearly worth less than £50,000. If that happens, the court at trial or on transfer may penalise the plaintiff and/or the plaintiff's solicitors in costs (see further pp 373 and 537); if the error was made dishonestly, eg in order to harass the defendant, the court may also simply strike out the proceedings, leaving the plaintiff to recommence in the correct court, subject to any limitation defence the defendant may by this time have acquired (see p 79). Simple costs penalties and/or striking out or transfer can also be imposed in non-personal injury cases (but as to the imposition of costs penalties under CLSA 1990, s 51(8) at present, see further p 373).

Taking 'wrong court' to mean 'geographically inappropriate court' (eg in certain landlord and tenant cases) the solution lies in transfer to the correct court and/or simple costs penalties against the plaintiff and/or his solicitors (see eg *Sharma v Knight* [1986] 1 WLR 757).

Different forms of originating process

An originating process is a document sealed by a court which commences proceedings in that court. Current rule-books contain a variety of such forms. Which one you choose affects the subsequent steps to be taken in those proceedings in order to get them to trial (if they ever get that far). In the High Court there are four basic forms of originating process: a writ, an originating summons, an originating notice of motion, or a petition. The writ is the method most frequently used in the Queen's Bench Division. The following cases must be commenced by writ:

(1) tort cases other than trespass to land;
(2) actions in which the plaintiff's claim is based on an allegation of fraud;
(3) actions in which the plaintiff claims damages for breach of duty (whether contractual, statutory or otherwise) where the damages claimed consist of or include damages in respect of death, personal injuries, or damage to property;
(4) patent actions; and
(5) other actions which are specifically required to be commenced by writ under any statute or any other rule, eg Admiralty actions *in rem* and probate actions (RSC Ord 5, r 2).

The originating summons is characteristic of the Chancery Division and the procedural route it prescribes is simpler than that for a writ action. It omits the so-called weapons of litigation (pleadings, automatic discovery, oral evidence) which are important only in contentious cases. RSC Ord 5, r 4 indicates the sort of case appropriate for this simpler procedure, namely proceedings:

(a) in which the sole or principal question at issue is or is likely to be one of the construction of an Act or of any instrument made under an Act or of any deed, will, contract or other document or some other question of law, or (*b*) in which there is unlikely to be any substantial dispute of fact, unless, in either case, the plaintiff intends to apply for summary judgment or for any other reason the proceedings are more appropriate to be begun by writ. Note that usually all claims of a contentious nature should be commenced by writ: *Re Sir Lindsay Parkinson & Co Ltd* [1965] 1 WLR 372.

RSC Ord 5, r 3 lists the proceedings which *must* be begun by originating summons. They are proceedings by which an 'application' is made to the High Court under any Act (such as the Trustee Act 1925 or the Law of Property Act 1925) where no other method of commencement is expressly authorised or required.

The remaining two types of originating process, motions and petitions, are very specialised. They are to be used only where the rules expressly so authorise or require. Examples of originating motions include certain non-contentious probate applications and also the application for what is known as judicial review, which is described on p 260. Examples of petitions include divorce cases, and bankruptcy and winding-up petitions. These cases are governed by separate procedural codes: the Family Proceedings Rules 1991 (outside the scope of this book), and the Insolvency Rules 1986 (see Chapter 26).

The county court also has four basic types of originating process: the *summons*, which is equivalent to the High Court writ; the *originating application*, which is used in cases which, if commenced in the High Court, would be commenced by originating summons; *petitions* (eg in divorce or bankruptcy cases) and *requests for entry of appeal* (eg against demolition orders or closing orders made by a local authority under the Housing Act 1985, s 269). The last two mentioned can only be used where an Act or rule so authorises or requires and are often subject to separate procedural codes.

In both courts, the procedure in each case depends directly upon the form of originating process used to commence it. Cases commenced by High Court writ or county court summons have to pass through several interlocutory stages on their way to trial. Cases commenced by originating summons (High Court) or originating application (county court) follow a simpler and faster route. These routes are summarised below. In county courts, there are two types of case which are not fully covered by the summaries: defended small claims (as to which see further p 279) and fixed date actions (as to which, see further p 255). In these two cases the procedure after commencement is determined as much by the nature of the case as by the form of originating process used to commence it.

Procedural tables

Actions commenced by High Court writ or county court summons

1 Issue

The form of originating process is usually prepared by the plaintiff's solicitors. It is issued when it is sealed ie officially stamped, at the court

office. As to the documentation on issue, see p 195 (High Court) and
p 238 (county court).

Normally, no leave to issue is necessary; for exceptional cases, see p 94
(concerning vexatious litigants) and p 142 (cases involving a foreign,
non-EU, element).

The date of issue is the vital date for the purpose of limitation law (see
p 79).

2 Service

As to the documentation on service, see p 204 (High Court) and p 250
(county court). In the vast majority of cases, service will be effected by
ordinary first-class post. In High Court cases and most personal injury
cases in the county court, the posting is normally done by the plaintiff's
solicitors. In other county court cases it is done by court clerks.

The writ or summons remains valid for service for four months
beginning with the date of issue (longer in some cases with a foreign
element; see further p 196). If, for some good reason, service is not
effected in that time, an extension of time may be granted (see further
p 205).

3 Defendant's response

In the High Court, the defendant must complete a form of *acknowledgment of service* and deliver it to the court office out of which the writ was
issued. The form enables the defendant to concede liability if he wishes,
and in some cases, if he does so, to obtain a delay upon enforcement
against him. The form also enables him, in some cases commenced
outside London, to apply for a transfer of proceedings to his local court
office.

In the county court, the defendant must deliver to the court office a
defence and/or a counterclaim or an admission making proposals as to
payment. Alternatively, if the plaintiff claims a fixed sum which the
defendant wants to admit in full, the defendant should send his admission
direct to the plaintiff.

All county court cases in which some decision by the court will have to
be made (eg defended cases and cases where there is a dispute about the
time or the rate of payment) are automatically transferred to the
defendant's home court (assuming of course they are not already
proceeding in that court).

In both courts, if the defendant fails to respond to service, the plaintiff
may, in most cases, enter judgment in default. As to the exceptional cases,
the deadlines and the documentation, see pp 212 and 247.

4 Pleadings stage

In the High Court, pleadings are served between the parties and are not
filed in court until the *setting down* stage (see below). The plaintiff's
pleading is called the statement of claim and may be indorsed on the writ,

or served with the writ or served later (eg after waiting to see if it will be possible to enter judgment in default without incurring the expense of pleadings). Failure to serve a statement of claim may lead (usually after many months if not years) to a dismissal for want of prosecution (as to which, see further p 364).

In the High Court, a defendant must serve a defence, usually within twenty-eight days of the service of the writ or fourteen days after service of the statement of claim, whichever is the longer. Any delay, eg just one day's delay, may lead to a judgment being entered in default of defence.

A High Court defendant who wishes to raise a counterclaim, must add the counterclaim to his defence. This will oblige the plaintiff to serve a defence to counterclaim. Any delay by the plaintiff in doing this, eg just one day's delay, may lead to a judgment being entered in default of defence to counterclaim.

In the county court, the pleadings are filed in court during the commencement stages (see above). The plaintiff's pleading, the particulars of claim, is stapled to or indorsed on the summons. The defendant has to send his defence and/or counterclaim to the court office, which then sends a copy to the plaintiff. If a counterclaim is raised, the plaintiff is not required to file or serve a defence to counterclaim (although it is usually wise to do so). If he does not, the defendant cannot obtain judgment in default of defence to counterclaim.

5 Close of pleadings

This is a notional date in the calendar of an action from which or to which certain time periods are measured. In the High Court, close of pleadings is deemed to occur fourteen days after the last pleading was served, the last pleading being either a defence, a defence to counterclaim or a reply (as to which, see p 164). In the county court, close of pleadings is deemed to occur twenty-eight days after delivery of a counterclaim, or fourteen days after delivery of a defence if there is no counterclaim.

6 Discovery of documents

In the High Court, lists of documents have to be served within fourteen days after close of pleadings, ie three or four weeks after the last pleading was served; inspection of non-privileged documents should be allowed seven days thereafter (see further p 394).

In the county court the parties get two weeks 'extra' in which to serve lists, twenty-eight days from close of pleadings, with inspection of non-privileged documents seven days thereafter. These two extra weeks replace the extra time allowed in the High Court timetable for the lodgment of an acknowledgment of service.

7 Directions

In most High Court cases, the plaintiff must take out a *summons for directions* within one month of close of pleadings (see further p 451). In most High Court personal injury cases, and most county court cases, certain *automatic directions* come into effect as from the close of pleadings (see further pp 465 and 472).

8 Exchange of evidence

In both courts, reports and statements made by the experts and other witnesses whom the parties are intending to call must be exchanged (ie disclosed simultaneously) within the deadlines fixed by directions (see further p 422).

9 Setting down

This old-fashioned term comes from the High Court and refers to cases being set down, ie put into, one or other of the lists of cases awaiting trial. In the High Court at present the parties are not given a fixed date for trial initially; instead the court keeps 'running lists'; after the case has been set down, the parties can then apply for a fixed date (a 'fixture', presumably a term drawn from league sports).

In the High Court, setting down involves the plaintiff delivering to the court within the time limit fixed by directions (see above) certain bundles of formal documents including in particular copies of the pleadings served. The plaintiff must also notify the parties that he has done so (see further p 483).

In the county court, setting down involves the plaintiff writing to the court requesting a trial date; the request should be made within the time limit fixed by directions (see above). There is no obligation to file documents at this stage and it is the court which notifies the defendant that this stage has been reached and what the date of trial is.

In both courts, a setting down fee is payable.

10 Trial bundles

After the setting down the parties must finalise their preparation of bundles of documents for use at the trial. These bundles should include in particular, the reports and statements made by the experts and other witnesses whom the parties are intending to call at the trial. The time limits for collaboration between the parties and for the lodging of these bundles is fixed by directions (see above).

11 Trial

Very few civil cases reach this stage. Of those that do, the usual mode of trial is by judge sitting without a jury. Evidence is given mainly in the form of experts and other witnesses attending in order to identify their signature on the report or statement previouly disclosed to the opponents and in order to answer any questions asked of them by the opponents by way of cross-examination.

Matters commenced by originating summons (High Court) or originating application (county court)

1 Issue

2 Service

Although the documentation is different, the procedure as to these steps is the same as in actions commenced by writ or county court summons.

3 Defendant's response

In the High Court, the defendant must lodge an acknowledgment of service but, if he does not, there is no provision for the plaintiff obtaining judgment in default.

In the county court, the defendant is in some cases required to file an answer to the originating application; in these cases, the obligation to do so will be stated in the notice of application served on him (see for example business tenancy applications and the prescribed form N8(2)).

4 Filing and serving evidence

In the High Court, once service has been acknowledged by the defendant (or one of them) the next stage is the filing and service of affidavits and exhibits which are intended to be used at the hearing. Within the next fourteen days, the plaintiff must file his evidence in court and serve copies of it on each defendant who has acknowledged service. Such a defendant has twenty-eight days from service of the originating summons in order to file his evidence and serve copies thereof on the plaintiff and on any other defendant who is affected thereby. The plaintiff then has a further fourteen days to file and serve evidence in reply. Parties must serve the copies on one another without requiring prior payment. Should it be necessary to do so, the court may make specific directions as to the filing and service of evidence (see generally RSC Ord 28, r 1A).

In the county court also, affidavit evidence is permissible if the hearing (see below) is to be in chambers or if fourteen days' notice is given to other parties and no notice of objection is received (CCR Ord 20, r 5). In practice, especially in the case of litigants in person, evidence at the hearing may be given orally.

5 Appointment for hearing

In the county court, this date is arranged by the court office at the time of issue. This date is recorded in the document given to the plaintiff at the time of issue and in the notice to the defendant which is stapled to the originating application. The originating application must be served at least twenty-one days before this date.

In the High Court, within one month after the time for filing and serving evidence, the plaintiff must obtain an appointment for the hearing of the summons and must give at least fourteen days' notice of the appointment to every defendant who has acknowledged service. The hearing takes place before the district judge. Many originating summonses can be finally determined by the district judge whose jurisdiction is set out in the rules, and, in the case of Chancery masters, in the practice direction currently in force (see Chapter 1). Chancery masters have no power to determine a question as to the construction of a document or a question of law (RSC Ord 32, r 14). If for any reason, a summons cannot be finally determined at the first hearing, the Chancery master/district judge can give such directions as to the further conduct of the proceedings as he thinks best adapted to secure the just, expeditious and economical disposal thereof (see generally RSC Ord 28, r 4). In particular, directions will be given for the exchange of witness statements if further evidence is to be adduced (see RSC Ord 38, r 2A and *White Book* 823).

For actions outside the district judge's jurisdiction the next stages are the setting down (as to which see the writ action notes) and ultimately the trial. The trial will be held before a judge sitting without a jury either in open court or in chambers. Evidence is normally given by affidavit, or written statement limited to those which were previously filed and served. If a party wishes to cross-examine an opponent's witness who has sworn an affidavit, the party can ask before the district judge at the first hearing for an order for the witness's attendance at the trial. Then if the witness fails to attend the trial the affidavit cannot be used as evidence without the leave of the judge (RSC Ord 38, r 2; CCR Ord 20, r 5). A witness whose evidence is in the form of a written statement must attend the trial as the statement is not evidence until the witness has sworn to the truth of the statement.

Commencement by the wrong form

Sometimes the plaintiff has no choice as to which form of originating process should be used. Even where there is a choice (usually between using a writ or an originating summons or their county court equivalents) the nature of the case may make one form more appropriate than the other. Whenever the plaintiff uses the wrong form or the less appropriate form, he must expect to pay any extra costs caused thereby. In many cases the simplest solution may be to terminate the action and begin again. However, sometimes this is not possible; the relevant limitation period may have expired or an overseas defendant who has acknowledged service may now wish to challenge the English court's jurisdiction (see p 212).

In the High Court, mistakes as to choice of originating process are never fatal to the action. They cannot render the action a nullity and the court has no power wholly to set aside the proceedings (RSC Ord 2, r 1). On the contrary it is possible to adapt any case to the most appropriate procedure. The change *from* originating summons procedure *to* writ procedure is made by applying under RSC Ord 28, r 8. This rule empowers the district judge to order that proceedings should continue *as if the action had been begun by writ*. If the district judge makes such an order he must then treat the hearing as if it were the hearing of a summons for directions and, eg, make orders as to discovery and pleadings.

An 'as if begun by' order might be sought in the following cases:

(1) a claim alleging fraud which therefore should have been started by writ (see RSC Ord 5, r 2: *Re Deadman* [1971] 1 WLR 426);

(2) an application under the Law of Property Act 1925 which could not have been started by writ but in which the defendant wishes to raise a counterclaim (see RSC Ord 5, r 3; Ord 28, rr 7 and 8).

There is no 'as if begun by' rule which turns a writ into an originating summons. However, a similar result is achieved by obtaining an order for *trial without pleadings* under RSC Ord 18, r 21. If the district judge makes such an order he must then treat the hearing as if it were the hearing of a summons for directions. It is usually convenient to prepare a statement of the issues in dispute: if the parties are unable to agree such a statement the district judge may settle it himself. As to the evidence to be given at the trial the district judge often gives leave for evidence by affidavit. An order under RSC Ord 18, r 21 also affects the third weapon of litigation present in writ procedure: there is no automatic discovery in actions to be tried without pleadings (see RSC Ord 24, r 2).

An application under RSC Ord 18, r 21, cannot be made where the writ includes a claim for libel, slander, malicious prosecution or false imprisonment, or a claim based on an allegation of fraud. These are the cases most likely to be tried by jury (see further p 463).

The county court rules as to commencement by the wrong form are much simpler. Where a party commences proceedings by summons which should have been commenced by originating application (or *vice versa*) the failure to comply with the rules constitutes an irregularity only and does not nullify those proceedings. The court can either allow them to continue in that form or adapt them to the correct form (CCR Ord 37, r 5 and see pp 3 and 109).

The role of solicitors

Relationship with the courts

The full title of the office of solicitor is 'solicitor of the Supreme Court' although, in fact, only a few members of the profession are directly employed by the courts as solicitors. The *Official Solicitor* and his team perform various duties including the representation of minors and mental patients in High Court cases (where there is no person willing or able to act) and the representation of persons sent to prison for contempt of court.

Nevertheless, the rest of the practising profession, although they receive no remuneration from the court, are officers thereof and are subject, therefore, to its summary jurisdiction and control (Solicitors Act 1974, s 50). The High Court can order that a solicitor's name should be struck off the roll of solicitors and can make orders summarily requiring solicitors to deliver up money or documents received or to pay compensation for loss suffered because of the solicitor's misconduct or neglect. Both the High Court and the county court can *inter alia* penalise solicitors in costs, disallowing payment between solicitor and client or ordering the solicitor personally to pay the costs of all parties (see generally *White Book* 3871 *et seq*; RSC Ord 62, r 11; CCR Ord 38, r 1(3); and *Davy-Chiesman v Davy-Chiesman* [1984] Fam 48 referred to below).

Relationship with clients and barristers

Litigation solicitors are not *employed* by their clients as such but *retained* by them to conduct the proceedings on their behalf and give them the benefit of professional skills and advice. Once a solicitor has notified the other party's solicitors of the retainer, they will in future correspond directly with that solicitor as it is then considered improper to communicate personally with the client. The solicitor has ostensible authority to accept service of documents on behalf of the client, to make admissions and arrangements as to the trial and, in certain circumstances, to compromise the proceedings (see generally Cordery on *Solicitors*; and as to compromise see p 33 above). As between solicitor and client, of course, the solicitor must ensure that he acts in accordance with the client's instructions. As a general rule a solicitor should never take any step without specific instructions from the client. Even where the client simply instructs the solicitor to 'get on with it and do whatever is necessary', the solicitor should still ensure that the client knows precisely what is being done on his behalf. Certainly one should never take an unusual step without specific instructions (see RSC Ord 62, r 15 and p 579).

The role the barrister plays in civil litigation is a limited one. The barrister's specialism is in trial procedure and evidence. The majority of civil cases end without a trial. Barristers also draft pleadings and other documents, and of course advise on difficult points of law or the *quantum* of damages in difficult or substantial cases. Generally speaking barristers may be instructed only by solicitors and not by the client direct. However, they speak for the client at the trial and may make admissions and compromises on the client's behalf. A barrister in court must always be attended at court by the instructing solicitor or the solicitor's clerk. As a matter of professional ethics the solicitor is personally liable to pay the barrister whether or not the solicitor has been put in funds by the client.

The duty of a solicitor retained by a client is an onerous one. Their relationship is of course fiduciary. Also, solicitors will be liable in negligence if they fail to act according to the high standards of skill and knowledge required of the profession. Proceedings against a solicitor may be framed in either contract or tort: *Midland Bank v Hett, Stubbs and Kemp* [1979] Ch 384; *Henderson v Merrett Syndicates Ltd* [1994] 3 WLR 761, HL. Allegations of misconduct or neglect concerning litigation are often dealt with summarily, the court deciding under its inherent jurisdiction whether to penalise the solicitor in costs (see above).

The question whether the solicitor is liable in respect of mistakes made by the barrister is a difficult one. Note first that 'as a general rule a solicitor acting on the advice of properly instructed counsel can hardly be said to be acting unreasonably, save perhaps in a very exceptional set of circumstances' (*per* Sachs J in *Francis v Francis* [1956] P 87). However the solicitor will be liable if he fails to instruct counsel properly, eg by failing to supply counsel with instructions as to a material fact of which the solicitor is aware (see 3 *Halsbury's Laws* (4th ed) para 1190). The solicitor will also be liable if, having the opportunity to do so, he fails to correct a mistake made by the barrister which is 'patent'or 'glaringly apparent' to any reasonable solicitor (see *Davy-Chiesman v Davy-Chiesman* [1984] Fam 48). In that case May LJ stated that 'a solicitor is in general entitled to rely on the advice of counsel properly instructed. However, this does not operate so as to give a solicitor an immunity in every such case. A solicitor is highly trained and rightly expected to be experienced in his particular legal fields. He is under a duty at all times to exercise that degree of care, both to client and the court, that can be expected of a reasonably prudent solicitor. He is not entitled to rely blindly and with no mind of his own on counsel's views.'

Lord Woolf's proposals for reform

In recent years, costs and delay have come to be identified as the two greatest faults in the civil process. There have been several inquiries and reports as to how these two faults can be remedied. The latest report, Lord Woolf's 'Access to Justice: Final Report, 1996' will fundamentally affect the conduct of civil litigation.

Currently, most solicitors charge clients according to an hourly rate. In such cases, time really is money. The more time which the solicitor can reasonably put in on the client's case, the more fees he is entitled to claim from that client.

Currently, 'litigation is in the hands of the parties'. Although rules of court provide procedural routes for cases to follow, it is up to the parties to decide whether and if so how quickly to proceed along those routes. Our system is adversarial; the court does not normally intervene to direct the parties except as to those questions which the parties decide to put to the court. This enables the rich, the legally aided and the insured to use interlocutory procedures aggressively in an attempt to frighten their opponents into submission.

Lord Woolf's report proposes:

A new approach to justice ...
An expanded small claims jurisdiction ...

A new fast track for cases up to £10,000, with strictly limited procedures, fixed timetables (20–30 weeks to trial) and fixed costs.

A new multi-track for cases above £10,000, providing individual hands-on management by judicial teams for the heaviest cases ...

In small claims cases there will be increased emphasis on reaching a decision involving only one attendance at court, or indeed by means of an adjudication on paper only.

In fast-track cases, ie, the majority of cases, the limitations on interlocutory proceedings will allow fewer opportunities to incur costs; discovery will be confined to the process we currently think of as the preparation of trial bundles other than witness statements; indeed, witness statements will be replaced by witness summaries; the instruction of experts will be severely controlled and the trial will be confined to a three-hour hearing with no oral evidence from experts. If fully implemented the fast-track recommendations will reduce lawyers' income from litigation. Correspondingly they will also reduce lawyers' responsibility for getting cases to the ideal result. This responsibility will be placed instead upon the court system.

In multi-track cases, ie the heavier county court cases and High Court cases, there will normally be two case management hearings; the first one will be convened after the defence is received and will attempt to identify the issues in dispute, fully explore the possibilities of settlement, including suggestions as to the use of ADR (see below) where this appears likely to be beneficial and, subject to that, decide what level of discovery is necessary and on which issues, and fix dates for the exchange of witness statements, and for other interlocutory applications and fix a provisional date or dates for the trial of the issues.

The second case management hearing in multi-track cases will take place just before the trial. The hearing will be conducted by the trial judge and the parties will be represented by the advocates instructed to represent them at the trial.

In all cases, the court will expect the parties and their lawyers to be co-operative rather then combative and costs penalties will be imposed on those who are not.

Many of the recommendations made in Lord Woolf's report have been recommended before. Indeed, some of them have been tried before. What is new is the expectation that, this time, the recommendations will be acted upon, and will be persisted in until they are fully accepted. Perhaps this is because, this time, the recommendations are in tune with the times. They are streamlined, unemotional, low-cost and user-friendly.

In similar vein, The Law Society has produced *Practice Management Standards* ([1995] *Gazette*, 26 May). These provide guidelines for the efficient working of solicitors' firms. So far as civil litigation is concerned they lay down sensible procedures to adopt concerning client contact and file management. For most firms, these written standards are recommended only; they are not compulsory. However, they are compulsory for firms which enter into a franchise agreement with the Legal Aid Board; they are required by the terms of their franchise to comply with them. Also bear in mind that many ideas that start off as best practice recommendations later become minimum standards for everyone.

The new approach to time

Emphasis upon the importance of reducing delays in order to avoid expense did not originate from Lord Woolf's Report. For several years now the courts and the rule committees have been taking an increasingly firmer hand against wastage and in favour of the just despatch of civil litigation. Although particular examples are itemised below it is convenient to start with the general guidance given by the Court of Appeal in *Mortgage Corporation Ltd v Sandoes* (1996) *The Times*, 27 December as to the future approach which litigants can expect the court to adopt to the failure to adhere to time limits contained in rules or directions of the court:

(1) Time limits laid down by the rules and directions given by the court were not merely targets to be attempted; they were rules to be observed.

(2) At the same time the overriding principle was that justice must be done.

(3) Litigants were entitled to have their cases resolved with reasonable expedition. The non-compliance with time limits could cause prejudice to one or more of the parties to the litigation.

(4) In addition the vacation or adjournment of the date of trial prejudiced other litigants and disrupted the administration of justice.

(5) Extensions of time which involved the vacation or adjournment of trial dates should therefore be granted only as a last resort.

(6) Where time limits had not been complied with the parties should co-operate in reaching an agreement as to new time limits which would not involve the date of trial being postponed.

(7) If they reached such an agreement they could ordinarily expect the court to give effect to that agreement at the trial and it was not necessary to make a separate application solely for that purpose.

(8) The court would not look with favour on a party who sought only to take tactical advantage from the failure of another party to comply with time limits.

(9) In the absence of an agreement as to a new timetable, an application should be made promptly to the court for directions.

(10) In considering whether to grant an extension of time to a party who was in default, the court would look at all the circumstances of the case including the considerations identified above.

Specific examples of the new approach

(1) Since 1990 the time for service of writs and most other forms of originating process is only four months (for exceptions, see p 112).

The plaintiff should not unreasonably delay service until the end of that period. If he does so and thereby gets into difficulties an extension of the period is likely to be refused (see further p 205 and *White Book* 6/8/4).

(2) Since 1994 the time for service of High Court interlocutory summonses has been (in most cases) not less than two days before the hearing and not more than 14 days after issue of the summons. Further, unless the subject-matter of the summons is wholly routine the applicant should seek at the outset to agree with the respondents a suitable time estimate and list of dates when both sides will and will not be available. Failure to do so may lead to costs penalties (see further p 537 and *White Book* 32/3/1).

(3) In the county court an intending plaintiff in a personal injury action who is unable to file the requisite medical report and statement of special damage at the time of issue and who applies *ex parte* for an extension of time in which to do so should explain in writing, usually by affidavit, the problem which had arisen and its cause (*Phillips v Taunton and Somerset National Health Trust* (1996) *The Times*, 15 August).

(4) Since 1989 the automatic directions which apply in most county court actions make provision for the automatic strike out of actions in which the plaintiff fails to request a date for trial in the time allowed (see further p 362 noting CCR Ord 17, r 11). Reinstatement is possible but before allowing this the court will consider various factors (see p 363 noting *Rastin v British Steel plc* [1994] 1 WLR 732). These factors require the legal profession to attain high standards of diligence throughout the litigation (*Jackson v Slater Harrison* [1996] 1 WLR 597 *per* Otton LJ at 601F, G) '[In] personal injury cases in the county court a new regime is in place, a regime under which the old leisurely and often rudderless way of conducting these usually simple cases will not be tolerated' *Gardner v Southwark LBC (Note)* [1996] 1 WLR 571 *per* Henry LJ. In *Perry v Wong* [1997] 1 WLR 381 Lord Bingham of Cornhill CJ stated that 'Ord 17, r 11 of the County Court Rules 1981, as substituted, does introduce a new and, as the court has held in the past, draconian regime with the obvious intention of attempting to eliminate the delays which have disfigured the conduct of litigation, particularly personal injury litigation, in the past ... [A rule requiring the making of a request nine months before the automatic strike out occurs] enables the court to summon the parties and impose a procedural timetable upon them which, indeed, this court would expect increasingly to be done.'

(5) Since July 1996 plaintiffs who fail to set down Queen's Bench actions within the time limit prescribed must apply for leave to set down. The application should be made *ex parte* to the district

judge who may require an *inter partes* summons to be issued (*Practice Direction (Action: Setting Down)* [1996] 1 WLR 1431).

(6) Since 1993 rules and directions laying down time limits for the exchange of witness statements have become routine. In the early days those time limits were often overlooked and trial judges frequently gave parties leave to adduce evidence which had not previously been disclosed. Such leave is not now given so readily (*Beachley Property Ltd v Edgar* (1996) *The Times*, 18 July: *Mortgage Corporation Ltd v Sandoes* (1996) *The Times*, 27 December, a quotation from which appears on p 121 above).

(7) Acting directly upon recommendations made in Lord Woolf's report judges now frequently make orders seeking to limit time and expense incurred by litigants concerning discovery of documents (see for example *Hoechst Celanese Corporation v BP Chemicals Ltd* (1997) *The Times*, 13 February) and the adduction of expert evidence (*Abbey National Mortgages plc v Key Surveyors Nationwide Ltd* [1996] 1 WLR 1534. Such orders should not be regarded as final. It is open to the parties to seek further orders on these topics as the case develops.

(8) Pre-reading of pleadings, skeleton arguments and certain other documents is now standard practice on many hearings before circuit judges, High Court judges and Court of Appeal judges. It also takes place in a growing number of proceedings before district judges in respect of applications going beyond formal or routine applications (see for example *White Book* 32/1–6/18 second paragraph; but woe betide those practitioners who lodge papers but later fail to inform the district judge if the matter then settles before the return day).

Unless orders

Another aspect of the new approach to time is the increasing willingness of judges to grant and to uphold unless orders made against litigants who fail to comply with a time limit imposed by a rule of court or by a previous direction made by the court. An unless order specifies the step to be taken by the erring litigant and also states the adverse consequences which will occur unless he does so. The order must state precisely the period within which the step is to be taken if the adverse consequences are to be avoided. It must either state the number of days *after* service of the order within which the step is to be taken; or state the hour and day *before* which it must be taken. The examples below derive from a *Practice Note* of 1986 set out in the *White Book* 3/5/5.

> Unless within 14 days of service of this order the defendant serves his list of documents the defence be struck out and judgment entered for the plaintiff with costs to be taxed if not agreed: plaintiff's costs of this application in any event.
> Unless by 4 pm on Friday 13 June 1997 the plaintiff requests the proper

officer to fix a day for the hearing the action shall be automatically struck with costs for the defendant to be taxed if not agreed: defendant's costs of this application in any event.

Today unless orders are more frequently applied for and granted than they used to be and this trend has received Court of Appeal approval at least in the case of county court actions governed by the automatic directions (*Downer & Downer Ltd v Brough* [1996] 1 WLR 575 at 582 D–G; *Whitehead v Avon County Council* (1997) *The Times*, 17 March *per* Waller LJ).

Even though such an order has been made the court still has power to extend the time limit and may even do so after the time limit has passed. However the court is unlikely to extend the time limit save in exceptional circumstances. In *Hytec Information Systems Ltd v Coventry City Council* (1996) *The Times*, 31 December Ward LJ set out the following principles which Lord Woolf MR described as general guidance applicable in most cases for the time being:

(1) An unless order was an order of last resort, not made unless there was a history of failure to comply with other orders. It was a party's last chance to put its case in order.

(2) Because it was the last chance, a failure to comply would ordinarily result in the sanction being imposed.

(3) That sanction was a necessary forensic weapon which the broader interests of the administration of justice required to be deployed unless the most compelling arguments were advanced to exonerate the failure.

(4) It seemed axiomatic that if a party intentionally or deliberately flouted the order he could expect no mercy.

(5) A sufficient exoneration would almost invariably require that he satisfied the court that something beyond his control had caused the failure.

(6) The judge would exercise his judicial discretion whether to excuse the failure in the circumstances of each case on its own merits, at the core of which was service to justice.

(7) The interests of justice required that justice be shown to the injured party for procedural inefficiencies causing the twin scourges of delay and wasted costs. The public interest in the administration of justice to contain those blights also weighed heavily. Any injustice to the defaulting party, although never to be ignored came a long way behind the other two.

Alternative dispute resolution (ADR)

For the solicitor, civil litigation commences when the client first seeks advice. Sometimes the most difficult job a solicitor has is to persuade the client *not* to fight an action. Often this advice will be unpalatable. The clients' pride or principles will not let them back down. But the old maxim is as true today as it has always been: don't go to law. Losing is not the only risk the client takes. Cases can take months to complete and years off one's lifespan. However confident the client is at the start, it is the opposing lawyer's job to sap that confidence. As the trial draws nearer doubts creep in, costs mount up and the nervous strain can become unbearable. Even if successful, the client may still be out of pocket. The costs order in his favour will not cover all the expense suffered. For example, the client cannot recover expenses or loss of earnings involved in attending the solicitor to give instructions: such losses can be recovered only when attending court as a witness. Further, a victory may be worthless if the opponent goes bankrupt, dies or simply disappears.

The solicitor's paramount duty in conducting civil litigation is to keep the door open for negotiations. Both before a case starts and throughout the interlocutory stage the solicitor must endeavour to compromise the claim on the best terms practicable for the client.

Litigation has never been an end in itself, it is a means to an end. The end here referred to is an enforceable result. In the past, claimants often started actions as a prelude to seeking a negotiated settlement, an enforceable contract setting out the parties' rights. There are several other means of achieving the same end, the two main ones being arbitration (in the hope of obtaining an 'award' which can later be registered as a judgment of the High Court) and mediation (in the hope of reaching an agreed settlement). The courts now recognise the importance of ADR and encourage its use (see further, the High Court's pre-trial checklist noted on p 489).

Although the different methods of ADR are described as being 'alternatives' to litigation, they can sometimes be employed in addition to litigation. For example, parties who need the litigious remedies of an interlocutory injunction and/or discovery can start an action, then get the remedies and only then turn to ADR.

A particular advantage which ADR may offer over litigation is the possibility of preserving or restoring goodwill between the parties to the dispute. Often, it is just as important to preserve a long-term business relationship as it is to insist upon strict legal rights.

Arbitration

Arbitration has one important feature in common with litigation. In litigation the judge gives a judgment which is binding on the parties. An arbitrator's decision (called an award) is likewise binding on the parties. Thus instead of going to court to have the judge impose a solution on the parties, the parties have gone before an arbitrator who has imposed a solution on them. Unless agreements provide to the contrary an arbitration is before one arbitrator although a contract with an arbitration clause can provide for however many arbitrators the parties think would be appropriate in the event of dispute (eg in a two-party contract, one arbitrator appointed by each party and an umpire appointed by the arbitrators).

Arbitration is thus very similar to having a contract dispute resolved before the courts, particularly if the dispute would have been assigned to the Commercial Court (see p 274) or designated as official referees' business (see p 270). Indeed CLSA 1990 and SCA 1981 permit, subject to conditions, both judges of the Commercial Court and official referees to act as arbitrators. At an arbitration hearing—unless the parties have agreed otherwise, the rules of evidence apply and because of the further need to state a case in writing (similar to pleadings) arbitration is often considered to be a specialist form of litigation.

The great advantage to the parties of arbitration over litigation is privacy. Trials are conducted in public; arbitration is in private. Large companies which are household names and therefore always newsworthy often find it more convenient for the company image to resolve disputes privately behind closed doors rather than in the public forum of a courtroom. Indeed many consider privacy to be the only advantage of arbitration. It is not cheaper for the work involved is much the same and indeed the arbitrator will also have to be paid (if the arbitrator is a judge the fees are taken in the High Court).

Another advantage which arbitration may offer is the possibility of appointing as arbitrator, a person who is skilled in the subject matter of the dispute; eg, a surveyor to arbitrate a rent review or a shipbroker to arbitrate a charterparty dispute.

Mediation

Mediation differs significantly from litigation or arbitration in that no solution is imposed on the parties. Mediation is a form of negotiation where a mediator facilitates a compromise between the parties themselves. Both sides attend mediation often simply to explore whether there is any prospect of compromise and without any real expectation of achieving one. Nevertheless a compromise can still emerge.

The mediation usually begins in a meeting at which both parties state their cases to the mediator and exchange views. They then move to separate rooms. The mediator visits each in turn reporting on offers and counter-offers, proposals and counter-proposals and obviously has to visit each side several times. If both sides are, or become, genuinely concerned to achieve a compromise, then one will usually be achieved.

The mediation form of ADR is not appropriate in all cases, eg:

(1) Cases in which there is no genuine dispute to be resolved, ie simple debt cases which are suitable for summary judgment (see p 221).

(2) Cases in which one party refuses to take part in any meaningful negotiations. Litigation is best here; it, unlike mediation, cannot be obstructed or blocked.

(3) Cases in which one party is financed by legal aid. Although legal aid will cover negotiations, it may not cover the extra fees payable in mediation.

Chapter 8

Service of Documents

Service of originating process

The expression 'originating process' covers High Court writs, county court summonses and other documents which commence actions or proceedings in court (see further pp 110 and 320). In this section and the last sections in this chapter, concerning service overseas, the words 'writ or summons' are used to refer to all types of originating process issued out of the High Court or county court respectively.

What was once a simple rule, all writs and summonses must be personally served, is now gone. Today most writs and summonses are served by post but there is a growing list of special cases and exceptions. In this section we describe the special provisions for service concerning minors and mental patients, corporations and partnerships. There are several other special cases, for example service on the Crown (as to which see RSC Ord 77; CCR Ord 42, r 7), service on members of Her Majesty's forces (as to which see *White Book* 65/2/7 and *Green Book* commentary to CCR Ord 7, r 10) and, in Admiralty actions *in rem*, the procedure by which a ship can be 'personally served' and arrested (as to which see RSC Ord 75, r 11: CCR Ord 40, r 5). We then consider the various alternatives open to a plaintiff: personal service, service by post, deemed service, service by county court bailiff and substituted service. In cases concerning service overseas and certain other cases with a foreign element, reference must also be made to the last sections of this chapter.

Minors and mental patients (RSC Ord 80, r 16; CCR Ord 10, r 4)

Where the defendant is a minor who is not also a mental patient the writ or summons must be served on 'one of his parents or his guardian' (county court) or 'his father or guardian' (High Court), or, if he has no parent/father or guardian, on the person with whom he resides or in whose care he is. Where the defendant is a mental patient the writ or summons must be served on the person who is authorised by the Court of Protection to represent him in the action, or, if there is no person so authorised, on the person with whom the mental patient resides or in whose care he is. The person these rules nominate for service is likely to become the defendant's guardian *ad litem*. As to minors and mental patients, see also Chapter 6.

Corporations

Companies Act 1985, s 725. In the case of a company registered under the Companies Act any document can be served by leaving it at or sending it by post to the registered office of the company. In the High Court, failure to serve at that address is an irregularity but does not nullify the proceedings and the court has a discretion whether or not to set aside such service (*Singh v Atombrook Ltd trading as Sterling Travel* [1989] 1 WLR 810). In the county court there is an alternative to service at the registered office (see below).

Companies Act 1985, s 695. In the case of a foreign company carrying on business in Great Britain a writ or summons can be served by leaving it at or sending it by post to any address in Great Britain which is registered by the company (under s 691) or which is being used by the company as an established place of business. As to the effect of registration of an address, see *Rome v Punjab National Bank (No 2)* [1989] 1 WLR 1211 (service still valid at that address even after the company has ceased trading in England and Wales) and *Boocock v Hilton International Co* [1993] 1 WLR 1065 (the correct person to whom to address the writ or summons). As to what amounts to the establishment of a place of business, see *South India Shipping Corporation Ltd v Export-Import Bank of Korea* [1985] 1 WLR 585 (activities incidental to the main business of the company may suffice).

RSC Ord 65, r 3; CCR Ord 7, r 14. In the case of other bodies corporate, such as local authorities or building societies, the writ or summons must be served on the mayor or other head officer or on the town clerk, clerk, treasurer or secretary. CCR Ord 7, r 14, also permits service on a company registered in England and Wales (ie not Scotland or Northern Ireland) 'at any place of business of the company which has some real connection with the cause or matter in issue'. This provision is of great convenience, especially to litigants in person, eg in cases in which the cause of action is alleged to have arisen in a local branch of a national retailer.

In the case of service by post under the Companies Act, delivery is presumed 'in the ordinary course of post' if there is proof of proper addressing, pre-paying and posting (Interpretation Act 1978, s 7 and see *Green Book* commentary to CCR Ord 7, r 14). The presumed date of service is the second working day after posting if first-class post was used or the fourth working day after posting if second-class post was used (Masters' Practice Direction, *White Book* 754: county court practice is similar). The presumptions are rebutted if the letter is returned by the Post Office undelivered to the company.

In the case of service by post on a mayor, town clerk, etc, the relevant rules as to class of post and presumptions applicable are those which relate to postal service on an individual (see overleaf).

Partnerships (RSC Ord 81, r 3; CCR Ord 7, r 13)

Where partners are sued in the name of their firm, service of a writ or summons on all the partners can be effected simply by serving it on any one of them or by serving it *at* their principal place of business within the jurisdiction or district of the court *on* the person having control of the business at the time of service.

In the High Court the plaintiff must give any person served under this rule written notice of the capacity in which he is being served: if no notice is given the person is deemed to be served as a partner. In neither court can the partnership rules for service be used if, to the plaintiff's knowledge, the partnership has been dissolved.

The partnership rules for service also apply to individuals trading under a business name or style.

Personal service

Personal service is effected by leaving the document in the possession of the person to be served (RSC Ord 65, r 2; CCR Ord 7, r 2). The server (often an inquiry agent employed by a solicitor, or a county court bailiff) usually hands the document to the person to be served whilst at the same time telling him what it is. 'Leaving' means 'causing to or letting remain (for however short a time)'. It does not necessarily involve the server departing without taking it with him although that is usually what happens (see further *Nottingham Building Society v Peter Bennett & Co* (1997) *The Times*, 26 February and see *White Book* 65/2/1).

Most writs and summonses are now served by post. Although personal service remains permissible in all cases, it is now appropriate only in exceptional cases such as cases of urgency or cases where the defendant is evading postal service (see p 219). However, if you do decide to use personal service, the writ must be served strictly in accordance with the rules (for an exceptional case where service not in accordance with the rules was nevertheless held to be valid see *Kenneth Allison Ltd v AE Limehouse & Co* [1992] AC 105).

Service on a Sunday

No writ, summons, judgment or other document sealed by a court can be served on a Sunday except, in a case of urgency, with the leave of a court: RSC Ord 65, r 10; CCR Ord 7, r 3. The county court rule similarly forbids service on Christmas Day and Good Friday.

Service of writ or summons by post on an individual

Service by post on companies has already been dealt with. The High Court rule for service by post on an individual is RSC Ord 10, r 1(2) which states:

A writ for service on a defendant within the jurisdiction may, instead of being served personally on him, be served—

(a) by sending a copy of the writ by ordinary first-class post to the defendant at his usual or last known address, or

(b) if there is a letter box for that address, by inserting through the letter box a copy of the writ enclosed in a sealed envelope addressed to the defendant.

In this rule 'a copy of the writ' means a 'sealed copy', ie a copy stamped with the court seal (RSC Ord 10, r 1(6)). In para (b) above 'a sealed envelope' has its normal meaning of an envelope with the flap glued down. The address will usually be a residential address, but this term is wide enough to include a business address at least in the case of a self-employed person (*Robertson v Banham & Co* [1997] 1 WLR 446). A business address may, perhaps, also suffice in the case of a defendant who is an employee (*Willowgreen Ltd v Smithers* [1994] 1 WLR 833; 'In most cases "the address" . . . will be the address at which the defendant ordinarily resides or works' *per* Thorpe J, *obiter*). 'Last known' means 'last known to the plaintiff' rather than 'last known to the general public' (see *Austin Rover Group Ltd v Crouch Butler Savage Associates* [1986] 1 WLR 1102 *obiter*). However, it must be or have been the defendant's address; service is irregular if the defendant has never lived or worked at the address in question (see *Willowgreen Ltd*, above).

Unless the contrary is shown a writ is presumed to have been served (ie come to the notice of the defendant) on the seventh day after the date on which the copy was sent or, as the case may be, inserted through the letterbox. If the defendant later proves that the writ never came to his notice, the presumption of service will be rebutted (*Forward v West Sussex County Council* [1995] 1 WLR 1469). As to the effect such a rebuttal upon any default judgment the plaintiff has in the meantime obtained, see p 219.

In computing the seven days RSC Ord 3, r 2(5) (see p 10) does *not* apply and therefore Saturdays and Sundays can be included in the reckoning. Contrast service by post on companies which need not be sent by first-class post and is presumed to be delivered in the 'ordinary course of post'.

In the county court service by post will automatically be effected by the court unless the plaintiff indicates that he wishes to effect personal service. The court clerk will send it by ordinary first-class post to the defendant at the address stated by the plaintiff in the summons or request. Service is deemed to be effected on the seventh day after posting (see generally CCR Ord 7, rr 9, 10).

In both courts service by post is effective when the writ or summons reaches the correct address (even if the envelope had been incorrectly addressed, *Austin Rover Group Ltd*, above) and comes to the knowledge of the defendant (even if he does not, in fact, visit that address, *Barclays Bank of Swaziland Ltd v Hahn* [1989] 1 WLR 506, HL, see below).

Evidence of such receipt may rebut the presumption of service on the seventh day after posting. It may be important for the plaintiff to rebut that presumption by proof that service in fact took place in less than seven days. For example, in *Barclays Bank of Swaziland Ltd* (above) the defendant departed these shores for Geneva and stayed there shortly after he had learnt that the writ had arrived at his English address. In *Hodgson v Hart District Council* [1985] 1 WLR 317, the writ was posted with a covering letter on 15 February 1985, only five days before it was due to expire. A date stamp impressed on the covering letter by the defence showed that it was received on 18 February 1985. The Court of Appeal rejected the defence argument that the writ was deemed to be served on 22 February 1985 (ie two days after its period of validity for service had expired).

Postal service of a writ or summons can also be effected on the persons designated for service in the rules relating to minors and mental patients and on a firm where a defendant or defendants are sued in a firm name.

For the position where a writ or summons is returned by the Post Office, undelivered to the defendant, see pp 220 and 250.

Deemed service

Where a defendant's solicitor indorses on the writ a statement that he accepts service on behalf of that defendant the writ is deemed to have been duly served on that defendant and to have been so served on the date on which the indorsement was made (RSC Ord 10, r 1(4); for an example of the indorsement see *White Book* 10/1/10). The corresponding rule for the county court (CCR Ord 7, r 11) differs slightly: the defendant's solicitor's statement need not be indorsed on the summons but must state an address for service.

Where a writ is not duly served on a defendant but he acknowledges service of it the writ is deemed to have been duly served on him and to have been so served on the date on which he acknowledged service (RSC Ord 10, r 1(5)). However, this deeming provision can be rebutted—even after both acknowledgment of service and a payment into court—by proof that the writ had not in fact been served (see *Towers v Morley* [1992] 1 WLR 511). In the county court a defendant is not required to acknowledge service. However CCR Ord 7, r 12, provides a similar deeming provision: where a summons has not been duly served but the defendant files an admission, defence, or counterclaim, the action may proceed as if the summons had been duly served.

A writ or summons is not deemed to be served under RSC Ord 10, r 1(5) or CCR Ord 7, r 12 in a case where the plaintiff can show that he has never made any attempt to serve at all. Thus where a defendant is sent a copy of a writ 'for information only' he cannot, by lodging an acknowledgment of service, start time running for the service of pleadings (*Abu Dhabi Helicopters Ltd v International Aeradio plc* [1986] 1 WLR

312). However, after that case was decided, there came RSC Ord 12, r 8A which enables a High Court defendant to serve a fourteen-day notice on the plaintiff requiring him either to serve the writ or discontinue the action.

Service by bailiff

In the county court, on payment of the prescribed fee, the plaintiff can request service of a summons by a bailiff of the court. Bailiff service is restricted to cases in which postal service has been tried and has failed. Using the bailiff is invariably cheaper than using an inquiry agent and, whereas the inquiry agent has to effect personal service on a county court defendant, the bailiff has other options. CCR Ord 7, r 10 provides that a bailiff can effect service of a summons by:
(1) inserting the summons, enclosed in an envelope addressed to the defendant, through the letter box at the address stated in the request for the summons; or
(2) delivering the summons to some person, apparently not less than sixteen years old, at the address stated in the request for the summons; or
(3) delivering the summons to the defendant personally.
Note that, in the first instance, the bailiff visits the address for the defendant given in the request for the summons, an address in respect of which postal service has failed. If the bailiff ascertains that the defendant has moved from there to another address within the district of the court he must attempt to effect service at that new address (CCR Ord 7, r 17). If the bailiff cannot trace the defendant or ascertains an address for him outside the district of the court a notice of non-service will be given to the plaintiff. The plaintiff must then consider, as the case may be, whether to employ an inquiry agent, to transfer the proceedings to another county court, or, if the cause of action arose in the district of this court, amend the request to give a new address for the defendant; the court office will then effect postal service at that new address. As a writ or summons is valid for service for four months only an application for renewal will be necessary if the defendant is not found quickly (see p 205).

Substituted service

Whenever it is impracticable to serve *any* document (not just writs or summonses) in the manner prescribed by the rules, an application can be made for leave to effect 'substituted service', ie service in some other manner the court may direct to bring the document to the notice of the party to be served (RSC Ord 65, r 4; CCR Ord 7, r 8).

When will service in the manner prescribed by the rules be impracticable? In the past the traditional examples were cases where a party was evading service ('keeping house closed') or where a party could not be traced but there were other persons with whom he had been in contact who could be traced (eg his spouse or employer or banker or solicitor). Mere absence abroad does not make service 'impracticable' unless of course the party went abroad to evade service, or cannot be traced.

As far as the service of writs or summonses is concerned the rules permitting postal service very much diminish the importance of substituted service. If a defendant's address is known the writ or summons can usually be sent to that address. If a defendant's address is not known but he can be traced elsewhere he can be served personally. If a defendant's address is not known and he cannot be traced elsewhere the plaintiff should seriously reconsider whether proceedings should be commenced in the first place. If you cannot find the defendant to effect service how will you ever enforce any judgment you obtain? There would be little point in starting an action unless, eg there are other defendants or the claim is in respect of a road accident and the plaintiff can enforce the judgment against an insurance company or the Motor Insurers' Bureau (see p 38).

If service in the manner prescribed by the rules is impracticable, what other method will the court direct? The usual methods are:
  (1) By post to the address of the party to be served (for documents such as injunctions which cannot otherwise be served by post; service will normally, be presumed 'in the ordinary course of post', *White Book* 754).
  (2) By post to the address of some person with whom the party to be served has been or is likely to be in communication. The court will allow this method only if it is likely to be successful in getting notice of the document to the party to be served. By way of exception, however, in an action arising out of a road accident the court may allow substituted service by post to the defendant's insurance company or to the Motor Insurers' Bureau (*Gurtner v Circuit* [1968] 2 QB 587 and see *White Book* 65/4/5).
  (3) By advertisement in a newspaper or journal. This method is allowed only in the rarest circumstances (see *White Book* 65/4/9 and *Green Book* commentary to CCR Ord 7, r 8).

An application for leave to effect substituted service is made to a district judge *ex parte* on affidavit showing why service in the normal manner is impracticable and stating the method of substituted service the deponent thinks most likely to bring the document to the knowledge of the party to be served (for a useful precedent, see Pyke and Oldham, *Practical County Court Precedents* (FT Law & Tax) Precedent 134). If an order for substituted service is made it will state the method of service to be used.

There are other rules similar in effect to the substituted service rules, by which the court can authorise alternative methods of service of a writ or summons (RSC Ord 10, r 2; service on agent of overseas principal; RSC Ord 10, r 4, CCR Ord 7, r 15; service in certain actions for possession of land).

Service of pleadings

In the High Court

In the High Court the service of pleadings should be effected by 'ordinary service', ie leaving the pleading at, or sending it by post to, the other party's 'address for service'. The plaintiff's address for service is stated in the writ; the defendant's address for service is stated in his acknowledgment of service. Service by document exchange is permissible as prescribed by RSC Ord 65, r 5(2A): where the address stated by the inteded recipient in the writ or acknowledgment of service (as the case may be) includes a document exchange number or where such a number is included on the notepaper of the intended recipient or of his solicitor.

Service by fax is permissible as prescribed by RSC Ord 65, r 5(2B): both parties must be represented by solicitors; the notepaper of the recipient solicitor includes a fax number and is not indorsed, eg 'fax number not for service of court proceedings'; as soon as practicable after the fax is sent a copy of the served document must be sent by one of the other approved methods of service otherwise the document is deemed never to have been served by fax.

Some solicitors include words on their notepaper which prohibit service by fax so as to make it more difficult for other solicitors to serve documents on them at the last minute. Even if the notepaper does not contain prohibiting words, a solicitor can nevertheless withdraw consent to service by fax at any time, simply by giving his opposing solicitor reasonable notice. In *Mayes v Gayton International* (1994) noted in *White Book* 65/5/9, a solicitor sent a fax to his opponent purporting to withdraw his consent to his opponent sending him documents by fax. This unco-operative fax was sent less than three hours before the expiry of an important deadline to which his opponent was working. Not surprisingly, it was held not to constitute reasonable notice.

If, for some reason, a party does not have an address for service but the action is nevertheless proceeding to trial (eg a Chancery action in which one of two defendants defaults in acknowledging service) pleadings and certain other documents need not be served on that party unless the court otherwise orders (RSC Ord 65, r 9).

Where, as is usual, pleadings are sent by post they are presumed to arrive in the 'ordinary course of post' if they were properly addressed, prepaid and posted. The presumed date of service depends upon the class of post used (see p 129). Where pleadings are left at a document exchange, the presumed date of service is the second working day following the day on which they were left. As to service by fax see above.

There is no restriction on serving pleadings on a Sunday. However, if a pleading is served outside certain hours (after 4 pm on a weekday, after 12 noon on a Saturday or at any hour on a Sunday) it is treated, for the purpose of calculating the time for the service of any subsequent pleading, as if it had been served on the next available working day (RSC Ord 65, r 7 and RSC Ord 65, r 5(2B) in the case of service by fax).

High Court pleadings are served only between the parties. If a summons for directions is taken out a full set of pleadings must be lodged with the court (Chancery Division) or made available to the court at the hearing of that summons (Queen's Bench Division, see further Chapter 20). In other cases (eg many personal injury actions where no application is made to vary automatic directions) no set of pleadings will be filed at the court unless and until the action is set down for trial.

In the county court

The county court system for the service of pleadings is much simpler. The original pleadings are filed at the court and a copy is then delivered to the other party. The plaintiff files his pleading (the particulars of claim) when the summons is issued. A copy of it is attached to the summons for service on the defendant. Within fourteen days of service (exclusive of the day of service) the defendant should deliver to the court any defence he intends to use. Once it is filed the court then sends a copy of it to the plaintiff.

Service of other documents

For documents such as High Court interlocutory summonses, county court notices of interlocutory applications and lists of documents (see Chapter 18) service may be effected by ordinary service (see above) including, in both courts, service *via* an approved document exchange if a solicitor's address for service includes a numbered box at such an exchange. If the party to be served has no address for service the document may be served by delivery to certain other addresses such as his last known address or the business address of the solicitor acting for him in those proceedings (see further RSC Ord 65, r 5; CCR Ord 7, r 1: in the High Court, in a very exceptional case, it may be appropriate not to serve interlocutory summonses or lists of documents on a party who has no address for service; see RSC Ord 65, r 9 above and *White Book* 65/9/1).

There are no specific County Court Rules permitting service by fax. In practice the High Court rule (see p 135) is followed relying on CCA 1984, s 76 (see p 2 and the *Green Book* commentary to CCR Ord 7, r 1).

For documents such as injunctions and applications in breach of an injunction personal service must be effected (see pp 294 and 609). If personal service is impracticable leave to effect substituted service may be granted (see p 133).

As to service of statutory demands, see p 621.

Note finally the rules forbidding service of court documents on a Sunday and certain other days (see p 130) and the High Court rule concerning service of documents outside certain hours (p 135 noting RSC Ord 65, r 7 which applies to all High Court documents except writs and other originating process).

Proving due service

Assume that a writ or summons is served but the defendant fails to acknowledge service, or in the county court, fails to serve a defence, or in a fixed date action, fails to attend on the return day. If the plaintiff wishes to obtain judgment in default or wishes to proceed with the action in the absence of the defendant it is necessary for him to prove that the writ or summons was in fact served and that therefore the defendant has been notified of the proceedings.

In the High Court, service of the writ is usually proved by filing an *affidavit of service* before the plaintiff takes the next step in the action. Of course no proof is necessary in cases of deemed service (where the defendant's solicitor indorses on the writ his acceptance of service on behalf of his client or the defendant lodges an acknowledgment). An affidavit of service must state by whom the writ was served, the day of the week and date on which it was served and also where and how it was served (RSC Ord 65, r 8). Where a writ is served by post under RSC Ord 10, r 1(3), the affidavit must contain a statement that:

(i) in the opinion of the deponent (or, if the deponent is the plaintiff's solicitor or an employee of that solicitor, in the opinion of the plaintiff) the copy of the writ, if sent to, or, as the case may be, inserted through the letter box for, the address in question, will have to come to the knowledge of the defendant within 7 days thereafter; and
(ii) in the case of service by post, the copy of the writ has not been returned to the plaintiff through the post undelivered to the addressee.

(For an example of this affidavit see fig 11 on p 216.)

In the county court, service of a summons within England and Wales is proved *either* by an affidavit of service sworn by the server *or*, if the summons was served through the court, by a certificate given by the bailiff or other court officer who effected service (CCR Ord 7, r 6). In the case of a default summons served through the court a *notice of service*, is sent to the plaintiff to enable him to calculate the earliest date for entry of a default judgment (CCR Ord 7, r 21). If the court fails to effect service the plaintiff is sent a *notice of non-service* (see fig 19, p 246) and further attempts to effect service must be made if the action is to proceed. In a fixed date action a successive summons may have to be issued fixing a later return day (CCR Ord 7, r 19).

The plaintiff will be given a *notice of doubtful service* where the bailiff's certificate indicates that (CCR Ord 7, r 18):

(1) he served the summons on some person other than the defendant at the defendant's residential or business address; and

(2) it is doubtful *when* the summons will come to the defendant's knowledge.

Thereafter if the defendant does not deliver an admission, defence or counterclaim, or in the case of a fixed date action, does not attend on the return day, the plaintiff has to satisfy the court that the defendant was given sufficient notice. In practice plaintiffs usually have no option but to treat a notice of doubtful service in the same way they would treat a notice of non-service.

Affidavits of service may also have to be filed at other stages of an action, eg in the High Court, to prove service of an interlocutory summons if the other party fails to attend at the hearing of that summons. However, in such cases, district judges will often accept informal evidence, eg a letter or copy letter on the serving solicitor's file, or will draw an inference of service if the other party has filed evidence in respect of the hearing. As to the proof of service of statutory demands, see p 621.

Service outside England and Wales

There are two basic sets of procedural rules concerning service outside England and Wales; cases governed by the Civil Jurisdiction and Judgments Act 1982 (CJJA 1982) in which service is permissible without leave; and other cases, in which leave to serve is required. In respect of any particular defendant there is no overlap between the two. However, both sets of rules may be applicable in some cases; for example, a tort action with two defendants where the CJJA 1982 governs service in respect of only one of them.

Civil Jurisdiction and Judgments Acts 1982 and 1991

The CJJA 1982 brought into force for the purposes of UK law the so-called European Judgments Convention of 1968 ('the Brussels Convention'), the full text of which is set out in a schedule to the Act. The Convention unifies to a large extent the private international law applicable in EU member states over a wide range of civil proceedings (for the excepted cases see p 142). The CJJA 1982 applies to all EU countries and the CJJA 1991 (which gave effect to 'the Lugano Convention') duplicates its provisions so as to bring within the same system all the European Free Trade Area countries (for an up-do-date list of countries covered see *White Book* 11/1/29 and 8-006).

The origins of the European Judgments Convention lay in a desire to attain reciprocal enforcement of judgments so promoting the 'free movement of judgments in Europe'. (This aspect is described on p 603.) However, before it was possible to agree recognition of judgments, it was necessary to agree the different bases of jurisdiction which the courts of each member state can claim. This was achieved as follows:

(1) The member states have agreed an elaborate system of rules defining the jurisdiction of their courts. (Some of these rules are summarised below.)

(2) The so-called 'exorbitant jurisdictions' claimed by different courts cannot be used against persons domiciled in a member state: thus the jurisdiction claimed by the English courts based on transient presence within this country (see p 142) is not available against defendants in countries covered by the Conventions.

(3) Where the Conventions supply a court with jurisdiction the plaintiff has a right to commence proceedings there: thus, in English cases, leave to serve overseas is not necessary and, save as between different parts of the UK, the doctrine of *forum non conveniens* (see pp 143 and 356) cannot be applied (see *Boss Group Ltd v Boss France SA* [1997] 1 WLR 351 *per* Saville LJ at 358 B–D).

(4) A court in which proceedings covered by the Conventions are commenced must, of its own motion, examine whether it has jurisdiction (Brussels Convention, Articles 19, 20).

(5) A court must decline jurisdiction if proceedings involving the same cause of action and between the same parties have already been commenced in the courts of another member state (Brussels Convention, Article 21). As to the exact date upon which proceedings in English courts are commenced for the purposes of this Article and Article 22, see *Dresser UK Ltd v Falcongate Freight Management Ltd* [1992] 2 QB 502. This provision does not apply as between the different courts of the UK (see further CJJA 1982, s 49).

(6) Litigants in an action before the courts in one member state may seek provisional and protective measures from the courts of another member state (see further, p 295 concerning *Mareva* injunctions).

Outline of some of the bases of jurisdiction under the Conventions

The primary basis of jurisdiction under the Conventions concerns the domicile of the defendant. Unless an alternative basis of jurisdiction applies a defendant domiciled in a Convention state must be sued in the courts of that state. There are however several alternative bases of jurisdiction. These provide what one might term 'non-exorbitant' bases of jurisdiction of the type which all courts have traditionally claimed. Thus a defendant domiciled in another member state may be sued in the English courts if:

(1) in a contract case, the contract was to be performed here; or

(2) in a tort case, the damage was sustained or the tort was committed here; or

(3) subject to Brussels Convention, Article 16 (see below), the defendant voluntarily submits to proceedings here.

As to some matters the Conventions give courts exclusive jurisdiction regardless of domicile. Thus, in an action concerning land, exclusive jurisdiction is given to the courts of the member states in which that land is situated. In contract actions, the contract may, in certain circumstances, confer exclusive jurisdiction upon a particular court. If the English courts have jurisdiction in these cases no leave to serve outside England and Wales is necessary for any defendant to that action, whether or not they are domiciled in a member state (see Brussels Convention, Articles 16 and 17).

Two matters not dealt with by the Conventions are supplied by the CJJA 1982. First, the Conventions do not define the concept of domicile; they merely regulate how questions of domicile are to be determined. Thus to determine whether a person is domiciled in the UK, the courts of all member states must use the relevant UK definition. To determine whether a person is domiciled in France, the courts of all member states must use the French definition. The position is made simpler by the CJJA 1982: for the purposes of the Conventions the English definition of domicile is assimilated to that used in other member states. Broadly speaking, an individual is domiciled in England if he is ordinarily resident here; a corporation is domiciled in England if it was incorporated here or if its central management and control is exercised here (ie a corporation may be treated as being domiciled in two countries: *The Deichland* [1989] 3 WLR 478).

The second matter supplied by the CJJA 1982 concerns the allocation of jurisdiction amongst the different parts of the UK. The CJJA 1982 makes such allocation by including a modified version of the Conventions under which the different parts of the UK are treated as if they were different member states.

Service outside England and Wales in CJJA cases

Commencement.   In the High Court, a writ can be issued without leave if it is indorsed under RSC Ord 6, r 7. The indorsement is in two parts. The first part requires the plaintiff to state that the High Court has jurisdiction under the CJJA 1982 (ie, as amended by CJJA 1991) in respect of the whole action. Such an indorsement cannot validly be made if, for example, the writ joins a non-EU and non-EFTA defendant unless all the claims in the writ relevant to that defendant come within the exclusive jurisdiction of the court (see Brussels Convention, Articles 16, 17). If the CJJA 1982 does not supply jurisdiction in respect of one defendant leave to issue is necessary as is leave to serve that defendant overseas.

The second part of the indorsement requires the plaintiff to state that no conflicting proceedings are pending in Scotland, Northern Ireland or another member state. If such proceedings are pending, leave to issue the writ is necessary. It will not be given if these proceedings are before a court in Europe (see Brussels Convention, Article 21, above). It may be given if these proceedings are before a court in Scotland or Northern Ireland if it is shown that the High Court is the more appropriate forum (see CJJA 1982, s 49).

If, by oversight, the plaintiff fails to indorse the writ under RSC Ord 6, r 7, see p 202.

In the county court, the request for the summons must certify that the court has jurisdiction under the CJJA 1982 for each claim made in the action and the particulars of claim must contain a statement very similar to the High Court indorsement (CCR Ord 3, r 3).

Service of writ or summons. This is permissible without leave if the defendant is domiciled in the UK or in any other member state, *or* if the court has exclusive jurisdiction under Brussels Convention, Article 16 or 17 (see above).

Methods and proof of service. These topics are not affected by the CJJA 1982. In all cases service of a writ or summons must be effected in accordance with the law of the country of service. In fact, in the majority of cases the plaintiff can request the court to arrange service through diplomatic or judicial channels. A completed form of request (see *White Book* 207, County Court Form N224 plus duplicate), two copies of the writ or summons and translations of all the documents to be served (in duplicate where required) have to be filed at the court office for onward transmission to the Foreign and Commonwealth Office. In the High Court it is also necessary to file copies of the form of acknowledgment of service modified as appropriate for an overseas defendant (see Oyez Form E28) with translations thereof. In the county court copies of the form of admission defence and counterclaim, plus translations, are required.

Where a writ or summons is served abroad through some official agency, service is proved by the certificate given by that agency (RSC Ord 11, r 5; CCR Ord 8, r 10).

Once parties have addresses for service in England and Wales, pleadings, interlocutory process and other documents can be served in their usual ways. No leave is necessary to serve interlocutory process outside England and Wales if the CJJA 1982 applies (RSC Ord 11, r 9; CCR Ord 8, r 4).

Time for acknowledging service (High Court). The number of days from service, to be stated in the writ, differs according to the country in which the writ is to be served. For writs to be served in a member state the number of days is twenty-one. For writs which are to be served in another country (eg on a non-EU and non-EFTA defendant in a case within Brussels Convention, Article 16 or 17) the number of days to be specified is as shown in the Extra Jurisdiction Tables set out in the *White Book* 902.

Time for delivering defence (county court). CCR Ord 8, r 1(3) provides similar time limits, twenty-one days for a summons served in a member state (thirty-one days for a summons served in non-European territory of a member state) and as 'fixed by the court' in other cases, usually by having regard to the Extra Jurisdiction Tables mentioned above. In fixed date actions (see p 255) the return day marked on the summons is always fixed by the court having regard to the distance of the country of service, whether it is inside or outside Europe (CCR Ord 8, r 1(4)).

Default judgments. Leave to enter judgment in default is necessary if the writ or summons was served outside England and Wales without leave. This provision will enable the court to consider whether it has jurisdiction (see Brussels Convention, Articles 19, 20).

It is important to note that leave to enter judgment in default is also necessary in the case of a writ or summons served in England and Wales if the defendant upon whom it was served is domiciled in Scotland, Northern Ireland or in any other member state. Imposing a leave requirement here enables the court to comply with the Brussels Convention, Article 3, which forbids use of our 'exorbitant jurisdiction' against EU and EFTA defendants (RSC Ord 13, r 7B; CCR Ord 9, r 6(4), and see p 139).

Service outside England and Wales in non-CJJA cases

The main categories of cases not governed by the CJJA 1982 are as follows:

(1) Proceedings which are outside the scope of the Brussels Convention—these include proceedings concerning revenue and customs, status or legal capacity of natural persons, matrimonial property rights (contrast maintenance orders), wills and succession, bankruptcy and winding up and analogous proceedings, social security and arbitration.

(2) Proceedings against non-EU and non-EFTA defendants *unless* in respect of them the Brussels Convention gives exclusive jurisdiction to the court under Articles 16 and 17 (see p 140).

If the CJJA 1982 does not apply, the first question to consider is whether the action falls within the jurisdiction of the English courts. It is convenient to mention here four general matters concerning cases containing some foreign element:

(1) The courts claim jurisdiction over—and therefore a writ or summons can be served without leave upon—any person 'present' in England and Wales, even if their presence in England is only temporary. (This, our so-called 'exorbitant jurisdiction', has been removed so far as concerns most European defendants served in this country: see p 139). However, if the English courts are not the most appropriate forum for the action the defendant can apply for a stay of action, thereby compelling the plaintiff to restart proceedings elsewhere (see p 356).

(2) If the defendant is not present in England or Wales the courts have jurisdiction over him only if:

(a) the court is given jurisdiction under a specific statute, such as the Civil Aviation (Eurocontrol) Act 1962; or

(b) the defendant voluntarily submits to the jurisdiction, eg by instructing English solicitors to accept service on his behalf; or

(c) the court assumes jurisdiction over the defendant on the grounds set out in the rules of court, and it grants leave to serve outside England and Wales.

(3) Where leave to serve outside England and Wales is granted the defendant can still object to the court's assumption of jurisdiction over him by applying to set aside the order granting leave (see further p 212).

(4) If an overseas plaintiff commences proceedings in this country the court has jurisdiction to hear any counterclaim against him in respect of a related matter (*Republic of Liberia v Gulf Oceanic Inc* [1985] 1 Lloyd's Rep 539 and the cases cited therein and *Metal Scrap Trade Corp Ltd v Kate Shipping Co Ltd* [1990] 1 WLR 115, HL).

(5) The service of a writ or summons outside England and Wales without leave in a case in which leave is required amounts to an irregularity of such importance that the court is unlikely later to waive or disregard it (*Leal v Dunlop Bio-Processes International Ltd* [1984] 1 WLR 874).

The application for leave

In the High Court it is necessary to make a combined application for leave to issue the writ as well as leave to serve it outside the jurisdiction. The application is made *ex parte* on affidavit which is entitled 'In the Matter of the Supreme Court Act 1981. And in the Matter of an intended action Between . . .' and which shows that:

(1) the defendant is or may probably be found outside England and Wales (naming the country in question);

(2) the plaintiff has a good arguable claim (as to which see *Seaconsar Far East Ltd v Bank Markazi Jomhouri Islami Iran* [1994] 1 AC 438); and

(3) one or more of the grounds set out in RSC Ord 11, r 1(1) apply (many of these grounds are similar to CJJA 1982 bases of jurisdiction, see p 139, save that they are discretionary, ie subject to the *forum non conveniens* doctrine, see below).

Drafts of the writ and statement of claim should be exhibited. It has been suggested that, because of its importance, the affidavit should be made by a solicitor rather than by a solicitor's clerk (see *White Book* 11/4/3).

In the county court no leave to commence proceedings is necessary. It is not normally possible to apply for leave to serve until the summons has been issued unless the court will accept an affidavit entitled in a manner similar to the High Court equivalent referring to 'an intended action'. The affidavit must:

(1) state (in the case of a fixed date summons) that in the belief of the deponent the applicant has a good cause of action; and

(2) show (in all cases) in what country or place the respondent is or may probably be found, whether the respondent is a UK national, and the grounds on which the application is made (a list of grounds, similar to the High Court list, is set out in CCR Ord 8, r 2(1), as to ground (c) see further CCR Ord 8, r 6(1)).

A High Court order granting leave will state the time within which the defendant must acknowledge service (as to which see *White Book* 902). The order must be drawn up by the plaintiff (see *Practice Form* 6, *White Book* 206). A county court order granting leave will, in the case of a default action, state the time in which the defendant must file an admission or defence, and, in any other case, fix the return day. The order will be drawn up by the court office (see Form N223).

In both courts, as to methods of service, requesting service by the court, and proof of service see p 141.

The defendant may later apply to set aside the order granting leave (RSC Ord 32, r 6; CCR Ord 8, r 12; and see p 212). On such an application the plaintiff must discharge the burden of proof that the order was correctly made and that England is clearly the most appropriate forum (*Spiliada Maritime Corp v Cansulex Ltd* [1987] AC 460, referred to on p 357).

Chapter 9

Drafting Pleadings, Affidavits and Witness Statements

Function of pleadings

Pleadings are the formal documents by which the parties state their cases. The trial is said to be 'on the pleadings'. This means that the pleadings show all the matters which have to be argued before and determined by the trial court. Listing all of the parties' claims and defences achieves several useful objects. Pleadings inform both or all sides of the nature of the case being alleged against them and so enable them to prepare properly for trial (*Farrell v Secretary of State for Defence* [1980] 1 WLR 172, HL). Pleadings disclose to the trial court the topics upon which the parties are seeking its decision. Ultimately pleadings provide a permanent record of all the matters involved in the action and thereby prevent further actions between the same parties. The consequence of saying that trial is 'on the pleadings' is that trial is limited by the pleadings. If a party omits to plead a matter he will be prevented from raising it at the trial (*Brunning v Odhams* (1897) 75 LT 602). If he pleads a matter too narrowly he will be prevented from relying on evidence tending to prove a wider allegation (*Esso v Southport* [1956] AC 218). Although both these difficulties may be avoided by amendment, leave to amend may be refused: even if granted the litigant will probably be penalised in costs. A pleading also limits a party's case in another way. Discovery and interrogatories are limited to the 'matters in question in the action', in other words the area of dispute disclosed by the pleadings.

The order in which pleadings are served

The plaintiff's pleading always comes first. In the High Court it is called the 'statement of claim'. In the county court it is called the 'particulars of claim'. In function and style these documents are almost identical: hereafter the expression 'the claim' will be used to refer to either of them. In both courts if the defendant wishes to defend he must prepare a 'defence'. If the defendant also wishes to claim remedies against the plaintiff his pleading is called a 'defence and counterclaim'.

Sometimes there are also subsequent pleadings: the plaintiff's 'defence to counter-claim'; the plaintiff's 'reply'; and (very rarely) the defendant's 'rejoinder' (see p 172).

Who should draft the pleadings?

The task of drafting pleadings involves forecasting the issues which will be raised at the trial. The persons best placed to do this are those who will be advocates at the trial. Thus, in theory, the plaintiff's advocate should be allowed to decide which claims he should raise and which parties should be brought before the court. The defendant's advocate should be allowed to decide which course the defence should take and whether there should be different defences for different defendants. You cannot expect the advocate to conduct the trial as he thinks best if his hands are tied by someone else's pleading.

In practice, experienced solicitors frequently settle their own pleadings whether or not they are entitled to or intend to, act as advocate in the case. Since the majority of cases settle (see p 33) the use of an advocate is usually unnecessary. If it becomes necessary the intended advocate could always be invited to consider the need for any amendment.

All practitioners make much use of precedent books such as Atkin's *Court Forms* and Bullen and Leake and Jacob's *Precedents of Pleadings*. Neither of these excellent books would claim to replace the expertise required in drafting pleadings. Rather they supplement it. The practitioner uses them as a guide to the essential ingredients of any particular pleading. The individual precedents should not be copied slavishly but 'should be varied, adapted or modified as may be necessary to meet the facts and circumstances which a particular case may require' (Bullen and Leake and Jacob, preface). The beginner cannot use precedent books properly until he has studied the formal requirements of pleading and has learnt what he can of the art of pleading.

Formal requirements of pleadings

Every professionally drafted pleading should:

1 *State the following matters:*
  (1) *The name of the court.* This is normally written at the top left-hand corner of the pleading. In the High Court one also states the name of the division to which the action is assigned: if the action is proceeding in a district registry the name of the district registry is also stated.
  (2) *The reference to the record of the action.* This is written in the top right-hand corner. The county court reference is the case number, written thus 'Case No KH61235'. The two letters show which court has issued the summons (every court has a unique

reference); the first number is the last digit in the current year. In the High Court the reference consists of three matters: the year in which the writ was issued, the initial letter of the first surname or business name stated in the title and the number of the action which is given when the writ is issued. The High Court reference should be written thus '1997-S-1234'.

(3) *The title of the action.*   In both courts this usually starts with the word 'BETWEEN' and sets out the full names of the parties. Sometimes the 'BETWEEN' section is preceded by an entitlement, eg 'In the Matter of the Trusts of the Will dated 1 March 1989 of John Smith Deceased' (see generally *Re Brickman* [1982] 1 All ER 336; *White Book* 6/1/9; CCR Ord 3, r 7).

No description of any party should be given unless the action involves minors or mental patients (see p 90) or, in an exceptional case, some description would aid understanding as to the identity of the party (*White Book* 736). By way of examples of exceptional cases consider 'Miss Hilary Law', 'Hilary Law (Spinster)', 'Hilary Law (Male)' 'Hilary and Law (a firm)', 'Hilary and Law (a trading name)', 'Hilary Law (Married Woman trading as Hilarious Holidays)'.

Where there are several plaintiffs or defendants, each name should be numbered and written on a separate line. Beside the name of the last party there should appear the single word 'Plaintiffs' or 'Defendants' as the case may be: there should be only one 'and' separating all of the plaintiffs from all of the defendants.

In the rest of the pleading the parties should be referred to only as 'the Plaintiff', 'the Defendant', 'the First Defendant' as the case may be.

(4) *The description of the pleading.*   That is to say, 'STATEMENT OF CLAIM', 'PARTICULARS OF CLAIM', 'DEFENCE' or as the case may be.

(5) *The name and business address of the party's solicitor.*   This is the party's address for service. CCR Ord 6, r 8 and Ord 9, r 19, further require the pleadings to be signed by the solicitor in his own name or in the name of his firm. In the High Court it is the writ which has to be signed, at the time of issue: RSC Ord 6, r 7 (see p 195).

(6) *The name of counsel, if the pleading was settled by him.*   Both the CCR and the RSC state that the pleading should be signed by counsel. This refers to the draft counsel gives to his instructing solicitors. The pleading is always re-typed and counsel's name is typed at the end.

2 *Be written in summary form,* thus:
(1) So far as convenient allegations should be divided into paragraphs numbered consecutively.

(2) Dates, sums and other numbers should be expressed in figures not in words. Note 'first', 'second', etc are always expressed in words unless they form part of a date, eg '1 March 1998'.

(3) If the necessary particulars of debt, expenses or damages are lengthy they should be set out in a separate document which is referred to in the pleading. In the High Court the particulars of debt, expenses or damages must be served separately if they exceed '3 folios', ie 216 words, each number being counted as one word: RSC Ord 18, r 12.

(4) It is sufficient to summarise the effect of a document or the purport of a conversation: the precise words should be quoted only if they are material.

(5) A party need not plead any fact which the law presumes in his favour unless the other party has specifically denied it in his pleading. Nor need he plead performance of a condition precedent since due performance is implied in every pleading.

Example

A landlord wishes to forfeit a lease for breach of a repairing covenant. Strictly speaking it is not essential to plead the service of a notice under s 146 of the Law of Property Act 1925: see *Gates v Jacobs* [1920] 1 Ch 567. In practice, however, it usually is pleaded.

3 Be written in archaic language?

We do not seriously suggest this though a few practitioners might. Sometimes the archaic style and rigid format of a pleading is enough to weaken the spirit of even the bravest opponent. Certainly a pleading should be bold, blunt and belligerent. Usually simple modern English is best for this purpose. Quaint-sounding legalistic expressions should be used only if they are necessary to ensure precision. The following examples can be used as a kind of legal shorthand:

'is and at all material times was ...'

'... the servants or agents of the Defendant acting in the course of their employment ...'

'By reason of the matters aforesaid ...'

'If (which is denied) ...'

'If (which is not admitted) ...'

'Further or alternatively ...'

'Further or in the further alternative ...'

But do not be quaint just for the sake of being quaint. The following expressions should always be avoided:

'... the Plaintiff was proceeding by foot in a northerly direction ...'

'... the Plaintiff did deliver the goods aforementioned unto the defendant'

'The defendant, before action, to wit, on 23 March 1997, tendered to the plaintiff the sum of £ ...'

This last is the beginning of a defence of tender before action as to which see p 160. For a modern precedent see Bullen and Leake and Jacob, No 1207, which begins 'On the ... day of ... 19 ..., before the issue of the writ herein the defendant tendered to the plaintiff the sum of £ ...'

Principles of drafting pleadings

The complete code of pleadings is to be found only in the High Court rules. RSC Ord 18 contains a distillation of the theories and art of pleadings propounded over the centuries. By comparison the code set out in the County Court Rules is meagre and incomplete. Since in our view there should be but one standard of pleading the rest of this chapter follows the High Court code, noting the County Court Rules only where they expressly differ. Four of the rules of RSC Ord 18 state what might be called the basic precepts of good pleadings: rr 7, 8, 12 and 13. The text of these rules and the excellent commentary on them in the *White Book* should be studied. For the present the following basic principles may be extracted.

(1) Pleadings must state facts only, not law or evidence.
(2) Pleadings must state only the material facts.
(3) Material facts must be pleaded with sufficient detail but without excessive detail.

The art of pleading lies in deciding *which facts* are material and in deciding *which details* are necessary.

Facts, not law or evidence

The modern system of pleading requires each party to state clearly the facts he is coming to the court to prove, not the legal consequences he intends to draw and not the evidence he intends to call. If litigants only pleaded law they would *conceal* the facts in issue. If a plaintiff could merely allege that 'The Defendant owes me £8,000' the defendant would be left to guess what facts the plaintiff was intending to prove at the trial. Does such an allegation relate to a contract or to a trust? Does it refer to something which happened days ago or years ago? The plaintiff should make these matters clear by pleading the facts he relies on, not just the legal conclusion he draws from them. For example, if the claim relates to goods sold and delivered he should plead the agreed price and the delivery of the goods. If in such a case the defendant could merely answer: 'The Defendant denies he is liable as alleged' it would be the plaintiff's turn to guess. Such a plea would be consistent with any of the following defences: that no agreement was made; that the agreement was invalid; that the agreement was for a different price; that no goods were delivered; and that the defendant has paid for them. By merely stating the legal result he contends for, the defendant would hide the facts upon which his defence is based.

If litigants pleaded evidence it would *obscure* the facts in issue. Assume that instead of alleging a delivery of goods a plaintiff alleged 'On 11 June 1997 a receipt for the delivery of the goods was signed by or on behalf of the Defendant.' Further assume that the defendant answers: 'On 11 June 1997 the Defendant was on holiday abroad and did not sign any such document and had not authorised anyone else to sign it.' Both these paragraphs raise entirely unnecessary issues. For the purpose of pleading it does not matter whether the plaintiff has a receipt or when the defendant went on holiday. The fact in issue is simply whether the goods were delivered and this is all the plaintiff should allege and is all the defendant should plead to.

The example of pleading evidence given above is an easy one. In practice however the line between fact and evidence is sometimes difficult, if not impossible, to draw. Sometimes you can plead facts only by pleading evidence: eg describing a document. Sometimes the detail necessary for a pleading (see the third principle) can be given only by stating 'the facts and matters relied on' in making the allegation. (The words in quotation marks come from the standard form of request for further and better particulars: see Chapter 10.) In cases in which it is doubtful whether certain matters are fact or evidence practitioners sometimes adopt the following pragmatic solutions: put in things you are scared to leave out; put in things that will look bad for your opponent.

The prohibitions against pleading law and evidence have each an important exception. First 'a party may by his pleading raise any point of law' (RSC Ord 18, r 11). Generally speaking points of law are taken only in defences. One way of contesting a claim is to plead an 'objection in point of law', the modern equivalent of the old 'demurrer'. For example, a defendant might in his pleading object that the claim discloses no cause of action because it alleges a promise unsupported by consideration or because special damage is essential to the cause of action and none is alleged. The distinction between pleading law only (which is not permitted) and pleading a point of law (which is) has been described thus: 'Pleading law tends to complicate the pleading and obscure the facts giving rise to the case being advanced; raising a point of law may define or isolate an issue or question arising on the facts as pleaded' (*White Book* 18/7/7). The exception does not *require* the defendant to plead his objection on point of law. At the trial he is free to argue any points of law which arise from the facts pleaded. However, the advantage of specifying the legal defence in advance is twofold:

(1) it puts the plaintiff on notice and therefore avoids the inconvenience of an adjournment at the trial (*cf Sheffield v Pickfords Ltd* (1997) *The Times*, 17 March);

(2) where the objection might dispose of the whole action it can be set down for trial as a preliminary issue thereby avoiding the delay and expense of preparing for a full trial (but see further p 456).

The second exception, ie to the rule against pleading evidence, concerns Civil Evidence Act 1968, s 11, which provides that a person's conviction for an offence can be used as evidence that he committed that offence. For example, in a road accident case the plaintiff might prove negligence on the part of the defendant simply by proving that as a result of the accident the defendant was convicted of careless driving. This simple item of evidence has the unique effect of reversing the legal burden of proof. Negligence by the defendant is presumed unless he can prove the contrary. It would be inconvenient, and perhaps unjust, if a defendant was not given fair notice of this burden before trial. Consequently RSC Ord 18, r 7A provides that, even though it is only evidence, the conviction must be pleaded before it can be proved. The statement of claim must contain particulars of the conviction, the court which made it and the date it was made, and must state the issue in the action to which the conviction is relevant. If the defendant wishes to deny the conviction or allege that it was erroneous or that it is not relevant, he must make the denial or allegation in his defence. By this means the High Court rule ensures that both parties obtain notice before trial of what their opponents are contending. The CCR does not contain a rule corresponding to RSC Ord 18, r 7A. However, in our view, the High Court practice should nevertheless be adopted. Failure to do so would risk expensive and time consuming adjournments (see further, *Green Book* commentary to CCR Ord 20, r 11).

Some practitioners say there is another exception to the rule against pleading evidence. In road accident cases one often sees pleaded as a particular of negligence a failure to comply with a specific provision of the Highway Code (see *Wells v Weeks (Practice Note)* [1965] 1 WLR 45). Strictly speaking such a particular is only evidence of negligence (see Road Traffic Act 1988, s 38).

Material facts only

In relation to claims, the expression 'material facts' has two meanings. Primarily it refers to those facts that it is essential for the plaintiff to prove in order to establish his cause of action. If he fails to plead any one of these facts his claim is bad and can be struck out unless amended. Thus in *Fowler v Lanning* [1959] 1 QB 426 it was held that a claim simply alleging 'the Defendant shot the Plaintiff' (giving details of the time and place and the injuries suffered) disclosed no cause of action since it was for the plaintiff to prove either intention or negligence on the part of the defendant: leave to amend was given (see also *Whall v Bulman* [1953] 2 QB 198).

Facts relating to the remedies the plaintiff seeks are material in the secondary sense of having an important bearing on the issues to be tried. For example, the plaintiff is entitled to plead facts supporting a claim for aggravated damages. Claims for exemplary damages are expressly required to be pleaded together with the facts relied on (RSC Ord 18, r 8(3); CCR Ord 6, r 1B). The same rules also apply to claims for provisional damages (for a precedent see Chitty & Jacob's *Queen's Bench Forms*, 21st ed (Sweet & Maxwell, 1986) No 1503). It is necessary to plead a claim for interest (RSC Ord 18, r 8(4); CCR Ord 6, r 1A; see further, below). As a matter of good practice a claim for loss of earning capacity (as to which see p 70) ought to be pleaded (*Chan Wai Tong v Li Ping Sum* [1985] AC 446). Where a plaintiff is claiming damages under the second rule in *Hadley v Baxendale* (1854) 9 ExD 341 it is usual to plead the defendant's knowledge of the circumstances giving rise to the special loss alleged. Where an injunction is claimed it is usual to include a paragraph stating that 'the Defendant threatens and intends, unless restrained from so doing, to continue to ....' (This last example is somewhat difficult to justify; it reads more like an accusation than a statement of material fact.)

Claims may also include 'introductory averments'. These are a paragraph or two explaining who the parties are, their occupations and their relationship to each other. Such facts help to introduce or explain the material facts even if they are not themselves material. Some introductory averments do contain matter it is essential to plead. A claim in a sale of goods action often states that 'The Defendants are and at all material times were wholesale dealers in ...'; it is essential to plead that the defendants were selling in the course of business if the plaintiff is relying on the implied terms as to quality or fitness. Similarly a county court claim for possession of land usually starts 'The Plaintiff is the freehold owner and is entitled to possession of the dwelling known as ...' This introductory averment clearly defines the land being claimed, a fact the plaintiff is expressly required to plead (CCR Ord 6, r 3).

Generally speaking a claim should not include facts which anticipate a particular defence. Such facts are material only if and when that defence is raised. Answering allegations before they are raised is 'like leaping before you come to the stile' (*Sir Ralph Bovey's Case* (1684) Vent 217, *per* Hale CJ). Anticipating a defence may put the plaintiff at a serious disadvantage; see *Gaston v United Newspapers* (1915) 32 TLR 143, noted on p 188. Assume, for example, that a plaintiff seeks damages for breach of a contract containing an exclusion clause which he thinks is invalid or inapplicable. To plead the clause and then try to explain it away would look weak. It would give the impression that the plaintiff thought the defence had some merit. It is better tactics to draft the claim omitting all reference to the clause. Then, if the defendant pleads it in his defence, the plaintiff's answers to it can be set out in a reply.

In *Sheffield v Pickfords Ltd* (1997) *The Times*, 17 March the defendants pleaded certain contractual clauses said to avoid or limit any liability they otherwise had. Under the Unfair Contract Terms Act 1977 the burden of proof as to reasonableness of these clauses fell upon the defendants. The plaintiff was held entitled to raise the issue of reasonableness at the trial even though she had not previously filed a reply to that effect. On the contrary Lord Woolf MR expressed the view that 'there were advantages in defendants setting out clearly and squarely that they contended that the contract provisions were reasonable. They could then take the course of requiring the plaintiff to clarify her position, to say whether or not she was taking the point. If she was taking the point, then the defendants were in a position to have the necessary evidence at the hearing to establish the matter.'

By way of exception it is usual to anticipate defences under the Limitation Act. (These defences are also exceptional in other ways: see p 161). It is poor tactics to allege a debt which accrued seven years ago without pleading the facts which, it is alleged, take the case out of the ordinary limitation period, eg that the debt was acknowledged two years ago (see p 83). In these cases the pleading would look weak if it did *not* anticipate. The important difference here is that until these additional matters are dealt with the plaintiff does not appear to have a valid cause of action (see generally, *Busch v Stevens* [1963] 1 QB 1).

Material facts in the defence

A defence may contain material facts in two forms. For the most part it comments on the facts pleaded in the claim, admitting or denying them as the case may be. Secondly, it may plead specifically any further facts the defendant relies on.

When a fact is admitted in a pleading it ceases to be 'in issue' and neither party has to advance evidence as to it at the trial. The defendant ought to admit 'plain and acknowledged facts which it is neither to his interest nor in his power to disprove' (*Lee v Button* (1879), *per* Malins VC). If he fails to do so he will cause avoidable expense and can expect to be penalised in costs whatever the outcome of the trial. Sometimes a plaintiff can make this costs penalty automatic by serving a notice to admit (see p 431). If admissions of fact amount to a clear admission of liability the plaintiff can obtain judgment on them without the necessity of a trial (RSC Ord 27, r 3; CCR Ord 17, r 6; and see pp 250 and 369). Where the defendant contradicts a fact alleged by the plaintiff he is said to 'traverse' it. He can do this by pleading a denial 'The Defendant denies ...' or by a less emphatic non-admission 'The Defendant does not admit ...' The latter form is used where the defendant is saying 'I am not in a position to know whether this is true or not so you prove it'. Facts can also be traversed 'by necessary implication': for example pleading facts inconsistent with the plaintiff's allegations.

Sometimes the defendant concedes that the plaintiff has a *prima facie* case, but intends to destroy it by proving additional facts by way of justification or excuse. In order to make clear the nature of such a defence the defendant should specifically plead the additional facts. Note the following examples:

(1) In contract actions: facts showing that the contract has been discharged or released or varied or was made only as agent for another.

(2) In debt actions: the defence of tender before action.

(3) In damages actions: facts relied on in mitigation of, or otherwise in relation to, the amount of damages.

(4) In negligence actions: facts showing that the defendant acted without negligence or that the injury was caused wholly or in part by the plaintiff or some third person (see the different points which arose in *Davie v New Merton Board Mills* [1956] 1 WLR 233, *Crook v Derbyshire* [1961] 1 WLR 1360, *Bills v Roe* [1968] 1 WLR 925, *Fookes v Slaytor* [1978] 1 WLR 1293).

(5) In assault and battery cases: facts showing the defendant acted in self-defence.

(6) In any action: equitable defences (eg undue influence or mistake), fraud, the Limitation Acts, any set-off, or facts in mitigation or damages. (Tender before action, defences under the Limitation Act and set-offs are dealt with in detail on pp 160–164.)

Inconsistent allegations

Any pleading may contain alternative and therefore inconsistent allegations of material facts. For example, in a contract action the plaintiff may allege that a promise he says the defendant made became a term of the main contract or alternatively formed the subject matter of a collateral contract. In the same action the defendant may allege in the alternative—(1) that he never made the promise, (2) that the promise was not broken, (3) that the plaintiff's cause of action is statute-barred. Of course if the pleadings contained too many inconsistencies they would fail in their object of clarifying the issues to be tried. The courts try to reduce the amount of inconsistency in two ways—by penalising in costs any party who multiplies the issues needlessly; and by striking out obviously fictitious or unsustainable allegations (*Remmington v Scoles* [1897] 2 Ch 1 noted on p 192, below, and *CH Pearce & Sons Ltd v Stonechester Ltd* (1983), noted in *White Book* 18/7/17).

There is one form of inconsistency that is never allowed. Co-plaintiffs or co-defendants cannot serve a joint pleading in which each sets up a conflicting case. This is bound up with the rules concerning representation at the trial. Generally speaking parties who serve a joint pleading must appear at the trial by the same advocate and must present a united case. If co-defendants wish to set up conflicting cases they can do so by serving separate defences. It is not possible for co-plaintiffs to serve separate claims (see notes on joinder of parties, p 96). If they disagree as to the facts to allege, one of them must be struck out from the claim in order to bring separate proceedings.

Sufficient but not excessive detail

A good pleading strikes a balance between two competing pressures: the need to give enough detail to inform the opponent of the issues being raised and the need to omit details which would only obscure those issues. In *Re Parton* (1882) 45 LT 756 Kay J summed this up by saying 'although pleadings must now be concise they must also be precise'. Of course the degree of detail necessary varies with the nature of the case. Striking the balance between 'not enough' and 'too much' is learnt only by practice and experience. However, some topics arise so frequently that there are now standard ways of pleading them. We list four of the more important examples.

Alleging an agreement

Describe briefly the nature of the agreement and state who were parties to it, the date it was made and whether it was oral or in writing or partly oral and partly in writing. If the agreement was under seal describe it thus: 'By a deed dated ...', otherwise state the consideration or state that the agreement was made 'for reward'.

Alleging negligence

List all the ways the loss or damage complained of can be explained as being caused by the opponent's negligence. Practitioners tend to use all the examples given in a relevant precedent and to add as many more as they can think of drawing on the particular facts of the case: eg an allegation that the opponent acted under the influence of drink (see *Bills v Roe* [1968] 1 WLR 925). It is important to make the list as complete as you can. The trial is limited to the pleadings, and therefore further particulars cannot be given at that stage without amendment, which is not always possible. To get over this practitioners often include a 'particular' of negligence of the most general nature as a kind of catch-all clause: for example 'Failed so to steer, slow down or stop the vehicle as to avoid the collision' or, in an action for injuries at work, 'Failed to provide or maintain a safe system of work'.

Alleging injury and loss

In personal injury claims full particulars of injury and loss are set out in two documents, a medical report and a statement of special damages claimed, both of which must accompany the plaintiff's pleading (see Chapter 11). In our view it is therefore sufficient if the pleading itself merely refers to those documents. Certain additional facts should also be pleaded, for example, the age or date of birth of the person injured, a fact the plaintiff is required to plead in High Court cases (*Practice Direction* [1974] 1 WLR 75), and future losses above and beyond what might be assumed from the figures set out (see *Domsalla v Barr* [1969] 1 WLR 630, loss of exceptional career prospects; *Chan Wai Tong v Li Ping Sum* [1985] AC 446, loss of earning capacity).

In contract claims for financial loss the claimant should give enough information to enable his opponent to estimate a payment into court.

Minute accuracy is not essential: the loss may be described as 'estimated'
or 'approx' (see *Perestrello v United Paint Co* [1969] 1 WLR 570).

Alleging a claim for interest

As to interest generally see p 15. The claim for interest should be
mentioned twice in the pleading; in the paragraphs and in the prayer for
relief at the end. In a damages claim interest is payable, if at all, in the
court's discretion under SCA 1981, s 35A or CCA 1984, s 69. In a
paragraph of the pleading specify the relevant statute and state that the
rates of interest, and the periods for which it is payable, are to be decided
by the court. The prayer for relief can then simply refer back to this
paragraph. (For examples see pp 166–170.) It has been suggested that a
plaintiff intending to claim an award of interest which is higher than that
usually awarded should say so in his pleading. In the paragraphs of the
pleading he should set out the special facts he relies on as justifying a
higher award (*Dexter v Courtaulds Ltd* [1984] 1 WLR 372, and see p 75).

In a debt claim interest may be payable either as of right or in the
court's discretion under the relevant statute. In the paragraphs of the
claim the plaintiff should state how his claim for interest arises (eg by
contract or by statute, specifying it), the full terms of any contractual
provision relied on and the date from which the interest is claimed. The
prayer for relief should specify the annual rate of interest being claimed,
the amount of interest in pounds and pence which has accrued before
commencement of proceedings and the daily rate at which it accrues. (For
examples see pp 170 and 199.)

Most debt claims end in a default judgment. If interest is pleaded in the
precise way described above, and if the rate of interest used is the
judgment debt rate or a contractually agreed rate, a plaintiff who is
entitled to a default judgment may enter final judgment for both the debt
and interest (and fixed costs): see further pp 212 and 247.

Claims, defences and replies

Drafting a claim

The material facts in the basic causes of action are familiar to everyone
and therefore claims alleging them follow certain well-recognised paths. A
negligence claim always covers four items: the incident complained of,
that the incident was caused by the defendant's negligence, the loss or
damage the plaintiff has suffered thereby and the claim for interest.
Depending on the complexity of the case the first three items may be set
out in three or thirty paragraphs. Sometimes they can all be included in a
single paragraph.

> *Example*
>
> On 1 March 1997 the Plaintiff was crossing Bishopthorpe Road,
> York when the Defendant so negligently drove his motor cycle that he

caused or permitted the same to collide with the Plaintiff causing the Plaintiff severe injuries, loss and damage:
Particulars of Negligence, etc
Particulars of Injury and Special damage, etc.

In a simple debt action one paragraph is almost always sufficient.

Example
   The Plaintiff's claim is for £12,000 the price of goods sold and delivered to the Defendant and for interest thereon from the date of delivery pursuant to section 69 of the County Courts Act 1984.

Particulars
1 March 1997: 40 lengths of cotton velvet 100 yards by 58 inches each, in colours specified in the Defendant's order dated 17 January 1997, at £300 per length £12,000
AND the Plaintiff claims, *etc*.

A claim alleging *breach of a term of contract* usually sets out six items:
   (1) the agreement and consideration;
   (2) the term alleged to have been broken;
   (3) breach of that term;
   (4) the consequences of breach (if any);
   (5) the loss the plaintiff has suffered thereby; and
   (6) the claim for interest.
Adapting that framework to a claim alleging *wrongful repudiation of a contract* the second and third items are replaced by a statement that the defendant 'wrongfully repudiated the agreement' (describing when and how this was done) and the fourth item will also state whether the repudiation was accepted by the plaintiff. As with negligence claims the number of paragraphs needed to set out the items in a contract claim depends upon the complexity of the case.

   Where the plaintiff relies on two or more causes of action arising from the same facts the familiar items of each should be woven together to prevent unnecessary repetition. However, if the plaintiff is raising causes of action based on different facts it is more convenient to keep separate the facts applicable to each.

   After the material facts have been pleaded the last substantial part of the claim is the prayer for relief. This is simply a list of the remedies the plaintiff is seeking and begins with the words 'AND the Plaintiff claims'. It should not be used to plead any material facts or to particularise any allegation of loss. In debt actions the prayer simply states the amount of the debt (plus interest). If the money claim is unliquidated the correct prayer is for 'damages': in county court claims it is convenient to state whether or not the damages claim exceeds £5,000 (which is the limit of the district judge's trial jurisdiction). If no such statement is pleaded the case is treated as falling within the trial jurisdiction of the district judge whatever its value (CCR Ord 6, r 1 (1A)).

Where the claim is for an injunction the full terms of the injunction should be set out. The plaintiff is entitled to claim remedies in the alternative or indeed different remedies against different defendants so long as the prayer makes this clear.

Example
'AND the Plaintiff claims

against the First Defendant
  (1)   Under paragraph 5 hereof £16,330

against both Defendants
  (2)   Under paragraph 6 hereof £1,322.28, alternatively, damages.
  (3)   An injunction to restrain the Defendants whether by them-selves, their servants or agents or otherwise howsoever from entering or using the coal yard or driving any motor vehicles into it.
  (4)   Under paragraph 9 hereof interest on such amounts and at such rate and for such periods as the Court shall think just.
  (5)   Costs.
  (6)   Further or other relief.'

Strictly speaking it is never necessary to claim items (5) and (6) though Chancery practitioners often include them, perhaps as a kind of finishing flourish (see *White Book* 18/15/4 and *Cargill v Bower* (1878) 10 ChD 502).

Drafting a defence

The clearest defence will answer the claim paragraph by paragraph. In other words it will deal in turn with each of the plaintiff's allegations, admitting or denying them as necessary, in the order in which the plaintiff pleaded them. Any additional facts can be inserted in their appropriate place in the story. When this method is followed it is possible to match up the pleadings and so locate precisely the facts in issue between the parties. The alternative method of drafting a defence is for the defendant to strike out on a separate path: pleading in chronological order all the material facts as he or she sees them, denying the plaintiff's major allegations, and concluding with a *seriatim* clause such as 'Save as hereinbefore specifically admitted the Defendant denies each and every allegation contained in the Statement of Claim as though the same were set out herein and traversed *seriatim*'. In practice defences often follow the paragraph by paragraph method and include a *seriatim* clause by way of double security. The alternative method of drafting mentioned is used only in particular cases; for example, in debt actions where the claim was in short form but the defendant has to plead the facts more fully in order to set out terms he alleges the plaintiff has broken; or in a case in which the claim is so unnecessarily long and complicated that to plead to it paragraph by paragraph would only add to the confusion.

Whichever method is used the defence should provide a complete account of the defendant's case. The High Court rules are very strict about this. RSC Ord 18, r 8, requires a defendant to plead specifically any additional facts he intends to rely on. RSC Ord 18, r 13, states that a defendant is deemed to *admit* any facts alleged in the statement of claim which he does not *specifically* traverse (ie contradict). The latter rule, called the rule of implied admissions, supplies against his interest any omissions the defendant has left in his pleadings. The rule has only one exception (and even that is rarely relied on); it does not apply to defences served by persons under disability (RSC Ord 80, r 8). In practice a second exception is allowed: *seriatim* clauses are an accepted method of traversing minor allegations (*Warner v Sampson* [1959] 1 QB 297).

Neither r 8 nor r 13 has any equivalent in the County Court Rules. The old CCR expressly stated that the delivery of a defence did not prevent the defendant relying on any further or other defence or counterclaim. This provision is not repeated in the current CCR. In *Tramp Leasing Ltd v Sanders* (1995) *The Times*, 18 April the Court of Appeal upheld the ruling of a county court judge not to allow an amendment of a defence during the final part of a trial. In his closing speech counsel sought to raise new defences of no consideration or past consideration. However, we respectfully doubt whether an amendment to the defence was necessary. In our view, the absence of any rule of implied admission still enables the defendant to raise unpleaded defences. However, we acknowledge that it would be unwise to assume that a poorer standard of pleading is sufficient in county court defences. If a defendant raises a point which takes the plaintiff by surprise the court can make appropriate orders for costs and adjournment.

Specific traverses

When pleading to a claim paragraph by paragraph, particular care must be taken with those paragraphs which allege several facts. Sometimes it is sufficient to use an expression such as 'Each of the allegations in paragraph [6] of the Statement of Claim is denied', but usually it is better to plead to each allegation separately. Different considerations apply to a paragraph which alleges a material fact of substance along with details and surrounding circumstances. The traverse of such a paragraph must deal with the point of substance clearly and unambiguously.

Example

Assume a statement of claim states '2. On 23 February 1997 the Plaintiff delivered the said goods to the Defendant's warehouse' and consider the following traverses:

(1)   'Paragraph 2 of the Statement of Claim is denied.'
(2)   'The Defendant denies that on 23 February 1997 the Plaintiff delivered the said goods to the Defendant's warehouse.'
(3)   'The Plaintiff never delivered any of the said goods to the Defendant.'
(4)   'The Defendant denies that the Plaintiff delivered the said goods or any goods to the Defendant as alleged in paragraph 2 of the Statement of Claim or at all.'

(1) does not specifically traverse the point of substance in paragraph 2 (the delivery of goods) and therefore would not be acceptable; (2) is worse, because it is over-specific and could be construed as meaning that the goods *were* delivered but on a different day (a plea such as this is termed a 'negative pregnant': see further p 188); (3) is the best traverse: it pleads only to the point of substance and traverses the details of time and place by necessary implication; (4) is the traverse most likely to be used in practice: the phrases 'or any goods' and 'as alleged ... or at all' are included to prevent the traverse being over-specific.

Special defences

In order to comply with RSC Ord 18, r 8, a defendant who intends to prove a positive case to defeat the plaintiff's claim must specifically plead the relevant facts in his defence. A list of such defences is set out on p 153. Most of them are very routine and ordinary (see for example contributory negligence). However, three of them call for more detailed discussion.

1 Tender before action

This defence can be raised only against a claim for a debt (this does not include claims falling within CCR Ord 1, r 10, county court negligence claims for the cost of accident repairs, see *John Laing Construction Ltd v Dastur* [1987] 1 WLR 686 and *Smith v Springer* [1987] 1 WLR 1720). It is an allegation that the defendant tendered the debt before the action was commenced. The defence carries the implication that the commencement of the action was unnecessary and therefore the plaintiff should pay the whole costs. In order to raise this defence the defendant must first pay into court a sum equal to, or exceeding, the amount alleged to have been tendered (see RSC Ord 18, r 16; CCR Ord 9, r 12).

At first sight it may seem odd that a defence of tender should ever be raised. One might ask, if the defendant *had* tendered payment surely the plaintiff would have accepted it? In practice the real dispute between the parties concerns the amount of the debt due.

Example

P sells and delivers wine to D for an agreed price of £5 per bottle. P says that 1,000 bottles were delivered and sends D an invoice for

£5,000. D says that only 800 bottles were delivered and sends P a cheque for £4,000. P returns the cheque and sues D for £5,000.

In this example the plaintiff will defeat the defence of tender before action if he can prove *any* of the following:

(1) The debt due exceeded the amount tendered.

(2) The plaintiff was not obliged to accept payment by cheque and, in returning the cheque, he did not waive his right to raise this objection. (Strictly speaking a cheque is not legal tender but in *Jones v Arthur* (1840) 8 Dowl 442 the plaintiff was held to have waived his right to object when he returned the cheque complaining only that it was not for the full sum due.)

(3) The tender was made conditional on the plaintiff acknowledging that no more was due (ie the cheque was sent 'in full and final settlement' or with some similar words). Even if the full amount was tendered the defendant cannot require the plaintiff to give up his right to query the calculation. However, if in the example above the defendant tendered £4,000 unconditionally or 'under protest that this is the full amount due' the plaintiff should have accepted it and sued only for the balance.

2 Defences under the Limitation Act

Defences under the Limitation Act are regarded as procedural rather than substantive. Accordingly the defendant must plead them if he wishes to rely on them (*White Book* 18/8/10). If a defendant fails to plead them he is treated as having waived the benefit of them, unless leave to amend can be given. One might describe these defences as 'special' in two other respects as well: they are the only objections in point of law which have to be pleaded, and they are the only defences it is usual for the plaintiff to anticipate in his claim (see p 153).

3 Pleas by way of set-off

'A set-off is a monetary cross-claim which is also a defence to the claim' (*White Book* 18/17/2). In other words it is a claim for money against a plaintiff which has dual effect. First, it is a claim, raisable by separate action or by counterclaim. Secondly, if raised in the plaintiff's action it has the additional effect of extinguishing his claim *pro tanto* (ie up to its value). Which monetary cross-claims have this dual effect depends on the substantive law and not upon the way a claim is pleaded. The distinction is important for three reasons: costs (see p 566); whether the cross-claim will prevent the plaintiff obtaining summary judgment (see p 227); and the effect of insolvency of either of the cross-claimants (see *Stein v Blake* [1996] AC 243).

There are three matters (set out below) which, in common parlance, lawyers usually call 'set-offs'. Strictly speaking only the first is a true set-off. The second was originally only a defence. The third was originally a cross-action in the courts of equity. These two have become pleas by way of set-off because of the reform of the courts and procedure made by the Judicature Acts 1873–75.

(*a*) *Mutual debt set-off.* Ever since the so-called Statutes of Set-off in 1729 and 1735 a claim for a debt can be set off against or extinguished by a debt the plaintiff owes the defendant 'in the same right'. Both claim and set-off must be for liquidated amounts.

> *Example*
> Alan and Bernard supply goods to each other. On 31 May 1996 Alan owed Bernard £60,000 and Bernard owes Alan £50,000. If Alan starts an action against Bernard his claim would be totally extinguished by the set-off: Bernard would also raise a counterclaim to obtain the balance of £10,000. If Bernard started proceedings first his claim could be partially extinguished.
>
> Assume Bernard dies and Colin, another trader, is appointed his executor. Colin personally owes Alan £10,000. If, as executor, Colin sues Alan for the £60,000 Alan could still set off £50,000 but not Colin's personal debt since that is not due 'in the same right'. *Semble* Alan could raise an ordinary counterclaim (*Re Richardson* [1933] WN 90 *per* Romer LJ).

(*b*) *Common law defence of abatement.* From early times where a plaintiff sues for the price of goods or services supplied the defendant has been able to 'set up', in diminution of the price, any claim he has for defects in quality of the goods or services supplied (*King v Boston* (1789) 7 East 481; *Mondel v Steel* (1841) 8 M&W 858). Although this plea is not a true set-off at common law (since it is for damages rather than a debt) it is treated as a defence in abatement of the plaintiff's claim. Since 1873 the defendant has also been able to raise the plea as a counterclaim, and therefore nowadays it has no significant difference from a true set-off. For sale of goods cases the plea has been made statutory: Sale of Goods Act 1979, s 53.

(*c*) *Equitable set-off.* Before 1875 equity would grant an injunction to restrain a plaintiff from insisting on his legal rights where it would be unconscionable for him to do so without taking into account cross-claims the defendant had arising out of the same subject matter. Since 1875 the administration of law and equity has been fused, and nowadays rather than issue an injunction the court will treat *related cross-claims* as defences extinguishing the plaintiff's claim *pro tanto*.

> *Example*
> P, a warehouseman, sued D for the agreed charges for storing D's vehicles. D claimed that, because of P's negligence, some of the goods had been lost or stolen from the warehouse. This cross-claim for

negligence amounted to an equitable defence thereby defeating an application for summary judgment (*Morgan v Martin Johnson* [1949] 1 KB 107).

P, a householder, sued D, a builder, for damages for failing to complete a building contract. D raised three cross-claims, *quantum meruit* for extra work done, damages for breach of contract by P and damages for trespass to D's tools (thrown away by P). All the cross-claims were held to be equitable set-offs. The cross-claims overtopping the plaintiff's claim by £10, the claim was dismissed, judgment for £10 was given on the counterclaim and a special order for costs made (*Hanak v Green* [1958] 2 QB 9).

P, a landlord, sued D, its tenant, for rent. D successfully pleaded, by way of set-off, damages for breach by P of its covenant for quiet enjoyment even though D's rent covenant provided for payment of rent 'without any deduction' (*Connaught Restaurants Ltd v Indoor Leisure Ltd* [1994] 1 WLR 501; contrast *Coca-Cola Financial Corporation v Finsat International Ltd* [1996] 3 WLR 849 in which it was held that there was a clear contractual exclusion of the right of set off).

The exact scope of the common law defence of abatement can now be regarded as being of academic interest only (*Sim v Rotheram Metropolitan Borough Council* [1987] Ch 216 *per* Scott J). It is a narrow common law version of the wide doctrine of equitable set-off. If equitable set-off is available, abatement is not needed (and see further, *Aectra Refining and Manufacturing Inc v Exmar NV* [1994] 1 WLR 1634). If, in the circumstances, equitable set-off is not available then it will also be impossible to establish abatement. There are certain exceptional types of transactions in which the law withholds both pleas: eg actions on dishonoured bills of exchange and certain related cases (see p 227); in actions for freight under a contract of carriage (*United Carriers Ltd v Heritage Food Group (UK) Ltd* [1996] 1 WLR 371 and the cases cited therein).

In some cases equitable set-off may also be available as a defence to a non-monetary claim, eg forfeiture or specific performance (*BICC plc v Burndy Corporation* [1985] Ch 232) or to a non-litigious remedy, eg a landlord's right to distrain for rent (*Eller v Grovecrest Investments Ltd* [1995] 2 WLR 278).

Pleading a set-off
A set-off can be pleaded as a defence, or as a counterclaim, or as both a defence and a counterclaim. There is serious disadvantage in pleading it only as a defence: the defendant would not be able to obtain a money judgment in his favour if the set-off exceeds the claim or if the claim is defeated by some other defence. There is no advantage to be gained in pleading it only as a counterclaim; the court can still give judgment only for the balance and make a special order as to costs (RSC Ord 15, r 2; CCR Ord 21, r 4; and see p 566). A professionally drafted pleading should always

raise the set-off as both a defence and a counterclaim. This can be done by adding a final paragraph to the defence such as: 'If necessary, the Defendant will rely upon his counterclaim in this action by way of set-off in extinction or diminution of the Plaintiff's claim.' The facts giving rise to the set-off can then be pleaded in a counterclaim drafted in the ordinary way.

Drafting a counterclaim

Normally the defence and the counterclaim are included in the same document, which is headed 'DEFENCE AND COUNTERCLAIM'. Then comes the subheading 'DEFENCE' and the paragraphs of the defence. Next comes the subheading 'COUNTERCLAIM' and beneath it the paragraphs of the counterclaim. The paragraphs are numbered in ascending sequence from the defence: if the last paragraph of the defence was numbered 6 the first paragraph of the counterclaim will be 7.

With one important difference the facts of the counterclaim are drafted in the same way as the facts of a statement of claim or particulars of claim. Thus a counterclaim alleging negligence will contain the four elements described on p 156: a counterclaim alleging breach of the terms of a contract will contain the six elements described. The only difference is this: if some of the material facts have already been pleaded to or stated in the defence there is no need to set them out again in the counterclaim. Instead state simply 'paragraphs ... to ... (inclusive) are repeated', then plead any additional facts and conclude 'AND the Defendant counterclaims ...'.

Forms of admission, defence and counterclaim

An example of these forms is given on p 251. They are served on the defendant with the summons and particulars of claim in county court cases. The defendant can either use the form supplied or file a pleading in some other form together with a copy for the plaintiff (CCR Ord 9, r 2). The court form would not normally be used by solicitors except in the simplest of cases. It is written in the form of questions, to be answered by a defendant acting in person.

Drafting a reply and/or defence to counterclaim

The plaintiff serves a reply if he wishes to plead to the defences raised. A reply is never compulsory and is rarely necessary. There is no need to serve a reply simply to deny the defences raised. In the absence of any reply these are deemed to be denied: in the High Court rules this is called an 'implied joinder of issue' (RSC Ord 18, r 14). A reply is served to comply with the requirement in RSC Ord 18, r 8 to plead any new facts the plaintiff intends to prove to defeat any defence, eg to 'confess and avoid' the defendant's case.

The rule of implied admissions does not apply with the same severity in the case of a reply. The plaintiff can make a 'general joinder of issue', for example, 'Save as hereinafter appears the Plaintiff joins issue with the Defendant on his Defence'. As with any other pleading the plaintiff is entitled to make alternative allegations.

Example
   In an action for damages for non-acceptance of goods the defendant admits that the plaintiff tendered delivery on the date alleged but says that the due date for delivery was two months earlier and therefore he was entitled to refuse the delivery. The plaintiff might reply: 'If, which is denied, it was a condition of the agreement that the last date for delivery was 30 September 1995, the defendant waived that condition and is not entitled to rely thereon. *Particulars* etc' (see Bullen and Leake and Jacob, Precedent No 1268).

However, the reply should not allege any facts which are inconsistent with the facts alleged in the claim (RSC Ord 18, r 10, the so-called 'rule against departure'). If after seeing the defence the plaintiff wishes to change his story he should do so by amending his first pleading (see *Herbert v Vaughan* [1972] 1 WLR 1128 and *Hannays v Baldeosingh* [1992] 1 WLR 395).

In the High Court a defence to counterclaim is compulsory if the plaintiff wishes to dispute the counterclaim: if the plaintiff fails to serve this pleading the defendant can get judgment in default (RSC Ord 19, r 8). A defence to counterclaim is drafted in the same manner as an ordinary defence. The High Court rule of implied admissions operates with all its usual severity: the plaintiff must specifically traverse (ie contradict) any allegation in the counterclaim which he does not wish to admit.

Where a plaintiff serves both a reply and a defence to counterclaim they must be included in the same document (RSC Ord 18, r 3). The document will have the general heading 'REPLY AND DEFENCE TO COUNTERCLAIM' and the two subheadings thereafter.

In the county court, the rules make no express provision for replies or defences to counterclaim and there is no provision for judgment to be entered in default of defence to counterclaim. However, if these pleadings are used, the costs reasonably incurred in respect of them may be claimed. Costs are, of course, discretionary. They will be disallowed if the court thinks the reply and/or defence to counterclaim served no useful purpose. In cases of doubt the plaintiff could ask the court to give a direction as to such pleadings (CCR Ord 13, r 2). In practice there is no longer any difference between High Court and county court pleadings and generally a reply and/or a defence to counterclaim should be filed and served in a county court where it would have been served had the case been in the High Court. [*continued on p 172*]

Fig 5a: Specimen statement of claim (QBD)

IN THE HIGH COURT OF JUSTICE   1996-D-No 3284

QUEEN'S BENCH DIVISION

(Writ issued 13th June 1996)

BETWEEN   CHARLES DIMWIT   Plaintiff
                                –AND–
                        NORTHDOWN COACHES PLC   Defendants

STATEMENT OF CLAIM

1. On 4th February 1996 at about 8 am the Plaintiff was standing at a bus stop situated in the High Street, Pethurst in the County of Sussex when a bus owned by the Defendants and driven by their servant or agent in the course of his employment stopped at the bus stop.

2. The plaintiff attempted to board the bus as a prospective passenger for reward, but while he was doing so the conductor thereof, acting in the course of his employment as servant or agent of the Defendants, sounded the bell as a signal for the driver to move the bus forward. The bus moved forward suddenly and the Plaintiff fell to the ground.

3. The matters complained of were caused by the negligence of the Defendants their servants or agents.

PARTICULARS

The conductor of the bus was negligent in that he
(1) sounded the bell as aforesaid without first ensuring that all persons on or in the act of boarding the bus, and in particular the Plaintiff, were in a safe position;
(2) failed to give any or any proper warning to the Plaintiff that the bus was about to move.

The driver of the bus was negligent in that he
(1) drove away from the bus stop without ensuring adequately or at all that it was safe to do so, and in particular that no passengers were still boarding the bus.
(2) drove off too fast and with a sudden jerk.

4. By reason of the negligence of the driver and conductor the Plaintiff suffered pain and injury, loss and damage, full particulars of which are set out in the medical report and the statement of special damages annexed hereto. The Plaintiff's date of birth is 28th December 1961.

5. In respect of damages awarded to him the Plaintiff is entitled to interest pursuant to section 35A of the Supreme Court Act 1981 for such periods and at such rates as to the Court shall seem just.

AND the Plaintiff claims
(1) Damages
(2) Under paragraph 5 hereof interest for such periods and at such rates as to the Court shall seem just.

JOHN DOE

SERVED on 11th July 1996 by Messrs Ross & Robert (ref AJS) of 27 Lundy Street London WC2A 1QA, the Plaintiff's Solicitors.

Fig 5b: Specimen defence (QBD)

IN THE HIGH COURT OF JUSTICE   **1996-D-No 3284**

QUEEN'S BENCH DIVISION

BETWEEN   CHARLES DIMWIT   Plaintiff
                                       –AND–
                          NORTHDOWN COACHES PLC   Defendants

DEFENCE

1. It is admitted that on the date and at the place mentioned in paragraphs 1 and 2 of Statement of Claim the Plaintiff while attempting to board a bus owned by the Defendants and driven by their servants fell to the ground. Save as aforesaid paragraphs 1 and 2 of the Statement of Claim are denied. In particular it is denied that the conductor rang the bell while the Plaintiff was attempting to board.

2. It is denied that the Defendants or any of their servants or agents were guilty of the alleged or any negligence or that the matters complained of were caused as alleged in the Statement of Claim.

3. Further or alternatively the matters complained of were caused wholly or in part by the Plaintiff's negligence.

PARTICULARS

The Plaintiff was negligent in that he
(1) boarded or attempted to board the bus while it was in motion;
(2) failed to hold on to the handrail or take any other sufficient steps to avoid falling into the road.

4. No admission is made as to the alleged or any pain or injury, loss or damage or as to any entitlement to interest.

5. Save as is hereinbefore expressly admitted each and every allegation in the Statement of Claim is denied as if the same were here set out and traversed seriatim.

RICHARD ROE

SERVED on 24th July 1996 by Messrs Giles, Shona & Co of 30 Percy Street Northdown NT3 0TT, Solicitors for the Defendant.

Note: The pleadings in figs 5a and 5b, which are taken from a College of Law tutorial question, show how a practitioner might make use of a precedent book. They are based on examples given in Atkin's Court Forms *but varied so as to emphasise a point which, according to the tutorial question, was the main issue between the parties: whether the bus was stationary when the plaintiff attempted to board it. Care must always be taken in the choice of language: one student pleaded in paragraph 1 of his statement of claim '... The Plaintiff boarded a bus but was thrown off by a jerk'.*

In this case consideration should be given to joining the defendants' employees as co-defendants (see p 98). It would be unnecessary to join them if, eg, the defendants or their insurers informed the plaintiffs that vicarious liability was not going to be contested. This often happens in practice.

Fig 5c: Specimen statement of claim (ChD)

IN THE HIGH COURT OF JUSTICE   **1995-G-No 321**

CHANCERY DIVISION

(WRIT issued 26th May 1995)

BETWEEN   BERNARD GREEN   Plaintiff
                                        -AND-
                            SLAPTON DISTRICT COUNCIL   Defendant

STATEMENT OF CLAIM

1. The Plaintiff is and at all material times was a promoter of professional wrestling contests.

2. By an agreement in writing dated 3rd April 1995 and in consideration of the sum of £2,500 per evening the Defendant agreed to allow the Plaintiff to use the premises known as Slapton Town Hall between the hours of 7 pm and 11 pm on Saturday 13 May 1995 and thereafter between the same hours each succeeding Saturday for the 1995 summer season (a total of 20 weeks) for the purpose of publicly presenting a series of programmes of professional wrestling contests.

3. After the Plaintiff had presented the first of the programmes in pursuance of the agreement, the Defendant by letter dated 20th May 1995 wrongfully purported to terminate the agreement.

4. Carrying out the intentions expressed in that letter, the Defendant has wrongfully excluded the Plaintiff from the Hall whereby the Plaintiff has suffered loss and damage.

PARTICULARS

The Plaintiff was compelled to cancel the second programme in the series and estimates his loss on that programme to be £23,000.

5. Further, in the circumstances, the Plaintiff is entitled to recover interest pursuant to section 35A of the Supreme Court Act 1981 on the amount found to be due to him at such rate and for such period as the court shall think just.

6. The Defendant threatens and intends unless restrained from so doing to continue to exclude the Plaintiff from the Hall whereby the Plaintiff apprehends the cancellation of further programmes with losses as described in paragraph 4 hereof.

AND the Plaintiff claims:

(1) An injunction to restrain the Defendant by its officers, servants, agents or otherwise howsoever from doing the following acts or any of them, that is to say:

(i) Preventing the Plaintiff from occupying and using Slapton Town Hall in accordance with the agreement in writing dated 3rd April 1995 and made between the parties hereto.
(ii) Taking any steps calculated whether directly or indirectly to impede the Plaintiff in occupying and using Slapton Town Hall in accordance with that agreement.
(2) Damages.
(3) Under paragraph 5 hereof, interest at such rate and for such period as the Court shall think just.
(4) Costs.
(5) Further or other relief.

JOHN DOE

SERVED *etc*

Fig 5d: Specimen defence and counterclaim (ChD)

IN THE HIGH COURT OF JUSTICE   1995-G-No 321

CHANCERY DIVISION

BETWEEN   BERNARD GREEN   Plaintiff
                                      -AND-
                            SLAPTON DISTRICT COUNCIL   Defendant

DEFENCE AND COUNTERCLAIM

DEFENCE

1. The Defendant admits paragraphs 1 and 2 of the Statement of Claim.

2. The Defendant admits that it terminated the agreement by its letter dated 20th May 1995 and subsequently excluded the Plaintiff from the Hall as alleged in paragraphs 3 and 4 of the Statement of Claim but denies for the reasons given hereafter that it thereby acted unlawfully or in breach of contract.

3. By clause 6 of the agreement the Defendant was entitled to bring the agreement to an end in the event of any breach by the Plaintiff of any of the conditions thereof.

4. By clause 4 of the agreement it was a condition of the agreement that the Plaintiff would not present any spectacle of a lewd or offensive nature.

5. The said condition was broken by the Plaintiff in that on 13th May 1995 in the course of the first programme in the series presented by the Plaintiff at the Hall one John Read, a contestant engaged by the Plaintiff, repeatedly made obscene gestures directed at the spectators attending the programme by raising 2 fingers in a provocative manner and pulling down his wrestling tights to expose his buttocks thereby prevoking a violent disturbance among the spectators.

6. By reason of the matters aforesaid the agreement was lawfully and effectively terminated by the Defendant by its letter of 20th May 1995.

7. No admission is made as to the alleged or any loss or damage.

8. In the circumstances the Plaintiff is not entitled to the relief claimed or any relief.

COUNTERCLAIM

9. The Defendant repeats paragraphs 1 to 6 of the Defence.

10. By clause 5 of the agreement the Plaintiff agreed to pay for any damage to the Hall and to any fittings and furniture which might occur during the hours of use thereof by the Plaintiff. In the course of the programme referred to in paragraph 5 hereof 2 chairs and 1 table of a total value of £340 and forming part of the furniture of the Hall were broken beyond repair.

11. By its letter of 16th May 1995, the Defendant claimed the said sum of £340 from the Plaintiff but the Plaintiff has failed to pay the same.

12. In respect of any sums awarded to it, the defendant is entitled to interest pursuant to section 35A of the Supreme Court Act 1981 at such rate and for such period as to the Court shall seem just.

AND the Defendant counterclaims.

    (1) Under paragraph 11 hereof, £340.
    (2) Under paragraph 12 hereof, interest at such rate and for such period as to the Court shall seem just.

SERVED *etc*   RICHARD ROE

Fig 5e: Specimen particulars of claim (Cty Ct)

IN THE AMSBURY COUNTY COURT   **Case No KH554321**

BETWEEN   BELLADONNAS (a firm)   Plaintiffs
–AND–
IAN PHILLIPS   Defendant

PARTICULARS OF CLAIM

The Plaintiffs' claim is for the sum of £3,275 being the balance of the price of goods sold and delivered to the Defendant and for interest thereon from the date of delivery pursuant to section 69 of the County Courts Act 1984.

PARTICULARS

Goods delivered: 9 May 1995	
1 Granville Stereo CD and Cassette Deck	£1,695.00
1 Granville Stereo Amplifier	£1,950.00
	£3,645.00
Less sum paid on account	£370.00
	£3,275.00

AND the Plaintiffs claim:
(1) £3,275 plus interest pursuant to statute at the rate of 8 per centum per annum equivalent to a sum of £34.56 for the period from 9th May 1995 to the date hereof (48 days), together making a total of £3,309.56.
(2) Interest as above from the date hereof at the rate of £0.72 daily until judgment or sooner payment.

DATED 27th June 1995   Pencharz and Reese, Plaintiffs' Solicitors of 21 Baron Road, Flint, where they will accept service of proceedings on behalf of the Plaintiffs

TO the Chief Clerk
AND TO the Defendant

Fig 5f: Specimen defence and counterclaim (Cty Ct)

IN THE AMSBURY COUNTY COURT   Case No KH554321

BETWEEN	BELLADONNAS (a firm)	Plaintiffs
	–AND–	
	IAN PHILLIPS	Defendant

DEFENCE AND COUNTERCLAIM

DEFENCE

1. By an oral agreement made on 9th May 1995 at the Plaintiffs' shop in Amsbury, the Plaintiffs, by their shop assistant, agreed to sell to the Defendant the goods described in the Particulars of Claim for the prices there stated whereupon the Defendant paid £370 on account and the goods were then and there delivered to him.

2. The Plaintiffs sold the goods in the course of business. In the circumstances it was an implied condition of the parties' agreement that the goods would be of satisfactory quality.

3. In breach of condition the goods delivered by the Plaintiffs were not of satisfactory quality in that the amplifier was incorrectly wired, the lead coloured brown being connected to the earth terminal.

4. On 10th May 1995 and in consequence of the breach the amplifier exploded when the Defendant first attempted to use it.

5. By reason of the matters aforesaid the amplifier was worthless and useless to the Defendant and the Defendant sets up the breach in extinction or diminution of the price claimed herein.

6. Further or alternatively the Defendant will rely upon his counterclaim herein by way of set-off in extinction or diminution of the Plaintiffs' claim.

7. In the circumstances the Plaintiffs are not entitled to the relief claimed or any relief.

COUNTERCLAIM

8. The Defendant repeats paragraphs 1 to 4 hereof inclusive.

9. As a consequence of the explosion the Defendant suffered loss and damage.

PARTICULARS

Cost of amplifier damaged beyond repair	£1,950.00
Value of carpet damaged beyond repair	£600.00
Cost of fitting new carpet	£117.50
	£2,667.50

10. In respect of damages awarded to him the Defendant is entitled to interest pursuant to section 69 of the County Courts Act 1984 for such periods and at such rates as to the Court shall seem just.

AND the Defendant counterclaims
(1) Damages
(2) Under paragraph 10 hereof interest for such periods and at such rates as to the Court shall seem just.

DATED 11th July 1995

TO the Chief Clerk
AND TO the Plaintiffs

The Alexander Thomas Partnership, Defendant's Solicitors of Tournament Buildings, Kelsey High Street, Amsbury, who will accept service of all proceedings on behalf of the Defendant at such address.

Drafting further pleadings

Almost invariably pleadings can be completed in three levels—claim, defence and reply. Further pleadings can be served only if leave is granted (RSC Ord 18, r 4; CCR Ord 13, r 2). Instead of granting leave the court is likely to invite the applicant to amend an earlier pleading. The names of the further pleadings show their ancient origins: the 'rejoinder', served by the defendant, the 'surrejoinder', served by the plaintiff, the 'rebutter', served by the defendant and finally the 'surrebutter', served by the plaintiff. These documents would be used to raise additional facts the party intended to rely on in answer to the immediately preceding pleading. In an exceptional case in the High Court a rejoinder might be allowed: usually only to do the work of a reply to defence to counterclaim. There is one case still within living memory in which the issues warranted pleadings on the old scale. In *Tito v Waddell (No 2)* [1977] Ch 106 a group of Banaban Islanders brought an action against the British Phosphate Commissioners in respect of mining agreements dating back to 1913. The pleadings, which were over 120 pages in length, ran to five levels ending with a surrejoinder.

Drafting affidavits

Litigation lawyers also have to acquire the skills necessary to draft affidavits. The function of an affidavit is fundamentally different from the function of a pleading. An affidavit is a sworn statement which can be used as evidence of the matters deposed to. In High Court writ-actions they are commonly used on interlocutory applications but can be used at the trial only if the court grants leave (see p 447). In the county courts affidavits can be used for any proceedings in chambers unless contrary provision is made (CCR Ord 20, r 5) and at the trial, if leave is granted (r 6), or if at least fourteen days' notice was given to the opponent and no notice of objection was made within seven days (r 7).

In both courts the affidavit should be sworn in the action and not, eg, before action or only for the purposes of another action. The original must be filed in the appropriate court office. Copies must then be served on the other parties. In the High Court the times for service are prescribed (see p 7).

Formal requirements

RSC Ord 41 and CCR Ord 20, r 10 provide that all affidavits must:
(1) state the title of the action;
(2) state the deponent's name, address and occupation; alternatively an affidavit sworn by, eg a solicitor or solicitor's clerk, may state his name and business address, the position he holds and the name of his firm or employer;

(3) state (if it be the case) that the deponent is, or is employed by, a party to the action;

(4) be expressed in the first person;

(5) be bound in book form and, whether or not both sides of the paper are used, the sides written on must be numbered consecutively;

(6) be divided into numbered paragraphs;

(7) give dates, sums and other numbers in figures and not in words;

(8) be indorsed with a note showing on whose behalf it is filed and the dates of swearing and filing.

A 1983 *Practice Direction* (*White Book* 41/11/1) gives lengthy details as to matters of form concerning affidavits. Note in particular the requirement to state on the first page of the affidavit and also on the backsheet (*a*) the party on whose behalf it is filed; (*b*) the initial and surname of the deponent; (*c*) the number of the affidavit in relation to the deponent; (*d*) the identifying initials and number of each exhibit to the affidavit (see further, below) and (*e*) the date when sworn. For example *2nd Dft: EW Jones: 3rd: Exhibits EWJ 3, 4 and 5: Sworn 24.7.97: Filed 2.8.97*. This annotation is also required on county court affidavits.

The final part of the affidavit (called the 'jurat') must state the date and place the affidavit was sworn and must be signed by the deponent and by the person before whom the affidavit is sworn (who will also sign and identify any exhibits to the affidavit, see below). Affidavits may be sworn before a solicitor or before senior clerks in the High Court or county court. Under the Oaths Act 1978 a deponent who objects to making an oath may instead 'affirm'. In such a case the opening words of the affidavit and the jurat would have to be drafted or altered accordingly. Any alteration in an affidavit has to be initialled by the person before whom it is sworn, or, if it is sworn before a clerk at the court office, stamped with the official stamp of that office.

A solicitor before whom an affidavit is sworn is entitled to charge fees as prescribed from time to time by statutory instrument (currently, £5 plus £2 per exhibit inclusive of any VAT payable). As to the inconvenience caused by rules of court forbidding a solicitor from administering an oath in any action in which he or his partners are instructed see p 6.

Once sworn, the affidavit should be filed in the appropriate court office (RSC Ord 41, r 9; CCR Ord 2, r 4). The party filing it will usually supply a copy of it for his opponent, whether because the rules of court so require or merely out of courtesy. Other parties may also obtain copies from the court office during office hours (High Court) or on written application (county court); RSC Ord 63, rr 4, 4A, 11; CCR Ord 50, r 10.

Content of affidavits

Some affidavits are standard form, eg an affidavit of service (p 216), or in support of an application under RSC Ord 14 (p 225), or in garnishee proceedings (see p 595). However, many others cannot be standardised and have to be drafted directly to the case in hand, eg an affidavit opposing an application under RSC Ord 14 or an affidavit in support of an application to set aside a default judgment.

There are seven points to bear in mind when setting out to draft such affidavits:

(1) *List the important points to be brought to the court's attention.* In sharp contrast to pleadings, affidavits should state the evidence relied on and should anticipate the opponent's case.

(2) *Then decide who should be the deponent: the person who can speak to most of the points from personal knowledge.* This will usually be the client. If not, it is appropriate to state in the affidavit what is the deponent's relationship (if any) to the client (director, employee, spouse, solicitor or whatever) and claim to be 'duly authorised to make this affidavit'.

(3) *Then divide the important points into numbered paragraphs written in the first person as if by the deponent.* The affidavit should be written in narrative form, facts being arranged in chronological order. In a lengthy affidavit covering a variety of different issues, it is sensible to include subheadings which will assist the reader; such subheadings may also add emphasis to the important points you wish to bring to the court's attention.

(4) *In the case of hearsay evidence state the source of information.* For example, 'I am informed by my client and truly believe ...' The source stated need not be an original source but, obviously, the affidavit may be more persuasive if it is (*Deutsche Ruckver-sicherung AG v Walbrook Insurance Co Ltd* [1995] 1 WLR 1017). Having drafted the affidavit read it through again. If there are too many of these 'informed by' passages you may well have chosen the wrong deponent. In the High Court, hearsay (ie a statement on information) is not permitted in an affidavit sworn for use at the trial unless leave is granted.

(5) *Condescend to particulars, state the deponent's means of knowledge and exhibit supporting documents.* Affidavits are evidence. The amount of detail they include marks the distinction between bare allegation and persuasive presentation. Unless the means of knowledge are obvious, always explain how the deponent came to learn the facts he states. If any of the facts arise from or are supported by documents, bring these documents into evidence by 'exhibiting' them to the affidavit: eg the deponent may refer to a written agreement between the parties and then state 'The agreement is now produced and shown to me marked "A".' In cases where there may be several affidavits, each with exhibits, it is customary to mark the exhibits according to the initials of the deponent and the number of the document. For example 'JB1' might identify the first exhibit in the affidavit of John Brown, 'MS2' might identify the second exhibit in the affidavit of Mary Smith.

(6) *A client stating matters of law should do so with the words 'I am advised and truly believe'.* Some practitioners still prefer to use the antique phrase 'I am advised and verily believe'. Verily, verily, we say unto you, beware! Audio-typists are often unfamiliar with this phrase; if you use it check that it is not typed as 'variably believe'.

(7) *If convenient to do so, conclude with a statement of the order sought.* These last two items do not relate to evidence and therefore, strictly, do not belong in an affidavit. However, it is often convenient to include them. The latter is usually redolent with phrases such as 'I respectfully request' and 'this Honourable Court'.

In practice the more difficult affidavits are often drafted by counsel. It is quite wrong to think that a barrister would draft a complex affidavit 'on spec' and then invite the solicitor to persuade someone to swear it. Counsel will insist upon being given a full proof of evidence from the intending deponent. Better still, if the affidavit is to be sworn by the client or solicitor, a conference with counsel can be arranged. (As to the rule against counsel interviewing witnesses other than client, solicitor and experts, see p 509). As with a pleading, counsel will sign the draft affidavit he gives to the solicitor. The solicitor will then have it retyped to be sworn by the deponent. Unlike a pleading, counsel's name should not appear on the final draft.

Drafting witness statements

Solicitors have always drafted witness statements, or proofs of evidence as they were often called. They were prepared for use by the advocate at the trial when examining witnesses 'in chief' (ie the question and answer session involving the witness and the advocate who called that witness). In the past, the legal professional privilege protecting these documents was maintained right up until the time the witness spoke the evidence in court. That way, the opponent's advocate would have the shortest possible amount of time to think up ways of attacking it or meeting it. A trial in those days was a high anxiety experience in which the advocates would proceed slowly in order to give themselves more time to 'think on their feet'.

Current practice is quite different. We now live in a world of 'cards on the table litigation' (see further p 427). The first major change towards this system occurred in 1974 when it became the practice in all cases, High Court and county court, to exchange expert evidence before trials. Since November 1992 the same has also been true of non-expert evidence. Advocates are now in a position to do most of their thinking in advance of the trial. Indeed, the fact that the parties exchange evidence may obviate the need for a trial altogether (see further p 429).

Before setting out to draft witness statements in the new regime it is as well to bear in mind their purpose and likely effect. The purpose indicated by the rules of court are the fair and expeditious disposal of the case and the saving of costs. Exchanging before trial all of the evidence which is likely to be called at that trial enables both parties to evaluate their prospects of success earlier than they otherwise could. By analysing the documents exchanged, each side can see more clearly exactly what the disputed issues are, what the evidence in chief upon them is likely to be and therefore what the result is likely to be. Parties whose cases are weak are not now able to bluff their opponents all the way up to the witness box as they used to do.

The exchange therefore increases the likelihood that the case will settle, so avoiding trial. If no settlement is reached, the exchange enables the parties to plan and develop fully their retaliation to their opponent's case (see later notes on further discovery, interrogatories, directions as to supplementary statements and cross-exmination at the trial). There is not much they can do to strengthen their own case; the evidence in chief which they are allowed to call is limited to the evidence set out in the experts' reports and the witness statements which they have exchanged (there are exceptions of course, see further p 429).

Although expert witnesses draft their own statements (ie their reports) non-expert witnesses don't. In most cases they would not know whether their evidence is wanted and, if it is, what the disputed issues are, and upon what topics they could give admissible evidence. Accordingly, the lawyers must draft the statements for them.

The best and most authoritative statement as to the form and content of witness statements is the commentary set out in the *White Book* at 38/2A/8 and at 878, para 3.7 of the *Chancery Guide*. The advice offered in this book is intended to highlight some particular points which may be helpful.

1 Identify all the issues upon which your client should seek to adduce evidence

In order to do this you will need to comb through the pleadings very carefully. One useful practice is to write in the margin beside each passage of the statement of claim or particulars of claim the letters 'A' (for *Admitted*), 'NA' (*Not admitted*), or 'D' (*Denied*). Then go through the defence, duplicating the annotation above against the relevant passages comprising the admissions, non-admissions and denials and then marking the other passages 'E' (for *Extra*), unless, most unusually, the plaintiff has subsequently admitted any of them (in which case, mark them 'A'). 'E' passages will contain those extra facts, the special defences or positive case which the defendant is relying on in order to defeat the claim (for examples, see p 153).

The plaintiff may have admitted some or all of the 'E' passages by serving a reply in order to 'confess and avoid' the defendant's defences (see p 164). If so, you will need to comb through that pleading also, marking each passage 'A' (for admissions by the plaintiff) or 'E' (in respect of any extras in the defence which are denied or not admitted in the reply) or 'R' (to represent extra facts which are alleged by the plaintiff in the reply).

The claim, defence and reply will now be annotated with the letters, A, NA, D, E and R. Later on, similar treatment will have to be given to the pleadings relating to any counterclaim. However, it is best to delay this task for the time being or you will end up with a totally confusing alphabet soup.

Applying the maxim 'He who alleges must prove' (see further p 421) the plaintiff should fully prepare to prove the 'NA' 'D' and 'R' passages. He should also consider what evidence he has contradicting the 'E' passages. In a road accident case, these are likely to be topics such as contributory negligence and failure to mitigate loss, topics upon which a failure by the plaintiff to lead evidence is bound to invite adverse comment.

The defendant should fully prepare to contradict the 'D' passages and prove the 'E' passages. He should also consider what if anything he can add by way of evidence to improve his case in respect of the 'NA' passages (as to which, see p 153).

Neither party need dwell upon the 'A' passages. Before you start drafting any particular statement, consider whether any further admissions have been made, or should now be sought, eg in correspondence or *via* a notice to admit (as to which, see p 431).

2 In respect of each witness whom it would be reasonable for your client to call on these issues, carefully interview them and then list all of the important points they can make

Who and how many people should you call? Although it is not easy to state this in theory, in practice it is normally obvious. As a general rule, don't call your opponent or anyone who is in your opponent's camp (eg your opponent's relatives or employees). Such people will normally be unwilling to give you an interview anyway. However, the more important reason is that it will be better for your client to have these people called by your opponent and cross-examined by your client's advocate; failure by the opponent to call these potential witnesses will give your advocate some very easy points to score by way of comment in the closing speech.

There are special points to bear in mind in the case of potential witnesses where the costs of interviewing and/or calling them is likely to be excessive (see p 431) and in the case of potential witnesses who are reluctant to give evidence (see p 487 which also deals with questions of when and how to interview witnesses, as does p 28).

How do you decide which witness should make each important point? Concentrate upon first hand evidence (as to hearsay, see below) and try to avoid irrelevancies, inadmissible opinions and pure conjecture.

What if there are several potential witnesses who could speak to one point and you have decided that it would be disproportionate to call all of them? Choose the ones who are best able to give important evidence on other issues. Also include the one whose evidence on this point will carry the greatest weight. Be wary of leaving out of your team anyone whose absence will generate adverse comment from the opponent's advocate. Of the potential witnesses you decide not to call, you could still prepare 'written statements' for them in respect of which you could give your opponent a hearsay notice (see further p 439).

3 For each witness, compose a statement in the form of an affidavit, but without any oath or jurat

Write it in the first person, in narrative form (as opposed to question and answer form) taking points in chronological order in clear straight-forward language. As to formal requirements, see the list given for affidavits on p 172. The last numbered paragraph of a witness statement should declare that the 'contents of this statement are true to the best of my knowledge and belief' and you should include spaces for the witness's signature and for the date of signature. A specimen witness statement is included overleaf (fig 6).

4 Send the draft statement to the witness for checking and signature

Ask the witness to read it through carefully and add to it and/or amend it as and where necessary and to date it and sign it. It is also desirable (but not in fact essential) to arrange, or ask the witness to arrange, for some responsible and creditworthy person to witness the signature.

If you receive back a document which is heavily and/or embarrassingly amended you will of course get it retyped and re-signed and witnessed. In other cases, consider whether the advantages to your client of not retyping etc outweigh the possible disadvantages. The advantages may be costs and/or a demonstration of how careful the witness has been and/or how objective and fair minded the original draftsman of the statement was.

5 Additional formalities if the witness is being called to give oral hearsay

For a definition of hearsay and a description of the notice requirements which apply to it, see p 436. It is unusual to rely upon hearsay evidence and even more unusual to rely upon oral hearsay; most hearsay is written.

However, assume that the unusual applies to your case, eg assume that an important remark was made to your client at the time of the event in question by a person you cannot now trace. You must draft, not only a witness statement to be signed by your client repeating the remark, but also a hearsay notice warning your opponent of your intention to rely upon this item or oral hearsay at the trial. The notice must be served on your opponent at the same time as the witness statement is served (see further p 443).

6 Review with your client, the effect which these draft statements will have on the prospects of success

Is there enough strength here to intimidate the opposition and/or discharge the relevant burdens of proof? If these drafts are served, how might the opponents respond to them? Are any of them unclear, ambiguous or evasive? Are there any inconsistencies between your chosen witnesses, or between their statements and your client's pleadings? Are there any inconsistencies between these statements and any other documents, eg discovered documents, correspondence between solicitors, interlocutory affidavits previously used in the action and newspaper reports? As to the witnesses themselves, what, if any, mud can be thrown at them by the opponents, eg criminal convictions or other items suggesting dishonesty or unreliability? It is easy to underestimate the importance of this review. In the current world of 'cards on the table' litigation, cases are often won or lost on paper.

Fig 6: Specimen witness statement

IN THE HIGH COURT OF JUSTICE   1995. S. No.99

QUEEN'S BENCH DIVISION

SOUTHCLIFFE DISTRICT REGISTRY

BETWEEN

SOUTHCLIFFE SPORTS AND WORKWEAR LIMITED   Plaintiff

and

ALTRAD SAFETY SHOES LIMITED   Defendant

WITNESS STATEMENT OF AMY JULIET GEORGE

1. My full name is Miss Amy Juliet George and I live at 25 Lavis Road, Christlethorpe, Guildshire CH4 4GS. I am employed as the Head of Quality Control of Altrad Safety Shoes Limited, the Defendant in this action.

2. The Quality Control Department of the Defendant is based at its factory premises in the Acomb Industrial Estate in Christlethorpe. I have been an employee of the Defendant, at all times working in Quality Control, for upwards of 12 years. I was promoted to Head of Quality Control in April 1991. My department has the equivalent of 5 full time quality controllers including myself plus one part time secretary.

3. Leather uppers of shoes produced at the Defendant's factory are subjected to 3 quality control measures.

4. The first measure is in respect of the raw materials. Shoe leather is purchased in the form of cured hides and each hide is subject to a visual check by the cutting machine operators. This check has proved very effective in the past. According to the records kept by my secretary which I have consulted, it produces an average rejection rate of approximately 5 per cent of all hides which are then returned to the supplying tannery.

5. Two further tests are carried out on the completed shoes before packaging. The checks are made in respect of batches. An average batch would be 25,000 pairs.

6. A ten per cent sample of each batch is subjected to a Ballisto Scan which is an industrial process. This would identify defective stitching, damage to soles and tears to or thinning of the leather upper. This test is carried out by my staff. If problems are identified, the explanation of which is not unique to the item scanned, the whole batch would be returned to the Stitching Department for sorting.

7. The third quality control measure affecting leather uppers is a visual appraisal of each batch. This appraisal is made by my staff. If problems are identified, the explanation of which is not unique to the item appraised, the quality controller would either subject a further sample to a Ballisto Scan and/or return the whole batch to the Stitching Department for sorting.

8. The quality control measures described above have been operated successfully throughout my period of employment by the Defendant. It is very rare indeed for a customer to complain about defective products. I do not think it likely that a substantial number of defective shoes could get through these measures.

Fig 6: contd

9. My department maintains full quality control records of all products sold during the immediate 6 year period. From these records I note that the shoes which are the subject of this action came from batch no. WSS 2291. This batch was subjected to each of the quality control measures described above.

10. Batch no. WSS 2291 comprised in total 26,500 pairs of shoes. So far as I am aware no complaints have been received about this batch other than the complaints now made by the Plaintiff in this action.

11. In my opinion any damage which has been suffered by the shoes sold to the Plaintiff is likely to have occurred after the shoes had left the Defendant's premises.

12. On December 14 1996 when I first learnt of the complaints which the Plaintiff is now making I telephoned the Plaintiff's Sales Manager, Mr Alexander Thomas, a gentleman I have corresponded with and spoken to by telephone on numerous occasions in the past in connection with other orders placed by the Plaintiff.

13. In my telephone conversation with Mr Thomas on December 14 1996 he told me that the complaints which the Plaintiff was making in respect of shoes received from the Defendant also applied to many other shoes received from other suppliers. He also told me that all of the affected shoes were stored together in the same part of the Plaintiff's warehouse in Southcliffe.

14. The contents of this statement are true to the best of my knowledge and belief.

    Dated   Signed

                                    in the presence of:

Chapter 10

Amending and Attacking Pleadings

Amendment

The rules relating to amendment are set out in RSC Ord 20 and CCR Ord 15. In both courts a party is given a limited right to amend without leave. In other cases leave of the court must be obtained unless the amendment can be made with the agreement of all parties.

Amending without leave

In the High Court a party can amend his pleading once without leave so long as he does so before deemed close of pleadings (ie before the expiry of fourteen days after the last pleading was served). The one amendment may be fairly small, such as altering one paragraph, or vast, such as rewriting the whole pleading. Two types of amendment by a plaintiff, namely altering the parties and altering the causes of action, also require amendment of the writ: they cannot be done without leave once the writ has been served. The position as to altering the causes of action is relaxed somewhat by RSC Ord 18, r 15. This rule allows the plaintiff to include in his statement of claim any cause of action mentioned on the writ *and* other causes which are inherent in those so mentioned. The rule also provides that the statement of claim may alter, modify or extend the claim for *remedies* indorsed on the writ (see p 196 and *Brickfield Properties v Newton* [1971] 1 WLR 862, below). Where an amendment is made without leave the other party may, within the next fourteen days, apply to the court to disallow it. The court will order the amendment to be struck out if it is satisfied that, had leave to amend been necessary, leave to amend would have been refused.

In most county court default actions (see p 239) and possession actions (see p 263) any party may file and deliver an amended pleading without any order at any time before the trial. In other fixed date actions the deadline is either the date of close of pleadings if the automatic directions apply (see CCR Ord 17, r 11(12) and p 466) otherwise the date of the pre-trial review (see p 476). However, in all county court cases, the court may later disallow the amendment or otherwise deal with it on such terms as may be just. There is no special restriction on altering causes of action but if, in a default action, the plaintiff raises a claim for some remedy other than the payment of money, the action must continue as if it had been commenced as a fixed date action. Amendments altering the parties to the action always require the leave of the court once the summons has been served (CCR Ord 7, r 17).

In both courts pleadings may be amended at any stage by agreement between the parties. In the High Court there must be a written agreement to that effect (RSC Ord 20, r 12; it is perhaps worth pointing out that you should never agree to amendments until you have seen them; for example, they may include the withdrawing of admissions previously made). In the county court the amendment is made by filing an amended pleading indorsed with the consent of every party to the proceedings (CCR Ord 15, r 2). Neither set of rules permits amendments by agreement which alter the parties to the action.

Seeking leave to amend

The basic principle as to amendment is this: a party has the *right* to amend his pleading to present his case as he thinks best. Amendment is not a privilege or favour allotted to him by the courts. Under the modern rules of procedure no case should fail merely for technical errors or omissions. There is only one limitation on this right: an amendment will not be allowed if it would work an injustice on the other party. In the majority of cases however, any injustice can be avoided by making a suitable order as to costs, including the costs of any adjournment caused. In *Clarapede v Commercial Union Association* (1883) 32 WR 263 Brett MR summed up this principle as follows: 'However negligent and careless may have been the first omission, and however late the proposed amendment, the amendment should be allowed if it can be made without injustice to the other side. There is no injustice if the other side can be compensated by costs.'

It is convenient to list the cases where leave to amend may *not* be granted. The main examples are as follows:

(1) Amendments which are futile, frivolous or proposed *mala fide*. See *White Book* 20/5–8/21 and 20/5–8/23.

(2) An amendment to withdraw an admission consciously made. See *Hollis v Burton* [1892] 3 Ch 226.

(3) Amendments sought at the trial. See *White Book* 20/5–8/11 and *Ketteman v Hansel Properties Ltd* [1987] AC 189. For a recent case in which leave to amend at the trial was given see *Beoco Ltd v Alfa Laval Co Ltd* [1995] QB 137 in which Stuart-Smith LJ stated 'As a general rule, where a plaintiff makes a late amendment as here, which substantially alters the case the defendant has to meet and without which the action will fail, the defendant is entitled to the costs of the action down to the date of the amendment.'

For a case in which leave to amend, to alter the name of the defendant, was given after judgment, see *Singh v Atombrook Ltd trading as Sterling Travel* [1989] 1 WLR 810, noted on p 129. In *Shell Chemicals UK Ltd v Vinamul Ltd* (1991) *The Times*, 7 March an amendment was ordered on the twenty-second day of the trial notwithstanding that further discovery might be required because of it.

(4) An amendment to raise a cause of action which accrued to the plaintiff only after the action commenced, unless the defendant consents. See *Eshelby v Federated European Bank* [1932] 1 KB 254 (see p 197 and compare *Tilcon Ltd v Land and Real Estate Investments Ltd* [1987] 1 WLR 46).

(5) An amendment adding (or substituting) a new party or raising a new cause of action after the expiry of the relevant limitation period. Generally speaking such amendments take effect from the date of the original writ (for possible exceptions concerning cases which become statute barred because of the Limitation Act 1939, see *Ketteman v Hansel Properties Ltd* [1987] AC 189).

Section 35 and the rules giving effect to it, RSC Ord 20, r 5, and CCR Ord 15, r 1, give the courts some limited powers to grant leave for late amendments. Where the relevant limitation period expired *after* the issue of the writ or county court summons, the court may grant leave to amend:

(1) to correct the name of a party even if this in effect adds a new party where the mistake sought to be corrected was a genuine mistake and the identity of the true party was never in doubt;

(2) to alter the capacity in which a party claims or counterclaims if the new capacity is one which that party had at the date of the claim or counterclaim or has since acquired;

(3) to add or substitute a new cause of action which arises out of the same facts or substantially the same facts as a cause of action which has already been pleaded.

If, notwithstanding the expiry of the relevant limitation period, the addition of a new party, or a new cause of action, is permissible under s 35, the addition 'shall be deemed to be a separate action and to have been commenced ... on the same date as the original action' (s 35(1); ie the doctrine of 'relation back' applies). Before deciding whether to grant leave, the court will take into account the extent to which delay has prejudiced the evidence available to the defendant (*Hancock Shipping Co Ltd v Kawasaki Heavy Industries Ltd* [1992] 1 WLR 1025).

The rules above-mentioned derive from the Limitation Act 1980, s 35 which is said to suppress any residual discretion the courts may have had to allow statute-barred claims to be raised by amendment in cases other than the three listed above. Does the statutory strait-jacket operate if the application for leave to amend was made *before* the relevant limitation period expired but was not heard until *after* it had expired? Yes, said the

Court of Appeal in *Welsh Development Agency v Redpath Dorman Long Ltd* [1994] 1 WLR 1409.

Examples

P, a landowner, sued D, an architect, in respect of building works, P copied the writ-indorsement and the statement of claim from a well-respected precedent book. The indorsement alleged only 'negligent supervision'. The statement of claim alleged 'negligent supervision' and 'negligent design'. The relevant limitation period expired. It was held that the latter cause of action was not inherent in the former (see RSC Ord 18, r 15) but leave to amend the writ was given because 'negligent design' arose from substantially the same facts as 'negligent supervision' (see *Brickfield Properties v Newton* [1971] 1 WLR 862 and see the facts of *Hancock Shipping Co Ltd*, referred to above).

P wished to sue their current landlords. The current landlords were a company ('Bass') for whom the former landlords ('Charringtons') acted as agents. Bass and Charringtons together formed part of a group of companies. P's solicitor wrongly believed that Charringtons were still the current landlords and commenced the proceedings solely against them. The relevant limitation period expired. It was held that the solicitor's mistake in commencing proceedings against Charringtons rather than Bass was one which could be corrected by amendment under ground (1) above (*Evans Construction Co Ltd v Charrington & Co Ltd* [1983] QB 810).

P wished to sue D and commenced proceedings intended to have that effect. By mistake the originating summons named D as plaintiff and P as defendant. D's solicitor spotted the mistake and refused to accept service. It was held that the mistake was genuine and not misleading and therefore could be corrected by amendment under ground (1) above even though the relevant limitation period had expired (*Teltscher Brothers Ltd v London and India Dock Investments Ltd* [1989] 1 WLR 770).

Section 35 of the Limitation Act 1980 and RSC Ord 20, r 5 do not apply where a contractual or substantive time limit (eg the Hague Rules) has expired (see *Payabi v Armstel Shipping Corp* [1992] 2 WLR 898).

Consequential amendments

When a pleading is amended the other parties to the action are entitled to make consequential amendments to any subsequent pleadings they have already served (see *Squire v Squire* [1972] Ch 391). In the High Court consequential amendments can be made without leave within fourteen days of the amendment to the earlier pleading. If the other parties do not take this opportunity it is assumed that they are relying on the original answer as an answer to the amended pleading.

Presumably similar principles apply in the county court. Bear in mind, however, that the right to make amendments without leave is much greater in the county court. Moreover, in the county court, the delivery of a defence does not, in our view, prevent the defendant relying on further or other defences (see p 159).

Amending other documents

A High Court writ can be amended once without leave at any time before deemed close of pleadings (but not as to causes of action or parties once it has been served). Generally speaking an acknowledgment of service can be amended only with leave. There is one exception to this: a defendant can without leave amend his acknowledgment to include or remove a 'notice of intention to defend' (see p 207) provided that, in the case of including a notice of intention to defend, he does so before judgment is entered (see generally RSC Ord 20, r 2, which also states that whenever an acknowledgment is amended a fresh acknowledgment must be lodged in the court office out of which the writ was issued). In the county court, if the defendant delivers an admission (see CCR Ord 9, r 17) the court may at any time allow him to amend or withdraw it on such terms as may be just (CCR Ord 9, r 2; eg a defendant who attends on the day fixed for disposal (see p 250) and satisfies the district judge that the delivery of the form of admission was a mistake). In both the High Court and county court, pleadings can be amended without leave as described above. Documents other than writs, acknowledgments of service and pleadings can be amended only with leave. As to amending further and better particulars see p 189. As to amending a judgment or order see the 'slip rule' (RSC Ord 20, r 11; CCR Ord 15, r 5) and p 519.

Practice on amendment of writs and pleadings

Amendments should usually be made in red. Re-amendments should be made in green, then violet, then yellow: see *Masters' Practice Direction No 20* (*White Book* 733) relating to amendment of writs and originating summonses. When a lengthy amendment has to be made consider retyping the whole document (see RSC Ord 20, r 10). This is usually better than trying to squeeze the new words onto the old form. The retyped document should include the superseded words, still legible, but struck out in the appropriate colour. If the amendments were drafted by counsel, counsel's name should be typed twice, the second time in red.

The Commercial Court has developed a more modern scheme for indicating amendments by varying the type of print used in a document rather than varying the colour of ink (see further *White Book* 72/A13). No doubt this will eventually become the standard practice in all cases.

All amended documents must be served (or, as practitioners usually say, 're-served') unless this is dispensed with. Note that in the High Court:

(1) amended documents must be indorsed with a statement such as 'Amended (*date*) under RSC Ord 20, (*r 3 or r 12*)' or 'Amended (*date*) pursuant to the order dated ...';

(2) when a writ, or a statement of claim indorsed on a writ, is amended without leave, a copy of the amended form must be filed at the Central Office or district registry (a similar rule applies in the county court, CCR Ord 15, rr 1, 2).

Costs of amendments

The costs of any amendment made without leave to a writ or county court summons or to any pleading are borne by the party making the amendment (RSC Ord 62, r 6; CCR Ord 38, r 1).

When leave to amend is given, whether as to pleadings, writs or other documents, that leave is frequently given 'on the usual terms' ie the party making the amendment is ordered to pay the opponents' costs of and occasioned by the amendment and the costs of any consequent amendment and the costs of the application to obtain leave to amend.

Seeking further and better particulars

If a party, whether plaintiff or defendant, fails to plead his case with sufficient detail, his opponent may seek particulars or further and better particulars as the case may be (RSC Ord 18, r 12; CCR Ord 6, r 7; Ord 9, r 11). 'The object of particulars is to enable the party asking for them to know what case he has to meet at the trial, and so to save unnecessary expense and avoid allowing parties to be taken by surprise' (*Spedding v Fitzpatrick* [1888] 38 ChD 410, *per* Cotton LJ).

An application for particulars should always be preceded by a request made by letter. The modern practice is to send a covering letter with a formal document headed 'Request for Further and Better Particulars of the (*pleading*)'. Similarly, any particulars given should be set out in a formal document headed 'Further and Better particulars of the (*pleading*) Pursuant to the Request (*or* Order of Master ...) dated ...' The document should incorporate the text of the request (see the illustration in fig 7). In the county court a party has to file the particulars as well as serve them on the other party.

If a party fails to give the particulars sought, an application can be made to the district judge, usually at the directions stage. In the High Court a request or order for particulars does not delay the deemed close of pleadings (RSC Ord 18, r 20).

An order for particulars will not be made before service of the defence unless the order is necessary or desirable, for example to enable the defendant to plead to specific issues rather than simply raise bare denials (*Shippam Ltd v Princes-Buitoni Ltd* (1983) noted in the *White Book* 18/12/20).

Fig 7: Specimen further and better particulars

IN THE ASTRID COUNTY COURT   **Case No 712345**

BETWEEN   GEOFFREY MICHAEL HAMILTON   Plaintiff
–AND–
DEREK DEACOCK   Defendant

FURTHER AND BETTER PARTICULARS OF THE PARTICULARS OF CLAIM

delivered pursuant to request dated 2nd May 1997

Under paragraph 2

Of the alleged implied warranty, state the facts relied upon as giving rise to such implication.

The Defendant sold the car in the course of his business as a seller of secondhand cars. The warranty was accordingly implied by the Sale of Goods Act 1979.

Under paragraph 3

(1) Of the alleged express warranty, state whether the same was oral or in writing. If oral, state when and by whom and to whom the same is alleged to have been made, and if in writing identify the document or documents.

The warranty was made orally by the Defendant to the Plaintiff on 27 March 1997.

(2) Of the allegation that the engine was more than 5 years old state the facts relied upon.

The defendant is not entitled to the particulars requested.

RICHARD ROE

DATED *etc*

The court usually has a discretion whether to order particulars. Sometimes an order will be made even in respect of an allegation it was unnecessary for a party to make (*Gaston v United Newspapers* (1915) 32 TLR 143, where, in a libel action, the court ordered particulars of an allegation made by the plaintiff which anticipated a defence of justification).

No particulars will be ordered of a simple traverse. If a litigant says 'no' his opponent should not ask 'what do you mean, no?' It is assumed that, if the litigant was intending to rely on any new facts justifying his negative he would have pleaded them (see RSC Ord 18, r 8). Different considerations apply to a traverse of a negative allegation. Such a traverse may amount to a 'negative pregnant', ie a traverse which contains or implies an affirmative; see the example given on p 160. In such a case the court can either strike out the traverse or order particulars of it to be given. Not every double negative contains or implies an affirmative. Two tax cases help to make clear the distinction.

In *IRC v Jackson* [1960] 1 WLR 873 the defendant 'denied that he failed to furnish particulars of his income without reasonable cause'. Particulars of this traverse were ordered.

In *Howard v Borneman* [1972] 1 WLR 863 by paras 7 and 8 of his statement of claim the plaintiff alleged that a tax tribunal (which had made a ruling against him) did not consider the documents he had sent them, did not decide the ruling correctly, did not meet to deliberate before ruling and did not deliberate. The defendants, the tribunal members, 'denied each and every allegation contained in paragraphs 7 and 8 of the Statement of Claim'. An application for particulars of this traverse was refused. The burden of proving the negative allegations was on the plaintiff and the traverse simply put him to proof and did not imply an affirmative. In effect the defendants were merely saying 'you prove where you say we went wrong'.

Sometimes difficulty is found in giving particulars of knowledge and the like. Assume a party intends to prove that his opponent 'knew' or 'ought to have known' a certain fact (see *Fox v Wood* [1963] 2 QB 601). He will often be unwilling, and perhaps unable, to narrow his case by particulars until discovery or even cross-examination. The High Court rules make only a very slight allowance here. Particulars of knowledge do not have to be included in the pleading, but should be given if the other party requests them. The particulars given usually list the facts and documents the party intends to rely on to prove his opponent's 'knowledge'.

Some particulars are expressly required, by statute or by other rules. In claims under the Fatal Accidents Act 1976 the plaintiff must give particulars of the dependants and particulars of their dependency on the deceased (s 2(4)). See also defamation actions (RSC Ord 82, r 3, particulars of any innuendo alleged and particulars of a 'rolled-up plea') and county court possession actions (CCR Ord 6, r 3; and p 263). If a party failed to obey these requirements his opponent should apply to set aside the pleading for irregularity rather than seek particulars (see p 2).

The terms upon which particulars will be ordered vary according to the circumstances. The basic order simply specifies the particulars to be given and fixes a time within which the party in default must file and/or deliver them. If he fails to comply a second order will be made, but this time providing penalties for non-compliance, eg striking out the part of the pleading of which particulars are sought, or terminating the action against the party in default. The penalty will not be imposed if the party *bona fide* attempts to comply with the order but still fails to give sufficient particulars (*Reiss v Woolf* [1952] 2 QB 557, but see further, *John Zink Co Ltd v Lloyds Bank* [1975] RPC 385, below).

Particulars served separately from the pleading do not come within the rules allowing amendment without leave. Note, however, two important qualifications. First, the order for particulars may allow for supplementary particulars to be given later: this would be appropriate where the particulars ordered are of facts peculiarly within the other party's knowledge (*Cyril Leonard & Co v Simo Securities* [1972] 1 WLR 80 where the defendants were ordered to give 'the best particulars they can give before discovery'). Secondly, leave to amend is almost certain to be given. Because of this, a practice has developed of serving without leave 'voluntary particulars', ie particulars altering or supplementing those already given. Although technically this practice is irregular it would normally be futile for the other side to complain of the irregularity. The court would not set aside the document if it thought that, had leave to amend been sought, leave would have been granted. As to delivery of voluntary particulars on setting down, see p 482. Consider also the possibility of using RSC Ord 20, r 12 or CCR Ord 15, r 2 (see p 183) as a means of altering particulars.

Striking out

Obviously this is the strongest attack a party can make on his opponent's pleading. Under RSC Ord 18, r 19, and CCR Ord 13, r 5, the court has power to order a pleading to be struck out on any one of the following grounds:

(*a*) *It discloses no reasonable cause of action or defence, as the case may be.* This ground raises an entirely legal question, namely 'Is such a cause of action (or is such a defence) known to the law?'. Since it is a legal question, no evidence as to facts is allowed: the court assumes the facts in favour of the party whose pleading is being attacked. (Indeed, in the High Court, if the applicant is prepared to admit for the purposes of the action the relevant facts alleged by his opponent, this application could also be brought under RSC Ord 14A; see p 231.)

Examples
In *Rondel v Worsley* [1969] 1 AC 191 a claim against a barrister for negligence in his conduct of a defence in a criminal trial was struck out on this ground (and ground (*b*)). (See now CLSA 1990, s 62.)
In *Sirros v Moore* [1975] QB 118 a claim against a Crown Court judge in respect of his judicial acts was struck out on this ground.
In *Evans v London Hospital Medical College* [1981] 1 WLR 184 the court struck out on this ground a claim against expert witnesses for negligence in respect of statements they had made in reports which had been sent to the DPP as part of the investigation of a possible prosecution. Witnesses, like judges and advocates, are normally immune from liability for their participation in court work. (As to the exact ambit of judicial immunity see *Re McC* [1985] AC 528; as to the liability of magistrates see CLSA 1990, s 108.)

(*b*) *It is scandalous, frivolous or vexatious.* This ground can be used where a party raises a claim or defence which, even if it is known to the law, is factually so weak, worthless and futile that the pleading can be regarded as 'frivolous or vexatious'. Evidence as to the facts is of course essential.

Example

In *Riches v DPP* [1973] 1 WLR 1019 the plaintiff alleged a claim for malicious prosecution against the defendant. One reason for striking it out was that the claim was indisputably statute barred (see also *Sparks v Harland* [1997] 1 WLR 143).

In *Blue Town Investments Ltd v Higgs and Hill plc* [1990] 1 WLR 696 the plaintiff claimed an injunction to restrain building work, but, because it was unwilling to give an undertaking as to damages (see p 284), the plaintiff decided not to seek an interlocutory injunction. On an application to strike out part of the plaintiff's claim (relying upon grounds (*b*) and (*d*) and upon the court's inherent jurisdiction, see below) it was held that the plaintiff's claim for an injunction to be granted at the trial was, on the facts, extremely weak but not wholly unarguable. However, Browne-Wilkinson V-C felt able to strike out that part of the statement of claim which claimed an injunction at trial unless the plaintiff was prepared to apply for an interlocutory injunction. He thought it vexatious for a plaintiff to put forward a weak and tenuous claim for an injunction at trial without being prepared to give an undertaking as to damages. However, that case was distinguished in *Oxy-Electric Ltd v Zainuddin* [1991] 1 WLR 115 where the plaintiffs were seeking to enforce a restrictive covenant: the plaintiffs had a seriously arguable case for a permanent injunction at trial and the case should not be stifled by a requirement to seek an interlocutory injunction and give an undertaking. (Failure to seek an interlocutory injunction to restrain building works may ultimately prevent the plaintiff obtaining a final injunction at the trial; see *Jaggard v Sawyer* [1995] 1 WLR 269 where the judge at trial awarded damages *in lieu* of a final injunction totalling £694.44.)

An allegation in a pleading is scandalous if it is both outrageous and irrelevant (see *Brooking v Maudslay* (1886) 55 LT 343, below). Usually only part of a pleading is struck out as 'scandalous'. If the whole pleading is scandalous it would be wholly irrelevant and therefore could be struck out as 'frivolous or vexatious'.

(*c*) *It may prejudice, embarrass or delay the fair trial of the action.* This ground would be appropriate where the pleading being attacked is so badly drafted as to be obstructive of any fair trial. Only rarely will a pleading be as bad as this.

Examples

In *Brooking v Maudslay* (1886) 55 LT 343 the plaintiff made allegations of dishonest conduct against the defendant, but further pleaded he sought no relief on that ground. The allegations were struck out as both scandalous and embarrassing.

In *John Zink Co Ltd v Lloyds Bank* [1975] RPC 385 the plaintiff served further and better particulars after being ordered to do so by a master. The particulars served still failed to make clear to the defendants the case they would have to meet at the trial. In the circumstances the court preferred to strike out the statement of claim on ground (*c*) rather than strike out for non-compliance with the master's order (and see *Butcher v Dowlen* [1981] 1 Lloyd's Rep 310).

(d) It is otherwise an abuse of the process of the court. Most cases for striking out come within grounds (*a*), (*b*) or (*c*). Ground (*d*) is the all-embracing ground for other cases of abuse and reveals the general principle behind the whole of the striking-out rule. The pleading complained of must be so bad as to amount to an abuse of the process of the court.

Examples

In *Remmington v Scoles* [1897] 2 Ch 1 the defence traversed allegations which the defendant had previously admitted on oath. The defence was struck out as being dishonest, put in merely to delay the plaintiff obtaining judgment.

It is an abuse to raise in subsequent proceedings matters which are *res judicata* or matters which could and should have been raised in earlier proceedings: *Yat Tung v Dao Heng Bank* [1975] AC 581. (As to the distinction between cause of action estoppel, which binds absolutely and issue estoppel, which permits of exceptions in special circumstances, see *Arnold v National Westminster Bank plc* [1991] 2 WLR 1177.)

In *Somasundaram v M Julius Melchior & Co* [1988] 1 WLR 1394 P had previously pleaded guilty on a charge of malicious wounding and had been sent to prison. P sued D, his former solicitors, alleging that they had been negligent in their conduct of his criminal case and in particular had pressurised him into pleading guilty. It is an abuse of the process of the civil court to use it to mount an attack on the correctness of a final decision made by another court. The claim was therefore struck out on ground (*d*) (and on ground (*b*)); the Court of Appeal judgment also considers the interrelation of this form of abuse with the immunity rule which protects advocates (see p 190) (see also *Walpole v Partridge & Wilson* [1994] QB 106 and *Smith v Linskills* [1996] 1 WLR 763).

Procedure

An application for striking out should be made to the district judge (by summons or on notice) as soon as possible after the offending pleading is served. It should not be left to the summons for directions or pre-trial review stage (contrast applications for further and better particulars). However some claims are revealed as being manifestly unsustainable only once the exchange of witness statements has taken place (as to which, see p 426). A striking out application relying on ground (*b*) at that stage may well be appropriate (see *Goodwill v British Pregnancy Advice Service* [1996] 1 WLR 1397). Where the pleading is settled by a lawyer a custom has developed of notifying the pleader a short time before applying to strike out. At first sight this may seem like a conspiracy against the lay clients. In fact the custom is both sensible and honourable. There is no point in applying to strike out if the opponent is able and intends to amend. Applications to strike out are always brutal. Lawyers should try to maintain a good-tempered relationship with each other. It would be harmful to the administration of justice if they allowed their relationship to be poisoned by the sort of anger and ill-will the lay clients may feel towards each other.

In *Williams and Humbert Ltd v W & H Trade Marks (Jersey) Ltd* [1986] AC 368 and *Friends' Provident Life Office v Hillier Parker May & Rowden* [1996] 2 WLR 123, it was emphasised that the striking-out procedure is primarily a summary procedure. It should not normally be used in cases requiring prolonged and serious argument. Sometimes it will be more appropriate for the applicant to seek a direction for the trial of a preliminary issue (but see further p 456).

Terminating the action following striking out

If the whole of a claim is struck out the action will usually be dismissed (for a case in which a general stay of action was granted, see *Sparks v Harland* [1997] 1 WLR 143). If the whole of a defence is struck out the court will usually enter judgment for the plaintiff on his claim: in a damages action the judgment will be for 'damages to be assessed' (and see p 213).

Striking out writ-indorsements etc

RSC Ord 18, r 19, and CCR Ord 13, r 5, also apply to general indorsements on writs, originating summonses and originating applications. They also give the court the coercive power to order a party to amend: in practice this power is used only in the most exceptional circumstances.

Striking out under the inherent jurisdiction

The High Court and the county court also have jurisdiction to strike out any document or action on the ground that it is an abuse of the process of the court.

In *Ernst & Young v Butte Mining plc* [1996] 1 WLR 1605 P sued D for unpaid professional fees of about £0.3 million and obtained a default judgment. D appealed to set aside that judgment in order to defend and raise a counterclaim for sums of about £1.9 million. P and D both then independently realised that, if the judgment was set aside, D could add to its counterclaim certain claims which D had already made against P in litigation in the USA for sums exceeding £100 million. Because of the relevant limitation period it was too late to raise these additional claims by way of fresh proceedings in England. The possibility of raising these claims by way of counterclaim in this action was never mentioned or even hinted at by either P's solicitor or by D's solicitor although each kept it at the forefront of their attention.

P's solicitor formulated 'plan A' and 'plan B'. Plan A was to negotiate a setting aside of P's default judgment with P having carriage of the order so enabling P to discontinue immediately thereby preventing D raising any counterclaim. Plan B was a vaguer fall-back plan involving resisting the application to set aside. P's solicitor successfully executed Plan A but the notice of discontinuance was later struck out as an abuse of the process of the court. D's solicitor mistakenly believed that P was not going to discontinue.

> 'Heavy, hostile commercial litigation is a serious business, it is not a form of indoor sport and litigation solicitors do not owe each other duties to be friendly (so far as that goes beyond politeness) or to be chivalrous or sportsmanlike (so far as that goes beyond being fair). Nevertheless, even in the most hostile litigation (indeed, especially in the most hostile litigation) solicitors must be scrupulously fair and not take unfair advantage of obvious mistakes [reference was then made to case law noted on p 405 below]. The duty not to take unfair advantage of an obvious mistake is intensified if the solicitor in question has been a major contributing cause of the mistake' (*per* Robert Walker J).

Similarly, the Court of Appeal has an inherent jurisdiction to strike out a notice of appeal if it was clear and obvious that the notice of appeal was hopeless (*Burgess v Stafford Hotel Ltd* [1990] 1 WLR 1215).

Chapter 11

High Court: Commencement, Default, Summary Judgment

Issue of writ

A writ is issued when it is *sealed*, ie when the court seal is stamped on the top left hand corner by the clerk at the court office or district registry out of which it is issued. It is necessary to submit at least three completed forms of writ for issue (one for the court, one for the plaintiff and one for each defendant). Two copies are sealed and returned. The third, which will be kept by the court as its record of the action, must be signed by the plaintiff or by or on behalf of his solicitor (see generally RSC Ord 6, r 7 and *White Book* 723). The writ can be issued by post, the plaintiff or his solicitor including in his letter a stamped addressed envelope (*White Book* 707). Before sealing the writ the clerk will check that it has been correctly completed and that the correct fee has been paid and will allot the distinguishing number to complete the reference to the record of the action (see p 146) and will also emboss the Royal Coat of Arms at the top (unless, of course, it is a law stationer's writ on which the Royal Coat of Arms is already printed).

Leave to issue a writ is not required except in certain, rare, cases, eg where the plaintiff has been declared a vexatious litigant (the leave of a judge being necessary: see p 94) or where the writ is to be served outside England and Wales (RSC Ord 6, r 7(1)): the leave of a district judge is required both to issue the writ and to serve it unless it falls within one of the exceptions (the most important of which is the CJJA 1982; see p 140).

One sealed copy of the writ is the plaintiff's official record of the action. The other sealed copy is for service on the defendant. Further sealed copies (called 'concurrent writs') will be issued if the plaintiff so requests (RSC Ord 6, r 6). When issued, a concurrent writ will be stamped 'concurrent': save as mentioned below it is valid for the purpose of service only for so long as the original writ is valid (RSC Ord 6, r 8). One particular example of an application for a concurrent writ is given in RSC Ord 6, r 6: where it becomes necessary to serve the writ outside England and Wales but the original writ was not validly issued for such service. In this instance the concurrent writ will attract a longer period of validity for service (six months rather than four months) from the date of issue of the original writ; RSC Ord 6, r 8 as amended in 1996).

The form of writ is prescribed. We illustrate two uses of it: the first a writ claiming a debt and issued out of the Central Office, the second a district registry writ claiming damages (see figs 8 and 9). The numbers in the margins of the writs refer to the notes beneath bold headings which follows this paragraph.

1 The court seal

The date included in the seal is important for three reasons: in calculating the time allowed for service of the writ (see p 204); for the purposes of the Limitation Act (see p 79); and with regard to the accrual of the plaintiff's causes of action (see below).

2 Indorsement of claim

RSC Ord 6, r 2, states—

> Before a writ is issued it must be indorsed ... with a statement of claim, or, if the statement of claim is not indorsed on the writ, with a concise statement of the nature of the claim made or the relief or remedy required in the action begun thereby ...

The Central Office writ illustrated is indorsed with a statement of claim: practitioners might refer to this as a 'specially indorsed writ' (an expression used in the pre-1965 rules of court). The district registry writ shows the alternative form of indorsement (a 'general indorsement') which must state both the nature of the claim *and* the remedies required (see *White Book* 6/2/2).

If a writ is 'generally indorsed' the plaintiff must then serve a statement of claim separately, either with the writ or before the expiration of fourteen days after the defendant gives notice of intention to defend (see p 207). A statement of claim served separately must state the date on which the writ was issued (RSC Ord 18, r 15(3): for an example see p 166). The 'general indorsement' forms the blueprint of what the statement of claim may contain (see p 182).

Accrual of plaintiff's cause of action

Obviously a plaintiff should not bring proceedings prematurely. He should sue only in respect of causes of action which have already accrued. However, this point is more technical than it might at first sight appear. A claim (unlike a defence or counterclaim) takes effect from the date of issue of the writ. A plaintiff cannot therefore include in his claim, whether by amendment or otherwise, any cause of action accrued to him only *after* that time.

Example

D borrows from P £50,000 and agrees to pay it back in ten monthly instalments of £5,000 plus interest. D fails to pay the second instalment. P starts proceedings immediately but before obtaining judgment the repayment dates for the third and fourth instalments pass without any payment by D. P cannot amend his writ to claim in respect of these further instalments (cf *Eshelby v Federated European Bank* [1932] 1 KB 254 and *Halliard v Jack Segal Ltd* [1978] 1 WLR 377).

In practice most loan contracts provide that if one instalment is in arrears the whole balance becomes due and payable, and the technicality is thereby avoided. If P's contract did not contain such a term, consider the following possible solutions (it must be said that only the first of them is really practical):

(1) P could start separate proceedings for the further instalments and then consolidate them (see p 101).
(2) P could obtain D's consent to the inclusion of the further claims (see p 3).
(3) If D raised a counterclaim P could raise the further instalments in a counterclaim to the counterclaim (see p 99).

3 The claim for interest

As to interest generally see p 15. A statement of claim, whether indorsed on the writ or served separately must contain any claim for interest (RSC Ord 18, r 8(4)). In view of this it is the better practice to state that there is to be a claim for interest in the general indorsement. However it is not fatal if the claim for interest is omitted from a generally indorsed writ: the subsequent statement of claim can still include the claim for interest. Alternatively, if judgment is entered in default of notice of intention to defend, the Court of Appeal has held that interest can nevertheless be included in the default judgment (*Edward Butler Vintners Ltd v Grange Seymour Internationale Ltd* (1987) *The Times,* 9 June; *White Book* 6/2/15).

4 Personal injury indorsement

When a personal injury action is commenced in the High Court the writ must be indorsed with a statement that the action is not one which, by art 5 of the High Court and County Courts Jurisdiction Order 1991, must be commenced in a county court (RSC Ord 6, r 2(1)(*f*) and see *White Book* 6/2/24) ie, a claim which has a 'value' of £50,000 or more (see p 107). False valuations made to enable proceedings to be commenced in the High Court will lead to either transfer or, in extreme cases, striking out (*Restick v Crickmore* [1994] 1 WLR 420). Almost invariably,

[*continued on p 202*]

Fig 8: Writ indorsed with statement of claim
(liquidated demand)

> Royal
> Coat of Arms
> Embossed here on
> issue of writ

IN THE HIGH COURT OF JUSTICE   1997–M–1020

QUEEN'S BENCH DIVISION

Between

1*

                    MASON-DIXON LIMITED   Plaintiff

                              and

                    ELEANOR RIGBY   Defendant

TO THE DEFENDANT   Eleanor Rigby

of   27 Shepherd Street, LONDON EC1 8QT

THIS WRIT OF SUMMONS has been issued against you by the above-named Plaintiff in respect of the claim set out on the back.

Within 14 days after the service of this Writ on you, counting the day of service, you must either satisfy the claim or return to the Court Office mentioned below the accompanying **ACKNOWLEDGMENT OF SERVICE** stating therein whether you intend to contest these proceedings.

If you fail to satisfy the claim or to return the Acknowledgment within the time stated, or if you return the Acknowledgment without stating therein an intention to contest the proceedings, the Plaintiff may proceed with the action and judgment may be entered against you forthwith without further notice.

Issued from the Central Office of the High Court this 1st day of September 1997.

NOTE: This Writ may not be served later than 4 calendar months (or, if leave is required to effect service out of the jurisdiction, 6 months) beginning with that date unless renewed by order of the Court*

I M P O R T A N T
Directions for Acknowledgment of Service are given with the accompanying form.

---

* See note 1 on p 196.

Fig 8: contd

STATEMENT OF CLAIM

2* The Plaintiff's claim is for the sum of £29,550.00 being the price of goods sold and delivered by the Plaintiff to the Defendant and for interest thereon pursuant to Section 35A Supreme Court Act 1981

Particulars

1997 January 26 to February 28	To goods comprising shop fittings and units sold and delivered to the Defendant full particulars of which have been given by invoice no. 86043 dated February 28 1997.

AND THE PLAINTIFF CLAIMS:

(1)   The said sum of £29,550.00

3*   (2)   Interest pursuant to statute at the rate of 8% per annum amounting to £1,198.80 for the period from February 28 1997 to date of issue (185 days)

(3)   Interest as above from date of issue until judgment or sooner payment at the daily rate of £6.48

Marian Hood for Hood & Leaford

5* (If, within the time for returning the Acknowledgment of Service, the Defendant pays the amount claimed and £239.25 for costs and, if the Plaintiff obtains an order for substituted service, the additional sum of £47.75, further proceedings will be stayed. The money must be paid to the Plaintiff, his Solicitor or Agent.)

THIS WRIT was issued by Messrs Hood and Leaford
of 7 Sherwood Street, LONDON EC4P 2EZ (ref AJS)

6* Solicitors for the said Plaintiff whose registered office is 12 Line Street, off Massachusett Drive, LONDON E1 4UP.

---

* *See note 2 on p 196 and notes 3, 5 and 6 on pp 197–203.*

Fig 9: Writ of summons (unliquidated demand)

COURT FEES ONLY

Writ of
Summons
[Unliquidated
Demand]
(0.6.r 1)

IN THE HIGH COURT OF JUSTICE   19 97 — .— No. 240

Queen's Bench Division

[Trafford   **District Registry]**

Between

ANGUS LAUDER   Plaintiff

AND

CHARLOTTE POPPY INGLE   Defendant

(1) Insert name   **To the Defendant (')** Charlotte Poppy Ingle

(2) Insert address   of (²) 10 Goodison Park, Southwich, Cheshire

This writ of Summons has been issued against you by the above-named Plaintiff in respect of the claim set out on the back.

Within 14 days after the service of this Writ on you, counting the day of service, you must either satisfy the claim or return to the Court Office mentioned below the accompanying **Acknowledgment of Service** stating therein whether you intend to contest these proceedings.

If you fail to satisfy the claim or to return the Acknowledgment within the time stated, or if you return the Acknowledgment without stating therein an intention to contest the proceedings, the Plaintiff may proceed with the action and judgment may be entered against you forthwith without further notice.

(3) Complete
and delete as
necessary

Issued from the (³) [Central Office] [Admiralty and Commercial Registry]
[Trafford   District Registry] of the High Court
this   1st   day of July   1997

NOTE: —This Writ may not be served later than 4 calendar months *(or, if leave is required to effect service out of the jurisdiction, 6 months)* beginning with that date unless renewed by order of the Court.

IMPORTANT

Directions for Acknowledgment of Service are given with the accompanying form

Fig 9: contd

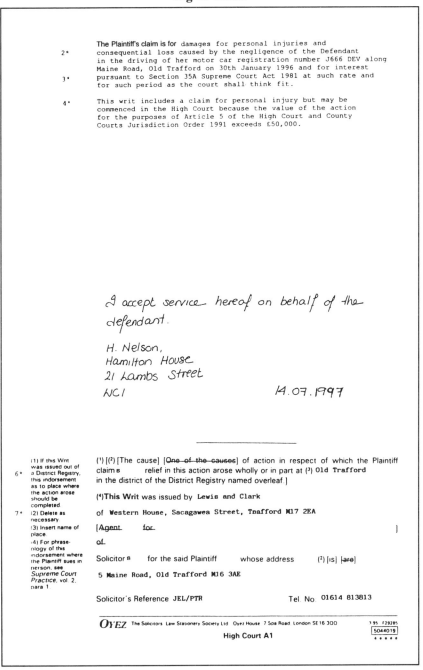

2* The Plaintiff's claim is for damages for personal injuries and consequential loss caused by the negligence of the Defendant in the driving of her motor car registration number J666 DEV along Maine Road, Old Trafford on 30th January 1996 and for interest

3* pursuant to Section 35A Supreme Court Act 1981 at such rate and for such period as the court shall think fit.

4* This writ includes a claim for personal injury but may be commenced in the High Court because the value of the action for the purposes of Article 5 of the High Court and County Courts Jurisdiction Order 1991 exceeds £50,000.

I accept service hereof on behalf of the defendant.

H. Nelson,
Hamilton House
21 Lambs Street
NC1   *14.07.1997*

(1) If this Writ was issued out of a District Registry, this indorsement as to place where the action arose should be completed.

6* (¹) [(²) [The cause] [One of the causes] of action in respect of which the Plaintiff claim s relief in this action arose wholly or in part at (³) Old Trafford in the district of the District Registry named overleaf.]

(2) Delete as necessary.

7* (⁴)This Writ was issued by Lewis and Clark

(3) Insert name of place.

of Western House, Sacagawea Street, Tnafford M17 2EA

(4) For phraseology of this indorsement where the Plaintiff sues in person, see Supreme Court Practice, vol. 2, para 1.

[Agent   for   ]

of

Solicitor s   for the said Plaintiff   whose address   (²) [is] [are]

5 Maine Road, Old Trafford M16 3AE

Solicitor's Reference JEL/PTR   Tel. No. 01614 813813

* *See note 2 on p 196 and notes 3, 4, 6 and 7 on pp 197–204.*
Reproduced by kind permission of the Solicitors' Law Stationery Society Ltd.

there will also be costs penalties for the plaintiff and/or his solicitor (see further p 375).

Further indorsements

In certain cases rules and practice directions specifically provide that other matters must be indorsed on the writ.

(1) The fourteen-day costs notice described below (RSC Ord 6, r 2(1)(*b*)).

(2) Where the plaintiff claims a debt expressed in a foreign currency, a statement of the current rate of exchange for that currency (*Practice Direction: White Book* 721).

(3) Where the plaintiff claims possession of land a statement as to whether a dwelling house is included, and, in all forfeiture cases, the name and address of any sub-tenant or mortgagee the plaintiff knows of who is entitled to claim relief against forfeiture (RSC Ord 6, r 2(1)(*c*)). If any such person is named, the plaintiff must send a copy of the writ to that person (RSC Ord 6, r 2(2)).

(4) Where the plaintiff claims possession of goods, a statement showing the value of the goods (RSC Ord 6, r 2(1)(*d*)).

(5) Where the plaintiff claims for wrongful interference with goods, a statement concerning the Torts (Interference with Goods) Act 1977, s 7 (RSC Ord 15, r 10A).

(6) Where a party is suing or being sued in a representative capacity, a statement showing that capacity (RSC Ord 6, r 3: for examples see Chitty and Jacob's *Queen's Bench Forms,* 21st ed (1986) No 31).

(7) Under CJJA 1982 a statement under RSC Ord 6, r 7 that the court has power to hear and determine the claim and that no proceedings involving the same cause of action are pending between the parties in Scotland, Northern Ireland or another convention territory (see further p 140). This indorsement removes the need to seek leave to issue a writ for service outside England and Wales. If, by oversight, a plaintiff failed to make this indorsement but stated a foreign address for the defendant the writ would be issued stamped with the words 'Not for service out of the jurisdiction'. The plaintiff would then have to go back to the court clerk with another writ-form, this time suitably indorsed, and obtain the issue of a concurrent writ.

5   The 'Fourteen-Day Costs and Stay' notice

Where the only remedy claimed by the plaintiff is a debt or liquidated demand the writ must be indorsed with this notice properly completed. The amount of costs allowed is prescribed by RSC Ord 62, Appendix 3. If the defendant makes full payment within fourteen days the plaintiff cannot claim any additional costs. However, if the defendant pays the fixed costs he or she (but not the plaintiff) is entitled to have the costs taxed (RSC Ord 62, r 7).

Although we use the expression 'fourteen-day notice' the period is in fact longer in cases where the writ is served outside England and Wales (see p 140 and 141).

The effect which the fourteen-day notice has on claims for interest has not been fully considered in a reported case. (For technical reasons the matters dealt with hereunder could not have arisen before April 1983 except on a claim for interest as of right.) Three propositions are set out which are derived from a 1983 *Practice Note* (*White Book* 6/2/15 and 971/3).

(1) *Effect on fixed costs.*   On a claim for a debt less than £3,000 the amount of the debt and the amount of pre-commencement interest claimed (at a contractually agreed rate or under SCA 1981, s 35A at the judgment debt rate) should be added together to determine how much fixed costs to specify in the fourteen-day notice.

(2) *Interest under SCA 1981 at higher rates.*   If, in an exceptional case, a plaintiff wishes to claim interest under SCA 1981, s 35A at a rate higher than the judgment debt rate, the fourteen-day notice may be deleted. This is because, in such a case, the total claim is not in respect of a liquidated demand; the interest must be assessed by the court whether or not it is expressed in the writ as a liquidated sum.

(3) *Cases in which post-commencement interest is not available.*   If a plaintiff claims, and gives precise figures for, interest at a contractually agreed rate or under SCA 1981, s 35A at the judgment debt rate, the fourteen-day notice must be indorsed on the writ. To obtain the stay of action the defendant must make full payment, including pre-commencement interest, within the time allowed. According to the 1983 *Practice Note* 'no further interest is payable'. We respectfully doubt the accuracy of this statement. The distinction it draws between pre-commencement interest and post-commencement interest seems arbitrary and does not take full account of SCA 1981, s 35A(3). In our view, a payment excluding post-commencement interest is part payment only; a plaintiff in such a case who considers it worth the trouble should be allowed to continue the action (and see p 215).

6   The address for service

Where the plaintiff sues by a solicitor, the plaintiff's address for service will be the business address of that solicitor or of the solicitor acting as agent. Where the plaintiff sues in person the address for service will be his residential address or, if that is not within the jurisdiction, he must give an address for service within England and Wales (see generally RSC Ord 6, r 5).

7 Indorsement as to place where cause of action arose

Most writs can be issued out of any High Court office (Central Office, Chancery Chambers or district registry). If the cause of action wholly or in part arose in the district of a district registry the plaintiff can commence the action there and may include this indorsement thereby preventing the defendant transferring the case to some other court office (see further p 207).

Service of writ

Methods of service

For rules as to service generally see Chapter 8. The writ must be served together with a form of acknowledgment of service in which the title of the action and its number have been entered (RSC Ord 10, r 1). Guidance notes for the plaintiff which are attached to the prescribed form of acknowledgment also require the completion or deletion of certain other parts of the form. Service of a writ without an accompanying form of acknowledgment of service is an irregularity but not normally an irregularity serious enough to merit the defendant applying to have the service set aside (*Tsai v Woodworth* (1984) *White Book* 12/1/3).

The rules permit deemed service where the defendant's solicitor indorses on the original writ a statement that he accepts service on behalf of his client (see p 132). Deemed service may be more convenient for the defendant in a case where, if it is not agreed to, a sealed writ and form of acknowledgment of service would be posted to an address distant from the defendant's solicitor. The defendant's solicitor's indorsement of acceptance does not of course obviate the need to lodge an acknowledgment of service at the court office. The defendant's solicitor should see to this at the same time as making the indorsement (*White Book* 10/1/12). An example of the indorsement is shown on p 201. We suggest that the wording should be qualified if the defendant's solicitor intends to complain of any irregularities in the issue or service of the writ.

Time for service

A writ remains valid for the purpose of service for four months beginning with the date of its issue. If the plaintiff serves the writ after that time without first applying to extend its validity the service is irregular and may be set aside.

> *Example*
> In *Trow v Ind Coope* [1967] 2 QB 899 the writ (then valid for twelve months), was issued on 10 September 1965 at 3.05 pm but was not served until 10 September 1966 at 11.59 am. The service was set aside

as irregular. It was held that the validity of the writ expired on 9 September 1966: the twelve-month period included the whole of the day of issue even though most of that day had elapsed before the writ was in fact issued.

Now that writs are valid for four months they must generally be served no later than the day before the corresponding date of issue four months hence; or if there is no such date, on the last day of the fourth month.

Examples
   A writ issued on 10 January must be served on or before 9 May. It is irrelevant that February is a short month.
   A writ issued on 1 June must be served on or before 30 September. It cannot be held over until 1 October on the ground that September has only thirty days.

The court can renew a writ (ie extend its validity) for any period not exceeding four months from the date when it would otherwise expire. The plaintiff can apply for a renewal even after the writ has expired and a renewed writ may be further renewed. The application is made to a district judge, *ex parte*, on affidavit showing some good reason justifying renewal. If the application is granted the period of the renewal will be marked on the original writ.

Applications for extension of time for service should normally be made before the expiry of the writ or within the four months following expiry. If you apply three months after expiry, the maximum extension you can get is one further month (unless the case is exceptional, see below). This is because, ordinarily, RSC Ord 6, r 8 allows only one extension, of up to four months from expiry of the writ, per application. The courts will not now, as they once did, grant two or more extensions 'back to back' on the same application (*Singh (Joghinder) v Duport Harper Foundries Ltd* [1994] 1 WLR 769 in which an application made five and a half months after the expiry of the writ was rejected).

In exceptional circumstances, an application for an extension bridging a period exceeding four months might be allowed under the wider rules of RSC Ord 2, r 1 (see p 2) or RSC Ord 3, r 5 (see p 9). *Ward-Lee v Lineham* [1993] 1 WLR 754 (referred to with approval in *Singh*, above) and *Kelliher v EH Savill Engineering Ltd*, noted in *White Book* 6/8/10, both indicate the circumstances exceptional enough to warrant departure from the ordinary rule; where the failure to serve in time was caused by mistakes on the part of the court office, not the plaintiff.

RSC Ord 6, r 8(2A) provides that on an application for renewal the court can extend the validity of a writ for up to twelve months if satisfied that, despite the making of all reasonable efforts *it may not be possible to serve the writ within four months*. Note that the wording of sub-rule (2A) looks to the future, not the past (see the words in italics above). It allows an extension up to twelve months in cases in which the court anticipates that the plaintiff will have problems locating the defendant within the *next* four months (because eg the defendant is overseas or untraceable). It does not help a plaintiff whose problems lie in the past, ie whose writ has already been expired for more than four months (*Singh*, above).

Renewals are fairly readily granted where the relevant limitation period has not expired since in such cases the plaintiff could always issue a new writ. (Indeed as a matter of costs it can sometimes be cheaper to issue a new writ.) However, if it is now too late to begin again the defendant has in a sense an accrued defence under the Limitation Act and therefore the 'good reason justifying renewal' will have to be stronger. Consider the following cases.

(1) *Failure to serve in time because defendant untraceable.* This reason was accepted in *Gurtner v Circuit* [1968] 2 QB 687 as a justification for granting three renewals extending the validity of the writ by twenty-seven months *in toto*. However, the difficulty in effecting service must extend over the whole four-month period. A renewal might be refused if the plaintiff made no attempt to effect service during, say, the first three months only to find, in the fourth month, that the defendant had just moved.

Since *Gurtner* the standard procedure in road accident cases where the defendant cannot be traced is to apply within the initial period of the writ's validity (ie the first four months) for substituted service at his insurer's address (see p 133).

(2) *Failure to serve because the defendant invited the plaintiff to defer service pending negotiations.* This reason was accepted in *North v Kirk* (1967) 111 SJ 793 and *Re Chittenden* [1970] 1 WLR 1618. However note that in *Easy v Universal Anchorage* [1974] 1 WLR 899 it was held that merely delaying service without the defendant's consent 'so as not to prejudice the possibility of a settlement' was not a sufficient reason. For a case in which it was held that the solicitor appointed by the insurers had impliedly consented to a delay in service, see *Hare v Personal Representatives of Mohammed Yunis Malik* (1980) 124 SJ 328.

The leading cases on the renewal of writs are *Kleinwort Benson Ltd v Barbrak Ltd (No 3)* [1987] AC 597 and *Waddon v Whitecroft-Scovill Ltd* [1988] 1 WLR 309. In *Lewis v Harewood* (1996) *The Times*, 11 March, *White Book* 6/8/4 Supplement, the Court of Appeal added a further gloss thereon which favours defendants in cases in which the application is made in respect of an expired writ. Before finally deciding questions concerning balance of prejudice or hardship the court should consider first, having regard to all the circumstances, possibly including questions of balance of prejudice or hardship, is there good reason to extend the time and has the plaintiff given a satisfactory explanation for his failure to apply before the validity of the writ expired (see further *Supreme Court Practice News*, Issue 4/96).

Acknowledgment of service

The first step the defendant takes in an action is the completion and return of the form of acknowledgment of service which will have been served with the writ. The defendant is given fourteen days after service of the writ (inclusive of the day of service) in which to acknowledge (a longer time is given in cases of service abroad, see pp 140 and 141). The prescribed form (1997 edition, illustrated in fig 10) requires the defendant to state the following information:

(1) *His full name.*

(2) *Whether he intends to contest the proceedings.* If the first or second box is ticked the defendant is said to have 'given notice of intention to defend'. If the third box is ticked the plaintiff can proceed immediately to judgment under Ord 13 (see p 212).

(3) *Whether he intends to apply for a stay of execution.* This arises only if the claim is for a debt or liquidated demand and if the defendant does not give notice of intention to defend (and see further pp 212 and 520).

(4) *If the writ was issued out of a district registry, whether he wishes to have the action transferred to the Central Office or to another district registry.* Note that the defendant can apply for a transfer only *if* the writ was issued out of a district registry *and if* the defendant's residence, place of business or registered office (if a limited company) is not within the district of the issuing district registry *and if* there is no indorsement on the writ that the plaintiff's cause of action arose wholly or in part within the district. The procedure on the defendant's application for a transfer is described on p 374.

The defendant has to return the form by handing it in at or by posting it to the court office or district registry out of which the writ was issued (as to which, see part 6 of the form which should be completed by the plaintiff, before service). Where the post is used the date of acknowledgment is the date the court receives it and not the date of posting (RSC Ord 12, r 1(5)). RSC Ord 12, r 1, further provides that a defendant company may return the form by employing a solicitor or any other person duly authorised to act on its behalf ('but except as aforesaid or as expressly provided by any enactment, such a defendant may not take steps in the action otherwise than by a solicitor'): and that if two or more defendants to an action acknowledge service by the same solicitor and at the same time only one form of acknowledgment of service need be used.

(5) *The signature of the defendant or his solicitor and the statement of an address for service.* As to the latter, see the notes as to address for service in fig 10 and compare the rules relating to the plaintiff's address for service (p 203 above).

[*continued on p 212*]

Fig 10: Acknowledgment of service of writ of summons

Guidance notes for the Plaintiff

Read these notes carefully
The notes explain what you have to do before this form is sent to ("served" on) the Defendant.

Form heading
You must fill in the heading of the form with:

- the action number,
- the name of the appropriate High Court Division, for example, Queen's Bench Division, Queen's Bench Division (Commercial Court), Queen's Bench Division (Admiralty Court) or Chancery Division, or
- if the writ issued in a District Registry, the name of the District Registry, and
- the names of the parties in the action (the "title") as they appear on the writ.

Part 3
If the claim is not for a fixed amount, you must delete part 3 and the notes relating to it.

Part 4
You must delete part 4 and the notes relating to it if the writ was:

- issued at any office in the Royal Courts of Justice (Strand, London), **or**
- issued at the District Registry for the area where the Defendant lives, carries on business, or, if a limited company, has its registered office, **and**
- the Plaintiff's cause of action arose in that area.

Part 5
Please leave blank for Defendant to complete.

Part 6
Return address
Write in the full address of the District Registry or office in the Royal Courts of Justice to which the form should be returned.

On the reverse of acknowledgment form
Plaintiff's (Plaintiff's solicitor's) details
Fill in your name and the address to which papers about the case should be sent. Detach these guidance notes before the form is sent to the Defendant.

Fig 10: contd

Guidance notes for the Defendant

Read these notes carefully
They will help you to fill in the form attached and tell you what other steps you need to take.

Act quickly
You have only a limited time to return the form. If you do not return the form promptly, the Plaintiff may obtain a court order against you. If the claim is for money, you could be ordered to pay the money immediately (called "entering judgment by default").

Help and advice
You can get help and legal advice from:
- a solicitor (who can fill in the form and return it to the court for you) or
- a Citizen's Advice Bureau.

They will also tell you if you qualify for help with your legal costs ("legal aid").
Staff at any District Registry or office in the Royal Courts of Justice (Strand, London) will help you to fill in the form.

Time for returning the form
You have **14 days** from the day you receive the writ of summons to **return the completed form to the court.** The day on which the 14 day period begins depends on how you received the writ (how it was "served" on you).
If the writ was:
- handed to you personally, the 14 days begins on the day you were given the writ;
- delivered by post, the 14 days begins 7 days from the date of the postmark;
- put through your letterbox, the 14 days begins 7 days from the day this was done.

If you are a limited company and the writ was delivered by post, the 14 days begins:
- on the second working day from the date of the postmark if first class post was used;
- on the fourth working day from the date of the postmark if the second class post was used.

If the writ was served on you at an address outside England and Wales, the writ will tell you how long you have to return the acknowledgment form.

(This prescribed form also comprises a fifth page upon which the name, address and other details of the plaintiff (or the plaintiff's solicitors) should be given – see the last guidance note for the plaintiff on p 208 above.)

Fig 10: contd

Filling in the form

Read these notes carefully.

They will help you to fill in the form opposite and tell you what other steps you need to take.

> You can use the same form of acknowledgment for two (or more) defendants provided the form makes this clear and they all wish to reply in the same way.

If you are **under 18 or suffering certain mental disorders** ("under disability") you must ask another person to act for you. That person can be any friend or relative who is over 18 and not a co-defendant in the same claim. But they must act on your behalf with the help of a solicitor. The solicitor must fill in the form of acknowledgment.

Part 1   Write in your full name. If your name was incorrect on the writ, add the words "sued as" followed by the name stated on the writ.

     If you are: • a person trading in a name other than your own, write in your name followed by the words "trading as" and the name under which you trade;

              • a partner in a firm, write in your name followed by the words "a partner in the firm of" and the name of the firm. **If you are sued as a partner but are not, say so.**

                 ⟶

Part 2   Tick the appropriate box to show whether you intend to contest all, or part, of the claim. **If you contest any part of the claim, read note 2 below on preparing your defence.** ⟶

Part 3   Should only be filled in if the Plaintiff is claiming a fixed amount of money and you do not contest the claim.

Part 3   Tick the appropriate box to show whether you intend to ask the court to make an order preventing the Plaintiff from enforcing any order for you to pay the amount claimed (called asking for a "stay of execution"). A stay of execution will allow you to pay the debt, perhaps by instalments. **If you wish to apply for a stay of execution, read note 3 below. This tells you how to make your application.** ⟶

Part 4   can only be filled in:

            • if the writ of summons was <u>not issued</u> in the Royal Courts of Justice or the District Registry for the area where you live, carry on business or have your registered office, <u>and</u>

            • the cause of the Plaintiff's action, or part of it, did not arise in that area.

Part 4   Tick the appropriate box to show whether you wish the case to be transferred to the Royal Courts of Justice (London) or to another District Registry. If you are unsure which is the District Registry for your area, staff at the District Registry which issued the writ will tell you. If the case is transferred, you will be told when this has happened and what your new case number is. The Plaintiff may object to the transfer; if so, there may be a hearing. ⟶

Part 5   Unless your solicitor is filling in the form on your behalf, you must sign the form and give an address to which court documents should be sent, and any reference, telephone or fax numbers. If you are being sued as an individual (that is in your own name rather than that of your firm or company) the address you give must be one in England and Wales. If you are a **limited company**, the form may be filled in by an **authorised officer** who must state his position in that company, or a solicitor. A solicitor may give his firm's address; an authorised officer must give the registered or principal office of the company. ⟶

What to do when you have filled in the form.

1. Return the form

Detach these guidance notes and send or take the acknowledgment form to the office in the Royal Courts of Justice or the District Registry which issued the writ.

2. Preparing the defence

If you contest the Plaintiff's claim, you must set out your reasons for doing so in writing (called a "defence"). You must send or take a copy of your defence to the Plaintiff (or the Plaintiff's solicitor). The time in which you have to do this will depend on whether you were given full particulars of the Plaintiff's claim (called a "statement of claim") with the writ.

If a statement of claim was **included** in the writ, or **accompanied it**, you must serve your defence within 14 days after the time for acknowledging service of the writ.

If a statement of claim is served on you **after** you received the writ, you must serve your defence 14 days from the date you received the statement of claim.

3. Applying for a stay of execution

If you agree that you owe the Plaintiff the amount of money claimed but want a stay of execution to allow you time to pay, you must issue a summons asking the court to make this order. Your summons must be accompanied by a sworn statement (an "affidavit") setting out details of your income and liabilities and any offer of payment you are making, for example, by instalments.

Copies of the form of summons and affidavit can be obtained from any firm of law stationers.

You must issue your summons at the appropriate office within 14 days of the court receiving your form of acknowledgment of service.

Fig 10: contd

Acknowledgment of Service of Writ of Summons

In the High Court of Justice   **19**   **No.**

                      Division

                      District Registry   Use black ink and capital letters

Plaintiff

Defendant

Part 1   (Your) (Defendant's)
           full name

Part 2   (Do you) (Does the Defendant)   the whole of the Plaintiff's claim? ☐
           intend to contest: part of the Plaintiff's claim? ☐
                                       none of the Plaintiff's claim? ☐

Part 3   If you (the Defendant) have said that you do not intend to
           contest the whole, or part, of the Plaintiff's claim will you
           (the Defendant) be asking the court for a stay of execution?   Yes ☐   No ☐

Part 4   (Do you) (Does the Defendant) wish to have the case transferred to:

                            the Royal Courts of Justice?   Yes ☐   No ☐
                            another District Registry?   Yes ☐   No ☐

           If to a District Registry, say which one

Part 5   I acknowledge that (I have) (the Defendant has) been served with a copy of the Writ of
           Summons

           Signed   Date
           Defendant (Solicitor for the Defendant) (Authorised officer)

           Address to which papers about this case should be sent:

           Solicitor's   Telephone   Fax
           Ref.   No.   No.

Part 6   When completed this form should be returned to:

Form High Court E22

Reproduced by kind permission of the Solicitors' Law Stationery Society Ltd

On receiving an acknowledgment of service the court staff will affix to it an official stamp showing the date of receipt, enter it in the records kept by the court, and post a stamped copy of it to the plaintiff's address for service.

RSC Ord 12, rr 7 and 8 make provision for the following cases: cases in which the defendant wishes to dispute the jurisdiction of the English courts *or* wishes to complain of any irregularity in the issue or service of the writ *or* wishes to challenge any *ex parte* order the plaintiff obtained which renewed the writ or gave leave to effect substituted service.

In such cases the defendant must acknowledge service and give notice of intention to defend. The defendant must then take out a summons to the district judge, within the time limited for the service of the defence (see p 233) applying for any order setting aside the writ etc as may be appropriate. As with other time limits in the rules the period in which the defendant must apply may be extended by the court, and may be so extended even after the period has expired (see pp 10 and 205).

An acknowledgment of service *does* amount to a submission to the jurisdiction of the English courts unless either the defendant gives notice of intention to defend and takes out a summons as described above or the defendant is given leave to withdraw the acknowledgment.

An acknowledgment of service does *not* amount to a waiver of any irregularity but, if the defendant does not give notice of intention to defend and take out a summons as described above, he will lose the opportunity to complain of that irregularity.

Judgment in default of acknowledgment

The title we use for RSC Ord 13 is for convenience only. It is important to note at the outset that RSC Ord 13 covers two possibilities: cases in which the defendant acknowledges service but fails to give notice of intention to defend and cases in which the defendant fails to lodge an acknowledgment of service and therefore of necessity fails to give notice of intention to defend. The expression 'judgment in default of notice of intention to defend' is sufficient to cater for both these cases but is in danger of being confused with 'judgment in default of defence' (RSC Ord 19).

The defendant is given fourteen days after service of the writ (inclusive of the day of service) in which to lodge an acknowledgment (a longer time is given in cases of service abroad; see pp 140 and 141). If by the end of that time the defendant has failed to lodge an acknowledgment, or has lodged an acknowledgment which does not give notice of intention to defend, the plaintiff can usually proceed to judgment (see *Remedies obtainable* below). However, at any time before the plaintiff enters judgment the defendant can without leave *either* lodge a late acknowledgment of service (RSC Ord 12, r 6) *or* amend his acknowledgment so as to give notice of intention to defend (RSC Ord 20, r 2; and see p 186).

Remedies obtainable

Under RSC Ord 13, rr 1, 2, 3 and 4, if the defendant fails to give notice of intention to defend, then after the 'prescribed time' (see below) the plaintiff may enter judgment in default *if* the writ is *only* indorsed with a claim:

(*a*) for unliquidated damages (other than provisional damages: see p 71); or

(*b*) for possession of land; or

(*c*) for a liquidated demand; or

(*d*) relating to the detention of goods.

The prescribed time means the fourteen days allowed for acknowledging service or the date, if earlier, an acknowledgment was lodged which did not include a notice of intention to defend (RSC Ord 13, r 6A).

In case (*a*) the plaintiff is entitled to enter only interlocutory judgment for damages to be assessed (under RSC Ord 37). In case (*b*) the plaintiff can enter final judgment and can proceed immediately to enforcement. The plaintiff can also enter final judgment in case (*c*), but bear in mind that the defendant may apply for a stay of execution. If the defendant lodged an acknowledgment stating that he intends to apply for a stay, the judgment is automatically stayed for fourteen days from the acknowledgment. If within these fourteen days the defendant issues and serves on the plaintiff a summons for a stay supported by the necessary affidavit (see p 520) the automatic stay is extended until the summons is disposed of (see generally RSC Ord 13, r 8).

In case (*d*) there are a range of courses open to the plaintiff: he can enter *either* interlocutory judgment for delivery of the goods or their value *or* interlocutory judgment for their value (in each case the assessment being made under RSC Ord 37) *or* he can apply by summons to a district judge for an order for the specific delivery of the goods, ie an order which does not give the defendant the option of paying their assessed value.

Assessment of damages or value

RSC Ord 37 provides that where judgment is given for damages or value to be assessed and no provision is made by the judgment for their assessment the plaintiff can make an appointment with the district judge for that purpose, giving at least seven days' notice of the appointment to the defendant. The hearing takes place 'in open court', (ie the public have a right to attend if they wish and an appeal from the district judge's decision lies directly to the Court of Appeal (RSC Ord 58, r 2). If the hearing is to be contested it may be convenient to convene a directions appointment first so as to obtain suitable directions as to evidence including expert evidence and discovery. At the assessment hearing the defendant cannot of course challenge the question of liability. However, he can contest issues of *quantum* including, if relevant, issues of contributory negligence. (*Maes Finance Ltd v A L Phillips & Co* (1997) *The Times*, 25 March).

It often happens that the assessment hearing, like the action, is not contested. Therefore, if you wish to avoid the trouble and expense of bringing your witnesses along to the appointment consider giving notice to your opponent of your intention to seek leave at the hearing to rely upon affidavit evidence (enclose copies) and ask your opponent to indicate whether that application will be opposed.

At an unopposed hearing the district judge may assess the costs immediately rather than ordering a taxation (see further pp 527 and 565). The assessed costs will perhaps comprise a sum equal to fixed costs on a default judgment in debt plus a further sum to cover the extra expenditure incurred by the assessment hearing.

In some cases the assessment will not be made by the district judge:
(1) where the district judge orders that the action shall proceed to trial (eg cases involving a difficult point of principle);
(2) where the district judge orders that the assessment shall be referred to an official referee (see p 270: this order is made especially in building contract cases or other cases involving lengthy matters of quantification);
(3) where RSC Ord 37, r 3, applies (see p 218).

Note that RSC Ord 37 is not limited to assessments in default cases. It can be used in many instances in which the plaintiff obtains interlocutory judgment for damages or value to be assessed, eg a summary judgment under RSC Ord 14 (see p 221) and a judgment on admissions under RSC Ord 27, r 3 (see p 369).

Multiplicity of claims or defendants

Two or more of the above-mentioned claims

Under RSC Ord 13, r 5, where the writ is indorsed with two or more of the above-mentioned claims (with or without interest) *but no other claim* the plaintiff may obtain judgment in respect of each claim as if it were the only claim made.

Examples

L sues T, his ex-tenant, for possession, arrears of rent, *mesne* profits and damages for breach of a covenant to repair. If T fails to give notice of intention to defend within the prescribed time L may obtain a combined final and interlocutory judgment (*mesne* profits are usually treated as a liquidated demand and therefore final judgment is given for them: *White Book* 13/4/5).

P sues D for the delivery of goods or the payment of their value and damages for their detention. If D fails to give notice of intention to defend within the prescribed time P may obtain interlocutory judgment for damages *and* value to be assessed.

RSC Ord 13, r 5, applies only to writs indorsed with claims, with or without interest, under (a), (b), (c) or (d) above, the common-law remedies. (An order for specific delivery of goods is in the nature of an equitable remedy but was first taken over by the common-law courts under the Common Law Procedure Act 1852. Note that it is discretionary and therefore is not obtainable without leave.)

Claims for interest

If the plaintiff has failed to claim interest in a statement of claim indorsed on the writ he cannot enter judgment in default in respect of it without first amending the writ and re-serving it; this would give the defendant a longer time in which to lodge an acknowledgment (contrast generally indorsed writs, as to which see p 196).

Assuming that interest has been claimed in the writ, if the plaintiff is entitled to enter interlocutory judgment for damages, he may also enter interlocutory judgment for interest thereon. (Since the damages must be assessed there is no point in the plaintiff pleading precise figures for interest in a damages case.)

If the plaintiff is entitled to enter final judgment for a debt he may also enter judgment for any interest claimed. However, if he claimed interest under SCA 1981, s 35A at a rate higher than the judgment debt rate (see p 16), the judgment for interest must be interlocutory only.

Turning now to the usual debt case in which the plaintiff has given precise figures for interest and has based them on a contractually agreed rate or, under SCA 1981, s 35A, on the judgment debt rate, final judgment may be entered for both the debt and the interest thereon up to the date of judgment. In such a case the plaintiff may also enter judgment for fixed costs. The plaintiff must not of course enter judgment for a sum greater than is due. If the defendant has made a part payment this should be taken into account in the judgment. On sums paid the plaintiff is not entitled to any interest for any period after that payment. The question therefore arises, how does one decide whether a part payment was made in respect of the debt, the interest thereon or the fixed costs? It benefits the defendant if the part payment is allocated to the debt rather than to the other sums. In practice, this is how the part payment will normally be allocated; the position is analogous to that dealt with in a 1933 *Masters' Practice Direction* (see *White Book* 13/6/3).

Claim for an equitable remedy or provisional damages

If the writ is indorsed with a claim for an equitable remedy (such as an account or an injunction) the plaintiff cannot obtain *any* remedy under RSC Ord 13 but is left to claim them in default of defence (but see further *White Book* 13/6/1, which is referred to on p 234).

[*continued on p 218*]

Fig 11: Affidavit of service of writ on individual by post

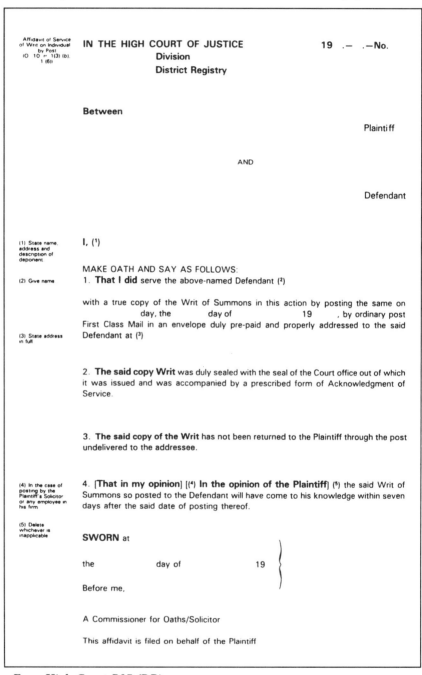

Affidavit of Service
of Writ on Individual
by Post
(O 10 r 1(3) (b),
1 (6))

IN THE HIGH COURT OF JUSTICE
Division
District Registry

19 .— .—No.

Between

Plaintiff

AND

Defendant

(1) State name,
address and
description of
deponent

I, (¹)

MAKE OATH AND SAY AS FOLLOWS:

(2) Give name

1. **That I did** serve the above-named Defendant (²)

with a true copy of the Writ of Summons in this action by posting the same on
day, the   day of   19   , by ordinary post
First Class Mail in an envelope duly pre-paid and properly addressed to the said

(3) State address
in full

Defendant at (³)

2. **The said copy Writ** was duly sealed with the seal of the Court office out of which it was issued and was accompanied by a prescribed form of Acknowledgment of Service.

3. **The said copy of the Writ** has not been returned to the Plaintiff through the post undelivered to the addressee.

(4) In the case of
posting by the
Plaintiff's Solicitor
or any employee in
his firm

4. **[That in my opinion]** [(⁴) **In the opinion of the Plaintiff]** (⁵) the said Writ of Summons so posted to the Defendant will have come to his knowledge within seven days after the said date of posting thereof.

(5) Delete
whichever is
inapplicable

SWORN at

the   day of   19

Before me,

A Commissioner for Oaths/Solicitor

This affidavit is filed on behalf of the Plaintiff

Form High Court B37 (DR)
Reproduced by kind permission of the Solicitors' Law Stationery Society Ltd.

Fig 12: Default judgment in action for unliquidated damages

Default judgment in action for unliquidated damages
(O 13, r.2.
O 19, r 3.
O 42, r 1.)

IN THE HIGH COURT OF JUSTICE   19   . —   . — No.
Queen's Bench Division

Between

Plaintiff

AND

Defendant

The   day of   19

(1) "notice of intention to defend having been given" or "defence having been served".

No(¹)

by the Defendant herein,

IT IS THIS DAY ADJUDGED that the Defendant

do pay the Plaintiff damages to be assessed.

The amount found due to the Plaintiff under this judgment having been certified

(2) "Official Referee's certificate" or "Master's certificate" or as may be.

at £   as appears by the (²)

filed the   day of   19 .

IT IS ADJUDGED that the Defendant

do pay the Plaintiff £   , and costs to be taxed.

The above costs have been taxed and allowed at £

as appears by a taxing officer's certificate dated the   day

of   19 .

Plaintiff's Solicitor

Form High Court D2
Reproduced by kind permission of the Solicitors' Law Stationery Society Ltd.

A default judgment under RSC Ord 13 (or RSC Ord 19: see p 234) is not available in a case where the plaintiff claims provisional damages (RSC Ord 37, r 8).

Two or more defendants

Under RSC Ord 13, rr 1, 2, 3 and 4, if there are two or more defendants only some of whom give notice of intention to defend, the plaintiff may enter judgment against those in default without prejudice to his right to proceed against the others. RSC Ord 37, r 3, provides that where in these circumstances the plaintiff obtains interlocutory judgment for damages or value to be assessed, the assessment will be made at the trial unless the court otherwise orders.

Defendant a minor or mental patient

A minor or mental patient cannot acknowledge service except through a guardian *ad litem*. Accordingly the plaintiff cannot enter judgment in default against him unless and until a guardian *ad litem* is appointed. RSC Ord 80, r 6, provides that if no acknowledgment of service is given for a minor or mental patient the plaintiff himself must apply for a guardian *ad litem* to be appointed.

Method of entering judgment

In most cases judgment under RSC Ord 13 can be entered without leave. The plaintiff delivers to the appropriate court office:
(1) the original writ;
(2) two copies of the form of judgment duly completed (see fig 12 above for claims for unliquidated damages);
(3) an affidavit of service (illustrated in fig 11 above), unless service was accepted by the defendant's solicitor, or the defendant lodged an acknowledgment;
(4) on a claim for possession of land the necessary certificate or affidavit referred to below.

   Leave to enter the judgment is required in the case of:
(1) proceedings against the Crown (RSC Ord 77, r 9) or against a foreign state (RSC Ord 13, r 7A);
(2) proceedings against a debtor or surety under a consumer credit agreement *if* a notice to re-open the agreement has already been given and a copy filed at the court (RSC Ord 83, r 3);
(3) an action in tort brought by one spouse against the other during the marriage (RSC Ord 89, r 2: under the Law Reform (Husband and Wife) Act 1962 the court has power to stay the action if it appears that no substantial benefit would accrue to either party from its continuance or if it could be more conveniently disposed

of by an application under the Married Women's Property Act 1882, s 17);

(4) actions for possession of land *unless* the plaintiff produces a certificate made by his solicitor (or, if acting in person, an affidavit) stating that the action is not a 'mortgage action' and does not involve the Rent Act 1977 (RSC Ord 13, r 4);

(5) in cases affected by the CJJA 1982 in which the writ has been served abroad without leave or has been served in England and Wales on a defendant domiciled in a country within the EU or EFTA (RSC Ord 13, r 7B).

An application for leave should be made by summons to the district judge.

Costs of default judgments

The rules allowing default judgments also allow judgment for costs. On final judgments the amount of costs is fixed (RSC Ord 62, Appendix 3, and see also *White Book* 746). On judgments which are wholly or in part interlocutory the plaintiff obtains an order for costs (to be taxed) at the assessment under RSC Ord 37. RSC Ord 13, r 6, permits an application (by summons to the district judge) for leave to enter a default judgment for costs in one specialised case: where the writ is indorsed with a claim for, eg an injunction, but it becomes unnecessary to proceed with the action and the defendant fails to give notice of intention to defend. (If the defendant does give notice of intention to defend but will not consent to an order for costs, see *Danesfield Securities Ltd v Sonuga* (1996) *The Times*, 31 December, noted on p 222, below.)

Setting aside default judgment

By RSC Ord 13, r 9, the court may on such terms as it thinks fit set aside or vary any Ord 13 judgment. The defendant is entitled to have a judgment set aside as of right if it was irregularly obtained: eg a final judgment for damages or a judgment obtained after some irregularity in issue or service—contrast cases where the irregularity is as to the amount claimed; see *White Book* 13/1/13 and *Ban Hin Lee Bank Berhad v Sonali Bank* (1988) noted therein. A defendant applies to set aside for irregularity by summons and although the affidavit in support need not disclose the defence it is prudent to do so because if the argument on irregularity is lost, the defendant can then seek to set aside on the merits (see below).

If the judgment is regular it will be set aside only *on the merits*: this has two important consequences:

(1) the defendant must, by affidavit, show some defence on the merits, ie some arguable defence or triable issue (*Evans v Bartlam* [1937] AC 473; *Alpine Bulk Transport v Saudi Eagle Shipping Co* [1986]

2 Lloyd's Rep 221 which suggests that a defendant has to show a somewhat stronger case to win a setting aside order than he would have to show to defeat a summary judgment application; see *White Book* 13/9/14);

(2) the court may impose terms, eg the payment into court of the whole or part of any money claimed in the action if the defence raised is shadowy (see p 228) and/or the payment of 'costs thrown away' (see p 570). As the defendant is in breach of the rules a payment into court may be required to ensure future compliance. If the defendant fails to comply with these terms the plaintiff can proceed to enforce the default judgment (RSC Ord 45, r 10). Any condition should be one with which the defendant can reasonably comply (*MV Yorke Motors v Edwards* [1982] 1 WLR 444, HL). To bring a successful appeal against conditions, the defendant must show that they are impossible (not just difficult) for him to fulfil and (on an appeal to the Court of Appeal) that the impossibility had been proved to the court below *Agyeman v Boadi* [1996] EGCS 14).

If, on an application to set aside, the court finds that there is no defence to part of the claim, the court will reduce the judgment and set aside as to the balance (*The Iran Nabuvat* [1990] 1 WLR 1115). The plaintiff thus retains the benefit of interest accrued under the Judgments Act 1838 from the date of the judgment in default on the amount of the reduced judgment.

What should happen if a writ is served by post, an affidavit of service is filed but after judgment is entered the presumption of due service is rebutted? Whether or not the judgment will be set aside depends upon how the presumption came to be rebutted. If, after judgment is entered, the writ posted to the defendant is returned through the post undelivered to the addressee RSC Ord 13, r 7(3) provides that the plaintiff must, before seeking to enforce the judgment, *either* file an affidavit stating the facts and requesting the judgment to be set aside, *or* apply *ex parte* to the district judge for directions (eg on affidavit evidence that, despite its being returned, the writ was in fact received by the defendant; in such a case the district judge will usually direct the plaintiff to re-apply by summons, to give the defendant the opportunity to be heard, see *White Book* 13/7/5). (Since this summons also has to be served, such an application to the district judge has little to recommend it unless the plaintiff has strong evidence that the defendant did receive the writ, eg incontrovertible evidence that the words 'gone away' written on the envelope are in the defendant's handwriting. Normally the better course for the plaintiff to adopt is to attempt to effect personal service, or, if appropriate, seek an order for substituted service. Sometimes however it will be crucial to prove the validity of the original service, eg where the relevant period for service has since expired, see p 132).

If the writ is not returned through the post the defendant will have to apply by summons to set aside the judgment: his affidavit in support ought to prove non-service and disclose some defence on the merits. In setting aside the judgment in such a case the district judge will not impose terms, or penalise the defendant in costs unless, exceptionally, it appears that the problem as to service was of the defendant's own making (and see further *White Book* 13/9/2).

If a judgment is set aside the plaintiff must return it to the court office to be marked with a note of the order (*White Book* 747).

In certain Queen's Bench Division cases it is now possible for parties to have a default judgment set aside by consent without a hearing (see further p 371).

Summary judgment under RSC Ord 14

The purpose of Ord 14 is to provide early judgment in those cases in which the defendant (or defendant to counterclaim) has no hope of success and any defence raised will merely have the effect of delaying judgment. The rule enables the court to grant summary judgment at an interlocutory stage without the delay and expense of a full trial if it is shown that no trial is necessary. It is important to distinguish this summary procedure from a summary trial. In a trial the judge inquires into the merits of the defence and decides whether it has been proved. Under Ord 14 the hearing is usually before a district judge. The task of the district judge is to determine whether there *ought* to be a trial. To defeat the application the defendant does not have to show a good defence but only an arguable defence or some other reason why there ought to be a trial (RSC Ord 14, r 3). Of course if judgment goes against the defendant it disposes of the case and is therefore treated as a trial judgment for the purposes of an appeal (see below).

Although originally limited to certain debt actions, Ord 14 is now of a very wide application. It can be used in almost any writ action in the Queen's Bench or Chancery Division. It can be used to obtain any remedy. (For some remedies there is an overlap with other rules—RSC Ord 43 (account); RSC Ord 113 (possession) as to which see p 264.) In practice however most cases brought under the rule are still debt actions. In many other cases Ord 14 would be inappropriate since the defendant will often be able to put up a defence which is arguable even if it is unlikely to be successful. For example, in a road accident case the defendant will usually be able to allege negligence by the plaintiff or some other defence going to causation. However, summary judgment was allowed in *Dummer v Brown* [1953] 1 QB 710 where the person injured was the passenger on a coach and the coach driver had already pleaded guilty to a dangerous driving charge. A similar decision was reached in *Bhowmick v Ward* (1981) CA (Civil Division) Transcript No 25 of 1982. In that case the Court of Appeal upheld an order for summary judgment in favour of a plaintiff whose vehicle had been forced to an emergency stop but who had then been hit from behind by the defendant's vehicle.

An application for summary judgment solely to obtain a final order for the costs of an action may be appropriate where eg the Plaintiff commenced the action seeking injunctions in respect of which the Defendant has given undertakings but refuses to pay the costs of action: see *Danesfield Securities Ltd v Sonuga* (1996) *The Times*, 31 December (and see p 219, above).

The only cases expressly excluded from Ord 14 are:

(1) claims or counterclaims which include claims for libel, slander, malicious prosecution or false imprisonment. In these cases the defendant may have a right to trial by jury, and therefore a right to trial. By way of exception to this exception, summary judgment is now available in fraud cases;

(2) where RSC Ord 86 applies (this is a separate rule for summary judgment for certain specific performance cases in the Chancery Division: see below);

(3) Admiralty actions *in rem*; and

(4) claims or counterclaims against the Crown (RSC Ord 77, r 7).

When to apply (RSC Ord 14, rr 1, 5)

The plaintiff can apply for summary judgment on his claim (or part of it) after the statement of claim has been served, and the defendant has given notice of intention to defend. These so-called prerequisites to Ord 14 usually involve no difficulty for a plaintiff. The statement of claim will usually be indorsed on the writ. If the defendant does not give notice of intention to defend the plaintiff can seek judgment in default. Difficulty arises only in claims for equitable remedies, such as injunctions, which are not obtainable under RSC Ord 13. Where he cannot use RSC Ord 13 or Ord 14 the plaintiff must instead wait a few more weeks to obtain judgment in default of defence. This gap in the rules is supplied in some cases by RSC Ord 86 (see p 230). The defendant can apply for summary judgment on a counterclaim (or part of it) after he has served his defence and counterclaim.

How to apply (RSC Ord 14, r 2)

The application is to a district judge in all cases except on claims for an injunction, when it is made to a judge. A summons must be issued, supported by an affidavit verifying the facts on which the claim is based and stating that in the deponent's belief there is no defence (except as to the amount of damages if that is so). The applicant must serve the summons (together with copies of the affidavit and any exhibits referred to therein) on the respondent not less than ten clear days before the return day. The forms of summons and affidavit are illustrated in figs 13 and 14.

The rule itself does not specify a time for service of the respondent's affidavit. However a notice included in the summons warns the respondent that, if he wishes to show cause against the application he should serve on the applicant a copy of any affidavit he intends to use at least three days before the return day. The only penalty imposed for failing to serve the affidavit in time is a penalty as to the costs of any adjournment caused. Respondents often produce their affidavit at the hearing although this practice 'should be avoided' (*White Book* 14/3–4/5). The district judge may order a respondent to produce any document or even, in an exceptional case, order attendance so as to be examined on oath (RSC Ord 14, r 4; *Sullivan v Henderson* [1973] 1 WLR 333).

Orders made in Ord 14 proceedings

At the hearing of an application by a plaintiff any one of the following orders may be made (similar orders may be made on an application by a counterclaiming defendant):

Judgment for the plaintiff (RSC Ord 14, r 3)
Unless the defendant satisfies the district judge that there is an issue or question which ought to be tried or that there ought for some other reason to be a trial of the plaintiff's claim, the district judge may give such judgment on the claim as may be just. (Although the rule says 'may', once it is clear that there is no triable issue or other reason for trial the district judge ordinarily 'will' give judgment for the plaintiff: *European Asian Bank AG v Punjab & Sind Bank (No 2)* [1983] 1 WLR 642.) If the judgment relates to only part of the claim the plaintiff may proceed with the action as to the rest (RSC Ord 14, r 8). On a claim for unliquidated damages the district judge will not normally assess the damages immediately. Unless the amount of damages is clear-cut (eg reasonable repair bills the plaintiff has paid) interlocutory judgment for damages to be assessed will be given; the plaintiff must later apply for the assessment under RSC Ord 37 (*Yarnold v Radio Wyvern plc*, CA (Civil Division) Transcript No 194 of 1985; see further p 213).

Raising a *bona fide* counterclaim on matters unconnected with the plaintiff's claim does not entitle the defendant to a stay of execution pending trial of that counterclaim (*Drake and Fletcher Ltd v Batchelor* (1986) 85 LSG 1232, see further *White Book* 14/3–4/13). Where the counterclaim *is* related to the plaintiff's claim (ie is an equitable set-off) see p 227 below.

If the defendant does not attend the hearing and has not acknowledged service of the summons the plaintiff will be required to file an affidavit of service (*White Book* 14/2/3). Any judgment given against a defendant who does not attend the hearing may be set aside or varied on just terms (RSC Ord 14, r 11).

[*continued on p 227*]

Fig 13: Summons under Ord 14 for whole claim

<table>
<tr>
<td>Summons under Order 14 for Whole Claim</td>
<td colspan="2">**IN THE HIGH COURT OF JUSTICE**
Queen's Bench Division</td>
<td>19 . — . —No.</td>
</tr>
<tr>
<td>(1) Master or District Judge.</td>
<td colspan="2">(^{1})</td>
<td>**District Registry**</td>
</tr>
</table>

Between

Plaintiff

AND

Defendant

(2) Insert either ''...the District Judge at the office of the District Registry situate at...'' or ''...the Master in Chambers in Room No. , Central Office Royal Courts of Justice, Strand London WC2A 2LL.''

Let all Parties concerned attend(^{2})

on   day, the   day of   19   , at   o'clock in the   noon on the hearing of an application on the

(3) The Defendant (or if against one or some of several Defendants insert names).

part of the Plaintiff   for final judgment in this action against(^{3})

(4) Or as the case may be, setting out the nature of the claim.

for the (^{4})amount claimed in the statement of claim with interest, if any, and costs.

Take Notice that a party intending to oppose this application or to apply for a stay of execution should send to the opposite party or his solicitor, to reach him in sufficient time to enable him to reply and in any event not less than three days before the date above-mentioned, a copy of any affidavit intended to be used.

Dated the   day of   19   .

To M

Solicitor   or Agent   for the Defendant

This Summons was taken out by

of

Solicitor   for the Plaintiff
[Agent   for

of   ]

Solicitor   for the Plaintiff

Form High Court S3

Reproduced by kind permission of the Solicitors' Law Stationery Society Ltd.

Fig 14: Affidavit on application under Ord 14

Filed on behalf of
Name of Deponent
No. of Affidavit
Date Affidavit sworn

Affidavit on Application under Order 14. Rule 2, by or on behalf of Plaintiff.

IN THE HIGH COURT OF JUSTICE   19   .—   .—No.

Queen's Bench Division

District Registry

Between

Plaintiff

AND

Defendant

I,

of

(1)   MAKE OATH AND SAY AS FOLLOWS:—

(1) "the above-named Plaintiff", or as may be.

1. The Defendant

(2) Is or are.
(3) Was or were.
(4) Me or the above-named Plaintiff or as the case may be.

(2)   , and (3)   at the commencement of this action, justly and truly indebted to (4)

in the sum of £   for the

The particulars of the said claim appear by the statement of claim in this action.

2. It is within my own knowledge that the said debt was incurred and is still due and owing as aforesaid.

or

(5) State source of information.

[2. I am informed by (5)

(6) State grounds of belief.

and/or I verily believe (6)

that the said debt was incurred and is still due and owing as aforesaid.]

3. I verily believe that there is no defence to this action [except as to the amount of the damages claimed].

(7) Delete if sworn by Plaintiff.

[4. I am duly authorised by the Plaintiff to make this affidavit.(7)]

Sworn at

the   day of   19   ,

Before me,

A Commissioner for Oaths

This affidavit is filed on behalf of the Plaintiff

Form High Court B34 (DR)
Reproduced by kind permission of the Solicitors' Law Stationery Society Ltd.

Table 2: Orders made in RSC Ord 14 proceedings

(Plaintiff's preference 1 to 4; defendant's preference 4 to 1)

Type of order	Circumstances in which made	Further proceedings	Costs of application
1 Judgment for plaintiff	Where no arguable defence or other reason why there ought to be a trial	If debt: final judgment, enforcement If damages: usually interlocutory judgment (RSC Ord 37)	Judgment with costs
2 Conditional leave to defend	Where only arguable defence is a sham or is raised *mala fide* (usual condition, payment into court)	District judge *must* treat hearing as if hearing of summons for directions District judge *may*: (1) transfer case to county court (if appropriate), (2) order trial by district judge or master (if parties consent)	Usually 'costs in cause'
3 Unconditional leave to defend	Where an arguable defence or other reason why there ought to be a trial (includes set-offs up to their value) (In some cases, not cheque actions, the court may instead give judgment with a stay of execution pending trial of counterclaim: see p 223)		
4 Dismissal of summons	Where: (1) Ord 14 application irregular, or (2) plaintiff knew defendant was entitled to unconditional leave to defend	Unless already served, defence must be served within next fourteen days: in other respects case returns to ordinary timetable	Summons dismissed with 'costs in any event' or 'costs forthwith' (see p 570)

Unconditional leave to defend (RSC Ord 14, r 4)

Unconditional leave to defend must be given whenever the defendant raises a triable defence (eg a substantial question of fact, a technical defence such as the Limitation Act or a set-off), or satisfies the district judge that for some other reason there ought to be a trial. For examples of 'other reasons' see *White Book* 14/3/9.

If the triable defence applies to only part of the plaintiff's claim the plaintiff may be given judgment for the balance. For example, if the defendant seeks to set off a sum which is or which is likely to be less than the plaintiff's claim he will only be given leave to defend *pro tanto* and the plaintiff will be given judgment for the excess. If the set-off exceeds the plaintiff's claim the defendant is, of course, entitled to full leave to defend. 'It therefore behoves a defendant to particularise the amount of his set off' (*White Book* 14/3–4/13).

Special position of equitable set-offs. Where the defendant raises an equitable set-off (see p 161) the court will usually give unconditional leave to defend up to the value of that set-off (see above and see *Morgan v Martin Johnson* [1949] 1 KB 107, noted on p 162 above). In times past, judgment was sometimes given with a stay of execution, possibly conditional upon the defendant making a payment into court. However, such orders are not now commonly made (see *United Overseas Ltd v Peter Robinson Ltd* (1991) *White Book* 14/3–4/13).

Special position of cheque actions. Traditionally the courts treat cheques, bills of exchange and promissory notes as cash. If a defendant had paid cash it would be too late for him now to raise a set-off or counterclaim to avoid payment. Accordingly, if he pays by cheque, etc, which is dishonoured the court will not permit any set-off or counterclaim either to prevent summary judgment (*Fielding & Platt v Selim Najjar* [1969] 1 WLR 357) or to stay execution of it (*Cebora v SIP (Industrial Products)* [1976] 1 Lloyd's Rep 271) unless there are exceptional circumstances. Examples of exceptional circumstances include:

(1) a *bona fide* denial of the validity of the cheque, eg denying the signature, or alleging that the amount of the cheque had been improperly altered;
(2) a *bona fide* allegation that the cheque was obtained by fraud;
(3) a *bona fide* allegation that the cheque relates to an illegal transaction, eg a gambling debt; and
(4) a *bona fide* allegation of a total failure of consideration, or a quantified partial failure of consideration.

The special rules for cheque actions have now been applied to the modern banking mechanism for handling what could otherwise be cash sales; the direct debit system (*Esso Petroleum Co Ltd v Milton* (1997) *The Times*, 13 February).

Conditional leave to defend (RSC Ord 14, r 4)

Leave to defend subject to conditions (eg security for costs or the payment into court of the whole or part of the sum claimed) may be given only where the district judge doubts the *bona fides* of the defendant (*Fieldrank v Stein* [1961] 1 WLR 1287) or is almost certain that the arguable defence raised is a sham or is bound to fail (*Ionian Bank v Couvreur* [1969] 1 WLR 781).

> *Example*
> P and D were dealers in cars. D sold P a second-hand Rolls-Royce which he said had been imported from America. In fact, the car was later repossessed by a UK finance company. P sued D for £23,250 and sought summary judgment. D's defence was that when selling the car to P, he had been acting as the agent of a foreign principal, but there was documentary evidence which contradicted this. D's defence was regarded as just sufficient to raise a triable issue but was shadowy and doubts arose as to its *bona fides*. D was given leave to defend conditional upon paying £3,000 into court within twenty-eight days: *MV Yorke Motors v Edwards* [1982] 1 WLR 444.

Moneys paid into court as a condition of the grant of leave to defend do not form part of the defendant's general assets should he later go bankrupt; the plaintiff is entitled to the money if he can prove his claim: *Re Ford* [1900] 2 QB 211. The court should not impose a financial condition which it is impossible for the defendant to fulfil. But this does not mean that, eg a person on supplementary benefit and receiving legal aid with a nil contribution, can never be ordered to pay substantial sums into court (see the facts of *MV Yorke Motors*, noted above and see further p 220).

In some cases, especially where very large sums of money are in question, the court may give the defendant the option of either paying money into court or providing a satisfactory bank guarantee for that sum (*Rosengrens Ltd v Safe Deposit Ltd* [1984] 1 WLR 1334).

Orders granting conditional leave to defend are not commonly made. They are appropriate only for those cases on the borderline between the two orders previously described. Where conditional leave to defend is appropriate the court has power to order that the defendant should make an interim payment to the plaintiff under RSC Ord 29, r 10 (*British & Commonwealth Holdings v Quadrex Holdings* [1989] 3 WLR 723).

Dismissal of the summons (RSC Ord 14, r 7)
The district judge may dismiss the summons if the case is not within Ord 14 (eg a libel action) or if it appears that the plaintiff knew that the defendant would be entitled to unconditional leave to defend. A dismissal differs from unconditional leave to defend in two respects:
  (1) the application of RSC Ord 14, r 6 (see below);
  (2) costs: where leave to defend is given the usual order for costs is 'costs in the cause' (ie they will be paid at the end of the action by the eventual loser); on a dismissal the district judge will usually
[*continued on p 230*]

Fig 15: Order under Ord 14 (conditional leave to defend)

IN THE HIGH COURT OF JUSTICE   1997-C-444
QUEEN'S BENCH DIVISION
EAST YORKSHIRE DISTRICT REGISTRY

District Judge Alexander in Chambers

Between

Jennifer Jane Marsh   Plaintiff

AND

Andrew Mark Seager   Defendant

Upon hearing the solicitor for the Plaintiff and counsel for the Defendant and upon reading the affidavits of the Plaintiff sworn 5th June 1997 and of the Defendant sworn 26th June 1997.

It is ordered that

Unless the Defendant pays £14,000 into court on or before 17th July 1997 the Plaintiff may enter final judgment against him for the amount claimed in the Statement of Claim plus interest and costs.

And it is further ordered that

If the said sum is so paid the Defendant may defend the action
and that the action be transferred to the Pocklington County Court
and that the Defendant shall have 14 days from the date of transfer in
which to file and serve his Defence.

Dated this 7th day of July 1997

order the plaintiff to pay costs and may, if the plaintiff is not legally aided, order him to pay the costs forthwith.

Directions for trial (RSC Ord 14, r 6)

If the district judge gives leave to defend (whether conditional or unconditional) or gives judgment with a stay of execution pending trial of a counterclaim he *must* then give directions as to the future conduct of the action as if the hearing were the hearing of a summons for directions. If appropriate he will order the transfer of the action to a county court (p 375). In London, the master may, if the parties consent, order that the action shall be tried by a master. This will mean the case will come up for trial faster than it otherwise would. Further directions are usually given simplifying the pleadings stage.

When giving directions the court will order that a statement of value of the action be lodged, and a copy served on all other parties, within a specified time (RSC Ord 14, r 6(3)). If the statement is not so lodged the action will be transferred to a county court.

Rule 6 does not apply if the master/district judge dismisses the summons. Herein lies the major difference between unconditional leave to defend and a dismissal. The former order is not a total loss to the plaintiff. At least he has got his case accelerated to the directions stage and this may save him several months on the time for trial. However, the plaintiff must not use Ord 14 simply to obtain this effect. If he does so when he knows the defendant would be entitled to unconditional leave the master/district judge will dismiss the summons with costs: the case then returns to the stage it had previously reached. Indeed the time of trial may even be delayed: the service of an Ord 14 summons extends the time for service of a defence (see p 233).

Appeals

On every order made under Ord 14 (whether in the Queen's Bench Division or Chancery Division) an appeal lies as of right to the judge in chambers. However, leave is required on an appeal from the judge in chambers to the Court of Appeal. (*NB* all former restrictions and exceptions which used to affect Ord 14 appeals have now been swept away.)

RSC Ord 86

This Order governs applications for summary judgment in certain claims and counterclaims for specific performance and related remedies. No overlap with RSC Ord 14 exists since if Ord 86 applies, Ord 14 does not. The only major differences between Ord 14 and Ord 86 are that under the latter order the plaintiff can apply for summary judgment without first serving his statement of claim and without waiting for the defendant to give notice of intention to defend. This enables a plaintiff to obtain a decree of specific performance even against a defendant in default of acknowledgment.

Unlike Ord 14 which is the general order for summary judgment, Ord 86 is very limited. It is limited to claims and counterclaims (*a*) in the Chancery Division (*b*) for specific performance (with or without an alternative claim for damages), or for rescission or for forfeiture or return of any deposit, (*c*) of agreements for the sale, purchase or exchange of any property (real or personal) or for the grant or assignment of a lease. These limitations are cumulative.

The order does not apply to cases which:

(1) are in the Queen's Bench Division; or
(2) do not concern the transfer of property (eg a building contract case); or
(3) concern the exchange of property in return for services (see *Doyle v East* [1972] 1 WLR 1080).

In each of these cases a decree of specific performance could be sought under Ord 14.

As with Ord 14, Ord 86 applies only to writ actions and cannot be used against the Crown. Basically the procedure under Ord 86 follows the Ord 14 procedure (summons, affidavit, hearing before district judge, orders made, directions for trial, appeals).

Disposal of case on point of law under RSC Ord 14A

RSC Ord 14A is best described as a hybrid between RSC Ord 14 (summary judgment, see above), RSC Ord 18, r 19 (striking out pleadings) and RSC Ord 33, r 3 (trials of preliminary points of law). However, it is convenient here to make comparisons and contrasts only with RSC Ord 14 (as to the others, see pp 190 and 456).

On an application under RSC Ord 14A, the district judge has power to determine any question of law or the construction of any document provided that:

(*a*) such question is suitable for determination without a full trial of the action, and
(*b*) such determination will finally determine (subject only to any possible appeal) the entire cause or matter or any claim or issue therein, and
(*c*) all parties have had an opportunity of being heard on the question or have consented to a ruling being given.

RSC Ord 14A is, therefore, narrower than RSC Ord 14 in two respects. First, it is restricted to questions of law or the construction of a document: defended summary judgment applications often turn upon questions of fact, eg the *bona fides* of the defendant's defence. Secondly, under RSC Ord 14A, the question for decision by the court must be one which will finally determine the action, in whole or in part or will finally determine an issue in the action which is the dominant feature of that action (as to the latter, see *Korso Finance Establishment Anstalt v John Wedge* (1994) *White Book* 14A/1–2/4). Summary judgment applications finally determine an action only if and to the extent that summary judgment is given: to the extent that leave to defend is given, the action is still proceeding to trial.

Now consider the respects in which RSC Ord 14A is wider than RSC Ord 14. It is a means of obtaining summary trial. If suitable questions arise as to some point of law or construction, the court does not merely consider whether those questions are triable; it actually decides them. One must beware of overstating the significance of this difference. Summary trial is not suitable for all questions of law or construction. Very often the questions will depend upon the underlying factual basis of the case from which other questions may arise. Even if that is not so, the parties will sometimes require the full trial process including especially discovery and directions as to expert evidence in order to argue the points of law or construction properly. Thus, in practice, RSC Ord 14A will be most commonly used to obtain rulings upon questions which are plain and obvious, points which perhaps could just as easily be determined under RSC Ord 14.

A much more significant difference between RSC Ord 14 and Ord 14A is that the latter can be used by defendants to obtain a summary dismissal of the plaintiff's claim. See, for example, *Associated Dairies Ltd v Baines* [1997] 2 WLR 364 which concerned a contractual dispute between a wholesale milk supplier and a milk roundsman. The defendant applied by summons under RSC Ord 14A for a declaration that part of the contract was void for non-registration under the Restrictive Trade Practices Act 1976. The dispute turned upon the meaning and application of s 9(3) of the Act. The defendant lost at first instance, won in the Court of Appeal but lost in the House of Lords.

There are also procedural differences between RSC Ord 14 and Ord 14A. For example, although both are usually sought by summons to a district judge, a ruling under RSC Ord 14A can also be made on an application made orally in the course of another application, or indeed by the court of its own motion during the course of that application (eg an application for an interlocutory injunction, or for further and better particulars).

Because in all RSC Ord 14A cases the questions raised are actually to be tried, ie finally determined (subject to rights of appeal) the court will always be most anxious to ensure that the respondent has had full opportunity to be heard on the question. Therefore, unless the application is to some extent consensual (as in *GS Fashions Ltd v B & Q plc* [1995] 1 WLR 1088 where the parties prepared an agreed statement of facts) the court is less likely to accept informal evidence of service of an RSC Ord 14A summons than it is in the case of other summonses (as to which, see p 138). An applicant under RSC Ord 14A should consider the desirability of attending the hearing armed with an affidavit of service of the summons so as to diminish the likelihood of an adjournment should the respondent fail to appear (see *White Book* 14A/1–2/6).

Pleadings, judgment in default of pleadings

Statement of claim

Unless it is indorsed on the writ the plaintiff must serve a statement of claim either with the writ or within fourteen days of the defendant's giving notice of intention to defend (RSC Ord 18, r 1). If the plaintiff fails to serve a statement of claim in time the defendant can apply to the district judge for the dismissal of the action for want of prosecution (RSC Ord 19, r 1; see p 364).

Defence

RSC Ord 18, r 2, allows the defendant a minimum of twenty-eight days after service of the writ in which to serve his defence or a longer time if the statement of claim is served late or if an application under Ord 14 intervenes or if the action is a derivative action (as to which see p 106). The full text of the rule is as follows:

(1) Subject to paragraph (2) a defendant who gives notice of intention to defend an action must, unless the Court gives leave to the contrary, serve a defence on every other party to the action who may be affected thereby before the expiration of 14 days after the time limited for acknowledging service of the writ or after the statement of claim is served on him, whichever is the later.

(2) If a summons under Order 14, rule 1, or under Order 86, rule 1, is served on a defendant before he serves his defence, paragraph (1) shall not have effect in relation to him unless by the order made on the summons he is given leave to defend the action and, in that case, shall have effect as if it required him to serve his defence within 14 days after the making of the order or within such other period as may be specified therein.

(3) Where an application is made by a defendant under Order 12, rule 8(1), paragraph (1) of this rule shall not have effect in relation to the defendant unless the application is dismissed or no order is made on the application and, in that case, paragraph (1) shall have effect as if it required him to serve his defence within 14 days after the final determination of the application or within such other period as may be specified by the Court.

(4) Paragraph (1) is subject to the provisions of Order 15, rule 12A(7) (derivative actions).

Note that the defendant gains no advantage from lodging an acknowledgment late (RSC Ord 12, r 6) and suffers no disadvantage by lodging it promptly. RSC Ord 18, r 2, does not *forbid* the defendant serving his defence if an Ord 14 (or Ord 86) summons is served on him. However if he does serve it, it would then be reasonable to agree with the plaintiff to defer the next step in procedure (discovery) until the summary judgment application has been dealt with. In practice, instead of serving the defence, the defendant often exhibits it to the affidavit seeking leave to defend as this may add weight to the defendant's case and help establish that the defence is *bona fide*.

Under RSC Ord 18, r 2(1) the defendant is required to serve a defence not only on the plaintiff but also on 'every other party to the action who may be affected thereby'. So, for example, defendants who serve separate defences on the plaintiff must also serve copies of those defences on each other.

If the defendant fails to serve a defence on the plaintiff in time the plaintiff may seek judgment in default under RSC Ord 19. But note that, as with RSC Ord 13, the defendant can cure his default without leave at any time before judgment is entered. The procedure for judgments in default of defence very much follows the RSC Ord 13 format. For the four common-law remedies, debt, damages, recovery of goods, recovery of land, RSC Ord 19 includes rules similar to RSC Ord 13 providing for judgment, with or without leave, final or interlocutory, and where there is multiplicity of claims, including interest, or multiplicity of defendants. (There are differences: the RSC Ord 13 rules requiring leave where the defendant is a foreign state and in certain cases affected by CJJA 1982 (see p 138) do not apply to judgments in default of defence.) The court copy of the form of judgment must be indorsed as follows:

> I/We, solicitors for the plaintiff certify that the time for service by the defendant prescribed by the rules of court or extended by order of the court or the consent of the parties has expired and that the defendant is in default in serving his defence within such time.
>
> Dated ....
>   Solicitors for the plaintiff

(*Practice Direction* [1979] 1 WLR 851. This indorsement is printed on the backsheet of the form illustrated on p 217 (fig 12).)

For cases in which an equitable remedy is claimed RSC Ord 19, r 7, states:

> (1) Where the plaintiff makes against a defendant or defendants a claim of a description not mentioned in rules 2 to 5, then, if the defendant or all the defendants (where there is more than one) fails or fail to serve a defence on the plaintiff, the plaintiff may, after the expiration of the period fixed by or under these rules for service of the defence, apply to the Court for judgment, and on the hearing of the application the Court shall give such judgment as the plaintiff appears entitled to on his statement of claim.
> (2) Where the plaintiff makes such a claim as is mentioned in paragraph (1) against more than one defendant, then, if one of the defendants makes default as mentioned in that paragraph, the plaintiff may—
>   (a) if his claim against the defendant in default is severable from his claim against the other defendants, apply under that paragraph for judgment

[*continued on p 236*]

Table 3: Default judgments

Nature of claim	Default of acknowledgment and/or notice of intention to defend (RSC Ord 13)	Default of defence (RSC Ord 19)
1 Common-law remedies *Debt*: final judgment *Damages*: interlocutory judgment *Recovery of goods*: interlocutory judgment *Recovery of land*: final judgment As to claims for interest see p 215	Obtainable without leave unless: (1) against the Crown, (2) consumer credit agreement and RSC Ord 83, r 3, applies, (3) husband and wife tort action, (4) recovery of land, no certificate or affidavit (see p 219); or (5) in certain cases affected by the CJJA 1982 (see p 138). In these cases leave must be sought by summons	Obtainable without leave except in cases (1) to (4) listed in column 2. In these four cases leave must be sought by summons
2 Where claim includes an equitable remedy	Not obtainable	Obtainable with leave (summons or motion)
3 Where provisional damages claimed	Not obtainable	Not obtainable
4 Where defendant is a minor or mental patient	Not obtainable unless and until a guardian *ad litem* is appointed	No special provision: see entries above

against that defendant, and proceed with the action against the other defendants; or

(b) set down the action on motion for judgment against the defendant in default at the time when the action is set down for trial, or is set down on motion for judgment, against the other defendants.

(3) An application under paragraph (1) must be by summons or motion.

(If the defendant is both in default of notice of intention to defend and in default of defence, the plaintiff must normally file an affidavit of service of the writ: RSC Ord 13, r 6.) In the Queen's Bench Division an application under r 7 is usually made by summons to the district judge or by summons to the judge if an injunction is claimed. In theory the rule also applies to a claim for a declaration, but in practice the court rarely gives declaratory relief except after a full argument (*Wallersteiner v Moir* [1974] 1 WLR 991): exceptionally the court will do so where the declaration affects only the defendants, or persons claiming through them, the case is clear and justice cannot be done if the declaration is omitted (*Patten v Burke Publishing Co Ltd* [1991] 2 All ER 821).

There is one special case to note. If the writ is indorsed with claims for both legal and equitable remedies the plaintiff can enter judgment in default *without leave* if he abandons his claims for the equitable remedies.

> *Example*
>
> In *Morley v Rightside Properties* (1973) 117 SJ 876, D agreed to sell land to P. P sued for specific performance and damages. D entered an appearance (the old equivalent of an acknowledgment of service) but was in default of defence. On learning that D had already sold the land to someone else P signed judgment without leave in the following form 'No defence having been served and the plaintiffs abandoning their claim to the other relief sought in the statement of claim it is ... adjudged that the defendant do pay the plaintiff damages to be assessed.' The Court of Appeal held the judgment regular and would only allow it to be set aside, on the merits, if D paid into court £23,000 within seven days.

Could this authority be used to allow a plaintiff, in similar circumstances, to obtain judgment under RSC Ord 13? The learned editors of the *White Book* think so (see 13/6/1).

There are no special rules concerning judgments in default of defence against minors or mental patients. Before the time of default of defence falls to be considered an application for the appointment of a guardian *ad litem* has to be made. If the person appointed guardian *ad litem* fails to serve a defence the plaintiff may enter judgment in default in the same way as he would have done had the defendant not been a minor or mental patient: ie usually without leave.

Judgment in default of defence is not available in a case where the plaintiff claims provisional damages (RSC Ord 37, r 8).

Defence to counterclaim

By RSC Ord 18, r 3, if the plaintiff is served with a counterclaim he does not wish to admit, he must serve a defence to counterclaim within the next fourteen days. By RSC Ord 19, r 8, if the plaintiff fails to serve a defence to counterclaim in time the defendant can enter judgment in default as if the counterclaim were an independent action.

Setting aside judgments given in default of pleadings

As with judgments under RSC Ord 13, any judgment in default of defence, etc, can be set aside or varied on such terms as the court thinks fit (RSC Ord 19, r 9), or, in certain circumstances, by consent (see p 371).

Chapter 12

County Court: Commencement, Default, Summary and Early Judgment

Commencement (CCR Ord 3)

To start an action in the county court the solicitor for the plaintiff must prepare the following documents:

(1) Either a completed form of request for a summons *or* the completed form of summons itself. The forms of request and forms of summons are available free of charge from any county court office.

(2) The particulars of claim plus one copy for each defendant.

(3) The appropriate plaint fee.

(4) A stamped, addressed envelope if the proceedings are being issued through the post.

(5) If the plaintiff is legally aided, notices of the issue of the civil aid certificate for service with the summons on each defendant. (In such a case the solicitor must, of course, also file the certificate itself; see p 52.)

(6) If the plaintiff is under disability, the necessary document, ie the next friend's written undertaking to be responsible for costs or an office copy of the order of the Court of Protection authorising the next friend to conduct the proceedings.

On receipt of the appropriate documents duly completed the court will draw up the summons (unless the solicitor has already done so) and seal it with the court seal. Nowadays it is only litigants in person who tender a request rather than the summons itself. Solicitors prefer to draw up the summons: it takes no longer than would preparing a request. Any document which has to be prepared by the court (eg a summons or an order) can now be prepared by the plaintiff or plaintiff's solicitor (CCR Ord 50, r 4A) and to do so produces an advantage to the client: by reducing the workload for the county court staff the prepared document will be dealt with much earlier than would otherwise be possible.

Unless the solicitor has asked the court to return the summons so that the solicitor can effect service (by post in a personal injury case (CCR Ord 7, r 10A) otherwise personal service, see p 130) the solicitor will not see the sealed summons. A sealed summons is retained on the court file and a sealed summons is served on each defendant but the plaintiff, or plaintiff's solicitor is not given a copy. Instead a 'notice of issue of default summons' is given to the plaintiff's solicitor, or, if proceedings are being issued by post, will be sent to the solicitor in the envelope provided. This notice of issue was formerly called a plaint note. It has the same importance as the original writ has in a High Court action. Duplicates can be issued without leave (CCR Ord 50, r 10 and compare the High Court rule, p 195). A solicitor's letter requesting the issue of a duplicate and dealing with the matters set out in Form N435 is usually sufficient.

If postal service fails (as to postal service effected by the court see p 131) and the summons is returned to the court undelivered to the defendant a notice of non-service (see fig 19) will be sent to the plaintiff together with a notice informing the plaintiff that it is now possible to request bailiff service to be effected. As to the methods by which service may be effected by a bailiff see p 133. There is an additional fee payable for bailiff service. Should the bailiff be unable to effect service (at the address stated in the request for the summons or at any other address within the district of the court which he may ascertain) a further notice of non-service will be sent to the plaintiff. Before requesting bailiff service the plaintiff's solicitor should ask the client whether he has reliable up-to-date information as to the defendant's present whereabouts. If a new address can be supplied, an amended request for the summons should be filed, without leave, stating that new address (CCR Ord 7, r 17). The court will then amend the summons and post it to that new address.

Default action

This is the form of action applicable when suing for a money claim, whether liquidated or unliquidated. The only money claims which are not brought by default action are Admiralty actions and actions in which some remedy, in addition to money remedies, is sought (see generally p 255).

Pleadings in a default action are usually in very simple form. Many litigants in person—particularly tradesmen—would merely send a copy of the unpaid account and in practice this is accepted as particulars of claim. Particulars drawn up by a solicitor should be in the usual professional form except that it is not usually necessary to provide a backsheet for pleadings in the county court. If the particulars of claim can be conveniently stated in just a few lines they can be indorsed on the summons itself (see fig 16).

Two forms of summons, N1 (fixed amount) and N2 (unliquidated), and a notice of issue of default summons in Form N205A are illustrated in figs 16–18. When completed, Form N1, which is for use in debt cases,

[continued on p 247]

Fig 16: Default summons (fixed amount)

County Court Summons	Case Number *Always quote this*

In the

County Court

The court office is open from 10am to 4pm Monday to Friday

Telephone:

Seal

This summons is only valid if sealed by the court
If it is not sealed it should be reported to the court
Keep this summons. You may need to refer to it

(1)
Plaintiff's full name address

(2)
Address for sending documents and payments
(if not as above)
Ref/Tel no.

(3)
Defendant's full name
(eg Mr, Mrs or Miss where known)
and address
Company no.
(where known)

What the plaintiff claims from you

Brief description of type of claim

Particulars of the plaintiff's claim against you

Amount claimed	
Court fee	
Solicitor's costs	
Total amount	
Summons issued on	

What to do about this summons

You have 21 days from the date of the postmark to reply to this summons
(A limited company served at its registered office has 16 days to reply)
If this summons was delivered by hand, you have 14 days from the date it was delivered to reply

You can

- dispute the claim
- make a claim against the plaintiff
- admit the claim and costs in full and offer to pay
- admit only part of the claim
- pay the total amount shown above

You must read the information on the back of this form. It will tell you more about what to do.

Signed
Plaintiff or plaintiff's solicitor
(or see enclosed particulars of claim)

N1 Default summons (fixed amount) (Order 3, rule 3(2)(b)) (11.95)   Printed by Satellite Press Limited

Fig 16: contd

If you do nothing	▶	**Judgment may be entered against you without further notice. This will make it difficult for you to get credit.**
If you dispute the claim	▶	Complete the white defence form (N9B) and return it to the court office within the time allowed. The notes on the form explain what you should do. It is not enough to contact the plaintiff by telephone or letter.
If you want to make a claim against the plaintiff (counterclaim)	▶	Complete boxes 5 and 6 on the white defence form (N9B) and return the form to the court office. The notes at box 5 explain what you should do.
If you admit all of the claim and you are asking for time to pay	▶	Fill in the blue admission form (N9A). The notes on the form explain what you should do and where you should send the completed form. You must reply within the time allowed.
If you admit all of the claim and you wish to pay now	▶	**Take or send the money including any interest and costs to the person named at box (2) on the front of the summons.** If there is no address in box (2), send the money to the address in box (1). You should ensure the plaintiff receives the money within the period given for reply. Read 'How to Pay' below.
If you admit only part of the claim	▶	Fill in the white defence form (N9B) saying how much you admit, and why you dispute the balance. Then **either:** Pay the amount admitted as explained in the box above; **or** If you need time to pay fill in the blue admission form (N9A) and return the form to the court office within the time allowed.

Costs

In addition to the solicitor's costs for issuing the summons, a plaintiff's solicitor is entitled to add further costs if the court enters judgment against you.

Interest on judgments

If judgment is entered against you and is for £5,000 or more the plaintiff may be entitled to interest on the total amount.

Registration of judgments

If the summons results in a judgment against you, your name and address may be entered in the Register of County Court Judgments. **This will make it difficult for you to get credit.** A leaflet giving further information can be obtained from the court.

Further advice

Court staff cannot give you advice on points of law, but you can get help to complete the reply forms and information about court procedures at **any** county court office or Citizens Advice Bureau. The address and telephone number of your local court is listed under 'Courts' in the phone book. When corresponding with the court, please address forms or letters to the Chief Clerk. Always quote the whole of the case number which appears at the top right corner on the front of this form; the court is unable to trace your case without it.

How to Pay

- **PAYMENT(S) MUST BE MADE to the person named at the address for payment quoting their reference and the court case number.**

- **DO NOT bring or send payments to the court. THEY WILL NOT BE ACCEPTED.**

- You should allow **at least** 4 days for your payments to reach the plaintiff or his representative.

- Make sure that you keep records and can account for all payments made. Proof may be required if there is any disagreement. It is not safe to send cash unless you use registered post.

- A leaflet giving further advice about payment can be obtained from the court.

- If you need more information you should contact the plaintiff or his representative.

Certificate of service
To be completed on the court copy only

Served on

By posting on

Officer

Not served on (reasons)

N1 Default summons (fixed amount) (Order 3, rule 3(2b)) (11/95)

Printed by Satellite Press Limited

Fig 17: Default summons (amount not fixed)

County Court Summons

Case Number *Always quote this*

In the

County Court

The court office is open from 10am to 4pm Monday to Friday

(1) Plaintiff's full name address

(2) Address for sending documents and payments *(if not as above)* **Ref/Tel no.**

Telephone:

Seal

This summons is only valid if sealed by the court
If it is not sealed it should be reported to the court

Keep this summons. You may need to refer to it

(3) Defendant's full name *(eg Mr, Mrs or Miss where known)* **and address Company no.** *(where known)*

What the plaintiff claims from you

Brief description of type of claim

Particulars of the plaintiff's claim against you

Amount claimed see particulars

Court fee

Solicitor's costs

Total amount

Summons issued on

What to do about this summons

You have 21 days from the date of the postmark to reply to this summons
(A limited company served at its registered office has 16 days to reply)
If this summons was delivered by hand, you have 14 days from the date it was delivered to reply

You can

- dispute the claim

- make a claim against the plaintiff

- admit the claim and costs in full and offer to pay

- admit only part of the claim

- pay the total amount shown above

You must read the information on the back of this form. It will tell you more about what to do.

My claim is worth £5,000 or less ☐ over £5,000 ☐

Total claim over £3,000 and/or damages for personal injury claims over £1,000

I would like my case decided by trial ☐ arbitration ☐

Signed
Plaintiff or plaintiff's solicitor
(or see enclosed particulars of claim)

N2 Default summons (amount not fixed) (Order 3, rule 3(2)(b)) (11.95)   *Printed by Satellite Press Limited*

Fig 17: contd

Please read this page: it will help you deal with the summons

If you dispute all or part of the claim

You may be entitled to help with your legal costs. Ask about the legal aid scheme at any county court office. Citizens Advice Bureau, legal advice centre or firm of solicitors displaying the legal aid sign.

- Say how much you dispute on the enclosed form for defending the claim and return it to the court office within the time allowed. It is not enough to contact the plaintiff by letter or telephone. The court will arrange a hearing and/or will tell you what to do next.

- If you dispute only part of the claim, you should also fill in the part of the form for admitting the claim and either pay the amount admitted to the court or make an offer of payment.

- If the court named on the summons is not your local county court, and/or the court for the area where the reason for the claim arose, you may write to the court named asking for the case to be transferred to the county court of your choice. You must explain your reasons for wanting the transfer. However, if the case is transferred and you later lose the case, you may have to pay more in costs.

How the claim will be dealt with if defended

If the total the plaintiff is claiming is £3,000 or less and/or the claim for damages for personal injury is worth £1,000 or less, it will be dealt with by arbitration (small claims procedure) unless the court decides the case is too difficult to be dealt with in this informal way. Costs and the grounds for setting aside an arbitration award are strictly limited. If the claim is not dealt with by arbitration, costs, including the costs of help from a legal representative, may be allowed.

If the total the plaintiff is claiming is more than £3,000 and/or he or she is claiming more than £1,000 for damages for personal injury, it can still be dealt with by arbitration if you or the plaintiff ask for it and the court approves. If your claim is dealt with by arbitration in these circumstances, costs may be allowed.

If you want to make a claim against the plaintiff

This is called a counterclaim.
Fill in the part of the enclosed form headed 'Counterclaim'. If your claim is for more than the plaintiff's claim you may have to pay a fee - the court will let you know. Unless the plaintiff admits your counterclaim there will usually be a hearing. The court will tell you what to do next.

If you admit owing all the claim

- If the claim is for more than £3,000 and/or includes a claim for damages for personal injury for more than £1,000, you may make a payment into court to compensate the plaintiff (see **Payments into Court** box). The figure of £3,000 includes interest claimed under contract but **excludes** costs and interest claimed under section 69 of the County Courts Act1984. Send a notice or letter with your payment, saying that it is in satisfaction of the claim. If the plaintiff accepts the amount paid, he is also entitled to payment of his costs.

- **If you need time to pay,** complete the enclosed form of admission and give details of how you propose to pay the plaintiff. You must reply within the time allowed. If your offer is accepted, the court will send an order telling you how to pay. If it is not accepted, the court will fix a rate of payment based on the details given in your form of admission and the plaintiff's comments. Judgment will be entered and you will be sent an order telling you how and when to pay.

- **If the plaintiff does not accept the amount paid or offered,** the court will fix a hearing to decide how much you must pay to compensate the plaintiff. The court will tell you when the hearing, which you should attend, will take place.

N2 Default summons (amount not fixed) (Order 3, rule 3(2)(b))

If you do nothing

Judgment may be entered against you. This will make it difficult for you to get credit.

General information

Court staff cannot give you advice on points of law, but you can get help to complete the reply forms and information about court procedures at any county court office or Citizens Advice Bureau. The address and telephone number of your local court is listed under 'Courts' in the phone book. When corresponding with the court, please address forms or letters to the Chief Clerk. Always quote the whole of the case number which appears at the top right corner on the front of this form; the court is unable to trace your case without it.

Costs

In addition to the solicitor's costs for issuing the summons, you may have more costs to pay if the court enters judgment against you.

Registration of judgments

If the summons results in a judgment against you, your name and address may be entered in the Register of County Court Judgments. **This will make it difficult for you to get credit.** A leaflet giving further information can be obtained from the court.

Interest on judgments

If judgment is entered against you and is for £5,000 or more the plaintiff may be entitled to interest on the full amount.

Payments into Court

You can pay the court by calling at the court office which is open 10am to 4pm Monday to Friday

You may only pay by:

- cash
- banker's or giro draft
- cheque supported by a cheque card
- cheque (unsupported cheques may be accepted, subject to clearance, if the Chief Clerk agrees)

Cheques and drafts must be made payable to HM Paymaster General and crossed.
Please bring this form with you.

By post

You may only pay by:

- postal order
- banker's or giro draft
- cheque (unsupported cheques may be accepted, subject to clearance, if the Chief Clerk agrees)

The payment must be made out to HM Paymaster General and crossed.
This method of payment is at your own risk.

And you must:

- pay the postage
- enclose this form
- enclose a self addressed envelope so that the court can return this form with a receipt

The court **cannot** accept stamps or payments by bank and giro credit transfers.

Note: You should carefully check any future forms from the court to see if payments should be made directly to the plaintiff

---

To be completed on the court copy only
Served on
By posting on
Officer
Not served on (reasons)

Fig 18: Notice of issue of default summons (plaint note)

Notice of Issue of Default Summons – fixed amount

N205A 239

To the plaintiff ('s solicitor)

In the **KINGSTON UPON HULL**

County Court

The court office at
KINGSTON UPON HULL COMBINED COURT CENTRE,
LOWGATE, KINGSTON UPON HULL HU1 2EZ
is open between 10 am & 4 pm Monday to Friday
Tel: 01482 586161

Case Number	*Always quote this*	

Plaintiff *(including ref.)*

Defendants

Issue date

Date of postal service

Issue fee

Your summons was issued today. The defendant has 14 days from the date of service to reply to the summons. If the date of postal service is not shown on this form you will be sent a separate notice of service (Form N222).

The defendant may either

- Pay you your total claim.
- **Dispute the whole claim.** The court will send you a copy of the defence and tell you what to do next.
- **Admit that all the money is owed.** The defendant will send you form of admission N9A. You may then ask the court to send the defendant an order to pay you the money owed by completing the request for judgment below and returning it to the court.
- **Admit that only part of your claim is owed.** The court will send you a copy of the reply and tell you what to do next.
- **Not reply at all.** You should wait 14 days from the date of service. You may then ask the court to send the defendant an order to pay you the money owed by completing the request for judgment below and returning it to the court.

For further information please turn over

Request for Judgment

- Tick and complete either A or B. Make sure that all the case details are given and that the judgment details at C are completed. Remember to sign and date the form. Your signature certifies that the information you have given is correct.
- If the defendant has given an address on the form of admission to which correspondence should be sent, which is different from the address shown on the summons, you will need to tell the court.

A ☐ **The defendant has not replied to my summons**

Complete all the judgment details at C. Decide how and when you want the defendant to pay. You can ask for the judgment to be paid by instalments or in one payment.

B ☐ **The defendant admits that all the money is owed**

Tick only one box below and return the completed slip to the court.

☐ **I accept the defendant's proposal for payment**

Complete all the judgment details at C. Say how the defendant intends to pay. The court will send the defendant an order to pay. You will also be sent a copy.

☐ **The defendant has not made any proposal for payment**

Complete all the judgment details at C. Say how you want the defendant to pay. You can ask for the judgment to be paid by instalments or in one payment. The court will send the defendant an order to pay. You will also be sent a copy.

☐ **I do NOT accept the defendant's proposal for payment**

Complete all the judgment details at C and say how you want the defendant to pay. Give your reasons for objecting to the defendant's offer of payment in the section overleaf. Return this slip to the court **together with the defendant's admission N9A** (or a copy). The court will fix a rate of payment and send the defendant an order to pay. You will also be sent a copy.

I certify that the information given is correct

Signed .... Dated ....

In the   **KINGSTON UPON HULL**

County Court

Case Number	*Always quote this*	

Plaintiff

Defendant

Plaintiff's Ref.

C Judgment details

I would like the judgment to be paid

☐ (forthwith) *only tick this box if you intend to enforce the order right away.*

☐ (by instalments of £ .... per month)

☐ (in full **by** ....)

Amount of claim as stated in summons (including interest at date of issue) ....

Interest since date of summons (if any) ....
Period .... Rate .... %

Court fees shown on summons ....

Solicitor's costs (if any) on issuing summons .....

Sub Total

Solicitor's costs (if any) on entering judgment

Sub Total

Deduct amount (if any) paid since issue ....

Amount payable by defendant

N205A *Notice of issue (default summons) and request for judgment (Order 3, rule (2) n.d)(1), Order 9, rules 3 and (6) (12.94)*   Printed by Satellite Press Limited

Fig 18: contd

─────────────── Further information ───────────────

- The summons must be served within 4 months of the date of issue (or 6 months if leave to serve out of the jurisdiction is granted under Order 8, rule 2). In exceptional circumstances you may apply for this time to be extended provided that you do so before the summons expires.

- If the defendant does not reply to the summons or if he delivers an admission without an offer of payment you may ask for judgment. If you do not ask for judgment within 12 months of the date of service the action will be struck out. It cannot be reinstated.

- You may be entitled to interest if judgment is entered against the defendant and your claim is for more than £5000.

- You should keep a record of any payments you receive from the defendant. If there is a hearing or you wish to take steps to enforce the judgment, you will need to satisfy the court about the balance outstanding. You should give the defendant a receipt and payment in cash should always be acknowledged. You should tell the defendant how much he owes if he asks.

- **You must inform the court IMMEDIATELY if you receive any payment before a hearing date or after you have sent a request for enforcement to the court.**

Objections to the defendant's proposal for payment

Case Number

Fig 19: Notice of non-service (general)

Notice of non-service (general)

In the
KINGSTON UPON HULL
County Court

Case Number	*Always quote this*	
Local Number		
Plaintiff		
Defendant		
Plaintiff's Ref.		

To the Plaintiff('s solicitor)

Take Notice that the   summons ☐
                          application ☐
                          order ☐

in this action has not been served for the reason ticked below:

1. The envelope addressed to the defendant has been returned by the Post Office marked:

Note: If you think that the defendant is still at the address you may ask for bailiff service there on payment of the appropriate fee.

"Not known at the address given" (see note) ☐

"Gone away" (see note) ☐

"No such address" ☐

"Insufficient address" ☐

2. The address is a registered office   • confirmation of address required ☐

     • an office copy of the company register confirming the address is required ☐

3. The bailiff is unable to trace the address given within the district of this court ☐

4. The defendant is not known at the address given ☐

5. The defendant is stated to have left the address given
   The defendant's new address (if known) is ....

   ....

6. Premises empty (and boarded up) ☐

7. Other reason (specify) ....

   ....

   ....

And the summons ☐

application ☐

order ☐

has been returned to the Home Court and any further correspondence should be sent there.

Dated

N216 - Notice of non-service (general) (Order 7, rules 6(2) and 10(4)) (1.95)   N216 239   Printed by Satellite Press Limited specifies the amount of the debt claimed, the court fee paid on issuing the summons and the amount of fixed costs which is payable in the event of the plaintiff obtaining a default judgment (see below) or the defendant paying the amount claimed. Fixed costs are not applicable to damages actions. Accordingly in Form N2 the entry 'Solicitor's costs' will be completed by the words 'to be taxed' (CCR Ord 38, r 18).

A default summons must be served within four months beginning with the date of issue. By CCR Ord 7, r 20(2) a summons can be renewed, on *ex parte* application to the district judge, for a further period of four months, (see generally the High Court practice, p 205).

If the summons is served by the plaintiff, or his agent, an affidavit of service must be filed (CCR Ord 7, r 6). If the summons is served through the court the bailiff or other officer who effected service completes a certificate of service whereupon the court sends the plaintiff a *notice of service* stating the date on which service was effected (CCR Ord 7, r 21). This notice enables the plaintiff to calculate the earliest date on which he can enter judgment should the defendant default in delivering a defence.

Summons production centre

Certain plaintiffs (eg water companies, finance companies, mail order companies or credit card companies) often wish to issue hundreds, sometimes thousands, of summonses at one go. This would place considerable strain on a particular county court. Accordingly, a 'summons production centre' has been in existence since December 1989 specifically to cater for the bulk issue of summonses. The centre is deemed to be part of the office of the county court whose name appears on the summonses which it issues. Plaintiffs or their solicitors issuing bulk summonses prepare the paper work in the usual way for issue in the correct county court. However, all such bulk summonses will in fact be issued by the summons production centre on behalf of the relevant county courts. The centre immediately notifies the appropriate county court that the summons has been issued and serves the summons by post. Thereafter all further steps are taken at or by the county court on whose behalf the summons was issued.

Special arrangements have to be made before plaintiffs or their solicitors can commence proceedings through the centre (see CCR Ord 2, r 8). Each centre user is given a distinguishing number or reference. Solicitors who wish to use the centre should consider CCR Ord 2, rr 6–12 and then apply to the Chief Clerk, Summons Production Centre, second floor, St Katherine's House, St Katherine Street, Northampton, NN1 1QP.

Obtaining judgment in default (CCR Ord 9)

The default action takes its name from the procedure which becomes available if the defendant does not respond in accordance with the instructions on the front of the summons, ie if the defendant does not within fourteen days after the service of the summons on him (exclusive of the day of service), pay to the plaintiff the total amount of the claim and any costs stated on the summons or deliver to the plaintiff an admission, or deliver to the court office a defence and/or counterclaim. When the fourteen-day period has elapsed the plaintiff is entitled to enter judgment which is done by simply filing the appropriate form of judgment. Note that the default judgment is not entered automatically. The plaintiff must enter judgment and, as in the High Court, if the plaintiff is slow in acting, the defendant can cure his default at any time without leave before the judgment is entered.

The forms of default judgment are different in debt claims and damages claims. (For this purpose, and for the purpose of fixed costs, a negligence claim for the cost of accident repairs is treated as a debt claim; CCR Ord 1, r 10.) No leave is necessary for the entry of a default judgment except in the case of certain types of defendant (the Crown, foreign states, persons under disability, tort actions between husband and wife (CCR Ord 42, r 5; Ord 9, r 6; Ord 10, rr 6, 8; Ord 47, r 3: compare High Court practice, p 218)) and in the case of a default judgment for money secured by a mortgage (CCR Ord 9, r 7).

Final judgment

On a debt claim the plaintiff enters final judgment for the debt plus fixed costs by completing a request Form N225A. It can be seen from this form that the plaintiff has complete freedom as to the form of judgment which he enters. It can be for a 'forthwith' judgment; payment of the whole sum on a stated date; or payment by instalments, the amount and frequency of which will be determined entirely by the plaintiff. Which form of judgment is entered may depend to some extent upon which method of enforcement it is proposed to use, a topic the plaintiff should consider before starting the action. Most creditors will wish to enter a 'forthwith' judgment so as to proceed immediately to enforcement proceedings such as execution against goods, garnishee orders or charging orders (see Chapter 24). By way of exception to the general rule a default judgment entered under CCR Ord 9, r 6(1) for payment forthwith is not served where a request for the issue of a warrant of execution has been made (CCR Ord 22, r 1(3)).

In the majority of debt cases, the entry of a final judgment in default is the easy part. It is the enforcement of that judgment that requires skill and expertise (see Chapter 24).

Interlocutory judgment

On a damages claim the plaintiff enters interlocutory judgment for 'damages to be assessed and costs' by completing a request in Form N234 (illustrated in fig 20). By CCR Ord 50, r 4A the plaintiff has the option of

Fig 20: Request for interlocutory judgment for damages to be assessed

---

IN THE   **COUNTY COURT**

Between _____ Plaintiff

                                             Case No.

And _____ Defendant

> **Request for interlocutory judgment for damages to be assessed**

Delete as appropriate. Insert name(s) of defendant(s) against whom judgment to be entered.

I request you enter judgment against _____
[by default] [the defendant having failed to comply with the conditions contained in the order in this action made on_____] for damages to be assessed and costs

[I request you to fix a date for the assessment of the damages and I estimate that the length of the hearing will be_____] [it will be necessary for the district judge to give directions before assessing the damages in this action]

When corresponding with the court, please address forms or letters to the Chief Clerk and quote the case number
The Court Office at

is open from 10 am to 4 pm Monday to Friday

N234 Request for interlocutory judgment of damages to be assessed (Order 9, rule 6(1) & (2) Order 22, rules 5(1) & (2) (2.95) *Printed by Satellite Press Limited*

---

preparing the judgment itself (in Form N17) instead of the request. As in the High Court, an interlocutory judgment determines the issue of liability in favour of the plaintiff but leaves open the question of *quantum* of damages. These have to be assessed at a subsequent hearing. The form of request and the form of judgment enable the plaintiff to seek, and the court to fix, the date for that assessment. If the plaintiff does not seek the fixing of the date (perhaps because he is not yet ready to prove his damages) the date for assessment will be fixed later and the plaintiff must give the defendant at least seven days' notice of it (CCR Ord 22, r 6(1)). In all cases the district judge has power to assess damages (CCR Ord 22, r 6(2)).

Awarding interest in default judgments

In a debt case, a plaintiff who has pleaded a claim for interest at a contractually agreed rate, or under CCA 1984, s 69 at the judgment debt rate (see p 16) and has given precise figures therefor, may enter final judgment for the total of the debt, fixed costs, and interest up to the date of the request for entry of the judgment (CCR Ord 9, r 8(1)).

In other debt cases (eg a claim for interest under CCA 1984, s 69 at a rate higher than the judgment debt rate) and in all damages cases the plaintiff can enter interlocutory judgment for interest to be assessed (CCR Ord 9, r 8(3)).

Setting aside default judgments

The CCR contain provisions similar to the High Court rules (see p 219) enabling the court to set aside a default judgment either 'as of right' or 'on the merits' as the case may be. Also, where the summons was served by post and eg it is returned by the post office undelivered to the defendant, the court may, of its own motion, set aside any default judgment entered and may give any directions it thinks fit (see generally CCR Ord 37, rr 3, 4, 5).

Delivery of admission, defence or counterclaim

On service the defendant receives not only the summons and particulars of claim but also the relevant form of admission, defence, or counterclaim. Form N9 accompanies a default summons for an unliquidated claim, and a fixed date summons; Form N9A (admission) and Form N9B (defence and counterclaim) both accompany a default summons for a liquidated claim. The court office will annex the relevant form(s) or supply them if the solicitor is to effect service. Form N9 is illustrated in fig 21.

A defendant who admits the whole of the plaintiff's liquidated claim and who requires time to pay will send direct to the plaintiff the completed Form N9A (which includes a statement of means). If the plaintiff accepts the defendant's offer he applies for judgment to be entered in the terms of the offer by completing appropriately Form N205A (see fig 18). If the plaintiff does not accept the offer he completes Form N205A or N225A accordingly and sends it to the court office with a copy of the defendant's admission and offer and gives reasons for rejecting the offer. The court staff will then fix the rate of payment and notify both parties. If either party objects to the rate fixed by the court staff the order will then be reconsidered by the district judge. If the case is not already in the defendant's local court the case will automatically be transferred to that court for any such reconsideration. If the defendant files an admission of the claim but makes no offer as to payment the plaintiff completes Form N225A in the appropriate manner and himself selects the form of the judgment exactly as he would do if judgment were being entered in default.

The decision on whether or not to accept an offer of payment is not one which a solicitor should take without instructions. Of course those doing a substantial volume of debt collecting work often have standing instructions from the client and know what to do without referring back in each individual case. In other cases the solicitor should advise rather than decide. Pragmatically the defendant's offer—unless preposterously

[continued on p 253]

Fig 21: Form of admission, defence and counterclaim

Form for Replying to a Summons

- *Read the notes on the summons before completing this form*
- *Tick the correct boxes and give the other details asked for*
- *Send or take this completed and signed form immediately to the court office shown on the summons*
- *You should keep your copy of the summons*
- **For details of where and how to pay see the summons**

What is your full name? (BLOCK CAPITALS)

Surname

Forenames

Mr ☐ Mrs ☐ Miss ☐ Ms ☐

How much of the claim do you admit?

☐ **All of it** *(complete only sections 1 and 2)*
☐ **Part of it** *(sections 1,2,3,4,5)* Amount £ :
☐ **None of it** *(complete sections 3,4 and 5 overleaf)*

Section 1   Offer of payment

I offer to pay the amount admitted on (date)

or for the reasons set out below

I cannot pay the amount admitted in one instalment

but I can pay by monthly instalments of £ :

Fill in the next section as fully as possible. Your answers will help the plaintiff decide whether your offer is realistic and ought to be accepted. Your answers will also help the court, if necessary, to fix a rate of payment that you can afford.

Section 2   Income and outgoings

a. Employment I am
☐ Unemployed
☐ A pensioner
☐ Self employed as
☐ Employed as a
My employer is
Employer's address:

b. Income *specify period: weekly, fortnightly, monthly etc.*

My usual take home pay £ :
Child benefit(s) total £ :
Other state benefit(s) total £ :
My pension(s) total £ :
Other people living in my home give me £ :
Other income *(give details)* £ :

In the   County Court

Case Number Always quote this

Plaintiff *(including reference)*

Defendant

c. Bank account and savings
☐ I do not have a bank account
☐ I have a bank account
The account is ☐ in credit ☐ overdrawn by £ :
☐ I do not have a savings account
☐ I have a savings account
The amount in the account is £ :

d. Dependants *(people you look after financially)*
Number of dependants
(give ages of children)

e. Outgoings
I make regular payments as follows:

	weekly	monthly		
Mortgage	☐	☐	£	:
Rent	☐	☐	£	:
Mail order	☐	☐	£	:
TV rental/licence	☐	☐	£	:
HP repayments	☐	☐	£	:
Court orders	☐	☐	£	:

specify period: yearly, quarterly, etc.

Gas £ :
Electricity £ :
Community charge £ :
Water charges £ :
Other regular payments *(give details below)*
£ :

Credit Card and other debts *(please list)*
£ :

Of the payments above, I am behind with payments to
£ :

continue on a separate sheet if necessary – put the case number in the top right hand corner

Give an address to which notices about this case should be sent to you Post code	I declare that the details I have given above are true to the best of my knowledge **Signed** *(to be signed by you or by your solicitor)* **Position** *(firm or company)* **Dated**

N9 Form of admission, defence and counterclaim to accompany Forms N2, 3 and 4 (Order 3, rule 3(2)(c)) (2.95)   *Printed by Satellite Press Limited*

Fig 21: contd

Case No.

Section 3 Defending the claim: defence	Section 4 Making a claim against the plaintiff: counterclaim

Fill in this part of the form only if you wish to defend the claim or part of the claim.

a.   How much of the plaintiff's claim do you dispute?

All of it ☐

Part of it ☐   *give amount*   £

If you dispute only part of the claim, you must complete sections 1 and 2 overleaf and part b. below.

b.   What are your reasons for disputing the claim?

Fill in this part of the form only if you wish to make a claim against the plaintiff.
If your claim against the plaintiff is for more than his claim against you, you may have to pay a fee. Ask at the court office whether a fee is payable.

a. What is the nature of the claim you wish to make against the plaintiff?

b. If your claim is for a specific sum of money, how much are you claiming?

£

c. What are your reasons for making the claim?

continue on a separate sheet if necessary – put the case number in the top right hand corner

Section 5   Arbitration under the small claims procedure

How the claim will be dealt with if defended

If the claim is worth £1,000 or less it will be dealt with by arbitration (small claims procedure) unless the court decides the case is too difficult to be dealt with in this informal way. Costs and the grounds for setting aside an arbitration award are strictly limited. If the claim is for £1,000 or less and is not dealt with by arbitration, costs including the cost of a legal representative, may be allowed.

If the claim is worth over £1,000 it can still be dealt with by arbitration if either you or the plaintiff asks for it and the court approves. If the claim is dealt with by arbitration in these circumstances, costs may be allowed.

Please tick this box if the claim is worth over £1,000 and you would like it dealt with by arbitration. ☐

Give an address to which notices about this case should be sent to you	**Signed** *(to be signed by you or by your solicitor)*
Post code	**Position** *(firm or company)*
	Dated

low—is usually better accepted rather than refused. A defendant who can afford £10 per week will probably pay £10 per week; the same defendant ordered to pay £20 per week will probably pay nothing. However in a borderline case the plaintiffs may leave it to the court staff to fix an appropriate rate of payment. Asking the district judge to reconsider such an order, however, will rarely be appropriate. The district judge is unlikely to overrule the court staff except where the order is clearly wrong or where further evidence not previously available is now produced. A hearing date is given for any reconsideration before the district judge and both sides can attend to make representations.

In a case where the defendant admits only part of the plaintiff's claim he should, within fourteen days of service of the summons, deliver to the court office an admission of liability together with, if he so wishes, a request for time for payment accompanied by a statement of means and if he wishes to defend part of the plaintiff's claim or to make a counterclaim he should also deliver a defence and/or counterclaim. The court will thereupon send notice to the plaintiff of the part admission. If the plaintiff accepts the amount admitted he will file a request in Form N225 whereupon the court will enter judgment for the amount admitted and costs. The judgment will be for payment by instalments in cases where the plaintiff has accepted the defendant's proposals for payment. Alternatively, if the plaintiff accepts the amount admitted but not the proposals for payment he must give reasons for the non-acceptance. The court staff will then consider the matter and determine the time for payment and enter judgment accordingly. Either party can apply for such a judgment to be reconsidered at a hearing before the district judge and proceedings will be automatically transferred to the defendant's home court if the judgment was not made in that court.

If the defendant has admitted part of the claim and the plaintiff does not accept the amount admitted, proceedings are automatically transferred to the defendant's home court where appropriate and a date for a pre-trial review will be given.

If the defendant in an action for damages delivers an admission of liability but disputes or does not admit the amount of the plaintiff's damages, the plaintiff may apply to the court for such judgment as he may be entitled to upon the admission and the court will give such a judgment which will normally be an interlocutory judgment for damages to be assessed and costs. If in such a case the defendant has offered to pay a specific sum which the plaintiff wishes to accept the procedure which follows is the same as that described above for cases where the defendant has admitted part of a plaintiff's liquidated claim.

In practice, the vast bulk of default actions will have been terminated by the methods discussed above, namely judgment in default or a judgment based on an admission and offer. It will be remembered, however, that the defendant has been given an invitation to defend and/or counterclaim. If the defendant accepts this invitation he must deliver a completed form (or a pleading in some other form) to the court within fourteen days of service of the summons. The court will then send a photocopy to the plaintiff. The action will now normally be governed by the automatic directions of CCR Ord 17, r 11 (see p 465). If appropriate the plaintiff might now apply for summary judgment (see below).

Finally in this section let us briefly consider how to approach the proceedings if consulted by a defendant. If the defendant admits the claim, obviously he should be invited to make a realistic offer as to payment. If he denies the claim a defence must be filed within fourteen days of service of the summons. A solicitor can of course complete and return to the court Form N9 or Form N9B as appropriate. A solicitor who does so will naturally keep a copy for the office file and there is no need to provide additional copies for the court. In all but the simplest cases, however, a solicitor will draft a defence in the professional form. It will then be necessary to deliver to the court the top copy plus additional copies for each plaintiff. One should never file the so-called 'holding defence' such as 'I deny this debt' (see p 158). In reality this is no defence at all and the court may ignore it altogether and allow judgment to be entered in default. Even if such a defence is not ignored but treated as a proper defence the action will now be governed by the automatic directions (see p 465). Further, one would expect the plaintiff to apply for summary judgment, or at the very least, for an order that a proper defence be filed with a direction that the defendant be debarred from defending if the order is not complied with.

It will be observed that the pleadings stage is conducted much more quickly in the county court than it is in the High Court. There being no equivalent to a 'general indorsement' (see p 196) the plaintiff cannot commence proceedings until he is ready to file the particulars of claim. There being no equivalent to an acknowledgment of service in the CCR the defendant has only fourteen days in which to file his defence and thereafter risks judgment in default. The time allowed for the defendant's solicitor to draft a proper defence will often be too short. In such a case the solicitor should seek a reasonable extension of time, either from the plaintiff or, if necessary, from the court. In practice, a solicitor acting for a plaintiff will usually grant one reasonable extension unless of course he has specific instructions to the contrary. If the plaintiff refuses to allow a reasonable extension the defendant should apply by notice to the district judge under CCR Ord 13, r 4 for an extension of time (and, probably, for the costs of the application).

Summary judgment

CCR Ord 9, r 14 is the county court equivalent of RSC Ord 14. The county court rule now applies to any action except:

(1) cases falling within the rules providing for small claims arbitration (see p 279);

(2) an action in which a claim is made for possession of land or in which the title to any land is in question;

(3) an action which includes a claim by the plaintiff for libel, slander, malicious prosecution or false imprisonment;

(4) an Admiralty action *in rem*.

Where the defendant in an action to which the rule applies has delivered at the court office a document purporting to be a defence, the plaintiff may apply to the court for judgment against the defendant on the grounds that, notwithstanding the delivery of that document, the defendant has no defence to the claim or to a particular part of the claim. An application must be supported by an affidavit verifying the facts on which the claim, or the part of it to which the application relates, is based and stating that in the deponent's belief, notwithstanding the document which has been delivered, there is no defence to the claim or the particular part of it. In a case where a date for a pre-trial review has been given (eg following a part-admission) the application for summary judgment will normally be heard at the pre-trial review. However, in most county court cases there is no pre-trial review and therefore a hearing date will be fixed for the summary judgment application. The plaintiff is required to serve notice of the application together with a copy of the affidavit in support, not less than seven days before the date fixed.

Order 9, r 14(5) expressly incorporates the High Court provisions (as to which see p 221) relating to showing cause, giving judgment, granting leave to defend whether conditional or not and granting summary judgment on a counterclaim.

The main difference now remaining between the High Court and county court concerns the stage at which the plaintiff will apply for summary judgment. In the county court summary judgment is available only if a defence is filed. This obviously limits the number of occasions when it will be used since, if that defence shows a triable issue, there would be no point in applying for summary judgment (in the High Court the application is usually made after notice of intention to defend has been given, but before any defence is served).

There is no equivalent of RSC Ord 14A (see p 231) in the county court (except for Business List actions in the Central London County Court; see further p 276).

Fixed date actions

All actions excluded from the definition of default actions (see CCR Ord 3, r 2 and see p 239) are classified as 'fixed date' actions. The most important examples are actions for the recovery of land and actions for the return of goods. Neither of these types of action fall within the rules providing automatic directions (see p 465). Other examples are actions for an injunction or other equitable remedy; these actions are usually governed by automatic directions.

In order to commence a fixed date action, the plaintiff prepares the appropriate documents listed on p 238, above (the forms of request and summons differ from those used in a default action). In recovery of land and return of goods actions the summons served on the defendant (several forms are prescribed) and the notice of issue of summons sent to the plaintiff (Form N206, illustrated in fig 22) have a 'fixed date' indorsed thereon. It will be observed from the notice of issue illustrated that the fixed date is either for the hearing itself or for a pre-trial review. A pre-trial review will not be fixed for an action for recovery of land unless the claim also includes a claim for some relief other than the payment of *mesne* profits, arrears of rent, or money secured by mortgage or charge. Thus, for example, where the plaintiff claims possession and rent arrears a fixed date will be given for the hearing, whereas if he claims damages for breach of covenant as well there will be a pre-trial review. In other cases, unless the court otherwise orders, the date given will be a date for a pre-trial review rather than the hearing itself.

In fixed date actions governed by automatic directions (see above) no 'fixed date' is given. Because of the automatic directions no pre-trial review is required and the automatic directions deal with the procedure for obtaining a hearing date. In these cases the name 'fixed date' hardly seems appropriate. Indeed the plaintiff may subsequently apply for a default judgment in these cases. If the defendant fails to deliver a defence within fourteen days of service the plaintiff can apply under CCR Ord 9, r 4A for judgment or directions. In practice very few fixed date actions are governed by automatic directions. Numerically speaking fixed date actions for recovery of land and return of goods swamp all others many times over.

The summons is served together with the particulars of claim and a form of admission defence and counterclaim (the forms for which vary). CCR Ord 7, r 20 applies (four months' duration of summons) but of greater significance is CCR Ord 7, r 10(5), which requires service not less than twenty-one days before the return day fixed (and see p 137 as to issue of successive summonses).

If the defendant delivers an admission the plaintiff can, in theory, apply before the return day fixed, for such judgment as he may be entitled to on the admission (CCR Ord 9, r 4). However the application must be made on notice to the defendant and thus, in practice, if the date already fixed is for a pre-trial review the plaintiff will have little real alternative but to wait until that day. Rule 4 does not apply to actions for recovery of land; in those cases the delivery of an admission merely limits the defendant's liability for further costs (CCR Ord 9, r 16).

If the defendant disputes liability he must within fourteen days of the service of the summons on him (inclusive of the day of service) deliver to the court a defence, using, if he wishes, the form supplied. The court will send a copy to the plaintiff. Despite this time limit the defendant may still serve a defence late at any time before the return day and, without

[continued on p 258]

Fig 22: Notice of issue of fixed date summons

Notice of Issue of Fixed Date Summons or Originating Application

Plaintiff

To the plaintiff('s solicitor)

In the
KINGSTON UPON HULL County Court

| Plaintiff's Ref. | |
| Date | |

The court office at

KINGSTON UPON HULL COMBINED COURT
CENTRE, LOWGATE,
KINGSTON UPON HULL HU1 2EZ
Telephone 01482 586161

is open from 10 am to 4 pm Monday to Friday
Please bring this notice with you to court

Case Number	Defendant(s)	Issue fee

The above case(s) was / were issued today and you must attend the

tick the appropriate box

☐ **Hearing** when the proceedings will be heard

Pre-trial review when the district judge will give directions for the determination of this action.
(If you intend to ask the district judge to give any particular direction, you must give notice of your intention to him and the defendant)

at

on   at   o'clock

Notes

- **Always quote the case number.**

- **You must inform the court IMMEDIATELY** If you receive any payment before the hearing date.

- Always bring this notice with you when you come to the court office for any purpose connected with your case(s). On the day of hearing bring all books and papers necessary to prove the claim.

- If judgment is entered, the defendant will be ordered to pay you or your representative.

- You should keep a record of any payments you receive from the defendant. At the hearing if you wish to take steps to enforce the judgment, you will need to satisfy the court about the balance outstanding. You should give the defendant a receipt. Payment in cash should always be acknowledged. You should tell the defendant how much he owes if he asks.

Proceedings after judgment
You must inform the court IMMEDIATELY if you receive any payment while a warrant or other enforcement is current and/or before any hearing date.

N206 239

N206 – Notice of issue (fixed date summons/originating application) (Order 3, rule 3(2)(d)(i) and 4(4)(c)) (12.94)   Printed by Satellite Press Limited delivering any defence, may even appear on the return day and dispute the plaintiff's claim (CCR Ord 9, r 9(2)). There are two sanctions which can be used against such a defendant:

(1) he may be ordered to pay the costs incurred in consequence of his delay or failure;

(2) the court may at any time before trial order the defendant to deliver a defence and may further direct that he shall be debarred from defending altogether unless the order is obeyed (CCR Ord 13, r 2(2)).

In a fixed date action governed by automatic directions (see CCR Ord 17, r 11 and pp 452 and 466) if the defendant fails to file a defence within the fourteen days the plaintiff can apply for judgment under CCR Ord 9, r 4A.

Judgment at the pre-trial review

In default actions a pre-trial review is convened where the defendant admits part of the claim but the plaintiff is unwilling to accept judgment for that part only, where third party proceedings are issued and in one or two other exceptional cases. As noted above some fixed date actions proceed straight to trial whereas in others the 'fixed date' is for a pre-trial review.

The district judge has a discretion to give judgment:

(1) In a fixed date action, if the defendant has not delivered an admission of defence and does not appear at the pre-trial review (CCR Ord 17, r 7). This rule corresponds to the High Court practice as to leave applications to obtain judgment in default of defence where some equitable remedy is claimed (see p 234). If, in a county court fixed date action, the plaintiff is also claiming damages he can obtain judgment which can be final if he is ready to prove *quantum* immediately. Note that, if the plaintiff is ready to prove *quantum* the assessment is made by the district judge.

(2) In any action, if the defendant has delivered a defence but does not appear at the pre-trial review and if the plaintiff is ready to prove his claim (CCR Ord 17, r 8). As above, if damages are claimed the judgment can be a final judgment if the plaintiff is also ready to prove *quantum* immediately.

It is important to note that the district judge's power to enter early judgment is discretionary and, in (2), is available only if the plaintiff is ready to prove his claim.

Actions may also be terminated at this stage by way of summary judgment, if the plaintiff has given due notice to the defendant (see p 254); by judgment on admissions (ie even though a defence was filed, see p 370); by the defendant being debarred from defending if he fails to deliver a defence as ordered at a previous hearing (see above); by striking out pleadings (see p 190); and by striking out the action if the plaintiff fails to appear (CCR Ord 17, r 5).

Chapter 13

Cases in which Special Rules Apply

Judicial review

RSC Ord 53 sets out the procedure for the exercise of the High Court's supervisory jurisdiction over inferior courts, tribunals or other bodies or persons charged with the performance of public duties and acts. By a single application a person can apply for any one or more of the following orders: the prerogative orders of *mandamus, certiorari* or prohibition, an injunction under SCA 1981, s 30 (restraining a person from acting in any office which he is not entitled to act), or a declaration or injunction against a public authority. The application may additionally include a claim for damages.

Order 53 provides a speedy means for determining issues of public and administrative law subject to certain protections (summarised below) which are given to statutory tribunals and public authorities and which are necessary for reasons of public policy. Where the applicant has rights under public and private law, judicial review is appropriate only in respect of the former (*R v East Berks Health Authority, ex parte Walsh* [1985] QB 152). It is an abuse of the process of the court to raise by way of an ordinary action claims which should be brought under Ord 53 (*O'Reilly v Mackman* [1983] 2 AC 237 in which actions by writ for declarations concerning decisions made by a prison disciplinary tribunal were struck out; *Cocks v Thanet District Council* [1983] 2 AC 286 in which proceedings alleging breach of duty under the Housing (Homeless Persons) Act 1977 were struck out).

Further in *Waverley Borough Council v Hilden* [1988] 1 WLR 246 it was held that the defendants, who were gypsies challenging a council's decision to seek an injunction restraining breach of enforcement notices, must apply for judicial review and could not raise the question of the reasonableness of the council's decision by way of defence. However, claims may be properly brought by ordinary action where issues of public law are raised only collaterally or peripherally (*Davy v Spelthorne Borough Council* [1984] AC 262, a damages claim alleging that negligent advice as to planning law had been given by officers of the planning authority) or where, although the principal issue is one of public law, the case also concerns private law rights, making proceedings under Ord 53 inappropriate (*Wandsworth London Borough Council v Winder* [1985] AC 461, in a possession action brought by a local authority, a defence alleging that notices of increase of rent previously given were *ultra vires* and void). The court would rarely allow an application where there is an alternative remedy available (eg a right of appeal from the decision in question: or a claim for unfair dismissal before an industrial tribunal, *R v Civil Service Appeal Board ex parte Bruce* [1988] 3 All ER 686). However, there are exceptional cases where the court will grant relief by way of judicial review without requiring the applicant to pursue the alternative remedy (*R v Chief Constable of Merseyside Police, ex parte Calveley* [1986] 2 WLR 144; delay in instituting disciplinary proceedings so serious that judicial review granted without requiring applicant to exercise right of appeal to Secretary of State).

Apart from the subject matter of the application the procedure by judicial review has two unusual features: the title of the action (proceedings are taken in the name of the Crown as in criminal proceedings) and the two-stage procedure it provides.

The first stage is the *application for leave* to apply. This stage is intended to eliminate at the outset frivolous or obviously untenable claims. It is made *ex parte* to a judge by filing in the Crown Office (a department of the Central Office) a notice in Form 86A and an affidavit as to the facts relied on. The judge will usually determine the application without a hearing (unless a hearing is requested in the notice) and a copy of his order will be sent to the applicant. The judge will grant the application if it discloses an arguable case for believing that:

(1) there has been a failure of public duty; and
(2) the applicant has sufficient interest or *locus standi* in the matter; and
(3) the application has been made promptly and in any event within three months from the date when grounds for the application arose or the case is one in which a late application should be allowed.

The time limit, the need for the applicant to obtain leave to proceed and the need for him to support that application by affidavit comprise the main protections afforded to statutory tribunals and public authorities by judicial review proceedings which they would not have in ordinary proceedings.

An application which is refused, or granted on terms, may be 'renewed' by lodging notice in Form 86B in the Crown Office within ten days of receipt of the judge's order. In a criminal cause or matter the application for renewal is made *ex parte* to a divisional court of the Queen's Bench Division whether or not any hearing has taken place before the judge. In a civil cause or matter the application for renewal is made *ex parte* to the judge in open court. However if a previous hearing has taken place no renewal is possible; the applicant may proceed by way of appeal to the Court of Appeal.

Having obtained leave to apply for judicial review, the second stage, the *application for judicial review* is made, in a criminal cause or matter, to the Divisional Court, in a civil cause or matter to a judge sitting in open court (unless otherwise ordered). In both cases the procedure is by way of originating motion entered for hearing within fourteen days of the grant of leave. Notice of motion must be served on all persons directly affected and, where the proceedings of an inferior court are impugned, on the clerk or registrar of that court. Unless the court granting leave otherwise directed, the notices of motion must be served at least ten days before the hearing. Affidavits will then be filed for use at the hearing, in preparation for which, interlocutory applications may be made to any judge or any Queen's Bench master. The time limit for the respondent's affidavit is fifty-six days (RSC Ord 53, r 6(4)).

Skeleton arguments have to be lodged during the second stage in all judicial review cases. The skeleton argument should include a list of issues, a list of propositions of law to be advanced and a chronology of events (as to this and further points on documentation see *Practice Direction (Crown Office List: Preparation for Hearings)* [1994] 1 WLR 1551).

If *certiorari* is sought the court may, in addition to quashing the inferior court's decision, remit the case with a direction to reconsider it. If a declaration, an injunction or damages are sought the court may, instead of refusing the application, order the proceedings to continue 'as if begun by' writ.

Judicial review is exclusively within the jurisdiction of the High Court (CCA 1984, s 38).

Interpleader proceedings (RSC Ord 17; CCR Ord 33)

Interpleader proceedings are appropriate where a person holding any money, goods or chattels is, or expects to be, sued by two or more rival claimants to the property. If he has no interest in the dispute he can apply for relief by way of interpleader, that is, a hearing at which the rival claimants will be made to interplead, argue against each other and not against him. Here are some typical examples:

(1) A car is left with a repairer or a warehouseman. The customer now claims it back, but so does a finance company, saying it is subject to a hire-purchase agreement with them.

(2) A solicitor receives a sum of money as the deposit on a contract for the sale of land. The money is now claimed by both the buyer and the seller.

(3) (*the most frequent example*) A sheriff enforcing a money judgment takes goods from a judgment debtor but a claim to the goods is made by some other person. The sheriff will notify the judgment creditor of the claim and, unless that person admits the claim, will start interpleader proceedings.

Interpleader proceedings have three unusual features. First, the role played by the applicant: he must be truly a disinterested party. Indeed he must provide an affidavit stating that he claims no interest in the money, goods or chattels (other than for his charges or costs), does not collude with any claimant and is willing to dispose of the property as the court may direct. (Note: a sheriff is not usually required to provide such an affidavit.) Secondly, the proceedings can be commenced either by an expedited form of originating summons or by an interlocutory summons. The latter is used when the applicant has already been sued by one or more claimants: it should be served on the plaintiffs and all other claimants. The court will then stay all proceedings in the action other than the interpleader proceedings. Thirdly, some interpleader proceedings may be summarily determined by the district judge. The district judge has such jurisdiction even if some claimants do not consent if the applicant is a sheriff or if the question at issue between the claimants is a question of law and the facts are not in dispute. (In other cases the district judge will usually order that an issue between the claimants be stated and tried, and may direct which of the claimants is to be plaintiff and which defendant.)

The county court's jurisdiction to hear interpleader proceedings derives from two sections of the CCA 1984, s 38 in the case of a 'stakeholder's interpleader' (see examples (1) and (2) above); and s 101 in the case of any goods (or the proceeds of sale thereof) seized under a warrant of execution. The procedure is governed by CCR Ord 33 and special forms of summons are prescribed, see Forms N88, N89 and see also Pyke and Oldham, *Practical County Court Precedents* (FT Law & Tax) Precedents 247–252). A stakeholder's interpleader can be determined by the district judge if it is within his ordinary jurisdiction (amount in dispute not exceeding £5,000). An interpleader in respect of goods seized in execution is sought by the district judge in person and therefore must be determined by a judge.

Possession actions

The county court has jurisdiction to hear any action for the recovery of land (CCA 1984, s 21) and therefore most such actions are brought there. Under CCA 1984, s 21 claims brought by a mortgagee for possession of a dwelling-house outside Greater London *must* be brought in the county court. County court actions for recovery of land constitute the main example of fixed date actions. However they require separate consideration here for six reasons:

(1) *The venue rule.* The action must be commenced in the court for the district in which the land or any part thereof is situated (CCR Ord 4, r 3).

(2) *The particulars of claim* to be filed at commencement must include the details required by CCR Ord 6, r 3. For mortgage actions see also CCR Ord 6, r 5 (see p 268).

(3) *Commencement.* Two forms of summons are prescribed: a general form and a form appropriate to claims for forfeiture for non-payment of rent, the notes to which explain how the defendant can obtain a stay of action by paying the arrears into court.

(4) *The delivery of an admission* does not enable the plaintiff to apply for judgment immediately as it does in other cases. Instead the plaintiff is given notice of the admission plus a copy and, thereafter, the costs of proving any fact which the admission renders it unnecessary to prove cannot be ordered against the defendant making the admission (CCR Ord 9, r 16).

(5) *The return day.* If the plaintiff seeks no remedies other than possession and the payment of *mesne* profits and arrears of rent or mortgage moneys the return day fixed on the summons will be for the trial of the action (CCR Ord 3, r 3(4)) in the district judge's court (see p 479); most mortgage actions are heard in chambers, CCR Ord 49, r 1). There will be no pre-trial review unless the district judge later decides to convene one (CCR Ord 17, r 10). If the plaintiff does seek some additional remedy (eg damages for breach of a covenant to repair) the return day will be for a pre-trial review unless the court otherwise directs (CCR Ord 3, r 3(3)).

(6) *The automatic directions* do not apply.

Many Rent Act cases and Housing Act 1988 cases may be commenced either by summons as described above or by a simpler procedure, ie an originating application supported by affidavit for a hearing before the district judge in chambers (Rent Act (County Court Proceedings for Possession) Rules 1981, *Green Book* 1363 and CCR Ord 49, r 6, *Green Book* 1543 and see *Procedural Table No 10, Green Book* 535).

Summary proceedings for the possession of land (RSC Ord 113; CCR Ord 24)

These rules provide a fast and economical procedure for cases in which the plaintiff is seeking an order for possession of land against persons who are unlikely to have any substantial defence. They are used mainly against squatters but can also be used against licensees of land whose licence has been terminated. They cannot be used against tenants holding over after the termination of the tenancy.

The unusual features of RSC Ord 113 and CCR Ord 24 are as follows:

(1) the action can be brought against occupiers whose names are unknown to the plaintiff;

(2) the rules provide for summary *trial* of the action;

(3) the rules allow summary execution of the order for possession;

(4) the automatic directions do not apply.

In the High Court, the proceedings must be commenced by a special form of originating summons to which acknowledgment of service is not required. This summons is addressed 'To [AB] and every other person in occupation of [etc]' or simply 'To every person in occupation of [etc]'. It must be supported by an affidavit stating the plaintiff's interest in the land, the circumstances in which the land has been occupied without licence or consent and in which his claim to possession arises, and stating that the plaintiff does not know the name of any person occupying the land who is not named in the summons.

The manner of service depends upon whether any defendant has been named in the summons. On named defendants a sealed copy of the summons, and a copy of the affidavit, must be served either personally, or by leaving or sending them to the premises or in such other manner as the court may direct. Where any person not named as a defendant is in occupation then (in addition to service on a named defendant where necessary) the copy summons and affidavit are served by affixing them to the main door or other conspicuous part of the premises and, if practicable, inserting through the letter box further copies in 'a sealed transparent envelope' addressed to 'the occupiers'. In a case where there are no premises (eg caravans trespassing in a field) service is effected by placing stakes in the ground at conspicuous parts of the occupied land to each of which is affixed a sealed transparent envelope addressed to 'the occupiers' containing copies of the summons and affidavit. (Note: because every copy summons for service has to be sealed be sure to prepare enough copies to take or send to the court when the summons is issued.)

On the issue of the summons an appointment is made for a hearing before the district judge to take place at least five days after the expected date of service in the case of residential premises and two days in the case of other land. In an urgent case the plaintiff may apply *ex parte* at or after the issue of the summons for an expedited hearing. Proceedings under RSC Ord 113 are now determined by a district judge (r 1A) who can, however, refer them to a judge if he considers they ought to be determined by a judge.

The hearing of the summons is a summary trial. Thus if the plaintiff proves his case the district judge *must* make an order for possession forthwith (see *GLC v Jenkins* [1975] 1 WLR 155; *McPhail v Persons, Names Unknown* [1973] Ch 447). The defendant cannot prevent summary judgment merely by raising a triable issue. However, if the defendant raises a substantial defence possibly requiring oral evidence the case is not suitable for summary trial. The court should instead give directions for a full trial, perhaps by making an 'as if begun by' order under RSC Ord 28, r 8 (see *White Book* 113/1–8/9).

A RSC Ord 113 order for possession is in special form. It provides that the plaintiff 'do recover possession' and is therefore enforceable *in rem*, ie against all occupiers of the premises, even those who may have entered possession after the action has commenced (and see *R v Wandsworth County Court, ex parte London Borough of Wandsworth* [1975] 1 WLR 1314 and the cases cited therein). By way of exception to the general rule an Ord 113 order can be enforced without first notifying all the occupiers of the land and (if the plaintiff applies within three months of the making of the order) without first obtaining the leave of the court. The writ of possession is in Form 66A.

The equivalent procedure in the county court is found in CCR Ord 24. In fact, outside London, it is usual to bring such actions in the county court. The principles governing the grant of the order are of course the same as in the High Court. The district judge now has full jurisdiction in county court cases just as he does in High Court cases.

Proceedings are commenced by originating application in Form N312 with an affidavit in support complying with the requirements of CCR Ord 24, r 2. The affidavit must be sworn by the applicant (a procedural error sometimes encountered is the affidavit having been sworn by the applicant's solicitor; this is not permitted). The affidavit must state the applicant's interest in the land; the circumstances in which the land has been occupied without licence or consent and in which the claim to possession arises and that the applicant does not know the name of any person occupying the land who is not named in the originating application.

The proceedings must be promptly served in accordance with the detailed requirements of CCR Ord 24, r 3, which corresponds with the High Court rules to service.

An order of possession is made in Form N36. To issue a warrant of possession no leave is required provided it is issued within three months of the date of the order. As in the High Court, because it is an order *in rem* the bailiff enforcing the warrant of possession is entitled to evict anyone he finds on the premises, whether or not that person was a party to the proceedings for possession (*R v Wandsworth County Court, ex parte London Borough of Wandsworth* [1975] 1 WLR 1314). Once an order for possession has been made it is not always necessary to issue fresh proceedings if other persons enter into occupation of the property. The correct procedure is to apply for leave to issue a warrant of restitution under CCR Ord 26, r 17. It was held in *Wiltshire County Council v Fraser* [1986] 1 WLR 109 that a warrant of restitution will issue to recover land from occupants who were neither parties to the original proceedings nor dispossessed by the original order, provided there is a plain and sufficient nexus between the order for possession and the need to effect further recovery of the land.

Interim possession orders

In the county court (but not the High Court) certain applicants who are entitled to proceed under CCR Ord 24, Pt I (see above) may instead seek an interim possession order under CCR Ord 24, Pt II. This provides a remedy similar to a mandatory interlocutory injunction (see p 288 and see the undertakings which the court must consider imposing on the applicant if the order is made, CCR Ord 24, r 12(4)). It compels the respondents to vacate the specified premises within twenty-four hours of the service of the order upon them. The order will also specify a return day for a hearing (ie the second hearing) at which the court may (amongst other things) make a final order for possession or discharge the interim possession order and allow the proceedings to continue as if begun under CCR Ord 24, Pt I.

There are several limitations on applications for interim possession orders in addition to those applicable to proceedings under CCR Ord 24, Pt I (eg that the respondent is not a tenant or ex-tenant). The three most important are: (i) the term 'premises' is defined to exclude open land; (ii) the proceedings must not include a claim by the applicant for any remedy other than recovery of land; (iii) the applicant must commence the proceedings within twenty-eight days of the date on which he first knew, or ought reasonably to have known, that the respondent, or any of the respondents, was in occupation.

Subject to those limitations, the proceedings should be commenced by originating application in Form N130, which includes a form of affidavit in support to be completed and sworn by the applicant. Within twenty-four hours of issue, a copy of certain documentation including a notice stating the date of the first hearing must be served by the applicant or his agent by fixing it to the main door or other conspicuous part of the premises etc.

Interim possession orders are enforceable by police action (ie by arrest and prosecution; see the prescribed form of order, Form N134). They are not enforceable by bailiffs (CCR Ord 24, r 13).

Mortgage possession actions

By CCA 1984, s 21, the county court has jurisdiction to hear and determine any action for the recovery of land.

By CCR Ord 21, r 5 (1)(c) the district judge has jurisdiction to hear and determine any action in which a mortgagee under a mortgage claims possession of the mortgage property.

AJA 1970, s 36 as amended in 1973 gives the court certain powers, if it appears to the court that in the event of exercising one of them the mortgagor is likely to be able within a reasonable period to pay off any arrears of capital and interest which have accrued. If so satisfied the court could then adjourn the proceedings or, on giving judgment, stay or suspend execution of the judgment or postpone the date for delivery of possession for such period as the court thinks reasonable. Any such adjournment or suspension etc can be made subject to conditions with regard to payment by the mortgagor as the court thinks fit, and the court has express power to vary or revoke any condition. Because of the 1973 amendment the court is concerned only with the actual arrears in instalments and should ignore the effect of any mortgage clause which makes the whole outstanding balance due and payable.

Particulars of claim in any action for recovery of land must comply with the pleading requirements of CCR Ord 6, r 3 (see p 263). In addition, actions under a mortgage must also comply with CCR Ord 6, r 5. The particulars of claim must therefore state the date of the mortgage; the amount of the advance; mortgage instalments; arrears and amount remaining due. It must also state what proceedings if any the plaintiff has previously taken in respect of the mortgage.

Particulars of claim must also state whether or not the mortgaged property is a dwelling-house and, if it is, whether there is any person on whom notice of the action is required to be served in accordance with the Matrimonial Homes Act 1983, s 8(3) and, if so, stating the name and address of that person. If the house had been purchased in joint names of husband and wife both would be defendants. If the house had been purchased in the sole name of one spouse then that spouse will be sole defendant. The Matrimonial Homes Act 1983 gives a statutory right of occupation to the non-owning spouse. In practice a Matrimonial Homes Act search is required in all cases. Where property is jointly owned by spouses obviously one could not register a charge and in any event it would be unnecessary. However, circumstances may have changed since the mortgage loan was granted. The borrowers could have been divorced, one of them could have married again and that new spouse could now be residing in the mortgaged property with the protection of an MHA land charge. Therefore in practice the district judge will insist on an MHA search in all cases.

The procedure on a mortgage possession action is by fixed date action which is listed for hearing before a district judge in chambers. Because the hearing is in chambers affidavit evidence is admissible under CCR Ord 20, r 5. The affidavit should be filed and a copy served on the defendant in advance of the hearing. At the hearing the mortgagees must produce the original mortgage (in the case of registered land this will involve production of the charge certificate as well) and the MHA search.

Sadly many defendants to mortgage possession actions fail to appreciate the court's willingness to help them to avoid eviction and therefore fail to attend the hearing. If the defendant does not attend there is no evidence of ability to pay and so the court's power to suspend or postpone under AJA 1970, s 36 will not arise. The order will be in Form N29 giving possession in twenty-eight days.

If a defendant does attend, whether in person or through a solicitor, what is a reasonable period for the purpose of the AJA? The first point to establish is whether the defendant has the ability to discharge the arrears by means of instalments paid over the remaining term of the mortgage. If so that period may well be the reasonable period to allow (*Cheltenham Gloucester Building Society v Norgan* [1996] 1 WLR 343. If however the defendant can discharge the arrears only by way of sale various other factors would come into play including the extent to which the mortgage debt and arrears were secured by the value of the property and the effect of time on that security (*National and Provincial Building Society v Lloyd* [1996] 1 All ER 630 and *Bristol and West Building Society v Ellis* (1996) *The Times*, 2 May).

In *Cheltenham and Gloucester plc v Krausz* [1997] 1 All ER 21 the Court of Appeal held that if a lender is entitled to possession and seeks an order for possession the court has no jurisdiction to withhold that remedy except (generally speaking) under s 36 of the AJA 1970 just described (ie on being satisfied that the mortgage debt and arrears will be paid off in full within a reasonable period). This decision seems almost wholly to negate the earlier decision in *Palk v Mortgage Services Funding plc* [1993] Ch 330, the court's power under LPA 1925, s 91 to order a sale by a borrower at a price insufficient to discharge the mortgage debt and arrears. It now seems that the *Palk* ruling is relevant only if eg the lender consents or decides not to seek an order for possession.

If a suspended order is to be made this will be in Form N31. It grants possession but suspends it so long as the current instalments plus so much per month off the arrears are paid.

Lenders in possession actions rarely seek an order for costs preferring instead to rely on an appropriate provision in the mortgage deed which will entitle them to add all legal costs to the amount of the outstanding debt. This contractual provision means that the full amount of the lenders' solicitors' 'solicitor and own client bill' will be added to the debt. The court has no power to order a losing litigant to pay costs on the solicitor and own client basis; the most generous basis on which the court can award costs is the indemnity basis (see p 527). Some district judges therefore include in the order made a provision requiring that the lender should notify the borrower within a stated period of time the amount of costs which they propose to add to the mortgage debt. If the defendant considers that these costs are unreasonable he may wish to exercise his rights of taxation under the Solicitors Act 1974, s 71. The county court has jurisdiction to tax the bill (Solicitors Act 1974, s 69(3) and see *Gomba Holdings v Minories Finance Ltd (No 2)* [1993] Ch 171).

Second mortgages securing loans not exceeding £15,000 made by secondary banks and finance houses are usually regulated agreements within the meaning of s 8 of the Consumer Credit Act 1974. In such cases the criteria of the Administration of Justice Act do not apply and instead the court must consider whether it is appropriate to make a time order under s 129 of the Consumer Credit Act 1974. The court can order such instalments, payable at such times as the court, having regard to the means of the debtor, considers reasonable. Time orders often allow a period exceeding the remaining period of the loan.

Mortgagees today prefer to seek an order for possession rather than issue foreclosure proceedings. Under an order for possession once the mortgage and the costs of re-sale have been recouped by the lender, any balance still remaining is paid to the borrower. This is not so under a foreclosure order because the whole equity of redemption is extinguished and the legal title will vest fully in the lender. Because of the draconian nature of foreclosure the courts are reluctant to grant it. Rather than abolishing the remedy outright procedural obstacles were placed in the path of foreclosure as long ago as 1925. In particular where a claim for foreclosure is brought, the court has power under s 91 of the Law of Property Act 1925, on the application of a person interested, to order sale instead of foreclosure. There is even power to re-open a foreclosure after an order absolute. Consequently foreclosure is no longer usually sought by most lenders and even those who still persist in pleading it cannot seriously expect to obtain it. Foreclosure is not possible in any event in the case of a regulated agreement under the Consumer Credit Act 1974 as s 113 prevents a lender from obtaining any greater benefit by enforcing security than he would have obtained if no security had been given.

Mortgage actions in the High Court are brought in the Chancery Division. The ordinary practice and rules of the Chancery Division apply save in so far as they are inconsistent with the particular requirements of RSC Ord 88. The action can be by a writ or originating summons but in fact are usually begun by originating summons. An action can be commenced in London or in a Chancery District Registry (as to which, see p 5) or in the district registry in which the mortgaged property is situated (RSC Ord 88, r 3).

Official Referees' Business (RSC Ord 36)

Under SCA 1981, s 68 'official referees' business' means those cases in which jurisdiction of the High Court may be exercised by such circuit judges, deputy circuit judges and recorders as the Lord Chancellor may from time to time nominate. The office and title of 'official referee' was abolished in 1972 but persons so nominated by the Lord Chancellor are referred to in the RSC (Ord 1, r 4) and in popular parlance as official referees. Official referees were first appointed under enabling provisions in the Judicature Acts 1873–1875. Initially their role was subordinate to that of the High Court judges. Questions raising complicated issues of fact could be referred to an official referee for inquiry and report or for the trial of an issue of fact. Questions of law and the discretion as to costs were reserved to the judge. This subordinate role lasted only until 1884 when legislative changes enabled cases (rather than questions) to be referred to them and empowered them to give judgments and to make costs and other orders. The power to refer questions for inquiry and report survives, but is now considered obsolete (*White Book* 36/1–9/23). Today the official referees' powers are defined by RSC Ord 36. They have the same jurisdiction, powers and duties (including the power of committal and discretion as to costs) as a High Court judge. Proceedings before an official referee are conducted as nearly as possible in the same manner as proceedings before a High Court judge, rights of audience being given to counsel, solicitors who have been granted higher rights of audience in civil courts and litigants in person. Thus, although official referees are circuit judges or recorders in status, they are equivalent to High Court judges in function (and see pp 12 and 509).

A list of the main classes of action which fall within the scope of official referees' business is given in the *White Book* 36/1–9/13. Typical examples are cases concerning civil or mechanical engineering, building or other construction work, most professional negligence claims (save those concerning doctors and lawyers), landlord and tenant disputes concerning repairing covenants, claims relating to the supply and use of computers and claims arising out of fires. Most cases involve complicated questions of fact, often of a scientific or technical nature. A high proportion of them concern numerous contracts and sub-contracts so giving rise to a multiplicity of defendants and third parties.

The caseload in the official referees' courts has increased in recent years. Since April 1989 there has been an official referees' registry under the supervision of a chief clerk and separate official referees' courts, both at St Dunstan's House, 133–137 Fetter Lane, London EC4A 1BT. There are eight circuit judges nominated to deal full-time with official referees' business and they are assisted by part-time 'official referee recorders'. Most of the official referees' business is conducted in London. Also, each circuit except the South Eastern, now has two circuit official referees. Cases are allocated to them by their local district registries.

The special features of procedure in the official referees' courts all stem from the complex nature of the caseload.

(1) The role played by the official referee in the interlocutory stages.
(2) The specialised forms of pleadings and directions as to evidence.
(3) The giving of fixed dates for trial at an early stage of proceedings and the specialised directions concerning trial.

Cases received by the official referees' courts

A plaintiff can commence a Chancery or Queen's Bench action as 'official referees' business' by marking those words, beneath the name of the division, on the writ or originating summons before it is issued. (Process is now issued at St Dunstan's House not the central office, see above.) In such a case all interlocutory applications will be dealt with by an official referee rather than by a district judge or master; this includes, where relevant, applications for leave to issue for service overseas (see p 138) and applications for transfer to another court or judge. Alternatively an action can be transferred to the official referees' courts, after commencement, on any party's application by summons to the district judge. For example, if a defendant is served with a writ not marked as official referees' business but the defendant considers that the case would be more conveniently dealt with as such, he should apply for transfer at the earliest opportunity after acknowledging service and, if appropriate, before serving the defence. Similarly a district judge may, of his own

motion, transfer a case to the official referees' courts if the parties consent
or have been given an opportunity of being heard on the matter. Cases
suitable to be dealt with as official referees' business are frequently
transferred at the summons for directions stage (see p 457) or for damages
to be assessed after a default judgment is entered (see p 214). Commencement in, or transfer to, the official referees' courts does not affect the right
any party may have to trial by jury (see further p 463).

The application for directions

In London the question which case should be dealt with by which
official referee is resolved by a rota clerk who allocates cases to official
referees in rotation (as to documentation see *White Book* 36/1–9/5). The
same official referee should, as far as possible, deal with all matters
arising in the action, ie interlocutory applications and the trial itself;
exceptions are made for applications concerning interim payments and
payments into court (as to which see pp 308 and 329). At a very early
stage of the case, the plaintiff must obtain an appointment for a hearing
before the official referee for directions. In cases *commenced* as official
referees' business the plaintiff must apply within fourteen days after the
date upon which a defendant acknowledges service giving notice of
intention to defend. In cases *transferred* to the official referees' courts the
plaintiff must apply within fourteen days after the date the case was so
transferred. If the action was commenced by writ the application is by
interlocutory summons served on the other parties; if the action was
commenced by originating summons notice of the hearing must be given
to the other parties (cf pp 6 and 110).

The hearing is treated as a hearing of a summons for directions (see
p 451). The parties are expected to be able to state the nature of the
claims and defences and assist the official referee in determining the
directions best adapted to secure the just, expeditious and economical
disposal of the action. Whenever possible the date and place of trial are
fixed by the official referee at this hearing. Most cases will involve expert
witnesses and long notice of a fixed date for trial gives them ample time
to arrange their affairs accordingly. Long notice also accommodates the
convenience of solicitors and counsel and reduces the likelihood of last
minute changes in counsel. Once the date for trial is fixed it cannot be
changed unless, in an exceptional case, the official referee gives leave.
Another argument in favour of fixing a date for trial early is that it
encourages the parties to redouble their efforts to negotiate a compromise.
As elsewhere in the High Court, most cases settle before trial.

Specialised orders and directions

Because of the complexity of the issues raised in most cases, there are
a variety of specialised orders and directions the official referee may

make so as to reduce the case to manageable proportions. An official referee is able to take a more robust attitude to directions than a master could. He will usually actively intervene and does not merely adjudicate upon the arguments of the parties. Whenever directions are given it is the duty of the court to secure all such reasonable admissions and agreements as can be secured and refusals to make reasonable admissions and agreements can be recorded with a view to a special order for costs being made at the trial (see p 456). Since the same official referee will conduct the trial and so decide upon costs this puts him in a strong position to ensure that his wishes prevail. Typical orders include the following:

(1) Directions for pleadings to be prepared in the horizontal format of a 'Scott Schedule'. This is a single document divided into columns. Some columns are for completion by the plaintiffs, listing their claims item by item; other columns are for the defendants, answering the claims item by item. Further columns may be included to plead matters arising as between defendants and as between defendants and third parties.

(2) Directions limiting the number of expert witnesses, requiring exchange of reports and requiring experts of like discipline to meet without prejudice with a view to agreeing technical facts and narrowing the issues in dispute (see further pp 32 and 426).

(3) Orders for exchange of signed witness statements, such statements to stand as evidence in chief.

(4) In lengthy cases, an order for a pre-trial hearing, to take place about three months before trial, at which the procedures and arrangements for trial can be sorted out. At that hearing counsel are encouraged to agree a list of issues and final directions for trial are given.

(5) Directions for trial such as an order that issues of liability be tried before issues of *quantum* (ie a split trial, see p 456) or orders dividing a large case into sub-trials, or orders that items in a Scott Schedule be agreed as representative of others and these issues be tried before the remainder of the issues.

All except (5) above are now 'common form directions' (see further, *White Book* 36/1–9/21). Indeed, directions (2), (3) and (4) are now standard form in virtually all civil cases.

Appeals from official referees

As in most High Court cases, leave is required to appeal interlocutory orders or final orders which relate solely to costs. Leave is also required to appeal against findings of fact made by an official referee (see further, RSC Ord 58, r 4). The previous limitations on the right of appeal on questions of fact were removed at the suggestion of the Official Referees' Users' Committee.

The full right of appeal on points of law is one of the most important advantages trial by official referee offers over arbitration. In cases dealt with by way of arbitration rather than trial the rights of appeal are now almost non-existent (see Arbitration Act 1979 and the cases thereon which will eventually be codified into statute; Arbitration Act 1996, s 69).

Proceedings in the Commercial Court (RSC Ord 72)

A 'commercial list' in the High Court, Queen's Bench Division has been in existence since 1895. Cases entered on the list were governed by a separate set of rules providing a simplified procedure more suited to the needs of the mercantile community with briefer pleadings and more expeditious trials before judges of special experience. By common usage the commercial list has come to be known as 'the commercial court' and the expression 'Commercial Court' is now used in the current rules and Practice Directions. Since 1987 there has been a combined 'Admiralty and Commercial Registry'.

By RSC Ord 72, r 1 'commercial action' is defined in very wide and archaic language. In practice, cases concerning the following topics are typical of the court's workload:

(1) the international carriage of goods;
(2) contracts relating to ships and shipping;
(3) insurance and reinsurance;
(4) banking, negotiable instruments and international credit;
(5) the purchase and sale of commodities;
(6) the operation of international markets and exchange;
(7) the construction and performance of mercantile contracts.

By RSC Ord 72, r 4, a writ or originating summons can be issued out of the Admiralty and Commercial Registry in London, by marking it in the top left hand corner with the words 'Commercial Court'; on issue it is thereupon entered in the commercial list. It is possible to issue a writ by fax out of the Admiralty and Commercial Registry when it is closed to the public (see RSC Ord 6, r 7A).

If an action has not been commenced in the Commercial Court it is possible to transfer it by applying to the judge under RSC Ord 72, r 5 (contrast official referees' business: orders of transfer to official referees can be made by any district judge or master).

In all cases entered in the commercial list interlocutory applications before trial are made to a judge, not to a master (contrast post-trial applications). With the approval of the judges a 'Guide to Commercial Court Practice' has been prepared and published: the full text is set out in the *White Book* 72/A1 to 72/A30.

Pleadings in an action in the commercial list must be in the form of points of claim, or of defence, counterclaim, defence to counterclaim or reply as the case may be and must be as brief as possible (RSC Ord 72, r 7). No further and better particulars are to be applied for or ordered in an action in the commercial list except such particulars as are necessary to enable the party to be informed of the case he has to meet or as are for some other reason necessary to secure the just, expeditious and economical disposal of any question at issue in the action.

Any party to an action in the commercial list can take out a summons for directions in the action before the pleadings are deemed closed (RSC Ord 72, r 8). However the normal time to issue the summons for directions in a commercial action is after the inspection of documents has been completed. For a form of standard directions, see *White Book* 72/A29.

Cases in the Commercial Court are usually complex and lengthy. Fixed dates are given and the action is normally ordered to be set down not later than three months before the fixed date. A checklist in a standard form (see p 489) is required to be lodged with the clerk to the Commercial Court not later than two months before the fixed date. If these checklists are not submitted, the clerk to the Commercial Court will refer the case to the judge in charge of the list to whom an explanation for the failure must be given and by whom penalties in costs may be imposed.

Although there are no special requirements concerning documents in the Commercial Court the volume and complexity of the documentation makes it particularly important to comply with the *Practice Direction* [1983] 1 WLR 922 (see p 173).

Normal trial procedure is varied at the hearing of an action in the Commercial Court (see *White Book* 72/A24). Of particular note is the fact that the plaintiff's counsel's opening speech is confined to a brief and uncontroversial summary of the commercial story, the issues and the oral evidence to be adduced with limited reference only to the most central documents. This is immediately followed by a similar brief statement from the defendant's counsel. Evidence is then called. Plaintiff's counsel normally makes a first full contentious speech dealing with the facts and law after the conclusion of the evidence. Documents are referred to as and when they become relevant to a party's case and evidence of all parties on a particular topic is heard before consideration of other topics. Evidence of expert witnesses is heard after the conclusion of the factual evidence.

Since 1990 there have been two new Queen's Bench lists in the district registries of Manchester and Liverpool and originating process for these lists can be marked with the name of the registry and the words 'The Mercantile List (Manchester)' or 'The Mercantile List (Liverpool)' as appropriate. In February 1997 two further lists were established; the 'Leeds Mercantile Court List' and the 'Newcastle upon Tyne Mercantile Court List'. RSC Ord 72 does not apply to such cases. However, the practice followed is in fact very similar (see *White Book* 72/31). The word 'Mercantile' is used simply to avoid confusion with the Commercial Court in London.

Since 1994 the county courts have also had a specialist court for commercial cases: the Central London County Court Business List, procedure as to which is governed by CCR Ord 48C and is similar to High Court procedure in many respects both general (an acknowledgment of service stage and no automatic transfers to the defendant's home court) and special (pleadings in the form of points of claim or defence etc, most applications, interlocutory or final, to be determined by the judge not the district judge). As to allocation of business between the High Court and the Central London County Court Business List, the figure above which suitability for trial in the High Court is presumed (see p 108) is increased from £50,000 to £200,000.

Business tenancy renewal applications

Business tenants enjoy security of tenure in respect of premises which they occupy for the purposes of their business. The law is contained in Pt II of the Landlord and Tenant Act 1954. Broadly, where a business tenant has complied with the terms of the tenancy, the Act gives security of tenure, or in a case where the landlord is able to terminate the tenancy, provides for compensation. 'Business' includes a trade, profession or employment and includes any activity carried on by a body of persons whether corporate or incorporate. Section 43 exempts certain tenancies. It is important to comply with the strict time limits. Time limits imposed by the Act are very short and the court has no discretion to extend them. Thus failure to comply with a requirement as to time is fatal and if it is the solicitor's fault the client will have an unanswerable claim in negligence.

A tenant enjoys security only in respect of premises occupied for the tenant's business. Thus, for example, if a tenant has sub-let part of the premises to another business tenant then the tenant will have no security of tenure in respect of the sub-let part but conversely the sub-tenant will have. Any application to the court for a new tenancy will be issued by the relevant tenant and must be against 'the competent landlord'. Where there is a multiplicity of sub-tenancies it will be necessary to ascertain who is 'the competent landlord' for the purposes of the Act (see s 44 and the Sched 6 definitions).

Whilst the tenancy still subsists (under the contractual term or because the tenant is holding over and enjoying the protection of s 24) either the landlord will serve a notice under s 25 or the tenant will serve a request under s 26.

A landlord's notice must be in the prescribed form and must be given to the tenant by the competent landlord not less than six months nor more than twelve months before the date of termination specified in the notice. It must require the tenant within two months after the giving of the notice to notify the landlord in writing whether or not he is willing is give up possession and state whether or not the landlord will oppose any application for the new tenancy and if so on which ground (the grounds are set out in s 30). A tenant's s 26 request can be used only where the tenant is holding under a tenancy granted for a term of years certain exceeding one year and cannot be used where a landlord has already served a s 25 notice. The request must state the date on which the new tenancy is to begin being not more than twelve months nor less than six months after the making of the request and cannot be earlier than the date on which the tenancy could have terminated at common law. It must also give the tenant's proposals as to the property to be comprised in the new tenancy, the rent to be payable and any other terms, eg duration.

The service of a s 25 notice or s 26 request must be followed by service of a counter-notice 'within 2 months' after the notice or request (ss 25(5), 26(6)). Failure on the part of the tenant to serve a counter-notice to a s 25 notice kills the tenant's right to apply to the court for a new tenancy (s 29(2)). Failure on the part of the landlord to serve a counter-notice to a s 26 request kills the landlord's right to seek to establish any grounds of opposition to the grant of a new tenancy (s 30(1)).

If the terms of a new tenancy are not agreed (and rarely in practice can they be agreed within the short time allowed) it will be necessary for the tenant to make an application to the court. The county court has equal jurisdiction with the High Court (s 63).

The tenant must issue an application to the court not less than two months nor more than four months after the giving of the s 25 notice or s 26 request as the case may be. In computing the period the 'corresponding date rule' is applied. Thus for example if the notice is served on the 30th of the month the time within which the tenant can make a valid application begins on the corresponding date (the 30th) two months forward and ends on the corresponding date (the 30th) four months forward. If any month in question does not have the corresponding date (February), the last day of that month is adopted instead (*Dodds v Walker* [1981] 1 WLR 1027, HL). If the last date for application falls on a date when the court office is closed (eg a Bank Holiday) an application is still in time if made on the next day (*Hodgson v Armstrong* [1967] QB 299). Procedure is by way of originating application (county court) or originating summons (High Court) and must comply with CCR Ord 43, r 6 or RSC Ord 97, r 6.

The application or summons as appropriate must be served on the competent landlord within two months of issue (CCR Ord 43, r 6; RSC Ord 97, r 6). The court can extend the period of service for a further period up to two months per application (and see further, p 205 where several of the cases referred to are in fact business tenancy renewal cases). If, after commencement, there is a change of competent landlord the action is not properly constituted until the new competent landlord is added as a party (*Piper v Muggleton* [1956] 2 QB 569).

In the county court the originating application for a new tenancy will be in Form N397. The first hearing will be for a pre-trial review.

In the county court the landlord must file an answer in Form N400 within fourteen days after the date of service of the application (CCR Ord 43, r 2 and CCR Ord 9, r 18). In the High Court the landlord must file an affidavit not less than four days before the date fixed for the first hearing of the summons (RSC Ord 97, r 7).

In both courts the response must state, *inter alia*, whether the landlord is a tenant under a lease having less than fourteen days unexpired at the date of termination of the tenant's tenancy and, if he is, details as to his immediate landlord and (in the county court) other superior landlords. If the landlord wishes to apply for an interim rent under s 24A in the county court the landlord's application must be made in the answer (*Thomas v Hammond-Lawrence* [1986] 1 WLR 456). In the High Court an application for an interim rent must be made by summons (RSC Ord 97, r 9A). If an application for interim rent under s 24A is made and the court determines such a rent it is payable from the date the application was made. In practice applications for interim rents are rarely heard as a separate issue but are normally dealt with at the hearing of the substantive application for a new tenancy itself. Especially after periods of high inflation, an interim rent may well be something between the current rent and the new rent ordered and therefore the practical effect of an interim rent application is often that there will be a partial backdating of the new rent ordered.

Most applications for new business tenancies are compromised. Proceedings have been issued merely because of the strict requirements of the statute but once the landlord's valuer and tenant's valuer get together it is usually possible for a new rent to be negotiated. If this is done then the new lease can simply be executed and the application to the court then discontinued. Alternatively, if a compromise is reached at the last minute, a consent order can be obtained.

The directions required at pre-trial review will depend on the ground of opposition of the landlord. If for example non-repair is alleged a schedule of dilapidations will be required. Directions will certainly be required as to expert evidence.

If acting for a tenant it is often essential to instruct an expert surveyor at an early stage with a view to obtaining advice as to the likely rent which the court would order under a new tenancy. It may be, for example, that if the new rent is to be substantially greater than the current rent the tenant simply could not afford to stay on and it would be pointless making the application to the court in any event.

If the landlord is opposing the grant of a new tenancy on one of the s 30 grounds it is usual to order trial of that issue as a preliminary point. This will avoid the need to call expert evidence as to rent at that hearing because if the landlord's opposition succeeds it will not be necessary for the court to hear such evidence. If, on the other hand, the landlord's opposition fails it will probably be possible to then agree terms or, failing that, a fresh hearing of the application can be arranged for the purpose of determining the terms of the new tenancy. The court's powers as to duration, rent and terms are contained in ss 33–35.

A new lease ordered by the court commences on the later of the dates specified in the s 25 notice or s 26 request or the date upon which the order for a new lease was made, or an appeal was heard plus three months plus twenty-eight days (ie the time allowed for any appeal or further appeal) (s 64).

Usually no order for costs is made (*Cairnplace Ltd v CBL (Property Investment) Co Ltd* (1984) 269 EG 542) but as ever costs will be in the discretion of the court. Business tenancy renewal applications are particularly susceptible to '*Calderbank* offers' (see p 329).

Small claims

In the county court, special rules apply to claims for £3,000 or less (£1,000 or less in the case of personal injury claims) unless the claim also includes a claim for possession of land. The rules and the *Green Book* commentary thereon refer to 'small claims arbitration'. This use of the term 'arbitration' has been judicially criticised (*Joyce v Liverpool City Council* [1996] QB 252 *per* Sir Thomas Bingham MR). The Arbitration Act 1996 does not apply in this context (see s 92 of the 1996 Act).

Small claims are commenced by default action in the normal way. Judgment in default will be obtained in the absence of a response from the defendant. If, however, a defence is filed the claim is automatically referred to arbitration under CCR Ord 19, r 3(1). The same occurs if a document is filed admitting liability but 'disputing or not admitting the amount claimed' (CCR Ord 19, r 3(4)). The district judge considers the documents filed, gives appropriate directions and fixes a time estimate for the arbitration hearing. Parties are given at least twenty-one days' notice of the hearing. Exceptionally (see CCR Ord 19, r 6(4)) a preliminary appointment will be convened. The district judge has the same powers on a preliminary hearing as he has on a pre-trial review. This includes the power to give early judgment discussed above.

The directions given by the district judge require each party to send to the other, not less than fourteen days before the hearing, copies of all documents in his possession and on which he intends to rely at the hearing and, not less than seven days before the hearing, a copy of any expert's report on which he intends to rely and a list of the witnesses whom he intends to call: a copy of the expert's report and the list of witnesses must also be filed at court.

Arbitration is intended to be quick, simple and convenient. The procedure is intended to be straightforward enough for a litigant in person without legal advice and with minimum assistance from the court office. Technicalities are avoided and many of the normal rules of litigation do not apply. CCR Ord 19, r 6 expressly states certain rules which do not apply to cases referred to arbitration namely Ord 6, r 7 (further particulars), Ord 9, r 11 (particulars of defence), Ord 14, rr 1(2), 3, 4, 5, 5A and 11 (discovery and interrogatories), Ord 20, rr 2 and 3 (notices to admit facts and documents), Ord 20, r 12A (exchange of witness statements), Ord 11, rr 1, 1A, 3, 4, 5, 7, 8 and 10 (payments into court) and Ord 13, r 1(8)(*a*) (security for costs). Instead, the district judge is, in effect, required to adopt an 'inquisitorial style' into the proceedings rather than the traditional 'adversarial style'.

The hearing itself is informal and the strict rules of evidence do not apply. Hearings are in private (usually the district judge's chambers) and evidence is not usually on oath. The arbitrator can adopt any procedure which he considers to be fair and which gives each party an equal opportunity to present his case. The arbitrator (having regard to whether or to what extent a party is represented) may assist a party by putting questions to the witnesses of other parties and will explain any legal terms or expressions used. At the conclusion the arbitrator states his award and gives reasons (see generally Ord 19, r 7).

In practice arbitration works well in consumer disputes or a dispute concerning a minor road accident with damage to property and no personal injuries. The issues of law involved are usually simple and the disputes are largely based on facts. Such cases can be argued by litigants in person without difficulty. Any inequality of representation (ie a claimant in person against an insurer's representative) can be remedied by the district judge's power to assist parties by putting questions for them and by explaining any legal terms used (CCR Ord 19, r 7(4)). The automatic reference to arbitration of such claims is intended to discourage legal representation. To this end CCR Ord 19, r 4 provides that no solicitors' charges will be allowed as between litigants in any small claim reference to arbitration except

> (*a*) the costs which were stated on the summons or which would have been stated on the summons if the claim had been for a liquidated sum;
> (*aa*) in proceedings which include a claim for an injunction or for an order for specific performance or similar relief, a sum not exceeding £260 in respect of the cost of legal advice obtained for the purpose of bringing or defending that claim;
> (*b*) the costs of enforcing the award, and
> (*c*) such further costs as the arbitrator may direct where there has been unreasonable conduct on the part of the opposite party in relation to the proceedings or the claim therein.

The first three exceptions listed above indicate the extent to which the cost of legal advice and assistance is considered justifiable in ordinary small claims. The costs of legal services are considered disproportionate to the issues arbitrated if those services go beyond help as to commencement, advice concerning equitable remedies and help as to enforcement *unless* exception (*c*) applies. Exception (*c*) concerns unreasonable conduct by the opponent, for example disgraceful, vexatious harassing behaviour which unnecessarily complicates and delays the arbitration.

The philosophy of disallowing full solicitors' charges in cases where the sums at stake are small has also been applied in cases which were *not* automatically referred to arbitration. For example a small claim in which the plaintiff overstated the value of the claim thereby obtaining trial rather than arbitration in circumstances in which he had no reasonable expectation of recovering more than the small claims limit (see *Afzal v Ford Motor Co Ltd* [1994] 4 All ER 720 in which in one of the cases dealt with a plaintiff who refused to proceed by way of arbitration was penalised in costs. Contrast *Smith v Vauxhall Motors Ltd* [1997] PIQR 19 where, in an action proceeding to trial, the plaintiff accepted a payment into court of £375; the district judge made an order for costs on Scale 1 on the basis that, objectively, her expectation of being awarded personal injuries damages exceeding £1,000 had been reasonable; this order was upheld by the circuit judge and by the Court of Appeal).

The automatic reference to arbitration does not remove the litigants' right to use legal representation, at their own expense, if they so wish. Further the CLSA 1990, s 11 permits a 'lay representative' and the Lay Representatives (Rights of Audience) Order 1992 gives a right of audience to a lay representative in small claims arbitrations (see further, *Green Book* 2026).

If, in a particular case, a litigant desires legal representation at all stages and with a full order for costs should he be successful, an application may be made for the reference to arbitration to be rescinded. If the reference is rescinded the claim will still be dealt with by the district judge (CCR Ord 21, r 5, see p 479) but by way of trial rather than by arbitration, and the successful litigant can expect to receive an order for costs on scale 1. However, the grounds for applying for rescission of a reference to arbitration are limited. The district judge can rescind the reference, either on application or of his own motion if satisfied (CCR Ord 19, r 3):

(a) that a difficult question of law or a question of fact of complexity is involved; or
(b) that a charge of fraud is in issue; or
(c) that the parties are agreed that the dispute should be tried in court; or
(d) that it would be unreasonable for the claim to proceed to arbitration having regard to its subject matter, the size of any counterclaim, the circumstances of the parties or the interests of any other person likely to be affected by the award.

In *Joyce v Liverpool City Council* [1996] QB 252 Sir Thomas Bingham MR stated that 'small claims arbitration procedure is no more, and no less, than a procedure for resolving low value claims, almost always by the district judge, with a minimum of formality and expense.' Recent case law and recent rule changes encourage the use of this procedure in most cases including employers' liability cases (*Afzal*, see above) and 'housing disrepair' cases in which tenants seek against their landlords modest damages and specific performance of repairing covenants (*Joyce*, see above). Rescission of the reference to arbitration is appropriate only in the borderline or exceptional cases. 'Difficult questions of law' and 'complex questions of fact' (see Ground (*a*)) connote those few cases in which the likely outcome of the case is not obvious to the layman.

Grounds (*b*) and (*c*) do not frequently arise in practice. Examples of Ground (*d*) include cases which it is unreasonable to arbitrate because they will affect other people, such as a test-action, or where the claim, though small, affects a continuing liability, such as a claim concerning service charges payable under the lease of a flat.

Arbitration in other cases

It is convenient to point out here that arbitration is by no means limited to small claims. Parties seeking the informality and finality it offers may apply for it in any action. Unless the court otherwise directs, an application may be made: in the case of a plaintiff, by notice incorporated in the particulars of claim; in the case of a defendant, by notice incorporated in any defence or counterclaim filed; in any case, on notice under CCR Ord 13, r 1. If an order referring the proceedings to arbitration is made (see Form N19) the procedure to be followed thereafter is identical to the small claims arbitration procedure (compare Forms N18 and N19). However if the claim exceeds £3,000 the rule restricting costs does not apply. The arbitrator will make the same order for costs as would have been made if the action had been tried (see generally CCR Ord 19, rr 2, 5).

Arbitrations are not always referred to the district judge. In any claim, small or large, the proceedings may be referred for arbitration by the circuit judge (subject to his consent) or by an outside arbitrator (subject to the consent of the parties: CCR Ord 19, r 5).

Chapter 14

Pre-trial Remedies

Interlocutory injunctions

An injunction is an order of the court either compelling a party to take specified steps (a mandatory injunction) or restraining him from taking specified steps (a prohibitory or negative injunction). An injunction granted after a trial is called a final or perpetual injunction. An interlocutory injunction is an order made before trial, if necessary even before the issue of proceedings, and is usually granted to keep matters *in statu quo* until the trial can be heard. An injunction, whether mandatory or prohibitory, whether final or interlocutory, can be granted to remedy an injury already suffered or *quia timet* to prevent an injury occurring.

A full interlocutory injunction may continue in force until 'judgment in the action or further order'. An interlocutory injunction granted on an *ex parte* application continues in force only for a short time thereby compelling an applicant who requires an order for longer to re-apply *inter partes*, ie after giving notice to the respondent. Even before the *ex parte* order expires the respondent may apply on notice for it to be discharged. Being of so short a duration injunctions granted *ex parte* are sometimes called 'interim injunctions'.

An interlocutory injunction is usually a temporary version of the type of injunction the applicant will seek at the trial and is thus only a provisional remedy. However, many injunction cases never get beyond the interlocutory stage. The parties are often content to accept the court's decision as a fair indication of what the trial judge would order. In exceptional cases the interlocutory order may amount to the full remedy sought by the action (*Cambridge Nutrition Ltd v BBC* [1990] 3 All ER 523; interlocutory injunction to restrain the broadcast of a programme listed for broadcast within the next few days) or may give the applicant a remedy which is a collateral to his trial remedies (eg *Mareva* injunctions and *Anton Piller* orders: see below). The principles applicable to the grant of these exceptional types of interlocutory injunction differ from the general principles laid down in *American Cyanamid v Ethicon* [1975] AC 396 (see below).

Undertaking as to damages

Since every interlocutory injunction is granted before trial and therefore before the merits of the case have been finally determined, the applicant is required to give an 'undertaking as to damages', ie a promise to pay his opponent compensation if the applicant later fails to establish his right to the injunction. The undertaking is enforced by an inquiry into what loss the respondent suffered because of the injunction. The assessment of damages is made on the premise that the applicant has covenanted with the respondent *not* to prevent the respondent doing that which he was restrained from doing by the terms of the injunction (*per* Lord Diplock in *Hoffman-La Roche v Secretary of State for Trade and Industry* [1975] AC 295). The undertaking is also enforceable by co-defendants who were not directly subject to the injunction but who have suffered loss because of it (*Dubai Bank Ltd v Galadari (No 2)* (1989) *The Times*, 11 October; *White Book* 29/1/12). The undertaking is given, not to the respondent, but to the court, which has a discretion as to whether or not to enforce it (*Cheltenham & Gloucester Building Society v Ricketts* [1993] 1 WLR 1545; and see *Goldman Sachs International Ltd v Lyons* (1995) *The Times*, 28 February; as to whether the inquiry should be conducted by a district judge see *Balkanbank v Taher* [1995] 1 WLR 1056 *per* Staughton LJ).

There are two exceptional cases where no undertaking will be required:
(1) Cases brought by the Crown, local authorities and similar law enforcement agencies acting in the public interest to enforce the law (*Hoffman-La Roche v Secretary of State for Trade and Industry* [1975] AC 295, above, *Director General of Fair Trading v Tobyward Ltd* [1989] 1 WLR 517 and *Kirklees Borough Council v Wickes Building Supplies Ltd* [1993] AC 227).
(2) Matrimonial cases not involving property rights (*Practice Direction* [1974] 1 WLR 576).

General principles upon which granted: *American Cyanamid v Ethicon*

In *American Cyanamid v Ethicon* [1975] AC 396 the House of Lords declared that so long as an action was not frivolous or vexatious the only substantial factor the court takes into account is the balance of convenience. In other words it should not prejudge the merits of the case, but should simply consider the nature of the injunction sought and ask: Would it hurt the plaintiff more to go without the injunction pending trial than it would hurt the defendant to suffer it? The matters for the court's attention and the order in which they are dealt with may be listed as follows:

1 Whether there is a serious question to be tried
The claim must not be frivolous or vexatious and must have some prospect of succeeding (see *Re Cable* [1975] 1 WLR 7; *Smith v ILEA* [1978] 1 All ER 441).

It is no part of the court's function at this stage to try to resolve conflicts of evidence on affidavits as to fact on which the claims of either party may ultimately depend nor to decide difficult questions of law which call for detailed argument and mature considerations. These are matters to be dealt with at the trial (*per* Lord Diplock in *American Cyanamid*).

In practice if questions of law do arise in proceedings before them, most judges cannot resist answering them (see *per* Lord Jauncey in *R v Secretary of State for Transport, ex parte Factortame Ltd (No 2)* [1991] AC 603, and see also determining questions of law arising on applications under RSC Ord 14A, p 231). In *Bristol & West Building Society v Marks and Spencer plc* [1991] 41 EG 139 an interlocutory injunction was refused on this factor (and *obiter* other factors, see p 288) because of the construction which the learned judge made of the meaning of the leasehold covenant upon which the plaintiff was suing.

2 Which way the balance of convenience lies

(1) Are damages an adequate remedy for the plaintiff and is the defendant able to pay them? If yes, the injunction will be refused: if no, you must next consider:

(2) Is the undertaking as to damages adequate protection for the defendant and is the plaintiff able to honour it? The plaintiff may be ordered to put up some security in case he fails to honour it, eg a bank guarantee or the payment of a specified sum into an account held in the joint names of the parties' solicitors (see further p 292). If the answer to question (2) is yes, the injunction will be granted: if no, you must next consider:

(3) The maintenance of the *status quo*. Where the other factors are evenly balanced the court prefers to maintain the *status quo*, ie the state of affairs prevailing before the last change if the plaintiff applies promptly after that change (*Garden Cottage Foods Ltd v Milk Marketing Board* [1984] AC 130 *per* Lord Diplock). Accordingly this factor is normally in the plaintiff's favour. But note that, unlike (1) or (2), it is never by itself conclusive and the relevant *status quo* will change if the plaintiff delays his application to the court.

(4) Other factors, including social and economic factors. In *American Cyanamid* itself, where a *quia timet* injunction was granted to restrain a threatened infringement of a patent, the court took into account the fact that 'no factories would be closed and no workpeople would be thrown out of work' because of the injunction. The court will also take into account the public interest in cases in which the injunctions will have some public or political significance going beyond the protection of merely private rights (*Beaverbrook Newspapers v Keys* [1978] ICR 582). There is no rule that, in such cases, the plaintiff is required to show more than

a serious question to be tried (*R v Secretary of State for Transport, ex parte Factortame Ltd (No 2)* [1991] AC 603).

(5) The relative strength of the parties' cases, ie the prediction which side will win. This is a factor of last resort and even then should be used only if the strength of one case is disproportionate. This factor has always been controversial. It underlies most of the exceptions to *American Cyanamid* which have been recognised (see below). In *Series 5 Software Ltd v Clarke* [1996] 1 All ER 853 Laddie J asserts strongly that Lord Diplock's famous *dicta* on this factor in *American Cyanamid* have not been properly understood. This assertion is supported by what Lord Diplock stated in *NWL Ltd v Woods* [1979] 1 WLR 1294 (see below) and by certain *dicta* of Lord Goff in *R v Secretary of State for Transport, ex parte Factortame Ltd* (No 2) [1991] AC 603.

The expression 'balance of convenience' has been criticised. In *Francome v Mirror Group Newspapers Ltd* [1984] 1 WLR 892 Sir John Donaldson MR described it as:

> an unfortunate expression. Our business is justice, not convenience. We can and must disregard fanciful claims by either party. Subject to that, we must contemplate the possibility that either party may succeed and must do our best to ensure that nothing occurs pending the trial which will prejudice his rights. Since the parties are usually asserting wholly inconsistent claims, this is difficult, but we have to do our best. In doing so we are seeking a balance of justice, not of convenience.

In *Cayne v Global Natural Resources plc* [1984] 1 All ER 225 May LJ described the expression 'balance of convenience' as a useful shorthand:

> but in truth ... the balance that one is seeking to make is more fundamental, more weighty, than mere 'convenience' ... [A]lthough the phrase may well be substantially less elegant, the 'balance of the risk of doing an injustice' better describes the process involved.

In *R v Secretary of State for Transport, ex parte Factortame Ltd (No 2)* [1991] AC 603 in which the House of Lords reaffirmed the *American Cyanamid* principles, Lord Bridge's speech included the following *dictum*:

> Questions as to the adequacy of an alternative remedy in damages to the party claiming injunctive relief and of a cross-undertaking in damages to the party against whom the relief is sought play a primary role in assisting the court to determine which course offers the best prospect that injustice may be avoided or minimised.

Exceptions to *American Cyanamid*

Several exceptions to the *American Cyanamid* principles as originally enunciated have been recognised or suggested. In our view the first three listed below are all varieties of the same exception; in cases where the injunction will pre-empt or obviate the need for a trial, the court should take into account the strength of the plaintiff's case. Although we list them as exceptions it has been explained that 'when properly understood' the *American Cyanamid* principles as originally enunciated cover at least the first two of them (see *per* Lord Diplock in *NWL Ltd v Woods* [1979] 1 WLR 1294).

1 Likelihood of defence under Trade Union and Labour Relations (Consolidation) Act 1992, ss 219—220

This is a statutory exception first made in 1975 shortly after *American Cyanamid* was reported. Under ss 219–220 of the Act certain conduct which would otherwise give rise to an action in tort is protected from such action if done 'in contemplation or furtherance of a trade dispute'. Section 221 as amended provides that if the respondent to an application for an interlocutory injunction claims a defence under ss 219–220 'the court shall, in exercising its discretion whether or not to grant the injunction, have regard to the likelihood' of his establishing the defence at the trial. This provision is one of the factors the court should consider when deciding which way the balance of convenience lies. It is not an overriding or paramount factor (*NWL Ltd v Woods* [1979] 1 WLR 1294). The weight to be attached to it depends upon the degree of likelihood that the defence will be established, ie the stronger the defence the less likely it is that an interlocutory injunction will be granted (*Hadmor Productions Ltd v Hamilton* [1983] 1 AC 191). The rationale behind s 221 may be explained as follows: industrial action is used by the defendant as a bargaining counter in negotiations with an employer; its effectiveness depends upon its being promoted immediately; if it is postponed the defendant is unlikely to be able to mobilise support later, once the initial furore has died down. Thus s 221 enables the court to take account of the fact that the grant of an injunction is tantamount to giving final judgment against the defendant (*per* Lord Diplock in *NWL Ltd v Woods*, above).

2 Where the injunction will finally dispose of the action

Interlocutory injunction applications are decided without a full investigation of the merits of either party's case. Thus the court is reluctant to give a plaintiff interlocutory relief which pre-empts the defendant's right to a trial.

> Cases of this kind are exceptional, but when they do occur they bring into the balance of convenience an important additional element (*per* Lord Diplock in *NWL Ltd v Woods* [1979] 1 WLR 1294).

In such cases, factor 2(5) (see opposite, p 286) is given increased importance (although it must not be treated as the sole consideration; *Lansing Linde Ltd v Kerr* [1991] 1 WLR 251). To obtain interlocutory relief the plaintiff must show a 'more than arguable case' or 'more than merely a serious issue to be tried'.

Examples

Parnass/Pelly v Hodges [1982] FSR 329, a passing-off action in which an interlocutory injunction would force the defendant to permanently damage his marketing strategy.

Cambridge Nutrition Ltd v BBC [1990] 3 All ER 523, an interlocutory injunction to prevent the broadcast of a programme on matters of topical interest to the general public.

Lansing Linde Ltd v Kerr [1991] 1 WLR 251, an interlocutory injunction to enforce a restrictive covenant in an employment contract in an action which could not be tried before the covenant had expired or almost expired (if such an action can be tried speedily, the general principles of *American Cyanamid* should be applied; see *Lawrence David Ltd v Ashton* [1989] ICR 123).

3 Interlocutory mandatory injunctions

The courts have always been reluctant to grant mandatory injunctions at an interlocutory stage. In some cases the injunction sought amounts to the whole remedy claimed in the action so bringing the case within the principles of the two previous exceptions (*Evans v BBC* (1974) *The Times*, 26 February; *Locabail International Finance Ltd v Agroexport* [1986] 1 WLR 657 *per* Mustill LJ). In other cases the court fears that, because it will alter and not preserve the *status quo*, a mandatory injunction is more likely to increase rather than reduce the risk of injustice (*Shephard Homes Ltd v Sandham* [1971] Ch 340, interlocutory order to pull down a fence; *Bristol & West Building Society v Marks and Spencer plc* [1991] 41 EG 139, an interlocutory order to re-open and keep open during shopping hours the side-doors of a store leading to and from an adjoining arcade of shops). In these exceptional cases a plaintiff may be required to show a high probability that his claim will succeed if he is to surmount the court's reluctance.

It is a mistake, however, to assume that every interlocutory mandatory injunction falls into these exceptional categories. On the contrary, many claims for such an injunction will not be pre-emptive of a trial. An injunction which compels the defendant 'until trial or further order' to continue a course of action which he has previously taken will maintain the *status quo* until trial. In such cases the ordinary principles of *American Cyanamid* should be applied: see for example *Garden Cottage Foods Ltd v Milk Marketing Board* [1984] AC 130, injunction sought to restrain interruption of supplies of bulk butter (in fact refused on *American Cyanamid* factor 2(1) (see p 285), damages an adequate remedy for the plaintiff); *Sky Petroleum Ltd v VIP Petroleum Ltd* [1974] 1 WLR 576, injunction granted restraining interruption of petrol supplies; *Worldwide Dryers Ltd v Warner Howard Ltd* (1982) *The Times*, 9 December, injunction restraining the defendants from 'refusing to continue supplying' certain machinery to the plaintiff.

Note that in each of these non-exceptional cases the injunction is worded in negative form even though it is positive in effect. In *Films Rover Ltd v Cannon Film Sales Ltd* [1987] 1 WLR 670, Hoffman J described cases such as these as being cases having a 'dynamic *status quo*': an order was granted in respect of a distribution agreement relating to seventeen films requiring the defendant to deliver to the plaintiff's solicitors forthwith certain negatives and other materials relevant to three of the films.

4 Where the defendant has no arguable defence

In *Official Custodian for Charities v Mackey* [1985] Ch 168, Scott J said that the *American Cyanamid* principles were not applicable in a case in which there is no arguable defence to the plaintiff's claim. Instead he placed reliance upon a nineteenth-century *dictum* of James LJ:

> Balance of convenience has nothing to do with a case of this kind; it can only be considered where there is some question which must be decided at the hearing (*Stocker v Planet Building Society* (1879) 27 WR 877).

In *Patel v WH Smith (Eziot) Ltd* [1987] 1 WLR 853 the plaintiff, whose title to the land in question was not disputed, obtained an interlocutory injunction to restrain trespass even though the acts complained of did not harm him.

> If there is no arguable case, as I believe there is not, then questions of balance of convenience, *status quo* and damages being an adequate remedy do not arise (*per* Balcombe LJ).

This approach appears to conflict with *American Cyanamid* factor 2(5): relative strength of parties' cases to be a factor (of last resort) in weighing the balance of convenience. Properly understood however there is no conflict. If there is no arguable defence the grant of an interlocutory injunction is an act of some generosity towards the defendant. In such a case the plaintiff is entitled to summary judgment under RSC Ord 14 and therefore is entitled to an injunction which is final. To seek an interlocutory injunction in such a case is to give the defendant two occasions not one on which to raise a defence. The approach is the same as that taken in cases in which interlocutory orders are sought vacating land charges or cautions (*Alpenstow Ltd v Regalian Properties plc* [1985] 1 WLR 721). The interlocutory order is in effect an order *nisi*. In most cases the drawing up of a final order, the order absolute, will be a formality.

5 Defamation and malicious falsehood

Where a plaintiff seeks an injunction to restrain defamation or malicious falsehood two basic rights conflict: the plaintiff's right to protection from unlawful injury to his reputation and the defendant's right to freedom of speech. For many years now the courts have resolved this conflict by holding that if the defendant *bona fide* intends to plead justification or fair comment on a matter of public interest the plaintiff cannot obtain an interlocutory injunction however strong his case (see *Fraser v Evans* [1969] 1 QB 349, *Harakas v Baltic Mercantile and Shipping Exchange Ltd* [1982] 1 WLR 958 and see *Khashoggi v IPC Magazines Ltd* [1986] 1 WLR 1412 in which the defendants intended to justify the 'common sting' of the allegations made against the plaintiff). Instead the plaintiff is left to claim remedies at the trial only, ie damages and a final injunction. These principles have not been affected by *American Cyanamid* (see *Herbage v Pressdram Ltd* [1984] 1 WLR 1160). A plaintiff can sometimes obtain an interlocutory injunction to restrain publication of *confidential* information (see *Francome v Mirror Group Newspapers Ltd* [1984] 1 WLR 892 where the plaintiffs' telephone had been tapped and their conversations were illegally recorded) and in cases of conspiracy to injure (*Gulf Oil (Great Britain) Ltd v Page* [1987] Ch 327; *Femis-Bank (Anguilla) Ltd v Lazar* [1991] 3 WLR 80) and cases in which the defendants have no arguable defence (*Coulson v Coulson* (1887) 3 TLR 846; *Kaye v Robertson* (1990) *The Times*, 21 March, and see above).

Procedure on applications

District judges have only limited jurisdiction to grant injunctions (see pp 6 and 12). Most applications are therefore made to a judge. In the High Court the procedure is governed by RSC Ord 29, r 1 and by practice directions: for Queen's Bench cases see *White Book* 32/1–6/5; for Chancery cases see *White Book* 850 and 856. Some standard forms of injunction have been published for use in all Chancery and Queen's Bench cases 'in the absence of good reason to the contrary' (*Practice Direction (Interlocutory Injunctions: Forms*) [1996] 1 WLR 1551 and for the forms themselves see *White Book* 947/3 second supplement p 147). Wherever possible a draft injunction should be provided on paper and also on disk (to facilitate the incorporation of any amendments made by the judge). In the county court the procedure is governed by CCR Ord 13, r 6.

Ex parte applications

An application can be made *ex parte*, ie without giving any formal notice to the opponent if two conditions are satisfied: that giving notice to the opponent would cause injustice to the applicant because of the urgency of the matter or because of the need to obtain a provisional remedy by surprise; and that the risk of damages to the opponent is either compensatable by damages or is clearly outweighed by the risk of injustice to the applicant if an order is not made *ex parte* (*Re First Express Ltd* (1991) *The Times*, 10 October).

In the High Court the writ (if any), the affidavit in support and papers relating to the application must if possible be delivered to the court office by a specified time during the working day preceding the day of application (in Queen's Bench, 3 pm; in Chancery, 12 noon). In cases of extreme urgency an application can be made *ex parte* to any judge either in court or at his home. Provision is made in both the High Court and the county court for emergency applications outside court hours, and lists of telephone numbers are issued to local law societies and to the police. In anticipation of an emergency each firm of solicitors should, of course, obtain these numbers in advance.

On any application made *ex parte* the applicant should explain why no notice to the opponent has been given (in the county court, see CCR Ord 13, r 6(3A)).

Under the Trade Union and Labour Relations (Consolidation) Act 1992, s 221(1) no *ex parte* application can be made against a person likely to raise the 'furtherance of a trade dispute' defence unless all reasonable steps have been taken to give that person notice and an opportunity to be heard. In other cases also it may be possible to give informal notice of the application to the opponent. In *Hunter & Partners v Welling & Partners* [1987] Gazette 341 (see also *White Book* 29/1/8) May LJ set out the proper procedure to follow should the respondent to such an application (an 'opposed *ex parte*' application) wish to challenge any order made. Before turning to the Court of Appeal he should first await the outcome of a full *inter partes* application for which evidence on both sides can be filed.

The application must be supported by an affidavit stating the relevant facts showing that an injunction is necessary and showing that the matter is urgent. If on an *ex parte* application it is not practicable to file an affidavit the injunction may be granted on other evidence, on the plaintiff's undertaking to file a verifying affidavit later. If the application is also made before the commencement of action the applicant will have to give a further undertaking to commence an action forthwith (in county court cases, see further, CCR Ord 13, r 6(4)). The order will be entitled 'In the Matter of an Intended Action between ...' (as to the full text of the standard form, see p 290). Breach of the last-mentioned undertaking is punishable as a contempt of court; alternatively the plaintiff's solicitors may be penalised in costs (*PS Refson & Co Ltd v Saggers* [1984] 1 WLR 1025).

The applicant should also produce copies of the writ or draft writ if any (High Court) and copies of the draft order sought (both High Court and county court). The injunction should specify precisely the acts the respondent must do or must abstain from doing (see *White Book* 29/1/6). The standard form text makes clear that a defendant who is an individual 'who is ordered not to do something must not do it himself or in any other way. He must not do it through others acting on his behalf or on his instructions or with his encouragement.' A similar explanation is also given for a defendant which is a corporation.

A party seeking an injunction *ex parte* owes a duty to disclose to the court all facts which are material to the proceedings. He must also make proper inquiries as to the material facts before making his application. How much, depends upon several factors including the degree of legitimate urgency and the time available (see generally *Brink's Mat Ltd v Elcombe* [1988] 1 WLR 1350). It is particularly important to draw the court's attention to any defences which the opponent has indicated (*Art Corporation v Schuppan* [1994] Gazette, 30 March, 36; *White Book* 29/1/33), and any facts bearing upon the value and enforceability of the undertaking as to damages which the applicant is required to give (see p 284). As to this, and as to the penalties for non-disclosure, see below.

Inter partes applications

In the High Court, Queen's Bench Division applications are made by summons to the judge in chambers (see p 5) and Chancery Division applications are made by motion to the judge in open court (see p 8). In some cases the parties agree to treat the application as if it were the trial of the action. A standard form is now prescribed for this (see further, p 290). County court applications are made to the judge, on notice, usually in open court (see CCR Ord 13, r 6(5) and, as to the jurisdiction of the district judge, see p 12).

Inter partes applications are made in cases which are not urgent and also in other cases, as a follow up to an *ex parte* application. *Ex parte* orders are often made for a limited time only thereby requiring the applicant to apply *inter partes* if he wishes to have it continued.

Before the hearing date for the application arrives each party files in court and serves upon his opponents copies of all the affidavit evidence he intends to rely upon. The tendency to file voluminous evidence should be resisted (see *Derby & Co Ltd v Weldon* [1990] Ch 48, *per* Parker LJ). If the documentation is intolerably heavy the court may, instead of granting an interlocutory injunction, seek instead to arrange an early trial date in order to consider what final injunction should be granted. In the High Court this would be achieved by the court making an order for an early trial (RSC Ord 29, r 5, in practice called an order for speedy trial) and by treating the hearing as if it were the hearing of a summons for directions (RSC Ord 29, r 7). In patent cases all applicants for interlocutory injunctions are now required to make some preparations for such an order (see *Practice Direction (Patents Court: Practice Explanation)* [1996] 1 WLR 1567).

As to the value and enforceability of the applicant's undertaking as to damages (see p 284) the court will take into account the applicant's financial standing and domicile. There are similarities here with an application for security of costs (see p 314). A bank guarantee or the payment of money into an account in the joint names of the parties' solicitors may be required from an overseas company; in *Ali Fahd Shobokshi Group Ltd v Moneim* [1989] 1 WLR 710 funds worth £25,000 were voluntarily paid into a Swiss account for this purpose. If the applicant is an insolvent company the liquidators may be required to give a personal undertaking perhaps up to a limited amount; in *Re DPR Futures Ltd* [1989] 1 WLR 778 the court accepted personal undertakings by the liquidators limited to £2 million, the estimated net assets of the company. In the case of an applicant who is an individual of limited means, the fact that his unsupported undertaking may be worthless is a factor, but not necessarily a decisive factor; in *Allen v Jambo Holdings Ltd* [1980] 1 WLR 1252 a legally aided plaintiff was granted an injunction without being required to put up any security.

It is only at an *inter partes* application that the court may be asked to rule upon allegations as to some material non-disclosure in previous *ex parte* applications. The usual penalty for material non-disclosure, whether inadvertent or not, is the discharge of the *ex parte* order (or, if it was limited to last only until the *inter partes* application, a dismissal of that application) together with a refusal to reimpose it immediately (see generally *Ali Fahd Shobokshi Group Ltd v Moneim* [1989] 1 WLR 710 and the cases cited therein, and as to orders limited to last only until the *inter partes* application, see *Dormeuil Freres SA v Nicolian International (Textiles) Ltd* [1988] 1 WLR 1362). However, the court has a discretion to maintain the injunction (or make a new order, if the *ex parte* order has expired) if satisfied that no injustice has been caused to the respondent (see *Brink's Mat Ltd v Elcombe* [1988] 1 WLR 1350 and *Lock International plc v Beswick* [1989] 1 WLR 1268).

A plaintiff who becomes aware of a material non-disclosure must bring it to the attention of the court and, if appropriate, seek a discharge of the order obtained (*White Book* 29/2–3/8).

A further consequence of a finding of material non-disclosure is the entitlement it will give the respondent to claim compensation under the applicant's undertaking as to damages (see p 284). An inquiry into what loss has been suffered may be deferred to be decided at or after the trial. (Compare and contrast *Lock International plc v Beswick* [1989] 1 WLR 1268 and *Columbia Picture Industries Inc v Robinson* [1987] Ch 38 where an award of £10,000 aggravated damages was made, at trial, subject to rights of set-off which the plaintiffs had for damages and costs ordered against the defendant.)

The order for costs likely to be made in cases of material non-disclosure depends very much on the particular circumstances of each case. In *Lloyds Bowmaker Ltd v Britannia Arrow Holdings plc* [1988] 1 WLR 1337 a *Mareva* injunction (see below) sought by the defendant against a third party was discharged with costs to be taxed and paid forthwith. In *Brink's Mat Ltd v Elcombe* [1988] 1 WLR 1350 the Court of Appeal upheld the judge's decision that the injunction should not be discharged and made 'no order as to costs'. In *Bir v Sharma* (1988) *The Times*, 7 December a *Mareva* injunction obtained by reliance on forged evidence was discharged and the plaintiff was ordered to pay costs forthwith on an indemnity basis (see p 527).

Serving the injunction

Both mandatory and prohibitory injunctions have to be drawn up, indorsed with a penal notice (for precedents see *White Book* 45/7/6 and County Court Form N77) and personally served on the respondent or, if a company, on the officers of the company against whom enforcement proceedings may later be taken (see generally RSC Ord 45, r 7; CCR Ord 29, r 1). Breach of an injunction is a contempt for which the respondent can be committed (as to the liability of directors and other officers of a company, see *Attorney-General for Tuvalu v Philatelic Distribution Corp Ltd* [1990] 1 WLR 926). A prohibitory injunction may be enforced by committal even before it has been served if the respondent was present when the injunction was made or was notified of it 'whether by telephone ... or otherwise' (RSC Ord 45, r 7(6); CCR Ord 29, r 1(6)).

Where an *inter partes* application is compromised on the basis of an undertaking given by the respondent *in lieu* of an injunction (see further p 610) it is nevertheless advisable for the applicant to have a formal order drawn up, indorsed with a suitable penal notice and served on the respondent (see *Hussain v Hussain* [1986] Fam 134 noted in *White Book* 45/5/3). As to the prescribed form of undertaking to be used, see p 290.

Mareva injunctions

High Court jurisdiction

SCA 1981, s 37 enables the High Court to grant injunctions 'in all cases in which it appears to the court to be just and convenient to do so'. Such an injunction can be made to restrain a party from moving overseas, or otherwise dealing with, assets located in England and Wales whether or not that party is a domiciled resident or present in England and Wales. The section thus provides statutory authority for the form of relief known as a *Mareva* injunction (following the decision in *Mareva Compania Naviera SA v International Bulkcarriers SA* [1975] 2 Lloyd's Rep 509) which is an injunction restraining a defendant from improperly disposing of his assets, or concealing, or moving them abroad thereby making himself 'judgment proof' and stultifying an action brought against him. Similar statutory authority is to be found for matrimonial cases in MCA 1973, s 37.

Under the Drug Trafficking Offences Act 1986 and the Criminal Justice Acts 1988 and 1993 the High Court has power to make 'restraint orders' in respect of assets which may later become the subject of a confiscation order following a conviction for certain offences (drug trafficking offences and certain other offences where the convicted person has benefited and has realisable assets exceeding £10,000 in value). Restraint orders are analogous to *Mareva* injunctions save that no undertakings as to damages (see p 284) are given; instead, there is a limited power to order compensation (see generally *Re Peters* [1988] QB 871; *Re R* [1990] 2 QB 307 and *Re O* [1991] 2 WLR 475).

Under CJJA 1982, s 25 a *Mareva* injunction can be granted in English proceedings brought solely for that purpose in a case in which the primary proceedings are being taken in the courts of another EU member state (and see further, p 139). If the defendant is domiciled in the UK, or in another member state, service overseas can be effected without leave under RSC Ord 11, r 1(2) (see *Republic of Haiti v Duvalier* [1990] 1 QB 202). If the defendant is not domiciled in the UK, or in any other member state, leave to serve overseas is necessary and may be granted under RSC Ord 11, r 1(1)(b), (CJJA 1982 (Interim Relief) Order 1997 negating the decision in *Mercedes Benz AG v Leindruch* [1996] 1 AC 285).

Under CJJA 1991, the High Court also has jurisdiction to grant *Mareva* injunctions in aid of cases proceeding before the courts of the EFTA states (Austria, Finland, Iceland, Norway, Sweden and Switzerland; see further *White Book* 11/1/29).

County court jurisdiction

The county courts have no general jurisdiction to grant *Mareva* injunctions (see generally County Courts Remedies Regulations 1991 noted in the *Green Book* commentary to CCA 1984, s 38). They may grant them only:

(1) in family proceedings.
(2) in order to secure the preservation, custody or detention of property which forms or may form the subject matter of proceedings (see p 305).
(3) in aid of execution of a county court judgment.

Exceptions are also made for any county court held by a judge who is a judge of the High Court or the Court of Appeal, and for certain proceedings in a patents county court and proceedings which will be or which are already included in the Central London County Court Business List (as to which, see p 276).

In other county court cases all applications for *Mareva* injunctions must be made to the High Court (see further p 381).

Importance of Mareva injunctions

The amount of court time spent on *Mareva* applications of one sort or another, and the amount of case law they have produced, is enormous. It is easy to see why this should be so. In many cases the grant or refusal or discharge of a *Mareva* injunction is determinative of the action. If the injunction is refused, or granted but later discharged, a plaintiff may perceive little point in continuing with the litigation. If the injunction is granted, and survives an *inter partes* hearing, the defendant may well concede defeat; the paralysing effect the injunction has on his business, and the injury to his reputation, may render futile any further opposition to the plaintiff's claim. It is not the purpose of a *Mareva* injunction to provide the plaintiff with a means of exerting pressure on a defendant to settle an action (*Camdex International Ltd v Bank of Zambia (No 2)* [1997] 1 All ER 728). However, in practice, that is often its effect.

With its growth of importance to litigants, so the *Mareva* injunction has grown in size. In the following five respects its availability has been increased over the years. The injunction can be granted:

(1) pre-trial or post-trial;

(2) against any defendant whether foreign-based or English-based;

(3) in respect of assets in this country or (if English assets are insufficient to cover the claim) in other countries (see *Derby & Co Ltd v Weldon (Nos 3 and 4)* [1990] Ch 65 and the cases cited therein);

(4) whether or not the defendant has assets in this country (see again *Derby & Co Ltd* above); and also

(5) against a plaintiff in respect of orders for interlocutory costs payable forthwith (*Jet West Ltd v Haddican* [1992] 1 WLR 487, the costs in question being the costs of unsuccessful *Mareva* proceedings which the plaintiff had pursued against the defendant; thus was the biter bit).

Applying for a Mareva injunction

The application must be made to the judge and is usually made *ex parte* and possibly even before the action has commenced. If practicable the papers to be used on the application should be lodged with the judge at least two hours before the hearing (*Practice Direction* of 1994, *White Book* 29/2–3/7).

There are in essence only three issues:

(1) whether the plaintiff has a good arguable case;

(2) whether the plaintiff can adduce sufficient evidence as to the existence and location of assets which the injunction, if made, would affect; and

(3) whether there is a real risk that the defendant may deal with those assets so as to render nugatory any judgment which the plaintiff may obtain.

Such matters should be decided on comparatively brief evidence (*per* Parker LJ in *Derby & Co Ltd v Weldon* [1990] Ch 48).

As to (1), the difference between 'good arguable case' and the *American Cyanamid* test of 'serious question to be tried' has been described as being 'incapable of definition' (*per* Parker LJ in the case just quoted). Mustill J once described 'a good arguable case' as 'one which is more than barely capable of serious argument, but not necessarily one which the judge considers would have a better than 50 per cent chance of success' (*Ninemia Maritime Corporation v Trave S GmbH* [1983] 2 Lloyd's Rep 600, a point which was not taken on the appeal, [1983]

1 WLR 1412; cf applications for leave to serve High Court proceedings outside the jurisdiction, p 143).

As to (2), the order sought should identify as precisely as possible the bank accounts or other assets to be affected by the injunction. The order will be confined to assets within England and Wales if they are of sufficient value to protect the plaintiff's claim; orders in respect of assets overseas are often said to be 'exceptional' (see *Derby & Co Ltd v Weldon (No 6)* [1990] 1 WLR 1139 *per* Staughton LJ). The injunction can be extended to cover bank accounts standing in the name of another person, eg the defendant's spouse, if there is evidence that the money held in the account belongs to the defendant (*SCF Finance Co Ltd v Masri* [1985] 1 WLR 876). If the defendant is the majority shareholder of a company which has substantial assets the injunction can also be made against that company which should be added as a co-defendant in the action (*TSB Private Bank International SA v Chabra* [1992] 1 WLR 231).

As to (3), a risk of dissipation etc may be shown in a variety of different ways: eg evidence of dishonest behaviour by the defendant, unreliability in the past, evasiveness in these proceedings (such as a willingness to retract admissions and/or rely upon implausible defences), statements of intent by the defendant, a lack of any established business reputation, or the possession of a poor reputation such as some types of off-shore companies have, a propensity to change domicile and/or move assets regularly and/or at short notice, having only weak or non-existent links with this country save for assets invested here, or being based in a country in which it is difficult to enforce English judgments.

Terms of the injunction

A *Practice Direction* of 1994 (*White Book* 29/2–3/7) contains standard forms of *Mareva* injunctions and *Anton Piller* orders for use in all cases 'save to the extent that the judge hearing a particular application considers there is a good reason for adopting a different form.' Revised forms were published in a *Practice Direction* of 1996 (see *White Book* 29/2–3/7 supplement and 974/3 second supplement p 138). The standard forms of *Mareva* injunction have three main components: certain undertakings given by the plaintiff; the order restraining the defendant from disposing of his assets (describing them in so far as the plaintiff can); and various provisos and limitations.

The undertakings will include, amongst others, the plaintiff's undertaking as to damages (see p 284) and an undertaking to indemnify any person upon whom notice of the order is served, in respect of any expenses and liabilities they may incur in seeking to comply with the order.

The restriction on the disposal of assets is worded so as to cover all assets (ie whether or not described) except to the extent that their total unencumbered value exceeds a specified amount. The value specified should take into account the value of the plaintiff's claim plus interest plus costs (*Atlas Maritime Co SA v Avalon Maritime Ltd (No 3)* [1991] 1 WLR 917). If an excessive amount is specified the plaintiff may later become liable to pay damages to the defendant under the undertaking in damages which must be given.

> [There] comes a point at which, if you open your mouth too wide, you run a substantial risk that there may be a claim against your client under the counter-indemnity (*per* Lord Donaldson MR in *Jet West Ltd v Haddican* [1992] 1 WLR 487).

The standard forms of injunction state the date up to and including which the order will remain in force (the return date). These are, of course, *ex parte* orders. An order made *inter partes* may endure until judgment or further order, or even sometimes 'until two weeks after the trial in this action or further order' (*Allied Arab Bank Ltd v Hajjar* [1988] QB 787).

The provisos and limitations will acknowledge any prior right any bank may have to set off against any of the defendant's assets they hold, the value of any loans they may have made to the defendant before the date of the injunction. They will also allow the defendant to draw reasonable living expenses and/or to pay debts in the ordinary course of business. They will give the defendant and anyone else affected by the order, liberty to apply (on notice) to set aside or vary the order, or to seek further directions. A worldwide *Mareva* injunction in standard form expressly states the extent to which the order operates unless and until it is recognised by the courts of the overseas country in question.

The injunction may also include various orders for discovery (see p 303).

Serving Mareva injunctions

A curious feature of the *Mareva* injunction is that, although it is made against the defendant, it may be effective only if notice of it is given to the bank, or other person in possession of the assets. They would be guilty of a contempt of court if, with notice of the injunction, they knowingly assisted in the disposal of the assets, whether or not the defendant has any knowledge of the injunction. Merely paying or handing over the asset in question to the defendant does not by itself amount to a contempt, even if it is done with notice of the injunction; to amount to a contempt, the bank or possessor of the asset must have notice of a probability that the asset would then be disposed of in breach of the injunction (*Bank Mellat v Kazmi* [1989] QB 541).

In one case, a conveyancing solicitor, given notice of a *Mareva* injunction which had been served on his client, failed to countermand two cheques which he had drawn on a client account and despatched to his client on the previous day. He was found guilty of contempt of court, ordered to pay £8,000 in compensation and suspended from practice for five years (see (1989) 39 LSG 48).

How can one enforce an order in respect of overseas assets, against a defendant who is himself overseas, and who has no assets in this country? It is unlikely that a foreign court would recognise and enforce an *ex parte* injunction made by the High Court: our courts will not recognise and enforce a foreign injunction (*EMI Records Ltd v Modern Music Karl-Ulrich Walterbach GmbH* [1992] 1 QB 115). Instead one should seek protective measures in the court local to the assets (in the case of EU member states, see their equivalent to our CJJA 1982, s 25; see p 295). Also, if there is proof of contempt by the defendant, the English court can bar his right to defend the English action (*Derby & Co Ltd v Weldon (Nos 3 and 4)* [1990] Ch 65).

Applications to discharge or vary the order

The injunction will be discharged if, at an *inter partes* hearing, the defendant provides sufficient security for the plaintiff's claim (*Allen v Jambo Holdings Ltd* [1980] 1 WLR 1252) or if the judge is satisfied that there is no sufficient risk of default (as in *Ninemia Maritime Corporation v Trave S GmbH* [1983] 1 WLR 1412) or that it was obtained as a result of material non-disclosure (see p 293). The plaintiff himself should apply for a discharge if he later decides not to proceed with his claim. Once a *Mareva* injunction has been granted, the plaintiff is under a duty to press on with his claim so that the defendant is subject to the order for the minimum amount of time necessary, and not kept in limbo (*Town and Country Building Society v Daisystar Ltd* (1989) White Book 29/1/34).

Alternatively, the defendant may apply to vary the provision made for reasonable living expenses, or to allow the payment of outstanding debts and payment of legal fees incurred in defending the proceedings. Before allowing such variations the court may require evidence that there are no other assets out of which the payments could reasonably be made (*A v C (No 2)* [1981] QB 961). There is a possibility that, once some assets are caught, the defendant may take steps to prevent further assets coming to England and may try to discharge out of the caught assets all subsequent trading debts, living expenses and legal costs. In order to check up on this, the court is willing to inquire into all the defendant's financial dealings including those made with subsidiary companies and parent companies (see *Atlas Maritime Co SA v Avalon Maritime Ltd (No 3)* [1991] 1 WLR 917; and see *DB Deniz Nakliyati TAS v Yugopetrol* [1992] 1 WLR 437). The court will not consent to any variation being made unless and until the defendant complies with any such discovery order (*Prekookeanska Plovidba v LNT Lines SRL* [1989] 1 WLR 753).

Variations may also be applied for by third parties intervening in the action such as persons whose claims the defendant has admitted in good faith and wishes to pay (*Iraqi Ministry of Defence v Arcepey Shipping Co SA* [1981] QB 65) or directors of a defendant company who apply to be added as co-defendants if eg the defendant company can no longer afford legal representation (*ALI Finance Ltd v Havelet Leasing Ltd* [1992] 1 WLR 455).

Applications for variation or discharge are properly made to the High Court judge even if the *ex parte* order was first made by the Court of Appeal (*Ocean Software Ltd v Kay* [1992] 2 WLR 633). In county court cases, the county court has power to vary an injunction made by the High Court if all parties are agreed on the terms of variation (County Court Remedies Regulations 1991, reg 3(4)(b)).

Variations may also be applied for in the case of 'restraint orders', eg to finance the costs of an appeal (see *Customs and Excise Commissioners v Norris* [1991] 2 QB 293).

Rights of third parties in the property attached

A person may apply as intervener to discharge or vary the injunction, eg by showing title paramount to the defendant (*Cretanor Maritime Co Ltd v Irish Marine Management Ltd* [1978] 1 WLR 966) or by showing that the order substantially interferes with their business rights (*Galaxia Maritime SA v Mineralimportexport* [1982] 1 WLR 539, the owners of a ship which was prevented from sailing because of an injunction in respect of the defendant's cargo on board). Successful interveners may be awarded their costs against the plaintiff upon the 'indemnity basis' (*Project Development Co Ltd v KMK Securities Ltd* [1982] 1 WLR 1470; *Capital Cameras Ltd v Harold Lines Ltd* [1991] 1 WLR 54).

Where a *Mareva* injunction relates to land no registration is possible under the Land Charges Act 1972, s 6(1)(a) 'writ or order affecting land ... for the purpose of enforcing a judgment ...' (*Stockler v Fourways Estates Ltd* [1984] 1 WLR 25), or, in our view, under s 5 as a 'pending land action' (see *Calgary and Edmonton Land Co Ltd v Dobinson* [1974] Ch 102). Query whether, if it is necessary to take further steps, the plaintiff should bring proceedings for an interlocutory order appointing a receiver (as to which see p 304). The order appointing a receiver is registrable under s 6(1)(b): the proceedings themselves may be registrable under s 5.

Precedents for various *Mareva* applications and orders and a detailed account of the law thereon are set out in Gee, *Mareva Injunctions and Anton Piller Relief*, 3rd ed (FT Law & Tax, 1995).

Anton Piller orders

These are orders compelling defendants to 'permit' the plaintiff's agents to enter the defendant's premises, search for and (in most cases) seize certain documents or property. The order is a special form of mandatory injunction. It does not amount to a search warrant and therefore no forcible entry of premises can be made. However, if a defendant fails to comply with the order he can be committed for contempt. Orders in this form are uniquely British; they are unknown in the rest of Europe and in the USA: see (1990) 106 LQR 173. The Civil Procedure Act 1997, s 7 places the courts' jurisdiction to make these orders on a statutory footing.

How to apply

The county court does not normally have jurisdiction to make *Anton Piller* orders (County Court Remedies Regulations 1991, the only exceptions are any county court held by a judge who is a judge of the High Court or the Court of Appeal and for certain proceedings in a patents county court and proceedings which will be or which already are included in the Central London County Court Business List (as to which, see p 276)). Most applications must therefore be made to the High Court; proceedings may be transferred to a county court after the application has been disposed of (as to which see further County Court Remedies Regulations 1991, reg 5(2) and, as to transfers, see p 381).

Given the limitations on the jurisdiction of district judges (see p 6) the application is usually made to a High Court judge. In order to secure the advantage of taking the defendant by surprise the application is invariably made *ex parte*, often before the main action is commenced. The application must be supported by evidence describing the premises and the relevant documents or property and showing strong evidence that serious harm or serious injustice will be suffered if the order is not made. The applicant will be required to give the usual undertaking as to damages. If practicable, the papers to be used on the application should be lodged with the judge at least two hours before the hearing (*Practice Direction* of 1994, *White Book* 29/2–3/7).

As with *Mareva* injunctions, *Anton Piller* orders are usually made pre-trial but can also be granted post-trial if necessary as an aid to execution of the judgment: see *Distributori Automatici Italia SpA v Holford General Trading Co Ltd* [1985] 1 WLR 1066.

Examples

In *EMI v Pandit* [1975] 1 WLR 302 P alleged that D was selling 'pirate records'. P obtained an order for the discovery of the names and addresses of D's suppliers (see the rule in *Norwich Pharmacal*, p 386). P had strong evidence that D's discovery was fraudulent and that certain documents had been forged: thus unless a further order was made P would suffer serious injustice. Order made compelling D to permit P's agents to enter, search, inspect and seize relevant documents and pirate records.

In *Anton Piller KG v Manufacturing Processes Ltd* [1976] Ch 55 P applied *ex parte* and pre-writ, showing that D had documents dishonestly acquired from P which would prove P's claim for heavy damages for breach of copyright and wrongful use of confidential information. There being strong evidence that these documents were likely to be copied and/or sent abroad an order authorising their seizure was made.

In *CBS United Kingdom Ltd v Lambert* [1983] Ch 37 there was strong evidence that the defendants, a husband and wife, were involved in the production and sale of pirate records and cassettes. If the plaintiff's claim were substantiated at trial they would be entitled to damages of about £105,000. As a result of certain inquiries (details of which were given) the plaintiffs believed that the first defendant, although in receipt of social security payments, had recently bought several expensive cars which he intended to hide from his creditors and dispose of for cash if the need arose. The Court of Appeal granted (1) an *Anton Piller* order, (2) a *Mareva* injunction, (3) an order requiring the defendants to disclose forthwith full details as to all their assets whether in this country or abroad including in particular details of all bank accounts and motor vehicles, and (4) an order to deliver up forthwith to the plaintiff's solicitor three cars which were specified in the order.

Anton Piller orders can be used in any type of action if the circumstances so warrant (see for example *Yousif v Salama* [1980] 1 WLR 1540, claim for commission under an agency agreement; *Emanuel v Emanuel* [1982] 1 WLR 669, ancillary relief in divorce proceedings). However, in practice, they are most commonly sought against alleged infringers, of copyright, patents, trade marks and the like.

Form of order

The standard form of *Anton Piller* order (*White Book* 29/2–3/7 Supplement) provides for it to be served by a supervising solicitor, an experienced solicitor familiar with *Anton Piller* orders who is independent of the plaintiff and the plaintiff's solicitors. The supervising solicitor must also (amongst many duties) 'offer to explain to the person served with the order its meaning and effect fairly and in everyday language', supervise the entry and search and later supply a written report to the plaintiff's solicitor (this is for the use of the judge on the return day).

If, before any search begins, the person served with the order wishes to seek legal advice and/or apply to the court to vary or discharge the order, he should still permit the supervising solicitor and the plaintiff's solicitors to enter the premises but otherwise may refuse entry to others and may refuse permission for the search to begin for a short time, not to exceed two hours unless the supervising solicitor agrees to a longer period.

Any publicity about the order and its execution could be extremely damaging to the defendant's reputation. Because this is so, the standard form of *Anton Piller* order contains an undertaking by the plaintiff not to inform third parties about the proceedings until after the return date.

Disclosure of information by the defendant

An *Anton Piller* order in standard form requires the defendant to disclose immediately, and later verify by affidavit, the whereabouts of any infringing articles and the names and addresses of any persons known by the defendant to be involved in the alleged wrongdoing (cf *Norwich Pharmacal* orders, p 386). However, in some cases a defendant may be entitled to refuse to disclose such information on the grounds that it may incriminate him. The privilege against self-incrimination has been removed in High Court 'infringement cases' (see SCA 1981, s 72, the types of proceedings being closely defined therein). Claims of privilege against self-incrimination are also restricted by the Theft Act 1968, s 31 in respect of all cases, High Court and county court, in which there is a real risk of a prosecution under that Act. In other cases, however, if the privilege is likely to arise, the order should contain an express provision preserving the privilege and requiring that the defendant should be informed of his right to take the point if he so chooses (*IBM United Kingdom Ltd v Prima Data International Ltd* [1994] 1 WLR 719). In an exceptional case, the defendant's protection from self-incrimination can be secured by other means (*AT&T Istel Ltd v Tully* [1993] AC 45; order made because the plaintiff had obtained the prior consent of the Crown Prosecution Service).

There is no privilege in respect of the risk of criminal proceedings in the courts of a foreign state. Proof that compliance with the order puts the defendant at serious risk of violent assault by his associates does not necessarily justify the discharge of the order (*Coca-Cola Company v Gilbey* [1995] 4 All ER 711; but see further on this point and on the previous point, p 391).

Enforcing orders for discovery

Subject to any questions of privilege against self-incrimination (see above) *Mareva* injunctions and *Anton Piller* orders often include a variety of discovery orders; eg as to nature, location and value of all assets wherever situated, details of bank and other accounts, nature and extent of shareholdings in specified companies, names and addresses of other alleged wrongdoers, the precise whereabouts of any documents relating to transactions in respect of which the plaintiff claims, and orders to deliver up documents such as share certificates, books of account, bank statements, etc. (As to the use by the plaintiff of any information gained by discovery, see p 392.)

In several cases the courts have considered what can be done to enforce these orders. In *Bayer AG v Winter* [1986] 1 WLR 497, injunctions were granted restraining a defendant from leaving the country and requiring him to deliver up his passports. In *B v B (Passport Surrender: Jurisdiction)* (1997) *The Times*, 1 April the court refused to make such orders where they were sought as enforcement measures in their own right; ie additional means of exerting pressure on the defendant to pay sums owed. These orders are perhaps the modern equivalent of the ancient writ of *ne exeat regno* which in most cases will be of too narrow a compass to be of use (see further *Allied Arab Bank Ltd v Hajjar* [1988] 2 WLR 942).

In *Bayer* it was said that, if a defendant refused to answer questions or gave answers which could be shown to be less than frank, the court had jurisdiction to order him to attend for cross-examination. The extent and scope of such a cross-examination has been doubted (see *Bayer AG v Winter (No 2)* [1986] 1 WLR 540, in which Scott J refused, as a matter of discretion, to make an order compelling attendance for cross-examination on affidavits filed in compliance with an *Anton Piller* order requiring disclosure of documents and details relating to the alleged sale of counterfeit chemicals). Cross-examination as to the existence and whereabouts of assets belonging to the defendant is far less controversial. RSC Ord 29, r 1A provides for such a cross-examination on affidavits filed in compliance with a *Mareva* injunction. The cross-examination may take place before a district judge or before an examiner of the court (as to which see p 447) and must take place in chambers and an official shorthand note or mechanical recording must be made. Even in *Mareva* proceedings cross-examination on a discovery affidavit is said to be exceptional (*Yukong Line Ltd of Korea v Rendsburg Investment Corporation of Liberia* [1996] 10 CL 68).

Interlocutory receivership orders

SCA 1981, s 37 (referred to above in connection with *Mareva* injunctions) also enables the High Court to make interlocutory orders appointing receivers 'in all cases in which it appears to the court to be just and convenient to do so' (see further *White Book* 30/1/2 and as to county court jurisdiction see p 108). In *Hart v Emelkirk Ltd* [1983] 1 WLR 1289, an interlocutory order was made appointing a receiver in respect of two blocks of flats. The flats were let on long leases under which the landlord had certain obligations to repair and insure and the tenants were required to pay ground rents and contribute to the costs of repair *via* a service charge. There was evidence that the current beneficial owner of the reversions to the leases had made no attempt to manage the block of flats, to collect rents and service charges, or to effect repairs or insurance for several years past and the properties had fallen into a condition which demanded urgent attention. Similar receivership orders have been made in *Daiches v Bluelake Investments Ltd* (1985) 82 LSG 3258 and in another case which has been reported on two related points; registration of a caution to protect the receivership order (*Clayhope Properties Ltd v Evans* [1986] 1 WLR 1223) and payment of remuneration to a receiver (*Evans v Clayhope Properties Ltd* [1987] 1 WLR 225). In *Parker v Camden London Borough Council* [1986] Ch 162, it was held that, in view of (what is now) Housing Act 1985, s 21 a receivership order should not be made against a local authority; however the council tenants were held to be entitled instead to an interlocutory mandatory injunction.

In our view the principles applied in these cases fully comply with the principles we describe as relevant to interlocutory mandatory injunctions (see p 288). In other words, if the receivership order will not finally dispose of the dispute between the parties (for an example see *Hart*, above) the ordinary principles of *American Cyanamid* should be applied. However if the receivership order will have consequences which are irreversible at a later trial (as in *Parker*, see below) the plaintiffs should be required to show a strong case.

In *Hart* the order which was granted merely filled the vacuum in estate management that had arisen. In *Parker* the relief granted related to a specific, short-term, problem: the local authority landlord's unwillingness to hire outside engineers to repair heating boilers which had broken down during a strike of its boilermen. It is also worthy of note that in both cases the persons liable as landlords appear not to have had any arguable defence (see p 289).

In *Derby & Co Ltd v Weldon (Nos 3 and 4)* [1990] Ch 65, interlocutory receivership was ordered in aid of a *Mareva* injunction and in *Derby & Co Ltd v Weldon (No 6)* [1990] 1 WLR 1139 further orders were made requiring the transfer of certain assets into the sole name of the receiver.

Interlocutory orders relating to property relevant to an action

Both the High Court and the county court can make, on such terms as may be just, a variety of orders relating to property which is the subject matter of the action or as to which any question may arise therein. The orders include orders for detention, preservation, inspection, the taking of samples, and experimentation or observation (RSC Ord 29, rr 2 and 3) or the delivery up of goods under the Torts (Interference with Goods) Act 1977, s 4 (RSC Ord 29, r 2A), the recovery of goods subject to a lien, usually on terms that the value of the lien be paid into court 'to abide the event of the action' (RSC Ord 29, r 6) and orders for the sale of goods, the subject matter of an action, which are perishable or which for any other good reason it is desirable to sell forthwith (RSC Ord 29, r 4). All the above-mentioned RSC are incorporated into the county court rules (CCR Ord 13, r 7).

Applications for these orders are made to the district judge and, normally, by summons or on notice. Orders for detention, etc, may authorise any person to enter upon any land or building in the possession of a party to the action (cf *Anton Piller* orders which are made in the High Court only and always on an *ex parte* application). In the High Court the district judge may, instead of determining the application, make an order for speedy trial and may treat the hearing as if it were the hearing of a summons for directions (see p 292).

Under RSC Ord 29, r 7A (which is also incorporated into the county court rules, see CCR Ord 13, r 7) orders for detention, etc, can be made pre-action (on an originating summons or originating application) or during a personal injury action (see further p 407) against persons who are not parties. Orders for these forms of inspection may provide for the costs of complying with the order. In the High Court these costs are allowed automatically unless the court otherwise orders (RSC Ord 62, r 3(12)).

There are two curious inconsistencies in the rules relating to inspection of property and discovery of documents. These inconsistencies are most clearly shown when the various rules are set out in the form of a table (see table 4 below). Two cases provide examples of the problems to which these inconsistencies can lead.

Table 4: Special orders for discovery of documents and inspection of property (High Court or county court)

Stage at which sought	Type of order	COLUMN 1 *Is the order available in all types of case?*	COLUMN 2 *Is the order available against non-parties?*
1 Pre-action	1 (a) Disclosure of documents (see p 408)	No. Limited to proceedings in respect of personal injury claims (see p 408)	No. Available only if the respondent is a likely party to such proceedings (see p 408)
	(b) Inspection of property (see p 305)	Yes	Yes
2 After the commencement of the action in which the application is made	2 (a) Disclosure of documents (see p 407)	No. Limited to proceedings in respect of personal injury claims (see p 407)	Yes
	(b) Inspection of property (see p 305)	No. Limited to proceedings in respect of personal injury claims (see p 407)	Yes

Huddleston v Control Risks Information Services Ltd [1987] 1 WLR 701 held that the statutory limitation, confining pre-action disclosure of documents to personal injury cases only, cannot be avoided merely by formulating the proceedings as a claim for 'pre-action inspection of property'. In that case the plaintiffs wished to examine a confidential report written by the defendants in order to see whether it libelled them. Hoffman J refused to make such an order. Pre-action inspection of property raises questions as to the physical object sought to be inspected ('the medium'). What the plaintiffs were seeking here was the information ('the message') which the report conveyed.

Douihech v Findlay [1990] 1 WLR 269 held that the statutory limitation, confining orders for inspection against non-parties to personal injury cases cannot be avoided merely by adding the non-party as a co-defendant. In that case the plaintiff's claim was for damages suffered because an antique cello which the defendant agreed to sell to the plaintiff was in fact stolen property and had to be returned to the true owner. The plaintiff wished to have the cello inspected by an expert valuer. Because the true owner refused to allow such inspection, the plaintiff had her added as a second defendant and sought orders for inspection under RSC Ord 29, r 2 (see above). Judge Dobry QC refused so to order following old authority that co-defendants cannot obtain orders for inspection against each other if there is no right to be adjusted between them.

We do not criticise the reasoning of either of these decisions. However we do criticise the random and arbitrary way the law operates in this area. Why should pre-action disclosure of documents be available in personal injury cases but not available in other cases? Why should inspection orders against non-parties be available in personal injury cases both before and after the issue of the writ but be available in all other cases only before the issue of the writ? In *Douihech* the plaintiff would have succeeded in obtaining an order for inspection (subject to the court's discretion) if he had applied under RSC Ord 29, r 7A(1) before issue of the writ. A law which refuses such an order if sought after issue is imposing upon litigants a procedural lottery which does it no credit. In our view the time has now come for SCA 1981, ss 33 and 34 to be amended to remove the limitation of some orders to personal injury cases (and see further p 387). The Civil Procedure Act 1997, s 8 gives the Lord Chancellor power to amend the statutes underlying the disclosure of documents rules. The amendments which we think are needed would be such as to enable us to give the answer *yes* in each of the entries in column 1 of table 4 above.

Pending such amendment, it is arguable that RSC Ord 29, r 7A(1) (normally called 'pre-action inspection of property') is not limited to pre-writ applications. Neither that rule nor the text of the statute upon which it is based (SCA 1981, s 33(1)) use the expressions 'pre-action' or 'before action'. Instead RSC Ord 29, r 7A(1) refers to 'subsequent proceedings in the High Court'. Does this mean that in *Douihech* the plaintiff might have obtained an order for inspection had he made his application by way of originating summons under r 7A(1) rather than by way of interlocutory summons, under r 2? We acknowledge that the expression 'subsequent proceedings' also appears in s 33(2) in a context which can only mean 'pre-action'. Subsection (2) deals with discovery orders against persons 'likely to be' parties to subsequent proceedings. There is no need for a special discovery rule for use against someone who is already a party. It is worth remembering however that subss (1) and (2) of s 33 do not stem from the same statutory origins. Subsection (1) re-enacts s 21 of the AJA 1969. Subsection (2) re-enacts s 31 of the AJA 1970; some inconsistency in their use of the expression 'subsequent proceedings' may therefore be explicable.

The arguments here presented in favour of construing r 7A(1) more widely, to cover more than just 'pre-action' inspection, cannot be described as strong. However they may provide a means of avoiding the result reached in *Douihech*, a result which, in our view, was manifestly unfair to the plaintiff.

Interim payments

An interim payment is an advance payment on account of any damages, debt or other sum (excluding costs) which a defendant, or a defendant to counterclaim, may be held liable to pay. The High Court rules for interim payments are set out in RSC Ord 29, Pt II. These rules also apply (with some modifications) in all county court cases in which the sum claimed or amount involved exceeds £1,000 (CCR Ord 13, r 12). The object of the rules is two-fold:

(1) In all claims for debts, damages, accounts or other financial remedies, to enable a claimant who has a strong case on liability (see the grounds for applying) to avoid the financial hardship which might otherwise be suffered because of any delay during the period between the start of the action and the completion of any negotiation or adjudication on *quantum*.

(2) In actions concerning the forfeiture of a lease where the tenant remains in occupation, to enable the landlord to obtain compensation for the tenant's occupation, either as *mesne* profits (if the forfeiture action is successful) or as rent (if it is unsuccessful).

Grounds for applying

RSC Ord 29, r 11 sets out three grounds for an interim payment in respect of damages, namely:

(1) that the respondent to the application has admitted liability; or

(2) that the applicant has obtained judgment against the respondent for damages to be assessed (eg a default judgment, a summary judgment or a judgment on admissions); or

(3) that if the action proceeded to trial, the applicant would obtain judgment for substantial damages against the respondent, or where there are two or more defendants, against any of them.

The three grounds for applying for an interim payment in respect of sums other than damages are as follows:

(1) that the plaintiff has obtained an order for an account to be taken as between himself and the defendant, and for any amount certified due on taking the account to be paid; or

(2) that the plaintiff's action includes a claim for possession of land, and, if the action proceeded to trial, the defendant would be held liable to pay to the plaintiff a sum of money in respect of the defendant's use and occupation of the land during the pendency of the action, even if a final judgment or order were given or made in favour of the defendant; or

(3) that, if the action proceeded to trial, the plaintiff would obtain judgment against the defendant for a substantial sum of money, apart from any damages or costs (see generally RSC Ord 29, r 12).

What is the position if the plaintiff has a claim for damages against two defendants sued in the alternative and he can show that he has a strong case against one of them but cannot, until trial, say which one? It seems that no interim payment can be awarded (*Breeze v R McKennon & Son Ltd* (1985) 32 BLR 41 *per* Croom-Johnson LJ; *Ricci Burns Ltd v Toole* [1989] 1 WLR 993; both cases construe the text of the rules more narrowly than seems necessary; see further *Structured Settlements and Interim and Provisional Damages* (1994) Law Com No 224, p 91).

What is the position if the plaintiff sues a single defendant in respect of alternative claims, one for damages (as to which see r 11) the other in debt (as to which see r 12), but cannot, until trial, say which claim will win? In *Shearson Lehman Brothers Inc v Maclaine Watson & Co Ltd* [1987] 1 WLR 480 the Court of Appeal took a broad approach to the construction of the relevant rules and awarded an interim payment.

If, in addition to multiple causes, there are also multiple defendants but not all of them are sued in respect of all causes, the court should carefully apportion the interim payments between each defendant and between each cause of action (*Schott Kem Ltd v Bentley* [1991] 1 QB 61).

How to apply

In the High Court a plaintiff can apply for an interim payment to the district judge, by summons, at any time after the writ has been served on the respondent to the application, and the time limited for that person to acknowledge service has expired (see generally RSC Ord 29, r 10). In the county court the plaintiff can apply to the district judge, on notice, presumably at any time after the time for defence has expired (CCR Ord 13, 17 and Ord 1, r 6). In both courts the application may be combined with eg an application for summary judgment or for judgment on admissions. In all cases the application must be supported by an affidavit which must:

(1) verify the amount of the damages, debt or other sums to which the application relates, and the grounds of the application;

(2) exhibit any documentary evidence relied on by the plaintiff in support of the application; and

(3) if the plaintiff's claim is made under the Fatal Accidents Act 1976, contain the particulars required by that Act (for Fatal Accidents Act particulars see p 189).

In the High Court the summons, and copies of the affidavit and exhibits must be served on the respondent at least ten clear days before the return day. In the county court the notice and evidence must be served at least seven clear days before the return day.

Where an application is made by a counterclaiming defendant, the above rules apply 'with the necessary modifications' (RSC Ord 29, r 18). No doubt this means the defendant can only apply for an interim payment after his counterclaim has been served on the plaintiff against whom the order is sought.

As to the law on recovery of social security benefits, see further p 313.

Strength of case to be shown

The plaintiff must prove the grounds of application relied upon up to the civil standard (balance of probabilities) and not up to the criminal standard (beyond all reasonable doubt). Given that there are degrees of probability within the civil standard (see p 421), interim payment cases come towards the top of the scale (*Shearson Lehman Brothers Inc v Maclaine, Watson & Co Ltd* [1987] 1 WLR 480).

An application for an interim payment of damages is often combined with an application for summary judgment (see p 221). The plaintiff hopes to obtain an order for damages to be assessed and, pending that assessment, an order for an interim payment payable immediately. If, in such a case, the plaintiff loses the summary judgment application because the defendant is given unconditional leave to defend, the plaintiff is also likely to lose the interim payment application. Such a plaintiff will not be able to establish any of the three grounds for an interim payment.

However, if the defendant is given only conditional leave to defend the court may specify, as the condition, the making of an interim payment: *British and Commonwealth Holdings plc v Quadrex Holdings Inc* [1989] QB 842; *Andrews v Schooling* [1991] 1 WLR 783. In the first of those cases, the Court of Appeal ordered an interim payment of £5 million and granted the defendant leave to defend on condition that that payment was made within twenty-eight days.

> I therefore reach the conclusion that [the defendant] has shown an arguable case which entitles it to leave to defend since the true position cannot be elucidated without a trial. However, I have the gravest reservations whether the defence will be successful ... The arguable defence now raised has all the

hallmarks of a lawyer's defence dredged up from the papers (*per* Browne-Wilkinson V-C in *British and Commonwealth Holdings plc*, above).

Defences to the application

There are up to three grounds upon which the respondent may contest the application:

(1) That the application is for some reason irregular (eg there has been some irregularity in the commencement of the action or in the documents by which the application is made; bear in mind that if the irregularity is merely technical the court may ignore it, see p 2).

(2) That the grounds of the application cannot be established (eg disproving that he admitted liability, or disproving that the applicant is likely to obtain judgment for a substantial sum against the respondents).

(3) In a personal injury action only, that the respondent is not a person falling within certain specified categories, namely:

(*a*) a person who is insured in respect of the claim or whose liability will be met by an insurer under the Road Traffic Act 1988, s 151 or under the MIB agreements (as to these, see further p 38); or

(*b*) a public authority; or

(*c*) a person whose means and resources are such as to enable him to make the interim payment.

This defence (set out in RSC Ord 29, r 11(2)) enables a respondent to plead poverty. It is important to note that this defence applies only in personal injury claims. In other cases, not concerning personal injuries, the impecuniosity of the defendant does not impose an absolute embargo on the making of an order for an interim payment. It is, however, a most important factor to be taken into account by the court when exercising its discretion whether so to order (see below).

The order for an interim payment

If the application is successful, the district judge can make an order for an interim payment of such amount as he thinks just after taking into account any relevant contributory negligence and any set-off, cross-claim or counterclaim on which the respondent may be entitled to rely. In the case of a damages claim the payment must not exceed 'a reasonable proportion of the damages which in the opinion of the court are likely to be recovered' (RSC Ord 29, r 11). In other words, the court must not risk over-paying the plaintiff.

An order for an interim payment may require payment in one sum or in specified instalments (eg in forfeiture actions, see p 308). The payment is normally made direct to the applicant, even if he is legally aided (it will be exempt from the statutory charge: see Legal Aid (General) Regulations 1989, reg 94). However, the court does have power to order payments into court to be dealt with under its control, eg where the plaintiff is a minor or mental patient (see generally RSC Ord 29, r 13).

The court has a discretion as to two questions, (i) whether to order an interim payment and (ii) if so, the amount. On question (i) no interim payment is appropriate if the issues are complicated or if difficult questions of law arise (*Schott Kem Ltd v Bentley* [1991] 1 QB 61) unless the circumstances are exceptional (*Chiron Corporation v Murex Diagnostics Ltd (No 11)* (1996) *The Times*, 15 March, noted below but as to question (ii) only). On question (ii) the court will seek to calculate what sum is indisputably due to the claimant and what sum is his opponent able to pay.

Examples

Shearson Lehman Brothers Inc v Maclaine, Watson & Co Ltd [1987] 1 WLR 480, primary claim in debt totalling £23.9 million, alternative claim for damages for non-acceptance calculated at a minimum figure of £7.2 million, valued by the defendant at £5.2 million; interim payment of £5.2 million ordered.

Ricci Burns Ltd v Toole [1989] 1 WLR 993, claim for approximately £70,000 likely to be successful against either of two defendants, an insurer and an insurance broker, but it was not possible to say which (see p 309; held *obiter* had an interim payment been permissible a payment of £50,000 namely two-thirds of the pleaded loss would have been appropriate, neither defendant having suggested that the amount claimed was inflated.

Chiron Corporation v Murex Diagnostics Ltd (No 11) (1996) *The Times*, 15 March, claims for many millions as to which expedition had been ordered, but that part was unlikely to be heard within eight months. Robert Walker J decided that £6.3 million was likely to be the minimum sum recoverable on this part: interim payment of £6 million ordered.

British and Commonwealth Holdings plc v Quadrex Holdings Inc [1989] QB 842, claim for over £100 million, interim payment of £75 million was reduced to £5 million on taking into account the resources of the defendant (see p 310).

Newton Chemical Ltd v Arsenis [1989] 1 WLR 1297, summary judgment given for accounts to be taken, estimated at over £33,000; defendant had negligible assets other than a half share in his matrimonial home, the half share being worth £13,500 net; not a suitable case for an interim payment.

The rules do not require an applicant to show any need for the interim payment. However, if the delay in assessment of damages is not likely to be substantial the court may be reluctant to exercise its discretion to grant an interim payment unless the plaintiff has some special reason for it; eg the payment of legal fees or the cost of private medical treatment or hardship caused by loss of earnings. The special reason need not relate to the claim.

> It should be noted that the plaintiff does not have to demonstrate any particular need over and above the general need that a plaintiff has to be paid his or her damages as soon as reasonably may be done. It will generally be appropriate and just to make an order where there will be some delay until the final disposal of the case (*Stringman v McArdle* [1994] 1 WLR 1653 *per* Stuart-Smith LJ).

In deciding the amount to award by way of an interim payment the court is entitled to take into account any payments into court which the defendant has made. The rule of secrecy as to payments into court (see p 341) does not apply to a court considering an interim payment application; it forbids disclosure only to the court at trial (*Fryer v London Transport Executive* (1983), *White Book* 29/11/4; court told that, in addition to an interim payment of £15,000 which had already been made voluntarily, the defendants had paid into court a further £48,000; the plaintiff successfully applied for a further interim payment to bring the total received up to £50,000).

If the district judge refuses to order an interim payment and no appeal is made or is successful, subsequent applications can be made upon cause shown, eg upon proof of change of circumstances (RSC Ord 29, r 10, and see p 652).

In cases affected by the law on recovery of social security benefits (see p 62) the making of an interim payment will bring that law into operation whether the payment is made voluntarily or under an order of the court. Therefore, in calculating how much to ask for by way of an interim payment, the plaintiff should take into account the sum the defendant is likely to deduct to pay to the DSS.

Further conduct of the action

On any application for an interim payment the district judge may give directions for the further conduct of the action and may (where applicable) treat the hearing as if it were the hearing of a summons for directions or pre-trial review (RSC Ord 29, r 14; CCR Ord 13, r 7).

Some rules affect the conduct of the parties after an interim payment has been made. An order for an interim payment *in respect of damages* prevents a High Court applicant discontinuing his claim or counterclaim unless he can obtain the leave of the court or the consent of all the other parties (RSC Ord 21, r 2(2A); in the county court, leave to discontinue is never required; see p 360). In both courts, where the respondent makes *any* interim payment, whether voluntarily or pursuant to an order, and later wishes to make a payment into court (see p 329) his notice of payment in must state that he 'has taken into account the interim payment', ie that his offer of compromise includes both the moneys paid into court and the interim payment (RSC Ord 29, r 16).

The fact that an interim payment has been made must not be pleaded and unless the respondent consents, or the district judge so directs, the trial court must not be told of it until all questions of liability and quantification have been decided (RSC Ord 29, r 15; cf the rule of secrecy concerning payments into court, p 341). When final judgment is given, the court can make such orders in respect of an interim payment (whether it was made voluntarily or pursuant to an order) as may be necessary to give effect to the trial court's determination, eg judgment for the balance and/or an order that one defendant refund moneys to another defendant (RSC Ord 29, r 17). Where the court has decided to make an award of interest some allowance must be made in respect of interest accruing after the date of the interim payment. In personal injury cases the interim payment is often set off against damages in the following order: special damages; then the pain and suffering and loss of amenity award; lastly, any future losses. This minimises the interest the defendant has to pay.

It sometimes happens that, even though he wins an interim payment, the plaintiff later loses the trial. In such a case the court has power to order the plaintiff to pay to the defendant a sum equal to the interim payment plus interest thereon from the date it was paid (*Wardens and Commonalty of the Mystery of Mercers of the City of London v New Hampshire Insurance Co* [1991] 1 WLR 1173 and see further [1992] 1 WLR 792).

Security for costs

An application for security of costs is a form of application which a defendant may in some cases make against a plaintiff (or, to be precise, a person in the position of plaintiff, see p 316). Its purpose is to ensure that, if the defendant defeats the action brought against him, he will have a fund available within England and Wales against which he can enforce any award of costs he may obtain. The principles governing security for costs applications share some similarities with applications for *Mareva* injunctions, which are, of course, applications sometimes made by plaintiffs against defendants (see p 294). In order to obtain an order of security for costs the applicant must show (i) that one or more grounds for security exist (see list below) and (ii) that, in all the circumstances it would be just to make an order.

As to question (i) RSC Ord 23, r 1 lists the following grounds (the list in CCR Ord 13, r 8 is shorter).

  (a) *the plaintiff is ordinarily resident out of the jurisdiction.* Two recent cases deal with the construction to be placed upon this ground so as to avoid any conflict with European Community law. An individual plaintiff who was a national of and ordinarily resident in another member state should usually be treated as if within the jurisdiction (*Fitzgerald v Williams* [1996] 2 WLR 447). A corporate plaintiff which was incorporated in and ordinarily resident in another member state should usually be treated as if it were an English company (*Chequepoint SARL v McClelland* [1996] 3 WLR 341 and see further, ground (*e*) below).

(b) *the plaintiff (not suing in a representative capacity) is a nominal plaintiff suing for the benefit of some other person and there is reason to believe that he will be unable to pay the costs if ordered to do so.*

(c) *the plaintiff's address is not stated in the writ or other originating process or is incorrectly stated therein.* However RSC Ord 23, r 1(2) states that no security will be ordered if the plaintiff satisfies the court that his failure or misstatement was made innocently and without intention to mislead.

(d) *the plaintiff has changed his address during the course of the proceedings with a view to evading the consequences of the litigation.*

(e) *the provisions of any enactment which empowers the court to provide security to be given for the costs of any proceedings.* The primary example here is the Companies Act 1985, s 726 which applies to a plaintiff which is an English registered company and there is reason to believe that it may not be able to pay the defendant's costs if it is ordered to do so. As to corporate plaintiffs incorporated in and ordinarily resident in another member state of the EU, see *Chequepoint SARL v McClelland* [1996] 3 WLR 341 and note (a) above. As to other statutory provisions for security for costs see *Green Book* 1583, 46, 758 and 1017.

As to question (ii), is it just to make an order, there are many factors which may have to be considered. For example, where impecuniosity is a relevant issue (see above) the court will take into account the value of any property within the jurisdiction, the strength of the plaintiff's claim, whether it is alleged that the plaintiff's impecuniosity was brought about by the conduct of the defendant, delay by the defendant in making the application and whether an order for security is being sought oppressively in order to stifle a claim (see further, *Kealy Developments Ltd v Tarmac Construction Ltd* [1995] 3 All ER 534 and *Danemark Ltd v BAA Plc* [1996] 12 CL 55). In *Simaan General Contracting Co v Pilkington Glass Ltd* [1987] 1 WLR 516 it was said that *Calderbank* offers (see p 329) can be taken into account but letters sent wholly 'without prejudice' cannot.

If residence outside the European Union (EU) is a relevant issue the court will take into account the value of any property within the EU (eg a statue, the subject matter of the action, lodged in a bank to the order of both parties' solicitors (*De Bry v Fitzgerald* [1990] 1 WLR 552) and the presence of co-plaintiffs who are resident here (*Slazengers Ltd v Seaspeed Ferries International Ltd* [1988] 1 WLR 221).

[I]t cannot be too emphatically stated that the impecuniosity of a personal plaintiff is never of itself enough to confer on the court a discretion to order security. It is not a ground in Ord 23, r 1(1) and section 726(1) of the Companies Act 1985, like its predecessor, only applies to limited companies. But I am, for my part, firmly of the opinion that it is a matter which the court may, and in a proper case should, consider in exercising a discretion where power to make an order is established [eg against plaintiffs resident in Norway] (*per* Bingham LJ in *Thune v London Properties Ltd* [1990] 1 WLR 562).

Applying for security of costs

Security for costs can be ordered only against a person *in the position of* plaintiff. However this would include a defendant who has raised a counterclaim going beyond merely defensive proceedings (*Procon (Great Britain) Ltd v Provincial Building Co Ltd* [1984] 1 WLR 557: counterclaim for Canadian £230 million, vastly exceeding the claim for sums due under a building contract; security of £6 million ordered against the defendant). A third party cannot obtain security from the plaintiff because the plaintiff is not 'in the position of' plaintiff *vis-à-vis* the third party (*Taly NDC International NV v Terra Nova Insurance Co Ltd* [1985] 1 WLR 1359).

The application should be made to the district judge, in the High Court by summons, in the county court on notice (see generally RSC Ord 23, CCR Ord 13, r 8). The traditional practice was to delay application until the directions stage. A more modern practice is to make two applications; the first at a relatively early stage to cover the costs up to directions (ie including costs incurred in interlocutory applications, investigating facts, instructing experts and making and receiving discovery); the second application at the directions stage to cover the costs of preparing for trial and trial. (Each application should, of course, be preceded by a request for security to be provided by consent.)

The application should be supported by an affidavit which sets out the applicant's case as to questions (i) and (ii) above and exhibits a draft bill of costs.

If security is ordered the district judge will specify the sum considered appropriate. If the order is made against a legally aided plaintiff, see Legal Aid (General) Regulations 1989, reg 123. Usually an order for the sum to be paid into court is more convenient than an order requiring the provision and agreement of a bond. The district judge may stay proceedings until the order has been complied with, or (following the practice which is preferred in the Commercial Court) specify a reasonable time for compliance and give the applicant liberty to apply in the event of default (see *White Book* 72/A11). Alternatively, the security may take the form of a personal undertaking given by the plaintiff's solicitor (*A Ltd v B Ltd* [1996] 1 WLR 665). The amount of security ordered may later be increased or reduced on proof of a material change of circumstances (*Gordano Building Contractors Ltd v Burgess* [1988] 1 WLR 890).

Security for the costs of an appeal

In the Court of Appeal security for costs is governed by RSC Ord 59, r 10, and can be ordered against an appellant whether he was plaintiff or defendant below (*White Book* 59/10/19). Insolvency or impecuniosity may justify the making of an order even against an individual, ie not just corporate appellants (*White Book* 59/10/20). The form of order for security is more stringent than that used in the courts below (see *White Book* 59/10/26) since urgency and expedition is especially important in the case of appeals (see p 661). Any failure by the respondent to apply for security promptly may lead to his application being turned down (*A Co v K Ltd* [1987] 1 WLR 1655).

If an order appealed to the Court of Appeal is an order for security for costs it is highly improbable that security for the costs of the appeal will be ordered or, if ordered, it is highly improbable that it will be ordered for an amount which the applicant cannot afford (*Smithfield Foods Ltd v Attorney-General of Barbados* [1992] 1 WLR 197 *per* Lord Ackner).

Costs orders in litigation funded by non-parties

In many cases one party, plaintiff or defendant, may be impecunious and the cost of his legal representation may be funded by a non-party, for example a close relative or friend, a trade union, or, especially in road accident cases, an insurer. In these examples the non-party providing financial support has a legitimate common interest with the supported party which derives from their relationship, be it family, social, contractual or otherwise. Less frequently litigation is financed illegitimately by an intermeddling mischief-maker; cf the old law of maintenance. In some cases the illegitimate intermeddling might be motivated by a contract between the supporter and the supported to share any proceeds of the litigation; cf the old law of champerty.

In 1967 conduct amounting to illegitimate intermeddling (maintenance and champerty) ceased to be criminal or tortious. However, contracts concerning such matters are still to be treated as contrary to public policy or otherwise illegal (Criminal Law Act 1967, ss 13, 14).

A basic principle of costs is that, in most cases, 'costs follow the event' (see further p 523). This has been described as a principle 'of fundamental importance in deterring plaintiffs from bringing and defendants from defending actions which they are likely to lose' (*Roache v News Group Newspapers Ltd* (1992) *The Times*, 23 November *per* Sir Thomas Bingham MR quoted in *Condliffe v Hislop* [1996] 1 WLR 753 at 762). This principle might be undermined if financial support is given to an impecunious party, even where that support is given legitimately, unless the supporter is willing to accept liability for the other side's costs if the supported party were to lose.

If, at the trial, a party whose case was financially supported by a non-party loses, the court may, in its discretion, order the non-party to pay the successful party's costs (*Symphony Group plc v Hodgson* [1994] QB 179). Such an order is almost inevitable where the financial support given is shown to amount to illegitimate intermeddling. In other cases no special order is necessary; the non-party frequently accepts liability and is willing to pay any costs the supported party is ordered to pay. In other words a non-party who *bona fide* wishes to support a litigant will not cease to support him just because he loses. In exceptional cases a non-party who has provided financial support legitimately may be excused from liability for the whole or part of the successful party's costs (*McFarlane v E E Caledonia Ltd (No 2)* [1995] 1 WLR 366 at 373, *Condliffe v Hislop* [1996] 1 WLR 753 at 759 C–D and *H Murphy v Young & Co's Brewery plc* (1997) *The Times*, 8 January).

In *Symphony Group plc v Hodgson* [1994] QB 179 it was said that a party who intends to apply for an order for costs against a non-party should, amongst other things, 'warn the non-party at the earliest opportunity'. Turning now to claims, especially defamation claims, a practice has grown up under which defendants, wherever they discover that the plaintiff has financial support, immediately seek an undertaking from the supporter to pay the defendant's costs if the claim fails. In *Condliffe v Hislop* [1996] 1 WLR 753 the Court of Appeal expressed the view that the practice (of seeking *and giving* undertakings) is not one to be in any way discouraged (at 763A–C).

The question arises what if any order can be made or is appropriate *pre-trial* if the supporter refuses to give an undertaking? Consider first cases in which financial support is being given to the claimant. In *Condliffe v Hislop* [1996] 1 WLR 763 it was held that no order for security of costs could be obtained, unless the case otherwise fell within the grounds listed in the rules of court. This is because those rules should be regarded as a complete and exhaustive code as to security for costs. It is for Parliament or the Rule Committees to add new categories to that code, not the courts. However, in *Condliffe* it was accepted that the court might achieve a similar result by ordering a stay of the supported party's claim unless and until a suitable undertaking is given. In that particular case no stay was ordered. The financial supporter there was the plaintiff's mother. She gave evidence that her only real asset was her house. Therefore, if she were to give a meaningful undertaking to the defendant that would or might disable her from continuing to give support to her son.

Orders staying claims have been made in two cases. *Broxton v McClelland* (1992, noted in *Condliffe v Hislop*) concerned a libel action financed by a French company which offered a limited undertaking. *Broxton* was decided before *Chequepoint SARL v McClelland* [1996] 3 WLR 341 which altered the law to some extent so far as companies incorporated within any EU state are concerned (see further p 315).

Secondly, *Grovewood Holdings plc v James Capel & Co Ltd* [1995] Ch 80 in which a stay was ordered in proceedings held to be champertous; no questions as to the giving of undertakings arose.

The most recent authority on these points draws back from the new law suggested in *Condliffe v Hislop*. In *Abraham v Thompson* (1997) *The Times*, 19 August, a differently constituted Court of Appeal expressed its disagreement with certain *dicta* in *Condliffe*. In *Abraham* the court stated that the proper time to consider adverse orders for costs against non-parties was at the end of the trial. Stays of action before then were appropriate if, eg, the action was not properly constituted or pleaded or was not brought *bona fide* in the sense of being vexatious, oppressive or otherwise an abuse. However, a stay of action should not be granted merely to provide security for costs in cases not covered by the security for costs rules.

In *Abraham v Thompson* at first instance, (1997) *The Times*, 15 May, it was held reasonable to infer that the plaintiff was being funded by off-shore trusts he had set up in order to divest himself of UK assets and avoid tax. Not knowing the identity of the trustees the defendants were unable to seek any undertaking from them. An order was made requiring the plaintiff to disclose the identity of any person who was financially supporting his claim. The defendants were held to have shown a sufficient prospect of obtaining a stay 'unless a sufficiently solid undertaking to answer for the defendants' costs' was given. However, as explained above, the Court of Appeal allowed an appeal against that decision.

Consider now what pre-trial relief is appropriate in cases in which financial support is being given to the defendant. Applications for security for costs and/or a stay of the applicant's own action are plainly inappropriate. Possibly some form of *Mareva* relief might be appropriate if the circumstances warranted it (see p 294 and see further *Grovewood Holdings plc v James Capel & Co Ltd* [1995] Ch 80 *obiter*).

Chapter 15

Third Party Proceedings

A defendant is not limited to defending. He can also attack by claiming remedies. Remedies against the plaintiff are sought by counterclaim (see Chapter 6). Third party proceedings are used to claim remedies against a person who is *not* already a party to the action. A defendant can bring them as an alternative to starting a separate action against the third party. In fact for many purposes third party proceedings are treated as if they were a separate action:

(1) the third party can raise a counterclaim against the defendant and/or bring in a fourth party;

(2) the third party proceedings do not directly involve the plaintiff; he cannot obtain judgment against the third party: the third party cannot counterclaim against him (see *Barclays Bank v Tom* [1923] 1 KB 221);

(3) the third party proceedings may continue even after the plaintiff's claim has been stayed (see *Stott v West Yorks Car Co* [1971] 2 QB 651, noted on p 353 below) or discontinued (see *Harper v Gray & Walker* [1985] 1 WLR 1196, noted on p 328 below).

The defendant reaps two benefits in bringing third party proceedings as opposed to starting a separate action. First, he obtains a saving of costs. Secondly, he ensures that his claim and the plaintiff's claim will be decided uniformly. The risk always present in bringing a separate action is that the different trial courts may come to inconsistent decisions on the same allegations.

If the plaintiff's claim were described as the 'main action' the third party proceedings could be regarded as a 'sub-action' arising out of it. They are brought to cover the possibility that the plaintiff may establish certain findings of fact against the defendant. In this 'sub-action' the defendant is saying to the third party 'If the plaintiff proves this against me I will then claim the following against you.' The sort of claims that can be raised by third party proceedings are very limited. Both the High Court rules and the county court rules allow only four types of claim (RSC Ord 16, r 1; CCR Ord 12, r 1):

(1) *A claim for contribution.* For example a road accident case in which P alleges negligence against D; D wishes to make T, another driver involved in the accident, contribute to any damages P may be awarded.

(2) *A claim for indemnity.* For example P sues D, a solicitor, alleging professional misconduct; D notifies T, his insurers, but they say that P's claim is not covered by the terms of their policy (see *Walker & Knight v Donne* (1976) *The Times*, 9 November). Third party proceedings against insurers are not normally used in road accident cases because in such cases P usually has a *better* right to claim against the insurers than D has; Road Traffic Act 1988, ss 151, 152, as to which see p 38.

(3) *A claim for a remedy which is similar to the remedy the plaintiff claims and which arises out of the same facts as the plaintiff's claim.* For example, a road accident case in which D, the driver, wishes to claim against T, the dealer from whom he bought the car, damages for breach of the implied term as to merchantable quality (T may also be a tortfeasor—see *Andrews v Hopkinson* [1957] 1 QB 229—enabling P to join him as a defendant and enabling D to raise claim (1) in the alternative).

(4) *A claim to have any question or issue arising out of the plaintiff's claim decided not only as between the plaintiff and defendant but also as between either or both of them and the third party.* For example where P sues D, a builder, for an injunction to restrain him from building on certain land and when D tells T, his customer, about P's claim, T says that if D stops building he will bring a breach of contract action against him. Note that in this example D claims no remedy against T. He merely wishes to bring about the effect, implicit in all the other grounds, that T will be bound by the findings of fact in P's claim.

What is the precise ambit of claim (3)? Consider the following problem.

> *Example*
> P, D and T are all drivers involved in a road accident. P sues D. Clearly D could take third party proceedings against T raising claims (1) and (4). Can he also raise claim (3) seeking compensation from T for his own injuries?

If one takes a narrow view of claim (3) and limits it to cases seeking to make the third party ultimately responsible for the plaintiff's claim, the answer to our question would be no. Such a view is consistent with the decision reached in *Myers v Sherick* [1974] 1 WLR 31. However, taking a narrow view of claim (3) in our example would lead to considerable inconvenience and delay. If D can get the necessary findings of fact against T why should he not also obtain damages?

If one takes a broader view of claim (3) the answer to our question would be yes. In *Kennet v Brown* [1988] 1 WLR 582, the facts of which are similar to our example, the district registrar, the judge and the Court of Appeal all took the broader view and assumed that the defendant could seek compensation for his own injuries. However, it would seem that, at least in the Court of Appeal, the question whether a broad or narrow view should be taken was not expressly argued and *Myers v Sherick* was not cited to the court. (*Kennet v Brown* was subsequently overruled on another point; see *Welsh Development Agency v Redpath Dorman Long Ltd* [1994] 1 WLR 1409.)

An alternative solution to the problem posed in our example would arise if D could also allege negligence against P: he could then counterclaim and add T as a defendant to counterclaim; see RSC Ord 15, r 2 and CCR Ord 9, r 15 and see further p 99.

Third party procedure in the High Court (RSC Ord 16)

The procedure is a shortened version of the writ procedure and is therefore similar to the procedure by originating summons.

Third party proceedings are possible only in cases commenced by writ or originating summons. RSC Ord 16 does not apply to cases commenced by originating notice of motion or petition (*Aiden Shipping Co Ltd v Interbulk Ltd* [1986] AC 965, *per* Lord Goff at p 981E).

Issue

After he has given notice of intention to defend the defendant can issue a third party notice in prescribed form. No leave is necessary if the action was begun by writ and the defendant *issues* the notice before he *serves* the defence. In an exceptional case leave to issue may be given even after the trial has started: see *Walker & Knight v Donne* (1976) *The Times*, 9 November.

Service

The notice must be served on the third party as if it were a writ, ie personal service or postal service, and only with leave if the third party is outside the jurisdiction (unless domiciled within the EU and CJJA 1982 applies, see p 138). The defendant must also serve copies of the writ and any pleadings already served in the action and a form of acknowledgment of service, amended so as to apply to a third party (see Oyez Form High Court E27). The defendant must also supply the plaintiff with a copy of the third party notice, if the plaintiff so requests (RSC Ord 66, r 3).

Acknowledgment of service

The third party must lodge an acknowledgment of service in the court office in which the action is proceeding, and must do so within fourteen days of service. If the third party does not acknowledge service or does not give notice of intention to defend he is deemed to admit any claim stated in the notice and will be bound by any judgment in the action, including a judgment by consent.

Summons for third party directions

Since the pleadings and discovery stages of the writ procedure are omitted the directions stage is reached immediately after the third party gives notice of intention to defend. The defendant must then take out and serve a summons for third party directions. This is true even in cases in which there are automatic directions for the plaintiff's claim (see p 452). If the defendant fails to serve a summons within seven days of the third party's acknowledgment the third party can apply either for directions or for a dismissal for want of prosecution.

The defendant's summons must be served on all parties to the action, ie including the plaintiff. At the hearing there is a variety of orders the master can make:

(1) *Dismissal of the summons.* This order has the effect of terminating the third party proceedings. It is appropriate where the defendant's claim is outside Ord 16, r 1, or cannot be conveniently tried with the plaintiff's claim (see *Chatsworth Investments v Amoco* [1968] Ch 665) or where the third party claim was commenced unfairly late (see *Courtenay-Evans v Stuart Passey & Associates* [1986] 1 All ER 932) or should be dismissed for want of prosecution (as to which, see p 364).

(2) *Order adding the third party as a defendant,* where either the plaintiff or the third party wishes to raise claims against the other.

(3) *Order substituting the third party as defendant or giving the third party leave to defend the plaintiff's claim,* for example where the third party agrees to indemnify the defendant.

(4) *Judgment against the third party,* for example on a third party claim in which, if it had been started by writ, the defendant could have obtained judgment under Ord 14. If the defendant's liability to the plaintiff still has to be determined the judgment against the third party might be 'a declaration that the said defendant is entitled to be indemnified by the said third party against any claim the plaintiff may establish herein and in respect of any costs ... liberty to apply for any further order which may be necessary to enforce such indemnity'. (See Chitty and Jacob, *Queen's Bench Forms*, 21st edn (Sweet & Maxwell 1986) No 218.)

(5) *Order for third party pleadings.* A Third Party Statement of Claim (served by the defendant) is not usually necessary on claims for contribution or indemnity where the issues can be clearly set out in the defence and the third party notice. However, an order might be made for a Third Party Defence (served by the third party).

(6) *Orders for discovery between the third party and the defendant or plaintiff.* Although there is no automatic discovery in third party

proceedings, the master can make such orders for discovery as are appropriate.

(7) *Directions for the trial of the third party issue.* The classic directions are 'that the said third party be at liberty to appear at the trial of this action and take such part as the judge shall direct and be bound by the result of the trial. And that the [third party issue] be tried at the trial of this action, but subsequent thereto.' Such directions enable discovery orders to be made directly between plaintiff and third party (see above).

If, for whatever reason, the plaintiff's claim is later determined without a trial (eg a judgment by consent, by default, under Ord 14, on admissions, or on acceptance of a payment into court) the defendant can apply, by summons to the district judge, for such judgment against the third party as the nature of the case may require (RSC Ord 16, r 7 and see p 353). Similarly, the third party could apply for judgment against the defendant (eg an order for costs) if, in the circumstances, that was appropriate.

Trial

Since the third party will be bound by the result of the plaintiff's claim he is allowed to 'appear and take such part as the judge shall direct'. Usually the judge will permit him to cross-examine the witnesses called by both the plaintiff and the defendant and sometimes may allow him to call a witness of his own.

Since the third party issue is decided 'at the trial but subsequent thereto' the plaintiff need not attend. Unless the third party was made a defendant the plaintiff is not entitled to enter judgment against him. Usually however the plaintiff will attend in order to make representations as to costs. The court has power to order costs between the plaintiff and the third party. Typical orders include the following:

(1) *Where the plaintiff wins against the defendant who in turn wins against the third party* the court may order that 'the defendant do pay the plaintiff ... costs ... the third party do pay the taxed costs the defendant is called upon to pay the plaintiff *and* the costs of defending this action *and* the costs of the third party proceedings'.

(2) *Where the plaintiff loses an action which rendered third party proceedings inevitable* the plaintiff will be ordered to pay all parties' costs (see *Thomas v Times Book Co* [1966] 1 WLR 911; although orders for costs can be made directly between plaintiff and third party, a third party is not entitled to apply for security for costs against the plaintiff: see *Taly NDC International NV v Terra Nova Insurance Co Ltd* [1985] 1 WLR 1359).

(3) *As in (2) but the plaintiff is insolvent or legally aided.* The defendant may be left to bear the third party's costs since as between them costs should be awarded as if the third party

proceedings were a separate action (see *Johnson v Ribbins* [1977] 1 WLR 1458).

The defendant cannot enforce any judgment he obtains against the third party until he has satisfied any judgment the plaintiff obtained against him (unless the court otherwise orders).

Third party procedure in the county court (CCR Ord 12)

Issue

In each of the following cases the defendant must apply for leave to issue (on notice to the plaintiff) and must file a copy of the proposed third party notice with his notice of application:

(1) a fixed date action;
(2) any default action in which a date for trial or pre-trial review has already been fixed;
(3) any default action in which automatic directions apply (see p 465) and in which the pleadings are deemed to be closed.

No leave to issue is necessary in a default action if the defendant issues the third party notice before, or at the same time as, he delivers his defence or counterclaim. Indeed, in a default action in which automatic directions apply a third party notice can be issued without leave at any time up to deemed close of pleadings.

It seems that there is no provision for third party procedure in cases commenced by originating application; see CCR Ord 12, r 1(1) referring to 'actions' and CCR Ord 3, r 1 and CCA 1984, s 147.

According to *Green Book Procedural Table No 7*, a defendant issuing a third party notice without leave should file three copies of the third party notice (one for the court, one for the third party and one to be sent to the plaintiff) and a full set of pleadings for service on the third party (see below).

In a default action, once a third party notice is issued, the plaintiff cannot enter a default judgment or a judgment on an admission (see p 250). Instead, the court will usually convene a pre-trial review or a further hearing thereof, the date and time for which will be specified in the third party notice (see fig 23 and see further, below).

Service

The third party notice, and copies of the summons, the particulars of claim and any defence or counterclaim must be served on the third party in accordance with the rules applicable to the service of the summons in a fixed date action (ie usually not less than twenty-one days before the return day). In the case of a notice issued without leave a copy of it must also be served on the plaintiff.

[continued on p 327]

Fig 23: Third party notice

IN THE .... COUNTY COURT

CASE No.

BETWEEN .... PLAINTIFF

AND .... DEFENDANT

AND .... THIRD PARTY

TO (THE THIRD PARTY) ....

TAKE NOTICE that this action has been brought by the plaintiff against the defendant and that the defendant claims against you

    (a)   that he is entitled to contribution from you to the extent of

or (b)   that he is entitled to be indemnified by you against liability in respect of

or (c)   that he is entitled to the following relief or remedy relating to or connected with the original subject matter of the action, namely

or (d)   that the following question or issue relating to or connected with the subject matter of the action should properly be determined as between the plaintiff and the defendant and the third party, namely

The grounds of the defendant's claim are —

If you dispute the plaintiff's claim against the defendant or the defendant's claim against you, you must within 14 days after the service of this notice upon you take or send to the court two copies of your defence.

AND TAKE NOTICE that you should attend at

on

at   o'clock when directions will be given for the further conduct of these proceedings.

If you fail to attend you may be deemed to admit:—

    (1)   the plaintiff's claim against the defendant; and

    (2)   the defendant's claim against you; and

    (3)   your liability to (contribute to the extent claimed)

           or (indemnify the defendant)

           or

    (4)   the defendant's right to the relief or remedy claimed in paragraph (c) above; and

    (5)   the validity of any judgment in the action;

And you will be bound by the judgment in the action.

DATED

Address all communications to the Chief Clerk AND QUOTE THE ABOVE CASE NUMBER
THE COURT OFFICE AT

is open from 10 a.m. to 4 p.m. Monday to Friday

N.15 Third Party Notice Order 12 Rule 1(1)

MCR 40428/3/8309676 350 4/82 TL

Delivery of third party defence

The third party must deliver a defence within fourteen days of the service of the third party notice. If he defaults the court may order him to serve a defence on penalty of being debarred from defending altogether (see CCR Ord 13, r 2).

Pre-trial review

In every case involving third party proceedings some sort of 'directions hearing' will take place, usually a pre-trial review of the whole action. This is true even in cases in which there are automatic directions for the plaintiff's claim.

When a third party notice is issued without leave (see above) the court office must fix a day for a pre-trial review and specify it in the third party notice itself (see fig 23). On an application for leave to issue a third party notice, the court, if it grants leave, must also give directions as to the further conduct of the action. Of course, at this hearing, the proposed third party will not be present. Therefore, directions will normally be given convening a pre-trial review and/or postponing any trial date or pre-trial review date already arranged.

Trial

If the third party does not appear at the trial he will be deemed to admit the claim stated in the notice and will be bound by any judgment, including a consent judgment, given in the action. This default penalty applies whether or not he has delivered a defence.

If the third party does appear he will be allowed to take such part therein as the court allows. Generally speaking the conduct of the trial, the orders (including orders for costs), and the restrictions on enforcement of judgment are the same as in a High Court action. As to the scale of costs applicable, see p 528 and CCR Ord 38, r 4(2).

Party and party proceedings (RSC Ord 16, r 8; CCR Ord 12, r 5)

A defendant can also make a third party claim against any other defendant (ie someone who *is* already a party to the action). In such a case leave to issue the notice is never required and, in the High Court, no acknowledgment of service is necessary if the recipient has already given notice of intention to defend the action. The case will then proceed to the hearing of a summons for directions or pre-trial review, as the case may be.

In order to distinguish it from an ordinary third party notice, any notice under RSC Ord 16, r 8 (or CCR Ord 12, r 5) can be correctly termed a 'party and party notice'. In practice, however, the only claim frequently made by such a notice is a claim for contribution and therefore these notices are often called 'contribution notices' (see for example *White Book* 16/8/1 and *RA Lister & Co Ltd v EG Thomson (Shipping) Ltd (No 2)* [1987] 1 WLR 1614). This alternative name would be incorrect in the case of eg a claim for indemnity. Also, one should take care never to confuse the formal notice under RSC Ord 16, r 8 (or CCR Ord 12, r 5) with an informal notice under RSC Ord 16, r 10 (or CCR Ord 12, r 7) which is called a 'written offer of contribution' (as to which see p 348).

Where two or more defendants are held liable for the same damage (whether their liability is in tort, contract, breach of trust or otherwise) the trial court has power to apportion the liability between them (Civil Liability (Contribution) Act 1978). Because of this power a defendant who wishes to claim contribution is not obliged to serve a formal notice on his co-defendants. However, it is always *desirable* to give some notice to the other parties, for example an informal notice such as a 'written offer of contribution' (see p 348). It is *prudent* to serve formal notice where one defendant learns that the plaintiff and other defendants are negotiating a compromise excluding him (see *Harper v Gray & Walker* [1985] 1 WLR 1196). It is *necessary* to give formal notice if one defendant wishes to obtain discovery orders against another defendant (see *Clayson v Rolls-Royce Ltd* [1951] 1 KB 746) or if the right to contribution itself is regulated by a contract between the defendants (see 1978 Act, s 7(3)) or, of course, if a claim is made for some remedy other than contribution, such as an indemnity or a declaration.

Fourth and subsequent parties (RSC Ord 16, r 9; CCR Ord 12, r 6)

By a similar procedure to that described above a third party may bring in a fourth party and a fourth party a fifth party and so on (see for example *Butterworth v Kingsway Motors* [1954] 1 WLR 1286). In the High Court no leave is necessary to issue such a notice if the action was begun by writ and the claimant issues his notice within twenty-eight days of the service of a notice on him. In the county court, the rules governing proceedings between a defendant and third party apply with any necessary modifications.

There are no special prescribed forms for use in proceedings under RSC Ord 16, rr 8, 9, or CCR Ord 12, rr 4, 5. In all cases the claimant has to amend the heading and text of the ordinary form which is headed 'Third Party Notice'.

Chapter 16

Payments into Court and *Calderbank* Offers

In any action for debt or damages the defendant is entitled, if he wishes, to pay money into court in satisfaction of the plaintiff's claim. Such a payment is perhaps the most important tactical step which the defendant can take once the action has started. It amounts to an attempt to *force* a compromise.

The compromise element is clear enough; if the plaintiff gives valid notice of acceptance the relevant cause of action is stayed and (usually) the plaintiff will be entitled to his costs to date. The forcing element becomes apparent if the payment is not accepted. Thereafter the plaintiff is taking a heavy risk as to costs. If, at the trial, the plaintiff fails to recover more than the money in court the judge is likely to make two orders for costs. First, the costs *up to* the date on which the plaintiff received notice of payment in will be awarded to the plaintiff. Secondly, the costs *from* that date will be awarded to the defendant. The plaintiff thus ends up paying a substantial proportion of both parties' costs even though he has won the action. If he fails to beat the payment into court then, in respect of all the proceedings after the payment was made, he, and not the defendant, is regarded as the losing party.

Making a well-estimated payment into court prevents a plaintiff pursuing inordinate or exaggerated claims at the defendant's expense. If the payment-in is accepted the defendant pays the costs to date and the litigation ceases as to that claim. If the plaintiff unsuccessfully seeks a higher award, he has to pay all the costs incurred since payment in. Although the plaintiff was justified in starting the action it was unreasonable for him to continue it once the appropriate offer of compromise had been made.

The system of making written offers known as '*Calderbank* offers' (following the Court of Appeal decision in *Calderbank v Calderbank* [1976] Fam 93) enables defendants to achieve a similar result in other cases where an offer of compromise cannot be made by means of a payment into court. For example, cases in which the plaintiff claims an injunction, or declaratory relief only, or any other claim for remedies other than debt or damages. The defendant sets out his offer of compromise in a letter addressed to the plaintiff and marked 'without prejudice save as to costs'. If the offer is accepted the action will come to an end. If it is not accepted but, at trial, the plaintiff fails to recover more than was offered, the trial court is likely to make orders for costs similar to the two costs orders described (see further p 348). In certain cases both tactics, payments into court and *Calderbank* offers may be employed, sometimes simultaneously, sometimes consecutively. This is explained further on p 348.

How to make a payment into court

In High Court cases in London the money is paid into the Court Funds Office. In district registry cases the money can be paid, either into the Court Funds Office direct, or into the district registry (which will remit the money to the Court Funds Office within one working day). In either case, cheques should be made payable to 'the Accountant-General of the Supreme Court'. In all High Court cases a copy of the writ and the documents illustrated in figs 24 and 25 must be produced (Court Funds Rules 1987, rr 15, 16). The defendant subsequently serves the latter document (the notice of payment-in) on the plaintiff and serves copies of it on every other defendant.

In the county court the money is paid into the appropriate court office accompanied by a notice stating that the payment is made in satisfaction of the plaintiff's cause or causes of action and stating the name and address of the defendant and the case number. The court then prepares and sends notices of payment-in to every other party (see fig 26). Of course, if he wishes to ensure that the matter is dealt with quickly, the defendant may prepare the notice of payment-in himself (and provide the court with sufficient copies) just as he would in a High Court case (CCR Ord 50, r 4A). County court defendants need never draw up a request for lodgment (fig 24). This will be done by the court staff, about three weeks later, if no notice of acceptance is received, when they remit the money to the Court Funds Office (see generally Court Funds Rules 1987, r 31). In county court cases cheques should be made payable to 'HM Paymaster-General'.

In both courts, money can be paid into court by post (see further *White Book* 1140 and *Green Book Procedure Table No 6*).

In all cases, it is necessary to ascertain the date upon which the plaintiff received the prescribed notice of payment-in. This is the date from which to measure his time limit for acceptance. Alternatively, if he does not accept the payment, this is the date from which he is at risk on costs should he fail to beat the payment-in.

In the High Court the defendant should effect service of the notice of payment-in by taking, posting or faxing it to the plaintiff's address for service (see p 203). To help the defendant prove the date of service, RSC

[continued on p 333]

Fig 24: Money lodgment (general)

Request for Lodgment In the _____ Division of the High Court

Please use BLOCK CAPITALS _____ **District Registry**

Full Action Title [   ]

Action or Case Number [   ]

Please ensure that you answer the relevant question(s) below. Otherwise this form may be returned to you.

Has a previous lodgment been made in this action? Yes ☐ No ☐ (Please Tick)

Has the hearing begun? Yes ☐ No ☐ (Please Tick)

Has a Certificate of Total Benefit been issued under Section 22 of the Social Security Act 1989? Yes ☐ No ☐ (Please Tick)

If YES, then a copy of the Certificate must accompany this Request for Payment into Court. If any subsequent deductions have been made from the sum to be lodged then a Certificate of Deduction must accompany this request.

We request the Accountant General to receive into Court for lodgment to the above account

£ [   ] which is paid in *(Complete relevant section below)*

A on behalf of [   ]

in satisfaction of the claim of subject to RSC O.22,r.1. [   ]

B on behalf of [   ]

against the claim of [   ]

with defence setting up tender subject to RSC O.22,r.1.

(Delete as appropriate)

C under Order dated [   ] copy attached/I do not have a copy because [   ]

D for the following reason [   ]

Signed _____   Name and address of other side's solicitors

Firm's name [   ] [   ]

Address (and/or DX code) [   ] [   ]

Solicitor for the [   ] [   ]

Ref. [   ] Dated [   ] Ref. [   ]

Note. Payments into Court are made to the Court Funds Office, 22 Kingsway, London WC2B 6LE, or by the DX system addressed to the Court Funds Office DX: 37965 Kingsway. Payments may be made by cheque or bankers draft and must be made payable to the ACCOUNTANT GENERAL OF THE SUPREME COURT. Please ensure that the cheque is crossed "ACCOUNT PAYEE".

NB. Cheques made out to anyone other than the Accountant General of the Supreme Court will be returned. Payments may also be made by cash *(payments in cash should not be made by post)*.

Date Stamp/Seal   For CFO use

Comments [   ]   A/c No [   ]

Placed B now/ + 21 days   inits

Date input [   ]   inits

Location Code [   ]   Bank Date/Receipt Number

Checked by [   ]   inits

Lodgment approved ___

Court Funds Office—Form 100 (Court Funds Rules 15 & 16)

OYEZ The Solicitors' Law Stationery Society Ltd, Oyez House, 7 Spa Road, London SE16 3QQ

High Court E33

1992 Edition 5.95 F29639 5050076

Form High Court E33

Reproduced by kind permission of the Solicitors' Law Stationery Society Ltd.

Fig 25: Notice of payment into court (High Court)

Notice of Payment
into Court
(O.22.rr 1,2)

IN THE HIGH COURT OF JUSTICE   19   .— .—No.
					Division

Between

					Plaintiff

				AND

					Defendant

Take Notice that —

(1) If by a particular
Defendant insert
name.

The Defendant (¹)

ha paid £			into Court.
The said £			is in satisfaction of [the cause of action] [all the causes
of action] in respect of which the Plaintiff claim [and after taking into account and
satisfying the above-named Defendant's cause of action for
					in respect of which he counterclaim]

					or

The said £			is in satisfaction of the following causes of action
in respect of which the Plaintiff   claim , namely,

[and after taking into account and satisfying the above-named Defendant's cause of
action for
					in respect of which he counterclaim]

					or

Of the said £			, £			is in satisfaction of the
Plaintiff's cause[s] of action for

[and after taking into account and satisfying the above-named Defendant's cause of
action for
					in respect of which he counterclaim]
and £			is in satisfaction of the Plaintiff's cause[s] of action for

[and after taking into account and satisfying the above-named Defendant's cause of
action for
					in respect of which he counterclaim].

[The Defendant has withheld from this payment into court the sum of
£			in accordance with paragraph 12(2)(a)(i) of Schedule 4 to the Social
Security Act 1989]

Dated the	.	day of			19 .

To

[					of

The Plaintiff's Solicitor			[Agent for

or Agent
[and to [				of

(2) If there are
co-Defendants a
copy of the notice
must also be
served upon their
Solicitors.

Solicitor for the Defendant (²) [			Solicitor for the Defendant
[

Form High Court B5

Reproduced by kind permission of the Solicitors' Law Stationery Society Ltd.

Fig 26: Notice of payment into court (Cty Ct)

IN THE   COUNTY COURT

BETWEEN   PLAINTIFF
                                                                 CASE No.
AND   DEFENDANT

To the Plaintiff

TAKE NOTICE that the defendant   has paid into court
the sum of £   in satisfaction of your claim in this section [or in satisfaction of
your cause of action for   [together with the
sum of £   for costs].

[In making this payment the defendant has taken into account and intends to satisfy his counterclaim]
[or his cause of action for

If you accept the payment made in satisfaction of your claim [or of the cause of action specified above]
you must give written notice of acceptance to the court and every other party within 21 days after
you receive this notice [or not less than 3 days before the day fixed for the hearing of this action]
[or before the hearing of this action begins] [or before judgment is given].

                                    DATED

Address all communications to the Chief Clerk AND QUOTE THE ABOVE CASE NUMBER
THE COURT OFFICE AT

is open from 10 am to 4 pm Monday to Friday

N.243   Notice to plaintiff of payment into court of part of claim or of whole of money claim
        where there is a claim for some other relief. Order 11, Rules 1(10), 3(1) & (2).

Ord 22, r 4.1(2) requires the plaintiff to acknowledge receipt within three days. The rule does not say what should be done if the plaintiff fails to acknowledge. However the matter is important enough to warrant the defendant pressing the plaintiff, eg demanding an acknowledgment and, if it is still not forthcoming, applying to the district judge under RSC Ord 2, r 2 (see p 3).

In the county court, the court will send the prescribed notice of payment-in to the plaintiff by posting it to his address for service. There is no obligation on the plaintiff to acknowledge receipt. Instead the court will record the date of posting from which the defendant can calculate the presumed date of receipt.

In both courts there is nothing to prevent the making of a payment into court as soon as the writ or summons has been issued. It is not necessary to await service or, in the High Court, the lodgment of an acknowledgment of service (*Towers v Morley* [1992] 1 WLR 511). Making a payment into court as early as possible advances the vital date for costs purposes and so maximises the costs pressure put upon the plaintiff.

What is covered by a payment into court

The payment into court is the 'bottom line' figure which is offered to the plaintiff in addition to, usually, all his reasonable costs to date. (In this context it is wrong to pay costs into court, see below.) What factors should the defendant have regard to when calculating the amount he wishes to offer? In this section we list five points for consideration. The more arithmetical and tactical aspects of these points will be described in later sections.

Multiplicity of claims

Where a plaintiff raises several causes of action the defendant can allocate parts of his payment into court in whatever way he chooses. He can either make a lump sum payment for the whole claim, or allocate separate sums for each cause of action, or allocate lump sums for some causes with separate sums for others. Usually the best policy is to pay in a lump sum for the whole claim because then the plaintiff cannot pick and choose which parts of the payment he will accept. The payment will be treated as a lump sum for the whole claim unless the notice given to the plaintiff specifically states to the contrary. If the joinder of causes of action in a lump sum payment unfairly prejudices the plaintiff, the court has power to order the defendant to specify separate sums for each cause (RSC Ord 22, r 1(5); CCR Ord 11, r 1(6)).

> *Example*
> In *Gable House Estates Ltd v The Halpern Partnership* (1993) Supreme Court Practice News, February 1994, P sued D1 (architects) and D2 (management contractors) in respect of a building dispute. P alleged two separate causes of action; one against both defendants and the other against D1 only. D1 made a payment into court in respect of both causes of action. The Court of Appeal ruled that D1 should not be required to apportion its offer of compromise between the two causes of action. The difficulty faced by P in this case was no more than the ordinary difficulty faced by any plaintiff when a lump sum payment into court was made.
> In *Walker v Turpin* [1994] 1 WLR 196 P1 and P2 alleged that D had broken agreements to sell them equal numbers of shares in *X Co*. Because of their previous dealings in shares in *X Co* it was likely that any damages recoverable by P1 would be calculated according to 1984 share prices and any damages recoverable by P2 would be calculated according to later share prices. D made lump sum payments into court in respect of both claims which totalled £110,000. P1 was prepared to accept £55,000 in settlement of his claim but P2 was not. D was ordered to apportion his offer of compromise as between the two claims. Because the lump sum offered related to two plaintiffs and not one, P1 and P2 'were placed in a difficulty which [they] ought not fairly to have to face'.

Note that claims under the Fatal Accidents Act 1976 and the Law Reform (Miscellaneous Provisions) Act 1934 are treated as being a single cause of action even though the money in court may be divisible between several people, ie the dependants of the deceased and/or the beneficiaries of his estate (RSC Ord 22, r 1(6); CCR Ord 11, r 1(7); and see further p 340).

Interests on debts or damages

As to the court's powers to award interest and the rates thereof, see p 15 and p 75. When calculating how much money to pay into court the defendant should include a sum in respect of any interest which he thinks the court would award if judgment were being given at the time of payment-in. The notice of payment-in given to the plaintiff (and other defendants) should state that the payment 'is in satisfaction of [all the causes of action] [the following cause of action] including any claims for interest thereon ...' (RSC Ord 22, r 1(8); CCR Ord 11, r 1(8)). However, there is nothing to be gained by apportioning the total sum as between compensation and interest.

If, later, a trial court has to determine whether the plaintiff has beaten the payment into court the trial court will not take into account any interest relevant to the period since payment-in (see p 329). Just because the court specifies separate sums in respect of compensation and interest it does not follow that the defendant should have done so as well.

Where counterclaim raised

Where a defendant who has raised a monetary counterclaim wishes to make a payment into court he may either pay in the gross value of the plaintiff's claim or the net value, ie the amount by which he thinks the claim will exceed his counterclaim. Whichever he does should be made clear in the notice of payment-in (RSC Ord 22, r 2; CCR Ord 11, r 1(9)). Almost invariably the best policy is to pay in the net figure. Note that in such a case the court has no power to order the defendant to bring the balance of the money into court.

Turning now to the counterclaim itself, the plaintiff can make a payment into court in respect of it as if he were a defendant in the action (RSC Ord 22, r 6; CCR Ord 11, r 8).

Recovery of state benefits

This is an important topic in most personal injury cases. As to the general law on recovery of state benefits see p 62. Where this law applies a defendant who makes a payment into court will become liable to make the relevant payments to the DSS within fourteen days of the money being paid out of court (ie only after the compromise or litigation is complete; Social Security Administration Act 1992, s 93(2), *Green Book* 1290).

It will normally be advisable for a defendant to obtain a certificate of total benefit before making a payment into court, and also to obtain a further certificate, if necessary, before making any subsequent increase in that payment. An up-to-date certificate will show the defendant the correct sum for him to deduct from the compensation he wishes to offer. He can then pay the balance into court and the notice of payment-in can be indorsed as follows: 'The Defendant has withheld from this payment into court the sum of £   in accordance with s 93 of the Social Security Administration Act 1992.' This indorsement is of importance if the payment into court is not accepted and the trial court later wishes to determine whether the plaintiff has beaten the payment-in (see p 329).

What steps are available to a defendant who does not have an up-to-date certificate of total benefit? The legislation permits him to make a payment into court but it will often be inadvisable for him to do so. If the payment is accepted and paid out the defendant will still have to make the relevant payment to the DSS (s 93(4) of the 1992 Act) the payment of a sum which, *ex hypothesi*, was not conclusively stated before he calculated his offer of compromise. Indeed s 93(4) requires him to apply for a certificate 'no later than the day on which the payment into court is made'.

The better course for such a defendant to take is to apply for a certificate of total benefit, and in the meantime, make a *Calderbank* offer (see p 329). Once the certificate is received he should then make the appropriate payment into court. The rules of court make express provision for *Calderbank* offers in such a case (RSC Ord 62, r 9(3); CCR Ord 11, r 10(3)). In order to obtain the maximum costs advantage from his offer of compromise it is necessary for the defendant to make the subsequent payment into court within seven days of receiving the certificate of total benefit.

Plaintiff's costs to date

Save in one case (CCR Ord 11, r 3(4) noted at the end of this section) a payment into court carries within it an implied offer by the defendant to pay all the plaintiff's reasonable costs up to the date of acceptance (see further p 339). This is so even if the notice of payment-in states, incorrectly, that the sum in court is inclusive of costs (*Stafford Knight & Co Ltd v Conway* [1970] 1 WLR 784). It is therefore important that the defendant should be warned about this implication before he makes his payment into court. It may be that the burden of costs which he would have to bear (ie his own as well as the plaintiff's) is such as to disincline him to offer any compromise. The burden is especially heavy whenever a payment is made, or increased, at a late stage in the proceedings (see further p 338).

Other costs matters about which the defendant should be advised before making a payment-in are the effect of a payment made in respect of some but not all of the causes of action and the effect of a payment made by some but not all of multiple defendants (see pp 339 and 340).

The exceptional case, in which the payment into court is inclusive of costs, is provided by CCR Ord 11, r 3(4), a rule which has no equivalent in the High Court rules. It enables a defendant in a debt action who acts promptly, to limit the plaintiff to fixed costs rather than taxed costs (see further as to fixed costs, p 565). Assume that the plaintiff claims in respect of debts which he alleges amount to £20,000. Further assume that the defendant pays £15,000 into court in satisfaction of that claim and that the plaintiff gives notice of acceptance. The defendant will not be liable for any further costs if he made the payment into court within fourteen days after service of the summons and if he also pays into court the sum in respect of fixed costs which is appropriate on a claim for £15,000.

Withdrawal of notice of payment-in

Although it is true that no leave of court is necessary to make or to increase a payment-in, such leave is necessary should the defendant later change his mind and seek to withdraw or to reduce the offer of compromise he has made (RSC Ord 22, r 1(3); CCR Ord 11, r 1(4)). To obtain leave the defendant must show matters such as fraud or mistake affecting the payment or show some sufficient change of circumstance such as a change in the law relevant to the action (*Cumper v Pothecary* [1941] 2 KB 58), or the discovery of new evidence in his favour (cf *Metroinvest Ansalt v Commercial Union Assurance Co Ltd* [1985] 1 WLR 513), or the fact that he has been ordered to make an interim payment (see p 308). Leave will not be granted so as to benefit an insolvent defendant's creditors; on the contrary, once a payment into court has been made, the plaintiff is to be treated as a secured creditor of the defendant to the extent of the payment in even though he does not wish to accept it (*Sherratt (WA) Ltd v John Bromley (Church Stretton) Ltd* [1985] QB 1038).

The defendant's object in seeking to withdraw his notice of payment-in is, usually, so as to obtain repayment of the money. Curiously an order for repayment to the defendant pre-trial is not expressly provided for in the rules. However, it seems that the courts have an inherent jurisdiction to make such order (*Sherratt*). Repayment to a defendant in a personal injury case terminates any obligation which the payment into court placed upon him concerning the recovery of state benefits (Social Security Administration Act 1992, s 93(7)).

Applications to withdraw a notice in order to obtain repayment are in practice rare and should, we think, remain so. Even if a sufficient change in circumstances does occur, entitling the defendant to apply he should consider very carefully before doing so. If he has no financial need for the return of his money he has nothing to gain but something to lose if he seeks leave to withdraw. The change of circumstance will prevent the plaintiff getting payment out (see below). However if the defendant withdraws his offer of compromise he will lose some of the costs advantages it gives him (see *Garner v Cleggs* [1983] 1 WLR 862 and see further, p 347).

Time limits for acceptance

The plaintiff first officially learns of the payment into court when he is given the prescribed notice. In the High Court he must acknowledge receipt within three days. In either court, if a single payment relates to more than one cause of action he can apply to have separate sums specified for each. These matters aside, he must consider whether he should accept any payment and so terminate the relevant causes of action or whether he should risk liability for further costs by going on to trial. If the payment was made before trial he is allotted a period of twenty-one days in which to make up his mind (RSC Ord 22, r 3; CCR Ord 11, r 3). During this period all parties should as far as possible avoid taking steps incurring further costs. Further preparations for battle should not be made (unless they are urgent or essential) while the plaintiff is considering the defendant's peace proposal and see *Hall v T Clarke Plc* (1997) Supreme Court Practice News, Issue 3/97 *per* Thorpe LJ.

If the plaintiff decides to accept he can normally obtain payment-out without leave simply by giving *notice of acceptance* to every defendant (and, in the county court, to the court office) so long as he does so within the twenty-one-day period and, in any case, before the trial begins (or, in the county court, not less than three days before the trial begins).

In the rare case of a payment being made or increased during the trial the High Court rules allow the plaintiff only two days in which to make up his mind. During those days he can obtain payment-out without leave so long as he gives notice of acceptance before the end of counsels' closing speeches. After the two days he cannot obtain payment-out unless the defendant consents. In the county court a fourteen-day period applies (county court cases are sometimes adjourned part-heard for several days or weeks) but the plaintiff cannot obtain payment-out without the defendant's consent once the trial court begins to deliver judgment.

As to acceptance of a payment into court after the relevant time limit has expired, see p 346.

If notice of acceptance is given within the time allowed

The acceptance of a payment into court within the time allowed has triple effect: the stay of all relevant causes of action, provision for the plaintiff's costs, and payment-out. In particular cases there may also be further consequences (see p 340).

Stay of all relevant causes

The relevant causes of action may or may not comprise the whole of the plaintiff's claim, and may or may not include any counterclaim. Which causes are stayed can be determined by looking at the notice of payment-in. Generally speaking no further proceedings in respect of these causes can be taken (though in a very exceptional case the court can lift the stay (see *Lambert v Mainland Market Deliveries Ltd* [1977] 1 WLR 825)). The stay does not prevent applications for costs and related matters (*Rookes v Barnard (No 2)* [1966] 1 QB 176). If the payment related only to some causes of action but the plaintiff abandons the rest he is also entitled to recover the costs reasonably incurred on the causes he has abandoned (*Hudson v Elmbridge Borough Council* [1991] 1 WLR 880). As presently worded the rules enable the plaintiff to achieve the same result as if the payment into court had been in respect of all causes of action and not just those specified by the defendant. In *Hudson* the Court of Appeal held that it had no power to disallow the costs of the abandoned causes of action despite the apparent injustice of this result.

A stay of all relevant causes of action will also bring to an end any further proceedings on these causes as regards any defendants sued jointly with or in the alternative to the paying party. This is considered further overleaf and in Table 5.

Provision for the plaintiff's costs

Where the plaintiff gives notice of acceptance within the time allowed and the action is thereby stayed (or some causes of action are stayed and the plaintiff abandons the rest) the plaintiff is entitled to have his costs taxed and paid (RSC Ord 62, rr 5(4) and 29(1); CCR Ord 11, r 3(5): where the stay includes a stay of counterclaim the defendant is correspondingly entitled to the costs of the counterclaim; RSC Ord 62, r 5(6); CCR Ord 38, r 1(3)). In both courts the plaintiff is entitled to draw a bill of the costs he has incurred 'up to the time of giving notice of acceptance'. This allows him to recover reasonable expenditure on steps taken to determine whether he should accept, eg seeking the advice of his solicitor and/or counsel.

In order to calculate any interest payable on costs (see p 535) the plaintiff is deemed to have an order for costs as from the date of his notice of acceptance (RSC Ord 62, r 5(1) as amended following the House of Lords' decision in *Legal Aid Board v Russell* [1991] 2 WLR 1300; CCR Ord 38, r 1(5)). If the costs remain unpaid after taxation the plaintiff may actually enter up judgment for them so as to proceed to enforcement (RSC Ord 45, r 15; CCR Ord 11, r 3(5)).

Payment-out

Payment-out can be obtained without leave by a plaintiff who gives notice of acceptance within the time allowed and who is of full age and not otherwise within the special cases listed below. In the High Court he must send a Request for Payment in prescribed form (see *White Book* 1210) to the Court Funds Office; in district registry cases a copy of the Request must also be sent to the district registry. In the county court no additional document is needed; the court office will act upon the notice of acceptance it received.

In some cases an order of the court authorising payment-out is required, eg:

(1) Where the payment was made by some, but not all, of the defendants sued jointly or in the alternative. Before granting leave the court may provide for the costs of the other defendants; a *Bullock* order or a *Sanderson* order may be appropriate (see p 97 and *West v Merseyside County Council* (1980) 77 LSG 679).

(2) Where the payment into court was made with a defence of tender before action (see p 160).

(3) Where the plaintiff is a minor or mental patient. In such cases the acceptance of the payment is valid only if it is approved by the court. If approval is given the moneys usually remain in court and are invested or otherwise dealt with for the benefit of the minor or mental patient.

(4) Where the payment was made in satisfaction of a claim under the Fatal Accidents Act 1976 or under that Act and the Law Reform (Miscellaneous Provisions) Act 1934, where more than one person is entitled to the money. The court will apportion the money as between eg the estate, the widow and the children.

(5) In the High Court, where the payment is accepted during the trial. This is usually possible only where the payment was made during the trial and accepted without leave within the very limited time allowed (see above).

An order for payment-out is obtainable on application to the district judge by summons (High Court) or on notice (county court). In some cases consent orders can be made without a hearing (see further p 371).

In recent years there has been a proliferation of cases concerning payments into court made by one of several defendants. We have classified the principles to be applied and have set them out in table 5. In doing so we have taken the liberty of re-explaining the result in *Hodgson v Guardall Ltd* [1991] 3 All ER 823. We respectfully suggest that this case reached the right result but for the wrong reasons, the learned judge being misled by a note in the *White Book* which Stuart-Smith LJ later criticised in two of the other cases. The reasoning relied on by the learned judge in *Hodgson* could never apply in county court cases (contrast the wording of RSC Ord 22, r 4(1)(a) and CCR Ord 11, r 4(2)(a)).

Further consequences

In High Court cases of libel, slander, malicious prosecution or false imprisonment, a party wishing to accept money paid into court in satisfaction of his claim can apply by summons to a judge in chambers for leave to make a statement in open court; the application can in fact be made before or after giving notice of acceptance (see generally RSC Ord 82, r 5).

In any case in which sums in respect of social security benefits have been withheld, the party who made the payment into court must, within fourteen days of being notified of the acceptance and payment-out, pay to the DSS the sum withheld and furnish his opponent with a certificate of deduction (see p 64).

As to the effect of acceptance after the time allowed has expired, see p 346.

Consequences if payment into court is not accepted

Transfer of money to a basic account

The Court Funds Rules 1987 have established two interest-bearing accounts: a basic account (formerly called a 'deposit account') and a special account (formerly called a 'short-term investment account'). The rates of interest payable on these accounts are fixed from time to time by directions of the Lord Chancellor (currently 6 per cent pa and 8 per cent pa respectively; see *White Book* 1262).

The payment into court will automatically be transferred to a basic account twenty-one days (or sometimes twenty-two days) after the effective date of lodgment. (In the case of a minor or mental patient the money will be transferred to a basic account at this time whether or not notice of acceptance has been given. If, later, the action is tried or a compromise is approved, any money to which he is entitled will be transferred to a special account, as at the date of the judgment or order. This gives the minor or mental patient the benefit of an advantageous rate of interest pending a decision as to the longer term investment strategy.)

As to payments-out of accrued interest see p 351.

The rule of secrecy

Except where there is a defence of tender before action (see p 160) the payment into court must not be pleaded and, if not accepted, the trial court must not be told of it until all questions of liability and quantification have been decided. The purpose of this rule is to prevent a premature disclosure which might unfairly prejudice the trial court's opinion of the case. If the rule is broken the judge has a discretion whether to order a new trial. But where any prejudice can only operate against the party who broke the rule, justice may demand that the judge should not order a new trial but should continue with the hearing himself.

[*continued on p 344*]

Table 5: Where payment into court is made by one of several defendants

	Defendants sued 'jointly'	Defendants sued 'in the alternative'	Defendants sued 'severally'
1 Causes of action			
2 Short definitions	One cause of action, multiple defendants alleged to be liable thereon	Multiple causes of action against multiple defendants all in respect of the same damage, it being anticipated that only one defendant may be found liable	Multiple causes of action against multiple defendants where the damage alleged against each is not precisely the same *or* where a finding of liability against one does not preclude a finding of liability against others
3 Examples	(*a*) Contract claim against three defendants trading in partnership (*b*) Running down action against a driver and the driver's employers (vicarious liability)	(*a*) Claim on a contract allegedly made by one defendant as agent for the other defendants (*b*) Running down action in respect of a three-car accident where plaintiff is unsure which driver was at fault (On these examples, see further p 97)	In respect of a building dispute, separate claims, some in contract, some in tort, against the architect, the builder, the subcontractors and the suppliers of the materials

Table 5: contd

Causes of action	Defendants sued 'jointly'	Defendants sued 'in the alternative'	Defendants sued 'severally'
4 Effect if plaintiff accepts payment into court made by one of three defendants	(a) Stay of action against all defendants (b) The whole costs of action are in the discretion of the court. For example the paying party may be ordered to pay one-third of the plaintiff's costs and the plaintiff may be ordered to pay all the costs of the other defendants	(a) Stay of action against all defendants (b) The whole costs of action are in the discretion of the court, eg the paying party may be ordered to pay all the plaintiff's costs and all the costs of the other defendants either directly (a *Sanderson* order) or indirectly (a *Bullock* order)	(a) The action still proceeds on the claims against other defendants. If the claims for damages against other defendants are overlapping, the plaintiff will be able to enforce any judgments later obtained only to the extent that they exceed the payment into court (b) Plaintiff has an automatic right to costs against the paying party but only in respect of his costs of the action against that party
5 Case authorities	*Scania (Great Britain) Ltd v Andrews* [1992] 1 WLR 578	*Hodgson v Guardall Ltd* [1991] 3 All ER 823; and see *Townsend v Stone Toms & Partners* [1981] 1 WLR 1153 *per* Eveleigh LJ at 1158H	*Hudson v Elmbridge Borough Council* [1991] 1 WLR 880; *QBE Insurance (UK) Ltd v Mediterranean Insurance and Reinsurance Co Ltd* [1992] 1 WLR 573; *Oak Tree Leisure Ltd v R A Fisk and Associates* (1997) *The Times*, 1 January

> Were it otherwise you would find that counsel [for the plaintiff] as soon as he
> felt the case was going against him, would apply to take the money out. He
> would say to himself: 'I will either get the money out or I will get a new trial
> before a different judge. And at that trial I may do better. Heads I win. Tails I
> cannot lose' (*per* Lord Denning MR in *Gaskins v British Aluminium* [1976] QB
> 524).

A similar rule of secrecy as to payments into court applies on appeals
to the Court of Appeal (RSC Ord 59, r 12A). In *H v A* (1983) *The Times*,
13 July a solicitor broke the rule by failing to delete references to the
payment which were made in the documents used on the appeal. The
appeal was adjourned so as to come before different judges and the
solicitor was personally penalised in the costs thrown away.

In the High Court there is an important exception to the rule of secrecy
in any case in which the issues of liability and *quantum* are being tried
separately (ie a 'split trial'; see p 456). At the end of the trial as to
liability, but before the question of costs has been decided, either party
can disclose to the court the existence of (but not the amount of) a
payment into court; see RSC Ord 22, r 7(2) as amended. Such a disclosure
may persuade the court to make an order for 'costs reserved' (see p 571
and, for a related matter concerning split trials, p 349).

As yet there is no equivalent to RSC Ord 22, r 7(2) in the county court
even though split trials are equally permissible there (CCR Ord 13,
r 2(2)(c)). Therefore, a defence advocate who wants an order for reserved
costs but cannot obtain it by consent, must employ what general
arguments he can and, if he is not successful, must seek leave to appeal
the costs order (see p 649).

In both courts, the rule of secrecy does not apply to applications for
interim payments (see further, *Fryer v London Transport Executive* (1983)
noted on p 313).

The effect on costs

At the end of the trial, the judge will announce his decision as to the
debt or damages awarded and as to any interest payable thereon. The
existence and amount of the payment into court must now be disclosed
and some arithmetic may be necessary to determine whether the plaintiff
has beaten it. If the judge has awarded interest it will be necessary to
calculate what interest would have been awarded had judgment been
given at the date of the payment-in. In determining whether the plaintiff
has beaten the payment into court the judge should not take into account
any interest relevant to the period since payment-in (see *White Book*
22/1/11). Also, in a personal injury case, where the notice of payment-in
specified a sum which had been withheld in respect of relevant state
benefits (see p 335) the court is required to treat the amount paid into
court as increased by the amount so specified (Social Security Administration Act 1992, s 93(2)(b), *Green Book* 1285).

If the plaintiff recovers more than the money in court, even one penny more, he has beaten the payment and will usually be entitled to his whole costs of the action. If he recovers a sum which is the same as or less than the payment he is penalised for his failure to accept, and the court will usually make the split orders described on p 329. The defendant is regarded as the successful litigant since the date of payment-in and is therefore entitled to his costs from that date unless, in an exceptional case, there is some reason good enough to deprive him of them.

What might amount to a reason good enough to deprive a defendant of the usual orders when he has made a successful payment into court? In *Smiths Ltd v Middleton* [1986] 1 WLR 598 the plaintiff was awarded little more than half the money in court. However, the judge felt that the defendant's conduct as to the matters disputed had been such as to make much of the litigation inevitable even though a large enough payment into court had been made. The judge awarded the plaintiff its costs up to the date of the first payment into court and made no order for the costs thereafter. This order was upheld on appeal.

In *Roache v Newsgroup* (1992) *The Times*, 23 November, *White Book* 62/5/5, the jury awarded, as damages for libel, £50,000, the exact sum paid into court. The plaintiff's pleading contained a standard form claim for an injunction against re-publication of the libel. The trial judge granted the injunction and considered this to be a suitable reason upon which to deprive the defendants of the usual orders for costs. The Court of Appeal disagreed; in their judgment the injunction was a token remedy only and should be ignored.

The fact that the payment into court was made at a very late stage does not, by itself, disentitle the defendant to the usual orders if the plaintiff fails to recover more. A pre-trial payment made less than twenty-one days before trial in the High Court, or made less than twenty-four days before trial in the county court, deprives the plaintiff of the full period allotted to him by the rules within which to decide whether to accept and still obtain payment-out without leave (see p 338). However, the rules give the defendant a right to make a payment into court at any stage of the action, even during the trial. Similarly, having made a payment into court he is entitled to make further payments by way of increase as often and as late as he wishes. Whether or not the payment was made late, the court is obliged to take into account both the fact of payment-in and the amount (*King v Weston-Howell* [1989] 1 WLR 579 and see *Bettaney v Five Towns Demolitions* (1971) 115 SJ 710; in both cases it was conceded that the plaintiff would not have accepted the amount paid in even if it had been paid in earlier).

The true penalty for making a very late payment into court is that it delays the vital date for costs purposes. The defendant's best policy in making payments into court is, the sooner, the better (see p 333).

Orders dealing with the money in court

If the plaintiff fails to prove his claim the action will be dismissed (with costs) and the defendant should apply for leave to withdraw his money from court: there is no possibility now of the plaintiff being allowed to accept it!

If the plaintiff proves his claim but recovers less than the money in court the defendant will be given leave to withdraw the excess of his payment. It does not follow that the balance will be paid out to the plaintiff. The defendant may ask for the damages awarded to be set off against the costs the plaintiff has to pay: see *Cook v Swinfen* [1967] 1 WLR 457.

If the plaintiff proves his claim and beats the payment into court he is entitled to full judgment for damages, costs, and, usually, interest. The judge will give him leave to take out the money in court in part satisfaction (see *Mills v Duckworth* [1938] 1 All ER 318).

As to payments-out of interest accruing on the money whilst in court, see p 351.

If plaintiff wishes to accept late

After expiry of the relevant time limits (see p 338) the plaintiff has no right to accept and obtain payment-out. Unless the defendant consents, the plaintiff must apply to the district judge by summons (High Court) or on notice (county court). Unless the defendant consents, no application can be made to the district judge or trial court, once the trial has begun (*Gaskins v British Aluminium Co Ltd* [1976] QB 524).

In the county court, the plaintiff should first give notice of acceptance (thereby staying the relevant causes of action, see p 339) and then seek an order for payment-out (CCR Ord 11, r 5). In the High Court it is possible to apply for an extension of the time limit for acceptance (*Proetta v Times Newspapers Ltd* [1991] 1 WLR 337) but the more usual application is to seek an order for payment-out under RSC Ord 22, r 5. The High Court rules do not expressly provide for any notice of acceptance or, indeed, any stay of action in such a case. However, according to RSC Ord 22, r 5, any payment-out under that rule before trial must be 'in satisfaction of the cause or causes of action in respect of which it was paid in'.

Before granting the order sought, the court will consider whether there has been a sufficient change of circumstances justifying an application by the defendant to withdraw his notice of payment-in (see p 337) or whether the defendant's chances of success in the action have substantially improved (*Proetta v Times Newspapers Ltd* [1991] 1 WLR 337; and see the *dictum* of Lord Denning which is cited therein).

If the plaintiff's application is successful, the court will usually make the split orders for costs described in p 329. After all, the plaintiff has, by accepting the payment into court, 'failed to recover more'. (For an exceptional case see *Seacroft Hotel (Teignmouth) Ltd v Goble* [1984] 1 WLR 939; although notice of acceptance was given within two days it did not fall within the relevant time limit because the notice of payment-in itself was not received more than two working days before trial; orders were made equivalent to those appropriate if acceptance had been made within the time allowed, as to which see p 339.)

Liability for costs incurred since payment-in is not the only disadvantage which the plaintiff suffers. Because he is accepting an offer previously made he will not receive any additional sum in respect of interest for the period since payment-in. Also, in a personal injury case in which deductions in respect of state benefits arise (see p 62) the defendant should seek an adjournment until an up-to-date certificate of total benefit is received. If the benefits paid since payment-in exceed the amount previously estimated by the DSS, the defendant must make a further deduction (Social Security Administration Act 1992, s 93(5), *Green Book* 1285). Thus the court is likely to order payment-out partly to the plaintiff and partly to the defendant (RSC Ord 22, r 5(2); CCR Ord 11, r 5(4)).

What happens if the plaintiff's application concerning late acceptance is dismissed? In the High Court the action will proceed to trial (unless the parties can agree some other compromise, presumably one less favourable to the plaintiff than the previous payment into court). Curiously, in the county court, the relevant causes of action will by this time be stayed (see p 346). Presumably the plaintiff will be permitted to withdraw his notice of acceptance and the stay will be lifted. What orders for costs would be appropriate (in either court) if the action now proceeds to the trial and the plaintiff, as he feared, fails to recover more than was paid into court? In our opinion it would be unfair to make the usual orders following a successful payment-in. Costs incurred since his failed application should not be attributed to his previous refusal to accept. Instead the court should make the same orders as it would have made if the defendant had withdrawn his notice of payment-in (see *Garner v Cleggs* [1983] 1 WLR 862); ie divide the liability for costs into three segments as follows:

(1) costs up to receipt of notice of payment-in, to be paid by the defendant;

(2) subsequent costs up to the date of the application concerning late acceptance, to be paid by the plaintiff;

(3) costs thereafter, to be paid by the defendant.

If he wishes to avoid (3) the defendant should seek to withdraw his previous payment into court in order to make a second, reduced, payment-in.

Procedure as to *Calderbank* offers

The purpose and effect of *Calderbank* offers are described at p 329. The simplest example is an action in which the plaintiff sues for an injunction to restrain the defendant from building upon two plots of land; the

defendant concedes that the plaintiff is entitled to an injunction in respect
of one plot but not the other. Obviously it would not be appropriate for
the defendant to make a payment into court to settle this action. Instead
he should write a letter to the plaintiff describing the injunction he is
prepared to consent to and marking his letter 'without prejudice save as to
costs'. In a county court case it is also necessary to file a copy of the
letter in the court office, placing it in a sealed envelope so that it will not
be shown to the trial court inadvertently. If, despite this offer, the action
proceeds to trial, the fact that such an offer was made must be kept secret
from the court until the question of costs falls to be decided. If the
plaintiff has failed to obtain an injunction greater than was offered, costs
are likely to be ordered as follows: costs up to the date of the offer, to be
paid by the defendant; costs after the time at which the offer should have
been accepted, to be paid by the plaintiff (see generally RSC Ord 22, r 14;
CCR Ord 11, r 10 and *per* Butler-Sloss LJ in *Gojkovic v Gojkovic* [1991]
3 WLR 621 at p 637A and *per* Waller J in *Chrulew v Borm-Reid & Co*
[1992] 1 WLR 176 at p 182G; and see the order made in *Platt v GKN
Kwikform Ltd* [1992] 1 WLR 465; as to the relevance of counter-offers,
see *C & H Engineering (a firm) v F Klucznik & Sons Ltd* (1992) *The
Times*, 26 March).

As with a payment into court, a party who has made a successful
Calderbank offer should not be deprived of his costs after the date of that
offer unless there are special reasons for doing so. However, the analogy
is not exact. The *Calderbank* offer is not as blunt an instrument as a
payment into court; it is often said that the court may consider more
closely the conduct of both parties than is usual in the case of a payment
into court (see *per* both of the learned judges mentioned above).
Especially in the case of an equitable remedy, such as an account, the
court may consider that the plaintiff was entitled to require some judicial
inquiry into his allegations whether or not the defendant has some time
previously begun to make reasonable offers of compromise (cf *Smiths Ltd
v Middleton* [1986] 1 WLR 598).

Making a *Calderbank* offer and a payment into court

A *Calderbank* offer cannot be used as a substitute for a payment into
court. The court must not take a *Calderbank* offer into account if, at the
time it was made 'the party making it could have protected his position as
to costs by means of a payment into court' (RSC Ord 62, r 9; CCR Ord
11, r 10 and see *Singh v Parkfield Group plc* (1996) *The Times*, 20
March). However, payments into court are applicable only in cases in
which an offer of compromise is directed at a simple issue of payment of
debts or damages. There are many other issues in respect of which
Calderbank offers can be used even in a debt or damages action.

Claims for contribution

In a running down action, claims for contribution may arise between
co-defendants and/or third parties. A defendant or third party can make a

'written offer' to those other parties specifying the fraction or percentage of the plaintiff's claim which he thinks he is liable to pay and reserving the right to bring the offer to the attention of the court at the trial. If the other parties argue unsuccessfully for some other apportionment, they will pay the costs of so arguing. Written offers of contribution are used in both the High Court and the county court; see RSC Ord 16, r 10 (under which the person making the offer must have acknowledged service) and CCR Ord 12, r 7 (under which the person making the offer must also file a copy of it in the court office). Both rules just quoted forbid the premature disclosure to the trial court of the existence of such offers.

As between defendants, written offers of contribution may take the place of 'party and party notices' (see p 327). Note also that a defendant may, in addition to serving a written offer of contribution, also make a full payment into court in respect of the plaintiff's claim.

Where split trial ordered

Where an order is made for the issue of liability to be tried separately and before any trial of the issue of *quantum* (ie an order for a split trial, see p 456) the defendant may, without prejudice to his defence, make a written offer to the plaintiff specifying the proportion of liability which he is prepared to accept. The offer, if not accepted, must be kept secret from the trial court until the question arises as to who should pay the costs of the trial as to liability (CCR Ord 11, r 10; RSC Ord 33, r 4A, a rule made several years before the system of *Calderbank* offers became of general application in civil cases). In addition to making a written offer on liability the defendant might also make a payment into court. As to the rule of secrecy affecting the payment into court where a split trial is held, see p 344.

Personal injury cases; recovery of state benefits

As to the general law on this topic, see p 62 and p 335. A defendant who has applied for but not yet received an up-to-date certificate of total benefit may either make a payment into court (in which case if it is accepted, he must still make a payment to the DSS) or make a *Calderbank* offer. If the offer is not accepted and at the trial the plaintiff fails to recover more, the defendant will be fully protected as to costs accruing after the date of his offer *if* he followed it up with an appropriate payment into court within seven days of receiving the certificate of total benefit. This very unusual example of a *Calderbank* offer is expressly provided for in RSC Ord 22, r 14 and CCR Ord 11, r 10.

Personal injury cases; provisional damages

RSC Ord 37, r 9 and CCR Ord 22, r 6A provide for the making of a *Calderbank* offer in respect of a claim for provisional damages. The offer must acknowledge the plaintiff's right to an award of provisional damages and must specify a sum of money payable immediately and must identify the disease or deterioration which will justify an application for an award of further damages. The plaintiff has twenty-one days in which to accept the offer. If he does so he must apply by summons for a formal order under RSC Ord 37, r 8(2). If the offer is not accepted it must not be disclosed prematurely to the trial court. The rules permit the defendant to make such an offer 'whether or not he makes a payment into court'.

Taxation of costs

RSC Ord 62, r 27 and CCR Ord 38, r 19A provide for the making of *Calderbank* offers in respect of a bill of costs to be taxed. Save in one important case (see below) a party liable to pay costs to be taxed can make a written offer to pay a specific sum in respect of those costs, making his offer 'without prejudice save as to the costs of taxation'. (In our opinion the sum offered should be expressed as being 'inclusive of profit costs, disbursements, the lodgment fee [if applicable] and any VAT payable'). The offer should be made before the expiration of fourteen days after the party making the offer has received his copy of the bill lodged for taxation. If the party receiving costs accepts the offer, he should then withdraw the bill if already lodged at court: no further taxing fee is payable.

If the offer is not accepted it must not be disclosed to the taxing officer until the costs of the taxation fall to be decided (the last item in the bill of costs). If the party receiving costs fails to recover more than was offered he must pay the costs of taxation and the taxing fee unless there are special reasons to the contrary. The fact that the offeror refuses to give a breakdown of the offer (specifying how much relates to profit costs and how much to disbursements) is not by itself a special reason to the contrary (*Chrulew v Borm-Reid & Co* [1982] 1 WLR 176).

The important exception referred to above is where the bill to be taxed relates to the costs of a legally-aided party. In such a case a taxation (a legal aid taxation) may be essential.

Claim for debt or damages in addition to other remedies

Which rules apply in a case in which the plaintiff alleges a single cause of action in respect of which he claims not only damages but also an injunction? What would be the effect of a payment into court in such a case? If the plaintiff gave notice of acceptance the action would be stayed; the plaintiff would not be entitled to pursue his claim for an injunction (*Hargreaves Construction v Williams* (1982) *The Times*, 3 July and see the opening words of CCR Ord 11, r 3).

If it is not accepted the trial court must take into account both the existence and the amount of the payment into court before exercising its discretion as to costs (RSC Ord 62, r 9; CCR Ord 28, r 1). The plaintiff will be entitled to recover his costs if he can show that he has obtained something of value which he could not have obtained except by going to a hearing (*Colgate Palmolive Ltd v Markwell Finance* [1990] RPC 197;

passing off; payment into court but no undertaking offered in lieu of the injunction sought; and see *Roache v Newsgroup* (1992) *The Times*, 23 November noted on p 345 above). In such cases a defendant who is prepared to submit to an injunction should make a *Calderbank* offer followed by an appropriate payment into court (compare RSC Ord 37, r 9, noted above).

Interest accruing on money in court

As already stated, money in court will automatically be transferred to a deposit account where it will earn interest (see p 341). The general principle to be observed is that such interest belongs to the defendant unless the trial court, or a district judge, makes a direction to the contrary. One example of a direction to the contrary might be a case in which the plaintiff has beaten a payment into court by a substantial margin and is allowed to take out of court all the money and accrued interest by way of part-satisfaction.

The general principle stated above is borne out in the Court Funds Rules by distinguishing between cases in which a plaintiff gives notice of acceptance within the three-week period allowed and is entitled to payment-out without an order, and other cases in which an order for payment-out is necessary (eg at trial or in cases of late acceptance).

In cases in which the plaintiff is entitled to payment-out without an order, no interest is payable by the Funds Office (that is to say, even if, having given notice of acceptance promptly, the plaintiff leaves the money in court for a few months). Where a payment into court was increased by a further payment, and the plaintiff then gives notice of acceptance of the increased sum, the defendant is entitled to the interest which accrued before the last increase was made. The Funds Office will pay such interest to him forthwith, without the need for any request or order (see generally Court Funds Rules 1987, rr 32 and 45).

In cases in which an order for payment-out is required in respect of the principal moneys, an order is also required in respect of any interest thereon. The same order for payment-out should therefore include a suitable direction as to accrued interest. If, by oversight, it is omitted, an application must be made to a district judge. Unless circumstances otherwise require the usual direction will be:

(1) interest accruing up to judgment or order goes to the defendant;
(2) interest accruing after the judgment or order follows the capital payment proportionately (see *Practice Note* of 1988, *White Book* 22/13/3).

How much to pay in or accept

How much one should pay in or accept is a topic which calls for a high degree of strategy. If the defendant pays in too little all the costs will go

against him. If the plaintiff holds out for too much he will have to pay all
the costs from payment-in. Each side has to try to predict what a trial
court would award. They should then include some safety margin to
guard against mishaps. For example, in a case where liability is admitted
the defendant should consider paying in, say, 10 per cent more than he
thinks the claim is worth. The plaintiff should be prepared to accept, say,
90 per cent of his valuation of the claim. Sometimes these safety margins
will have the beneficial effect of bringing the parties to a compromise
neither of them would otherwise have considered.

Example
   D values a claim at £10,000 including interest. He may be well
   advised to pay £11,000 into court. In the same case P's valuation of the
   claim plus interest is £11,500. Allowing him the same 10 per cent safety
   margin he ought to accept anything over £10,350.

In this example each party's valuation of the claim is within 20 per
cent of the other party's valuation and, therefore, they are likely to reach
a compromise. The cases which still go to trial after a substantial
payment-in are usually those where the parties disagree over some
fundamental element such as remoteness, contributory negligence or the
like. In practice, there is usually a very large discrepancy between the
money in court and the judge's award.
   So far we have suggested a safety margin of 10 per cent. But is this
enough or too much? What further discount is appropriate if liability is
not admitted? Also, how accurately can the parties determine what the
trial court may award? These matters will depend on the particular
circumstances of each case. And they are matters on which the litigants
are entitled to skilled advice from their solicitors (see further p 36).
   A style some defence solicitors use takes maximum advantage of the
pressure which a payment into court places on the plaintiff. Paying into
court a sum which is less than the plaintiff is entitled to but which is, they
hope, more than he dares refuse—a 'sub-minimum payment'. Many
plaintiffs, especially fee-paying plaintiffs, will accept such a payment if it
is finely judged. All civil litigation and civil negotiations are conducted
under pressure of cost. Usually such pressure bears most heavily on the
weaker party, who is usually the plaintiff. The exception is the
legally-aided plaintiff. This plaintiff is less likely than others to accept a
sub-minimum payment and is more likely than others to go to trial and
recover a larger sum. They can afford to be braver. Although they risk
losing all their compensation to the statutory charge (see p 53) they have
little else to lose should the decision go against them.
   Some defendants calculate that, should they meet a plaintiff of
above-average bravery who will not accept a sub-minimum payment, they
can always make an increase later on. Herein lies the weakness inherent
in sub-minimum payments. An increase is always disadvantageous to the

defence. It delays the vital date for costs consequences. It gives the plaintiff the upper hand in negotiations: by increasing their payment the defence appears to be crumbling and the plaintiff feels his decision to reject the original payment has been proved right.

For one final point on the amount to pay in consider the following problem:

> *Example*
> P, a pedestrian, was injured in the collision of two cars, driven by D and T respectively. P sues D. D thinks that he and T were equally responsible for the accident and joins T as a third party. D wishes to make a payment into court. If D and T can agree on a figure and how to apportion it between them they can make a full payment into court. But what happens if T will not agree?

In such a case the defendant is in a dilemma. There is no point in paying into court what he regards as his share of liability. The plaintiff could not accept part-payment since to do so would terminate his cause of action. If the defendant makes no payment into court he will ultimately suffer judgment for the full amount plus costs, which he may or may not be able to recoup from the third party. In *Stott v West Yorks Car Co* [1971] 2 QB 651 the defendant resolved this dilemma by making a full payment into court by himself. When the plaintiff gave notice of acceptance it was held that the third party proceedings should continue as if they had been started by a separate action. In the third party proceedings the defendant would, of course, have to justify the figure by which he compromised the plaintiff's claim.

Legal aid

Legal aid and its effect on orders for costs is described in Chapters 3 and 23. There are three special points to note when advising a legally-aided plaintiff who has received a notice of payment-in.

(1) *Whether to accept.* The decision may not rest solely with the plaintiff. If he refuses to accept a payment which his advisers consider adequate his solicitor should report the position to the Area Director before proceeding further (see p 53, Civil Legal Aid (General) Regulations 1989, reg 70 and *Legal Aid Handbook 1996/97*, pp 104, 105; as to a similar obligation placed upon barristers see *Legal Aid Handbook 1996/97*, p 585).

(2) *Payment-out.* This must be made to the plaintiff's solicitor, or, if none, to the Legal Aid Board. This protects the Legal Aid Board which has a statutory charge for its costs over all moneys (or other property) recovered or preserved for a legally-aided party.

(3) *Failure to recover more*. If a legally-aided plaintiff fails to beat the payment into court he is likely to lose all his compensation; if the defendant's costs do not extinguish it (see p 346 noting *Cook v Swinfen* [1967] 1 WLR 457), the statutory charge will. Consider also the position of the defendant. Can he obtain an order for costs against the Legal Aid Board?

> *Example*
>   A defendant pays into court £9,000 which is not accepted. At the trial the plaintiff, who is legally aided, fails to beat the payment and obtains judgment for only £4,000. The defendant's costs since payment exceed £4,000.

The Legal Aid Act 1988, s 18 allows an order to be made against the Legal Aid Board if *inter alia* the proceedings are 'finally decided in favour of' the defendant (see further p 57). In *Kelly v London Transport Executive* [1982] 1 WLR 1055 (the facts of which were similar to the example) it was held that, despite the judgment for damages in favour of the plaintiff the defendants were substantially successful in the action and accordingly the proceedings were 'finally decided' in their favour. (However, no order under what is now s 18 was made since the defendants, a large public corporation with a deficit in 1980 of £175 million, would not suffer 'severe financial hardship'.)

Payments into court for other purposes

Not every payment into court is made with an offer of compromise, permitting the plaintiff to accept and terminate the action. The convenience of using the court as a collecting bank for the parties is so great that other uses for it have been found. Two important examples are described below (see also security for costs, recovery of money by minors and mental patients, and the payment into court of trust funds).

Payment into court under order

A defendant may be required to pay money into court as a term of conditional leave to defend under RSC Ord 14 or CCR Ord 9, r 14 or where a default judgment is set aside 'on the merits'. In the High Court, a defendant making such a payment must give notice of it to the plaintiff and to every other party (RSC Ord 22, r 8). However the payment is not a payment 'in satisfaction' and thus the notice given will not be the usual notice of payment-in and, of course, the plaintiff will have no right to 'accept' and obtain payment-out. The money will be kept in court to abide the event of the action. The county court rules do not require notice to be given to the plaintiff or other parties in this instance. Indeed it is they who must notify the court if a payment into court is misdirected to them (CCR Ord 11, r 1A and Ord 22, r 9).

In certain cases, a defendant who has made a payment into court under order may later convert that payment, or if he so wishes convert part of it, into a payment 'in satisfaction'. This is achieved by giving the court and the plaintiff a 'notice of appropriation' (see Chitty and Jacob's *Queen's Bench Forms*, 21st ed (Sweet & Maxwell, 1986) Nos 386, 387). In the county court, notice of appropriation can be given whether the money was originally paid into court to prevent the entry of a summary judgment or to obtain the setting aside of a default judgment (see CCR Ord 11, r 9). The High Court rule is more limited: notice of appropriation may be employed there only if the money was originally paid in to prevent the entry of a summary judgment (RSC Ord 22, r 8(3); in other cases the court can give leave to allow notice of appropriation in respect of money paid *to another person* (rather than into court) to abide by the event of the action (RSC Ord 22, r 8(4) as amended in 1994).

Payment with a defence of tender before action

In order to raise this defence (described on p 160) the defendant must first pay the money into court (see RSC Ord 18, r 16; CCR Ord 9, r 12). The nature of this payment differs in three respects from the usual payment 'in satisfaction'. First, the defence must be pleaded; the rule of secrecy does not apply. Secondly, the plaintiff cannot get payment out of court without the court's leave; if leave is granted he will usually be made to pay all the costs of the action. Thirdly, if at the trial the plaintiff fails to disprove the defence, he has not merely 'failed to recover more': his action will be dismissed with costs (*White Book* 18/16/1).

Chapter 17

Termination without Trial

The overwhelming majority of civil actions do not go to trial. There are many ways in which that expense can be avoided. Some of them are dealt with elsewhere in this book (eg default judgments, summary judgments, striking out pleadings etc, stay on acceptance of payment into court). In this chapter we list certain other methods of termination and two related topics which are not termination as far as the action is concerned but are included here for convenience (Change of Solicitor and Transfer to Another Court).

Defence application for stay of action

The courts have a very wide discretion to stay proceedings. Sometimes the stay operates as a temporary interruption only. Sometimes it amounts to a final termination of the action. Even in the latter case however, the action is best regarded as being 'not dead but merely sleeping' (contrast discontinuance and dismissals, as to which see below). The stay may later be removed and the action revived (see *White Book* 5207, 5210). In the meantime other parties may be added as co-defendants (*RA Lister & Co Ltd v EG Thomson (Shipping) Ltd (No 2)* [1987] 1 WLR 1614) even against the wishes of the original parties (*Rofa Sport Management AG v DHL International (UK) Ltd* [1989] 1 WLR 902).

Grounds for a stay

Forum non conveniens

Subject to the provisions of the CJJA 1982 (see below) the court will grant a stay of action if it is satisfied that there is another available forum which is clearly or distinctly more appropriate than the English forum; the disadvantages if any which the plaintiff may suffer if prevented from invoking the English jurisdiction will not normally be determinative provided that the court is satisfied that substantial justice will be done in that forum. The fact that some proceedings have already been commenced in the foreign court (*lis alibi pendens*) is an additional factor to be taken into account, but not a conclusive factor (see generally *Spiliada Maritime Corp v Cansulex Ltd* [1987] AC 460).

Under this doctrine, the burden of proof as to the appropriateness of the English or foreign court rests upon the defendant if process is served upon him in England; alternatively, the burden rests upon the plaintiff if he was required to obtain leave to serve overseas (as to which, see p 138). As a general rule the issue of appropriateness has to be proved having regard to the circumstances subsisting at the date of application, ie the date of issue of summons by the defendant. Evidence of circumstances subsisting at the date of the hearing will not normally be relevant (*Mohammed v Bank of Kuwait and the Middle East KSC* [1996] 1 WLR 1483).

The doctrine of *forum non conveniens* does not apply as between the different parts of Europe which are within the EU or EFTA in cases in which the relevant treaties apply (see p 138). But what is the position if the only forum alternative to England is the court of a non-EU and non-EFTA country? In two Queen's Bench Division cases it was said that, if the European Judgments Convention supplies the English court with jurisdiction that court will normally have no discretion to stay proceedings on the basis of the *forum non conveniens* doctrine whether or not it thinks that another forum would be more appropriate (*S & W Berisford plc v New Hampshire Insurance Co* [1990] QB 631) and whether or not proceedings have already been commenced in that forum (*Arkwright Mutual Insurance Co v Bryanstone Insurance Co Ltd* [1990] QB 649). However, these *dicta* were disapproved by the Court of Appeal in another case, *Re Harrods (Buenos Aires) Ltd* [1992] Ch 72). It must be at least arguable that the Convention was not relevant in the *Harrods* case, a Companies Act petition for a 'buy-out' order under s 459 of the Companies Act 1985, alternatively a winding-up order; see Article 1 of the Convention which was mentioned, but only briefly, by Dillon LJ (at p 92C).

It is convenient to include in this section mention of a related matter, applications for injunctions restraining the commencement or continuation of actions in foreign courts. For example, an English case where proceedings (on a matter not covered by the CJJA 1982) have been commenced, or threatened, in a foreign court and the defendant, or potential defendant, in those proceedings asks the English court for an injunction which in effect requires his opponent to stay, or not commence, the foreign action. Here, it is not enough for the applicant (the defendant or potential defendant in the foreign proceedings) to show that England is the more appropriate forum. He must also satisfy the court as to two matters:

(1) that the foreign proceedings complained of are in the circumstances vexatious or oppressive; and
(2) that the injunction will not deprive the plaintiff in the foreign proceedings of any advantages in that forum of which it would be unjust to deprive him.

See generally *Société Nationale Industrielle Aerospatiale v Lee Kui Jak*
[1987] AC 871 and, for a recent example *Airbus Industrie GIE v Patel*
(1996) *The Times*, 12 August. In both cases cited injunctions were granted
restraining a party from continuing proceedings commenced in the courts
of Texas.

Reference to arbitration

The following notes apply to written arbitration agreements. Under the
old law (Arbitration Act 1950, s 4 where still applicable) the court has a
discretion to grant a stay of action in certain cases so as to enable the
parties to resolve their dispute by arbitration, as previously agreed. It has
long been the law that the party seeking the stay (ie the defendant or
defendant to counterclaim) has to apply to the district judge promptly, ie
before serving any pleading or taking any other step in answer to the
claim other than (in the High Court) acknowledging service. However, in
respect of arbitrations commenced after January 1997 or arbitrations not
yet commenced the relevant statute is the Arbitration Act 1996. This
contains three provisions (sections 9, 86 and 91) which replace the letter
of the old law but not its spirit. The full text of the new Act is set out in
the *White Book* 5891–5893/112 supplement.

Under s 9 (now in force) the court 'shall grant a stay' if the application
is made promptly (as to which see s 9(2) and see old law above) *unless*
the respondent (ie the plaintiff or counterclaiming defendant) can show
that the arbitration agreement is 'null and void, inoperative or incapable
of being performed'.

A different attitude is taken in the case of domestic arbitration
agreements (defined in s 85: in a nutshell, agreements in which all parties
are UK based). In these cases a stay of action is not so easily obtained.
The plaintiff or counterclaiming defendant has additional grounds upon
which to rely; the existence of 'other sufficient grounds for not requiring
the parties to abide by the arbitration agreement' (s 86 when in force:
check *White Book* 5893/86 supplement).

Although they differ in extent both s 9 and s 86 favour arbitration over
litigation. Contrast the law applicable to consumer arbitration agreements
so far as they apply to money claims within the small claims limit of the
county court (as to which see p 279). In these cases s 91 of the 1996 Act
extends the application of the Unfair Terms in Consumer Contracts
Regulations 1994 in order to declare arbitration clauses in such cases
'unfair'.

An application for a stay of proceedings under the Arbitration Acts
1950 or 1996 must, of course, be made in the court in which those
proceedings are pending (as to the 1996 Act, see the High Court and
County Courts (Allocation of Arbitration Proceedings) Order 1996).

In the High Court and in cases in the Central London County Court
Business List applications governed by the new law must be made on the

new multi-purpose form 8A (RSC Ord 73 r 4 as amended, CCR Ord 48C
as amended: for the form itself see *White Book* para 31A supplement).

Other grounds for a stay

Many other examples of stays of action are noted or referred to
elsewhere in this book. Consider, for example, the following:

(1) applications under the rule in *Edmeades v Thames Board Mills*
    [1969] 2 QB 67 (see p 30);
(2) applications in cases covered by the Law Reform (Husband and
    Wife) Act 1962 (see p 218);
(3) where partners suing in a firm name fail to comply with a written
    demand for a written statement of names and addresses of the
    persons constituting the firm (see p 92);
(4) where the plaintiff's claim discloses no reasonable cause of action,
    or is frivolous or vexatious, or is otherwise an abuse of the process
    of the court (see p 190);
(5) a stay until the plaintiff pays the costs of an earlier action on the
    same subject matter which was discontinued (see p 360); and
(6) on a joint application where a compromise has been reached, eg a
    '*Tomlin* order' (see p 371).

Another topic which is often confused with a stay of action is a stay of
execution; this is dealt with on p 520.

Discontinuance and withdrawal

Consider the plight of a plaintiff who, having started proceedings, now
finds that he has overstated his case, or has sued the wrong defendants, or
finds that he cannot now produce the evidence which is vital to his case
(see eg p 447). If he now wishes to abandon his proceedings, in whole or
in part, he can do so by serving notice on the defendants (see generally
RSC Ord 21; CCR Ord 18: broadly speaking the notes beneath also apply
on discontinuance of a counterclaim). In the High Court no form of notice
is prescribed. In the county court the plaintiff should use Form N279 and
must deliver a copy to the court office. The plaintiff must then pay the
defence costs incurred in the matters discontinued. If he wishes to avoid
this costs penalty he must apply to the district judge for leave to
discontinue. He will avoid the penalty by showing eg that the dispute has
since become academic and therefore the discontinuance is not a defeat or
an acknowledgment of likely defeat (*Barretts & Baird (Wholesale) Ltd v
Institution of Professional Civil Servants* (1988) *White Book* 21/2–5/12.
An alternative procedure to consider for a plaintiff who wishes to
terminate proceedings with an order for costs in his favour is to seek
summary judgment under RSC Ord 14 (*Danesfield Securities Ltd v
Sonuga* (1996) *The Times*, 31 December).

Discontinuance by the plaintiff terminates the action (in whole or in
part) without the expense of trial and judgment. However, it does not

affect anything in the nature of a claim made by the defendant against the plaintiff which has been recognised or directed by the rules and becomes part of the record, or which has been filed in court (*The Saxicava* [1924] P 131, *per* Bankes LJ).

Examples
   Discontinuance of the plaintiff's claim will not affect any counter-claim raised: RSC Ord 15, r 2; CCR Ord 21, r 4.
   In *Artoc Bank Trust Ltd v Prudential Assurance Co Ltd* [1984] 1 WLR 1181 the plaintiffs (tenants) commenced an application by originating summons claiming a new tenancy under the Landlord and Tenant Act 1954. The defendants (landlords) took out an interlocutory summons under RSC Ord 97, r 9A claiming an interim rent. The plaintiffs discontinued their action but, nevertheless, the defendants' summons survived. (Cf *Thomas v Hammond-Lawrence* [1986] 1 WLR 456, a county court case on a similar point, in which the claim for an interim rent was raised in the landlord's answer to the tenant's originating application.)

A notice of discontinuance may later be struck out as an abuse of the process of the court and the action reinstated (*Ernst & Young v Butte Mining plc* [1996] 1 WLR 1605, noted on p 194, above).
   Discontinuance is not, by itself, a bar to a subsequent action on the same subject matter (unless, in the High Court only, the court so orders: see below) but a subsequent action may be stayed until the costs of the discontinued action have been paid (RSC Ord 21, r 5; CCR Ord 18, r 2). Also, the right to re-litigate may be affected by a contract made between the parties such as a contract of compromise (see p 370).
   In one respect High Court and county court procedures differ fundamentally. In the High Court, once fourteen days have elapsed after the service of the defence (or, in proceedings by originating summons, after the service of the defence affidavit evidence) the plaintiff can discontinue only if the court grants him leave (special provision is made for the calculation of the time limit where there are two or more defendants: as to cases in which an interim payment has been ordered, see p 313). This leave requirement is imposed to prevent a discontinuance which would unfairly prejudice the defendant. There are two types of unfair prejudice to consider: costs and the possibility of future proceedings. The High Court can protect the defendant as to both these items *either* by granting leave on terms providing for costs and providing that no other action shall be brought *or* by refusing leave and forcing the plaintiff to a trial (*Fox v Star Newspapers* [1898] 1 QB 636; [1900] AC 19, where the application for leave was made at the trial).
   In the county court leave to discontinue is never required. On the contrary, even at the trial a county court plaintiff still has the ancient right of 'non-suit', ie the right to withdraw the case from court in order to

bring fresh proceedings (see generally *Clack v Arthurs Engineering Ltd* [1959] 2 QB 211; as to the abolition of this right in High Court cases see *Fox v Star Newspapers*, above). 'The power of non-suit is useful in the county court, particularly where the plaintiff is acting in person and does not understand the niceties of procedure or the law of evidence' (see generally, *Green Book* commentary to CCR Ord 21, r 2).

A defendant may withdraw his defence (in whole or in part) at any time, without leave. In the High Court he may amend his acknowledgment of service to cancel his notice of intention to defend (see p 186). However, leave to withdraw the acknowledgment itself is always required (RSC Ord 21, r 1).

It seems that leave is always necessary to discontinue third party proceedings, at least in High Court cases (see *Chapman v Chief Constable of South Yorkshire* (1990) *White Book* 21/2–5/10; in the county court, see CCR Ord 12, rr 2 and 3).

Dormant actions

In the High Court, where an action has lain dormant for one year or more any party who desires to proceed must give not less than one month's notice of his intention to proceed (RSC Ord 3, r 6) to any party who has an address for service and who is not in default as to acknowledgment of service (RSC Ord 65, r 9).

> *Examples*
>
> P serves a writ on D who does not lodge an acknowledgment of service. P waits one year before deciding to seek judgment in default. He need not give D any notice of intention to proceed (*Randall Rose & Phillips v Becchio* (1990) noted in *White Book* 3/6/1).
>
> If instead, D had acknowledged service but failed to serve a defence, P must first give one month's notice to D. Had P decided to seek such judgment after eleven and a half months he could have applied immediately in the ordinary way. In such circumstances he would not need to give notice of his intention to proceed. A notice given *before* the year has elapsed would not validate any step taken *after* it had elapsed (*Suedeclub Co Ltd v Occasions Textiles Ltd* [1981] 1 WLR 1245).

The rule applies to any step in the action which the other party might wish to oppose. However, it does not apply to a summons to dismiss for want of prosecution (see generally *White Book* 3/6/1) or to the late taxation of costs (RSC Ord 62, r 30(6)).

In the county court the position is substantially different. Dormant actions are struck out automatically in two cases. First, CCR Ord 9, r 10 which applies to all default actions (for a definition of which, see p 239). If twelve months have elapsed since the date of service and the plaintiff has not within that time applied for any default judgment available or responded to any part admission or request for time for payment, the action must be struck out and no enlargement of the period of twelve months can be given (see eg *Webster v Ellison Circlips Group Ltd* [1995] 1 WLR 447). The wording of the rule plainly prevents reinstatement of the action. If the relevant limitation period has now expired there would be little point in commencing a second action. In personal injury cases the court sometimes has power to disapply limitation periods but that is not so in 'second action cases' (see further p 88).

CCR Ord 9, r 10 has no effect where the defendant delivers a defence which admits carelessness but denies that any damage resulted (*Parrott v Jackson* (1996) *The Times*, 14 February and see further p 370). In such a case the plaintiff should instead comply with the automatic directions in order to bring the case to trial (as to which, see CCR Ord 17, r 11 below).

The operation of CCR Ord 9, r 10 is prevented if the parties agree to extend generally the time for delivery of a defence or if the plaintiff or defendant successfully applies for an extension of time before the twelve-month deadline expires (*Heer v Tutton* [1995] 1 WLR 1336). In respect of agreed extensions, the Master of the Rolls stated:

> ... it would be repugnant to ordinary principles if the court were to accede to the application of a defendant asking the court for an order penalising the plaintiff for not doing what the defendant had agreed, if not asked, that he should not do.

The other county court rule which deals with striking out dormant actions is CCR Ord 17, r 11(9). In any default or fixed date action in which automatic directions are given the plaintiff must (unless a date has already been fixed) request the court within six months of close of pleadings, to fix a date for trial (see p 468). That action will be automatically struck out if no such request is made within fifteen months of close of pleadings, or, if the direction is varied by the court, within nine months after the expiry of the period fixed by the court (*Perry v Wong* [1997] 1 WLR 381, no penalty even though the request is made 'late', ie after the time allowed for a request (usually six months) so long as it is made before the full period, usually fifteen months expires). Under this rule (if not CCR Ord 9, r 10) the striking out is automatic. No bells are rung, no orders made, the dormant action simply dies in the filing cabinet. Death occurs because of a double-fault by the plaintiff or his solicitors; failing to request a trial date in time and failing to apply for an extension of that time limit. The automatic penalty does not apply if the plaintiff does seek an extension of time in advance, even if the court refuses to grant it (*Ferreira v The American Embassy Employees' Association* [1996] 1 WLR 536, holding that an application for extension of time impliedly includes a request for a date to be fixed).

Post mortem, a plaintiff who wants the court to lift the penalty must apply for 'reinstatement', the leading case authority upon which is *Rastin v British Steel plc* [1994] 1 WLR 732. In that case the Court of Appeal held that the court does have a discretion to reinstate cases struck out under Ord 17, r 11(9). However, that discretion should not be exercised solely upon the principles ordinarily applied on applications for extensions of time, nor upon the principles applicable to applications for dismissals for want of prosecution (see below). Instead the court should consider:

(1) Has the plaintiff shown that (except for his failure to comply with the automatic directions) he has prosecuted the case with at least reasonable diligence and that his failure to comply with the automatic direction is excusable.

(2) More general factors including prejudice (if any) suffered by the defendant, alternative remedies available to the plaintiff, expiry of the limitation period, admissions of liability and payments into court.

The automatic strike out rule has been described as 'a crude remedy the effects of which have not been wholly beneficial' (*Grovit v Doctor* [1997] 1 WLR 640 *per* Lord Woolf). Most practitioners would choose much harsher language. In many thousands of cases the rule has caused enormous expense, confusion and delay. It has also spawned hundreds of appeals to the Court of Appeal, many of which are noted below. There have been many calls for reform. The Court of Appeal has more than once stated its preference for a completely different rule; a rule which obliges the court to take a proactive role and, in appropriate cases, fix the trial date at an early stage without waiting for a request. Despite all this no rule amendments have as yet been made. Perhaps because that is so the Court of Appeal has now in effect restated the rule and practice. In *Bannister v SGB plc* (1997) *The Times*, 2 May, the Court of Appeal has provided in a single judgment comprehensive guidelines for resolving automatic strike out problems. In future cases practitioners will find it more useful to read this case than to read the rule itself. *Bannister* also tells the reader, whether practitioner or judge, how to avoid strike out problems in the first place.

Gardner v Southwark London Borough Council (Note) [1996] 1 WLR 571 provides a useful illustration of the reinstatement principles and shows that delays by the defendant do not excuse delays by the plaintiff. In *Gardner* both sides had been dilatory in taking steps to prepare the case for trial which they did with little or no reference to the timetable set out in the automatic directions (see p 467). Discovery took place eight months late and witness statements were not exchanged until after the case had been automatically struck out in March 1993. In May 1993 when the plaintiff requested a date for trial the defendants informed the court that they were not ready for trial. It was held that the plaintiff had failed to act with due diligence and therefore the case should not be reinstated. The fact that the defendants were similarly at fault did not help the plaintiff (see further p 121). Different considerations apply where a plaintiff has been misled, to his detriment, by a mistake made by a court clerk in completing forms N450 (see p 467). In *Williams v Globe Coaches (a firm)* [1996] 1 WLR 553 plaintiffs took steps late but within the deadlines indicated on the forms N450 they had received; the Court of Appeal allowed reinstatement without applying the *Rastin* principles.

Whether or not reinstatement is possible, the court will still have a discretion as to costs; cf *Rookes v Barnard (No 2)* [1966] 1 QB 176 concerning orders for costs after a stay of action and *Hoskins v Wiggins Teape (UK) Ltd* [1994] PIQR P377.

An automatic strike out under CCR Ord 17, r 11 does not by itself prevent or render contumelious (see p 365) a second action on the same cause of action (*Gardner v Southwark London Borough Council (No 2)* [1996] 1 WLR 561). However as to that second action the plaintiff may have problems as to limitation (see pp 79 and 88) and as to costs liabilities from the first action.

CCR Ord 17, r 11 and its automatic strike-out provision has no application in cases in which judgment for damages to be assessed has already been entered, even if the district judge, when giving directions for the assessment hearing states 'the automatic directions to apply' (*Gomes v Clark* (1997) *The Times*, 27 March). Instead the district judge should either fix the date for a hearing or make an 'unless order' staying further proceedings if a request for a hearing date was not made within a specific time (see further as to 'unless orders' p 123).

Finally on CCR Ord 17, r 11 strike-outs note two reported decisions where the plaintiffs were tardy but escaped the death penalty because the county courts in question made orders which the Court of Appeal criticised as being inconsistent with current practice; *Downer & Downer Ltd v Brough* [1996] 1 WLR 575 where the court made old-fashioned 'set down when ready' orders; and *Whitehead v Avon County Council* (1997) *The Times*, 17 March where the court ordered a simple stay of action under the rule in *Edmeades v Thames Board Mills* [1969] 2 QB 67 (see p 30). In order to maintain consistency with the automatic directions an order could have been made 'staying the action pending a medical examination of the plaintiff by [Dr X], that examination to take place by (a date), and the plaintiff to be obliged to apply by (a further date) to fix a date for trial from which the nine-month period shall run under CCR Ord 17, r 11(9).'

A third county court rule provides for cases which become dormant after the date of hearing of the proceedings has been adjourned generally; if no party applies within twelve months to fix a new date, the court may give a fourteen-day warning notice to the parties (Form N250) after which the action or matter may be struck out (CCR Ord 13, r 3).

Dismissal for want of prosecution

In the High Court there are several rules under which the defendant can apply for the dismissal of the action for want of prosecution, eg RSC

Ord 19, r 1, default of statement of claim; Ord 25, r 1, default of summons for directions; Ord 34, r 1, default of setting down. The court also has an inherent jurisdiction to dismiss wherever the plaintiff is in breach of a time period imposed by an order of the court (see for example p 189). These principles are adopted and applied in the county court (see CCA 1984, s 76, and p 2). Unlike eg default of defence, a dismissal for want of prosecution is never granted automatically on the plaintiff's failure to obey a rule or order. The cases fall into two categories (see generally *Birkett v James* [1978] AC 297, *White Book* 25/1/5). These principles also apply in High Court cases commenced by originating summons (*Halls v O'Dell* [1992] 2 WLR 308).

(1) *Where delay is intentional and contumelious (ie impertinent or abusive of the court).* For example, issuing a writ for libel merely to prevent the defendant discussing matters thereby made *sub judice* and with no real intention of proceeding to trial (the so-called 'gagging' writ for libel: see *Wallersteiner v Moir* [1974] 1 WLR 991), or breaking a peremptory order of the court (see below). In *Hytrac Ltd v Conveyors International Ltd* [1983] 1 WLR 44 a delay in serving the statement of claim for a period of approximately six weeks was held to be 'inordinate' in the circumstances and the action was dismissed under RSC Ord 19, r 1. However, the case appears to have been decided on the basis that the proceedings themselves, rather than the delay, were an abuse of the court's process; the relevance of delay lay in making this abuse manifest and in giving the court the occasion to act upon it; see further p 388.

(2) *Where delay is inordinate, inexcusable and prejudicial to the defence.* There is also, usually, a fourth requirement; the defendant has to show that the relevant limitation period has expired. The case law on each of these four requirements is now voluminous.

Inordinate delay

'Inordinate' delay is usually reckoned in years and months rather than weeks. The relevant period to consider is that following commencement of proceedings. However, the longer the delay before commencement, the greater is the obligation upon the plaintiff to proceed quickly (*Biss v Lambeth, Southwark and Lewisham Area Health Authority* [1978] 1 WLR 382). Long delay before issue of the writ will have the effect of any post-writ delay being looked at critically by the court and more readily being regarded as inordinate and inexcusable than it would have been if the action had been commenced promptly (*Department of Transport v Chris Smaller (Transport) Ltd* [1989] 2 WLR 578, HL *per* Lord Griffiths).

Inexcusable delay

Here, the faults of solicitor and counsel are no excuse; whether the plaintiff has an alternative remedy against his solicitor is not relevant (*Birkett*, above). The fact that the defendants became insolvent rendering further proceedings futile does not excuse inordinate delay (*Claremont Construction Ltd v GCT Construction Ltd* (1983) 80 LSG 1795). Mere inaction on the part of the defendant does not excuse or waive the plaintiff's delay. The defendant is entitled to 'let sleeping dogs lie'. However, if the plaintiff suddenly stirs and gives one month's notice of his intention to proceed (as to which, see p 361) a defendant who wishes to apply for a dismissal should do so within that month. If he does not, he is at risk of losing his opportunity to apply altogether. Once the plaintiff takes the next step it will be too late to complain of previous wants of prosecution (see *Trill v Sacher* [1993] 1 WLR 1379 at p 1391A–C).

The plaintiff may have some excuse if he can show that, despite the delay, the defendant has encouraged him to continue or re-continue the action; such conduct by the defendant is something which the court can take into account in exercising its discretion as to whether to dismiss the claim. However, it is now clear that such conduct by the defendant does not constitute an absolute bar, preventing the defendant from obtaining a dismissal for want of prosecution; see *Roebuck v Mungovin* [1994] 2 AC 224, overruling *County & District Properties Ltd v Lyell (Note)* [1991] 1 WLR 683. In *Mungovin* the action had stood still for about four years. The defendants then wrote to the plaintiff's solicitors asking for certain information and documents concerning *quantum*. The plaintiff's solicitors replied saying (amongst other things) that an accountant had been instructed to prepare a schedule of special damages. However, nothing of substance was sent by the plaintiff's solicitors until another year had elapsed. The House of Lords ruled that the defendants' actions were minor as compared to the inordinate delay by the plaintiff and could not have lulled the plaintiff into any major additional expense. The action was dismissed.

Prejudice

The defendant must show overall serious prejudice including more than minimal additional prejudice resulting from post-writ delay (*Birkett v James per* Lord Diplock). The court should look at the totality of the post-writ delay; on this issue it matters not whether the limitation period has or has not expired so long as that delay has caused the prejudice (*Rath v CS Lawrence & Partners* [1991] 1 WLR 399). Cases depending upon oral evidence are especially prone to suffer by delay; witnesses may die or disappear; their memories may fade. The defendant's obligation to prove prejudice may be discharged by direct evidence of prejudice or, in some case, by inference (*Shtun v Zaleska* [1996] 1 WLR 1271, CA, not following a stricter test suggested by Roch LJ in *Hol–nagold v Fairclough Building Ltd* [1993] PIQR P400). Further, the court is not limited to considering only prejudice affecting the conduct of the trial. Even if liability is admitted and only *quantum* remains to be tried, the defendant may suffer serious financial prejudice (*Department of Transport v Chris Smaller (Transport) Ltd*, above; *Hayes v Bowman* [1989] 1 WLR

456, CA; *Antcliffe v Gloucester Health Authority* [1992] 1 WLR 1044). The anxiety suffered by being involved in protracted litigation will not by itself justify a dismissal unless it is truly exceptional; for example, anxiety caused to defendants having an action hanging over their heads for eleven and a half years with professional reputations at stake (*Biss*, cited with approval in *Department of Transport*).

Expiry of limitation period
If the relevant limitation period has not expired, a dismissal for want of prosecution would not by itself prevent the plaintiff issuing a fresh writ the very next day. In *Bailey v Bailey* [1983] 1 WLR 1129 an action was struck out because of 'unintentional delay'. As to part of the claim the relevant limitation period expired during the interval between the issue of the defendant's summons to dismiss and the hearing of that summons. The day before expiry the plaintiff issued a fresh writ for that part of her claim, thereby escaping the consequences of the dismissal of the first action.

Because of the possibility of re-commencement the court will not dismiss the action if to do so would merely amount to a costs penalty and may delay the trial further. Thus it may only aggravate and not mitigate the prejudice suffered by the defendant. (Cases which have been dismissed during the currency of a limitation period are considered below.)

Consider the plight of a defendant who is being prejudiced by inordinate and inexcusable delay but the relevant limitation period is still current. Rather than seek a dismissal he should apply for a peremptory order, ie an order commanding the plaintiff to take the next step in the action within a specified time. Breach of this order would be regarded as 'contumelious' entitling the defendant to re-apply for dismissal. To avoid the need for a re-application the peremptory order may be made in the form of an 'unless order', ie an order dismissing the action unless the plaintiff takes the next step within a specified time (see further p 123 and see the note on *Grovit v Doctor* [1997] 1 WLR 640, below).

If an action is terminated following a breach of a peremptory order, any new action on the same matter may be struck out as an abuse of the process of the court even though it was commenced within the current limitation period (*Janov v Morris* [1981] 1 WLR 1389.

Dismissal before expiry of limitation period

Birkett v James [1978] AC 297 does not create an absolute bar to the dismissal of an action within the limitation period. The court should take into account whether the delay is contumelious (see above) and, in other cases, the likelihood of the plaintiff availing himself of his legal right to issue a fresh writ (*Birkett v James per* Lord Diplock; *Wright v Morris* (1988) Court of Appeal, noted in *the White Book* at 25/1/7). Also, there may be a dispute as to whether the limitation period has expired. A dispute such as this can be more conveniently resolved if and when a second action is started (*Barclays Bank plc v Miller* [1990] 1 WLR 343). Moreover the claim may include several causes of action, some now time-barred some not; dismissal will finally dispose of the time-barred causes for all practical purposes; it will also enable the defendant to seek his costs to date and to seek a stay of any subsequent action until these costs are paid (*Hicks v Newman* (1989) unreported, quoted with approval in *Barclays Bank plc v Miller* [1990] 1 WLR 343).

Possible reform of the *Birkett v James* principles

Birkett v James puts the onus on the defendant to show why an action should be dismissed because of delays. Over the years since it was decided lawyers acting for delaying plaintiffs have shown great ingenuity in resisting these applications; see for example *County and District Properties Ltd v Lyell (Note)* [1991] 1 WLR 683 and subsequent cases thereon (later overruled by *Roebuck v Mungovin* [1994] 2 AC 224) and *Hornagold v Fairclough Building Ltd* [1993] PIQR P400 (now re-explained in *Shtun v Zaleska* [1996] 1 WLR 1271). A new line of resistance is now emerging in cases involving two or more defendants: *Kincardine Fisheries Ltd v Sunderland Marine Mutual Insurance Ltd* (1997) *The Times*, 12 February (prejudice must be shown in respect of each defendant seeking dismissal; the multiplicity of defendants may make it harder for them to characterise the delays suffered as being inordinate or inexcusable).

Some may argue that these lines of resistance have caused a huge volume of litigation. It is at least equally arguable that these lines are the product of rather than the cause of such litigation. Whichever view is taken, the *Birkett v James* principles do not now stand comfortably with current practice as to case management and the new approach to time generally (as to which, see p 121). In *Kincardine Fisheries Ltd* (above) Colman J complained that the application before him had itself taken up an inordinate amount of time. The need to analyse the facts of the case and the evidence available in order to apply the *Birkett v James* principles 'gave rise to an unduly complex and time consuming process of case management'.

In *Grovit v Doctor* [1997] 1 WLR 640, the defendants invited the House of Lords to reconsider the *Birkett v James* principles. In his speech in that case Lord Woolf indicated as a possible preference the awaiting of more widespread reform of the civil process (eg the Woolf reforms).

> In the meantime both the court and defendants have the means to achieve greater control over delay. Defendants do not need to wait until there has been inordinate delay before applying for peremptory orders (although they are under no obligation to do this). The Courts should more readily make 'unless orders', that is, orders that an action should be struck out unless certain steps

are taken at certain times. The advantage of such an order is that it places the onus on the plaintiff to justify the action being allowed to continue whereas in the case of an application to strike out the onus is on the defendant to show the action should be struck out.

Judgment on admissions

By admitting a fact a litigant can usually save costs by obviating the need to call evidence as to that fact. Parties ought to admit all those facts which they have no hope of disproving (see p 153). Indeed the rules of court provide two ways in which one party can oblige his opponent to make reasonable admissions or be penalised in costs (see pp 431 and 457. Admissions are usually made in the pleadings since it is the function of these to define the area of dispute. Parties may further limit that area later by amendment (see p 182), discontinuance or withdrawal (see p 359), cancellation of a notice of intention to defend (see p 186), or by making written admissions at any time (RSC Ord 27, r 1; CCR Ord 20, r 1, used typically after a notice to admit facts has been served, see p 431).

Under RSC Ord 27, r 3, the High Court has power, where a party has made admissions of fact, to give his opponent such judgment as he may be entitled to without waiting for the determination of any other questions between the parties. If the relief claimed is an injunction the application must be made to the judge. In other cases the application should normally be made by summons to the master, unless, in the Chancery Division, some good reason justifies an application by motion to the judge (*Practice Direction* [1984] 1 WLR 447). The applicant must show a 'clear admission', ie must prove the words or circumstances he relies on and must demonstrate that they amount to an admission by his opponent. Subject to that the admission may be:

(1) an express admission in a pleading;
(2) an implied admission in a pleading (except in actions against minors or mental patients: (see p 159));
(3) any written admission;
(4) even an oral admission: but these are often difficult to prove as being 'clear admissions'.

At the hearing the defendants may seek leave to withdraw their admission. The principles to be applied in such cases are set out in *Gale v Superdrug Stores plc* [1996] 1 WLR 1089; the court should treat the request as if it were an application for leave to amend a pleading (as to which, see p 182).

If a defendant in a damages action admits the claim the plaintiff will obtain judgment under RSC Ord 27, r 3, for 'damages to be assessed'; the assessment is governed by RSC Ord 37 (see p 213). In order that a plaintiff may obtain judgment in a negligence action the defendant must have admitted both that he was negligent and that the plaintiff thereby suffered damage: an admission of the negligence only is not sufficient

(*Rankine v Garton* [1979] 2 All ER 1185 followed in *Parrott v Jackson* (1996) *The Times*, 14 February). In damages actions an application under RSC Ord 27, r 3, might be combined with an application for an interim payment (see p 308).

The county court equivalent to RSC Ord 27, r 3, is CCR Ord 17, r 6, allowing judgment to be entered at a pre-trial review (an application for judgment will, it seems, prevent the rule leading to automatic strike out from applying; see *Bannister v SGB plc* (1997) *The Times*, 2 May). County court cases otherwise within the small claims rules (see p 279) are automatically referred to arbitration not trial if the defendant files 'a document admitting liability ... but disputing ... the amount claimed' (see CCR Ord 19, r 3(4)). Remember also the form of admission, defence and counterclaim county court defendants are given (see p 250). At a trial in the county court, if the defendant appears and admits the claim, the case may be dealt with by the district judge even where the amount in dispute exceeds £5,000 (CCR Ord 21, rr 3 and 5).

Compromise

This is of course the solicitor's primary object in any civil action. Technically a solicitor usually has power to compromise a claim once the action has been commenced: counsel has power to compromise during the trial (see generally *White Book* 4613). However, these powers should never be relied on. The decision to compromise should always be that of the client, advised but not pressurised by his lawyers (and see further p 36).

If the parties conclude a compromise any rights of action they had will be replaced by rights under the contract of compromise. A contract expressed to be 'in full and final settlement' covers all claims arising from the alleged causes of action including claims for losses which the parties had not anticipated would be incurred (*O'Boyle v Leiper* [1990] Gazette, 14 March, 36). The terms of the compromise should always provide for the costs incurred. There are several ways of terminating proceedings after compromise, eg:

(1) *Discontinuance by consent.* This is possible in the High Court only. The parties file a joint notice at the court office, or, if the action has already been set down for trial in London, with the head clerk of the Crown Office (Queen's Bench Division) or the cause clerk (Chancery Division); see generally RSC Ord 21, r 2(4). In a legal aid case the assisted party's solicitor can then obtain a legal aid taxation by producing the notice of discharge of the civil aid certificate to the relevant taxing office (Civil Legal Aid (General) Regulations 1989, reg 107).

(2) *Judgment by consent.* This can be obtained, at trial from the judge, before the trial from the district judge (see generally *White Book* 4606 *et seq* and as to appeals see p 653). The judgment might perhaps

include a stay of execution so long as instalments are paid in accordance with the contract of compromise.

In the Queen's Bench Division and in the county court it is possible for parties who have come to terms to obtain many forms of consent judgments and orders without the necessity of a hearing before a judge or district judge. This is governed by RSC Ord 42, r 5A and CCR Ord 22, r 7A which is in similar terms. Both set out all the various forms of judgments and orders to which they apply: examples include stays of execution (see p 520), the setting aside of default judgments (see p 219) and the payment-out of money in court (see pp 339 and 346). Further examples are described below (stays of action, *Tomlin* orders, transfers to a county court). There are several types of proceedings to which these rules do not apply; note in particular (in either court) proceedings in which one or more parties is a litigant in person or a person under disability, proceedings relating to a claim for possession of residential property, any High Court proceedings in the Commercial Court or before an official referee, any county court proceedings relating to the custody of a child or maintenance or to financial provision for a spouse or child.

(3) *Stay of action.* This can also be obtained from the trial judge or, earlier, from the district judge or under RSC Ord 42, r 5A or CCR Ord 22, r 7A where they apply. In a simple money action this method would be used if eg the defendant's solicitor was in funds and undertook to pay the plaintiff. (If the plaintiff is legally-aided the payment must be made to his solicitor or to the Legal Aid Board; see Civil Legal Aid (General) Regulations 1989, reg 87.)

If the terms of compromise involve more than the simple payment of money a stay in the form of a *Tomlin* order might be made, ie a stay of action on terms set out in a schedule to the order with liberty to restore if necessary for the purpose of carrying such terms into effect (for a precedent, see *Green Book* commentary to CCR Ord 21, r 2). It is important to note that a *Tomlin* order is not a money judgment and thus cannot be enforced as such and does not carry interest under the Judgments Act 1838 or CCA 1984, s 74 as the case may be (see *White Book* 4616 and p 517). Also, if any costs are to be taxed, the order (and not the schedule) should provide for taxation so as to comply with RSC Ord 62, r 29(5) and (6) or CCR Ord 38, r 20(1).

Compromise of minor's or mental patient's money claim

RSC Ord 80, r 10, and CCR Ord 10, r 10, provide that in any action in which money is claimed by or on behalf of a person under disability no settlement, compromise or payment and no acceptance of a payment into court shall be valid without the approval of the court. The application for approval is made to the district judge by summons (High Court) or on notice (county court). In a difficult case a written opinion from counsel should be produced. If the district judge feels the compromise figure is too low he may adjourn the hearing to let the parties negotiate a compromise for a higher sum. The sum proposed should take into account the value of the claim on a full liability basis, the chances of success and/or the strength of a defence of contributory negligence and the interest on the award which a trial court would have ordered. For a full account of the procedure to be followed see *White Book* 80/10–11/4 and as to the documentation to use see *White Book* 329 *et seq*, 759 and County Court Form N292. If a compromise is approved the compensation, if not already in court, will be paid into court (see Court Funds Office Form 200, *White Book* 1209). In the case of a minor plaintiff the next friend should obtain from the court office before the hearing copies of Court Funds Office Forms 319 and 320 (*White Book* 1224 and 1225). The latter will be used by the district judge at the hearing to lay down the investment policy to be adopted for this fund until the minor attains full age (see the *Green Book* commentary to the Court Funds Rules 1987, r 34). In the case of a mental patient an order is usually made transferring the money to the Court of Protection.

The terms of the compromise, and thus the court's order, will usually make provision for costs. Unless these costs can be agreed, there will have to be a *taxation inter partes* (see p 527). There may also have to be a *solicitor-and-own-client taxation* of the bill of the solicitor acting on behalf of the minor or mental patient (unless the court otherwise orders or unless that solicitor waives any further costs; see p 577). The order for costs should direct payment to be made to the plaintiff (ie the next friend) and not into court.

It will be appreciated that many civil claims are compromised before proceedings are begun. If it is intended so to compromise a minor's or mental patient's money claim a simple application can be made to obtain the court's approval: in the High Court by originating summons in expedited form; in the county court by originating application. Some claims are too small to merit the cost of any court proceedings, however simple. In such cases the defendant's insurers may make payments direct to the parents in return for an indemnity by them should proceedings on the claim be commenced in the future.

Change of solicitor

To his opponents, the consequence of a party acting by solicitor are twofold. First, his solicitor's business address will be the party's address for service (see p 135). Secondly, the signing by the solicitor ofthe writ, acknowledgment of service or county court pleading notifies the opponents of the costs the party may claim (and see *White Book* 67/3/1). In the High Court the solicitor acting for a party is said to be 'on the record'. In both High Court and county court other parties are entitled to treat him as the solicitor for that party until given notice to the contrary.

If a party instructs a new solicitor, the new solicitor must file notice of change of solicitor at the appropriate court office and serve copies on the former solicitor and on every other party to the action (see generally RSC Ord 67; CCR Ord 50, r 5). In the High Court the copies must be indorsed with a memorandum stating that it has been duly filed. Contrast the county court practice under which the filed notice has to contain a certificate that the copies of the notice have been duly served. Similar procedures apply if a party, having previously employed a solicitor, intends in future to act in person, or if a party, having previously acted in person, now wishes to act by solicitor. In the county court there is no need for a notice of the appointment of a solicitor merely to act as advocate at the trial.

A problem arises for the solicitor if his client withdraws instructions or if the solicitor withdraws from the retainer (permissible only for good cause and upon reasonable notice, eg where the client has persistently failed to give adequate instructions or has failed to put the solicitor in funds; and see Solicitors Act 1974, s 65). Unfortunately it not infrequently happens that the client is slow to appoint a new solicitor or give notice that he is acting in person. It is important for the solicitor that the court and the other parties should be notified of the change. Thus the rules of court allow the solicitor to apply for an order declaring that he has ceased to act for that party; the solicitor will have to establish sufficient grounds for the order. In the High Court or county court the application is made by summons, or on notice, served on the party (it need not be served on any other party; *Re Creehouse* [1983] 1 WLR 77). In the Court of Appeal the application is made by motion. The order obtained must be filed in the appropriate court office and copies served on the other parties (in the county court the court office sees to this). The costs of the application may be recoverable from the client (see *Green Book* commentary to *Craftlake Ltd v Welch and Hayes* (1989) unreported). In respect of his costs a solicitor is entitled to a lien over papers and chattels (see further, *White Book* 3884).

Where a legally-aided party's certificate is discharged or revoked (see p 58) his solicitor must file at court and serve on the other parties notice of that discharge or revocation (Civil Legal Aid (General) Regulations 1989, reg 83). Such discharge or revocation automatically determines the solicitor's retainer once he has sent to the court office and served on the other parties a notice in prescribed form. Accordingly it is not necessary to obtain an order in the form mentioned above.

Transfer to another court

Transfer between district registries or between a district registry and London

The district judge has general power to order such transfer on such terms as he thinks fit. Orders can be made on the application of any party or indeed by the district judge of his own motion, without any application being made (see RSC Ord 4, r 5 and, in Queen's Bench cases, *White Book* 718). Further, in certain cases a defendant to a writ issued in a district registry can, by his acknowledgment of service, apply for an order transferring the case to another court office (see p 207). If he so applies the plaintiff then has eight days in which to object to the making of such an order. If the plaintiff does not object the district judge will make an order accordingly. If the plaintiff does so object the district judge will notify the parties of a time and place for the hearing of the defendant's application (see generally RSC Ord 4, r 5(3)).

Transfer between divisions of the High Court

The theory and practice relating to the allocation of business between the divisions of the High Court is described on p 4. The large overlap of business between the Queen's Bench Division and the Chancery Division often gives the plaintiff a free choice as to which division to commence in. Often the most important factor influencing the plaintiff's decision is his estimate as to which division is likely to provide him with the quickest interlocutory stage and the earliest trial date.

Once an action has been allocated to a particular division it can later be transferred to another division on application under RSC Ord 4, r 13 to the division of the court presently seised of the case (in Queen's Bench cases see *White Book* 717). Some good reason would have to be shown justifying a transfer. For example, where the action has been commenced in an inappropriate or less appropriate division (see p 4) or where transfer is needed to enable the action to be consolidated with an action in another division (see p 102). Speed of trial is not by itself a justifiable ground for transfer (*Barclays Bank plc v Bemister* [1989] 1 WLR 128). Thus plaintiffs who wish to 'division shop' for the quickest division can do so only before commencement. What should they do if they later regret their choice and would prefer to continue the action elsewhere? There are two possible applications.

If the need for urgency becomes apparent early enough, an application should be made at the directions stage (see p 452) for 'an order for a speedy trial'. If such an order is made the parties must, within one week of setting down, apply to the clerk of the lists for a fixed date for trial: the existence of an order for a speedy trial is one of the factors the clerk must take into account in hearing that application (see *Practice Direction* of 1981, para 8, *White Book* 34/4/1).

The second possible application to consider only arises after the action has been set down and a date fixed which dissatisfies one or both parties. An aggrieved party can apply to the judge in charge of the lists for an order for an expedited hearing. The judge will consider the need alleged, and whether the appropriate degree of expedition can be found without transfer. If not, the judge will inquire of the heads of other divisions whether an earlier trial could be obtained by transfer; if it can he will make the necessary order for transfer (see generally *Barclays Bank plc v Bemister* [1989] 1 WLR 128).

Transfer from High Court to county court

Under CCA 1984, s 40 the High Court has power to transfer the whole or any part of any High Court proceedings to such county court as the High Court considers convenient to the parties.

This section is all embracing; it covers any proceedings currently in the High Court. It is convenient to classify such proceedings into three categories.

(1) Cases which should not have been commenced in the High Court; eg a personal injury action if the value of the action is less than £50,000 (see p 108). In such a case the High Court must transfer the proceedings a to county court, or, if it is satisfied that the plaintiff knew or ought to have known of the requirement to commence such cases in a county court, must order transfer or striking out (s 40(1) as construed in *Restick v Crickmore* [1994] 1 WLR 420 noted on p 197).

(2) Cases which could only be commenced in the High Court; eg an action for libel or slander (CCA 1984, s 15(2)) or equity proceedings such as an action for specific performance of a contract for the sale of land at a price exceeding £30,000 (see p 108). In this category of cases there is no rule requirement for the filing of statements of value at various stages of the proceedings.

(3) Cases which can be tried either in the High Court or in the county court; eg almost any contract or tort claim (including personal injury claims), however high, or low, the value of the action (see below). It is in this category of cases that the High Court rules require the filing of statements of value at various stages of the proceedings; failure to comply with these rules may, or sometimes must, lead to transfer (see below).

How questions of transfer may arise

A transfer may be ordered by consent without a hearing if RSC Ord 42, r 5A applies (see p 371) or on an application made (by summons to the district judge) by any party at any stage of the action. A transfer may also be ordered where no application is made, the court raising the matter of its own motion. RSC Ord 107, r 2 provides that no transfer will be ordered unless the parties consent or unless the parties have had an opportunity of being heard on the issue (certain transfers 'in default of statement of value' are excepted from this rule; see below). A *Practice Direction* of 1991 (*White Book* 34/4/7) sets out the procedure by which parties may be given such an opportunity. No appointment will be made to consider the question of transfer unless one of the parties expressly requires one. If, at any stage of an action, it appears to a judge or district judge that the proceedings must be transferred (or struck out) or ought to be transferred, he will direct the court staff to give notice of the proposed transfer (or striking out) to all parties. This requires the parties to serve a notice of objection within fourteen days if they wish to prevent such an order being made or if they dispute that the county court specified in the court's notice is the most appropriate county court.

In what circumstances is the court likely to give notice under this *Practice Direction?* In what circumstances will the court be able to form a view as to transfer without either party having applied for it? The most likely example is at the setting down stage. All proceedings set down in the Queen's Bench Division are considered by a district judge who will peruse as necessary the documentation lodged on setting down and review the question as to the most suitable court for trial. The district judge may then order that the action shall remain in the High Court *or* direct that a notice of proposed transfer (or striking out) be given to all parties *or* refer the question as to transfer to the judge in charge of the lists in that court for him to decide whether any notice of proposed transfer (or striking out) should be given (*Practice Direction*, para 4). In cases falling within category (3) above this review by the district judge is expressly anticipated by the rules in cases in which no statement of value was filed on setting down (RSC Ord 34, r 3(1B)).

The question of transfer will also arise at the hearing of a summons for directions, transfer being one of the matters which the district judge is required to consider at that hearing, whether or not the parties raise it (see p 455). The question may also arise during the course of any other interlocutory hearing, eg the hearing of a summons to set aside a default judgment (see p 219) or the hearing of an application for an interim payment (see p 308). The likelihood of this is increased in the case of all private room appointments for hearings before a Queen's Bench master. The form prescribed for requesting such a hearing (see *White Book* 711) requires the applicant to state 'VALUE OF CLAIM (or, if unliquidated, the approximate sum the plaintiff reasonably expects to recover)'.

If the question of transfer arises during the hearing of a summons and all parties are then before the court, they will be given an opportunity to be heard on the question immediately, the court dispensing with the need to give prior notice. Alternatively, if eg one of the parties is not then before the court, notice of proposed transfer (or striking out) may be given to all parties, including the absentee (*Practice Direction*, paras 2, 3). There is no need to give notice to the absentee or to anyone else when the question is considered at the hearing of a summons for directions (RSC Ord 107, r 2(1B)).

There are two other circumstances in which transfer to a county court is provided for:

    (*a*) In cases listed in category (3) above, failure to file a statement of value in breach of an 'unless order' made under RSC Ord 14, r 6(3) (see p 230). Neither RSC Ord 107, r 2 nor the *Practice Direction* of 1991 apply in this case (see r 2(1B), and para 12 of the *Practice Direction*).

(b) In any case in which the High Court has granted an *Anton Piller* order or *Mareva* injunction in respect of proceedings commenced in a county court and the application for such relief has now been disposed of (see pp 294, 301; query whether either RSC Ord 107, r 2 or the *Practice Direction* of 1991 apply in such a case; presumably they do not).

Criteria relevant to questions of transfer

Article 7 of the High Court and County Courts Jurisdiction Order 1991 lists four criteria or factors which the court should take into account on questions of transfer. Strictly, they apply only to cases falling within category (3) above but presumably they also will be applied by analogy in cases falling within category (2) above. They do not apply to family proceedings within the meaning of Pt V of the Matrimonial and Family Proceedings Act 1984 or to proceedings within the Admiralty jurisdiction of the county court (art 12). Also, special provision is made for High Court cases in which the Crown is a party (art 11).

In summary the four criteria are financial substance, importance, complexity and speed of trial. The High Court and County Courts Jurisdiction Order also sets out certain presumptions. The four criteria just listed are applicable in cases in which no presumption applies, and also in cases when one or other party is seeking to rebut a relevant presumption.

The presumptions turn upon a quite separate factor, 'value'. In actions for debt or damages this factor is fairly easy to calculate; 'value' means the amount which the plaintiff reasonably expects to recover *without adding* any expectation as to an award of costs or of interest in the court's discretion (see p 16) and *without deducting* any sum in respect of recoverable state benefits (see p 62) or contributory negligence (unless admitted) or debts owed to the defendant (unless admitted).

In actions for relief other than debt or damages 'value' means, for the purposes of the presumptions, that sum which the plaintiff can reasonably state to be the financial worth of the claim to him. For example, in a possession action the value might be the difference between the value of the land with vacant possession and the value of the land burdened by the difficulties and uncertainties of the present litigation; an alternative measure might be the extra cost and expense of any delay which the plaintiff is likely to suffer because of the need to cancel development plans pending the litigation (consider an alleged ex-tenant shopkeeper whose refusal to quit is delaying a billion pound development scheme). In a case concerning lease renewal under the Landlord and Tenant Act 1954, Pt II, 'value' might be the relocation costs which the tenant will be put to if he fails to obtain an order for the new lease.

In our view when calculating value in a damages action the plaintiff is justified in assuming a 'strongest case scenario'; ie the maximum sum likely to be awarded. When calculating value in the sense of 'financial worth' the plaintiff is justified in assuming a 'worst case scenario'; assume that the defendant will be as awkward, as unwilling, destructive and attacking as he can be.

If the value of an action cannot be expressed in terms of financial worth to the plaintiff, the claim has 'no quantifiable value' and the presumptions as to value will not come into effect; consider for example claims for declarations as to the rights of members of a private tennis club or political body.

In the case of multiplicity of causes (eg a claim for debts and possession or claims for damages by two passengers injured in a road accident) one must consider the aggregate value of the claims. However, if any of the claims in the action has no quantifiable value (see above) the presumptions as to value will not come into effect.

The presumptions as to value

If 'value' is less than £25,000 the proceedings are presumed suitable for trial in the county court unless, in an exceptional case, other factors relevant to the four criteria, render High Court trial more suitable.

If 'value' is £50,000 or more the proceedings are presumed suitable for trial in the High Court unless they were commenced in the county court or unless other factors, relevant to the four criteria, render the case equally suitable for trial in the county court. (Where transfer to the Central London County Court Business List is contemplated, see p 276.)

If 'value' is £25,000 or more but less than £50,000 there is no presumption as to place for trial. The court must simply apply the four criteria.

Applying the criteria

The first criterion is financial substance; what is the case really worth? The court, unlike the plaintiff, will not make a 'strongest case' or 'worst case' valuation. For example, according to the High Court and County Courts Jurisdiction Order 1991 the financial substance of the action includes the value of any counterclaim (art 7(5)(a)). The 1991 Order does not state whether the value of a counterclaim (if any) should be taken into account by way of addition (swelling 'financial substance') or by way of subtraction (reducing 'financial substance'). Presumably the answer depends upon whether the counterclaim is 'related to the plaintiff's claim,' ie is a set-off properly so called (see p 161).

After value or financial substance the next two factors are *importance* and *complexity*: see art 7(5) of the High Court and County Courts Jurisdiction Order 1991 which states:

(a) whether the action is otherwise important and, in particular, whether it raises questions of importance to persons who are not parties or questions of general public interest;

(b) the complexity of the facts, legal issues, remedies or procedures involved.

One may assume that, in most cases, the greater the importance and complexity, the more likely it is that the case is suitable for trial in the High Court. Importance and complexity may, if above average, rebut the presumption that cases under £25,000 are suitable for trial in the county court. However, cases of below average importance or complexity may be tried in the county court even if value is £50,000 or more.

No doubt litigants wanting High Court trial will strive to emphasise the importance and complexity of the case. Those wanting a county court trial will strive to emphasise how minor and straightforward the proceedings are. These factors can be used to rebut the presumptions as to value, where they apply. Above average importance or complexity may carry the smallest value cases to a High Court trial. Below average importance and complexity may carry even a six figure case to a county court trial.

The *Practice Direction* of 1991 (*White Book* 34/4/7) states that actions including one or more of the following types of case, whether by claim or counterclaim, may be considered important and therefore suitable for trial in the High Court.

(1) Professional negligence.
(2) Fatal accidents.
(3) Fraud or undue influence.
(4) Defamation.
(5) Malicious prosecution or false imprisonment.
(6) Claims against the police.

The fourth criterion or factor is *speed of trial,* or, more exactly '(d) whether transfer is likely to result in a more speedy trial of the action'. Whether this factor favours trial in the High Court or in the county court obviously depends upon the relative state of the lists etc in both courts.

Article 7 further states that no transfer shall be made solely upon the grounds of sub-paragraph (d). Thus, in many cases it will be a make-weight factor only. It cannot by itself justify a transfer, although it may be used to bolster a case based also on other factors. However, it does have some power of inertia. It may by itself prevent the transfer of a case which is otherwise suitable for transfer.

Consequences of transfer

Before specifying the county court to which the proceedings are to be transferred, the High Court is required to take into account the convenience of the parties and also any other persons likely to be affected (such as witnesses) and must also take into account the state of business in each of the two courts (s 40(4)). In the case of an order transferring an action from the Queen's Bench Division to a county court the party having the 'carriage of the order' (usually the plaintiff) or, sometimes, the court itself (see below) must prepare and file certain documentation at the High Court office for onward transmission to the county court office

(*Master's Practice Direction* 9, *White Book* 719). Thereafter for all purposes save one the action is now a county court action. The one exception is the right of appeal (if any) from the order of transfer itself. If such a right exists, eg to a High Court judge, it may be executed even after the transfer is complete (s 40(5)). Contrast an appeal made against a High Court order which was made by a district judge *before* the question of transfer arose. In *Kings Quality Homes Ltd v A J Paints Ltd* (1997) *The Times*, 24 April an order concerning joinder of parties was made in the High Court shortly before the case was transferred to the county court; after transfer, an appeal from that order was properly made to a circuit judge.

In two of the 'default of statement of value' cases provided for in the rules (following a hearing order under RSC Ord 14 or before the hearing of a summons for directions; contrast the third default case provided for in the rules, RSC Ord 34, r 3(1B) at setting down) the court staff will deal with the documentation on transfer (*White Book* 723). The *Practice Direction* of 1991 states as follows:

> Any party not in default either as to lodgment or service of such a statement of value [under RSC Ord 14, r 6(2) or under RSC Ord 25, r 6(2A)] and who objects to transfer to a county court or to the particular county court must apply *on notice in the county court to which the proceedings have been transferred* within fourteen days of receipt by him of notice of the transfer (*Practice Direction*, para 12, emphasis added).

In other words, the proper method of challenge is an application for an order setting aside the transfer, rather than an appeal against the transfer.

On being entered in the county court records, the further procedure in the action is governed by CCR Ord 16, r 6 and the automatic directions under CCR Ord 17, r 11 if the action is one to which that rule applies (see p 452) to the extent that they do not conflict with any directions actually given in the case in the High Court (CCR Ord 17, r 11(1A)). Depending on the degree to which the case has already been prepared, the court office may fix a day for the trial or a day for a pre-trial review. The court office must fix a day for trial if the case was transferred after it had been set down in the High Court or if a request for a day to be fixed is made under the automatic directions (CCR Ord 16, r 6(1A)).

In transferred cases which are subject to automatic directions in the county court (see p 452) the pleadings are deemed to be closed fourteen days after the date of transfer (CCR Ord 16, r 6(1A)). As to the exact date of transfer, see p 466.

Transfer from county court to High Court

Under CCA 1984, s 41 an application can be made *in the High Court* under RSC Ord 107 for the transfer to the High Court of the whole or part of any proceedings in a county court. An order can be made if the

High Court considers it 'desirable'. This provision is important in county court cases in which the High Court is asked to grant an *Anton Piller* order or a *Mareva* injunction (see p 294). In almost every other case an application for transfer to the High Court is better made under s 42. Under CCA 1984, s 42 the county court may, either of its own motion, or on the application of any party, order the transfer of the whole or part of any proceedings to the High Court if it thinks fit. In cases which should not have been commenced in a county court (eg many equity cases in which the relevant capital value exceeds £30,000 and jurisdiction was not obtained by agreement) the court must order transfer or, if satisfied that the plaintiff knew or ought to have known of the need to commence in the High Court, must order transfer or striking out (as to which cf *Restick v Crickmore* [1994] 1 WLR 420, noted on p 197).

In cases which could have been commenced either in the High Court or in the county court (eg personal injury actions apart, any contract or tort claim, however high or low the value of the action) the court will apply the presumptions as to value and the criteria, financial substance, importance, complexity and speed of trial, as defined and discussed above. However, the presumption applicable where 'value' is £50,000 or more operates slightly differently in cases commenced in the county court. Any case, even a seven figure case, is suitable for trial in the county court if it was commenced there unless the county court expressly orders otherwise (see the 1991 Order, art 7(4)(a) and compare and contrast the wording of art 7(3)(a)).

Any application for transfer should be made to the district judge on notice supported by a statement showing whether or not the value of the action exceeds £25,000 (CCR Ord 16, r 9). If an order is made it may specify that transfer is to be made to the Central Office or to a particular district registry (see Form N278). The procedure thereafter is governed by CCR Ord 16, r 10 and, in the High Court, by RSC Ord 78 (county court sends papers to High Court, High Court gives notice of transfer, defendants must acknowledge service of that notice whereupon plaintiff may take out a summons for directions or summons for summary judgment under RSC Ord 14). The transfer does not affect any right of appeal to the county court judge, from the district judge's order directing the transfer (see s 42(4)).

Both ss 41 and 42 apply to proceedings commenced in the county court and also to proceedings transferred under s 40.

Transfer from one county court to another

In some cases proceedings will be transferred from one county court to another automatically, ie without any order being made directing transfer. The cases all concern default actions (see p 239) presently before a court other than the defendant's home court (see p 112); they will be automatically transferred to his home court if:

(1) In the case of a debt action a defence is filed (and see further p 253).

(2) In the case of a debt action, an application is made to set aside a judgment obtained in default of defence (see p 253).

(3) In any default action (ie whether debt or damages) after a 'paper disposal' by court staff, if either party applies on notice for the order as to rate of payment to be reconsidered by a district judge (see p 250).

In other cases the court has general power to order transfer from one county court to another if satisfied that the proceedings could be more conveniently or fairly heard and determined in that other county court (CCR Ord 16, r 1; and see p 110; proceedings commenced in the wrong court). In multi-party litigation transfers will be ordered as a matter of good sense and good administration to particular courts which can provide specialised listing arrangements for them. In *Horrocks v Ford Motor Co Ltd* (1990) *The Times*, 15 February, *White Book* 34/5/4, proceedings commenced in Brentwood County Court by plaintiffs who were 'shopping' for the speediest forum, were transferred to Liverpool County Court, where the alleged causes of action arose.

Under CCR Ord 16, r 4 orders for transfer can be made by the court of its own motion or on the application of any party. Applications should normally be made on notice to all other parties. However, applications can be made *ex parte* in writing (eg by letter) if the applicant does not reside or carry on business within the district of the court. If the applicant is a defendant (eg in a damages action proceeding in a court which is not his home court) he must file his defence before applying. If the applicant is a plaintiff, the action must have been automatically transferred on the filing of a defence; in other cases plaintiffs can apply only on notice (see generally CCR Ord 16, r 4(2)). If an *ex parte* application is made the respondents will usually be given the opportunity to make representations in writing before any order is made.

Procedure on transfer is governed by CCR Ord 16, r 4.

Costs in cases transferred between courts

Unless a specific order is made to the contrary, wherever a case is transferred between courts the costs both before and after transfer are in the discretion of the court to which the proceedings are transferred. In cases moving from the High Court the possibility of a costs penalty under SCA 1981, s 51 should be considered (see p 527).

Transfer of judgments between courts for the purposes of enforcement

Under CCA 1984, s 40 any High Court judgment is enforceable in the county court as if it were a county court judgment. The procedure to be followed is governed by CCR Ord 25, r 11. Similarly, under CCA 1984, s 42 any county court judgment is enforceable in the High Court as if it were a High Court judgment.

To effect transfer the plaintiff must obtain a certificate of judgment from the county court (see CCR Ord 25, r 13) and deliver it to the High Court (see further *Masters' Practice Direction* 32, *White Book* 745).

Transfer to the High Court for the purposes of enforcement should not normally be obtained in cases in which execution against goods will be sought and the judgment debt outstanding is less than £1,000 (see High Court and County Courts Jurisdiction Order 1991, art 8 (as amended in 1996); and see p 592). In other cases, transfer to the High Court for the purposes of enforcement gives the plaintiff two potential benefits: interest on the judgment debt (not available in the county court in the case of debts less than £5,000; see p 18) and the opportunity to obtain enforcement against chattels enforced by a sheriff's officer rather than by a county court bailiff (see p 592). After transfer for the purposes of enforcement under either s 40 or s 42, an application for any stay of execution must be made in the 'enforcement court'. However, applications to set aside, correct, vary or quash the judgment must still be made in the 'judgment court' and the relevant statutory provisions as to appeals from that court will continue to apply (see s 40(6), (7) and s 42(5), (6)).

Chapter 18

Discovery

Definitions

'Discovery' used in the strict sense is the disclosure by one party to another of the existence of relevant documents which are or have been in his possession, custody or power. The disclosure may be general, ie a list of all documents (see further p 394) or particular, ie in respect of some previously specified document or class of document (see further p 406). The party receiving discovery then has the right (subject to the court's discretion: see p 388) to inspect such of the documents his opponent still has as are not privileged. In practice the term 'discovery' is often used to include both the disclosure and the subsequent inspection.

The word 'discovery' is used in an old-fashioned sense which can be misleading. It refers to the act of 'uncovering' or revealing and not, as one might expect, to the act of 'finding out'. Thus, if A discloses a document to B, A is the person who 'discovers' the document, not B.

For the purposes of discovery 'document' includes any artefact which records information, including for example audio tapes (*Grant v Southwestern and County Properties* [1975] Ch 185) or a computer database (*Derby & Co Ltd v Weldon (No 9)* [1991] 1 WLR 652). Documents are relevant if they relate to 'any matter in question' in the proceedings, a term obviously wide enough to cover all documents which, directly or indirectly, assist or damage either party's case. 'Inspection' means examination and carries with it the right to take copies. Inspection is not confined to mere ocular inspection (*Grant v Southwestern and County Properties*, above). As to the taking of copies of documents which can be photocopied, the party producing them for inspection can be required to supply copies in return for an undertaking as to reasonable or proper payment (see further pp 405 and 411).

The party making discovery may object to producing for inspection *privileged documents*, using this expression to include:

(1) confidential correspondence between a client and his legal advisers for the purposes of obtaining legal advice and also documents prepared with a view to litigation (legal professional privilege);

(2) documents tending to criminate or expose to a penalty; and

(3) documents the inspection of which would be injurious to the public interest.

Note that there is no privilege from discovery, only from inspection (save for a limited exception in certain Crown cases: RSC Ord 77, r 12(2); CCR Ord 42, r 12(1)). However, when describing privileged documents in a list of documents a party can give them a general description only so as not to reveal indirectly their contents (see further p 402, and, as to challenging a claim of privilege, see p 419).

'Interrogatories' are questions answerable on oath which any party may serve on his opponent (as to whether leave to serve is required, see p 411). In the first instance the answers are given by affidavit. If the party interrogated omits to answer some of the questions or gives insufficient answers the court may order a further answer to be given either by affidavit or by oral examination. Alternatively the party serving the interrogatories can sometimes serve a request for further and better particulars of the answers given (see p 417). Although the interrogatories proposed must be relevant to the action the definition of 'relevance' is very wide. The questions may relate to any matters which go to support the interrogator's case or to impeach or destroy his opponent's case (*White Book* 26/1/2). Thus answering interrogatories is just another form of discovery and is sometimes called 'discovery of facts'.

Origins and purpose

Discovery and interrogatories originally formed one remedy, 'discovery', granted by the Court of Chancery to assist litigants in preparing their claims or defences in any civil action in any court. Discovery (in either of its forms) is not intended to provide early disclosure of the evidence that will be brought at the trial. It involves much more than that. The party making discovery must disclose *all* his relevant documents and must answer *all* questions properly put to him 'however disagreeable it may be ... however contrary to his personal interests, however fatal to the claim upon which he may have insisted' (*per* Lord Langdale MR in *Flight v Robinson* (1844) Beav 22). Thus discovery may *forearm* the recipient as well as *forewarn* him.

> In plain language, litigation in this country is conducted 'cards face up on the table'. Some people from other lands regard this as incomprehensible. 'Why', they ask, 'should I be expected to provide my opponent with the means of defeating me?' The answer, of course, is that litigation is not a war or even a game. It is designed to do real justice between opposing parties and, if the court does not have *all* the relevant information, it cannot achieve this object (*per* Sir John Donaldson MR in *Davies v Eli Lilly & Co* [1987] 1 WLR 428).

Today the main purpose of discovery is to enable parties to evaluate better the strength of their case in advance of the trial and so to promote the compromise of disputes and the saving of costs. Many actions settle after discovery has taken place. The process causes the parties to concentrate their minds on the issues in dispute and also gives their solicitors an opportunity to meet and talk casually about settlement. The *scope* of the remedy, however, is still limited by the original purpose for which it was developed. Before 1851 a party to an action at law could not be called as a witness in that action. By granting discovery equity assisted litigants to elicit *from their opponents* admissions, information and documents that the common law prevented them from obtaining by *subpoena*. Despite the reform of the common law procedure, discovery is still limited to this area. It is not a general remedy for the collection of information, though in recent years piecemeal attempts have been made to make it so (see AJA 1970 now consolidated in SCA 1981 and CCA 1984; *Norwich Pharmacal v Customs & Excise* [1974] AC 133, below). Consequently the present scope of the remedy is not always logical.

Scope of the remedy

No discovery against mere witnesses

The remedy of discovery (in both its forms) is obtainable only against persons properly joined as parties to an action. Information cannot be obtained from strangers to the dispute except by calling them as witnesses at the trial. It is improper to join a stranger as a party merely for the purpose of obtaining discovery (*Elder v Carter* (1890) 25 QBD 194).

> It has been clear at least since the time of Lord Hardwicke that information cannot be obtained by discovery from a person who will in due course be compellable to give information either by oral testimony as a witness or on a *subpoena duces tecum*. Whether the reasons justifying the rule are good or bad it is much too late to inquire: the rule is settled (*per* Lord Reid, *Norwich Pharmacal*).
>
> The mere witness rule has lost a great deal of its importance since the Common Law Procedure Act removed the bar to persons interested in giving evidence, but it still has significance (*per* Viscount Dilhorne, *Norwich Pharmacal*).

Two exceptions have been made to the rule. In *Norwich Pharmacal* itself a limited order for discovery (of the identity of alleged wrongdoers) was made against defendants who were not personally liable for the wrongdoing complained of but who had facilitated its commission. The plaintiffs had no other means of finding out the identity of the wrongdoers and therefore if the order had not been made there would never have been a trial to which they could call the present defendants as witnesses.

A much more important exception to the 'mere witness' rule has been made by statute. Under SCA 1981, s 34 and CCA 1984, s 53 (replacing provisions first made by the AJA 1970), any party to proceedings in respect of personal injuries or death can apply for *disclosure of documents by non-parties*, for example, hospitals or vehicle manufacturers who have documents which would otherwise only be obtainable at a trial (as to procedure, see pp 407 and 409). The purpose of the provision is to assist parties to compromise their dispute in the light of full information without the necessity of a trial. A discovery such as this is 'entirely contrary to every rule relating to discovery which has ever existed' (*per* Lindley LJ in *Elder v Carter* (1890) 25 QBD 194 above).

The statutory extension of discovery first made by the AJA 1970 appears to have been entirely successful and so it is difficult to see why it should be limited to personal injury litigation. The Civil Justice Review supported the current trend towards greater openness in litigation (1988 Cm 394, p 43). At present however, until the evidence at trial is called, the only 'cards on the table' (see *dictum* of Sir John Donaldson MR, above) are those which were previously in the hands of the parties. Further documents, from the hands of witnesses, may be revealed for the first time at, or just before, the trial (see p 488). A litigant is not required to give discovery of documents which have never been in his possession, custody or power even if he could have obtained them by request at any time had he so wished (*Theodore v Australian Postal Commission* [1988] CLY 2831). Nor can his opponent obtain an order compelling him to obtain them (*Dubai Bank Ltd v Galadari (No 6)* (1992) *The Times*, 14 October, CA).

In *Omar v Omar* (1996) noted in *Supreme Court Practice News* Issue 4/97, the Court of Appeal found itself compelled by the mere witness rule to set aside a *subpoena duces tecum*. It was held that, because the *subpoena* did not describe the documents sought with sufficient particularity, the party who issued and served it was in effect seeking discovery against a witness. It was noted that, in some other common law jurisdictions some limited discovery against a witness is now permitted. Peter Gibson LJ expressed the hope that on some future occasion the House of Lords might follow this lead.

Discovery limited to matters relevant to existing dispute

Discovery does not license a party to subject his opponent to a general inquisition. He can use it only to elicit information relating to an existing claim or defence raised. He cannot use it for a 'fishing expedition', ie seeking discovery merely in the hope of finding some claim or defence to raise.

Example

In *Barham v Lord Huntingfield* [1913] 2 KB 193, P alleged that D had slandered her by words spoken to her servant and to other unnamed persons. P wished to serve interrogatories asking D if he had repeated the words to any person or persons other than the servant, and if so to specify the person and the times, identifying each occasion. The Court of Appeal disallowed the interrogatories, Farwell LJ declaring them to be 'as striking an example of fishing interrogatories as I have ever seen:

counsel admitted this, but contended that there was no objection to fishing interrogatories. I do not agree with him'.

In *Rofe v Kevorkian* [1936] 2 All ER 1334, D denied that he was liable for the price of certain drawings sold to him as originals on the ground that they were merely copies. The Court of Appeal refused to allow an interrogatory asking the plaintiffs when, where and from whom the seller acquired the drawings. The interrogatory was held to be 'a fishing interrogatory by a man who is trying to make a case and has not already the evidence which would justify him in making the case' (*per* Greer LJ).

Plaintiffs must not use *Anton Piller* orders (see p 300) as a means of finding out what sort of charges they can make. Improper use of an *Anton Piller* order is a grave matter justifying the court in dismissing the plaintiff's action as abusive of the court's process. This is the effect of the Court of Appeal decision in *Hytrac Ltd v Conveyors International Ltd* [1983] 1 WLR 44 (in which the plaintiff's action against seven of the eleven defendants was dismissed because of delay in serving the statement of claim; see further p 365 and *per* Goulding J in *Greek City Co Ltd v Demetriou* [1983] 2 All ER 921).

Under SCA 1981, s 33 and CCA 1984, s 52 a prospective party to personal injury litigation can obtain *pre-action disclosure of documents* (as to procedure, see pp 408 and 416).

> This power to order discovery before proceedings are commenced is certainly not one which should be used to encourage fishing expeditions to enable a prospective plaintiff to discover whether he has in fact got a case at all ... a prospective plaintiff who proposes to make application for discovery under [section 33 of the SCA 1981 should] formulate the nature of his allegations and his claim in writing ... before launching any application under the section (*per* Buckley LJ in *Shaw v Vauxhall Motors* [1974] 1 WLR 1035).

Similarly a party cannot seek discovery of documents or facts merely to find out the names of his opponent's witnesses (*Knapp v Harvey* [1911] 2 KB 725) or to seek information merely as to the credit of possible witnesses: *Thorpe v Chief Constable of Greater Manchester Police* [1989] 1 WLR 665 (documents); RSC Ord 26, r 1(3); CCR Ord 14, r 11 (interrogatories).

Discovery only as necessary to dispose of the action fairly or save costs

This is the governing principle of discovery and is written into all the rules of court (RSC Ord 24, rr 2(5), 8 and 13(1); Ord 26, r 1(1); CCR Ord 14, rr 8 and 11). Since it is an equitable remedy discovery is never granted as of right. The court has a discretion and can make such orders as are appropriate to prevent the remedy being used oppressively. On applications for discovery the burden is placed upon the respondent (ie the objecting party) to satisfy the court that discovery is not necessary either for disposing fairly of the action or for saving costs (RSC Ord 24, r 8; CCR Ord 14, r 8). Contrast High Court applications for inspection; under RSC Ord 24, r 13 it is for the applicant to satisfy the court that an inspection order is necessary (see *Dolling-Baker v Merrett* [1990] 1 WLR 1205 *per* Parker LJ). The difference between the rules means that, in High Court cases, orders for discovery are more readily obtainable than orders for inspection. In the county court the same rule governs both discovery and inspection; under CCR Ord 14, r 8 the burden is normally upon the respondent to satisfy the court that discovery or inspection is not necessary; the burden switches to the applicant only on applications for the production of a document to the court, rather than to the parties (r 8(2)). However, the difference between the rules of both courts should not, in our view, lead to a difference in result in many cases.

Disallowing discovery

The court will disallow discovery which would unfairly prejudice the respondent's rights, eg discovery and/or inspection of documents relating to trade secrets (*White Book* 24/5/16). The court will also disallow interrogatories which are prolix or which do not precisely formulate the question asked (*White Book* 26/1/3) or interrogatories which the respondent could answer only by consulting an expert and repeating his opinion (*Rofe v Kevorkian*, noted on p 388: 'Is it not the fact that the said goods were made in the 18th or 19th century?').

Discovery of documents or facts (ie interrogatories) may be rendered unnecessary if the respondent can supply the information sought by some other means, eg giving particulars, making admissions or exchanging witness statements. Indeed, the service of interrogatories before witness statements have been exchanged will almost always be premature (*Det Danske Hedeselskabet v KDM International* [1994] 2 Lloyd's Rep 534; see further p 413).

Limiting discovery or permitting it only on terms

Where the information sought is so voluminous as to impose excessive inconvenience or expense upon the respondent, the court may limit discovery to certain specified documents, classes of documents or matters in question (RSC Ord 24, rr 2(5) and 3(3); CCR Ord 14, r 1(3)) or postpone discovery until after determination of some preliminary issue (RSC Ord 24, r 4; CCR Ord 14, r 8) or in some cases permit discovery only upon terms as to costs (RSC Ord 24, r 7A(5); CCR Ord 13, r 1(8)(a) and r 7(1)(g)). If a 'split trial' has been ordered (as to which, see p 456) the court should limit discovery to the issue of liability only, unless there are special circumstances (*Baldock v Addison* [1995] 1 WLR 158; and see further, the *Practice Direction* of 1995 noted on p 489).

Disallowing inspection

If a document is shown to be privileged the court must not order inspection. However, it does not follow that, if a relevant document is not privileged, the court must order inspection of it. The court has a discretion enabling it to take into account other factors so as to ensure the fair disposal of the action. For example, consider the case of documents which, although not privileged, are confidential; the court may inspect them itself and disallow inspection by the applicant if it thinks that the documents are of insignificant weight or value to the applicant (*Science Research Council v Nassé* [1980] AC 1028). The court may also disallow inspection of any document which is not in the possession, custody or power of the respondent if eg the respondent has made a genuine attempt to obtain it for inspection (see *Rafidain Bank v Agom Universal Sugar Trading Co Ltd* [1987] 1 WLR 1606).

There is another objection to production which should be considered. It has been suggested that the court may disallow inspection of a document which is favourable only to the party making discovery of it. In other words the court will not compel a party to display his 'winning cards' if, perhaps for reasons of delicacy, he chooses not to rely on them at any stage of the proceedings (*Air Canada v Secretary of State for Trade* [1983] 2 AC 394, *obiter* and see *Derby & Co Ltd v Weldon (No 7)* [1990] 1 WLR 1156 at p 1178E). This objection to production is, perhaps, more theoretical than practical. In our view the document in question is still relevant and therefore discoverable in the strict sense; its existence must be disclosed.

Permitting inspection of documents only on terms

Where production for inspection is likely to cause excessive expense, the party seeking inspection may be required to give security for costs (CCR Ord 13, r 1(8)(a)).

In the case of a document over which the respondent claims a lien, although the court has power to order production for inspection, the order may be conditional on the applicant paying into court a sum equal to the value of the lien (*Woodworth v Conroy* [1976] QB 884, where in fact no such condition was imposed).

In the case of a computer database, Vinelott J in *Derby & Co Ltd v Weldon (No 9)* [1991] 1 WLR 652 listed several difficulties which the court should have regard to before fixing the terms upon which inspection may be ordered; eg safeguards will be necessary to exclude inspection of irrelevant or privileged material, to avoid corruption of the information stored and to minimise interference with the respondent's everyday use of the computer.

In the case of confidential documents which are not privileged, can the court impose terms preventing their inspection by the client in person? The making of confidential reports, especially hospital reports and records, may be inhibited if it were thought that they might later be read by non-professional eyes. In *McIvor v Southern Health Board* [1978] 1 WLR 757 the House of Lords overruled earlier Court of Appeal cases which limited discovery of medical reports to the applicant's medical advisers. However, it seems that the court can limit inspection to medical advisers *and* legal advisers, the client in person still being excluded. See for example *per* Lord Denning in the Court of Appeal decision in *Science Research Council v Nassé* (above, this point not being taken in the House of Lords); the court may limit production to selected persons 'for instance ... the counsel and solicitors on their undertaking that it should go no further'. This discretion is now provided by statute in the case of *pre-action* and *non-party discovery*; see SCA 1981, ss 32(2)(b) and 34(2)(b); CCA 1984, ss 52(2)(b) and 53(2)(b).

Orders preventing the disclosure of information to a client have been made in four other cases: *Church of Scientology v DHSS* [1979] 1 WLR 723 (to protect informers from harassment; and see *Ventouris v Mountain* [1991] 1 WLR 607, allegations that inspection could lead to violence, intimidation, interference with witnesses and destruction of evidence); *Arab Monetary Fund v Hashim* [1989] 1 WLR 565 (to conceal the identities of persons overseas implicated in currency offences said to be punishable by death); and *Black & Decker Inc v Flymo Ltd* [1991] 1 WLR 753 (to prevent a business rival gaining commercial advantage from inspecting the design documents and drawings of an intended new product). In each of these cases the purpose of the restrictions imposed was to prevent confidential information which a party had been compelled to disclose being used for a purpose extraneous to the action. This aspect of discovery is dealt with in greater detail below (see overleaf).

Any discovery made normally conclusive

Sworn statements made by a party making discovery are normally conclusive. If, by affidavit, he states that certain documents are irrelevant or if he objects to producing documents or answering interrogatories on grounds of privilege the court is reluctant to go behind his oath unless there is strong reason to do so.

> Although it gives great advantages to a statement on oath which may be unscrupulous, and it may be unadvisable to give such weight to the oath of a party deeply interested, yet many inconveniences would follow from not adopting that rule (*per* Denman J in *Bewicke v Graham* (1881) 7 QBD 400).
> This ... is really founded not upon any artificial or arbitrary rule of the courts but upon the very nature of things ... it is obviously beyond the power of any court to order a party to swear particular facts when he is determined to swear the contrary (*per* Watkin Williams J in *Bewicke*).

This being so, a heavy burden is placed upon solicitors to ensure that their clients appreciate at an early stage of the litigation both the duty of discovery and its width and the importance of not destroying documents which might have to be disclosed (*Rockwell v Barrus* [1968] 1 WLR 693). Indeed the solicitor owes a duty to the court to examine his client's documents himself to ensure that full disclosure is made (*Woods v Martins Bank* [1959] 1 QB 55). If the client will not permit this, or insists on giving imperfect discovery, it is the solicitor's duty to withdraw from the case (*Myers v Elman* [1940] AC 282).

The court's unwillingness to go behind the discoverer's oath has substantially diminished, especially in recent years. There are now several ways of attacking a party's discovery; see further p 418.

Discovery granted only for purposes of action

Parties and their solicitors receive discovery of documents on a strict undertaking that they will make use of them only for the purposes of that action and not for the purposes of any other action or for any collateral purpose (*Home Office v Harman* [1983] 1 AC 280). The undertaking is implied whether the court expressly requires it or not (*Riddick v Thames Board Mills Ltd* [1977] QB 881, 896). Although it is intended for the benefit of the other parties, the undertaking is not in fact given to them but to the court. This enables the court to control the position, imposing sanctions for breach or threatened breach if necessary and releasing or modifying the undertaking if appropriate.

Breach of undertaking

In *Home Office v Harman* [1983] 1 AC 280 a solicitor who had received copies of documents discovered by the opposing party, passed them to a journalist in order to assist him to write a newspaper article about them. The solicitor was found guilty of contempt of court. In fact no penalty was imposed upon her because she had honestly believed that she had been entitled to do what she did (the documents having been read out in court, see further p 394).

In *Riddick v Thames Board Mills Ltd* [1977] QB 881 the plaintiff claimed damages for libel in respect of a document which he had obtained by way of discovery in an earlier action for wrongful dismissal. The libel action was struck out as an abuse of the process of the court. 'I see no reason why [the plaintiff] could not have done justice to himself—and to the company—by amending his writ in the [earlier] action to add the claim which he ... is making in this action', *per* Stephenson LJ.

In *Distillers Co (Biochemicals) Ltd v Times Newspapers Ltd* [1975] QB 613 an interlocutory injunction was granted against the defendants restraining them from publishing an article based on copies of documents which had been obtained from the plaintiff by way of discovery in a negligence action concerning the drug thalidomide.

Release or modification of the undertaking

In *Crest Homes plc v Marks* [1987] AC 829 it was held that, in an exceptional case, the court may release or modify the undertaking so as to permit use of discovered documents for the purposes of other proceedings if the applicant could demonstrate 'cogent and persuasive reasons' to that effect and if 'the release or modification will not occasion injustice to the person giving discovery' (*per* Lord Oliver with whose speech all the other law lords agreed). In *Crest* the plaintiffs had commenced two actions against the defendant, the first in 1984 and the second in 1985. In both actions the plaintiffs obtained *Anton Piller* orders plus related discovery orders. As a result of the *Anton Piller* order in the 1985 action the plaintiffs obtained documents which, they alleged, should have been disclosed to them in their 1984 action. The implied undertaking was released to the extent necessary to enable them to use information (documents and some affidavits) obtained in the 1985 action in support of proceedings for contempt of court in the 1984 action.

> In substance the 1984 action and the 1985 action are a single set of proceedings—a circumstance emphasised by the order that the two should be heard together—and the fact that, because, for reasons good or bad, Crest's claim has been prosecuted by the issue of the two writs instead of one, the court's leave is required for the use of the documents obtained under the 1985 order is the merest technicality. To accede to Crest's application will, in these circumstances, cause no injustice to the appellants nor will it detract from the solemnity and importance of the implied undertaking (*per* Lord Oliver).

In *Apple Corp Ltd v Apple Computer Inc* [1991] Gazette, 22 May, 34, *White Book* 24/14A/1 there were parallel proceedings in relation to the same dispute before the High Court and before the European Commission. The desirability of ensuring that each tribunal should have the same materials for consideration constituted 'cogent and persuasive reasons' and an order was made releasing the implied undertaking in respect of certain documents which had been discovered so as to allow the applicant to deploy them in the proceedings before the European Commission.

Sometimes discovery orders are made specifically for the purpose of providing the applicant with information in order to assist him in bringing other proceedings; in such cases there is no restriction on the applicant using the information for that purpose unless the court expressly requires it. For example, in *Sony Corp v Anand* [1981] FSR 398 the plaintiffs wished to commence proceedings against persons whose identity had been disclosed to them by a *Norwich Pharmacal* order (see p 409); it was held that no application for release from the implied undertaking was required in that case. In *Derby & Co Ltd v Weldon* [1990] Ch 48 a *Mareva* injunction was made in respect of overseas assets (see p 294). It was held that a discovery order given in aid of it should contain an express undertaking by the plaintiffs not to use the information gained without first obtaining the leave of the court. It was expected that the plaintiffs would wish to commence parallel proceedings in countries in which assets were located. The English court wished to control the commencement of such proceedings in order to protect the defendants from oppression by exposure to a multiplicity of proceedings.

Cesser of undertaking

Rules of court made in 1987 state that the undertaking (whether given expressly or impliedly) ceases to apply to a discovered document '...

after it has been read to or by the Court, or referred to, in open court, unless the Court for special reasons has otherwise ordered...' (RSC Ord 24, r 14A, CCR Ord 14, r 8A, negativing part of the House of Lords decision in *Home Office v Harman* [1983] 1 AC 280). There have not been many cases reported as to these rules (see *White Book* 24/14A/1). Two important questions still remain largely unanswered. First, the breadth of meaning the courts will give to the words 'read... or referred to, in open court'; eg will a 500 page report cease to be protected if counsel makes a one-line quotation from it or a fleeting reference to it? Secondly, case law as to what amounts to 'special reasons' justifying the court to 'otherwise order' so maintaining protection for documents even if they are read out in full in open court; presumably the grant or refusal of such an order will often depend upon the amount of publicity the proceedings are likely to attract and the likelihood and extent of injury to the owner of the document if the order is refused.

By requiring an undertaking not to use information obtained by discovery except in furtherance of the current proceedings, the court recognises that discovery amounts to a serious invasion of privacy which can be justified only in so far as it is absolutely necessary for the achievement of justice between the parties. Discovery is obtained by, or by the threat of, compulsion. The public interest in privacy and confidentiality demands that this compulsion should never be pressed further than is necessary for disposing fairly of a cause or matter. For other ways in which the court may restrict the use of information obtained by discovery, see p 390.

Discovery of documents by list

Automatic discovery in the High Court

In most actions begun by writ general discovery occurs automatically, ie without an order being made (see generally, RSC Ord 24, rr 1, 2). Within fourteen days after close of pleadings (see p 113) the plaintiff and defendant must exchange lists of all the relevant documents which are or have been in their possession, custody or power. The form of list is prescribed (see further p 398). It contains two schedules. The first schedule lists the documents presently in the party's possession, custody or power and is subdivided into Part 1, documents he will allow his opponent to inspect, and Part 2, documents he objects to producing for inspection. The second schedule lists the documents which have been but are not now in his possession, custody or power. In the body of the list the party must state, of the documents in Schedule 1, Part 2, the ground upon which the objection to production for inspection is made (usually, privilege) and, of the documents in Schedule 2, when he last had them, what has become of them and in whose possession they now are. The last part of the list should specify a time and place at which the other party may inspect and take copies of the documents in Schedule 1, Part 1. The place specified is usually the office of the solicitor acting for the party serving the list. The time specified must be within seven days of the service of the list: RSC Ord 24, r 9. If the party fails to complete this part of the list, or specifies an unreasonable time or place for inspection, the court will make an order for inspection: RSC Ord 24, r 11 (see p 419). Originally, lists of documents always had to be sworn. This is no longer the case. However, if he so wishes, the party receiving the list may serve, on the party whose list it is, a notice requiring him to make a verifying affidavit. If such a notice is served, the party whose list it is must, within the next fourteen days, make such an affidavit, file the original in court and serve a copy of it on the party by whom the notice was served (see further as to verifying affidavits on pp 397 and 418).

Limiting automatic discovery

The parties may agree to dispense with or limit automatic discovery, or indeed extend the time for it to take place (the time for a summons for directions is then extended accordingly: RSC Ord 25, r 1(3)). Alternatively any party may apply by summons to the district judge for an order postponing or dispensing with discovery by all or any of the parties or limiting discovery to certain specified documents or classes of documents or matters in question. (As to limiting discovery where a split trial is ordered, see *Baldock v Addison* [1995] 1 WLR 158 and see p 389 above).

High Court cases in which there is no automatic discovery

RSC Ord 24, r 2 does not apply to proceedings without pleadings (eg originating summons cases), third party proceedings or proceedings to which the Crown is a party (RSC Ord 77, r 12). In road accident cases the defendant is not required to make discovery unless the court so orders (see RSC Ord 24, r 2(2) which applies to all road accident cases whether or not damages for personal injuries are claimed). In road accident cases the defendant is unlikely to have any relevant documents except privileged documents; note that the plaintiff must still serve a list, although in personal injury cases the plaintiff's list is limited to documents relating to special damages (see above).

Automatic discovery in the High Court is restricted to documents 'relating to any matter in question between' the parties serving the lists. Therefore it does not normally take place between co-defendants unless, in an exceptional case, some question or issue in the action has to be decided as between them. However, under RSC Ord 24, r 6, a defendant who has served a list of documents on the plaintiff must supply a copy of that list, free of charge, to any co-defendant who so requests. The list supplied must fix a time and place for inspection by the co-defendant (see RSC Ord 24, r 9).

Automatic discovery in the county court

In most default actions and fixed date actions general discovery occurs automatically, ie without an order being made, because of the rules as to automatic directions set out in CCR Ord 17, r 11 (see further p 465). The form of list used in the county court is illustrated in fig 27 (see p 399). Like the High Court form, it contains two Schedules with the First Schedule divided into two Parts. However, it does not contain any notice to inspect the documents listed in Schedule 1 Part 1 (see CCR Ord 14, r 3). Thus the party serving the list must include details of the time and place for inspection either in his covering letter or in a separate document. ('Take notice that the documents listed in Schedule 1 Part 1 of the [*party's*] list may be inspected at the office of the solicitors for the [*party*] at [*address*] on [*date*] by prior appointment or at any time during usual business hours'.)

Limiting automatic discovery

As in the High Court, the parties may agree to dispense with or limit automatic discovery or extend the time for it to take place. Alternatively any party may apply to the district judge on notice for an order postponing or dispensing with discovery by any or all of the parties or limiting discovery to certain specified documents or classes of documents or matters in question (CCR Ord 17, r 11(5)). In any action in which liability is admitted and in road accident cases claiming damages for personal injuries, the lists to be served by each party should be limited to documents relating to the amount of damages (CCR Ord 17, r 11(5)).

County court cases in which there is no automatic discovery

There is no automatic discovery in any case commenced by originating application or in any of the default actions or fixed date actions which are excepted from the rules as to automatic directions (CCR Ord 17, r 11(1), the excepted cases are considered in p 476) or in any proceedings to which the Crown is a party (CCR Ord 17, r 11(6)).

As in the High Court the rule providing for automatic discovery restricts it to documents 'relating to any matter in question between' the parties serving the lists. Therefore lists are not normally served between defendants unless, in an exceptional case, some question or issue in the action has to be decided as between them. The county court has no rule equivalent to RSC Ord 24, r 6 (see above). However, the automatic direction requires the making and serving of lists 'on every other party' (see CCR Ord 17, r 11(5)(a)). Also, the county court rules provide for a system of voluntary discovery under which one party may request another party to make discovery without any order being made (CCR Ord 14, r 1(2); cf the procedure concerning further and better particulars).

Order for discovery by list

In any action, High Court or county court, an application can be made to the district judge by summons (High Court) or on notice (county court) for an order compelling any other party to make and serve on the applicant a list of documents 'relating to any matter in question in the cause or matter' (RSC Ord 24, r 3) or 'relating to any matter in question in the proceedings' (CCR Ord 14, r 1(1); contrast the more restricted wording, quoted at pp 395 and 396 above, which is used in both courts in relation to automatic discovery). In the county court the application should be preceded by a written request for discovery (see above). In both courts the discovery ordered may be limited to certain specified documents or classes of documents or matters in question. The list served must be in a prescribed form and must contain a notice fixing a time and place for inspection. In addition the court may, at the same time or subsequently, order the respondent to make and serve a verifying affidavit.

In what circumstances would a party need to apply for an order for discovery by list? There are three important examples:

(1) cases in which the respondent was not required to make discovery automatically and has refused or failed to make discovery voluntarily;

(2) cases in which the respondent was required but has failed to make discovery automatically—in this instance the applicant may also seek penalty orders (see p 419);

(3) cases in which automatic discovery has already taken place and the applicant now wishes to obtain a 'further and better list'; these cases are dealt with in p 418.

Verifying affidavits

In all High Court cases in which automatic discovery is made, any party who serves a list can be required to verify it on affidavit if due notice is given (see p 395). In all other cases, High Court and county court, any party who serves a list can be requested to verify it on affidavit; however he is not required to do so unless the court so orders.

In both courts the same form of affidavit is used; see *White Book* 22 and County Court Form N265(1). It is important to note that, unless the court has otherwise ordered, the obligation to make the affidavit is personal to the party whose list it is: this obligation cannot be delegated (*Clauss v Pir* [1988] Ch 267). *Semble* in the case of a company, the affidavit should be made by an appropriate officer of the company, such as the Company Secretary, cf the practice as to interrogatories, p 414.

Requiring or requesting one's opponent to make a verifying affidavit is a useful tactic for several reasons. At the very least it should jolt the opponent into ensuring that full discovery is given; swearing false oaths may give rise to penalties for perjury or contempt of court. If, having received discovery, you have cause to believe that your opponent is likely to have other relevant documents not yet disclosed you should tell him so when seeking the affidavit; that may save the costs of an application for further discovery (see p 418).

The making of a verifying affidavit may impede the opponent relying on additional documents at the trial. There used to be a rule which automatically prevented parties relying at trial on documents which they should have, but had not, disclosed. Their previous statement on oath was taken as conclusive (see p 391). That automatic rule has now gone but it is still the usual practice at trial for the judge not to allow reliance on documents in such circumstances (see *Rafidain Bank v Agom Universal Sugar Trading Co Ltd* [1987] 1 WLR 1606 *per* Nourse LJ).

Drafting a list of documents

The documents to be listed are those which are now, or at some previous time were, in the client's 'possession, custody or power': as to the meaning of this expression see *White Book* 24/2/3. The documents which are presently in the client's possession, custody or power should have been collected in, of course, by the solicitor as soon as possible after receipt of instructions (see p 25).

The list 'must enumerate the documents in a convenient order and as shortly as possible but describing each of them, or in the case of bundles of documents of the same nature, each bundle, sufficiently to enable it to be identified' (RSC Ord 24, r 5; county court practice is similar). The layout of a list has already been described (see p 394) and a specimen list is illustrated in fig 27 opposite. It is convenient to divide any further discussion, in the same way the documents are divided, according to the three sections of the list.

Schedule 1, Part 1

Here you should list documents which are now in the possession, custody or power of the client and which he will allow the opponent to inspect. This will include, for example, letters received from opposing solicitors and copies of any letters sent in reply. Series of letters and other linked documents should always be arranged in convenient bundles. This will keep the list 'as short as possible' (see the High Court rule quoted above). There is little point in seeking to 'bury' problem documents in a morass of unnecessary listings; at least in the High Court, such conduct may be penalised in costs (see *White Book* 24/5/2).

Schedule 1, Part 2

Here you should list documents in the client's possession, custody or power which he objects to producing for inspection. The ground of objection relied on must be specified. For examples of different grounds to consider, see p 384. In practice, the most common ground is legal

[*continued on p 402*]

Fig 27: List of documents

List of Documents

Plaintiff Geoffrey Michael Hamilton

Defendant Derek Deacock

In the	
ASTRID County Court	**County Court**
Case Number Always quote this	KH 712347

(1) Delete words in brackets if list is sent in response to automatic directions (O17 r11)

(2) Insert date

The following is a list of documents which contain information about matters in dispute in this case which are or have been in my possession(¹). [They are sent in response to your request dated(²)   19   .]

Schedule 1 PART I

(3) List and number here in a convenient order the documents (or bundles of documents if of the same nature, eg invoices) in your possession which you do not object to being inspected Give a short description of each document or bundle so that it can be identified and say if it is kept elsewhere i e bank solicitor

I have in my possession the documents numbered and listed here. I do not object to you inspecting them(³).

1. Entries in the Defendant's Purchase Ledger for 2nd March 1997.

2. Entries in the Defendant's Sales Ledger for 27th March 1997.

3. Letter from Plaintiff to Defendant dated 10th April 1997.

4. Copy letter from Defendant to Plaintiff dated 13th April 1997.

5. Copy letter from Defendant to Plaintiff dated 17th April 1997.

6. Letter from Plaintiff's solicitors to Defendant dated 27th April 1997.

7. Bundle of letters from Plaintiff's solicitors to Defendant's solicitors numbered 1 to 6 and dated 6th May 1997, 21st May 1997, 12th June 1997, 2nd September 1997, 21st September 1997 and 24th September 1997, respectively.

8. Buundle of copy letters from Defendant's solicitors to Plaintiff's solicitors numbered 1 to 5 and dated 7th May 1997, 22nd May 1997, 9th June 1997, 3rd September 1997 and 22nd September 1997, respectively.

9. Pleadings, court documents and copies thereof common to both parties.

N.265 List of documents
O 14 r 1(5)

[P.T.O.

Fig 27: contd

Schedule 1 PART II

(4) List and number here, as above, the documents in your possession which you object to being inspected

I have in my possession the documents numbered and listed here but I object to you inspecting them([4]).

1. Confidential correspondence and communications between the Defendant's solicitors and the Defendant for the purposes of giving or obtaining legal advice; copies of the above; Instructions to and Advice of Counsel including drafts and copies; statements and proofs of witnesses and other correspondence and documents brought into existence solely for the purposes of this action.

2. Entries in the Defendant's Purchase Ledger and Sales Ledger other than those parts thereof described in Part 1 above.

(5) Say what your objections are

I object to you inspecting these documents because([5]): —

As to the documents numbered 1 above, they are by their nature privileged from production.

As to the documents numbered 2 above, those parts of the documents as will be sealed or covered up for the purpose of this action do not relate to any matter in question in this action.

Fig 27: contd

Schedule 2

(6) List and number here, the documents you once had in your possession but which you no longer have when this list is served. For each document listed say when it was last in your possession and where it is now

I have had the documents numbered and listed below, but they are no longer in my possession(6).

1. The originals of the copy letters referred to in items 4,5 and 8 of Schedule 1 Part 1 all of which were last in the Defendant's possession custody or power on their respective dates when they were posted to their respective addressees.

All the documents which are or have been in my possession and which contain information about the matters in dispute in this case are listed in Schedules 1 and 2.

(7) "Plaintiff" or "Defendant"

(8) Insert date

Signed(7): (Solicitors for the Defendant)   Dated(8):

Reproduced by kind permission of the Solicitors' Law Stationery Society Ltd.

professional privilege. If different grounds are relied on for different documents they should be arranged and listed in separate bundles. It is proper to give each bundle a general description only so as not to reveal indirectly their contents (see *White Book* 24/5/3). The standard phrases often adopted in the case of legal professional privilege are very generalised (see fig 27). On this head of privilege only, the claim for privilege is treated as being in itself a sufficient description of the documents in question and therefore it is not now the practice to bundle and number legal professional privilege documents (*Derby & Co Ltd v Weldon (No 7)* [1990] 1 WLR 1156). In the case of other heads of privilege, and all other objections to production, it is advisable to be more specific (see *Alfred Crompton Amusement Machines v Commissioners of Customs and Excise* [1971] 2 All ER 843).

Parties may, if they wish, group all the 'without prejudice' letters and copy letters together and list them in Schedule 1, Part 2 (as to 'without prejudice' see p 34). In most cases there will be no advantage in doing so; all the parties to the action will have participated in the 'without prejudice' correspondence and so will already have a complete set of letters and copy letters on their correspondence files. There would be an advantage in listing 'without prejudice' correspondence in Schedule 1, Part 2 if you wanted to keep them secret from any other parties to the action who had not participated in that correspondence. In *Rush & Tompkins Ltd v Greater London Council* [1989] AC 1280 the plaintiffs negotiated a compromise with one defendant but the action was still proceeding between them and a second defendant. The plaintiffs listed their 'without prejudice' correspondence with the first defendant in Schedule 1, Part 2 and their claim of privilege from inspection by the second defendant was upheld even though the documents were no longer privileged as between themselves and the first defendant.

Should discovery be given of documents in respect of which a genuine doubt arises as to whether or not they are relevant? The most advisable course is, give discovery of every document unless it is clearly irrelevant. Group any documents of doubtful relevance together in convenient bundles, list them in Schedule 1, Part 2 and specify the claim of irrelevancy as the ground of objection to production. The solicitor's duty to the court has already been described (see p 391). The current trend is in favour of 'cards face up on the table'. Also point out to the client the adverse consequences which silence now may lead to. Will a later request for a verifying affidavit cause embarrassment? Should the opponent later ask questions about these documents, what would the client reply? If that answer was tested by an application for further discovery (see p 419) would not the client's failure to speak earlier (in what is, *ex hypothesi*, a borderline case) not seem suspicious, possibly even slippery?

As to listing a document only part of which the client objects to producing, see p 404.

Schedule 2

Here you should list documents which have been, but are not now, in the client's possession, custody or power. This often comprises little more than the original letters, written by or on behalf of the client, copies of which have already been listed in Schedule 1, Part 1. In respect of each document or class of documents listed here it is necessary to state (so far as is known) when they were last in the client's possession, custody or power, what has become of them and in whose possession they now are. The purpose is to enable the parties receiving discovery to continue their investigations elsewhere. Of course, even if they can locate the present whereabouts of the documents, they will not be able to compel production of them from a 'mere witness' (see p 386) unless the action is a personal injury action (see p 407) until the commencement of the trial (see p 488).

Documents created before litigation contemplated

No legal professional privilege attaches to documents, even though they are relevant, if they were brought into existence before the possibility of litigation ever arose (eg pre-accident maintenance reports on vehicles) or brought into existence by strangers to any possible litigation (eg medical reports made by the casualty department at which a road accident victim received treatment). If these documents later come into the possession, custody or power of a party they are discoverable even though that party obtained these documents solely for the purposes of the present litigation (*Ventouris v Mountain* [1991] 1 WLR 607, an original diary kept by a potential witness; as to inspection of this document, see p 391). An exception is made for eg a collection of documents obtained by a solicitor, the production of which would betray the trend of advice given about the litigation (*Ventouris*, above, *obiter*; *Dubai Bank Ltd v Galadari (No 7)* [1992] 1 WLR 106). Subject to that exception, a non-privileged document does not become privileged merely because it has been handed to a solicitor for the purposes of an action.

Copies of non-privileged documents

Copies of documents are generally treated as being in no better or worse position than originals. For example, copy correspondence is discoverable (in Schedule 1, Part 1) just as the originals are (in Schedule 2); expert reports, and copies thereof sent to counsel, will all be referred to in Schedule 1, Part 2. Should a different rule apply if the original document is not within the possession, custody or power of a party but a copy of it has been obtained by or prepared by his solicitors solely for the purposes of the litigation? Several recent cases have answered, firmly, no. The general rule as to copy documents applies. If an original document is not privileged a copy of it does not, without more, become privileged even if that copy was prepared by a solicitor solely for the purposes of an action. As before, an exception is allowed for copy documents the production of which would betray the trend of legal advice given about the litigation (see generally *Dubai Bank Ltd v Galadari* [1990] Ch 98, a copy document sent to the defendants' solicitors by a potential witness; *Dubai Bank Ltd v Galadari (No 7)* [1992] 1 WLR 106; *Lubrizol Corporation v Esso Petroleum Ltd* [1992] 1 WLR 957).

Continuing obligation to make discovery

In High Court cases once discovery takes place (whether automatically or by order) the party making discovery is under a continuing duty to disclose after-acquired documents (RSC Ord 24, r 1). This duty continues until the proceedings are concluded (*Vernon v Bosley (No 2)* [1997] 1 All ER 614). If further documents should later come into the client's possession, custody or power, further discovery should be made, either informally, by letter, or formally, by making and serving a supplementary list. Failure to do so may prevent reliance on those documents at the trial (see p 398). No further discovery is appropriate if the additional documents all fall clearly within legal professional privilege. If asked, any court would dispense with further discovery of these. Failure to ask the court may be considered a 'judicious irregularity' (see p 3; and see *Vernon*, above at pp 628a and 639j).

Is there a continuing obligation to keep one's discovery up to date in county court cases? The absence of any rule equivalent to RSC Ord 24, r 1 makes the position unclear. However it seems strongly arguable that CCA 1984, s 76 (see p 2) remedies the position.

Production for inspection

The time and place for inspection should be specified in the list itself (see further pp 395 and 396). Inspection comprises examination and the taking of copies (see p 384). Ideally the person carrying out the inspection should be supervised at all times. All the documents listed in Schedule 1, Part 1 should be made available. Before it takes place the party allowing inspection should check through these documents to confirm that no privileged documents have accidentally been included. Mistakes made before inspection can always be corrected, by removing the privileged document and by serving an amended list if necessary.

If privilege is claimed for part, but not the whole, of a document you should cover up ('seal up') the parts which the client does not wish to be disclosed. In such a case the list of documents previously made should have specified this document in both parts of Schedule 1. The opponent is entitled to be told in advance that only some parts of this document will be made available for inspection and that the party making the list objects to producing the rest and the grounds upon which the objection is based (see generally *G E Capital Corporate Finance Group Ltd v Bankers Trust Co* [1995] 1 WLR 172).

What happens if mistakes as to listing and/or inspection are not spotted by the party making discovery and the opponent sees and takes copies of privileged documents? The general rule is that the privilege is lost by waiver, even though the waiver was unintended. However, in some cases the court may still grant injunctions to prevent the opponent using any information so obtained 'for the purposes of pleading, evidence, cross-examination or otherwise overtly for the purposes of the action' (see *Guinness Peat Properties Ltd v Fitzroy Robinson Partnership* [1987] 1 WLR 1027).

(1) where the inspection of the document in question was obtained by fraud;

(2) where, *at the time of inspection*, it was obvious to the party inspecting the document that he had been permitted to see it only by reason of a mistake;

(3) where, at the time of inspection, the fact that a mistake had been made would have been obvious to a reasonable person who had the qualities of the person inspecting (ie, in most cases, the hypothetical reasonable solicitor).

In the first two cases equity acts to prevent one party knowingly taking advantage of an obvious mistake; his knowledge of that mistake precludes him from asserting that the privilege has been waived (*Derby & Co Ltd v Weldon (No 8)* [1991] 1 WLR 73). As to the third case, see *Pizzey v Ford Motor Co* (1993) *The Times*, 8 March and *IBM v Phoenix International* [1995] 1 All ER 413. In both of these cases the solicitor receiving inspection was surprised to be shown the document in question but inferred that the opponent's action was deliberate, not a mistake. In *Pizzey* an injunction was refused. In *IBM* an injunction was granted.

Provision of copies of documents

In the case of a document which is 'capable of being copied by photographic or similar process' a party required to produce it for inspection may also be required to supply a true copy of it (see generally RSC Ord 24, r 11A, CCR Ord 14, r 5A). The right to require copies is subject to three qualifications. Written notice must be given. The notice must contain an undertaking to pay 'reasonable charges' (High Court) or 'proper charges' (county court, see further, below). Thirdly, the notice must be served 'at or before the time when inspection takes place'. The party on whom a valid notice is served must then supply the documents requested within the next seven days.

It is important to note that the time limits imposed by these rules are very short. A party will normally need to see the documents in question before deciding which to have copied: in such a case a decision will have to be made and a notice given immediately, at the time of inspection. The other side will then have to set about preparing the copies virtually at once: in a large commercial case the number of documents to be copied may run into thousands. These time limits are subject to RSC Ord 3, r 5, or CCR Ord 13, r 4, as the case may be, enabling the court to grant extensions of time in such cases and on such terms as it thinks just.

Consider now the provisions as to the payment of reasonable or proper charges for the copies supplied. An account of the charges claimed has to be prepared and sent together with the copy documents. In the county court the maximum sum which can be claimed is fixed by CCR, Appendix A, item 4 (currently 25 pence per A5 or A4 page and 50 pence per A3 page). In both courts these charges are usually paid on receipt of the copies in question. The party who later wins judgment and costs at the trial will be able to claim a refund in his bill of costs. In fact, however, he is only entitled to claim that sum which it was reasonable to incur in photocopying charges (see further p 527). If the taxing officer decides that the winner required more copy documents than was reasonable, the unreasonable cost would be disallowed.

It would be foolish to assume that, just because you can require your opponent to supply copies, it is not worthwhile for you to attend at your opposing solicitor's office to inspect them. Unless the documents are very few in number, you will need to see them before deciding which to obtain copies of. The cost of attending for inspection may be recoverable from the opponent as part of the general costs of the action, should your client subsequently win the action. Also, when inspecting the documents you may see other things which may not be apparent from copies, eg creases, pencil marks, punctures made by pins or paper clips. The person given the task of preparing copies for you may not carry it out meticulously; words written on the reverse of some letters may be accidentally missed. Attending for inspection may provide an opportunity to negotiate in person with your opposite number.

There is no obligation to supply copies of documents which cannot be photocopied, eg video tapes or audio tapes.

Disclosure of particular documents

The four different procedures for discovery now to be considered are all applications to the court seeking discovery by way of affidavit rather than by way of list. In the first three to be described the affidavit sought is an 'affidavit of documents', ie an affidavit in which the deponent states whether any document, or any class of document, specified or described in the application is or has at any time been in his possession, custody or power and, if it is not still in his possession, custody or power, when he parted with it and what has become of it.

Assuming it discloses a document the respondent's affidavit does not have to fix a time and place for inspection. Indeed the affidavit may state that the document is not relevant or is privileged from inspection. The applicant can seek inspection by using the 'notice to produce' procedure described below.

The content of the affidavit sought in the last application to be described in this section, the rule in *Norwich Pharmacal*, is very specialised. It is a hybrid between an affidavit of documents and an 'affidavit in answer', the method by which interrogatories are usually answered (see p 417).

Disclosure by parties during the action

The procedure on this application is governed by RSC Ord 24, r 7 or CCR Ord 14, r 2 which is in similar terms. The application is made to the district judge by summons (High Court) or on notice (county court), describing the particular document or class of documents of which discovery is sought. The application must be supported by an affidavit stating the deponent's belief that the document or class of document described is relevant and is likely to be, or to have been, in the respondent's possession, custody or power. If persuaded that the applicant has made out a *prima facie* case as to relevance and likely possession, the court will order the respondent to make and serve on the applicant, within a specified number of days, an affidavit of documents as described above. Unless some other point was also decided at the time of the application the costs of the application are usually reserved (*White Book* 24/7/2; as to reserved costs see p 571).

As to inspection and the provision of copies of any documents disclosed, see pp 410 and 405 respectively.

Why would parties to an action make this application for discovery? In most cases they can more easily seek automatic discovery or voluntary discovery and obtain a list of documents from their opponents. Applications under these rules are normally made after obtaining a list, by way of further discovery (see p 418).

Disclosure by non-parties

As a general rule it is not possible to obtain orders for discovery from a 'mere witness' (see p 386). This application for discovery forms an exception to that rule which was made by SCA 1981, s 34 and CCA 1984, s 53. The sections apply only to claims in respect of personal injuries or death, but this expression has been given a wide interpretation so as to include a claim against a solicitor for failing to commence a personal injury action against a hospital in time (*Paterson v Chadwick* [1974] 1 WLR 890; contrast the interpretation given to similar words in the Limitation Act; *Ackbar v Green* [1975] QB 582, *Howe v David Brown Tractors Ltd* [1991] 4 All ER 30 and *Walkin v South Manchester HA* [1995] 1 WLR 1543).

The procedure on this application is governed by RSC Ord 24, r 7A(2) which also applies in county court cases (CCR Ord 13, r 7) with the necessary modifications (CCR Ord 1, r 6). The rule lays down a variation of the procedure under RSC Ord 24, r 7 and CCR Ord 14, r 2, namely, an application to the district judge, by summons (High Court) or on notice (county court), requiring an affidavit in support. If successful an order for an affidavit of documents will be made and this may later generate a 'notice to produce' for inspection and/or a request for the provision of copies. The only differences are in the method of serving the summons or notice of application on the non-party, and, possibly, in the order for costs.

The summons or notice of application must be served on the non-party as if it were a writ or county court summons. There are no special requirements for service in respect of any other respondents to the application.

Unless the court otherwise orders, the person against whom an application under r 7A is made is entitled to his costs of the application and the costs of complying with any order made (RSC Ord 62, r 6(9); CCR Ord 38, r 1). The order for discovery may be made conditional on the applicant's giving security for those costs (r 7A(5)). (For precedents of an application, affidavit and order see Style and Hollander, *Documentary Evidence*, 5th edn (FT Law & Tax, 1995) pp 470–472.)

Pre-action disclosure of documents

This is an application under SCA 1981, s 33 or CCA 1984, s 52, as the case may be. Like applications for disclosure against non-parties, it is limited to claims in respect of personal injuries or death (but, as to pre-action disclosure only, see further, Civil Procedure Act 1997, s 8, noted on p 307). These two applications are governed by the same rules (RSC Ord 24, r 7A; CCR Ord 13, r 7). Pre-action disclosure differs from disclosure by non-parties in two respects. First, it is not possible to obtain an order for pre-action disclosure against a 'mere witness'. The procedure is available only to a person who is 'likely to be a party' to a subsequent action in respect of personal injuries or death and even then only against any other person 'likely to be a party' to that action. The procedure enables a prospective plaintiff to find out, before commencement of a personal injury action, whether or not such an action has much chance of success. Accordingly, the expression 'likely to be' has been construed as meaning 'may' or 'may well be' dependent on the outcome of the disclosure (*Dunning v United Liverpool Hospitals Board* [1973] 1 WLR 586). However, the application should not be used merely to 'fish' for a case. A prospective plaintiff seeking pre-action disclosure is first required to state his claim in writing (*Shaw v Vauxhall Motors Ltd* [1974] 1 WLR 1035, an applicant injured at work, seeking disclosure by his employer of vehicle maintenance reports; see the *dictum* of Buckley LJ quoted on p 388: the letter suggested has since come to be known as the 'Shaw letter').

The second difference, between pre-action disclosure and disclosure by non-parties, concerns the form of application which must be used. Pre-action disclosure must be sought by originating summons in expedited form (High Court) or originating application (county court). In all other respects the procedure is the same (see above as to the evidence in support needed, the order made, costs and inspection; in the county court see also CCR Ord 13, r 7(3) which states that the affidavit in support of the application must additionally show that the county court has jurisdiction to hear the subsequent action).

In practice, pre-action disclosure of documents is not frequently encountered, except in medical injury cases. The current restriction of pre-action disclosure to claims in respect of personal injuries and death cannot be evaded by treating the documents sought as 'property' and applying for pre-action inspection of property (*Huddleston v Control Risks Information Services Ltd* [1987] 1 WLR 701 noted on p 306).

Action for discovery: the rule in *Norwich Pharmacal*

This is a form of discovery of a very special kind. It derives from the inherent jurisdiction of the court rather than from the RSC (*Norwich Pharmacal Co v Commissioners of Customs & Excise* [1974] AC 133 and see *White Book* 24/1/4). It relates to discovery of information (names and addresses of alleged wrongdoers) relevant to a future action. It can be sought against a person whether or not he is personally liable for the wrong complained of so long as he has become mixed up in the wrongdoing so as to facilitate its commission. The order the court makes need not be limited to discovery of documents: it may include discovery of facts (cf interrogatories).

For several years now *Norwich Pharmacal* orders have been a standard ingredient in virtually every *Anton Piller* order made (see further, p 300). Two recent cases indicate further judicial development of the principles (*P v T Ltd* (1997) *The Times*, 7 May, order against a former employer requiring it to disclose the identity of persons whose allegations of gross misconduct against the plaintiff led the defendant to summarily dismiss the plaintiff without pay; *Abraham v Thompson* (1997) *The Times*, 15 May, noted on p 319).

An application for a *Norwich Pharmacal* order can be sought in both the High Court and the county court by ordinary interlocutory proceedings therein (High Court summons, county court notice of application) if the applicant is also claiming other remedies against the respondent.

A High Court case in which the plaintiff seeks no other remedy against the defendant, ie an action purely for discovery, could be brought simply by originating summons, to be dealt with by a district judge.

There are two restrictions to note concerning the jurisdiction of the county court to make *Norwich Pharmacal* orders.

(1) The county court has no jurisdiction to hear an action brought solely for discovery; *Norwich Pharmacal* orders can be made in the county court only if they constitute an ancillary claim in an action otherwise within the court's jurisdiction (see CCA 1984, s 38).

(2) Parties applying for a *Norwich Pharmacal* order often wish to obtain, in the same application, an *Anton Piller* order, an order which the county court has no jurisdiction to grant (see p 300). A combined application for the two orders has to be made to the High Court.

As to the use of information obtained under a *Norwich Pharmacal* order see p 392.

Production for inspection

RSC Ord 24, r 10 and CCR Ord 14, r 4 set out the procedure by which inspection can be obtained of documents referred to in an affidavit of documents. The same procedure applies to affidavits of documents obtained by way of an application for disclosure by non-parties and pre-action disclosure (RSC Ord 24, r 7A(8)). If the affidavit discloses a document, notice can be served on the party making the affidavit requiring him to produce that document for inspection.

The person served with the notice must reply to it within four days either stating a time and place for inspection (within the next seven days after reply) or stating the grounds upon which he objects to producing the document. If he fails to reply, or fixes a time or place for inspection which is unreasonable, or if in the opinion of the court his objection to production is not justified, the court can make an order for its production (RSC Ord 24, r 11(1); CCR Ord 14, r 5(1)). *Semble* a party seeking an order for production for inspection should first ensure that the affidavit of documents is or has already been filed in court (see RSC Ord 41, r 9; CCR Ord 20, r 10).

RSC Ord 24, rr 10 and 11(1) and CCR Ord 14, rr 4 and 5(1) apply to documents referred to in any affidavit, pleading, or witness statement; the rules are not limited to affidavits of documents. The exercise of this power in respect of eg affidavits in support of an interlocutory application, might in some circumstances be justifiable on the basis that the reference to the document renders prior discovery of it unnecessary: important examples here are the affidavits filed in respect of *Mareva* or *Anton Piller* applications, applications made many months before discovery by list is likely to take place. In some circumstances it might be justifiable as a way of giving other parties the same advantage they would have received if the document referred to had been fully set out in the pleading or affidavit. It enables the other parties to check for themselves whether the reference to the document was full enough to be fair and whether any inference or conclusion drawn by the reference was justifiable. It follows that, in such cases, the court has power to order production even if the document in question is not in the possession, custody or power of the respondent (*Rafidain Bank v Agom Universal Sugar Trading Co Ltd* [1987] 1 WLR 1606). There must, however, be a direct allusion to the document (*Dubai Bank Ltd v Galadari (No 2)* [1990] 1 WLR 731).

Under RSC Ord 24, r 11(2) and CCR Ord 14, r 5(2) an order for production for inspection can be made in respect of any document even if it has never been discovered or referred to in a pleading, affidavit, or witness statement. This should be regarded as a residuary power, held in reserve for use in the most exceptional cases only. It is limited to documents which are within the respondent's possession, custody or power (cf *Black & Decker Inc v Flymo Ltd* [1991] 1 WLR 753; the actual decision in that case, concerning documents referred to in a witness statement, has been subsequently overtaken by an amendment to RSC Ord 24, r 10 to cover witness statements).

Provision of copies

RSC Ord 24, s 11A and CCR Ord 14, r 5A (noted on p 405) state that a notice requiring copies of documents to be supplied can be served by 'Any party who is entitled to inspect any documents under any provision of this Order [ie RSC Ord 24 or CCR Ord 14, as the case may be] or any order made thereunder.' Save, as mentioned below, the right to require copies therefore applies to any document which is capable of being copied by photographic or similar process and which is the subject of an order for production or for which a time and place for inspection have been fixed in response to a notice to produce. The exceptions are county court applications for disclosure by non-parties and pre-action disclosure; these do not relate to any provision of 'this order' ie CCR Ord 14.

Interrogatories

The High Court rules on interrogatories are set out in RSC Ord 26. These rules are also applicable in all county court cases except small claims which stand referred to arbitration (CCR Ord 14, r 11 and as to small claims see p 279; as to a restriction on interrogatories in certain actions for libel and slander see RSC Ord 82, r 6).

Interrogatories without order

Any party may serve interrogatories (as described below) on any other party, requiring them to be answered within a specified period of time, not being less than twenty-eight days from the date of service. There is no time limit on the right so to serve interrogatories. Whenever possible they should be served at or before the directions stage; if not served until later there may be penalties in costs if court applications then follow.

Often, however, the interrogatories will arise from information obtained only after the directions stage, eg from the receipt of witness statements where these have been ordered to be exchanged.

The party on whom the interrogatories are served must then either (1) within the time period specified answer the interrogatories, such answer being on affidavit or, (2) within fourteen days of service, apply to the court for the interrogatories to be varied or withdrawn. On such an application the court can make such order as it thinks fit including an order that the party who served the interrogatories must not serve further interrogatories without order.

If the party served with interrogatories fails to apply to the court and fails to answer the interrogatories the party who served them can apply for judgment in default. The court may at that stage dismiss the action or order that the defence be struck out and judgment be entered accordingly, or indeed may take no action if eg the interrogatories have already been answered or are now shown to be unnecessary or unfair, or if the information sought is instead supplied by other means (see *Maxiplus Ltd v Lunn* (1992) *The Times*, 27 February, *White Book* 26/6/1 and 26/6/4).

Interrogatories without order may be served on a party not more than twice. (Presumably, if three defendants wish to serve interrogatories on one plaintiff, they must either combine their requests or race against each other.) In calculating the number of times interrogatories are served, no account is taken of interrogatories required to be answered pursuant to an order (including for this purpose an order made following an application to vary or withdraw the interrogatories). Interrogatories without order cannot be validly served on the Crown.

Ordered interrogatories

An application for leave to serve interrogatories can be made in any case; eg on a third or subsequent occasion, or against the Crown. A copy of the proposed interrogatories must be served with the summons or notice by which the application is made. In deciding whether to give leave the court must take into account any offer to supply the information by other means, eg giving particulars, making admissions or producing documents. Ordered interrogatories do not use up the number of times interrogatories without order may be served (twice).

Drafting interrogatories

The questions asked

The interrogatories served must relate to a 'matter in question' between the parties and must be necessary either—(*a*) for disposing fairly of the cause or matter, or (*b*) for saving costs. As previously noted the expression 'relating to any matter in question' is wide enough to include matters which are only indirectly relevant (see p 384). However, the rules specifically outlaw any questions which relate merely to the evidence the recipient is intending to call or merely as to the credit of potential witnesses (see p 388). Also the questions must be couched in plain language and must be capable of being answered by the recipient (see p 389).

A rich seam of information and guidance as to drafting interrogatories is to be found in *Det Danske Hedeselskabet v KDM International* [1994] 2 Lloyd's Rep 534 (specifically approved by the Court of Appeal in *Hall v Selvaco Ltd* (1996) *The Times*, 27 March).

> Oppressive interrogatories will be strongly discouraged and attempts to interrogate at a late stage before the trial will be unlikely to receive judicial support unless clearly justified. Suitable times to interrogate (if at all) will probably be after discovery and after exchange of witness statements.
>
> There are ... some very specific yardsticks which it is worth bearing in mind:
>
> First, unless the answers are essential for the preparation of the requesting party's case for trial and cannot reasonably be expected to emerge from requests for further and better particulars and further discovery or witness statements, interrogatories will not normally be ordered. For this reason the service of interrogatories before witness statements have been exchanged will almost always be premature.
>
> Secondly, information which is relevant to matters in issue only in the sense that it may lead to further inquiry or that questions about it could be asked in cross-examination at the trial will not be essential information for the purposes of the first consideration.
>
> Thirdly, requests for information which, although it may be relevant to matters in issue, can be provided only by means of detailed research or investigation which the party interrogated would not otherwise carry out for the purpose of preparing for trial will hardly ever qualify as being necessary either for disposing fairly of the cause or matter or for saving costs.
>
> Fourthly, hypothetical questions should not normally be asked.
>
> Fifthly, requests for information ascertainable by cross-examination at the trial are inappropriate unless the party questioning can establish that it is essential for the proper preparation of his case that such information is made available to him before trial, in the sense that if the matter is left until cross-examination at the trial that party will, or probably will be irremediably prejudiced in his conduct of the trial or the trial may be unduly interrupted or otherwise disorganised by the late emergence of the information (*per* Colman J).

To this excellent advice we would suggest some tactical do's and don'ts to consider when deciding what questions to ask.

Do ask questions which will reveal details which

* your opponents are attempting to conceal by, eg the use of vague words in the statements;
* you can disprove later (ie tangle them up in their webs of deceit).

Don't ask questions which

* would help your opponents to embellish or improve their story;
* would be better saved for use in a surprise attack when cross-examining (eg questions such as 'if that was the case, why didn't you ...?').

Interrogatories are usually drafted as questions in the form of an inquiry (ie ending with a question mark). However, on occasions a question in the form of a demand may be more convenient. By way of example, consider the interrogatories administered by the defendants in *McKenna v Cammell Laird Ship Repairers Ltd* (1989) *The Times*, 11 May, a county court personal injury action. Some of the interrogatories served in that case sought information about other claims for compensation which the plaintiff may have made.

> 6. Has the plaintiff made a claim against any other person in respect of industrial deafness?
> 7. If the answer to 6. is 'yes', what was the result of that claim? In particular has the plaintiff received any compensation from such person and, if so, when and in what sum?

Question 7 could also have been phrased as follows:

> 7. If the answer to 6. is 'yes', supply details of each claim made including in particular the dates in question and the amounts of any compensation received by the plaintiff as a result.

Questions to avoid are those which are irrelevant, or vague, fishing, prolix (ie unduly long-winded) or otherwise oppressive (ie unfair).

Formal requirements

A note at the end of the interrogatories must specify three things:

(1) A period of time (not being less than twenty-eight days from the date of service) within which the interrogatories are to be answered, must be specified.

(2) Where the party to be interrogated is a company ('body corporate or unincorporate which is empowered by law to sue or be sued whether in its own name or in the name of an officer or other person') the interrogatories must specify the officer or member 'on whom the interrogatories are to be served'. (*Query*: interrogatories are always served on parties; should the words just quoted be replaced by the words 'by whom the interrogatories are to be answered'?) In the case of companies, usually the name of the company secretary will be given. He is bound to make all reasonable inquiries, including if appropriate, inquiries of past officers of the company, so as to reveal what is known to the company; in many cases it will be convenient to set out in the affidavit, information as to the inquiries made (*Stanfield Properties Ltd v National Westminster Bank plc* [1983] 1 WLR 568).

(3) Where the interrogatories are to be served on two or more parties, or are required to be answered by an agent or servant of a party, the interrogatories must specify which questions must be answered by each party or (as the case may be) which must be answered by an agent or servant, and in that instance must also specify which agent or servant. Although, if necessary, orders can be made

[continued on p 417]

Table 6: Applications for discovery and interrogatories: procedure

RSC and CCR provision	How to apply	Evidence in support	Method by which made	How to obtain copies
1 Application for discovery by list (RSC Ord 24, r 3; CCR Ord 14, r 1)	To district judge by summons (High Court) or on notice (county court)	Show general discovery necessary, eg list of documents already received is obviously incomplete (an application for a further and better list)	List of documents (perhaps verified by affidavit)	When inspecting (see List) and/or from opponent
2 Application for disclosure of particular documents (RSC Ord 24, r 7; CCR Ord 14, r 2) between litigants in any action, usually as further discovery after exchange of lists	To district judge by summons (High Court) or on notice (county court)	Affidavit (1) describing the document or class and (2) stating why deponent believes it is relevant and is likely to be in respondent's possession	Affidavit of documents	When inspecting (see Notices to Produce) and/or from respondent
3 Disclosure by non-parties (RSC Ord 24, r 7A; CCR Ord 13, r 7): limited to personal injury or death claims	To district judge by summons (High Court) or on notice (county court) served on non-party as if it was an originating process	Affidavit, as for **2**	As for **2**	*High Court* As for **2** *County court* When inspecting (see Notices to Produce). No right to require copies from respondent

Table 6: contd

RSC and CCR provision	How to apply	Evidence in support	Method by which made	How to obtain copies
4 Pre-action disclosure (RSC Ord 24, r 7A(1); CCR Ord 13, r 7): limited to applications between likely parties to a personal injury or death claim	To district judge by originating summons in expedited form (High Court) or originating application (county court)	Affidavit, as for 2 and (3) stating the grounds upon which it is alleged that the parties are likely to be parties to subsequent proceedings in which a personal injuries or death claim is likely to be made and (4) in the county court only, showing that the court has jurisdiction in the subsequent proceedings	As for **2**	As for **3**
5 Action for discovery (rule in *Norwich Pharmacal*) limited to application *for* discovery of the identity of alleged wrongdoers *against* persons who facilitated the wrongdoing	*High Court* Originating summons if no other remedy claimed. Otherwise writ plus summons to district judge *County court* Not applicable unless other remedies claimed against respondent; not appropriate if applicant also seeks *Anton Piller* order	Affidavit describing the wrongdoing, how it was facilitated by the respondent and stating why respondent is likely to know the wrongdoer's identity	Affidavit stating the relevant names and addresses to the best of respondent's knowledge and exhibiting any relevant documents	Not applicable
6 Ordered inter-rogatories (RSC Ord 26, r 4; CCR Ord 14, r 11): where no right to serve without order	To district judge by summons (High Court) on notice (county court) plus copy of proposed questions	Show that the proposed questions are relevant, clearly worded and fair	Affidavit in answer	Not applicable

against an agent or servant, ideally, that person should first be given an opportunity to be heard (*Harrington v Polytechnic of North London* [1984] 1 WLR 1293, *Norwich Pharmacal* orders against fourteen named lecturers requiring them to make affidavits stating, where known, the identity of persons shown in certain photographs, such persons having allegedly taken part in an unlawful picket).

Ideal time for service of interrogatories

Generally speaking, interrogatories should not be served before the exchange of witness statements and experts' reports has taken place.

> Interrogatories should not be regarded as a source of ammunition to be routinely discharged as part of an interlocutory bombardment preceding the main battle. The interrogator has to be able to show that his interrogatories, if answered when served, would serve a clear litigious purpose by saving costs or promoting the fair and efficient conduct of the action (*Hall v Selvaco Ltd* (1996) *The Times*, 27 March, *per* Sir Thomas Bingham, Master of the Rolls).

An example of circumstances in which early service of interrogatories does serve a clear litigious purpose is provided by *UCB Bank plc v Halifax (SW) Ltd* (1996) *The Times*, 15 July (questions as to certain assumptions and other matters which the defendant's valuer had in mind when preparing his valuation evidence).

The affidavit in answer

Unless the court otherwise orders, the interrogatories must first be answered on affidavit. There is no prescribed form of affidavit. If the person to be interrogated claims that answering any interrogatory would invade his privilege or would be injurious to the public interest he must make the objection in his affidavit in answer.

If the person to be interrogated answers insufficiently, or wrongly claims privilege, the district judge may order him to make a further answer either by affidavit or on oral examination.

In the case of interrogatories served without order, there is an alternative. The party who served the interrogatories may serve a request for further and better particulars of the answer given. Presumably any such particulars supplied must also be by affidavit but this is not expressly stated in the rules. The rules do, however, state that a request shall not be treated as service of further interrogatories so as to use up the number of times interrogatories without order can be served.

An answer is insufficient if it is inconclusive, ambiguous or devious. 'In considering whether a further answer should be ordered, the question to be decided is whether the answer is sufficient, and not whether it is true' (*White Book* 26/5/3). A claim of privilege is normally conclusive unless it can be shown to be clearly bad (*White Book* 26/5/3).

Further discovery and inspection

What can you do if you suspect that your opponent will not, or has not, made complete discovery, or is objecting to produce for inspection documents you have a right to inspect? The first step will usually be to raise this matter in correspondence as soon as possible. If that does not work, there are four procedures to consider.

Applying for a verifying affidavit

The procedure concerning verifying affidavits is summarised on p 397. Its value to you is as a threat to your opponent should he eg fail to discover some relevant documents, or make unjustified claims of privilege. The affidavit must be made by the opponent in person. False oaths or affirmations are punishable as perjury and as contempts of court.

In the High Court, if discovery takes place automatically (see p 394) before the directions stage (see p 452) you should request a verifying affidavit as a preliminary step to making any of the other applications here listed. In other cases, eg county court cases, verifying affidavits are compulsory only if ordered. If you also require an order for a list, a combined order for a list verified by affidavit will at least concentrate the opponent's mind on the need to be comprehensive (see p 402). However, if you have already received a list which you can attack in other ways you should do so; in this instance, time may not permit a preliminary order for a verifying affidavit.

Applying for a further and better list

This is a particular example of further discovery obtained by way of the procedure under RSC Ord 24, r 3 or CCR Ord 14, r 1 described on p 397. It is a much stronger attack on your opponent since it may cause him to incur a costs penalty as well as a loss of face. However, orders for further and better lists are not frequently granted. To obtain one it is necessary to demonstrate that the first list received was obviously incomplete. Such incompleteness can be demonstrated only from the following matters (*White Book* 24/3/5):
   (1) from the list itself (eg it omits a schedule);
   (2) from the documents referred to in the list (eg a party discloses a letter which begins 'Further to your letter of 1 March' but the letter of 1 March is not disclosed);
   (3) from admissions made by the party making discovery (whether in his pleading or otherwise);

(4) from other documents showing that the party making the list had misconceived his obligation to make full discovery where it is likely that, had he conceived his obligation correctly, further documents would have been disclosed.

If the applicant cannot by these methods show that the earlier list was incomplete, but nevertheless has reasonable grounds for believing that his opponent does have some further document, the proper application is for an order under the rules next mentioned.

Order for disclosure under RSC Ord 24, r 7 or CCR Ord 14, r 2

The procedure on this application is summarised on p 407. An application under these rules is the method of obtaining further discovery which is most commonly used in practice. It is not necessary to show more than a *prima facie* case for saying that some other document or class of documents is likely to be relevant and likely to be in the respondent's possession. The courts are less willing today than they once were to treat the respondent's discovery as the final word on the matter (see pp 391–392).

Challenging objections to production

Your opponent may have given discovery of a document but, either at the same time or later, may have objected to producing it for your inspection. Objections to production which are commonly made are described earlier in this chapter. For present purposes they may be summarised as cases where the respondent claims that the document is privileged (see p 384) or subject to public interest immunity (see p 385) or confidential and of minimal value to the applicant (see p 385). The party who received discovery can challenge these objections by seeking an order for inspection under RSC Ord 24, r 11 or CCR Ord 14, r 5 (see p 410). The court also has power to order production of the document to the court for it to inspect privately for the purpose of deciding whether the claim or objection is valid (RSC Ord 24, r 12; CCR Ord 14, r 6). Unhappily for the applicant, a claim of privilege is normally upheld if the documents are clearly described and the claim appears soundly based (*White Book* 24/13/2). Claims of public interest immunity and irrelevancy are easier to attack if the applicant can make out a strong case for believing that the document is important to him (*Air Canada v Secretary of State for Trade* [1983] 2 AC 394) it being the court's job to determine whether the immunity applies.

Default in making discovery or answering interrogatories

If a party fails to comply with any requirement to make discovery, produce documents, supply copy documents or answer interrogatories, the court may make such order as it thinks just, including dismissing the action or striking out the defence and giving judgment as the case may be (RSC Ord 24, rr 11A, 16; CCR Ord 14, rr 5A, 10). This power is designed to secure compliance rather than to punish (*Husband v Drummond* [1975] 1 WLR 603). Ultimately the court will make an 'unless order', ie that the action be terminated against the party in default unless he complies with his obligation within a fixed time limit (as to which see p 123).

The destruction of discoverable documents justifies the immediate striking out of a claim or defence if the destruction has rendered a fair trial impossible or if the destruction was done deliberately and contumaciously (*White Book* 24/16/1, and see further cases cited in the *Green Book* commentary to CCR Ord 14, r 10).

In addition to the power mentioned above, the court may punish for contempt any party who disobeys an order of the court relating to discovery or production of documents or interrogatories which has been served upon him or upon his solicitor. Failure to supply copy documents would not, by itself, amount to a contempt of court.

Any order made under RSC Ords 24 and 26 and CCR Ord 14 may subsequently be revoked or varied on sufficient cause being shown (RSC Ord 24, r 17; Ord 26, r 8; CCR Ord 14, r 12).

Chapter 19

Evidence

The law of evidence specifies which party must prove the facts in issue, the types of evidence admissible to prove them and the way in which that evidence may be adduced.

Which facts are in issue depends partly on the substantive law and partly on the state of the pleadings (ie some of them may have been admitted). Generally speaking the burden of proof rests on the party who asserts the fact, ie 'he who alleges must prove'. In a civil case, therefore, the burden of proof is usually on the plaintiff. There is at least one important exception: where pursuant to the Civil Evidence Act 1968, s 11, the plaintiff relies on the defendant's conviction by a criminal court (see p 150).

Identifying the party upon whom the burden of proof lies assists the parties in preparing their evidence for trial and may affect the question, which party has 'the right to begin' (see p 510). However, only very exceptionally are cases determined according to the burden of proof. Judges should make findings of fact in relation to matters before them, if they can. From these facts they should consider what inferences it is appropriate to draw. It is only in an exceptional case (eg where the facts proved are so meagre, or do not cover adequately all the alternative possibilities and no adjournment is appropriate) that the judge should decide on the basis that the burden of proof has not been discharged (see *Morris v London Iron and Steel Co Ltd* [1988] QB 493 and the cases cited therein). Deciding cases by reference to the burden of proof has been described as 'very often the last refuge of the "don't knows"' (Staughton LJ in *De Bry v Fitzgerald* [1990] 1 WLR 552).

The standard of proof in civil cases is said to be 'on the balance of probabilities'. However, the balance referred to is not fixed in an arithmetical way. The level of probability which has to be shown varies in proportion to the importance of the subject-matter in dispute:

> Perhaps we should recognise that our time-honoured phrase is not a happy one to express a concept which, though we all understand it, is very elusive when it comes to definition. In the criminal law the burden of proof is usually expressed in the formula 'the prosecution must satisfy you so that you are sure that the accused is guilty'. The civil burden might be formulated on analogous lines, 'the plaintiff (or the party on whom the burden rests) must satisfy the

court that it is reasonably safe in all the circumstances of the case to act on the evidence before the court, bearing in mind the consequences which will follow' (*per* Ormrod LJ in *Re JS (a minor)* [1981] Fam 22).

There are three types of evidence: oral evidence, documentary evidence (ie the production of documents), and real evidence (ie the production of physical objects for the inspection of the court). Procedural rules as to each of these are considered below. Next come the procedural rules on hearsay evidence, evidence by affidavit and evidence by deposition.

Oral evidence

The basic rule is that witnesses must attend the trial and give oral evidence on oath from the witness box (RSC Ord 38, r 1; CCR Ord 20, r 4). The witness will give evidence in chief and the opponent will then have the opportunity to cross-examine. There can then be re-examination of the witness by the advocate who called him. Although this remains the basic rule its operation is now substantially affected by the pre-trial procedures which have to be followed. The trend towards greater openness in litigation has resulted in a major re-organisation of the way in which evidence at civil trials has to be prepared and presented. In all cases, High Court and county court, the parties are required to give early disclosure of the evidence they are intending to rely upon (see p 426). A witness statement which has previously been disclosed will often replace some or all of that witness's examination in chief (for exceptions, see below). In many cases, directions are made requiring parties to file in court any experts' reports they have exchanged so enabling the trial judge to read them in advance of the trial (contrast witness statements of non-experts, as to which see *White Book* 72/A17 para 14.7).

Early disclosure of experts' reports

The significance of expert evidence lies in the admissibility of the opinions of the expert on matters falling within his expertise. (Opinion evidence is also admissible in other circumstances, eg the opinion of a criminal court as to the guilt of a person convicted of a crime, see p 150; opinion evidence by a non-expert given as a way of conveying relevant facts such as identity, speed of vehicles, and drunkenness.) Whether a witness is qualified to express expert opinion is not normally a practical problem in civil cases. Each party will retain the most experienced and illustrious expert they can afford.

The relevant rules as to early disclosure of experts' reports are RSC Ord 38, rr 36–44 all of which are either reproduced or incorporated into the county court rules by CCR Ord 20, rr 27, 28, with the necessary modifications (CCR Ord 1, r 6).

The rules of court provide that, subject to certain exceptions, no expert evidence may be adduced at the trial unless the party seeking to adduce it has previously applied to the court to determine whether and to what extent he should be ordered to give his opponents early disclosure of the substance of his expert's evidence and has complied with any direction given. The exceptions include actions in which automatic directions are given (see p 452), or where the trial court grants leave (*Cable v Dallaturca* (1977) 121 SJ 705), or where the other side consent to the admission of the evidence and, in the county court, cases in which no defence or answer has been filed and small claims which are sent for arbitration rather than trial (see p 279).

Where an application under the expert evidence rules is necessary it will normally be made at the directions stage. In a sense the applicant is applying for an order against himself. Bear in mind, however, that the other parties also have to apply in respect of their experts and disclosure is normally ordered on a mutual basis. Nothing in the rules requires the disclosure of evidence which it is not proposed to use at the trial. Since this is so, the rules do not injuriously affect any party's legal professional privilege in those reports which were obtained with a view to litigation.

Example

P obtains a medical report which is unfavourable to his case. Subsequently P obtains another report from another doctor. The second report is favourable to P's case. P is entitled to go to trial relying only upon the evidence of the second doctor and giving early disclosure only of the second report. P need make no specific mention of the earlier unfavourable report (as to discovery of privileged documents see p 402).

In effect the rules provide that if a party intends to waive his privilege by calling the expert at the trial he may be required to waive his privilege earlier so that the evidence will not take his opponent by surprise at the trial.

Presumption in favour of early disclosure

The relevant rules of court provide that, where any application is made concerning early disclosure of experts' reports, the court must order early disclosure 'unless the Court considers that there are special reasons for not doing so' (RSC Ord 38, r 37; CCR Ord 20, r 28). If these special reasons apply only to part of an expert's evidence the court may still order early disclosure of the remainder of that evidence (RSC Ord 38, r 39; CCR Ord 20, r 28).

What could amount to special reasons justifying non-disclosure? Current practice is now strongly in favour of 'openness', of 'cards on the table' litigation. Examples of special reasons recognised in the past (where fraud is pleaded or where there is a real risk of dishonest trimming of evidence) are not regarded as sufficiently convincing today (*Khan v Armaguard Ltd* [1994] 1 WLR 1204). It is possible that the court's discretion not to order disclosure is a residual discretion only, preserved by the rule makers out of caution and unlikely ever to be exercised.

RSC Ord 38, r 37 makes special provision for one case. A plaintiff in an action for personal injuries is not required to disclose a further medical report if he proposes to rely at the trial only upon the report previously provided by him at the time of serving his statement of claim (see p 155). Of course, in such a case, early disclosure by the plaintiff of other, non-medical, expert evidence would still be appropriate.

Steps following the order

If an order for early disclosure is made, the court will specify a time by which 'the substance of the (expert's) evidence ... in the form of a written report or reports' should be disclosed to the other parties. Usually the same time limit will be given in orders for disclosure affecting other parties' experts, ie the mutual disclosure will take place simultaneously. This is intended to prevent one side enjoying the unfair advantage of seeing their opponent's reports before they disclose their own. However, in an exceptional case, an order for sequential disclosure can be made if the circumstances so require (*Kirkup v British Rail Engineering Ltd* [1983] 1 WLR 1165: negligence claim against employers alleging deafness caused by the plaintiff's exposure to excessive noise during the course of his employment since 1952; expert engineering evidence necessary ranging over many years and many factory sites; plaintiff ordered to disclose his report first, the defendants to disclose theirs within forty-two days thereafter).

Plaintiffs in personal injury actions usually 'go first', ie serve a copy of their medical report together with their pleading (see further p 155). If, at the directions stage, they disclose a further medical report they must also serve an up-to-date 'statement of special damages claimed' (see p 467).

The 'substance' of the expert's evidence has been held to include all the opinions the expert has expressed on the matters within his expertise. Indeed, to disclose less may be self-defeating since the experts' opinions carry weight only to the extent that they are seen to be independent and impartial. In *Whitehouse v Jordan* [1981] 1 WLR 246 solicitors and counsel were criticised for disclosing a medical report from which the embarrassing passages had been edited out. In *Kenning v Eve Construction Ltd* [1989] 1 WLR 1189 a consulting engineer wrote a report which was favourable to the case of the parties instructing him but added a covering letter drawing attention to two further points (not at that stage pleaded by the opponents) which were unfavourable: it was held that, if reliance was placed upon this expert, both the report and the letter should be disclosed.

In the past many practitioners have invited experts to edit their reports themselves on the basis that it is necessary to disclose only the evidence the expert intends to give, not all the evidence the expert might give. This policy must now be substantially reviewed and in many cases abandoned following the very clear guidance given by Cresswell J as to the duties and responsibilities of expert witnesses in civil cases. In particular the expert should not omit to consider material facts which could detract from his concluded opinion. In cases where the expert could not assert that his report contains the truth, the whole truth and nothing but the truth without some qualification, that qualification must be stated in the report (see generally *The Ikarian Reefer* [1993] 2 Lloyd's Rep 68).

A doctor preparing a report will usually take a 'history' from the person examined ie in accident cases, details of the accident, in all cases, a list of symptoms and dates when they first appeared. The history taken is often set out in the report. The expert opinions expressed are not of much value except in relation to it. In the multi-party litigation concerning the drugs 'Ativan' and 'Valium', some of the medical reports disclosed did not set out the history relied on but referred instead (without details) to a history prepared by the plaintiffs' solicitors. It was held that, if insufficient detail was included in or sent with the report, the defence were entitled to request 'details of the full relevant medical history of the plaintiff relied on by the plaintiff's doctor for the purpose of preparing the report served with the [pleading] in so far as that history is derived from a written document supplied to that doctor which has not already been disclosed'; the plaintiff is not obliged to disclose the actual document submitted to the doctor, although that will usually be the most suitable course to take (*B v John Wyeth and Brother Ltd* [1992] 1 WLR 168; contrast the position concerning documents referred to in affidavits and witness statements as to which see p 410 and RSC Ord 24, r 10 and CCR Ord 14, r 4; those rules have recently been extended to cover witness statements but still do not cover experts' reports).

There are certain formality requirements and other procedural rules which apply to experts' reports if they are disclosed under automatic directions (see further p 428).

Use of reports at trial

The following points apply in both High Court and county court cases (RSC Ord 38, rr 41, 42, 43; CCR Ord 20, r 28).

If either party calls as a witness an expert whose report has previously been disclosed pursuant to a direction of the court, that report may be 'put in evidence' (ie 'taken as read') at the commencement of the expert's examination in chief.

What should happen if at, or just before, the start of a trial, one party who had not previously disclosed an expert's report now does so and seeks leave to call that expert? Would such leave be granted? Leave has been refused in two cases (*Thake v Maurice* [1986] 2 WLR 337; *Associated Newspapers plc v Insert Media Ltd* [1990] 1 WLR 900, a point not taken on the appeal, [1991] 1 WLR 571). However, in both of these cases the opponent was not calling, and had not prepared, any expert evidence relevant to the same issues. If, however, the opponent is intending to call relevant expert evidence, leave will often be granted subject to a suitable costs penalty. If both sides want to call an expert it is difficult to imagine a judge hearing an expert from one side only.

Practice: agreeing expert evidence

The experts most commonly employed in civil actions are medical experts. The practice of exchanging medical reports and seeking to agree them is fully discussed in Chapter 2. As there stated, a real dispute between medical experts is rare. One way of resolving the dispute is to convene a 'without prejudice' meeting in an effort to identify differences. The court has power to direct the parties to convene such a meeting; see RSC Ord 38, r 38. This power arises in all cases (it is not limited to High Court cases) and in respect of all experts (it is not limited to medical experts).

Early disclosure of evidence of non-experts

The relevant rules as to early disclosure of statements of witnesses, other than expert witnesses, are set out in RSC Ord 38, r 2A and CCR Ord 20, r 12A (county court small claims (see p 279) are expressly excluded). We call these witnesses 'non-experts'; they may also be referred to as 'factual witnesses'.

The rules just referred to provide that the court shall direct any party to serve on other parties, on such terms as the court shall think just, written statements of the oral evidence which the party intends to lead on all issues of fact, or on any specified issues of fact which are to be decided at the trial. A party who fails to comply with an order for early disclosure of witness statements will not be entitled to adduce any evidence to which the order related unless the court gives leave. The order must be made 'for the purpose of disposing fairly and expeditiously of the cause or matter and saving costs'. It is noteworthy that these two elements, fair (and expeditious) disposal and cost-saving are stated conjunctively: they are not alternative purposes as they are under various discovery rules (see p 388).

The order for early disclosure can be made 'at any stage'. However, as with expert witnesses, the ideal time will usually be at the directions stage and in the High Court, this is one of the matters which the court is required to consider at that stage whether or not the parties raise it (see p 455). Exchange of witness statements is now included in the automatic directions which govern most county court actions and most High Court personal injury actions (see pp 467 and 473).

How to draft witness statements is considered in Chapter 9 above (see p 175). When should witness statements be drafted? In most cases, given the very short time allowed for exchange (see p 467) the task cannot be left for any substantial time after the close of pleadings. Experienced litigators will apply the 'one bite of the cherry' policy and try to do as much of the work as they can when first interviewing the witnesses. This practice is especially important in the case of plaintiffs so as to minimise the costs threat which an early payment into court can impose (see p 329).

Are there any circumstances in which early disclosure might be inappropriate? Given the current policy in favour of 'cards on the table litigation', already discussed in relation to disclosure of experts' reports (see p 423), the answer must be very few. However, consider, for example, cases where such disclosure would be oppressive, either as to expense, or because there is cause for believing that the identity of witnesses should not be revealed. In some cases a party may be unable to obtain a written statement from an intended witness, eg because that witness is presently untraceable or is unwilling to co-operate with the party intending to call him. In cases such as these the court may make a direction that the party intending to call that witness should provide the other party with the name of the witness and (unless the court otherwise orders) a statement of the nature of the evidence intended to be adduced from that witness (RSC Ord 38, r 2A(5); CCR Ord 20, r 12A(5)). In deciding whether (and how) to exercise its powers, the court will take into account:

(a) the extent to which the facts are in dispute or have been admitted;
(b) the extent to which the issues of fact are defined by the pleadings;
(c) the extent to which information has been or is likely to be provided by further and better particulars, answers to interrogatories or otherwise (RSC Ord 38, r 2A(1); CCR Ord 20, r 12A(1)).

Steps following the order

If an order for early disclosure is made it should specify a time by which the witness statement should be served; possibly the same time by which expert reports should be served. The order will usually provide for mutual disclosure, ie an exchange of statements taking place simultaneously rather than in sequence (RSC Ord 38, r 2A(4)(c); CCR Ord 20, r 12A(4)(c)). However, a direction is also made sometimes permitting the service of supplementary statements by a later date if, on seeing the opposing statements, the parties wish to call additional witnesses or raise additional points. It is not necessary or desirable to serve supplementary statements merely to contradict the opponent's evidence; evidence to this effect is better given orally.

In an exceptional case the court may direct that witness statements are to be served sequentially rather than simultaneously. For example, a plaintiff may be ordered to reveal his evidence first if he has pleaded his case in the widest possible terms, so concealing the true nature of the case he is intending to prove.

> The normal rule should be that the exchange of witness statements shall be simultaneous. This is, I think, inherent in the concept of an 'exchange' ... But if either party shows any reluctance to 'come clean', the district judge has power to order that the exchange of witness statements be wholly or partially sequential ... thereby tying the party to a particular case ... before the other party has to prepare his own witness statements. If an order for the service by all parties of witness statements within the same period of time is silent as to whether or not the service is to be simultaneous, it should be so construed, but it would be better to state this expressly (*Mercer v Chief Constable of the Lancashire Constabulary* [1991] 1 WLR 367 *per* Lord Donaldson MR).

Another example of sequential disclosure arises where a party seeks leave to serve supplementary statements in order to improve or add to the statements he has already disclosed. In *Williams v Alpha Mechanical Handling and National Power* [1996] Current Law (November) 77 Moses J allowed one party a second attempt to get his evidence in order, presumably subject to a suitable costs' penalty.

Witness statements served under a direction of the court or under an automatic direction must be dated and (usually) signed by the witness and must include a statement by him that the contents are true to the best of his knowledge and belief. Also, the statement must sufficiently identify any documents referred to therein (as to inspection of such documents, see p 410). An unsigned statement can be relied on only if some good reason exists justifying the service of an unsigned statement, which reason must be specified by letter accompanying the statement (RSC Ord 38, r 2A(4)(a), (b); CCR Ord 20, r 12A(4)(a), (b)). Curiously, these formality requirements (date, signature and certificate of belief) also apply to experts' reports if those reports are disclosed under automatic directions (RSC Ord 25, r 8(2) and CCR Ord 17, r 11(3A)).

The court order may require the parties to file in court copies of all the statements thus disclosed. The court is not likely to permit parties to amend the statements save in the most exceptional cases. The appropriate way to alter or withdraw part of the statement is for the witness himself to do it, orally, in the witness box.

Because of directions for exchange of witness statements more cases are being won or lost on paper, ie without there being any trial to which these witnesses are called. Thus the old-fashioned gladiatorial style of advocacy is becoming outmoded. Instead of waiting to hear the opponent's evidence, you can read the witness statements he discloses. Instead of waiting to puncture that evidence by cross-examination, use interrogatories (see p 411) to attack any points in those statements which appear ambiguous, evasive or devious. The current policy in favour of 'cards on the table litigation' makes it far more likely that the parties will agree a compromise. This is because, once all the cards are placed face up on the table, there is no longer much point in playing them. Usually everyone can see which side will win; the side which has most of the high cards and trumps.

Use at the trial

Assume that a full exchange of witness statements has been made but nevertheless the case proceeds to trial. What is the position if a witness who gave a statement is now put into the witness box? The statement will usually stand as the evidence in chief of that witness (see p 511). You should not let this happen to your witness too quickly. It is better to get him settled into the witness box with a few friendly questions first so that he can find his voice before the cross-examination begins.

What questions can you ask him? The rules state that the party calling the witness cannot lead any evidence from that witness the substance of which was omitted from the written statement. In other words, the witness statement must be exhaustive, must cover every point you wish to raise from that witness by way of examination in chief. To this rule there are three exceptions:

(1) Evidence as to 'new matters' which have arisen since the statement was served on the opponent.
(2) Cases in which the consent of other parties or the leave of the court is obtained.
(3) Matters which, by specific direction, are excluded from the obligation to give early disclosure.

Exception (1) permits questions asking the witness to comment upon statements which have already been made on oath by other witnesses. Exception (2) will be most frequently sought in respect of points overlooked before, or points contradicting facts previously declared in the witness statement. In our view the advocate is entitled to be allowed one or two additional questions in every case. No matter how careful you are in preparing a statement you are almost bound to want to make some finishing adjustments. However, the consent or leave, if granted, is likely to be on terms providing for an adjournment if that is necessary to enable the opponent to reconsider the position, and on terms providing for the costs of and occasioned by the adjournment.

In some cases the opposing party may wish to object to the disclosed statement claiming that it contains, eg inadmissible opinion evidence. An objection such as this is best made after the witness has been sworn and the disclosed statement has been put in evidence (*White Book* 38/2A/9 para 14.7). If the objection is first raised between the parties before trial some suitable annotation of it may be made on the copies of the witness statement prepared for use at the trial (see the practice in the Commercial Court, *White Book* 72/A17 para 14.7). An aggrieved party might also consider serving a notice to admit in respect of the admissibility dispute (as to notices to admit, see opposite).

Whether or not a statement is to stand as the evidence in chief of the witness, any other party may raise it or any part of it in the cross-examination of that witness.

An order that a witness statement should stand as evidence brings the content of the statement into the public domain. Thereafter, during the course of the trial any person (ie whether or not a party) may request the judge (orally or in writing) to direct that the witness statement in question should be certified as open to inspection. The grounds upon which the judge may refuse to make such a direction are limited. If a direction is made a certified copy of the witness statement will be prepared and held available for inspection and copying by any person, during office hours, until the end of seven days after the conclusion of the trial (RSC Ord 38, r 2A(12)–(15); CCR Ord 20, r 12A(12)–(15); and see further *Practice Direction* [1992] 1 WLR 1157).

What is the position if, after exchange of witness statements, one of those witnesses is *not* called? For example, if the plaintiff's solicitor gives the defence a witness statement of John Smith, but later fails to call Smith as a witness. Perhaps the defence was surprised that the plaintiff intended to call him and were happily awaiting the opportunity to get his evidence by way of leading questions rather than in chief. Now that the plaintiff has decided not to call him, can the defence call him? In our view, if they are able to trace him and, if necessary, summons him, they will be allowed to rely upon his evidence even though, technically, they are in breach of the rules in that they will not have given the plaintiff a witness statement in respect of him.

What is the position if they cannot trace him? Can they adduce in evidence the witness statement the plaintiff gave them? A hearsay question arises but this is easily dealt with either by giving due notice or by obtaining the leave of the court (see generally p 440). A more difficult question concerns legal professional privilege. Plainly the witness statement was obtained by the plaintiff 'with a view to litigation'. Therefore it was, at least initially, a privileged document. Is it still privileged? The answer depends upon whether John Smith is being relied upon as an expert and, if not, upon which of two conflicting cases is correct.

In the case of expert evidence the privilege is lost by disclosure; see s 2(3) of the Civil Evidence Act 1972 and RSC Ord 38, r 42.

In the case of non-expert evidence there are conflicting decisions at first instance (*Fairfield-Mabey Ltd v Shell UK Ltd* [1989] 1 All ER 576, *Youell v Bland Welch & Co Ltd (No 3)* [1991] 1 WLR 122). Although the point is by no means an easy one, it seems that the later case is the more reliable, ie once the witness statement is served any privilege previously attached to it ceases (and see further *Balkanbank v Taher* (1994) *The Times*, 19 February). In practice, this problem can be easily sidestepped by ensuring that all witnesses in respect of whom witness statements are exchanged are in fact subpoenaed to attend the trial (see further p 489).

Notice to admit

The cost of preparing witness statements and calling witnesses can sometimes be excessive. What can be done if your opponent refuses to make reasonable admissions in his pleading and therefore forces you to incur heavy expense? The rules make three provisions: first, interrogatories (see p 411). Secondly, where a summons for directions or a pre-trial review is held, the district judge may record in the order for directions any refusal to make reasonable admissions (see p 456). Thirdly, the notice to admit procedure. This is often the best solution to try, though unfortunately it is not used frequently enough in practice. Any party may, without leave, serve on his opponent a notice specifying certain facts or specifying a certain part of his case. The notice calls upon the opponent to deliver a written admission of the facts, or the part of the case, so specified within fourteen days (in the county court, seven days). Any admission so made is for the purposes of the action only, can be used only by the person serving the notice and can be amended or withdrawn if the court so allows (see generally RSC Ord 27, r 2; Ord 62, r 6(7); CCR Ord 20, r 2; although the notice can now be used to require the opponent to admit a part of the case (and not merely facts) the CCR still describe it as a 'notice to admit facts').

The sanction behind the notice is that, if the recipient does not admit the matters it specifies but they are subsequently proved at the trial, he will bear the costs of so proving them and any costs occasioned by and thrown away as a result of his failure to admit (ie his own costs relating to these facts) whatever the outcome of the action, unless the court otherwise orders. Unless the party upon whom the notice was served is legally aided, the trial court may assess the costs in question immediately (ie without taxation, see further p 523) and may order the payment of the sum assessed forthwith (RSC Ord 62, r 7(6); CCR Ord 38, r 17B). If not assessed by the trial court, they will be assessed by the taxing officer and deducted from the general costs of the action unless the party upon whom the notice was served is entitled to and requires the drawing of a bill of those costs (cf CCR Ord 38, r 19(3)).

Example

In a road accident case D has a good defence on negligence but decides also to deny that he was involved in the accident. P serves a notice to admit facts establishing that D was involved in the accident. D does not admit them. At the trial the judge finds that D was involved but was not negligent. The judge therefore dismisses P's claim with costs.

Nevertheless D must, unless the court otherwise orders, reimburse P in the costs incurred in proving the accident and will not be entitled to recover the costs he incurred in trying to disprove it. P should ask the trial court to assess the costs in question immediately. Alternatively, the taxing officer may assess them, either by consent of both parties or because CCR Ord 38, r 19(3) applies.

The court should be asked to 'otherwise order' and so lift the penalty in cases where the person serving the notice is abusing the system and trying to get an advantage in costs on matters which his opponent had good grounds for not admitting (see *Lipkin Gorman v Karpnale Ltd* [1989] 1 WLR 1340, 1390 reversed on a different point [1991] 2 AC 548).

Example
  In a breach of a contract action D has good defences on both breach and measure of damages. P serves a notice requiring D to admit that she was in breach of contract. D does not admit it. At the trial the judge finds that there was a breach of contract by D but that it was a technical breach only, and also finds that all P's loss is too remote. The judge therefore awards nominal damages and orders P to pay costs (see p 518). D should consider whether to ask the judge to 'otherwise order' as to the costs of proving the breach of contract so as to prevent them being deducted from the costs she receives.

In the High Court the time limit for serving a notice to admit is not later than twenty-one days after the setting down of the action; in the county court the time limit is not later than fourteen days before the trial. In practice of course it is always desirable to serve any notice as soon as possible.

Documentary evidence

A party who intends to put in a document at the trial should seek to anticipate and deal with any questions concerning the authenticity and availability of that document. Various statutes and rules of court make provision as to both these topics. The purpose for which documents are normally adduced, as evidence of any facts stated therein, is postponed to the separate section entitled Hearsay Evidence (see p 436).

Is the document authentic?

Section 9 of the Civil Evidence Act 1995 provides that records of a business or public authority can be authenticated (ie proved genuine) by a document purporting to be a certificate signed by an officer of that business or public authority. The absence of an entry in the records of a business or public authority can be proved by an affidavit of an officer of the business or public authority to which the records belong. These provisions apply to all 'businesses' and public authorities, whether or not they or their proprietors are parties to the action in which the records are adduced. Also, s 9 provides definitions of 'business' and 'officer' (and other terms) which are very wide. However the section also gives the court an overriding power in all cases to 'direct that all or any of the above provisions of this section do not apply in relation to a particular document or record, or descriptions of documents or records' (s 9(5)).

As to evidence of bank ledgers, eg to prove the payment of a debt, see also the Bankers' Books Evidence Act 1879 which statute is summarised in the *Green Book* commentary to CCR Ord 20, r 11.

What of documents to which s 9 does not apply (eg personal letters and diaries) or in respect of which s 9 has been disapplied (see s 9(5))? Section 8 of the 1995 Act states that documents containing statements which are admissible as evidence in civil proceedings (and this includes hearsay statements nowadays) can be 'authenticated in such manner as the court may approve'. It is usual to call as a witness the person who created the document. Alternatively look for someone who eg saw it being written or who can identify the handwriting.

Is proof of authenticity required?

Does your opponent require you to prove that your document is not a forgery? Find out by serving a *notice to admit documents*. This is a notice requiring your opponent to admit, for the purposes of the action, the authenticity of the documents specified in the notice. The time limit for serving the notice is, in the High Court, within twenty-one days after setting down and, in the county court, not less than fourteen days before the trial.

A recipient who does not wish to admit the authenticity of the documents listed in the notice must give *notice of non-admission* within the next twenty-one days (in the High Court) or within the next seven days (in the county court). A party who fails to give such notice of non-admission is deemed to admit the authenticity of the documents unless the court otherwise orders (RSC Ord 27, r 5; CCR Ord 20, r 3). If a party gives notice of non-admission but the authenticity of the documents is later proved, the party who failed to admit authenticity may be penalised in costs under RSC Ord 62, rr 6, 7 or CCR Ord 38, r 17B described above.

Documents proved or purporting to be not less than twenty years old which are produced from proper custody are presumed to be authentic unless the contrary is shown (see Evidence Act 1938, s 4). In the county court this presumption is extended to all documents, whatever their age, if they appear to be genuine and no objection is taken to their admissibility (CCR Ord 20, r 11). In the High Court the corresponding provision is somewhat different. Where discovery takes place a party on whom a list of documents or affidavit of documents is served is deemed to admit the authenticity of the documents thereby discovered unless he denies their authenticity in his pleading or unless he serves notice of non-admission within twenty-one days after inspection (RSC Ord 27, r 4).

Is the document available?

You cannot prove authenticity of a document without producing it to the court or producing 'a copy of ... [it] or of the material part of it' (s 8(1) of the 1995 Act). In the case of copies it is immaterial for *this purpose* (authenticity) whether the copy produced was taken directly from the original or is a copy of a copy (s 8(2) of the 1995 Act). In the case of a good quality photocopy the number of removes there are between the copy produced and the original may be immaterial for all purposes. With other types of copy (carbon copies, handwritten copies, poor quality photocopies) the number of removes there are between the copy produced and the original may well be material on other issues—although authentic, is it accurate; repetition may lead to mistakes, omissions and distortions by the copier.

The availability of the document or a copy thereof is important whether or not authenticity is in dispute. If you want the court to look at it then first you have got to show it. If a party wishes to put in evidence a document which is in his possession, no problem of availability arises. If a party wishes to put in evidence an original document which is not in his possession he could serve a *subpoena duces tecum* on the possessor of it (see p 487). However, if the original is in the possession of his opponent it would usually be embarrassing to call the opponent as a witness. In such a case it is sufficient to serve on him a notice to produce. If at the trial the opponent does not produce the original there is no direct penalty on him, but the judge may draw an adverse inference, and the party serving the notice can then adduce secondary evidence of the document, perhaps a copy of it or oral evidence as to its contents (see generally RSC Ord 27, r 5; CCR Ord 20, r 3(4)).

> *Example*
> In a county court possession action where it is necessary to prove a notice to quit the original will have been served on the defendant and the plaintiff will have only a copy of it. He should therefore serve a 'notice to admit and produce'. The notice requires the defendant both to admit that the plaintiff's copy is a true copy and to produce the original at the trial.

In some High Court cases a notice to produce is deemed to be served. Where discovery takes place the person making discovery is deemed to be on notice to produce documents he discovered as being in his possession, custody or power (RSC Ord 27, r 4).

Practice: agreeing documents

In practice the position is much more straightforward than a reading of the rules might at first suggest. Solicitors should always do everything possible to narrow down the area of dispute and agree as much as possible. Rules made in both courts require parties to consider in advance of trial what documents they wish to place before the court at trial. One party, usually the plaintiff, is given the task of filing in court indexed and paginated bundles of the documents which either or both parties wish the court to see. These rules and the procedures to follow in preparing bundles are set out in p 492.

Real evidence

Real evidence is said to consist of 'material objects other than documents produced for inspection of the court' (Phipson, *Law of Evidence*). Obvious examples include the bringing to court of a machine which a plaintiff factory worker claims has injured him; or the production of office equipment which a plaintiff buyer claims is not of satisfactory quality. Where the object is not in the possession of the party wishing to produce it to the court he can get an order for its 'detention' or 'custody' (see p 305). Usually, however, the matter is dealt with by agreement between the parties. At the trial it will be necessary to call a witness to identify the object, which will then become an exhibit in the action. This is one of the exceptional cases in which leading questions (see p 514) can be asked during examination in chief ('Is this the machine?'). The associate, or court clerk, will then take charge of it and mark or label it (RSC Ord 35, r 11; CCA 1984, s 76).

Oral evidence and documents usually contain assertions of fact, made either expressly or impliedly, which the judge is invited to accept. Real evidence is different. Here, the judge is invited to reach conclusions on the basis of his own observations, not other people's. It is therefore possible to argue that real evidence is not limited to material objects. It includes a visit made by the judge to view, eg the scene of a road accident; recorded television pictures taken by security cameras in a bank, eg in a civil action against an alleged bank robber; or the reconstruction of an event to which an action relates, eg an industrial process, to demonstrate to the court how injuries were caused (and see generally *Cross & Tapper on Evidence*, 8th edn (Butterworths, 1995) pp 49–55).

The court can compel parties to supply facilities to enable a reconstruction to be made (*Ash v Buxted Poultry Ltd* (1989) *The Times*, 29 November, *White Book* 29/2–3/1; defendant-employer ordered to allow the plaintiff to make a video recording showing the nature of the work done by the plaintiff, in respect of which he claimed damages for personal injuries). Can the court compel a witness to take part in a reconstruction? Presumably the sanction would be committal for contempt of court for disobedience. In our view the answer to the question posed is no. A witness can be compelled only to answer questions and to state facts. The position would be different however if the witness in question was also a party to the action. In that instance the judge might draw an adverse inference from his refusal to co-operate (cf *Armory v Delamirie* (1722) 1 Stra 505).

Hearsay evidence

Hearsay evidence is evidence of an oral or written statement which was made out of court and which is relied on in court to prove the truth of the matters stated (*cf* Civil Evidence Act 1995, s 1(2) set out opposite). The layman's definition of hearsay (the repetition by one person of what another person said or wrote) is incorrect and misleading. The purpose for which the repetition is adduced is crucial. It is hearsay only if it is adduced in order to prove the truth of the matters stated.

Example

Smith, giving evidence at the trial of a road accident claim declares 'I saw the bus careering across the pavement. Some weeks later my friend Jones told me that he had been a passenger on the bus and had seen a dog run out into the road, thus causing the driver to swerve. I wrote all this down in the statement I gave to the police.'

The first sentence is clearly not hearsay. Smith is making a statement in court of facts he personally perceived (or, to be more precise, of facts he claims he personally perceived). The second sentence is hearsay on the question whether the accident was caused by a dog: Jones can give original evidence on this and so perhaps should be called to do so. However, Smith's repetition of what Jones said (or, rather, what he claims Jones said) is original evidence that Jones spoke such words. Smith claims to have personally perceived Jones speaking them. This repetition could be useful evidence if eg Jones, on being called as a witness, denies any personal knowledge of the accident. Note, in such an event, Smith's evidence is still hearsay on the question whether the accident was caused by a dog (but see further, Civil Evidence Act 1995, s 6 and p 444).

The third sentence refers to a previous written statement by Smith. It was not made in court in these proceedings and so would be hearsay if it was adduced to prove the truth of the matters it states. (In any case, since Smith is giving evidence, his previous statement is superfluous unless, eg he is allowed to use it to 'refresh his memory'; but see further Civil Evidence Act 1995, s 6 and p 444).

The law relating to hearsay in most civil cases is governed by the Civil Evidence Acts of 1968 and 1972 or the Civil Evidence Act of 1995 and by rules of court made thereunder, namely RSC Ord 38, rr 20–34, and CCR Ord 20, rr 14–26. This edition of this book covers only the new law. All its relevant sections and rules of court are now in force but they do *not* apply to proceedings:

(a) in which directions have been given, or orders have been made, as to the evidence to be given at the trial or hearing, or

(b) where the trial has begun

before 31 January 1997.

For the statutes and rules of court which do apply to the excepted cases reference may be made to earlier editions of this book.

The Civil Evidence Act 1995 sets out a new law relating to hearsay which is most clearly explained without making constant comparisons and contrasts with the old law. New readers should therefore skip the rest of this paragraph which is aimed at readers who are familiar with the old law. Our intention here is to list just three points which should minimise the number of questions beginning 'But what about ...' which such readers might otherwise ask as they read through the new law.

(1) The rule against hearsay is abolished. If they want to, litigants can adduce hearsay evidence whether oral or written, whether first degree, second degree or worse. There are notice requirements for them to obey but these are not in substance any different from the notice requirements relating to any other evidence being adduced, eg the requirements concerning the exchange of witness statements and experts' reports.

(2) Admissions and confessions, which used to form an exceptional case exempt from the old notice requirements, are not exempted from the new notice requirements. The current 'cards on the table' philosophy applies to all evidence, whether or not hearsay and whether or not admissions or confessions.

(3) Evidence which is inadmissible for some other reason is not now made admissible just because it is adduced in a hearsay form. Hearsay evidence, just like other evidence may be attacked as being, eg, irrelevant (ie non-probative) whether factually or legally (eg inadmissible opinion evidence) or as being evidence adduced from a source which is not competent to give evidence (eg persons of very young age or persons who are mentally defective).

Text of the Civil Evidence Act 1995 sections 1 to 4

1. Admissibility of hearsay evidence

(1) In civil proceedings evidence shall not be excluded on the ground that it is hearsay.

(2) In this Act—

(a) 'hearsay' means a statement made otherwise than by a person while giving oral evidence in the proceedings which is tendered as evidence of the matters stated; and

(b) references to hearsay include hearsay of whatever degree.

(3) Nothing in this Act affects the admissibility of evidence admissible apart from this section.

(4) The provisions of sections 2 to 6 (safeguards and supplementary provisions relating to hearsay evidence) do not apply in relation to hearsay evidence admissible apart form this section, notwithstanding that it may also be admissible by virtue of this section.

2. Notice of proposal to adduce hearsay evidence

(1) A party proposing to adduce hearsay evidence in civil proceedings shall, subject to the following provisions of this section, give to the other party or parties to the proceedings—

(a) such notice (if any) of that fact, and

(b) on request, such particulars of or relating to the evidence,

as is reasonable and practicable in the circumstances for the purpose of enabling him or them to deal with any matters arising from its being hearsay.

(2) Provision may be made by rules of court—

(a) specifying classes of proceedings or evidence in relation to which subsection (1) does not apply, and

(b) as to the manner in which (including the time within which) the duties imposed by that subsection are to be complied with in the cases where it does apply.

(3) Subsection (1) may also be excluded by agreement of the parties; and compliance with the duty to give notice may in any case be waived by the person to whom notice is required to be given.

(4) A failure to comply with subsection (1), or with rules under subsection (2)(b), does not affect the admissibility of the evidence but may be taken into account by the court—

(a) in considering the exercise of its powers with respect to the course of proceedings and costs, and

(b) as a matter adversely affecting the weight to be given to the evidence in accordance with section 4.

3. Power to call witness for cross-examination on hearsay statement

Rules of court may provide that where a party to civil proceedings adduces hearsay evidence of a statement made by a person and does not call that person as a witness, any other party to the proceedings may, with the leave of the court, call that person as a witness and cross-examine him on the statement as if he had been called by the first-mentioned party and as if the hearsay statement were his evidence in chief.

4. Considerations relevant to weighing of hearsay evidence

(1) In estimating the weight (if any) to be given to hearsay evidence in civil proceedings the court shall have regard to any circumstances from which any inference can reasonably be drawn as to the reliability or otherwise of the evidence.

(2) Regard may be had, in particular, to the following—

(a) whether it would have been reasonable and practicable for the party by whom the evidence was adduced to have produced the maker of the original statement as a witness;

(b) whether the original statement was made contemporaneously with the occurrence or existence of the matters stated;

(c) whether the evidence involves multiple hearsay;

(d) whether any person involved had any motive to conceal or misrepresent matters;

(e) whether the original statement was an edited account, or was made in collaboration with another or for a particular purpose;

(f) whether the circumstances in which the evidence is adduced as hearsay are such as to suggest an attempt to prevent proper evaluation of its weight.

Contents of a hearsay notice

RSC Ord 38, r 21 and CCR Ord 20 r 15 provide that a hearsay notice must

(a) *State that it is a hearsay notice*   Make this part of the title of the document (see fig 28 on p 441).

(b) *Identify the hearsay evidence and (c) identify the person who made the statement which is to be given in evidence*   In the case of written hearsay (eg a letter) the person to be identified is the person whose document it is (eg the person who wrote the letter or, if it was written or prepared by a secretary, the person who adopted it by signing it). In many cases (eg business records) this person may be identified by job description rather than by name.

In the case of oral hearsay the person to be identified is the speaker (not the hearer). In the case of second degree (or multiple degree) hearsay two persons (or multiple persons) will have to be identified. For example, if the hearsay is a letter written by C recording something A had said to B which B had reported to C, A, B and C would all have to be identified (see the example illustrated in fig 28 on p 441).

The rules of court only require the hearsay to be 'identified'. It is not essential for the notice to set out the details of it or, if it is written, to provide a copy of it. In practice however it is almost inevitable that full details of the hearsay will be supplied before trial. If it is written hearsay, discovery obligations may apply to it (see p 384) and/or questions as to the authenticity of the writing may arise pre-trial (see p 432). If the hearsay is going to be adduced orally at the trial it is likely that a witness statement setting out the hearsay will have to be exchanged before trial.

(d) *State why that person will (or may) not be called to give oral evidence*   This relates to one of the factors affecting the weight (if any) to be given to the hearsay evidence; see s 4(2)(a) of the 1995 Act and see p 446.

(e) *If the hearsay evidence is contained in a witness statement, refer to the part of the witness statement where it is set out*   Consider the example of this illustrated by fig 6 (on p 180) and fig 28 (on p 441).

The rules of court also state that a 'hearsay notice may deal with the hearsay evidence of more than one witness', ie a litigant need not produce a separate notice for each item of hearsay evidence. Our specimen notice (fig 28 on p 441) shows how one item of evidence may contain more than one item of hearsay. (As to the words in quotation marks above, a pedant might criticise that final word, 'witness'. Presumably it means the person who made the hearsay statement, ie the person who 'will (or may) not be called to give oral evidence'.)

Failure to serve the notice, or to serve the notice in time (as to which see 443), does not of course invalidate the hearsay evidence but it may lead to penalties concerning adjournments and/or adverse costs orders and it may be taken into account as a matter adversely affecting the weight to be given to the evidence (see s 2(4) and see further p 446).

The opponent's response to a hearsay notice

There are three responses which might be made to a hearsay notice. First, an opponent might wish to seek leave under s 3 of the Act (see p 438) to call the person who made the hearsay statement solely for the purpose of cross-examining that person as to the contents of the statement. An opponent might want so to cross-examine if he thinks that the person who made the hearsay statement will be available to give oral evidence and that, if he is so called, the contents of his hearsay statement can be diminished or destroyed by means of cross-examination. As to the difference between cross-examination and examination in chief see p 514. Calling someone merely to cross-examine them is primarily a method of destruction of evidence. It removes or neutralises what your opponent wants to rely on. It does not add anything positive in support of your own case. As such it is exempt from the ordinary rules as to exchange of witness statements (ie pre-trial disclosure of evidence you intend to rely on at the trial).

In order to invoke s 3 it is necessary to apply to the court within 28 days after service of the hearsay notice. That deadline is such that, in most cases, the application will have to be made to the district judge (see 'Pre-trial rulings', below).

The concept of calling a witness solely for the purpose of cross-examination on a hearsay statement is novel and it remains to be seen how much use will be made of it in practice. Probably not much. Consider first the position of the person whose case is supported by the hearsay statement ('A'); if the evidence is important and the witness is available A's first instinct should be to call the maker of the statement to give original, sworn evidence. Why rely upon secondhand unsworn evidence? (See further p 446.) If the reason is that the evidence would be destroyed by the calling of the witness A's only hope in serving hearsay notice must be that his opponent ('B') is an idiot and/or will be badly advised.

Now consider the position from the point of view of the other party ('B'). It is true that, on receiving a hearsay notice his first instinct will be to oppose it, ie, invoke s 3 where the hearsay is important and the

[continued on p 442]

Fig 28: Specimen hearsay notice

IN THE HIGH COURT OF JUSTICE   1995. S. No 99

QUEEN'S BENCH DIVISION
SOUTHCLIFFE DISTRICT REGISTRY

BETWEEN

SOUTHCLIFFE SPORTS AND WORKWEAR LIMITED   Plaintiff

AND

ALTRAD SAFETY SHOES LIMITED   Defendant

Hearsay Notice

TAKE NOTICE that at the trial of this action the Defendant intends to put in evidence

(1) A written statement dated 20 October 1996 and made by Miss Amy Juliet George. Miss George will not be called to give oral evidence on behalf of the Defendant because in July 1997 she emigrated to Apia, Western Samoa. So far as the Defendant is aware her full postal address is All Saints Anglican Church, PO Box 16, Apia, Western Samoa.

(2) An oral statement which was made by Mr Alexander Thomas to Miss Amy Juliet George on December 14 1996. The substance of Mr Thomas's statement is set out in paragraph 13 of the written statement of Miss Amy Juliet George referred to in paragraph (1) of this notice. Mr Thomas will not be called to give oral evidence on behalf of the Defendant because on 14 December 1996 Mr Thomas was and, so far as the Defendant is aware, still remains, an employee of the Plaintiff. Further, Mr Thomas's residential address, past or present, is not known to the Defendant.

Served on 17 July 1997 by Olivia, Isobel, Callum and Toby (ref FLD) of 14 Square Street London WC2A 5PP, DX 806402 Bloomsbury, the Defendant's solicitors

---

[Editor's Note: Assume that Miss George later returns to England and the Defendant seeks to call her as a witness at the trial. Technically, they would need leave to do so if, pre-trial, they had failed to disclose her witness statement in compliance with any directions made and deadlines set for the exchange of witness statements.]

maker of the statement is available. However he would be well advised to consider carefully whether he can diminish or destroy the evidence by cross-examination. There is a danger that, if he calls the maker of the statement but the cross-examination is not effective B will have improved A's case, not weakened it. What means are available to B to destroy the evidence by cross-examination? To a large extent this is the subject matter of the second response which might be made to a hearsay notice, serving a counter-notice.

In what circumstances will the court refuse to grant leave under s 3 thereby in effect compelling B to seek to destroy the statement by means of examination in chief rather than cross-examination? Perhaps the best example here will be the case in which the person who made the hearsay statement is a friend, relative or employee of the recipient of the hearsay notice. In such circumstances the court might take the view that parties should not be permitted to ask leading questions of persons who are clearly within their own camp and therefore may be biased towards them anyway. In such circumstances it is more appropriate to let the other party rely upon the hearsay if he wishes to and let him ask the leading questions and confront the maker of the statement with that statement if he gives sworn evidence inconsistent with it (see further p 444).

RSC Ord 38 r 23 and CCR Ord 20, r 17 require the recipient of a hearsay notice to serve a counter-notice if he wishes to attack the credibility of the person who made the hearsay statement. The usual ways of attacking credibility involve the making of allegations concerning bias, previous convictions or previous inconsistent (ie, contradictory) statements. Witnesses in court can be asked to admit these faults and, if they do not, evidence as to them can then be adduced (see further 'Previous statements of witnesses' below). These are the occasions when a cross-examination can 'contradict the answer to a credit question' (see generally *Cross & Tapper on Evidence*, 8th edn (1995) Chapter 6, VI and VII especially pp 331–340).

The rules of court make no provision as to the form and contents of a counter-notice. Presumably therefore it can be in the simplest form '. . . we wish to attack the credibility of [name]'. Other rules and directions govern the obligation (if any) to disclose in advance what form that attack will take. In most cases no advance disclosure will be necessary. Sworn testimony on the credibility issue is a 'new matter' so avoiding the rules requiring early disclosure of witness evidence (see p 429). Documentary evidence is admissible on the credibility issue without the need for any hearsay notice in respect of it (s 5(2) of the 1995 Act).

Examples
    A serves on B a hearsay notice identifying a statement made by C which statement A intends to produce at trial because C is now dead. B serves a counter-notice simply declaring his wish to attack the credibility of C but does not state how or in what way. At the trial B could:

(i) ask questions of other witnesses tending to show that C was biased (eg questions revealing some love or financial interest between A and C or revealing some grudge C felt he had against B). These questions need not be indicated in any witness statements B previously served.

(ii) produce a letter C wrote to B which flatly contradicts the statement relied on by A. B would have to produce this letter to A before trial only if:

    (1) B has discovery obligations to A and this letter does not fall within legal professional privilege.

    (2) B wishes to use this letter not merely on the credibility issue: B wishes to produce it as evidence of the truth of the statements it contains.

    (3) B wishes to obtain pre-trial rulings as to the authenticity of the letter (see s 8(1)).

The third response which may be made to a hearsay notice is to request further particulars 'of or relating to the evidence' (see s 2(2)(b) of the 1995 Act, set out on p 438). This provision gives the recipient of an incomplete notice a simple means of attaching the notice. In exceptional cases it may also enable recipients to seek further details of the evidence itself (eg those rare cases of written hearsay where the document in question has not been produced or those unusual cases of oral hearsay in proceedings in which there is to be no exchange of witness statements.

Time limits for notices and counter-notices

In the vast majority of cases (ie cases where one or more parties serve witness statements in compliance with directions to that effect) hearsay notices should be served at the same time as the witness statements. In most other cases the time limit prescribed for the service of a hearsay notice is, in the High Court, within *28 days after* the setting down and, *in* the county court, not less than *28 days before* the day fixed for trial (see generally RSC Ord 38, r 21 and CCR Ord 20, r 15; the county court rule specifically covers witness statements served pursuant to automatic directions; presumably the position is the same in the High Court; and see further as to late service of defences in the county court, p 254).

In all cases the time for service of a counter-notice is within 28 days after service of the hearsay notice (see generally RSC Ord 38, r 23 and CCR Ord 20, r 17).

The time limit for applying for leave to call a witness solely for cross-examination on hearsay evidence is also within 28 days after service of the relevant hearsay notice. The application must be made 'on notice'. In the High Court this means by summons to a district judge if the hearsay notice was served more than 28 days before the trial.

Pre-trial rulings as to hearsay evidence
Applications may be made to the district judge by summons (in the High Court) or on notice (in the county court) if, for example,

(i) Any questions arise as to the manner of proof of authenticity of documents relied on as hearsay (see s 8 and p 432).

(ii) A recipient of a hearsay notice wishes to invoke s 3 of the 1995 Act ie calls the person who made the hearsay statement solely for the purpose of cross-examination on that statement (see p 440). In such a case the court may give such directions as it thinks fit to secure the attendance of the statement maker and as to the procedure to be followed (RSC Ord 38, r 23(3) and CCR Ord 20, r 16(3)).

(iii) One party seeks an extension of time for the service of a hearsay notice or of a counter-notice or an extension of time for the making of an application invoking s 3 (see above).

(iv) In the county court, a defence is served less than 28 days before the trial and a party wishing to rely on hearsay evidence seeks an adjournment or such other directions as may be appropriate (CCR Ord 20, r 15(5) the exact meaning of which is not easy to follow) when is a party 'required to give a hearsay notice').

Cases in which hearsay notices are not required

(i) Cases excluded by agreement between the parties (see s 2(3) of the 1995 Act).

(ii) Evidence authorised to be given by or in an affidavit (RSC Ord 38, r 21(3) and CCR Ord 20, r 15(3) and see p 447).

(iii) In probate actions, statements alleged to have been made by the deceased (RSC Ord 38, r 21(3) and CCR Ord 20, r 15(3)).

(iv) Hearsay evidence produced for the purpose of attacking or supporting the credibility of a person whose hearsay evidence is relied on (s 5(2) of the 1995 Act).

(v) County court cases in which no defence is filed (see CCR Ord 20, r 15(5) and consider for example cases determined at the pre-trial review, see p 258 or possession actions, see p 263).

(vi) Small claims arbitrations in the county court (as to which see p 279; CCR Ord 20, r 14(3)).

(vii) In personal injury actions, HMSO copies of the Ogden Tables (see s 10 of the 1995 Act, not yet in force, and see p 70).

(viii) Hearsay evidence which is admissible under s 7(2) and (3) of the 1995 Act (a ragbag of 'common law exceptions' the most important of which concerns public documents and records).

Previous statements of witnesses
This topic is covered by s 6 of the 1995 Act. Subsection (2) states that, subject to exceptions: 'A party who has called or intends to call a person

as a witness in civil proceedings may not in those proceedings adduce evidence of a previous statement made by that person'. This is, because, ordinarily, the duplication of sworn testimony and previous statements would add nothing of value. Extraordinary circumstances in which the duplication is allowed include the following.

  (i) Where a witness uses a document to 'refresh his memory' in the witness box in circumstances where that is permitted (see *Cross & Tapper on Evidence* 8th ed (1995) pp 284–294). In these circumstances the document used does not necessarily become a separate item of evidence in the case.

 (ii) Where the written statement is a witness statement previously disclosed to other parties and is adopted by the witness when giving evidence or is treated as his evidence (s 6(2) proviso). In these circumstances also it is the sworn testimony that forms the evidence. The written statement is used solely to save time at the trial.

(iii) Where the court grants leave (s 6(2)(a)). This exception enables the court to relax the ordinary rule when appropriate. For example at the trial of a road accident claim one party might call as a witness someone who, at the time of the accident, made a statement containing important and lucid evidence as to the accident, which statement was later disclosed as a witness statement. However, because of his age or other health problems and the time lapse between the accident and the trial the person called may not now be competent to give sworn evidence. The trial court might give the party who called him leave to switch from the oral testimony to the written hearsay. There is therefore no duplication of witness and statement here.

(iv) Where in cross-examination it is suggested that the sworn testimony has been fabricated ('concocted') and, in re-examination of the witness the written statement is used for the purpose of rebutting that suggestion (s 6(2)(b)).

Item (iv) above forms part of the law concerning 'previous consistent statements' as to which see *Cross & Tapper on Evidence* 8th ed (1995) pp 304–306. In theory the re-examiner (ie the party who called the witness) might also ask the trial court for leave under s 6(2)(a) to use the previous statement as hearsay evidence as well. More often than not however the written statement will not add anything of value to the sworn testimony. It is therefore not worth seeking leave.

Section 6 also deals with the very different rules which apply when one party relies on the sworn testimony of a witness and an opponent relies on a previous statement made by that witness. The previous statement must therefore be a '*previous inconsistent statement*', ie something which contradicts the sworn testimony; see the example given on p 436 and see further *Cross & Tapper on Evidence* 8th ed (1995) pp 321–323. Consider the following examples

(i) 'A' serves a hearsay notice on 'B'. B obtains the leave of the court under s 3 to call the person who made the hearsay statement so as to cross-examine him as to it (see p 440).

(ii) A calls a witness to give sworn evidence. In cross-examining that witness B attacks his credibility by 'confronting him with his previous inconsistent statement' (as to which a procedure is set out in the Criminal Procedure Act 1865, ss 4 and 5). The purpose of this attack is to neutralise or destroy the evidence A relies on from this witness (Counsel in a closing speech: *That witness is not worthy of credence Your Honour. First he says one thing, later he says the opposite. He blows about like a weather vane*).

The cross-examiner may if he wishes rely on the previous inconsistent statement as hearsay evidence supporting the cross-examiner's case. However, this may involve penalties as to adjournment and/or costs if such reliance now takes the other side by surprise (eg if the previous inconsistent statement was never identified to them pre-trial during discovery or by means of a hearsay notice). On the other hand, the cross-examination might have been so wholly effective that the witness now adopts his previous statement, thereby making an adjournment unnecessary (witness in a sobbing voice: '*Yes, yes, you're right. What I've sworn so far today is a pack of lies. What I said in that letter is the truth. May the Lord Above forgive me*').

Weight and credibility of hearsay evidence

A list of factors, to be taken into account by the court when estimating the weight (if any) to be given to hearsay evidence, is set out in s 4 of the 1995 Act (see p 438). There are three points we wish to emphasise here.

(i) Words or actions tantamount to admissions (whether hearsay or not) have always been regarded as carrying extra probative force on the basis that people do not usually speak falsely against themselves (contrast self-serving statements or acts).

(ii) The first of the factors specified in s 4 considers whether there is any justification for reliance upon hearsay evidence rather than original evidence. Remember that a party giving a hearsay notice has to specify the reason why the maker of the hearsay statement will or may not be called to give oral evidence. In practice there are six reasons which, if true, may indicate circumstances in which the use of hearsay evidence is legitimate or justifiable: the maker of the hearsay statement is dead, overseas and unwilling to return, unfit to attend trial, untraceable, unlikely to remember the details of his statement (eg routine business records made by various clerks such as pre-accident health records) or a person who may be reluctant to repeat his statement because of bias (see further p 442, the 'exception' to s 3).

(iii) The party relying on hearsay should not under-estimate the importance of proving the reason specified in case his opponent denies it. You should always clarify this issue in advance of trial. Simple steps to take are to serve on the opponents a notice requiring them to admit this aspect of your case (see p 442).

At first sight it may be thought that hearsay evidence is preferable to first hand oral testimony. Hearsay evidence is 'cut and dried': it has no surprises; and if it is contained in a document it usually saves the expense of calling a witness. In practice the preference lies entirely the other way. The value of first hand evidence is the weight and credibility the courts traditionally attach to it. Hearsay evidence by its nature is second hand evidence. First hand evidence from a witness who can be tested in cross-examination will almost always be the more persuasive. The standard of proof in civil cases is on a balance of probabilities. A trial judge faced with conflicting evidence has to decide which is probably the more accurate. If he has received first hand evidence from, say, the plaintiff, and only hearsay evidence from the defence he may well feel bound to give judgment for the plaintiff. Do not therefore assume that it is correct to put in a hearsay statement wherever it is possible to do so. It will usually be better to call the witness.

Evidence sworn out of court

What can a party do if one of his witnesses will be unable to attend the trial? Perhaps he is going into hospital or intends to go abroad. If his evidence is of marginal value only or merely corroborates (ie supports) other, highly probative, evidence it might be put in as a hearsay statement, or, even better, by agreement with the other side. If his evidence is vital and cannot be agreed with the other side it is usually best to call him even if this involves adjourning the trial until he is available or paying his travelling expenses (in a legal aid case clearance would be required for taking this step). There are two other possibilities. One might seek leave to put the evidence in by affidavit (RSC Ord 38, r 2; CCR Ord 20, rr 6, 7). Being a sworn statement, this may carry more weight than a hearsay statement, but it still deprives the other side of the opportunity to cross-examine. Indeed the court may forbid the use of an affidavit if the other side reasonably requires the production of the witness for cross-examination (see *White Book* 38/2/6). The court will not usually make an order for evidence by affidavit 'where the evidence will be strongly contested and its credibility depends on the court's view of the witness, eg, the evidence of an eye-witness in a running-down action' (*White Book* 38/2/1).

Another possibility is to obtain an order for the examination of the witness (RSC Ord 39, r 1; CCR Ord 20, r 13). This does offer the opportunity to have the witness cross-examined. The examiner appointed (often a barrister or a district judge, see *Re Brickman* [1982] 1 All ER

336) usually fixes a convenient time and place for the examination: advocates for each side can attend and the evidence is taken in the usual way. A deposition is prepared for use at the trial. The examiner can make a special report to the court concerning eg the conduct of the witness in giving his evidence. 'In some cases video recordings have been used to record evidence . . for use in English courts' (*J Barber & Sons v Lloyd's Underwriters* [1987] QB 103 *per* Evans J).

If the person to be examined is outside England and Wales the High Court can issue letters of request to the judicial authorities of that country for them to take the examination or an order can be made for examination by British consular authority (usually only in the case of countries with whom a Civil Procedure Convention has been made: the Convention countries are listed in *White Book* 39/2–3/3). In High Court cases the order is usually made at the directions stage; as to the documentation to prepare see *White Book* 28 *et seq*. In county court cases the application for an order for examination of a witness outside England and Wales has to be made to a High Court Queen's Bench master. RSC Ord 107, r 3, governs the procedure. The *Green Book* commentary to CCA 1984, s 56, shows the title of the originating summons by which the application is made.

Taking the evidence of a witness overseas can be both time consuming and expensive. Modern technology now provides an alternative. The court has power to direct that, at the trial, the evidence of the overseas witness can be given through a live television link (RSC Ord 38, r 3; CCA 1984, s 76; presumably in order to take the evidence, the trial court will adjourn to premises which are equipped with a video conferencing suite). Of course the giving of evidence in this way depends upon the willingness of the overseas witness to take part; the English court cannot compel him to do so. However if, after the order is made, the witness unexpectedly refuses to take part, the trial could be adjourned and an order made at that stage for the issue of letters of request etc (*Garcin v Amerindo Investment Advisors Ltd* [1991] 1 WLR 1141 in which an order for evidence by television link was made after the trial of the action had already started).

Advice on evidence

If a solicitor is intending to brief counsel to appear at the trial it is usually essential to obtain a written advice from counsel before the conclusion of the directions stage. The advocate at the trial has the task of presenting the case to the judge and must be consulted on the evidence which he will wish to call in order to do so. It is just as important to obtain a detailed and comprehensive survey of all the evidence even if the solicitor intends to conduct the case personally. In large or difficult cases it will often be appropriate for the solicitor to seek a second opinion on evidence.

In this chapter we have set out the various evidential matters which must be considered when preparing for trial, and one of our purposes in doing so is to enable solicitors to draw proper instructions to counsel to advise on evidence. It is not enough to say to counsel, 'Herewith the papers—please advise on evidence.' The instructions should contain all the relevant documents including:

(1) Witness statements of the client and all potential witnesses
(2) Medical and other expert evidence commissioned by the solicitor and client
(3) Any evidence, expert or otherwise, received from the opponents
(4) Pleadings
(5) Correspondence
(6) Copies of all police reports, notes from inquests etc
(7) Any interlocutory orders
(8) Any photographs or plans
(9) Opinions from counsel already received
(10) Any other documents which the solicitor feels may be relevant (to enable counsel to determine their relevance).

The instructions should summarise the issues and state clearly what it is necessary to prove and how it is proposed to prove it.

Sometimes the advice on evidence will be very short because the case has been properly prepared by the solicitor and counsel is simply able to record his agreement with his instructing solicitor's suggestions. Often, however, counsel will be able to suggest shortcuts or additional matters which should be proved.

We have already pointed out that much can and should be done by agreement with the other side—eg agreed bundles of correspondence, agreed medical reports. Sometimes counsel will suggest special reasons why this should not be done in a particular case or, conversely, reasons why something should be agreed when it is not normal to do so. We submit, therefore, that an advice on evidence should be sought as soon as possible after it becomes clear that the case must proceed to trial and, preferably, before the directions stage is reached. Thus, at a directions hearing (or a hearing to vary the automatic directions) all appropriate orders can be sought to give effect to counsel's advice.

Advising on evidence is one of counsel's most important functions and it is essential to make proper use of it. Evidence matters apart, at this stage counsel should not be asked to 'advise generally' but may be asked to deal with specific points. If, for example, advice on *quantum* is also required this must be made clear in the instructions. In addition to the points already considered ask counsel if he would like a conference with the client before advising in writing. In a complex case ask if leading counsel should now be employed.

The advice must be carefully studied. It is sensible to tick off each paragraph as it is attended to. Always go back to counsel for further advice if anything happens which may cause counsel to change his view of the case—eg if a witness statement subsequently disclosed by the other side contains points which were not anticipated. In particular, ensure that all directions which counsel requires are obtained at the directions stage. If an order is made refusing to grant the direction counsel wants refer back to counsel immediately to consider appealing against that order.

Chapter 20

The Directions Stage

The directions stage of an action occurs after the close of pleadings and before the action is set down (High Court) or before a date for trial is requested (county court). In the High Court the directions stage is marked by the taking out of *summons for directions* or, in some cases, by the coming into operation of certain *automatic directions* or *standard directions*, as explained below. In the county court the directions stage is usually marked by the coming into operation of certain *automatic directions* or, in exceptional cases, by the court convening a *pre-trial review*.

As partly explained above, there are many different types of directions stages. In this chapter we shall concentrate upon the High Court summons for directions and the county court automatic directions and then deal with the various alternative or exceptional provisions in both courts. The table overleaf provides a quick reference to all the possibilities we shall cover.

In the county court, some cases have no directions stage: actions for recovery of land and originating applications in which, on commencement, a date for trial is specified.

Summons for directions (High Court)

The hearing of the summons for directions was originally intended to provide a 'thorough stocktaking' of the action (*White Book* 25/1/1). The district judge looks back over the preparations for trial the parties have made, gives directions for any further preparation necessary and then looks forward to the trial and gives directions on evidential matters and on the time, place and mode of trial.

In some cases the summons for directions is *pre-empted*: the district judge will treat as a summons for directions a summons issued for some other purpose (for two examples see pp 230 and 313). In some cases the summons for directions is *precluded* by the rule giving automatic or standard directions (see pp 465 and 472).

[*continued on p 453*]

Table 7: Different types of directions stage

IN THE HIGH COURT	IN THE COUNTY COURT
1 Summons for directions In all writ actions except cases falling within the following paragraphs **2 Automatic directions** In all personal injury actions except Admiralty actions and medical negligence cases **3 Standard directions** In writ actions in the Chancery Division if the parties so agree **4 Order for directions by consent** In Queen's Bench Division cases if the parties so agree **5 Cases which do not have a directions stage** (a) Summary proceedings commenced by originating summons, eg proceedings against 'squatters' (see p 264) (b) Other cases commenced by originating summons which can be finally determined at the first hearing (see p 116)	**1 Automatic directions** (a) In all default actions and fixed date actions with some exceptions such as defended small claims (see p 279) and others, referred to in the following paragraphs (b) In all actions transferred from the High Court (subject to any directions given by the High Court) **2 Pre-trial review** (a) In all actions expressly excepted from para 1(a) unless proceeding directly to trial. Cases within this sub-paragraph include debt actions in which a part admission is made but is not accepted and cases in which the possibility of jury trial should be considered (see p 479) (b) Cases commenced by originating application in which a pre-trial review is expressly provided for by the rules, eg lease renewal applications under the Landlord and Tenant Act 1954, Pt II (see p 276) (c) Third party proceedings (whether or not automatic directions will also take effect) (d) Any case in which a pre-trial review is required by the district judge **3 Cases which do not have a directions stage** Fixed date actions and originating applications in which, on commencement, a date for trial is specified, eg actions for the recovery of land (see p 263) and summary proceedings against 'squatters' (see p 264)

Issue of summons

Where it has not been pre-empted or precluded, a summons for directions must be taken out, usually, within one calendar month of deemed close of pleadings or within fourteen days of automatic discovery if the time for automatic discovery was extended by consent or by order. However, RSC Ord 25, r 1(7) enables any party, if he so wishes, to take out a summons for directions immediately upon, or at any time after, an acknowledgment of service is lodged giving notice of intention to defend. This provision is intended to enable the parties and the court to speed up the pre-trial processes of any action where it is necessary and proper to do so (see *White Book* 25/1/3).

The primary duty to issue the summons usually falls on the plaintiff. Although the defendant can do it, in practice he often prefers to do nothing and then after an inordinate delay to apply to dismiss the action for want of prosecution (see p 364), unless for example he has raised a counterclaim he wishes to get to trial. The primary duty to issue the summons falls on the defendant only if the action is proceeding on a counterclaim only.

Filing a statement of value

One of the questions to be considered at the hearing of the summons for directions is whether or not the case should be transferred to a county court for trial. This question often turns upon the application of the presumptions and criteria set out in the High Court and County Courts Jurisdiction Order 1991 (see generally p 373). In order to assist the court when making this consideration, the rules require that, in most cases, one party (usually the plaintiff) must file a *statement of value* in court and serve copies of it upon all the other parties. The deadline for doing so is 'not later than the day before the hearing of the summons for directions' (RSC Ord 25, r 6(2A)). The cases to which this rule applies are those in which the High Court and county court have concurrent jurisdiction for the purpose of trial, eg all contract and tort claims (except libel or slander) however high or low the value of the claim and whether or not a claim is made for damages in respect of personal injuries (see further, p 375 and note (3) therein).

The practice form of statement of value for use in the QBD is illustrated in fig 29. Briefly 'value' in this context means the financial worth of the remedies claimed by the party filing the statement (see further p 373).

The obligation to file and serve the statement of value usually falls upon the plaintiff whether or not it was the plaintiff or defendant who took out the summons. The obligation to file and serve the statement of value falls on the defendant only if the case is proceeding solely as
[*continued on p 455*]

Fig 29: Statement of value

Statement of the value of the action for the purpose of Article 7 of the High Court and County Courts Jurisdiction Order 1991 (Form No. Pf 204)

IN THE HIGH COURT OF JUSTICE   19   . —   . —No.

Queen's Bench Division

District Registry

Between

Plaintiff

AND

Defendant

(1) Insert Master or District Judge

(2) Insert Central Office or District Registry as appropriate

To the(¹)

of(²)

STATEMENT OF THE VALUE OF THE ACTION

(Tick appropriate box)

☐ The value of this action for the purpose of Article 7(3) of the High Court and County Courts Jurisdiction Order 1991 is not less than £25,000;

OR

☐ The value of this action is less than £25,000 but by reason of one or more of the criteria mentioned in Article 7(5) of that Order it is suitable for determination in the High Court;

OR

☐ The action is for relief other than a sum of money but the Plaintiff can reasonably state that it is of financial worth to him of not less than £25,000;

OR

☐ The action is for relief other than a sum of money but the Plaintiff cannot reasonably state that it is of financial worth to him of not less than £25,000 but by reason of one or more of the criteria mentioned in Article 7(5) of that Order it is suitable for determination in the High Court;

OR

☐ The action has no quantifiable value but by reason of one or more of the criteria mentioned in Article 7(5) of that Order it is suitable for determination in the High Court;

OR

☐ The action is suitable for trial in a county court.

Dated the   day of   19 .

Signed

(3) Delete as appropriate

[Solicitor for the Plaintiff/Defendant/Party Acting in Person](3).

OYEZ The Solicitors Law Stationery Society Ltd   Oyez House   7 Spa Road   London SE 16 3QQ   7 91 F20480

HC B89   5048916
• • •

Reproduced by kind permission of the Solicitors' Law Stationery Society Ltd.

respects a counterclaim. In this case of course, it is the value of the counterclaim which must be stated.

The sanction behind this requirement to file and serve is that, in the case of non-compliance 'the Court shall at the hearing of the summons for directions order the action to be transferred to a county court' (RSC Ord 25, r 6(2A)).

Presumably, the philosophy underlying this sanction is that all cases should be tried in the county court unless and until they are shown to be suitable for trial only in the High Court. Nevertheless, it does seem to us a somewhat heavy handed sanction. Is it really fair or sensible to order the transfer of all cases in which the plaintiff fails to file and/or serve the statement, whether that failure was by accident, and easily remedied, or by design and contumaciously persisted in?

What should the court do if, at the hearing, the plaintiff apologises for his breach of the rule, explains that he did so merely through inadvertence and now produces the missing statement and/or now serves copies of it upon the defendants? Must the case still go to the county court? In practice, most district judges would avoid the literal application of the rule by extending the time for filing and serving the statement (see RSC Ord 3, r 5, p 9). If, because of the non-compliance, it was necessary to adjourn the hearing the district judge might also penalise the plaintiff in the costs thrown away by the adjournment.

In London, notwithstanding the terms of the rule, the preferred practice is that the statement of value should be handed to the master at the start of the hearing (see *White Book* 25/6/1).

What should the court do if the plaintiff breaches the rule deliberately and it is the defendant who protests against transfer and wishes to show that the case is suitable for trial in the High Court only? Must he make that argument before the county court district judge on an application for re-transfer? Or would the High Court district judge allow the defendant to file the statement of value to avoid transfer even in a case where the obligation falls upon the plaintiff? Alternatively, in order to avoid the literal application of the rule, would the High Court district judge extend the time limit for the plaintiff and make a peremptory order, perhaps in the 'unless' form, relying upon the court's inherent jurisdiction to strike out proceedings which are an abuse of the process of the court (see p 123 and p 193)?

Matters which must be considered at the hearing

In addition to the matters that will be raised by each party, there are certain matters which the district judge is required to consider without request (RSC Ord 25, rr 3 and 4). These are:

(1) Whether the writ-indorsement and pleadings are in proper form or ought to be amended. (At the hearing the parties should be able to

produce copies of the pleadings should the district judge ask to see them; in some district registries the parties are required to deliver such copies to the court at the time the summons is issued.)

(2) Whether notices should be served or directions given concerning hearsay evidence (see p 437).

(3) Whether directions should be given concerning medical or other expert evidence (see p 422).

(4) Whether a direction should be given under CCA 1984, s 40 transferring the case to a county court (see p 375 and see *De Souza v Lansing Linde Ltd* (1993) *White Book* 5523, in which the Court of Appeal upheld an order transferring a personal injury action to a county court even though the plaintiff valued his claim at £200,000).

(5) Whether an order should be made requiring that some issues be tried before others, ie an order for a split trial. Such orders are being made more frequently now because of the enormous savings in costs which often result. For example, if the issues of *liability* and *quantum* are ordered to be tried separately, liability first, it often turns out that the second trial, on *quantum*, is unnecessary. Where the plaintiff wins on liability, *quantum* is often agreed without the need for a further hearing. Where the plaintiff loses on liability no issues of *quantum* arise. As to payments into court and *Calderbank* offers with regard to split trials, see p 349.

The court may also order the trial of a preliminary point of law. This differs from a split trial in that, on a preliminary point of law, no findings of fact are made. However, this can cause considerable difficulties, especially when the ruling is taken on appeal before the trial is heard. In *Tilling v Whiteman* [1980] AC 1 Lord Scarman described orders for preliminary points of law as 'too often treacherous short cuts. Their price can be delay, anxiety and expense'. (The treachery stems from the fact that, because of disputes of fact, the preliminary point may not turn out to be determinative of the action; in this respect, contrast applications under RSC Ord 14A, noted on p 231.) Preliminary points of law, in contrast to split trials, are not normally ordered. However if they are ordered, the appellate courts should nevertheless be reluctant to intervene (*Ashmore v Corporation of Lloyd's* [1992] 1 WLR 446, HL).

(6) Whether a variety of directions concerning the presentation of evidence at the trial *vis-à-vis* evidence by affidavit (see p 447), limitations on the number of expert witnesses (see p 459) and directions regulating the method by which particular facts may be proved and the use of plans and photographs (see p 462).

(7) Whether directions should be given as to the preparation of a court bundle of documents for use at the trial (see p 492).

(8) Whether the parties have made all reasonable agreements and admissions (RSC Ord 25, r 4). The district judge is under a duty to secure all such agreements and admissions. The order for directions may record any agreements and admissions so made and also may record any refusal

to make a reasonable agreement or admission. Refusals are recorded with a view to a special order as to costs being made at the trial. (One agreement the district judge does not have to seek is the limitation of the parties' rights of appeal, although if such an agreement is made it may be recorded in the order.) The purpose of RSC Ord 25, r 4 is to require the district judge to limit the areas of dispute between the parties as far as is reasonably possible. To facilitate the process RSC Ord 25, r 6, provides that the parties should attend the hearing prepared to give the district judge all such information and to produce all such documents (other than privileged documents) which the district judge may reasonably require.

Form of summons

The form of summons is illustrated in fig 30, p 460 below. Its text includes in draft most of the directions commonly sought by *either* party to the action. Some of these directions will not be relevant in a particular case and where this is so the numbers (but not the text) of unused paragraphs should be struck out (see further p 465). Any directions not provided for on the form can be asked for either by completing paragraph 18 or by continuing on a blank sheet of paper (which is required to be sealed along with the summons when the summons is issued).

We now comment on each of the paragraphs of the prescribed form.

1 Consolidation
This topic is considered in Chapter 6.

2 Transfer to official referee
Under RSC Ord 36, r 3, either party can apply for transfer to an official referee, ie a circuit judge nominated under SCA 1981, s 68. In practice this is a matter which should be considered and dealt with long before the directions stage (see generally p 270).

3 Transfer to county court
This topic is considered in Chapter 17 (see p 373). Before the hearing commences, the district judge and the defendants should have received the plaintiff's statement of value (see p 453). At the hearing, the plaintiff may be called upon to justify this statement and/or may give further information, ie whether his estimate of value amounts to £50,000 or more. The district judge may have to consider the four criteria, financial substance, importance, complexity and speed of trial, in order to determine as follows:

    (a) *If the plaintiff's estimated value of his claim is less than £25,000* whether the presumption *in favour* of transfer to the county court is rebutted.

(b) *If the plaintiff's estimated value of his claim is £50,000 or more* whether the presumption *against* transfer to the county court is rebutted.

(c) *If the plaintiff's estimated value of his claim lies between £25,000 and £50,000 or if the claim has no quantifiable value* whether the case is more suitable for trial in the High Court or the county court (ie no presumptions apply).

4 and 5   Amendments

This is one of the matters which the district judge must consider whether or not it is raised by the parties (see above). The principles upon which leave to amend is granted are referred to in Chapter 10.

6   Further and better particulars

The principles have already been discussed (see p 187). The practice is first to request the further and better particulars by letter. If no, or no adequate, further and better particulars are given, the usual practice is to delay applying for an order until the summons for directions. The court will not usually order further and better particulars prior to this stage. If a complex or substantial dispute arises as to further and better particulars it may be appropriate to deal with all the other matters raised on the summons apart from this item and then adjourn the hearing to a fixed date. This is particularly appropriate if the pleadings were settled by counsel and one or both parties wishes to instruct counsel to attend the adjourned hearing in order to justify counsel's request for (or refusal to give) particulars.

7 and 8   Discovery and inspection of documents

This should take place before the summons for directions is heard. It is included on the prescribed form of summons to deal with exceptional cases where the rules do not require automatic discovery (see p 395), where a party has failed to comply with the rules, where further discovery is necessary (and see also RSC Ord 25, r 1(7)).

9   Interrogatories

The marginal note on the summons here reminds us that most interrogatories are served and answered without the need for any application to the court; see further p 411.

10   Retention, preservation and inspection of property

For example, preservation of a ladder which, it is alleged, caused the accident of which complaint is made. In practice, such matters will have been dealt with by agreement, or long before the summons for directions (see p 305).

11 Witness statements

RSC Ord 38, r 2A states that, at the hearing of a summons for directions in a writ action, the court 'shall direct every party to serve on the other parties, within fourteen weeks (or such other period as the court may specify) thereafter and on such terms as the court may specify, written statements of the oral evidence which the party intends to adduce on any issues of fact to be decided at the trial'. Directions may make different provisions with regard to different issues of fact or different witnesses. For example, in an appropriate case, directions may be made which also provide for amended statements or supplementary statements to be served after the first exchange. The possibility of such directions being appropriate emphasises the importance of the skill of taking witness statements (see pp 27 and 428) and the desirability of taking advice on evidence before, rather than after, the directions appointment (see p 448).

A direction for exchange of witness statements will always specify a deadline by which it is to be accomplished. In the High Court such a deadline, if fixed by a specific direction, cannot be extended by agreement between the parties (RSC Ord 38, r 2A(2) disapplying Ord 3, r 5(3); contrast agreements concerning witness statements and experts' reports being exchanged under automatic directions).

12A Expert evidence: numbers and disciplines

The usual order places a limit upon which types of experts and how many experts can be called. The limit is not in fact binding; the trial judge may permit different or additional experts to be called at the trial. This limit does not fetter either party's right to call witnesses; neither does it fetter the discretion of the taxing officer (see White Book 38/4/1 and the cases there cited).

12B Expert evidence: exchange of statements

As with other witness statements it is standard practice now to specify time limits for exchange; see further p 426.

13 Definition and reduction of issues to be tried

An order made on this paragraph requires the parties to seek to agree within a specified time limit a list of main issues to be tried and to seek to eliminate or reduce the issues to which expert evidence is directed; See further as to these topics pp 426 and 431 respectively.

14 and 15 Lodgment of checklists and court bundle

A Practice Direction of 1995 makes clear that an order will be made on this paragraph in virtually all cases; see further pp 489 to 496. The checklist itself is illustrated in fig 32, p 490 below.

[continued on p 462]

Fig 30: Summons for directions pursuant to Ord 25

Summons for
Directions,
pursuant to
Order 25

IN THE HIGH COURT OF JUSTICE   19   . —   . —No.
Division

Master   **Master in Chambers**

Between

Plaintiff

AND

Defendant

Let all parties concerned attend the Master in Chambers in Room No.   Royal Courts of Justice, Strand, London WC2A 2LL on   day, the   day of   19   , at   o'clock in the   noon on the hearing of an application for directions in this action:

1. Consolidation. This action be consolidated with the actions whose numbers are given below and that action number   shall be the leading action.
Action No.
Action No.

2. Transfer to Official Referee. This action be transferred to an Official Referee, and that the costs of this application be costs in the cause.

3. Transfer to the County Court. This action be transferred to   County Court under section 40 of the County Courts Act 1984, and that the costs of the action, including this application be in the discretion of the County Court.

4. Amendment of Writ. The Plaintiff have leave to amend the writ as shown in the document initialled by the Master and that service of the writ and the Defendant's acknowledgment of service do stand and that the costs of and occasioned by the amendment be the Defendant's costs in any event.

5. Other Amendments. [The Plaintiff have leave to amend the Statement of Claim] [The Defendant have leave to amend the Defence (and Counterclaim)] [The Plaintiff have leave to amend the Reply (and Defence to Counterclaim)] as shown in the document initialled by the Master, and to re-serve the amended pleading within   days on all parties, to this action.
Any party who has already served a pleading in response to the pleading to be amended may serve a consequential amended pleading as advised within   days and all costs of and occasioned by such amendments shall be the [Plaintiff's] [Defendant's] costs in any event.

6. Further and Better Particulars. [The Plaintiff serve on the Defendant] [The Defendant serve on the Plaintiff] within   days the Further and Better Particulars of h pleading specified in the document initialled by the Master.

Fig 30: contd

7. Discovery of Documents.

(1) All parties are reminded of their duty to make discovery of documents within 14 days of close of pleadings in accordance with O.24 r. 2.

(¹)All parties serve upon all other parties lists of documents within days [and verify such lists by affidavit]. The obligation to serve lists is limited as follows:

8. Inspection of Documents.

There be inspection of documents within   days of service of lists [filing affidavits in verification of lists].

9. Interrogatories.

(2) This paragraph of the Summons for Directions applies to "ordered interrogatories" within the meaning of O.26 r. 1(4).

(²)The [Plaintiff] [Defendant] to answer on oath [by its proper officer] those interrogatories administered to h   by the [Plaintiff] [Defendant] and initialled by the Master within   days.

10. Preservation of Evidence.

The [Plaintiff] [Defendant] to retain and preserve safely the following items pending the trial of this action:

The [Plaintiff] [Defendant] to give facilities for inspection by parties, legal advisers, experts of the item(s) retained upon 7 days' written notice to do so.

11. Witness Statements.

Every party shall within   weeks serve upon every other party statements signed by those witnesses of fact upon whose evidence it is intended to rely.

12A. Expert Evidence (numbers and disciplines)

Every party shall have leave to adduce expert evidence at the trial limited as follows:

(a)   To the following disciplines:

   (i)

   (ii)

   (iii)

AND

(b)   To one witness in respect of any one discipline

AND

(c)   To those witnesses whose signed statements have been exchanged in accordance with the order under 12B(a) below.

Fig 30: contd

12B. Expert Evidence (exchange of statements).	(a) Every party shall serve their statement ordered under 12A(a)(i) on or before and their statement ordered under 12A(a)(ii) on or before and their statement ordered under 12A(a)(iii) on or before

[AND] [OR]

(b) The limitation at 12A(c) be dispensed with as concerns witnesses expert in the following disciplines:

13. Definition and Reductions of Issues to be Tried. (3) Failure by any party to comply with this order is liable to be considered separately from other matters concerning costs both as concerns the parties and their legal advisers.	Within weeks of the completion of those steps ordered at 11 and/or 12 of this order or within weeks of setting down, whichever be the earlier, every party shall communicate with every other party and use their best endeavours both to define the main issues to be tried **and** to eliminate or reduce the issues to which expert evidence is directed([3]).
14. Lodgment of Check Lists.	All parties shall lodge in Court with the Listing Officer no later than 2 months before the date for trial a duly completed check list in Form PF77.
15. Lodgment of Court Bundle.	The Plaintiff shall lodge a single Court Bundle of documents such as conforms to RSC O.34 r.10(2)(a)–(c) and the Practice Direction entitled ''Case Management'' dated 24th January 1995.
16. Pre-Trial Review.	The estimate of length of trial being in excess of 10 days, the Plaintiff shall apply to the Master for a pre-trial review within days of the lodgment of a check list under paragraph 14 of this order. In default of the Plaintiff complying with this requirement any other party may apply or the Master may appoint such a review of h own motion.
17. Skeleton Argument.	Every party shall lodge a single copy of its skeleton argument not less than 3 clear days before the hearing of the action or any application of substance by a Master.

Fig 30: contd

18. Other Directions.

(4) The party issuing this Summons should set out any other direction(s) which he or she invites the Master to make.

19. Trial Directions.

[NOTE: Parties are reminded of their duty to provide the Master with accurate information required to make realistic directions for the trial of the action. Underestimates of time may **not** be corrected by the Listing Officer, but must be the subject of an application to a [Judge] [Master]. Costs wasted through inaccurate information are likely to fall on professional advisers personally.]

Trial: [Judge alone] [Judge and Jury].

Listing Category: A or B or C.

[Estimated length: To be set down within   days [and to be listed with and tried immediately after (before) action 19   ,   , No.   ].]

20. Liberty to Restore.

There shall be liberty to restore the Summons for Further Directions.

21. Costs.

The costs of this application to be costs in the cause.

Dated the   day of   19   .

To Messrs

of

Solicitors for the Defendant(s)

This Summons was issued by

of

Solicitors for the Plaintiff(s)

Solicitor's Reference

OYEZ The Solicitors' Law Stationery Society Ltd, Oyez House, 7 Spa Road, London SE16 3QQ

1995 Edition
11.95 F30745
5054169
* * *

High Court S30(PR)

16 and 17 Pre-trial review and skeleton arguments

Provision for a pre-trial review (ie by the trial judge) is appropriate in cases estimated to last more than ten days. Provisions for lodging skeleton arguments are appropriate in all cases. As to both see further pp 489 and 505.

18 Other directions

Here the marginal notes invite the party issuing the summons to set out any other directions which may be appropriate. Consider the following examples.

(1) *Security for costs.* The court has a discretionary power to order a plaintiff to give security for the defendant's costs where the defendant can establish one or more of several grounds requiring security (see generally RSC Ord 23). This topic is considered in Chapter 14 (see p 314). The usual practice these days, if security cannot be agreed, is for the defendant to make two applications; the first at or shortly after acknowledging service in order to obtain security up to the directions stage; the second at the directions stage seeking security in respect of the whole action up to and including the trial.

(2) *Plans and photographs.* The usefulness of plans and photographs was discussed in Chapter 2. Often it is not possible to present the case adequately without using plans and photographs and thus their incorporation in the evidence at the trial is essential. Ideally, plans and photographs will already have been agreed with the other side and formal agreement can be recorded on the summons for directions. The general rule is that photographs and plans are not receivable in evidence unless submitted to the other side for approval at least ten days before the trial (RSC Ord 38, r 5). As in practice photographs and plans should be prepared at a very early stage, it should normally be perfectly clear what orders are required on the summons for directions.

(3) *Evidence of particular facts.* RSC Ord 38, r 3 empowers the district judge (or the trial court) to make directions regulating the method by which particular facts may be proved; for example reliance at trial upon an affidavit containing hearsay evidence, or, in respect of a fact which is a matter of common knowledge, by production of a specified newspaper which contains a statement of that fact. The subject matter of the rule is largely overtaken by changes in the law of hearsay (see p 436). Its main use today is as a costs-saving device confined to the proof of matters which are largely formal, or peripheral to the main issues in the action (see further *Arab Monetary Fund v Hashim (No 7)* [1993] 1 WLR 1014 approving *H v Schering Chemicals Ltd* [1983] 1 WLR 143; and see the *Green Book* commentary to the equivalent county court rule, CCR Ord 20, r 8). It has also been invoked to authorise the presentation of evidence *via* modern technology, live television link (*Garcin v Amerindo Investment Advisors Ltd* [1991] 1 WLR 1140, noted on p 448).

RSC Ord 38, r 7 provides a notice procedure concerning the citation of English cases in which questions of foreign law were decided. In English courts, questions of foreign law are treated as questions of fact which can be proved by expert evidence. Before 1972 the decision of an English court on a question of foreign law could not form a precedent for other cases in which the same question arose. Questions of foreign law had to be proved afresh by an expert in each case. This was altered by the Civil Evidence Act 1972, s 4. Previous English cases in which questions of foreign law were decided can now be used as evidence if *inter alia* notice is given to all other parties in the action.

RSC Ord 38, rr 3, 4, 5 and 7, described in this and the paragraphs numbered (1) and (2) above are all matters which the district judge is required to consider at the hearing of the summons for directions (see further, p 455).

19 Trial directions

There is considerable freedom in choosing the trial centre where a trial can take place. It must not be thought that an action commenced in the Central Office must be tried in London and an action commenced in a district registry must be tried in the district of that registry. In most cases it will be obvious which is the most convenient place for trial having regard to the addresses of the witnesses, parties, counsel and solicitors (frequently in that order of preference). The district judge also considers the convenience of the court. For example, even if all parties desire trial in, say, Liverpool, that centre's lists may be too full and the district judge might order trial in Manchester. Where the choice of forum is not obvious it is both customary and courteous for the plaintiff to discuss the question with the defendants.

A direction must also be given as to the *mode* of trial. The most common direction is 'judge alone'. In practice the jury has all but disappeared in civil cases: see *H v Ministry of Defence* [1991] 2 QB 103 and the cases cited therein. Trial by judge and jury is ordered only for cases falling within the SCA 1981, s 69(1), ie cases in the Queen's Bench Division *if* there is in issue a charge of fraud against the party who applies for jury trial, or a claim for defamation, malicious prosecution, or false imprisonment *and if* an application is made before the mode and place of trial has been fixed. Even then the court may order trial by judge alone if the trial will involve any prolonged examination of documents or accounts or any scientific or local investigation which cannot conveniently be made with a jury (as to which see *Taylor v Anderton (Police Complaints Authority intervening)* [1995] 1 WLR 447 and *Aitken v Preston* (1997) *The Times*, 21 May).

Under SCA 1981, s 69(3), the court has a residual discretion to order trial by judge and jury in any other case if the court thinks fit; eg a personal injury action in which a claim for exemplary damages is made (*H v Ministry of Defence*, above *obiter*) or a false imprisonment case in which the application is made after an order for trial by judge alone has been fixed (*Cropper v Chief Constable of South Yorkshire Police* [1989] 1 WLR 333). However, not many further examples of this residual power are likely to arise; the wording of s 69(3) emphasises that the normal mode of trial for actions outside s 69(1) is trial by judge alone.

Another topic concerning mode of trial which must be considered is whether an order should be made providing for some issues to be tried before others, ie an order for a split trial (for a precedent, see fig 31). If such an order is made, different modes and places of trial may be provided for each issue or segment of the trial (RSC Ord 33, r 4).

The listing category must be stated. Category A applies to cases of great substance, great difficulty or of public importance. Few cases come within this category. Category B applies to cases of substance or difficulty. Category C applies to all other cases (but note that many cases which would otherwise fall within this category are more likely to be transferred to the county court for trial under CCA 1984, s 40). When judicial manpower is short, category B and C cases are the ones more likely to be listed for trial by a deputy High Court judge.

The parties are required to estimate the length of the trial. Clearly the plaintiff should estimate only how long his case will take, and should ask the defendant for his own estimate so that the two can be added together. It is vitally important to ensure that an accurate estimate of the length of trial is given. The inexperienced should ask counsel to indicate in his advice on evidence how long he estimates the case is likely to last. As to keeping one's estimate up-to-date see fig 32 and see p 485.

Finally in this section the district judge will state the number of days within which the case should be set down for trial. Obviously this can only be done when everything else has been considered. Setting down is usually ordered within a period of twenty-eight to fifty-six days after the exchange of evidence.

20 Liberty to restore

As to the meaning of this term see *White Book* 4605. The parties are required to treat the summons for directions as the culmination of the preparatory stage. If, after the order for directions has been made, a party wishes to make a further interlocutory application that party must restore the summons giving at least two clear days' notice of the application to the other parties. Any such application is made at the applicant's peril as to costs unless there is a reasonable excuse for not applying earlier.

21 Costs

It will be noted that the prescribed form of summons assumes that the order for costs will be 'in the cause' (see p 570). Only in exceptional circumstances would it be otherwise.

Fig 31:   Notice under summons for directions

IN THE HIGH COURT OF JUSTICE   1997——No.

QUEEN'S BENCH DIVISION

BETWEEN   Plaintiff
                            —AND—
                                                          Defendant

   TAKE NOTICE that the above-named defendant intends to apply at the hearing
   of the summons for directions herein for an order that the issues of the liability
   of the defendant to the plaintiff, and of the liability of the plaintiff in respect
   of the counterclaim in this action, be tried separately from and before any trial
   as to issues of damage.

DATED the   day of   1997
TO
Solicitors for

Defendant's directions

Initially a summons taken out by a plaintiff seeks only those directions the plaintiff requires. If the defendant wishes to seek any further directions he does not take out a separate summons. In this one instance the defendant is allowed to use the opponent's summons. Not less than seven days before the hearing he must serve on the other parties a notice specifying the directions he seeks in so far as they differ from the directions already sought on the summons (see fig 31). If the district judge grants any of the additional directions he will complete the relevant paragraphs on the summons. This is one reason why the person taking out the summons should strike out the numbers only and not the text of any unused paragraphs.

The order for directions

Immediately after the hearing, the plaintiff should draw up the order for directions and produce it to the court office together with a copy (see p 8 and RSC Ord 42, r 5). A copy of the order should then be served on any defendant who failed to attend the hearing (see *White Book* 25/1/11).

In practice, it often happens that the parties can agree all the directions which they consider appropriate. In such cases the plaintiff can apply for a consent order for directions by post with a request that, if the order is made as drawn, the directions appointment should be cancelled. Before making an order for directions by consent the district judge will require to see the pleadings and will consider what further or other directions are appropriate (see RSC Ord 25, r 3 above and see *White Book* 711).

Automatic directions in the county court

Since October 1990 automatic directions have applied in almost all county court cases. CCR Ord 17, r 11 provides that, at the close of pleadings (defined below) a list of routine directions comes into effect without there being any hearing at which they are considered and without there being any order for directions drawn up to specify them. The underlying purpose of CCR Ord 17, r 11 is to streamline and simplify the preparation of virtually all county court cases (for the exceptions, see pp 452 and 476). In some cases, of course, one or other party may wish to apply for a direction which varies or adds to those which take effect automatically and this is provided for in r 11(4), described in p 469. The automatic directions also apply in cases transferred to the county court from the High Court subject to any specific directions which may have been made whilst the case was in the High Court (CCR Ord 17, r 11(1A)).

Importance of close of pleadings

The date from which automatic directions take effect ('the trigger date') is the date the pleadings are 'deemed to be closed'. This expression is defined to mean fourteen days after delivery of a defence if there is no counterclaim; otherwise twenty-eight days after delivery of a defence and counterclaim (CCR Ord 17, r 11(11)). In cases against two or more defendants who do not deliver a joint defence, the trigger date is calculated from the date of the last defence to be delivered. If it is never delivered the trigger date never arrives and parties wishing the action to proceed according to a timetable should apply for appropriate directions (see *Bannister v SGB plc* (1997) *The Times*, 2 May. In the case of High Court actions transferred to the county court, the trigger date runs from the delivery of the relevant papers to the county court.

The trigger date is the date from which to calculate the time limits within which the parties must take many of the steps in the action which are specified in the automatic directions.

What happens if the defendant fails to deliver a defence? In a default action the plaintiff will instead be entitled to enter judgment in default, or on admission as the case may be; if however the defendant has admitted only part of the plaintiff's claim and the plaintiff notifies the court that he does not accept the amount admitted the court will fix a pre-trial review (see further p 476). In a fixed date action to which the rule for automatic directions applies (see pp 255 and 452) the plaintiff may apply to the district judge on notice for judgment or directions; whichever he applies for the district judge may give such judgment or directions as he thinks fit: CCR Ord 9, r 4A. This rule is headed 'Judgment in default in fixed date action', so apparently mixing the two types of county court action—default actions on the one hand and fixed date actions on the other. In fact the distinction between the two types of action remains largely intact. CCR Ord 9, r 4A does not apply to possession actions or the other fixed date actions expressly excepted from the automatic directions rule. Even in the fixed date actions to which it does apply CCR Ord 9, r 4A does not entitle the plaintiff to enter judgment without leave and even if he seeks leave, does not promise him that he will get it; the court may instead treat the hearing as a directions appointment (see further p 478).

What do the automatic directions provide?

County Court Form N450 sets out full and explicit guidance on the content of automatic directions and on the steps which the parties must take in order to comply with them. A copy of this form is usually sent to litigants in person (whether plaintiff or defendant) as soon as a defence is filed. What follows in this section is our, shorter, summary which is intended for legal eyes. You will also find a checklist of the automatic directions set out in table 8 on p 470.

(a) Discovery and inspection

Each party must make general discovery, ie make and serve on every other party a list of all relevant documents which are or have been in their possession, custody or power. In two cases general discovery is limited to disclosure by all parties of documents relating to the amount of damages; actions in which liability is admitted and personal injury actions concerning road accidents (compare and contrast the High Court rules; see p 473).

The lists must be served within twenty-eight days of close of pleadings with inspection seven days thereafter.

(b) Expert evidence

A party intending to adduce expert evidence at the trial must, within ten weeks, disclose relevant reports to the other parties. In personal injury actions the plaintiff need not produce a further medical report unless he is intending to rely upon expert medical evidence going beyond the report filed with his particulars of claim (see p 424). However, if he does produce a further medical report, he must also produce an up-to-date statement of any special damages claimed.

The current county court rules provide for the disclosure of expert evidence to be made upon a mutual basis, ie simultaneously (CCR Ord 17, r 11(3A) and Ord 20, r 12A(4)(c)). You should take care not to give your opponent the unfair advantage of seeing your expert evidence before his expert's report has been written. You should refuse to disclose expert reports except upon the mutual basis and, if the opponent will not co-operate, apply for further directions. The position is to some extent different in personal injury cases: there, so far as medical evidence is concerned, plaintiffs always go first by disclosing a medical report together with their pleading.

At the trial the number of expert witnesses which each party can call is limited. Unless the court otherwise orders or all parties agree, each side is limited to two experts of any kind, or, in a personal injury action, two medical experts and one expert of any other kind (as to the effect of such a direction see further p 459).

(c) Exchange of witness statements

A party intending to adduce any other (ie non-expert) oral evidence must, within ten weeks, serve on the other parties written statements of all such oral evidence. As to the form and content of written statements, see p 492. If more than one party is intending to call non-expert evidence the written statements must be exchanged simultaneously (CCR Ord 17, r 11(3A) and Ord 20, r 12A(4)(c)).

(d) Photographs and sketch plans

Photographs, sketch plans and, in personal injury actions, the contents of any police accident report book are 'receivable in evidence at the trial' (ie without calling as a witness the photographer, draughtsman or police officer) and must be agreed if possible. As to the purpose and significance of this direction see p 492. The direction does not by itself permit reliance upon hearsay evidence. If a party desires to rely upon eg a witness statement set out in a police accident report book instead of calling the witness in person, the usual hearsay notice procedure should be used (see p 437 and see *McSorley v Woodall* [1995] PIQR P187).

(e) Fixing the date for trial

Unless a date for trial has already been fixed the plaintiff must, within six months, request the court office to fix a date. This automatic direction is subject to an automatic sanction. If no such request is made before expiry of an extra period (defined below) the 'action shall be automatically struck out'. The extra period before this striking out occurs is nine months after the last date upon which a request could have been made on time, ie fifteen months after the deemed close of pleadings or, if the court has previously varied the automatic direction to allow the plaintiff more (or less) time, nine months after that extended (or reduced) period. The precise date upon which the automatic strike-out occurs is known as 'the guillotine date'. No notice of striking out is given to the parties either before or after it happens. However, once the plaintiff becomes aware of it he can apply for reinstatement (see p 362).

The direction to fix a date for trial also applies in fixed date actions unless they are expressly excepted from CCR Ord 17, r 11 (see pp 263 and 452). This means that the label 'fixed date action' is wholly misleading in some cases. If the action is subject to the automatic directions rule no date is fixed on the issue of the summons (CCR Ord 3, r 3). Instead CCR Ord 17, r 11(12) provides that any reference in the rules to the return day must be construed as a reference to the date pleadings are deemed to close.

(f) Estimate of length of trial and number of witnesses

The parties must seek to agree a note giving an estimate of the length of the trial and the number of witnesses to be called. Whether it is agreed or not the plaintiff must file such a note when requesting a date for trial.

Orders varying the automatic directions

Automatic directions are, by their very nature, routine provisions only. They are designed to cover the average breach of contract or running down action which is likely to be ready for trial within about six months. If, in a particular case, some special provision or longer time allowance is needed, the time to say so is now. Applying for changes or adjournments later may lead to costs penalties against transgressing parties or their representatives (see further p 537). In times past it was thought that a directions hearing before a district judge was a convenient occasion for the court and parties to undertake a 'thorough stocktaking of the action' (see p 451). In most county court cases the current philosophy is quite different. In order to streamline and simplify civil procedure the rules now place a heavier burden upon the parties to carry out a full 'case appraisal' on up to three occasions before trial.

(1) On commencement; which court? See pp 109 and 375; this appraisal is made mainly by the plaintiff.
(2) At the directions stage; what variations are needed?
(3) In preparations for trial; agreeing and supplying the appropriate documentation (see p 492).

On each occasion failure to make the right decisions can lead to costs penalties for the parties or their representatives (see further p 537).

In this section we must consider the case appraisal needed at the directions stage. A checklist of automatic directions is set out overleaf as is a checklist of possible variations to automatic directions. If in a particular case you consider that some further or other direction is necessary, you should first seek to agree it with your opponent. If you can agree it, an application can be made by post or *ex parte* for an order by consent. If you cannot agree it, an application can be made on notice (see p 14). If, whether by consent or after a hearing, a particular direction is made, the automatic directions will still apply but, of course, will now take effect subject to the further or other direction specifically made (CCR Ord 17, r 11(2)(b)).

Directions which have the effect of slowing down the timetable of the action are not now readily granted even where they are sought by all parties. The district judge must be persuaded that the delay is unavoidable, ie necessary to ensure proper preparation. If he is persuaded that some delay is unavoidable the district judge will next consider why such delay has arisen and if appropriate will make a penalty order as to costs (cf *Boyle v Ford Motor Co Ltd* [1992] 1 WLR 476).

[*continued on p 472*]

Table 8: Automatic directions checklist (county court)

Topic	Action	Deadline
(a) Discovery and inspection	Serve upon every other party lists of documents specifying a time and place for inspection	Serve lists within 28 days of close of pleadings and allow inspection within 7 days after serving the list
(b) Expert evidence	Disclose reports setting out the relevant opinions of the experts intended to be called	Within 10 weeks of close of pleadings
	In personal injury actions plaintiffs disclosing an additional medical report must also serve an amended statement of special damages claimed, if appropriate	
(c) Exchange of witness statements	Serve written statements of the oral evidence intended to be called on any issues of fact to be decided at the trial	Within 10 weeks of close of pleadings
(d) Photographs, sketch plans and (if relevant) police accident report book	Disclose any such documents you are intending to produce at trial and seek to agree them and/or seek to agree any such document disclosed by any other party	No deadline
(e) Fixing date for trial	Plaintiff must request court office to fix a date for trial	Within 6 months of close of pleadings (action automatically struck out after a further 9 months)
(f) Estimate of length of trial and number of witnesses	Seek to agree a note of these matters with all parties. Plaintiff to file such a note (whether or not agreed) when requesting a date for trial	Date upon which the plaintiff contacts court office under (e) above

Table 9: Checklist of variations to automatic directions

		See page
1	Further and better particulars of opponent's pleadings?	187
2	Order for further pleadings, eg Reply and/or Defence to Counterclaim?	165
3	Orders limiting or increasing discovery?	396
4	Is extra time needed for discovery or for inspection?	467
5	Orders relating to interrogatories?	411
6	Orders for the preservation and/or inspection of property?	305
7	In personal injury actions, stay of action unless and until plaintiff submits to a medical examination reasonably required by the defence?	30
8	Is extra time needed in which to obtain and disclose expert evidence?	470
9	Order making disclosure of expert evidence sequential?	424
10	Order increasing, alternatively, reducing, the limit on numbers of expert witnesses?	467
11	A without prejudice meeting of experts?	426
12	Order dispensing with exchange of witness statements, or alternatively, requiring sequential disclosure?	427
13	Security for costs or further security for costs?	314
14	Is an order transferring the proceedings to arbitration appropriate?	282
15	Transfer to the High Court or alternatively to another county court?	380
16	Direction for trial by jury? See CCA 1984, s 66.	463
17	Order for a split trial?	456
18	Order relating to trial documentation, eg provision of skeleton arguments, chronology of events, etc?	495
19	Is extra time needed before a date for trial can be fixed? Consider trial documentation and availability of witnesses.	468
20	Is this a suitable case in which to arrange a pre-trial hearing conducted by the trial judge and attended by the trial advocates?	489

NB This checklist is not exhaustive. Are there any further directions needed as to other matters?

The case appraisal appropriate at the directions stage is not limited to considering what further or other directions to seek. There are several other matters which must also be considered; in particular:

(1) Is an application for summary judgment appropriate (see p 254) or any other attacking application (see p 190) such as striking out?

(2) What agreements and admissions should you strive for (see p 479 and CCA 1984, s 79) and how should they be recorded?

(3) Are any amendments (see p 182) to your pleadings necessary?

(4) Obtain renewed instructions as to documents, possible sources of evidence and the client's willingness to compromise and/or make or accept a payment into court.

Special cases in the High Court

High Court personal injury actions

RSC Ord 25, r 8 sets out automatic directions for all High Court personal injury actions; ie personal injury claims by plaintiffs said to exceed £50,000 (see p 197), cases transferred to the High Court (see RSC Ord 25, r 8(5)) and counterclaims in respect of personal injuries (see RSC Ord 1, r 4). However, the rule does not apply to Admiralty actions or any action where the pleadings (whether claim or counterclaim) contain an allegation of a negligent act or omission in the course of medical treatment (see RSC Ord 25, r 8(5)).

As in the county court, automatic directions set out routine provisions only. Each party should consider what further or other directions should be sought (cf the checklist of possible variations, see p 471). In the cases to which r 8 applies neither party is required to take out a summons for directions (RSC Ord 25, r 1(2)(j)). However, in our view, if an application to vary or add to the automatic directions is appropriate it can be most conveniently made on the forms illustrated in figs 30 and 31. If this is done it will also be necessary for the plaintiff to file a statement of value and serve copies thereof on the parties not later than the day before the hearing of the summons (see p 454 and fig 29).

We now comment briefly on each of the High Court automatic directions. There is of course a striking similarity between them and the routine provisions of the county court.

(a) Discovery

The automatic discovery rule applies but is varied in two cases. Where liability is admitted and in all road accident cases, the discovery is limited to disclosure by the plaintiff of any documents relating to special damages. The expressions 'road accident' and 'documents relating to special damages' are defined in para (4) of the rule.

It is convenient here to state the combined effect of this direction and RSC Ord 24, r 2(2) and to compare and contrast the automatic

Table 10: Automatic discovery in road accident cases (*quantum*)

Court	Claims alleging personal injury	Claims alleging property damage only
High Court	P must give D a list of documents but can give a list limited to the issue of *quantum* of special damages D is not obliged to give P any list of documents at all	P must give D a list of documents relating to ALL relevant issues (eg liability and *quantum*) D is not obliged to give P any list of documents at all
County court	P and D must exchange lists of documents but each can give lists LIMITED to the issue of *quantum* of damages	P and D must exchange lists of documents relating to ALL relevant issues (eg liability and *quantum*)

directions applicable in most county court cases (see p 467). This is best done by means of a table, see table 10, above.

(b) Early disclosure of expert evidence

A party intending to adduce expert evidence at the trial must, within fourteen weeks, disclose relevant reports to the other parties. The reports must be agreed if possible. If they are not the parties are at liberty to call as witnesses the experts whose reports have been disclosed. However, the number of experts each party may call is limited to two medical experts and one expert of any other kind.

Paragraph (2) of the rule states that if more than one party intends to adduce expert evidence the reports shall be disclosed by mutual exchange, medical for medical and non-medical for non-medical within the fourteen weeks provided or as soon thereafter as the reports on each side are available.

As in county court personal injury claims, a plaintiff need not produce a further medical report unless he is intending to rely upon expert medical evidence going beyond the report, a copy of which was served with his statement of claim (see p 424). However, if he does produce a further medical report, he must also produce an up-to-date statement of any special damages claimed (RSC Ord 25, r 8(1A)).

(c) Exchange of witness statements

A party intending to adduce any other (ie non-expert) oral evidence must, within fourteen weeks, serve on the other parties written statements of all such oral evidence. As to the form and content of written statements, see p 175. This automatic direction is in all respects identical to its county court equivalent save that the deadline for exchanging written statements (and experts' reports) is extended to fourteen weeks not just ten weeks as it is in the county court.

(d) Photographs, sketch plan, police accident report book
The items listed above are 'receivable in evidence at the trial' (ie without calling as a witness the photographer, draughtsman or police officer) and must be agreed if possible (see further pp 468 and 492).

(e) Place of trial
Subject to two exceptions (see below) the place of trial will be, in the case of a Central Office action, London, and in the case of a district registry action, the trial centre designated for that district registry (as to which see *White Book* 4808). The exceptions are: cases in which the parties agree in writing as to a different venue; and cases in which the Crown is a party; these must be tried in London unless the Crown consents to or requires trial elsewhere.

(f) Time of trial, listing category, mode of trial
The action must be set down within six months, must be listed as a Category B case and will be tried by judge alone. The primary obligation as to setting down falls upon the plaintiff (see p 482). When the action is set down the court may direct a hearing to determine whether the action is suitable for transfer to a county court: see p 484.

(g) Estimate of the length of trial
The court must be notified, on setting down, of the estimated length of the trial.

Standard directions by consent in Chancery actions

RSC Ord 25, r 9, provides that, if, in a Chancery action, the parties agree in writing that the only directions required are as to the mode of trial and the time for setting down, certain *standard directions* will come into operation. The agreement is valid only if made within one month of close of pleadings (see p 113). Such an agreement will save the parties the time and expense of taking out a summons, attending thereon or writing to the court, and drawing up an order for directions. It is stated in the *White Book* 25/9/1 that 'solicitors should satisfy themselves that counsel is content with the pleadings and discovery before adopting this procedure'. We would respectfully add that the solicitors should also consider these topics for themselves (see p 119). The agreement does not prevent the court making further directions, or indeed alternative directions, at least in respect of trials in Birmingham, Bristol or Cardiff.

As to the place of trial, para 1(e) of RSC Ord 25, r 8 applies (ie save in Crown cases, the local trial centre or as the parties may agree). However, if the relevant trial centre is Birmingham, Bristol or Cardiff the plaintiff, or other party having the conduct of the action, must forthwith lodge copies of the pleadings in the court office in which the action is currently proceeding; this enables the court to consider whether to make an alternative direction as to the place of trial, or a further direction by which the action would be released for trial by a circuit judge.

The mode of trial is by judge alone, and the action must be set down within six months of the agreement. As to setting down para 1(g) of RSC Ord 25, r 8 applies (ie on setting down the court must be notified of the estimated length of the trial).

Given the current rules on exchange of witness statements (see p 426) the parties should, presumably, seek to agree a regime similar to the automatic direction (see p 473; RSC Ord 25, r 9 was not in fact amended at the time the current rules on exchange of witness statements were introduced).

Cases commenced by originating summons

The summons for directions rule, RSC Ord 25, is limited to actions begun by writ. The procedure which governs actions begun by originating summons is set out in RSC Ord 28 (summarised in p 115) under which directions are to be given at the first hearing of the summons, unless the case is one which can be finally determined at that first hearing.

Official referees' business and patent actions

Specialised forms of action, such as cases commenced or ordered to be tried as official referees' business (see further p 270) and actions for the infringement of a patent, are expressly excluded from the summons for directions rule (see RSC Ord 25, r 1(2)(g) and (h)). Also excluded are actions in which an application for transfer to the Commercial Court is pending (RSC Ord 25, r 1(2)(f)). However, in this instance the exclusion is temporary only. The summons for directions rule will apply once that application is determined, whether in favour of or against transfer to the Commercial Court; as to procedure in the Commercial Court, see p 274.

Deemed summons for directions

In six cases the summons for directions rule is, or may be, pre-empted, the district judge treating as a summons for directions a summons which was issued for some other purpose. In the first three cases listed below the pre-emption is mandatory, the court being required to treat the hearing in question as the hearing of a summons for directions. In the other three cases listed below the court has a discretion as to whether or not to pre-empt the summons for directions stage (see generally RSC Ord 25, r 1(2)).

(1) Actions in which summary judgment was sought, whether under RSC Ord 14 (see p 221) or under RSC Ord 86 (see p 230) and leave to defend is given.

(2) Actions in which an order for trial without pleadings is made (see p 117).

(3) Actions in which an order is made for the determination of an issue before any discovery of documents occurs.

(4) Actions in which the court refuses to make an order for trial without pleadings (see p 117; in these and the next two cases the court has a discretion whether or not to pre-empt the summons for directions rule).

(5) Actions in which application is made for interlocutory injunctions (see p 283) or other interim orders affecting property (see p 305) or, in our opinion, interim payments (see p 308 and note RSC Ord 25, r 1(2)(d) and RSC Ord 29, rr 7 and 14).

(6) Actions in which a summary order for the taking of an account has been made (see RSC Ord 43, r 1).

Special cases in the county court

There are many exceptions to CCR Ord 17, r 11, the automatic directions rule in the county court, the relevant text of which appears in p 480. In most (but not all) of them the case will be listed for a pre-trial review either when proceedings are commenced or, in default actions, when a defence is filed or when some other step in the action is taken. Some of the exceptions can be explained on the basis that specific directions are likely to be required (administration of a deceased's estate, Admiralty actions, interpleader proceedings, actions triable by jury, partnership actions, patent actions, contentious probate actions, representative proceedings (see p 103) and tort actions between spouses (see p 218)). A further group of exceptions can be explained on the basis that the cases in question can often be finally determined at a directions hearing (actions concerning regulated consumer credit agreements, delivery of goods or the recovery of income tax). It is convenient to comment separately upon each of the remaining exceptions.

Part admission not accepted by the plaintiff

The court office will fix a date for a pre-trial review in a default action in which the defendant has admitted liability for a sum less than the full sum claimed and the plaintiff has notified the court that he does not accept the amount admitted (CCR Ord 9, r 3(9), Ord 17, r 11(1)(o) and see p 253). Presumably such cases are excepted from the automatic directions rule in order to enable the court to consider whether any special directions are required. At the pre-trial review the district judge must endeavour to secure that the parties make all such admissions and agreements as ought reasonably to be made by them and the district judge may record in his order any admission or agreement so made and any refusal to make an admission or agreement (CCR Ord 17, r 2).

Third party proceedings

The court office will fix a date for a pre-trial review in any action in which third party proceedings or analogous proceedings have been commenced. Notice of the hearing date will then be given to every party, including the plaintiff. In this instance the action is governed by automatic directions and also any directions made at the pre-trial review (CCR Ord 17, r 11(1)(p)).

Actions proceeding directly to trial

Actions proceeding directly to trial do not have a directions stage (ie are not governed by the automatic directions or given a pre-trial review) unless, in an exceptional case, either the court or the parties specifically requests a pre-trial review (as to which, see below). The most important examples here are actions for the recovery of land (as to which see p 263).

Proceedings referred for arbitration

There are neither automatic directions nor a pre-trial review in any small claim (as to which see p 279). However, the court may, in an exceptional case, convene a preliminary hearing.

The exception which applies to proceedings referred for arbitration is not limited to small claims (CCR Ord 17, r 11(1)(c)). In any case, whatever its value, the automatic directions as to fixing a date for trial and so on, will cease to apply once arbitration has been decided upon as the appropriate method of disposal.

Originating applications

The automatic directions rule is limited to default actions and fixed date actions. The procedure which governs cases commenced by originating applications depends upon the nature of the return day fixed by the court office at the time of commencement (trial or pre-trial review, see p 115). For example in business tenancy renewal applications the first return day given will usually be for a pre-trial review (CCR Ord 43, r 2(2) and see p 276).

Ad hoc pre-trial reviews

Under CCR Ord 17, r 11(4) the court may, in any action to which the automatic directions would otherwise apply, make an order that a pre-trial review should be held instead. There is more to this than just a variation of the automatic directions. If an order is made under CCR Ord 17, r 11(4) the automatic directions cease to apply. Instead all the 'foregoing provisions of this Order ... apply' (CCR Ord 17, r 11(2)(a)). The foregoing provisions referred to are summarised in the next section of this chapter.

The court can make an order under CCR Ord 17, r 11(4) either on the application of any party or indeed of its own motion. Such an order is likely to be made if one or both parties are litigants in person and, either from the pleadings or from other indications, there is reason to suspect that the case will not be properly prepared for trial without a directions hearing. It often happens that, although a case may seem very routine to the court and to any opposing solicitor, it is an uncharted sea to the litigant in person. For such a person automatic directions, ie directions which are for him unwritten and unexplained, could be disastrous.

CCR Ord 17, r 10 gives the court similar power to convene a pre-trial review in cases which would not otherwise have one. For example, an action for recovery of land in which the issues raised on the pleadings suggest that the question of giving pre-trial directions ought to be considered.

There are also three occasions in the county court when an interlocutory application on some other matter may turn into an *ad hoc* pre-trial review.

   (1) In a fixed date action to which the automatic directions rule applies, where the plaintiff applies for judgment in default of defence but the district judge considers it more appropriate to give directions (CCR Ord 9, r 4A and see p 466).
   (2) Where an application for summary judgment is made but leave to defend is given (CCR Ord 9, r 14(4) and see p 255).
   (3) Where an application is made for an interim payment (CCR Ord 13, r 12(4)).

Except in cases falling outside the automatic directions rule (see p 476) a hearing conducted under the rules just cited is usually no more than a variations hearing rather than a full pre-trial review. In other words the automatic directions would still apply subject to any specific directions given by the court (CCR Ord 17, r 11(2)(b)) unless of course an order under CCR Ord 17, r 11(4)(a) was made.

Conduct of a pre-trial review

Pre-trial reviews are convened in many cases excepted from the automatic directions rule (see p 476) in certain cases commenced by originating application (see p 115 and in other cases where an *ad hoc* pre-trial review is ordered (see above). In this section we summarise the rules governing such cases (CCR Ord 17, rr 1–4 and 9). We have already described the district judge's powers to give early judgment on a pre-trial review (see p 258). Here we shall deal with the pre-trial review only in so far as it corresponds to the directions stage in a High Court action.

On a pre-trial review the district judge must consider the course of the proceedings and give all appropriate directions. He must endeavour to secure that the parties make such agreements and admissions as are appropriate. Every party must, so far as is practicable, apply for any direction required on the pre-trial review in preference to applying at any other time. The usual notice of application must be filed and copies must be given to the other parties (see p 14).

In broad terms all the matters discussed in the context of the summons for directions apply to a pre-trial review. Only six items call for special comment:

(1) The district judge's jurisdiction to try cases is governed by CCR Ord 21, r 5, that is to say claims where the defendant fails to appear or admits the claim, claims not exceeding £5,000 (claims not exceeding £3,000 will usually be arbitrated rather than tried), all actions for recovery of land including mortgage possession actions, any other claims by consent of the circuit judge and the parties. One must also bear in mind the rule affecting pleadings (see Chapter 9); the district judge has jurisdiction to try all damages actions unless the plaintiff states, in the particulars of claim or otherwise, that the value of the claim exceeds £5,000 (see CCR Ord 6, r 1(1A)).

(2) The equivalent jury trial provision is CCA 1984, s 66.

(3) As to agreements not to appeal, see CCA 1984, s 79.

(4) At the pre-trial review the court must make a direction as to exchange of witness statements (CCR Ord 20, r 12A and consider the equivalent High Court rule, noted on p 459).

(5) The district judge must give directions as to the date of trial. Often the simplest and most convenient thing to do is to duplicate the automatic direction as to the date of trial. In order to do this effectively the court's order should spell out plainly and precisely what the parties are to do and when they are to do it. A shorthand expression such as 'automatic directions to apply' is both undesirable and ineffective so far as the automatic strike-out is concerned. In order to impose a sanction for failure to request a date in time the court's order should be framed as an 'unless order' (as to which, see p 123).

(6) As with all interlocutory orders in the county court, any order made on a pre-trial review will be drawn up and served by the court office. However, except in *ad hoc* pre-trial reviews (see opposite) it often happens that both parties can agree all the directions which they consider appropriate. In such cases the district judge will usually accept letters

from both parties reciting the order required and without any attendance. Rather than receive two identical letters however, the court would prefer one side to draw up the agreed order and send it to the court. The court can then seal it and use it as the order thus saving time by avoiding the need for a court clerk to prepare it. However, as with consent orders varying automatic directions, the district judge will not make the order sought if he has cause to doubt whether it is appropriate in all the circumstances (see p 469).

CCR ORDER 17, RULE 11(1) and (1A)

(1) This rule applies to any default or fixed date action except—

(a) an action for the administration of the estate of a deceased person;
(b) an Admiralty action;
(c) proceedings which are referred for arbitration under Order 19;
(d) an action arising out of a regulated consumer credit agreement within the meaning of the Consumer Credit Act 1974;
(e) an action for the delivery of goods;
(f) an action for the recovery of income tax;
(g) interpleader proceedings or an action in which an application is made for relief by way of interpleader;
(h) an action of a kind mentioned in section 66(3) of the Act (trial by jury);
(i) an action for the recovery of land;
(j) a partnership action;
(k) an action to which Order 48A applies (patent actions);
(l) a contentious probate action;
(m) [revoked]
(n) an action to which Order 5, rule 5 applies (representative proceedings);
(o) an action to which Order 9, rule 3(6) applies (admission of part of plaintiff's claim);
(p) an action on a third party notice or similar proceedings under Order 12;
(q) an action to which Order 47, rule 3 applies (actions in tort between husband and wife).

(1A) This rule applies to actions transferred from the High Court as it applies to actions commenced in a county court but (without prejudice to paragraph (2)) where directions have been given by the High Court, directions taking effect automatically under this rule shall have effect subject to any directions given by the High Court.

Chapter 21

Final Preparations for Trial

Order for directions

In the High Court, unless automatic or standard directions were given under RSC Ord 25, rr 8 and 9, this order must be drawn up (usually by the plaintiff) and complied with. If the other side is dilatory in complying with the order, consider what steps to take. In particular, a plaintiff should take out a summons for judgment in default of compliance with the order for directions: a defendant can issue a summons to dismiss the action for want of prosecution (see p 364).

In county court cases in which a pre-trial review was held, the court office draws up the order for directions. You must still take any steps which may be necessary to ensure that you and your opponent have complied with it.

In both courts, if automatic directions (see pp 465 and 472) or standard directions (see p 474) apply, you must take any steps necessary to ensure that you and your opponent have complied with them.

Further directions

Further directions can be sought even after the order for directions has been made, but this is frowned upon and it is highly likely that the applicant will have to pay the costs of the application, regardless of the outcome of the trial itself. Sometimes, however, there will be exceptional circumstances justifying a further application for directions, eg where a defendant dies an order substituting his personal representatives may be sought.

Double-check the advice on evidence

Go back to the advice on evidence and be satisfied that everything is in order and that you are now in a position, not only to set the case down for trial, but also to draw the brief. Consider also whether it is necessary to obtain any further advice at this stage, whether on evidence or on any other matter. One would hope that the answer is no but it is right to double-check the matter.

Setting down (High Court writ actions)

This must be done by the plaintiff in the court office appropriate to the place of trial and within the time stated in the directions. A time period specified in an order runs from the date of the order itself—not from the date when the order was actually drawn up. A plaintiff seeking to set down an action late must first obtain the leave of the court. In London the application should be made *ex parte* to the practice master (*Practice Direction* of 1996, *White Book* 737 Supplement). If the plaintiff does not set down, a defendant can do so or can apply to have the action dismissed (RSC Ord 34, r 2). As to the time period specified in automatic directions or standard directions, see pp 474 and 475.

To set a case down for trial you must tender the correct setting down fee (as to which see *White Book* 1001 *et seq*) and also deliver to the appropriate court office (as to which see the directions applicable) a request for setting down plus two identical bundles of copy documents (not originals). These bundles should be typed or printed single-sided on A4 ISO paper of durable quality having a margin of at least 3.5 centimetres and should include an index and backsheet (*White Book* 34/3/2, RSC Ord 66, r 1). Each bundle must contain (see *White Book* 975):

(1) the writ;
(2) the pleadings;
(3) any request or order for particulars and the particulars given;
(4) any interrogatories and answers thereto;
(5) all orders made in the action except only any order relating only to time;
(6) in proceedings which both the High Court and the county court have jurisdiction to try, a statement of value (see pp 375 and 454).
(7) a note, to be agreed if possible, giving an estimate of the length of the trial and stating the list in which the action is to be included (as to lists see *White Book* 34/4/1 for Queen's Bench actions set down in London, 34/4/3 for Queen's Bench actions set down out of London and, similarly, 34/4/5 and 34/4/6 for Chancery cases in London and out of London); if the note cannot be agreed the bundles must contain a note from each party;
(8) any third party notice and certain other third party documents (*White Book* 34/3/2; the defendant should supply the plaintiff with copies, see 34/3/5 and RSC Ord 66, r 3);
(9) if one or more parties are legally aided, any notice of issue of certificate served and also any notices of amendment thereto (see Civil Legal Aid (General) Regulations 1989, reg 50(2)).

The bundles should be firmly secured together (see *Practice Direction* of 1983, para 13, *White Book* 41/11/1, on this and other important details;

White Book 34/3/2 specifies the use of 'green tape or secure plastic binding'). One bundle is for use by the judge at the trial, the other is the official court record. In cases being set down for trial out of London, the plaintiff (or other party setting down the action) must also lodge a statement (as illustrated in fig 32) which sets out several matters concerning the current state of readiness for trial. Practitioners often refer to this statement as a certificate of readiness but this is a misnomer. Certificates of readiness were abolished in 1987.

A party who sets down an action for trial must, within twenty-four hours, notify the other parties that he has done so (RSC Ord 34, r 8: note this rare use by the rules of hours rather than days or weeks).

Once the action has been set down any subsequent interlocutory applications may be made to the court office in which the action was set down even if the action was transferred there merely for setting down (RSC Ord 34, r 5). The applications most commonly made at this stage will probably be to the clerk of the lists concerning the possible hearing date. It is the duty of all parties to an action entered in the list to furnish without delay to the clerk of the lists all available information as to the action being, or being likely, to be settled or anything affecting the estimated length of trial. In particular, if the action is settled or withdrawn the clerk must be notified immediately and the record withdrawn: this includes a settlement effected by accepting a payment into court (see generally RSC Ord 34, r 8).

It is desirable, before actually setting the case down for trial, to discover the likely waiting time. There is no way of knowing precisely when the case will be heard, as inevitably this depends on the progress of other cases already in the list. Nevertheless, some rough estimate can be given, and if it is a short period it would be as well to prepare the brief (see below) before setting down. In the Queen's Bench Division there will be a minimum wait of twenty-eight days in non-jury cases (*White Book* 34/4/2); contrast jury cases which may come on for trial almost immediately after setting down (*Practice Direction (Jury List: Setting Down)* [1995] 1 WLR 364). In the Chancery Division various target hearing dates have been set for various types of case (eg cases estimated to last more than ten days, nine months from setting down; cases estimated to last three days or less, three months from setting down; see *White Book* 34/4/5).

An issue which the court may raise after setting down, whether or not the parties wish to raise it, is the possibility of transferring the case to be tried in a county court; as to this, see further p 376.

Once the action has been set down it is possible to apply for a fixed date for trial. A common reason for obtaining a fixed date is the necessity to call expert witnesses. Fixing a date usually delays rather than speeds up the time of trial. However, if, at the directions stage, 'an order for a speedy trial' was obtained, this is a factor to which the clerk of the lists is required to pay regard when arranging the hearing date (see further as to this, and as to applications for an expedited hearing, p 374).

Once a hearing date has been fixed there are two applications which might later be made; the first is liked by the court, the second is usually loathed. To vacate a fixed date in order to return to the general list when the reasons why a fixed date was granted can no longer be justified (eg fixture made for the convenience of expert witnesses and the expert evidence has now been agreed). Parties have been described as being under a duty to make this application in these circumstances (*Practice Statement* (1988) *The Times*, 15 April). The other possibility is an application to adjourn the hearing to a later date. If the hearing date is imminent this application has to be made to the judge in charge of the lists and is not likely to succeed even if this is made by consent of all parties. If the order is made it may be on terms that the costs thrown away will be paid by the solicitors personally on an indemnity basis (*Practice Statement*, above and see *Boyle v Ford Motor Co Ltd* [1992] 1 WLR 476, referred to on p 469).

Fixing date for hearing (county court actions)

In county court actions in which the automatic directions apply the plaintiff must, within six months of the close of pleadings, request the court office to fix a day for the hearing (see p 468). When making this request the plaintiff must file a note, which must be agreed if possible giving an estimate of the length of the trial and stating the number of witnesses likely to be called. There is no need to file bundles of copy documents in county court cases; the court file will already contain copies of most of the documents in question; others are filed at a later stage (see p 492). There is no need for any separate application for a fixture in the county court; unlike the High Court, the county court does not have running lists of cases awaiting trial; all cases are fixtures.

The county court automatic direction described above also differs from High Court setting down in two other respects. Failure to request a date in county court cases may eventually lead to an automatic striking out (see p 468). Also, it seems that, if the plaintiff fails to request a date, the defendant cannot do so in his place unless he so permits (*Bannister v SGB plc* (1997) *The Times*, 2 May). For example, if the defendant wishes to obtain a date for trial of a counterclaim, he must first obtain a specific direction enabling him to do so (see, again p 468).

In some county court cases, the court office will fix a date for hearing without waiting for either party's request for it to do so. This happens in cases such as actions for recovery of land in which the trial date is usually fixed at the time of commencement and is stated in the summons (see p 263). Also, in cases in which a pre-trial review is held (see p 476) CCR Ord 17, r 9 requires the court office to fix a date, and give notice

[*continued on p 487*]

Fig 32: Statement on setting down action for trial (out of London)

IN THE HIGH COURT OF JUSTICE 19 . — . —No.

Queen's Bench Division

 District Registry

Between

 Plaintiff

 AND

 Defendant

(1) Or "Directions
pursuant to
Order 25 Rule 8
have"
(2) State and give
reasons for any
omissions.

1. The Order made on the Summons for Directions has(^{1}) been complied
with [except that (^{2})

 ]

In particular *(delete or amplify as necessary)*

(3) Or "have not"

(a) medical reports have(^{3}) been submitted for agreement;

(b) medical reports have been agreed, [agreement of medical reports has been
refused and it is expected that medical witnesses will be called to give evidence
at the trial];

(c) plans and photographs have (^{3}) been agreed.

 [P.T.O.]

Fig 32: contd

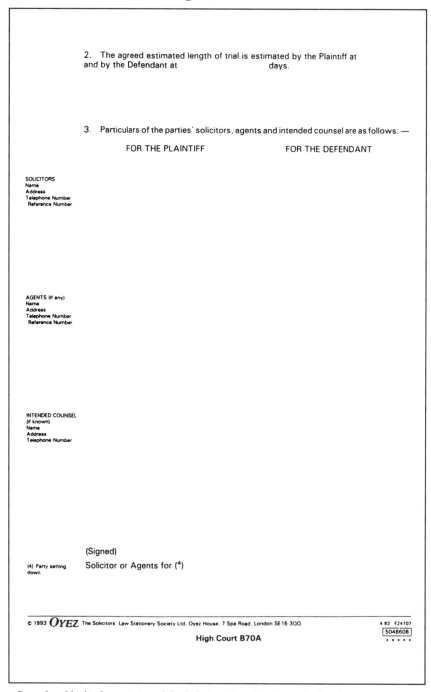

2. The agreed estimated length of trial is estimated by the Plaintiff at
and by the Defendant at   days.

3. Particulars of the parties' solicitors, agents and intended counsel are as follows: —

FOR THE PLAINTIFF   FOR THE DEFENDANT

SOLICITORS
Name
Address
Telephone Number
 Reference Number

AGENTS (if any)
Name
Address
Telephone Number
 Reference Number

INTENDED COUNSEL
(if known)
Name
Address
Telephone Number

(Signed)

(4) Party setting   Solicitor or Agents for (⁴)
down.

© 1993 OYEZ The Solicitors' Law Stationery Society Ltd, Oyez House, 7 Spa Road, London SE16 3QQ   4 93 F24707
                                                                                                       5048608
High Court B70A   * * * * *

Reproduced by kind permission of the Solicitors' Law Stationery Society Ltd.

thereof to the parties, immediately upon the completion of the pre-trial review, or as soon as practicable thereafter, unless of course the district judge makes some other direction, eg a direction duplicating the automatic directions as to fixing dates (see p 479).

Notification of client and witnesses

Immediately after the case has been set down—or in the county court a hearing date obtained—the client and witnesses should be told. If it is not possible to give a precise hearing date they should be given as good an estimate as is possible and should be told that nearer the time you will contact them again with the precise date, time and place of trial. As to the last detail mentioned, do not forget to inform clients and witnesses of the address of the trial court and give them suitable directions as to how to get there.

Consideration must be given to the issuing of a *subpoena* (RSC Ord 38, r 14) or, in a county court action, a witness summons (CCR Ord 20, r 12). The penalties for breach are: in the High Court, committal (see *White Book* 52/1/11); in the county court, a fine (see CCA 1984, s 55 and CCR Ord 34, r 2). There is little practical difference between a *subpoena* and a witness summons, and although we use the expression *subpoena* below, it can be taken that, save as to service, the comments equally apply to a witness summons in a county court action.

If a witness will not attend court of his own free will obviously he must be served with a *subpoena*. However, the *subpoena* is not restricted to such occasions. Indeed it is well worth reconsidering whether to call a witness who, despite every proper encouragement, remains reluctant to give evidence. Such a witness may know, but be unwilling to tell you, that if he is called he is bound to be a poor witness for your side. There are a variety of dangers to beware of with reluctant witnesses. A witness who gave you false information before may be unwilling to retract it now but knows that he will do so if placed on oath. Another danger is that a witness who is reluctant now may become a hostile witness later. Even worse, he may become a hostile witness who does not display that hostility in the witness box, ie he may destroy your case by giving false evidence but with an appearance of frankness, innocence and detachment.

There are two vital tasks for the solicitor to perform. First, find out what the witness will really say if called; work on this should begin, of course, from the very first time the witness is contacted. Secondly, if you decide to call him, use tact, diplomacy and charm to persuade him that he ought to attend. Many honest people do have to be persuaded to enter the witness box. Who would relish the prospect of being examined and cross-examined in court?

In our view you should make it your general practice to use *subpoenas* in the case of almost every witness (except expert witnesses) as an aid to persuasion. And you should tell witnesses that the *subpoena* is an order issued by the court to guarantee the availability of all the important witnesses whose evidence the parties wish to rely on. In other words, you should put the responsibility for the forcing element of the *subpoena* where it belongs; on the legal system and not on the client.

Even if you do not adopt the strategy we have just recommended, there are three particular instances in which a *subpoena* should be served, even on a willing witness. Police officers, who, by convention, do not take sides in a civil dispute and therefore will not give evidence unless compelled to do so. Witnesses who may otherwise have difficulty getting time off work. And expert witnesses; in almost every case they will have other appointments on the day fixed for trial which they made before the trial date was known. A *subpoena* may make it easier for them to break those appointments. Expert witnesses do not fall within the general practice we have recommended. However, it is always courteous to ask a medical expert or other expert if he would prefer to be served with a *subpoena* for the trial.

There are two basic forms of *subpoena*: the *subpoena ad testificandum*, where the witness is required to attend and give evidence, and the *subpoena duces tecum* where the witness is also required to produce documents at the trial. Although a separate *subpoena duces tecum* is required in respect of each witness required to produce documents, a *subpoena ad testificandum* can relate to more than one witness. However, in practice it is often preferable to issue a separate *subpoena* for each witness, for each has to be served separately (ie given a copy of it and shown the original if they ask to see it).

A *subpoena duces tecum* must specify the documents required to be produced. Sometimes, such a *subpoena* is used merely to obtain those documents and prove their authenticity; the witness producing them is not relied upon to give any other evidence in the action. In such circumstances a practice has grown up of specifying a trial date for production of the documents which is earlier than the date fixed for the rest of the trial (*Khanna v Lovell White Durrant* [1995] 1 WLR 121).

A *subpoena* must be served personally and the witness must be tendered 'conduct money', ie a sum of money sufficient to cover his expenses and subsistence in coming to court. He is entitled to be paid later for his loss of income incurred through doing so. It is always desirable, when informing a witness that the case has been set down, to add that he will be paid his expenses for attending the trial. In the county court a witness summons can be served through the court by post: the witness must be given travelling etc expenses plus a first instalment towards his witness allowance (£8.50 or £6 for a police officer, see further p 541).

To issue a *subpoena* in the High Court the party needs a *praecipe*, and a completed form of *subpoena*. Service of the *subpoena* is invalid unless effected within twelve weeks of issue and not less than (usually) four days before the expected date of trial. In the county court the applicant must file a request in Form N286 for a witness summons. If postal service is desired, the applicant must complete the certificate for postal service printed on the back of the request. The summons must be served not less than (usually) four days before the date fixed for trial; a summons will not be issued less than seven days before that date.

A witness summons is not valid for service outside England and Wales. If a witness is to be served in Scotland or Northern Ireland a *subpoena* can be issued if leave is obtained; in High Court cases see *White Book* 38/14–19/8; in county court cases an application must be made to a Queen's Bench master in London; see RSC Ord 38, r 19.

Problems sometimes arise when a party relies upon his opponent to call as witnesses those persons in respect of whom he serves witness statements, but the opponent later decides not to call one of these persons (see the conflicting cases referred to on p 430). In order to minimise or avoid such problems we recommend the following practice. After the exchange of checklists (see below), write to your opponent asking him to state whether he is intending to serve *subpoenas* on any of the witnesses he is intending to call and if so specifying which. The letter should also state that, if the information requested is given, this may avoid the expense of two *subpoenas* being served on the same witness.

Service of notices

We have already discussed the possible need to serve notices under the Civil Evidence Act or to serve notices to admit, or notices to admit and produce documents (see pp 431 and 434). In the High Court the time limit for doing so runs from the date of setting down. In the county court the time limited is counted back from the date fixed for trial.

Pre-trial checklist

A *Practice Direction* 1995 (*White Book* 973/1) extends to all Queen's Bench and Chancery Division cases an obligation to use a pre-trial checklist originally devised only for Commercial Court cases (see fig 32). The purpose here is to enable the court 'to assert greater control over the preparation for and conduct of hearings than has hitherto been customary'. Paragraph 5 of the checklist requires the parties to list the names of the experts and other witnesses they intend to call. As to this, the *Practice Direction* requires them to 'use their best endeavours to agree which are the issues or main issues, and ... so far as possible ... reduce or eliminate the expert issues'.

As to paragraph 8 of the checklist, the *Practice Direction* refers to pre-trial reviews being conducted by the trial judge and attended by the trial advocates ideally in the period between eight weeks and four weeks before the date of the trial. The *Practice Direction* further states that, in

[*continued on p 492*]

Fig 33: Pre-trial checklist

IN THE HIGH COURT OF JUSTICE   **19** .— .—**No.**

Division*

Between

Plaintiff

AND

Defendant

Date of trial:

Party lodging check list:

Name of Solicitor:

Name(s) of Counsel for trial:
                    (if known)

SETTING DOWN.
1. Has the Action been set down?

PLEADINGS.
2. (a) Do you intend to make any amendment to your pleading?

(b) If so, when?

INTERROGATORIES.
3. (a) Are any interrogatorie outstanding?

(b) If so, when served and upon whom?

EVIDENCE.
4. (a) Have all orders in relation to expert, factual and hearsay evidence been complied with? If not, please specify what remains outstanding.

(b) Do you intend to serve [seek leave to serve] any further report or statement? If so, when and what report or statement?

(c) Have all other orders in relation to oral evidence been complied with?

(d) Do you require any further leave or orders in relation to evidence? If so, please specify and say when you will apply.

(1) List the names.   **5.** (a) What witnesses of fact do you intend to call?(1)

Fig 33: contd

(1) List of names.   (b) What expert witnesses do you intend to call?([1])

(c) Will any witness require an interpreter? If so, which?

DOCUMENTS.
6. (a) Have all orders in relation to discovery been complied with?

(b) If not, what orders are outstanding?

(c) Do you intend to apply for any further orders relating to discovery?

(d) If so, what and when?

7. Will you not later than seven days before trial have prepared agreed paginated bundles of fully legible documents for the use of Counsel and the Court?

PRE-TRIAL REVIEW.
8. (a) Has a pre-trial review been ordered?

(b) If so, when is it to take place?

(c) If not, would it be useful to have one?

(3) The answer to this question should ordinarily be supported by an estimate of length signed by the Counsel to be instructed.

LENGTH OF TRIAL.
9. What are Counsels' estimates of the minimum and maximum lengths of the trial ([3])?

(4) See the Practice Direction dated 10.12.93.

ALTERNATIVE DISPUTE RESOLUTION (ADR.)([4])
10. Have you or Counsel discussed with your client(s) the possibility of attempting to resolve the dispute (or particular issues) by ADR?

11. Might some form of ADR procedure assist to resolve or narrow the issues in this case?

12. Have you or your client(s) explored with the other parties the possibility of resolving this dispute (or particular issues) by ADR?

(5) Solicitor.   Signed([5])

Dated this   day of   19   .

NOTE: This check list must be lodged not later than two months before the date of hearing with copies to the other parties.

cases estimated to last more than ten days, a pre-trial review should be applied for or in default may be appointed by the court.

Unless the court otherwise orders, each party must send a completed checklist to the court listing officer (or equivalent) no later than two months before the date of trial. The checklist itself requires parties to serve copies on the other parties.

The checklist also affects the summons for directions (see p 459) and further steps (see p 505 (skeleton arguments) and p 510 (procedure at trial)).

Plans and photographs

RSC Ord 38, r 5 states as follows:

> Unless, at or before the trial, the Court for special reasons otherwise orders, no plan, photograph or model shall be receivable in evidence at the trial of an action unless at least 10 days before the commencement of the trial the parties, other than the party producing it, have been given an opportunity to inspect it and to agree to the admission thereof without further proof.

The purpose of this rule is to prevent the action being plagued by the delay and expense which may occur if, at the trial, the other parties are taken by surprise by the plan, photograph etc and ask for time to examine it and test its accuracy. RSC Ord 38, r 5 has no direct equivalent in the county court system other than the rule requiring the lodging of a bundle of documents on which either party 'intends to rely or wishes to have before the court' (CCR Ord 17, r 12 and see below). In both courts see also the automatic directions where relevant (see pp 465 and 472). In the county court, and probably also in the High Court, the most likely penalty for failing to seek prior agreement as to plans, photographs etc is a penalty in costs.

As to what might or might not amount to a 'special reason' justifying a party to ask the court to 'otherwise order', see *Khan v Armaguard Ltd* [1994] 1 WLR 1204 and at p 424 above.

Lodging bundles of documents including witness statements

In most cases, High Court and county court, rules of court have been made placing obligations on the plaintiff to prepare and lodge at court copies of all the documents intended to be used or referred to at the trial by either the plaintiff or the defendant (see generally RSC Ord 34, r 10 and CCR Ord 17, r 12). The rules also place obligations on the defendant to give the plaintiff advance notice of his requirements and also some obligations to agree certain documents (witness statements and expert reports) where possible. Strict time limits are imposed on each party (see below). Delay or failure which subsequently causes expense and/or adjournments will no doubt lead to penalty orders for costs (see pp 469 and 537).

In both courts the term 'plaintiff' in these rules sometimes means 'defendant' and, we assume, *vice versa*. In other words, where an action is proceeding solely as to a counterclaim, the obligations are reversed; it is the counterclaiming defendant who must prepare and lodge the bundle and the plaintiff who must collaborate therein. Where an action is proceeding as to both a claim and a counterclaim it will sometimes be appropriate for separate sets of documentation to be prepared and lodged, some by the claimant, and some by the counterclaimant.

In the High Court rule only the term 'defendant' includes other parties entitled to be heard at the trial, eg third parties. In other words some collaboration must also occur between plaintiff and third party. The county court rule differs on this point (contrast RSC Ord 34, r 10(5) and CCR Ord 17, r 12(5)).

Collaborating on the preparation of documentation is one thing, but why do the rules require that documentation to be lodged at court in advance of the trial date? Obviously, this is to enable the trial judge to read the documents before trial, if time permits. However, witness statements (as opposed to experts' reports) are not normally read by the judge in advance without an express invitation to do so (*White Book* 72/A17, para 14.7).

Cases to which the rules apply

The High Court rule applies to all cases proceeding to trial in the High Court, whether commenced by writ or by originating summons.

The county court rule is similarly worded save in one vital respect; it applies to all cases proceeding to trial in the county court (including often, cases transferred from the High Court) *except* cases which are subject neither to automatic directions nor to directions made at a pre-trial review (CCR Ord 17, r 12(1)). In other words, bundles of documents including witness statements do not have to be lodged in actions for recovery of land or other actions or matters which, from commencement, proceed directly to trial (see p 477).

The deadlines

In the High Court, the defendant must contact the plaintiff at least fourteen days before the date fixed for the trial (or, if the proceedings are entered in a running list, within three weeks of the defendant's receiving notice of entry in that list) and must identify to the plaintiff those documents which he wishes to be included in the bundle. The plaintiff must get the bundles prepared and lodged at least two clear days before the date fixed for trial. (Even in a case entered in a running list the parties normally receive more than two days' notice of the expected start date.)

In the county court, the deadline for the defendant is the same, fourteen days before the day fixed for the hearing, but the deadline for the plaintiff is different. The plaintiff must get the bundles prepared and lodged at least seven days before the day fixed for the hearing.

Number, form and content of bundles

In High Court cases the plaintiff should lodge a bundle of documents, prepared in the same format as the bundles lodged on setting down (see p 483) containing copies of:

(1) *Witness statements which have been exchanged and expert reports which have been disclosed together with an indication of whether the contents of such documents are agreed.*

If a dispute arises as to admissibility or relevance of any parts of the statements or reports and the matter cannot be resolved by agreement, some suitable annotation should be made in the margins beside the paragraphs objected to (cf Commercial Court practice, *White Book* 72/A17 Supplement).

(2) *Those documents which the defendant wishes to have included in the bundle and those documents the plaintiff wishes to include.*

Documents falling into these categories will often comprise, eg correspondence between the parties, correspondence between the parties' solicitors, contractual documents if relevant. By way of limitation, the High Court rule requires each party to select those documents which they consider to be 'central to' that party's case. In some cases it may be open to doubt whether plans and photographs fall within this limitation. However, we would suggest that they normally should be included unless to do so would lead to obvious inconvenience (see also p 492).

The High Court rule does not expressly require the plaintiff to index or paginate these documents, nor does it require the parties to seek to agree their contents or authenticity. However, in our opinion, failure to take such obvious steps to simplify and streamline the proceedings could well lead to costs penalties for the parties or their lawyers (see p 537). Ideally, correspondence should be arranged consecutively with the oldest letters on the top and the newest on the bottom. Although this is inconvenient from the compiler's point of view, it makes things much easier from the reader's point of view, especially in the case of letters running to more than one page. In the case of handwritten letters it is usually convenient to obtain a typed version and use that by way of substitution, if that is agreed, otherwise, by way of addition.

What happens if, by mistake, the plaintiff includes in the bundles privileged documents which he did not wish to reveal? Would their inclusion amount to a waiver of privilege? The answer to this question is probably yes although each case will depend upon its own special facts. In *Derby & Co Ltd v Weldon (No 10)* [1991] 1 WLR 660 a plaintiff who had made such a mistake was unsuccessful in its claim for an injunction against the defendants restraining them from using the information accidentally leaked. Mistakes as to trial documentation are more likely to lead to loss of privilege than are mistakes as to discovery and inspection (as to which see p 405.

(3) *Where a direction has been given under RSC Ord 25, r 3(2), a note agreed by the parties or, failing agreement, a note by each party giving (in the following order)—*
   (a) a summary of the issues involved
   (b) a summary of any propositions of law to be advanced together with a list of the authorities to be cited, and
   (c) a chronology of relevant events.

The inclusion of documents such as these in the bundle, whether it is done by order or merely by agreement, will often further simplify and streamline the proceedings at trial. They are considered further overleaf.

The county court rule requires plaintiffs to prepare and lodge *a paginated and indexed bundle comprising the documents on which either of the parties intends to rely or which either party wishes to have before the court at the hearing (cf para (2) above).*

Plaintiffs must also file two other bundles each containing copies of documents which, in High Court cases, are included either in the bundle lodged on setting down or in the bundle lodged just before trial:

(a) Any request for particulars and the particulars given and any answer to interrogatories (cf p 482).
(b) Witness statements which have been exchanged and experts' reports which have been disclosed, together with an indication of whether the contents of such documents are agreed (cf p 494, opposite).
(c) If one or more parties is legally aided, any notice of issue of certificate served and any notices of amendment thereto (cf p 482).

Preparing extra bundles for use by the parties

The party compiling the bundles will usually prepare multiple copies of them. His own requirements will often be for at least four copies in addition to those which will be lodged in court; ie three copies for counsel, solicitor, and witness respectively and a spare copy for use by the client should he attend, or by any other person should accident or mishap spoil their first copy.

It is proper also to ask the opponents how many copies of each bundle they would like (as to negotiating the cost of supplying such copies cf p 406). What can be done if the compiler unreasonably refuses to supply other parties with copies even though reasonable terms as to payment are offered? The alternatives are, either obtain permission to copy the bundles lodged in court (see RSC Ord 63, r 4 and CCR Ord 50, r 10) or, preferably, serve a written request for a copy together with an undertaking to pay the proper charges required (RSC Ord 66, r 3; CCA 1984, s 76).

Specific directions concerning the rules as to trial documentation

In both courts, the district judge may give further or different directions as to the documents to be lodged. The ideal time to apply for such directions is during the directions stage. However, directions can also be made later, even after any bundles of documents have been lodged (RSC Ord 34, r 10(3); CCR Ord 17, r 12(4)).

By way of example of directions which might be obtained at the directions stage consider:

(1) A direction requiring the provision of copy bundles to other parties.

(2) In heavy cases, directions bringing forward the deadlines for collaboration and directions requiring the compiler to provide, at specified times before the bundles have been lodged, copies of some documents to opponents and permitting those opponents to serve a second, supplementary list of documents which they wish to have included.

(3) A direction providing for the inclusion of additional documents in the bundles. In the High Court this is one of the matters which must always be considered at the hearing of a summons for directions (see p 456). In the county court you should seek a specific direction as to this possibility if you want to ensure that the costs of preparing and agreeing the documents may be included in the costs of the action. In a particular case the inclusion of all or any of the following may facilitate the trial:

(a) a summary of the issues involved;

(b) a summary of any propositions of law to be advanced together with a list of the authorities to be cited;

(c) a chronology of relevant events;

(d) a list of the names of witnesses, companies, and employees mentioned in the other documents;

(e) in very heavy cases a reading guide as used in patent actions (see *White Book* 859);

(f) in cases mainly turning upon matters of expert opinion (eg certain medical negligence cases) lists of published works and journals which each expert relied upon when making his report (*H v Shering Chemicals Ltd* [1983] 1 WLR 143; *Naylor v Preston Area Health Authority* [1987] 1 WLR 958 *per* Sir Frederick Lawton).

Choice of advocate

Who should be chosen to conduct the case on behalf of the client at the trial; the solicitor who conducted the litigation leading to trial, another advocate from the same firm, or a barrister or a solicitor-advocate from another firm? When advising on this question the solicitor is under a duty to act in the best interests of the client (Solicitors' Practice Rules 1990, r 1(c)). Further, r 16B prohibits solicitors from making it a condition of providing litigation services that advocacy services shall also be provided by that solicitor or by the solicitor's firm or the solicitor's agent. This, the so-called *rule against tying-in*, is intended to ensure that the advocacy services provided by a firm have to be a bonus which clients of that firm can use if they want to, not a burden they have to put up with.

Rule 16B of the Solicitors' Practice Rules also states that a solicitor who provides both litigation and advocacy services:

> shall as soon as practicable after receiving instructions and from time to time consider and advise the client whether having regard to the circumstances including: the gravity, complexity and likely cost of the case;
> (i)   the gravity, complexity and likely cost of the case;
> (ii)   the nature of the solicitor's practice;
> (iii)   the solicitor's ability and experience;
> (iv)   the solicitor's relationship with the client;
> the best interest of the client would be served by the solicitor, another advocate from the solicitor's firm, or some other advocate providing the advocacy services.

Law Society guidance on this rule specifies two matters to be emphasised to the client, (*i*) who to choose and (*ii*) the likely cost. It further suggests that, in respect of advocacy likely to last more than half a day, the advice to the client should be evidenced by a note on the file *and* in a letter to the client.

Drafting the brief for trial

The brief for trial is perhaps the most important document which the solicitor has to draft. It is the set of instructions which will be sent to the advocate chosen to present the case at trial. It must inform that advocate about every aspect of the case which may be mentioned at the trial. The trial is the culmination of all the effort that has gone into the case, and the brief is the final document in preparation for the trial. Clearly, it must be given the detailed thought, time and attention which such a document so obviously requires.

Implicit in the act of drafting a brief is the assumption that the advocate chosen to conduct the case at trial is not the same person who previously had the conduct of the case. Does this assumption still hold good now that the vast majority of civil trials are conducted in the county courts, courts in which solicitors have full rights of audience? In our opinion it does. Not every litigator is an advocate, using the term advocate here to mean someone who has experience of and has specialised in the presentation of cases at trial. The skills needed by a trial lawyer are not likely to be needed or studied by most litigators even if they regularly undertake advocacy in interlocutory hearings. Furthermore, even if the same lawyer is going to both prepare and present a case we still think that a 'brief' of sorts should be drafted if only as part of the lawyer's preparation for trial.

A brief should begin by listing all the copy documents sent with it; ie witness statements and/or proofs of evidence, pleadings, medical reports, other experts' reports, agreed bundles of documents, all opinions of counsel previously received, all relevant notices and orders. It should not include everything in the case file; eg previous instructions to counsel and long forgotten interlocutory summonses which are no longer of any relevance.

Do not send original documents to your advocate. It used to be said of barristers that 'Those [documents] they don't lose, they scribble on'. Instead your advocate should be supplied with good copies. Keep the originals, and also copies of every new document you send so that you can discuss the case intelligently with the advocate over the telephone if necessary and, of course, so that you are still able to conduct last-minute negotiations.

The number of documents sent with the brief is usually extremely large. Gone are the days when it was possible to enclose them all within large sheets of paper tied up in pink ribbon. These days the documents are usually sent in one or more ringbinder files arranged with cardboard dividers for ease of reference. Some of the documents may have been sent to the advocate previously (eg pleadings and medical reports with instructions to advise on *quantum*) and so may already be housed in a ringbinder file. Other documents will have to be copied now, eg opinions and notes previously delivered by the advocate; or prepared now, eg proofs of evidence.

Usually, all the evidence which you intended to rely upon will have been disclosed to your opponent, in the form of witness statements or expert's reports, several weeks before you draft the brief. However, it is still often necessary for you to prepare proofs of evidence for each of your witnesses. The proofs should deal with any 'new matters' (see p 429) and should set forth any relevant comments upon the witness statements and reports relied upon by the opponent (see p 428).

Office practice varies as to whether the brief itself is included in the ringbinder files. It is more convenient for the administrative staff if it is and their convenience is important if high efficiency is to be maintained. However, this should not be the decisive factor. The convenience of the advocate is the more important, even at the expense of causing the administrative staff some inconvenience. Most advocates prefer the brief to be kept separate, ie a bundle of pages stapled together, the pages being either A4 ISO or A3 ISO, which is twice the size of A4 ISO. The advantages of the large paper are that it is readily identifiable and it prevents the brief from being of inordinate length and yet still leaves ample margins for the advocate to make manuscript notes and comments.

The brief should be as full and as explicit as the circumstances demand. If there are any matters as to which you are unsure whether you should put them in or leave them out, the wisest course is to put them in. This leaves it to the advocate to decide their relevance and importance.

A specimen brief to counsel is set out in fig 34. We appreciate that some practitioners will be surprised, or perhaps outraged, by our decision to abandon the traditional style in which both the solicitor and the advocate are referred to throughout in the third person: eg 'Instructing Solicitors are much obliged to Counsel for the assistance which Counsel has already given them on this matter'. In our view the use of the third person adds nothing except archness and obsequiousness. As far as we know, nobody uses it when speaking to counsel. Why then should it be used when writing to them? We think that the traditional style has as much usefulness as the traditional pink ribbon and the barrister's wig. All three should disappear within the next few years.

Delivering a brief to counsel

In the specimen brief illustrated in fig 34, the plaintiff has the benefit of a legal aid certificate. Thus the backsheet should be indorsed with the legal aid reference number and a copy of the certificate should be included together with any amendments thereof or any specific authorities to incur costs (Civil Legal Aid (General) Regulations 1989, reg 59). Had this not been a legal aid case it would have been advisable to negotiate the fee in advance with counsel or with counsel's clerk.

The Bar's 'Written Standards for the Conduct of Professional Work: General Standards' states that '3.2 A barrister is not considered to have accepted a brief or instructions unless he has had an opportunity to consider it and has expressly accepted it'. Thus, a day or two after delivering the brief the solicitor should telephone counsel's chambers to agree the fee. Under the Code of Conduct of the Bar of England and Wales (1990) it is not now necessary for brief fees to be agreed in advance or marked on the brief. However, in our view it will usually be wiser to agree it in advance, and to get the client's approval of it (see p 580) and (bearing in mind para 3.2 quoted above) get counsel or his clerk to confirm expressly acceptance of the brief at that fee.

In an ideal world briefs would always be delivered at least two weeks before the date fixed for trial (and see further, p 505).

It has always been the rule that, once the brief has been delivered, the full fee is payable even if the case should subsequently settle. Since 1967 it has been agreed that, in such a case 'counsel may accept no fee or less than the agreed fee' (see *White Book* 62/A2/11) and many will do so. However, the fact remains that they cannot be obliged to do so unless an agreement to that effect was obtained before delivery. This can provide a useful negotiating point for a plaintiff. It enables him to impose a deadline on offers of compromise 'after which date the brief for trial will have to be delivered'; those acting for the defendant will appreciate what this means.

It is important to note that, although counsel can insist on the full fee if he so wishes, the solicitor is under a duty to seek to re-negotiate that

[continued on p 505]

Fig 34: Specimen brief to counsel

IN THE KNAVESMIRE COUNTY COURT					Case No KL712345

BETWEEN

PETER GERALD CHISHOLM					Plaintiff

–AND–

ANNA THOMASINA WHITE					Defendant

BRIEF FOR THE PLAINTIFF

Copy documents enclosed:

BLUE LEVER ARCH FILE with dividers containing at:

A   Writ and pleadings
     Statement of Special Damages (to date of trial)
B   Police Accident Report
C   Exchanged witness statements
D   Statement of Brian Bates plus hearsay notice
E   Interrogatories without Order, served by the Defendant
     Plaintiff's affidavit in answer
F   Opinion on *Quantum*
     Note on Conference as to medical evidence and provisional damages
     Advice on Evidence
G   Order for Transfer

BLUE WALLET FILE containing bundles of copy documents filed at court including:

   (i) Agreed bundle of medical reports
  (ii) Agreed bundle of correspondence
 (iii) Agreed photographs of the scene of the accident
 (iv) Photographs of the bicycle (referred to in the Plaintiff's proof of evidence)
  (v) Answers to interrogatories (also at E)
 (vi) Legal aid certificate and notice of issue.

The Facts

1.   We act for PETER GERALD CHISHOLM, the Plaintiff in this action in respect of which he has obtained legal aid (see at (vi) above).

2.   The action was commenced in the High Court in 1994 and transferred to the Knavesmire County Court earlier this year.

3.   The Plaintiff's proof of evidence sets out in detail what happened at the time of the accident. You will find it easier to follow the proof if you refer to the plan on page 8 of the Police Accident Report (see at B). Under the automatic directions this plan is receivable in evidence at the trial. Several copies have been prepared.

4.   The accident occurred on 7 March, 1994 at the junction of Mill Lane with Church Lane. Mill Lane is a narrow road along which traffic travels in both directions. It is joined from the east by Church Lane which is a one-way road. Vehicles turning out of Church Lane must either turn left into Mill Lane or right into Heath Road (as Mill Lane now becomes). As the road changes its name from Mill Lane into Heath Road, the road itself now becomes one-way.

5.   Vehicles coming along Church Lane and intending to turn (left) into Mill Lane often take the corner at excessive speeds. Sometimes they take the bend at such a speed as to cross the centre white line of Mill Lane. This fact is agreed by the Defendant (see in wallet file, letter dated 31 August, 1994, page 12 in the agreed bundle of correspondence).

Fig 34: contd

6. The Plaintiff was riding his bicycle northwards along Mill Lane with Church Lane on his right. He was going fishing. He was carrying his fishing rods across his back and his fishing basket was balanced on the handlebars in front of him. As he was approaching the junction with Church Lane (he of course would have right of way) he was aware that a car began to overtake him. This car was driven by the Defendant. As it was next to the Plaintiff the car swerved inwards knocking the Plaintiff off his bicycle and causing injuries.

The Issues

7. The Defendant subsequently maintained (see, in wallet file, the agreed correspond-ence—in particular the letter dated 14 April, 1994) that she was forced to pull in as a 'red van' had come from Church Lane into Mill Lane on the wrong side of the road, causing the Defendant to pull in tight so as to avoid a collision with it, and so causing the collision with the Plaintiff instead. At first the Defendant's insurers suggested that the Plaintiff should proceed against the driver of the red van and/or his employer. Unfortunately the driver of the van did not stop. He was not, of course, involved in a collision himself and may not have realised what happened. The registration number of the van is not known. We have made such inquiries as we can to find this driver, in particular inquiries of the Post Office and also of two local firms, of roofing contractors and electricians, which are known to use red vans. Our inquiries have not traced the driver in question or his employers. No doubt we would have joined this driver in these proceedings had he been traced. However, we have at all times taken the view that this is principally a matter of concern to the Defendant rather than us and that the Plaintiff can still succeed in his action against the Defendant alone.

8. Although the Defendant was prosecuted for driving without due care and attention she was acquitted. This acquittal has no doubt influenced the Defendant's insurers in their decision to contest these civil proceedings. We were not instructed by the Plaintiff until just after the criminal trial was concluded and therefore do not have a transcript of those proceedings. Although a conviction against the Defendant would, of course, have helped the Plaintiff, we think that the civil action can still succeed without it having regard to the differing standards of proof between the two cases.

9. We took the view, with which you agreed and settled pleadings accordingly, that the Defendant should not have been overtaking the Plaintiff at that time as it was clearly unsafe to do so. There are six particulars of negligence pleaded in the Plaintiff's Statement of Claim, but this is the first and paramount allegation of negligence.

10. In her Defence, the Defendant denies negligence and seeks to blame both the unidentified driver of the red van and the Plaintiff. The allegation against the Plaintiff is that he was unable to steer his bicycle properly as it was over-loaded. Although this will be denied, we have advised the Plaintiff that he should be prepared, at least for negotiating purposes but probably also at the trial itself, for some reduction to be made for contributory negligence in this respect.

11. The Defendant's solicitors have asked us (see, in the wallet file, the letter dated 22 February, 1995, page 38 in the agreed bundle of correspondence) to produce at the trial the bicycle and all the fishing gear the Plaintiff had with him at the time. These we will bring to court as items of real evidence. We have already inspected these items. The bicycle is a full size racing cycle with 27 inch wheels. The fishing basket measures (in inches) 24 × 18 × 18. The Plaintiff is only 5 feet 2 inches tall and clearly would sometimes have found some difficulty in controlling his bicycle with such an obstacle immediately in front of him. However, in our submission, this is not the issue. The issue is whether the Plaintiff's inability to exercise complete control over his bicycle in any way contributed to the accident. At the time of the collision he was riding in a proper manner and was not wobbling. The Plaintiff's unsteadiness, if any, does not appear to have contributed to the accident. In the statement she made to the police officer (see at B, page 4 of the Police Accident Report) the Defendant made no allegation about the way in which the Plaintiff was riding.

12. Nevertheless it may be argued that, because of any general unsteadiness in his cycling, the Plaintiff's reaction to an emergency took longer than it would otherwise have done. We have informed the Plaintiff that, on this basis, he should be prepared to concede something for contributory negligence and have suggested a reduction of

Fig 34: contd

10 per cent should his claim be successful in other respects. In your Opinion on *Quantum* (see at F) you expressed general agreement with our view but recommended a higher reduction and suggested 15 to 20 per cent. You will recall discussing this matter with the Plaintiff in person at our conference (see at F, the Note of Conference made by the trainee solicitor who attended upon you and the Plaintiff on that occasion).

13.   Some weeks ago the Defendant served some Interrogatories without Order (see at E). This would seem to have been done more for the sake of appearances than with the expectation of finding out weaknesses in our evidence. Two of the questions relate to the Plaintiff's experience as a cyclist. The others relate to his exact position in the road at the time of the accident. We hope that, by his affidavit in answer (also at E) the Plaintiff has been able to turn these interrogatories to his own advantage.

The Evidence

14.   We have, we hope, taken all the steps which you suggested in the Advice on Evidence (included at F). The principal evidence will be that of the Plaintiff himself. In addition there is a short statement by Brian Bates (see at D) who witnessed the accident whilst on a holiday to this country. Mr Bates has long since returned home, to Canada, and a hearsay notice has been served on the Defendant (also at D). This statement may be useful even though Mr Bates seems to place the blame on the driver of the unidentified red van. His statement is useful to us because he expressly states that 'the cyclist was proceeding in a proper manner'. The statement was prepared by Canadian solicitors instructed and paid with the authority of the legal aid office.

15.   Correspondence which we have had with our Canadian agents suggests as follows:

  (i) Whilst Mr Bates has not the slightest antagonism or hostility towards the Plaintiff neither has he any sympathy for him.
  (ii) Mr Bates is it seems a hard-headed hard-talking man who may have struck up something of a relationship with the Defendant.
  (iii) In addition to signing the statement Mr Bates repeatedly told our Canadian agents that he 'would in no way speak against the lady'.

16.   As you requested in the Advice on Evidence, we have discussed with the Plaintiff whether he thinks it is worth going to the expense of arranging for Mr Bates to give oral testimony: such expense may well cause, or increase, any statutory charge on any damages recovered. The Plaintiff has decided not to take that risk. Mr Bates has been invited to travel to England at his own expense in order to give evidence but, not surprisingly, has declined to do so. He has told us that he is not intending to return here on holiday within the foreseeable future.

17.   For the sake of appearances, even though the Plaintiff does not wish to call Mr Bates, we nevertheless applied for legal aid approval to pay Mr Bates's travelling and other expenses. In the circumstances we are happy to be able to report that this application was (as we expected) unsuccessful.

18.   We have not as yet received a witness statement or a hearsay notice from the Defendant in respect of Mr Bates. We have written again to Mr Bates telling him of the date of the trial and asking him whether his previous plans not to visit England this year have changed. If we receive any reply to that letter we will of course send a copy to you.

19.   In our opinion the Plaintiff is likely to be quite an impressive witness. He is a straightforward, open and patently honest person. You will see from his proof of evidence (included at C) and from the agreed medical reports (in the wallet file) that he has at all times remained cheerful and optimistic about his recovery and shows not the slightest hint of 'compensationitis'.

20.   There are several points upon which it may be useful to cross-examine the Defendant. In particular, upon her decision to overtake the Plaintiff's bicycle at that junction, on the fact that she has lived in the area for upwards of ten years and so will be aware of the junction in question as being an accident black spot (as noted above, paragraph 5,

Fig 34: contd

this fact has been admitted) and on her experience of driving in this country. We understand that the Defendant is of Spanish origin. She first obtained a full English driving licence only three years ago. Information has reached us that she is prone to quick temper and sudden and dramatic attitudes. In contrast to the Plaintiff she is not likely to make a good witness.

21. As far as we know there are no other witnesses to the accident. Our only other evidence will be the bicycle and fishing tackle, as noted above in paragraph 11.

Medical Evidence

22. The medical evidence has been agreed. In accordance with the suggestion you made in the Advice on Evidence, Mrs Martin, the consultant orthopaedic surgeon involved, will attend court to give evidence to help with the elucidation of some of the medical problems involved in this case.

23. At the date of the accident the Plaintiff was aged 48: his date of birth is 6 February, 1946. In the accident he sustained an extremely serious injury to his right knee. The knee joint was disrupted: there was gross damage to the ligaments of the knee controlling the knee joint. He spent three months in plaster. Six months after the accident Mrs Martin carried out an operation which she hoped would help to repair damage to the knee. The Plaintiff was an in-patient for three weeks; he was in plaster from hip to ankle for six weeks. He returned to hospital twice per week thereafter for physiotherapy. Unfortunately the operation was not successful; the knee did not get better, but remained painful and not stable.

24. A second attempt to repair the damage was made in 1996, two years after the accident. Again the Plaintiff was in plaster from hip to ankle for six weeks. Unfortunately, yet again, the operation was not a success; the knee remains painful and not stable. Mrs Martin, who is a leading orthopaedic surgeon specialising in knee injuries, has stated that she can do no more for him.

25. The agreed medical reports are included in the wallet file. The Defendant's consultant, Mr Swift, agrees with everything in Mrs Martin's report, the only substantial point of difference between them being Mr Swift's suggestion that the Plaintiff has inhibited his recovery by gaining ten pounds in weight. Having regard to the Plaintiff's reduced mobility and his previously active life, it is hardly surprising that he has put on weight and this point is clearly not going to be pursued.

26. The Plaintiff remains then with a very serious injury. An artherodesis will be required in (now) 14 to 19 years' time. The only hope for the Plaintiff is that, between then and now, the operation to perform an artho-plasty may become sufficiently developed. An artherodesis simply freezes the joint, leaving the patient with a stiff leg whereas, if the artho-plasty can be successfully developed for a knee joint, it would restore that joint to working order. Such an operation is now common in the case of hips but is virtually unknown in the case of knees.

27. You will recall that, at one time, we were on the point of amending the claim to claim provisional damages. In the end, you advised the Plaintiff in conference (see the Note of Conference included at F) that it was not appropriate to do so. The medical evidence in this case is best regarded as final. Mrs Martin can give evidence not only of what has happened in this case but can also forecast the Plaintiff's deterioration in health and mobility in future years. We should proceed on the basis of the known medical knowledge under which it seems more than likely that an artherodesis will in due course have to be performed. We respectfully agree and support your advice on this matter. Further, that advice has clearly been vindicated by Mr Swift's acceptance of Mrs Martin's opinions. A claim for provisional damages, even assuming that we could obtain leave to amend now, would only reduce the compensation payable and not increase it.

28. The effect which the injuries have had upon the Plaintiff's recreational and social life are fully dealt with in his proof of evidence (see at C). He was a keen sportsman. He used to jog daily and was a regular competitor in marathon and half-marathon road races. This is now impossible because of the permanent injury to his leg. His other hobby, fishing, is largely unaffected.

Fig 34: contd

29. In August 1996 the Plaintiff was told that he was then fit to return to light work and he did so. Until he retired from the army at the age of 45 the Plaintiff had served in the Royal Corps of Signals and had risen to the rank of sergeant. On retirement from the army he obtained a job in a workshop as a repairs engineer for an office equipment firm. This job is secure and there is no claim for loss of future earnings.

Quantum

30. In your Opinion on Quantum (see at F) you advise that the Plaintiff should expect to receive, if his claim is wholly successful, compensation in the region of £24,000 to £28,000 for general damages for pain and suffering and loss of amenity and you set out various reports of cases and other information upon which your opinion was based. This advice is wholeheartedly agreed and accepted by us. Unfortunately however we have not yet had any sensible discussions with the Defendant's solicitors on *quantum* and so, unusually, we are unable to say what their attitude is likely to be.

31. Your Opinion also deals with the likelihood that the Plaintiff will be awarded compensation for loss of earning capacity and it sets out the law thereon. On the basis of your Opinion we have advised the Plaintiff, and he accepts, that his damages on this head will not exceed the pain and suffering and loss of amenity award (bearing in mind the type of injury, the type of work and his age). The award is likely to fall within the scale £9,350 (current gross annual salary) and £28,000 (see above) and will probably be at the lower end of that scale.

32. Although it was not possible to agree general damages or liability with the Defendant's solicitors we have been able to agree special damages without prejudice to the remaining issues. An up-to-date statement of them is included at A, which you will observe totals £6,108 net.

33. There has been no payment into court in this case. However, we will be extremely surprised if no last-minute negotiations take place and the Plaintiff has been warned to expect a 'door-step offer'. The Plaintiff did apply for an interim payment. Unfortunately the application came on before a rather timid District Judge and was unsuccessful.

Interest and Costs

34. The usual claim for interest having been pleaded, the Plaintiff will be entitled to interest on any sums awarded to him in accordance with the principles laid down in *Pickett v British Rail Engineering Ltd* [1980] AC 136 and *Wright v British Railways Board* [1983] 2 AC 773. We will make the necessary calculations at the trial.

35. As there has been no payment into court, the Plaintiff is not at risk on that score. There are no special applications to make regarding costs. The usual orders will be required and in any event an order for a legal aid taxation will be needed. If his claim succeeds the Plaintiff will also require an order for standard costs against the Defendant, High Court scale down to the date of transfer (see at G) and county court scale 2 thereafter. If his claim for compensation should fail it may be possible to restrict or limit the Plaintiff's liability for the Defendant's costs. The Omnia Refutanda Insurance plc are in reality instructing the Defendant's solicitors and the fact that the Plaintiff has a legal aid certificate indicates that he is of limited means and will have the usual protection of the Legal Aid Act 1988, s 17.

36. The trial is fixed for 10.30 am on Monday 14 July, 1997. We will be at court with the Plaintiff by 9.30 am for a final conference. Mrs Martin will, at her own request, be served with a witness summons and will also be available at court in good time.

You are briefed to appear for the Plaintiff at the trial of the action.

fee. In the absence of any evidence of such re-negotiation the taxing officer is likely to reduce the amount claimed in the solicitor's bill (*Greenslade on Costs* (FT Law & Tax), para 1.49). The re-negotiation should obviously take into account any work already done on the brief and any work lost because this brief was accepted.

The brief fee covers only the first day of the action and thereafter counsel will be entitled to a 'refresher' for each subsequent day of the trial. Thus refreshers should also be agreed in advance where the case has been estimated to last more than one day. A refresher usually amounts to one half or two thirds of the brief fee unless the brief fee is very substantial. Think of it like this; the refresher fee is counsel's daily rate. If it is half the brief fee, the brief will cover two days' work, one for preparation, the other for presentation. If it is two thirds of the brief fee, the brief covers one and a half day's work; a half day of preparation and the first day of the trial.

Do not forget the client whose case it is. Having delivered the brief it is a good idea to write, telling the client that this has been done, and confirming that it is now simply a question of waiting for the trial date.

Getting everybody to court

As soon as the precise hearing date and time is known the client and witnesses must be notified. They should also be sent reminders, at the very latest, a week or two before the hearing date arrives. This may have to be done by telephone, or personal messenger rather than by letter.

Skeleton arguments and list of cases to be cited

In High Court cases, a *Practice Direction* of 1995 (see p 489) requires each party to lodge a skeleton argument with the court (and to copy it to other parties) at least three clear days before the hearing. Skeleton arguments should not, without leave, exceed twenty pages of double spaced A4 paper and should cite the main authorities relied on. Although the *Practice Direction* does not apply to the county court the same practice will normally be appropriate there also.

Further when the trial is to take place in the county court or in a court outside London advance arrangements have to be made in order to ensure that the judge will have available copies of any law reports likely to be cited.

Last minute changes as to counsel

One of the most distressing aspects of civil litigation, for both the instructing solicitor and the client, is that sometimes counsel who has been advising in the case, has seen the client in conference, and has been adequately briefed well in advance, is then not free to present the case on the date fixed for trial. If counsel is 'part heard' in a different case obviously he cannot stop in the middle of it to conduct yours; consequently your brief will have to be 'returned'. In practice counsel's clerk will do everything possible to avoid this. Often he is successful and counsel is able to take the brief, the instructing solicitor knowing nothing of the agonies and manoeuvrings of counsel's clerk to bring that about. Sometimes he will fail and, much to your client's dissatisfaction, the brief has to go to a different barrister. It is a good general rule for an instructing solicitor never to accept a substitute barrister who is junior to the one originally briefed. The client will be disappointed anyway that the chosen barrister is not free to conduct his case, and that disappointment should not be compounded by replacing your counsel of ten years' experience with one of ten weeks.

The responsibility for appointing counsel belongs to solicitors, not to counsel's clerks. Where a brief has to be 'returned' counsel's clerk should so inform the solicitor to enable him to exercise complete freedom of choice as to whom to give it to. In practice this is not always possible, particularly as counsel's clerk will have kept the brief until the last minute in the hope that the chosen counsel will be free. Here much turns on the relationship between the individual solicitor and counsel's clerk. When he telephones to explain what has happened counsel's clerk may well suggest a substitute barrister from the same chambers. If the solicitor is satisfied as to the competence of the barrister then he can safely allow him to take the brief. Where a brief has to be 'returned' it is often advantageous if substitute counsel can be found in the same chambers, if only because the substitute counsel may at least have the opportunity to talk to your original counsel.

The practice of returning briefs is unfortunate, and if it happens too often instructing solicitors should seriously consider whether they should continue placing work with the chambers concerned. It must be at least arguable that counsel have the same professional duties with regard to returning briefs for trial as they have with regard to returning briefs for appeals assigned to the short warned list (as to which, see p 665).

Incapacity or death of judge

Solicitors should consider with their clients the risk of loss and expense which would be suffered if the trial were to be delayed or aborted because the judge becomes incapacitated or dies. In such cases the Lord Chancellor may, if he thinks fit, make some reimbursement of additional costs incurred by parties to the action (AJA 1985, s 53, *White Book* 5473, a scheme which also applies to interlocutory proceedings before district judges).

The Law Society has recommended an insurance scheme called 'Judicial Delay Insurance' details of which are available from the Law Society or from their insurance brokers.

Chapter 22

The Trial

Rights of audience

Section 27 of the Courts and Legal Services Act 1990 sets out five classes of person who have, or who may be given, rights of audience:

(1) professional advocates duly authorised by the General Council of the Bar, The Law Society or other bodies designated by Order in Council;

(2) persons authorised by an order or statute;

(3) persons authorised by a court in relation to proceedings before the court;

(4) litigants in person;

(5) solicitors' clerks (and corresponding employees of other professional advocates) in proceedings which are being heard in chambers.

Litigants in person

Litigants in person (see (4) above) are best treated as having rights of audience in all cases in all courts (for a curious exception see *Re McKernan* (1985) *The Times*, 26 October). A company of course has no 'person'; to appear in open court it must retain professional advocates (see (1) above), but a judge (especially in the county court) may allow some other person, for example the company secretary, to speak for it (see (3) above and see *ALI Finance Ltd v Havelet Leasing Ltd* [1992] 1 WLR 455).

A litigant in person is entitled to bring to the court a friend to take notes, quietly make suggestions and give advice. The court is entitled to know that the person sitting beside the litigant is an adviser (as opposed to, eg a party in another case or a spectator sitting in the wrong place). The court may also wish to know whether the adviser is likely to be called as a witness and whether the adviser is intending to claim or exercise any right of audience and if so under what category (see generally *R v Leicester City Justices, ex parte Barrow* [1991] 2 QB 260).

Barristers and solicitors

Barristers have full rights of audience in all cases and in all courts.

Solicitors have full rights of audience in all cases and in all courts except in hearings in open court in the High Court unless, in respect of a particular solicitor, The Law Society has granted that solicitor a Higher Courts advocacy certificate. Thus, for most solicitors, their rights of audience in High Court open court hearings are limited to formal and unopposed applications (*Practice Direction (Solicitors' Rights of Audience)* [1986] 1 WLR 545), certain bankruptcy cases (*Re Barnett* (1885) 15 QBD 169), judgment summons hearings in the Family Division (*Shaw v Shaw* (1983) *The Times*, 6 August) and hearings in open court before district judges on assessments of damages (*White Book* 35/7/4 and see p 213).

Solicitors' clerks and others

Solicitors' clerks have full rights of audience in cases heard in chambers in the High Court and county courts (but not in certain family proceedings).

Clerks who are Fellows of the Institute of Legal Executives also have rights of audience in respect of formal and unopposed applications in open court in the county court (CCA 1984, s 61).

Officers acting for local authorities in possession actions, and similar actions, have rights of audience in the county court, whether in open court or in chambers, in so far as the proceedings in the action are heard by the district judge (CCA 1984, s 60).

CLSA 1990 gives the Lord Chancellor power to make orders relaxing the restrictions on rights of audience in certain types of county court proceedings. The first such order made is the Lay Representatives (Rights of Audience) Order 1992 (SI 1992 No 1966, set out in the *Green Book* commentary to CCR Ord 19, r 1). This order authorises 'any person' to exercise rights of audience in small claims automatically referred to arbitration (see p 279) *unless and until* judgment is entered *if* the party represented also attends the hearing in question.

The role of the advocate's support team

Even if the main work at the trial is to be conducted by a specialist advocate it may still be advisable to have another professional also in attendance to provide proper support. Indeed in High Court and county court cases it is at the moment professional misconduct for a solicitor not to be present or represented whenever a barrister is briefed (*Guide to Professional Conduct of Solicitors* 1996, p 326). However, this may soon be changed to match the corresponding rule in the Bar's code of conduct which permits barristers, in certain circumstances, to agree that no solicitor or clerk need attend (*Code of Conduct of the Bar of England and Wales* 1990, para 608).

The support team's first task is to ensure that everyone is at the right court at the right time. The client and witnesses will probably be nervous.

The second task is to tell them what to expect and to set about quietly reassuring them. In civil cases this task can be shared with the specialist advocate, whether that person is a solicitor or a barrister. Barristers are permitted to discuss cases with a potential witness if *inter alia* the witness is the lay client, a character witness, an expert witness or a witness in respect of whom the barrister has been supplied with a proper proof of evidence (*Code of Conduct of the Bar of England and Wales* 1990, para 607; the above is a brief summary of the gist of this paragraph only; as to barristers interviewing witnesses and taking proofs of evidence in the absence of a solicitor or clerk, see paras 607 and 609).

It is particularly important to tell a witness what will happen when he enters the witness box. The clerk of the court will administer the oath or, if preferred, the form of solemn affirmation. The first advocate to ask him questions will be the one who wanted this witness to attend. The witness may well be handed a copy of the statement he made previously and asked to say whether its contents are true. Alternatively, the advocate may ask him a series of questions about the topics covered in that statement. The witness will then be asked questions by the advocate for the other party.

A witness should be told that whenever he is asked a question, whether by an advocate or by the judge he should give it as short an answer as possible. A 'yes' or 'no' is ideal, but, if the question cannot be answered in such simple terms, he should use as short a sentence as he can manage. Follow-up questions will be asked if necessary. It is vitally important that the witness giving evidence should not lose his temper and become embroiled in an argument with an advocate. This can never do any good and may do serious harm. It is a good idea to tell the witness to keep his eye on the judge, who is usually taking a note of the evidence. In any event, even when the question is not from the judge the answer should always be given to the judge. Witnesses often worry about what to call the judge. In the High Court the judge should be addressed as 'My Lord' or 'My Lady'; in the county court or official referees' court the judge should be addressed as 'Your Honour'. If you think this sort of formality would over-worry the witness just tell him to call the judge 'sir' or 'madam': no judge would object to this from a witness. Always explain the lay-out of the court to the client and witnesses so that they know who is who among the court officers and what their functions are.

In the High Court the solicitor usually has to fill in a form before the case is called on for trial giving his own name, the name of his firm, the name of counsel briefed to appear, the name of the case and the names and addresses of all witnesses to be called. In the county court advocates not already known to the judge usually hand in a note of their name.

Unlike criminal trials, whilst the case is going on there is no reason why the witnesses should not sit in the court. The other side will object if they do not want this to happen, but will have to have cogent reasons for excluding the witnesses. Most witnesses prefer to sit in rather than wait outside. Obviously the client will be present throughout anyway.

Whilst the case is going on, the support team should take a *verbatim* note of the evidence given. This is particularly important when the advocate is conducting a cross-examination and is unable to take his own *verbatim* notes. So far as is possible, take a *verbatim* note of everything that happens, and record the times.

In the county court the proceedings will be tape-recorded 'if the judge so directs' (CCR Ord 50, r 9B). If no such recording is made it is the duty of the advocate to ensure that a *verbatim* note is taken of the judgment. This will be invaluable if it is subsequently decided to appeal.

In the High Court, an official shorthand writer will be present or the proceedings will be tape-recorded 'unless the judge otherwise directs' (RSC Ord 68, r 1). Thus, usually there is an official record of the judgment (a copy of which can be obtained on payment of the prescribed fee—which is surprisingly high). It is still desirable for the advocate to take a *verbatim* note of the judgment. Again, this is particularly important if an appeal is to be considered because there is usually some delay before the official record is available.

The client will want to be present throughout the trial, but a witness may not. When such a witness has given his evidence the advocate should ask the court to release him. It is necessary to find out in advance whether the witness will wish to be released. The solicitor will also have told the witness beforehand to send a note of his net losses and expenses in attending court. Expert witnesses do not usually need reminding.

Procedure

At the start of the hearing the judge may give directions as to which party should speak first ('the right to begin') and as to the order of speeches if there are more than two parties. In an action tried without a jury, directions may be made dispensing with opening speeches or putting time limits on them (see generally RSC Ord 35, r 7; CCR Ord 22, r 5A and see p 489). It is now possible for proceedings to be conducted very briskly indeed; the judge first putting questions to each advocate in turn and then immediately requiring them to call their witnesses.

In the rest of this section we describe what is the current practice of trial procedure in cases in which no directions are made under the rules cited above.

The plaintiff's advocate has the right to begin unless the burden of proof of *all* issues lies on the defendant. The advocate begins by making an opening speech outlining the facts and indicating areas of dispute, the legal principles involved, and the areas where a ruling will have to be made. Frequently the pleadings, the agreed photographs, plan and documents are gone through. Both parties may then be invited to amplify briefly any skeleton arguments previously lodged (see further p 505 and the *Practice Direction* of 1995 noted on p 489). The first witness for the plaintiff will then be called. It is customary (though not essential) to call the plaintiff first. Each adult witness will take the oath or make a solemn affirmation. Child witnesses are at first questioned by the judge to determine whether they are competent to give evidence, either sworn (*R v Hayes* [1977] 1 WLR 234) or unsworn (Children Act 1989, s 96).

Where early disclosure of witness statements has taken place (see p 426) the court may allow that statement, or part of it, to stand as the evidence of that witness (see p 429). The trial judge is not required to so order, even where a direction to that effect has already been obtained (*Cole v Kivells* (1997) *The Times*, 2 May). Before the witness enters the box the opposing advocate should indicate whether there are any passages he is content to accept as the evidence of that witness or whether he requires some or all topics to be examined in the traditional way by non-leading questions and answers. The defence advocate is likely so to require if, eg it is hoped that the witness will not repeat on oath some of the things he said in his statement; on other matters his sworn evidence may contradict what was previously said; wherever factual evidence is strongly contested both advocates may prefer the traditional method so giving the judge the sight and sound of the witness thereby demonstrating the strength (or weakness) of his credibility. In other cases the traditional examination will be unnecessary; the witness, especially an expert witness, may be unlikely to be timid or fall into contradiction; or the evidence may be circumstantial or inferential only, its value depending more on interpretation than credibility.

Once the first question session, the examination in chief is concluded, the witness will be cross-examined by the defence advocate and then, if necessary, re-examined by the plaintiff's advocate. This procedure is then repeated with the other witnesses the plaintiff calls. The order in which the witnesses are to be called will have been decided upon at the time the advice on evidence was obtained (see p 448).

When all the plaintiff's witnesses have been called, the advocate for the defendant has the right, if he is calling evidence, to open his case. County court and High Court procedure differ here (see generally RSC Ord 35, r 7, and the *Green Book* commentary to CCR Ord 21, r 2). In the county court a defence advocate who elects to make an opening speech is not entitled to make a closing speech, except with leave of the court. The practice as to whether or not leave is usually given differs in different county courts. The advocate should be careful to ascertain the practice in the particular court in which he is to appear. The defendant's witnesses will be called in the same way as the plaintiff's advocate's, ie the defendant first and then other witnesses, each being examined, cross-examined and, if necessary, re-examined. At the conclusion of the evidence the defendant's advocate and then the plaintiff's advocate may make closing speeches.

Civil trial procedure differs from criminal trial procedure in three important respects:

(1) *Submission of no case to answer.* In a criminal trial the submission is made to the judge: if it fails the jury will later give a verdict on all the evidence. In a civil trial without a jury a defendant who makes such a submission is usually barred from calling evidence: *Alexander v Rayson* [1936] 1 KB 169. Were this not so the judge might be embarrassed by having to make a premature ruling on the plaintiff's evidence (and see *Cross & Tapper on Evidence*, 8th ed (Butterworths, 1995) p 193). In practice the civil judge always warns the defendant as to the consequences before the defendant addresses him on the submission.

(2) *The right to the last word.* Except where the defendant began or where the defendant calls no evidence, the advocate for the plaintiff has the last word in a civil case. Contrast criminal cases, and see Criminal Procedure (Right of Reply) Act 1964. Since civil trials rarely involve juries the advantage is minimal. In his closing speech the plaintiff's advocate should summarise his own submissions and answer his opponent's submissions. If he raises a point of law not previously raised his opponent may make a further speech in reply, but only in relation to that point. The closing speech for the plaintiff rarely needs to be a long one. If the judge has already decided to find in favour of the plaintiff he will tell plaintiff's advocate that he need not address him. If a judge tells you that he does not wish to hear you then you have won. Losers make the longest speeches.

(3) *Curtailing wasteful oral hearings.* A variety of rules and procedures in civil cases increases the likelihood of oral hearings being conducted more speedily and efficiently; exchange of witness statements (see p 426), written summaries of issues etc (see p 495), pre-reading of trial documentation by the judge (see p 493), flexibility as to advocates' speeches (see p 510), and the avoidance of unnecessary examination in chief where witness statements have been exchanged (see p 429).

In the future some further improvements in civil trial procedure are likely to be introduced. Trial procedures currently adopted in the Commercial Court already differ from general Queen's Bench cases in several significant respects (see p 274). The differences are important given the trend in recent years for new ideas to be introduced in the specialist courts first before being extended to all cases. The official referees' courts are also experimenting with new procedures (see p 270) in particular the order in which witnesses are called. Why should the witnesses always be grouped according to the party calling them? Given that expert reports and witness statements have already been exchanged, everybody will know what every witness is expected to say. Thus, why not group the witnesses according to the issues instead? For example, assume that, in a building dispute which is likely to last six weeks, one issue turns upon the chemical analysis of the cement mix used. Each side is intending to call an expert witness on this issue and expert reports have been exchanged. What is to be gained by dividing the testimony of these two witnesses by three or more weeks? It is much more convenient if one expert follows the other one into the witness box.

Coping with disasters

Even in a well-run practice things may occasionally go wrong. For example, on arriving at court it is discovered that a vital notice has not been served, or even that the witnesses have not been notified to attend the trial. If a blunder has occurred, then, unless the situation can be retrieved by agreement with the other side, the solicitor must explain to the court quite frankly what has happened, ask for an adjournment, and accept the responsibility. The solicitor can expect some form of admonition from the judge and will almost certainly be expected to pay personally the costs 'thrown away' (see further p 537).

If, when the case is called on, no-one from either side appears the action will be struck out, but the judge may reinstate it later. If only one side fails to attend the trial may proceed and judgment can be entered and a claim or counterclaim can be dismissed (see generally, RSC Ord 35, r 1; CCR Ord 21, rr 1 and 3). Any judgment made in the absence of one party may be set aside on such terms as the court thinks just (RSC Ord 35, r 2; CCR Ord 37, r 2). However, a defendant who deliberately stays away from a hearing is unlikely to succeed on an application to set aside judgment, even if he has an arguable defence (*Shocked v Goldschmidt* (1994) *The Times*, 4 November).

CLSA 1990, s 12 enables the High Court or county court to impose fines on parties or their representatives who fail to appear, or fail to give the court due notice of their desire to cancel a hearing, or of their inability to appear at it. The latecomer or non-attender must, of course, be given an opportunity to be heard before any fine is imposed. The maximum fine at present is £1,000. This sum may well be payable in addition to any penalty order made in respect of any costs which have been wasted (see p 537).

The art of advocacy

Some simple instructions can be given for those who aspire to be good advocates. First, read *The Technique of Persuasion* by Sir David Napley, 4th ed (Sweet & Maxwell, 1991). What follows in this section is only a short introduction to a very large topic. However, no-one should think that advocacy can ever be properly learned from books. You should attend court as much as possible where you will see how it should be done; and, unfortunately, sometimes, how it should not be done. A third instruction for the aspirant is to start off with the easy cases, particularly work in chambers.

Preparation

The key to successful advocacy is preparation. Thus, the litigation solicitor, even if he has no intention of ever appearing as an advocate, must know something of the art of advocacy otherwise he will not be able to brief his chosen advocate properly.

The advocate must get his points across. However, he must have decided beforehand which points he wants to make and the order in which he must make them. A useful and efficient practice here is to prepare and disclose to the opponent and the court a note of written submissions and skeleton arguments. This practice is becoming more and more frequently used at trials (see p 505) on appeals (see p 663) and even in small claims arbitrations (see p 279). (In most interlocutory hearings you will have no reason to, and no opportunity to, lodge written submissions in advance of the hearing. You can often, however, begin your part of the proceedings by handing to the court and to your opponent a shortlist of the submissions you are about to make. Curiosity alone will ensure that everyone reads it, even if they pretend not to.)

Examination in chief

Start with questions as to the witness's name, address, relationship to the parties or proceedings and, if an expert witness, qualifications. Where a statement made by this witness has previously been disclosed to the other parties, you will often show the witness a copy of that statement, get him to confirm that it is his statement and to authenticate any documents referred to in the statement (eg letters he wrote and received). If appropriate you might then invite the judge to confirm that the statement may stand as the evidence of this witness in this case. However, before so addressing the judge you should ask the witness a couple of additional simple questions in order to let him settle into the witness box and find his voice before the cross-examination begins. Also, almost invariably, there will be one or two topics upon which you will seek his testimony which are not covered in his statement; as to whether you will be permitted to raise these topics, see p 429.

What happens if your opponent asks you to examine the witness in the traditional question and answer method (see p 511)? For the beginner this is the advocacy skill which is the most difficult to learn. This is because, on disputed matters, one cannot ask one's own witness leading questions, that is, questions which prompt the witness or which assume a fact not yet proved. Thus one cannot normally ask one's landlord-client the question 'Did the tenant pick up a hammer and smash the furniture?' Neither can you ask 'what did the tenant do after he had picked up a hammer and smashed the furniture?' The technique is to lead the witness through undisputed matters—for example name, are you the plaintiff, did you grant a monthly tenancy to the defendant, did you visit the premises last November?—and then ask a general question such as 'what do you remember particularly about that occasion?' If that does not obtain the desired response try another general question such as 'what complaint do you now make against this tenant?' Once the witness has started upon the desired topic one keeps him there by asking how, when, why, type questions: How did you react to that? When did that happen? Why did you do that? The question most frequently asked once the witness is giving relevant evidence is 'And then what happened?'

During the examination in chief the opposing advocates should remain seated and silent. They should listen carefully for any questions which are objectionable, eg questions which lead the witness or questions raising irrelevant issues (questions about other persons, other places, other times or questions about the witness's non-expert opinions).

If a question is asked which you wish to object to, or if the witness strays into irrelevance, how should you make an objection? Please do not use the Hollywood method (*Objection, your Honour!*). Simply stand up and state politely 'That is not evidence'. The other advocate should then at least pause. When he or she does so you should resume your seat, unless the judge addresses you.

Cross-examination

The true test of an advocate is his or her proficiency in the skill, or art, of deadly cross-examination; the ability to destroy the evidence of an opposing witness by asking a series of piercing, puncturing, pulverising questions. An experienced advocate will execute a staged campaign which has frequently been tried and tested on other witnesses and which has been thoroughly adapted and prepared so as to undermine this particular witness. The opening shots are aimed at his confidence; next, several barrages of questions will cause the witness to accept a series of facts damaging to his previous testimony; the final round is often the question 'And yet you still say ... ' which receives a doubtful, embarrassed, and crestfallen reply. Proficiency in this skill still requires years of practice even though, because of exchange of witness statements it is now so much easier to plan almost every question in advance.

When planning your questions for cross-examination, try to identify the aspects of this witness's evidence which are most vulnerable to attack. Generally speaking the weaknesses which the evidence may have, and which it is your job to expose, are ambiguity, insincerity, faulty perception and erroneous memory. In practice most of your best scores will come from the weaknesses of faulty perception and erroneous memory. The most likely weaknesses in the evidence of experts are somewhat different: ambiguity (ie more than one opinion on the matter is tenable); insincerity (the expert is not stating honest independent opinions but has descended into the arena); and faulty perception (look for omissions in his report; it is normally easier to cross-examine on what is not there rather than on something which is there).

Beginners usually find that the skill of cross-examining is, at first anyway, the easier skill to acquire. This is because, in cross-examining, you are allowed to ask leading questions. Cross-examination is essential because a failure to challenge evidence given in chief implies acceptance of it. The perceived problem about cross-examination is the difficulty in aggressively questioning someone whose evidence you think is unshake-able. The danger is that aggressive cross-examination may be counter-productive; it may appear to strengthen rather than weaken your opponent's case.

One way of contesting the opponent's evidence without damaging the merits of one's own case is by formulating the question 'I put it to you that ...' Thus 'I put it to you that an important part of the evidence you have given here today is untrue. I put it to you that, in the plaintiff's presence, you did pick up a hammer and smash the furniture.' This formulation does challenge the evidence strongly but prevents you becoming embroiled in an argument you may not win and, therefore may appear to lose.

Everyone will agree that the 'I put it to you' formulation is nowadays considered old fashioned and stagey but these are not necessarily fatal faults. Its staginess makes it more uncomfortable for the witness to answer than for you to ask. On the other hand one common weakness of this formulation is that it almost invariably compels the witness to stick to what he said before. In the result he just repeats his evidence.

An alternative method is to say, eg 'You know that my client has said ...'. If nothing else it will involve a repetition of your own side's evidence rather than the other side's evidence. It also puts pressure on the witness to find some middle ground to adopt, ie to retract or qualify what he previously said. This formulation is, however, best confined to putting your client's case to a witness. On the whole, questions in cross-examination should be just that; questions, not statements. Also, it is unprofessional to seek to browbeat the opposing witnesses or to subject them to an argumentative and overbearing assault.

A common mistake of beginners is to try to comment on the evidence as each point is scored. The proper place for comment is in your closing speech. And do not do what so many do; seek to get in some comment indirectly by asking the witness that one question too many; the one which explains away any comment you might otherwise have been able to make.

Examples

In a contract action: Was that letter the first time you complained? (*Yes.*) You didn't complain before, then? (*I tried to telephone many many times but your client's phone has been disconnected.*)

In a road accident case: Your mother was also a passenger, wasn't she? (*Yes.*) But she hasn't come to give evidence for you today has she? (*She wanted to. But she suffered a massive stroke three weeks ago. She's still in hospital.*)

On a claim for a debt which the defendant says he repaid, in cash, on meeting the plaintiff in the street: Do you often walk about with £4,000 in cash in your wallet? (*Yes.*) Show me how much you've got in your wallet today. (*Witness produces over £4,000 in cash.*)

Re-examination

Re-examination of your witness has two purposes. It can be used to restore your own witness's credibility. For example, where it has been suggested in cross-examination that he would not have had a clear observation of certain matters, you can ask questions demonstrating the amount of detail he can recall. Re-examination can also be used to allow your witness to explain points made in cross-examination which seem adverse but in fact are not; you see this especially when the cross-examiner has insisted upon a yes or no answer and your witness replied 'Yes but'. Re-examination must be confined to matters arising out of the cross-examination. Leading questions should not be asked.

Judgment

After the closing speeches the judge will deliver his judgment. He will sometimes adjourn to the following day before doing so, particularly if the hour is late, and sometimes he may expressly reserve judgment, in which case the parties will be told at a later date when to attend to hear the judgment delivered.

After judgment has been given there are several formal applications which may have to be made.

(1) The successful advocate will ask for final judgment to be entered (strictly speaking this is not necessary: it dates from ancient rules of court, long since amended). High Court money judgments are usually payable forthwith (see *White Book* 42/2/2). County court money judgments provide for payment within fourteen days unless the judge otherwise orders (CCR Ord 22, r 2); consider applying for payment forthwith. In both courts the payment must be made direct to the judgment creditor, and not into court (unless the judgment otherwise provides).

(2) On a claim for debt or damages interest may be awarded in the judgment (see generally pp 15 and 75). The calculations are best done immediately: you should take a pocket calculator along for this purpose. In the High Court every judgment creditor is also entitled to interest on the judgment at the statutory rate (at present eight per cent *per annum*)

under the Judgments Act 1838, s 17, until the debt is paid. Interest under this statute runs from the date upon which the amount of the judgment debt was finally assessed or agreed (*Thomas v Bunn* [1991] 1 AC 362; a different rule applies to orders for costs; there interest runs from the date costs were awarded, ie after taxation the interest is calculated retrospectively, *Hunt v RM Douglas (Roofing) Ltd* [1990] 1 AC 398). In the county court similar rules as to judgment interest have been made for all judgments of £5,000 or more (see p 18).

(3) The successful advocate will ask for costs (possibly 'to be taxed if not agreed'). In the county court the judge will specify the relevant scale of costs (see p 528): also, he may certify that on taxation the district judge shall not be bound by the amounts appearing in that scale (see p 529). The general principle is that 'costs follow the event', ie are ordered against the loser. Where the 'event' is a technical win only the judge may make no order as to costs between the parties or may award costs against the winner (see eg *Alltrans Express Ltd v CVA Holdings Ltd* [1984] 1 WLR 394, contract action for damages, the decision in which would not establish any independent legal right; nominal damages of £2 awarded against the defendants; the defendants were regarded as the successful parties and costs were awarded to them).

(4) A ruling may now be sought in respect of the costs of any interlocutory application which were 'reserved' (see p 571).

(5) Where a payment into court has been made an application for payment out should be made and directions should be sought as to the interest which will have accrued on the money whilst in court (see p 351).

(6) Any advocate appearing for a legally-aided party must apply for a legal aid taxation (see p 573).

Associate's certificate (High Court)

RSC Ord 35, rr 10 and 10A provide that at the conclusion of the trial of any action in the Queen's Bench Division the associate in attendance at the trial (ie the clerk of the court) must make a certificate in which he certifies:
  (1) the time actually occupied by the trial (this is for the information of the taxing officer: see Chapter 23 on Costs);
  (2) any order made by the judge under RSC Ord 38, r 5, allowing the admission in evidence of a plan, photograph or model despite a failure to give notice (see p 492), or under r 6 which deals with the revocation or variation of certain orders as to evidence;
  (3) every finding of fact by the jury, where the trial was with a jury;
  (4) the judgment given by the judge;
  (5) any order made by the judge as to costs.
  (6) any opinion expressed by the judge that the proceedings should have been commenced in a county court (see further p 537).

In a district registry case the certificate should be collected from the associate immediately after the hearing, together with the copy bundle of pleadings that was lodged with the court when the case was set down. In cases tried in London the certificate and pleadings are automatically sent to the solicitor entitled to draw up the judgment and need not be collected in person.

RSC Ord 35, r 12 makes it the duty of every party who has put in an exhibit at the trial to apply to the associate immediately after the trial for the return of that exhibit, and to preserve it as far as practicable in case it should be needed in the event of an appeal.

Drawing up and entering the judgment

In the Queen's Bench Division the successful party should draw up the judgment and enter it in the books of the court. He must produce the associate's certificate and, if he is the plaintiff, the original writ (see generally RSC Ord 42, r 5, and *White Book* 744). Until the judgment has been drawn up it cannot be enforced, costs cannot be taxed and money cannot be taken out of court (as to statutory interest under the Judgments Act 1838, see p 517).

In the county court, strictly it is for the court to draw up the judgment. There are several prescribed forms of judgment in the *Green Book* and if the order made can be suitably recorded in such a form this will be done by the court staff. However, if there is no suitable prescribed form the court staff will sometimes request the successful party's solicitor to draw up the judgment as he would have had to do in a High Court case.

Amendments of judgments or orders

RSC Ord 20, r 11, states that 'Clerical mistakes in judgments or orders, or errors arising therein from any accidental slip or omission, may at any time be corrected by the court on motion or summons without an appeal.' (Compare CCR Ord 15, r 5, which is in similar terms.) This rule is known as the 'slip rule'. Although mainly used to correct mistakes made when drawing up a judgment or order, it can also be used to correct other errors and omissions in expressing the manifest intention of the court (see *White Book* 20/11/1). The court also has 'an inherent power to vary its own orders so as to carry out its own meaning and to make its meaning plain' (*White Book* 20/11/1; and see *Pearlman v Bernhard Bartels* [1954] 1 WLR 1457, amendment of proceedings including the judgment to describe the defendant as 'Josef Bartels trading as Bernhard Bartels').

Once a judgment has been drawn up and perfected, the slip rule does not extend so as to permit the judge to alter his decision even if he subsequently regrets it; the proper solution in such a case is to exercise any right of appeal there may be (*R v Cripps, ex parte Muldoon* [1984] QB 686). On the other hand, no slip rule power is needed if a judge changes his mind *before* his order is drawn up and perfected (*Pittalis v Sherefettin* [1986] 1 QB 868).

Applications under the slip rule are often made with regard to High Court default judgments where the error was not that of the court but emanated from an accidental mistake made by a solicitor (*Navimprex Centrala Navala v George Moundreas & Co SA* [1983] Gazette 1143, default judgment entered for a sum $63,400 more than was due).

Stay of execution

A stay of execution is an order preventing the successful party proceeding to enforcement. Generally speaking, there are only three sorts of cases in which a stay of execution might be considered.

(1) *Pending an appeal and in the county court, pending an application for a new trial.* Observe that the service of a notice of appeal or application for a new trial does not of itself operate as a stay (RSC Ord 59, r 13; CCR Ord 37, r 8). An application has to be made to the trial court either at the time it gives judgment or subsequently on notice. If necessary a further application can be made to the Court of Appeal. The applicant has to persuade the court that a stay is necessary. For example, he may show that, without a stay of execution, he would be ruined and that he has an appeal which has some prospect of success (*Linotype-Hell Finance Ltd v Baker* [1993] 1 WLR 321).

(2) *Pending trial of a counterclaim.* A stay may be granted in these circumstances if the judgment was entered on a claim without a trial and a related counterclaim still remains to be tried, eg a summary judgment (see p 227). A stay will be refused if the judgment in question was obtained at a trial, unless the circumstances are exceptional (*Schofield v Church Army* [1986] 1 WLR 1328).

(3) *Where the judgment debtor is unable to pay.* In the High Court a party against whom a money judgment is entered can apply under RSC Ord 47, r 1, either to the court at the time the judgment is given or later by summons to a district judge. An application made by summons must be supported by an affidavit disclosing the debtor's income, his assets and any other liabilities he has. The summons and a copy of the affidavit must be served on the judgment creditor at least four clear days before the return day. The usual form of order granting a stay requires the debtor to pay the judgment debt by specified instalments. An order under RSC Ord 47, r 1 prevents the creditor enforcing the judgment only by writ of *fi fa* (described on p 592). However, all the other methods of enforcement require an application to the court in any event (as to the effect on insolvency proceedings, see p 632).

In the Queen's Bench Division a stay of execution by consent is now obtainable in certain cases without leave (see further p 371). In cases of urgency it is possible to obtain a stay *ex parte*. In such a case, if a writ of *fi fa* has already been issued (see p 592) it is most important to inform the sheriff of this stay as soon as possible (*White Book* 47/1/2).

In the county court a judgment debtor who wants time to pay should ask the trial court to order payment by instalments (cf Form N30). The proper application to make after the judgment has been given is an application to the court staff under CCR Ord 22, r 10 for a variation of the rate of payment (see p 606).

Chapter 23

Costs

Of the many problems the litigation solicitor has to deal with, problems concerning costs are often the most difficult and the most time-consuming of all. There are many reasons why this should be so. First, whether the actions concern road accident claims, breach of contract or probate, most litigation is about money. Many parties are dissatisfied with what they receive, or have to pay. They are likely to feel the same dissatisfaction about the other money element in the action, costs. Secondly, most clients expect to win. No matter how carefully their solicitor advised them, no matter how pessimistic he told them to be, they still expect, at the end of the day, to win: and not just win partially or mainly, they expect to win outright, totally and completely. Such expectations are often unrealistic. (See further on these two topics, p 20, the first interview.) Thirdly, the orders for costs the court makes between litigants deal with only one aspect of the subject. There are others, in particular, the obligations as to costs between the solicitor and the client. Each aspect of costs raises questions of reasonableness. But what is reasonable from one standpoint may be quite unreasonable when viewed from another standpoint.

> *Example*
> The clients, a well-known up-market department store, are sued by a customer who claims to have been sold a joint of meat which was rotten. The damages claimed by the customer are as nothing compared to the injury which will be done to the clients' reputation if they lose this case. Acting on instructions, their solicitor retains England's most illustrious and fashionable barrister, with whose clerk a brief fee of £10,000 is agreed. After a two-hour trial in the county court, the customer's claim is dismissed with costs.

Is it reasonable for the barrister to expect the solicitor to pay the £10,000 brief fee? If so, is it reasonable for the solicitor to pass that cost on to the clients? Is it reasonable for the clients to look to the losing plaintiff in respect of such a fee? These three questions (for the answers, see p 588) each raise different issues which will be considered below.

Fourthly, the law as to costs, which is part principle, part arithmetic and always multi-faceted, is one of the most, if not in fact the most, arcane, cold and dense areas of English law. It is also one of the most fluid and constantly changing areas of law. Consider for example the following dictum concerning a ruling as to whether joint appellants should be able to recover the costs of separate representation in the House of Lords:

> What then is the proper approach? As in all questions to do with costs, the fundamental rule is that there are no rules. Costs are always in the discretion of the court, and practice, however widespread and long standing, must never be allowed to harden into a rule (*per* Lord Lloyd of Berwick in *Bolton Metropolitan District Council v Secretary of State for the Environment* [1995] 1 WLR 1176).

Costs between litigants

General principles

Both in the High Court and in the county court the court's power to award costs is discretionary (RSC Ord 62, r 2; CCR Ord 38, r 1). As between litigants the general principle is 'costs follow the event', ie the loser will be ordered to pay the winner's costs and will be left to bear his own (see p 517). The general principle sometimes gives way in particular circumstances. For example, the court may award the winner only a proportion of his costs (see p 567) or his costs from or up to a specified stage of the proceedings (see the split orders for costs made when a plaintiff fails to beat a payment into court, see p 329). Sometimes the court may make no order as to costs, in which case each party will be left to bear his own. Sometimes the winner may have to pay the loser's costs of certain matters. For example, costs of any amendment made without leave; the costs of an application for the extension of a time period obtained; the costs of proving facts specified in a notice to admit facts; the costs of proving the authenticity of a document where he served a notice of non-admission (see p 433). In each of these examples the penalty is imposed automatically unless the court otherwise orders (RSC Ord 62, r 6; CCR Ord 38, r 1). Lastly, the winner may be ordered to pay the loser's costs (see cases cited on p 517) and/or any costs arising from 'misconduct or neglect', eg where the order for directions recorded a refusal to make reasonable agreements or admissions (see p 456; RSC Ord 62, r 10; CCR Ord 38, rr 1 and 19A; and see further p 537).

In certain cases the court's discretion as to costs is *restricted*: it can only be exercised subject to certain limits, thus:

(1) Trustees, personal representatives and mortgagees are entitled to recoup their expenses from the trust fund or mortgaged property. They can also recoup any costs they are ordered to pay unless the court otherwise orders, which it can do only if the fiduciary has acted unreasonably or, in the case of trustees and personal representatives, has

acted for his own benefit rather than for the benefit of the fund (RSC Ord 62, r 6; CCR Ord 38, r 1).

(2) Under the Slander of Women Act 1891 words spoken or published which impute unchastity or adultery to any woman or girl are actionable without proof of special damage. But the plaintiff can recover no more costs than damages unless the judge certifies that there were reasonable grounds for bringing the action.

(3) Under the Legal Aid Act 1988, s 17, no costs can be recovered from a legally-aided party until the court has determined the extent of his liability, which cannot exceed the amount (if any) which it is reasonable for him to pay having regard to all the circumstances including the means of both parties and their conduct in connection with the dispute (see generally p 55, and note the courts' power to order costs of successful defendants out of the legal aid fund).

(4) The Rent Act 1977, s 141, and the Housing Act 1985, s 110, provide that a person who takes proceedings under those Acts in the High Court which could have been brought in the county court is not entitled to recover any costs: in these cases the court cannot otherwise order.

Definition of costs

RSC Ord 62, r 1(4) states as follows:

> References to costs shall be construed as including references to fees, charges, disbursements, expenses and remuneration and, in relation to proceedings (including taxation proceedings), also include references to costs of or incidental to those proceedings.

Costs between litigants typically include court fees, remuneration for solicitors and counsel, and witness allowances. The words 'of or incidental to ... proceedings' permit the inclusion of costs which were usefully incurred in anticipation of proceedings, eg the letter before action and the cost of collecting evidence such as the police accident report, and also costs incurred in negotiations held in an attempt to settle the proceedings (see generally *Re Gibson* [1981] Ch 179). The phrase 'costs of or incidental to those proceedings' also marks an important difference in the definition of costs as between litigants and the definition of costs as between a solicitor and his own client and as between a solicitor and the legal aid fund. As between litigants, the winner is entitled to recover from the loser only that part of his solicitor's bill as relates to the action (the so-called *costs of action*). The solicitor's right to remuneration is not so limited. The solicitor of a fee-paying client is entitled to remuneration for all work properly done for that client whether or not it is in respect of items reclaimable from the loser. Similarly a solicitor acting for an assisted person is entitled to remuneration for all work covered by the legal aid certificate, including work upon items which are not costs of action. Consequently it often happens that the costs *payable by* the loser do not provide a full refund of the costs *payable to* the winner's solicitor.

Examples of these differences are given below (see p 572 and p 580). The potential existence of such differences, and the potential difficulties there may be in enforcing costs orders, should be thought of as the 'nuisance value' of the action and should be borne in mind in any negotiations for a compromise.

Costs against non-parties

The court's discretion as to costs is wide enough to permit, in an exceptional case, the making of an order against persons who are not parties to the action. Even in the exceptional cases, the person against whom the order is made will usually have some substantial connection with the proceedings, eg as the next friend or solicitor of one of the parties (see p 91 and p 537) or as a party to separate proceedings which are heard at the same time (*Aiden Shipping Ltd v Interbulk Ltd* [1986] AC 965) or a person who has maintained (ie provided funds for) unsuccessful proceedings, whether lawfully (eg a trade union assisting a member suing his employer) or unlawfully (see generally *McFarlane v E E Caledonia Ltd (No 2)* [1995] 1 WLR 366). Guidance as to the principles to be applied in the exceptional cases is given in *Symphony Group plc v Hodgson* [1994] QB 179 (and see *White Book* 62/2/7).

In multi-party litigation a 'costs sharing order' may be made. This is an order under which lead actions (ie test cases) are selected. Where parties to those actions incur costs, either personally or through the legal aid fund, all other parties with a common interest (ie all the other plaintiffs or defendants as the case may be) will become liable to contribute rateably to those costs on a *per capita* basis. The order is made pre-trial but expressly excludes any fetter on the trial court's powers and indeed contains a liberty to apply to vary the order before trial if circumstances alter (eg some parties abandon the litigation before trial or negotiate individual compromises with the common opponent); see generally *Ward v Guinness Mahon plc* [1996] 1 WLR 894 and see also the legal aid rules on multi-party litigation, *White Book* 4199/1).

Indemnity principle

An order requiring one party to pay another party's costs is an order to *indemnify* the other party only. The indemnity is often imperfect in that it may not cover every item which the other party is bound (by contract) to pay his own solicitor. The loser often pays the winner a sum which is *smaller* than the sum the winner pays to his own solicitor (see p 580). Because of the indemnity principle the loser can never be required to pay *more* than the winner is obliged to pay. This is because the order for costs belongs to the winner; it does not belong to the winner's solicitor.

Examples

In *Gundry v Sainsbury* [1910] 1 KB 645, the plaintiff, a labourer, was awarded £15 damages for injuries sustained by the bite of a dog. The

plaintiff had expressly agreed with his solicitors that he would not have
to pay them any costs. It was held that, having incurred no costs in
pursuing his claim, the plaintiff could recover none.

In *British Waterways Board v Norman* (1993) 26 HLR 232, as a
result of a private prosecution the British Waterways Board was fined
£2,000 for statutory nuisance and ordered to pay the complainant
£1,500 compensation. The complainant was of very limited means. No
legal aid is available for private prosecutions. Her solicitors knew of
her circumstances, did not discuss costs with her, did not comply with
the written professional standards as to costs (see p 21) and only
expected to be paid by her if (as they assumed) her case was successful
and she was awarded costs. On these facts it was found that there must
have been a contingency fee agreement between her and the solicitors
and, such agreement being void and unenforceable, no costs order
could be made against the British Waterways Board.

The indemnity principle is now subject to three important inroads or
exceptions. First, it has always been the case that, so long as the winner
is subject to a potential legal obligation to pay his solicitor's costs, full
costs can be recovered from the loser even if the winner was in fact
maintained by someone else (eg his employer, *R v Miller* [1983] 1 WLR
1056) or even if the solicitor never expected to call upon that potential
obligation.

> If ... it is made clear that the client is liable for costs irrespective of the
> outcome of the proceedings, there can be no objection to the solicitor agreeing
> that such liability need not be discharged until the outcome of those
> proceedings, if any, is known. At that stage, provided it has not formed part of
> the basis of the agreement with the client, it would be open to the solicitors, if
> the circumstances warranted it, to decide not to enforce their right to be paid,
> in the event that some or all of their costs were unrecovered from the other
> party to the proceedings (*per* Tuckey J in *British Waterways Board v Norman*
> above).

The second inroad or exception to the indemnity principle is the Civil
Legal Aid (General) Regulations 1989, reg 107B under which costs orders
in favour of an assisted party can be taxed at normal rates and then
'belong' to the assisted party's solicitor to the extent that they exceed the
prescribed rates (see further, p 573).

The last inroad or exception which must be mentioned here is the new
law on conditional fee agreements. In the limited areas of civil practice to
which this law applies (ie personal injury, insolvency and proceedings
before the European Commission of Human Rights and the European
Court of Human Rights) an agreement between solicitor and own client
similar to the one inferred by the court in *British Waterways Board v
Norman* (above) is no longer void and unenforceable.

Taxation of costs

The party receiving costs is entitled only to his 'taxed costs', ie that part of his expenditure which is assessed and approved by the taxing officer of the court (RSC Ord 62, r 3(4); CCR Ord 38, r 1; for exceptions 'agreed costs', 'assessed costs', and 'fixed costs', see pp 565 *et seq*). Orders for costs may be made at various stages throughout the action (see pp 568 *et seq*). However, unless, in a particular case, a specific direction to the contrary is made, all these orders will be taxed together, at the conclusion of the proceedings (RSC Ord 62, r 8; CCR Ord 38, r 1). The amount of costs which will be allowed on taxation depends upon the *basis* on which the taxation is made and upon the *scale* of costs applicable to the case.

Basis of taxation

There are only two bases of taxation upon which the costs may be awarded between litigants (see generally RSC Ord 62, r 12; CCR Ord 38, r 19A). The *standard basis* which is defined as 'a reasonable amount in respect of all costs reasonably incurred and any doubts [as to questions of reasonableness] shall be resolved in favour of the paying party'. And the *indemnity basis* which is defined as 'all costs ... except insofar as they are of an unreasonable amount or have been unreasonably incurred and any doubts [as to questions of reasonableness] shall be resolved in favour of the receiving party'. (The use of the word 'doubts' in these definitions does not alter the standard of proof on questions as to costs: it is the usual civil standard, proof on a balance of probabilities. One should treat the references to doubts as indicating upon which party falls the burden of proof; see further p 531.)

The distinction between the two bases lies in the question who is to get the benefit of the doubt on any questions of reasonableness. Accordingly on costs as to which there is no doubt there will be no difference whichever basis is used. On the other hand, where there is doubt, the costs in question will be 'taxed off' if the standard basis is used but will be left in if the indemnity basis is used. Examples of doubts which may arise include the following:

(1) the use of leading counsel (*White Book* 62/A2/9);
(2) the quantum of counsel's fees (*White Book* 62/14/1 and 62/A2/11);
(3) the number and length of attendances on client and witnesses;
(4) the status of fee-earner (senior solicitor, assistant solicitor, legal executive etc) which it was reasonable to employ;
(5) the hourly rate and mark-up (see p 533) which it is appropriate to award.

From the receiving party's point of view the indemnity basis is to be preferred since it will give him the benefit of any doubts. However, in practice this basis is awarded only in exceptional cases (and see *Billson v Residential Apartments Ltd* [1992] 1 AC 494). Exceptional cases include major test cases (see Chapter 6), cases in which the paying party's conduct is considered to have been wholly unmeritorious (*House of Spring Gardens Ltd v Waite* [1991] 1 QB 241) or oppressive (*Singh v Observer Ltd* [1989] 2 All ER 751) or in contempt of court (*Midland Marts Ltd v Hobday* [1989] 1 WLR 1143). The standard basis is the one which, as its name implies, will ordinarily be used in most cases. Costs will be taxed on the indemnity basis only if the court awarding costs expressly so directed (RSC Ord 62, r 3(4); CCR Ord 38, r 1). Costs will be taxed on the standard basis in each of the following cases:

(1) no order for costs was required (eg where a case terminates on the acceptance of a payment into court);
(2) the order specifies the standard basis;
(3) the order is silent as to the basis to be used;
(4) the order specifies a basis other than the standard basis or the indemnity basis (RSC Ord 62, rr 3(4), 12(3); CCR Ord 38, r 1).

The last entry in the list just given shows that, as between litigants there are only two bases upon which costs can be awarded. Indeed no other bases are defined in the rules. RSC Ord 62, r 12(3) specifically prohibits judges from attempting to turn back the clock and awarding costs between litigants on any of the old bases. If today a judge decides, whether by accident or by design, to award a party 'costs on party and party basis' or 'utmost costs' this sub-rule will steer his order back to modernity by converting his order into an order for costs on the standard basis. When acting for the winning party, the best order for taxed costs you can get against the losing party is an order which specifies the indemnity basis: any other order for taxed costs will be on the standard basis.

Scale of costs

The basis of taxation tells you, eg which letters, instructions to counsel and attendances at court the party receiving the costs can claim for and limits, in general terms, the amounts which can be claimed. The scale of costs applicable to the case tells you how those items should be set out in the bill and, sometimes, specifies in pounds and pence how much can be claimed for these items. In the High Court there is only one scale, RSC Ord 62, Appendix 2. No pounds and pence figures are given in this scale: the actual amount which may be allowed for any item is entirely within the discretion of the taxing officer (as to how that discretion should be exercised, see further p 532).

In the county court there are three scales of costs. Which one applies in a particular case may be specified in the order for costs. If the order does not specify it, the scale is determined:

(1) In default actions (see p 239) by the amount of money recovered (if the plaintiff wins) or by the amount claimed (if the defendant wins); CCR Ord 38, r 4 (for details of the scales see below).

(2) In other actions, as the district judge on taxation thinks fit; CCR Ord 38, r 4(7).

As to (1) above, CCR Ord 38, r 3 specifies as follows:

Sum of money	*Scale applicable*
Exceeding £25 but not exceeding £100	lower scale
Exceeding £100 but not exceeding £3,000	scale 1
Exceeding £3,000	scale 2

The lower scale is rarely encountered in practice. Such cases and cases within scale 1 are usually arbitrated not tried and therefore subject to a rule which severely restricts costs (see p 280). In actions for recovery of land (see p 263) it is customary to specify scale 1 if an order is made for costs to be taxed (as opposed to assessed, as to which see p 565). Most of the items on scale 1 are subject to maximum figures upon the amounts which can be claimed for these items in pounds and pence (scale maxima). This is explained further, below.

Scale 2 is the top county court scale. It adopts wholesale the High Court rules concerning scales of costs, such as the absence of scale maxima. Because this is so, there is a single costs regime for all civil cases where the amount in dispute exceeds £3,000, regardless of where the cases are commenced or tried.

The pounds and pence allowed under scale 1 are set out in the CCR, Appendix A. By way of example we illustrate Item No 9 of the Appendix:

Scale 1

9.   £100–3,000

Interlocutory attendances etc: Attending at court, or in chambers, on an interlocutory or any other application to judge or [district judge] in the course of or relating to the proceedings including time travelling thereto—   not exceeding
(a) without counsel £106.00
(b) with counsel £8.50–27.50

The sum allowed will be assessed just as it would be in the High Court (CCR Ord 38, r 5 and see below). In two cases the taxing officer (the district judge) may, if he thinks fit, allow a sum larger than is prescribed by scale 1 (CCR Ord 38, r 9):

(1) where the trial judge grants a certificate to that effect, either at the trial or on application made on notice within fourteen days of the order for costs; and

(2) where, on taxation, the district judge is satisfied that, in all the circumstances, the prescribed sums are inadequate *and* no contrary direction has been made by the trial judge. Note that the mere refusal by the trial judge to grant a certificate under (1) does not by itself amount to a contrary direction for this purpose (*Trusler v Tudor* (1980) 77 LSG 405).

Outline of procedure on taxation and review

In a High Court case in London the taxation of a bill exceeding £30,000 is conducted by a taxing master; smaller bills are taxed by a principal or senior executive officer of the Supreme Court Taxing Office. Outside London and in the county court the taxation is usually conducted by the district judge however large or small the bill; however the rules do make provision for authorising certain principals or senior executive officers who have gained relevant experience whilst working in court offices in London, Birmingham, Bristol, Cardiff, Leeds, Liverpool or Manchester.

To obtain a taxation in the High Court the party receiving costs must:

(1) commence proceedings and obtain a taxing reference number (as to the three-month time limit, see p 536);

(2) lodge his bill of costs together with certain papers;

(3) pay the appropriate lodgment fee (see *White Book* 1011 supplement); and

(4) within the next seven days, send a copy of his bill to the paying party and notify the court that he has done so.

Unless the court otherwise directs the papers to be lodged and the order in which they are to be bundled are as set out in RSC Ord 62, r 29. The papers comprise most if not all of the party's file plus any accounts delivered ('vouchers') in respect of disbursements. In district registries the practice varies: some follow the practice of the Supreme Court Taxing Office; others make local Practice Directions, simply requiring the lodging of the party's case file plus vouchers without any pre-bundling of its contents.

In the Supreme Court Taxing Office, the taxing officer usually peruses the papers before the hearing. In an effort to save time at the hearing, the paying party usually files in court and serves on the receiving party 'Points in Issue' indicating what items are disputed, the reason relied upon and if appropriate the reduced figure he suggests. Such points should not exceed more than a few lines per item (*Practice Note (Supreme Court Taxing Office)* of 1995, *White Book* 62/C/3A). If a reply is appropriate (usually it is not) it should be equally brief. If necessary, directions may be given in advance of the hearing, eg for the filing of affidavits or the lodging of further documents. At the hearing, the taxing officer will allow or 'tax off' (ie disallow or reduce) each item in the bill. After a short period a certificate of taxation is issued.

In the county court and in district registries, there are two important differences:

(1) In county court cases (only) the receiving party must also lodge a copy of the bill and it is the court which sends this to the paying party.

(2) A taxation as between litigants is usually made without a hearing unless either party requests one. No appointment for a hearing is made in the first instance. The court sends a notice to the paying party (together with the copy bill) informing him of his right to request a hearing and specifying the time limit for doing so. If he does not request a hearing a similar notice will later be sent to the

receiving party together with a statement of the sum which has been provisionally taxed.

The procedure for reviewing a taxation is now largely the same in both High Court and county court (RSC Ord 62, rr 33–35; CCR Ord 38, r 24). A party who is dissatisfied with the taxing officer's decision must state the objection in writing within twenty-one days (fourteen days in the county court) and request the taxing officer to reconsider his decision in respect of that item. (In the High Court a review of the decision of a principal or senior executive officer will be conducted by a taxing master or district judge.) After the review or reconsideration has been held the taxing officer will notify each party of his decision and his reasons for it. Any party dissatisfied with that decision may, within fourteen days, apply to the judge for a further review. On a review by the judge, it is usual for him to be assisted by two assessors, one of whom will be a taxing officer and the other a practising solicitor nominated by The Law Society.

A fuller explanation of SCTO practice is set out in the *SCTO Guide* (obtainable from the Royal Courts of Justice Accounts Office or from the SCTO itself, price £3) the full text of which will be included in future supplements to the *White Book*.

Factors relevant in taxations

As to each item of cost for which sums of money are claimed, the taxing officer has to decide three questions.
(1) Was that cost actually incurred?
(2) If so, was it reasonable to incur it?
(3) If so, is the sum claimed for it reasonable in amount?

As to question (1) the burden of proof is on the party receiving costs. The item of costs will be taxed off if the taxing officer is not persuaded that that item was incurred *or* if the taxing officer is satisfied that the item did not cause the party any expense, eg the solicitor waived his fee in respect of it. A litigant cannot recover from another litigant more money than he is liable to pay (see generally on this, see p 525).

As to questions (2) and (3) the burden of proof is on the party receiving costs if the standard basis applies, but is on the party paying costs if the indemnity basis applies. The fact that the two bases differ in this respect can be demonstrated in two ways. First, by the placing of the benefit of the doubt in each definition. Secondly, by the narrowness or width of each definition: standard basis includes only 'a *reasonable* amount in respect of all costs *reasonably* incurred'; the indemnity basis, which is broader, includes 'all costs *except* those [which are unreasonable]'.

A party claiming costs is required to disclose privileged documents to the court on taxation. To some extent this amounts to a waiver of privilege *vis-à-vis* the other party. However, the taxing officer has to be fair to both parties and will try to maintain the protection normally afforded by privilege if he can do so without depriving the paying party of an opportunity to raise a *bona fide* challenge. Where questions arise as to a particular document (whether or not relied upon by the receiving party) the receiving party may be put to election; either to allow inspection by the opposing party or to concede the opposing party's allegations as to that document (*Silverstone Records Ltd v Mountfield* (1994) *White Book* 60/20/2). Occasionally the taxing officer will have to allow inspection of a privileged document by the paying party or by his solicitor only; but such disclosure is for the purposes of taxation only and privilege can subsequently be reasserted (*Goldman v Hesper* [1988] 1 WLR 1238).

If the answer given to question (2) is 'no' the item will be taxed off whichever basis is used. If the answer given to questions (2) and (3) is 'yes' the full amount claimed will be allowed whichever basis is used. It is only where the answer to either question is 'I am in doubt' or 'I am not sure' that there will be a difference between the two bases. A phrase which we used earlier bears repeating: where there is no doubt there is no difference. But what happens if there is a doubt? The three possible answers are as follows: the doubtful item will be taxed off; or, a reduced amount will be allowed for it; or, despite the doubt, the full amount claimed for it will be allowed. Which answer should be given where is most easily demonstrated by the use of a flow diagram (see fig 35).

On question (3) when deciding the amount in pounds and pence the taxing officer has a discretion. Rules of court explain how that discretion should be exercised.

In the High Court

RSC Ord 62, Appendix 2, Part I, para 1 states as follows:

Amount of costs

> **1.** (1) The amount of costs to be allowed shall (subject to rule 18 and to any order of the Court fixing the costs to be allowed) be in the discretion of the taxing officer.
>
> (2) In exercising his discretion the taxing officer shall have regard to all the relevant circumstances, and in particular to—
>> (a) the complexity of the item or of the cause or matter in which it arises and the difficulty or novelty of the questions involved;
>> (b) the skill, specialised knowledge and responsibility required of, and the time and labour expended by, the solicitor or counsel;
>> (c) the number and importance of the documents (however brief) prepared or perused;
>> (d) the place and circumstances in which the business involved is transacted;
>> (e) the importance of the cause or matter to the client;
>> (f) where money or property is involved, its amount or value;
>> (g) any other fees and allowances payable to the solicitor or counsel in respect of other items in the same cause or matter, but only where work done in relation to those items has reduced the work which would otherwise have been necessary in relation to the item in question.

(3) The bill of costs shall consist of such items specified in Part II as may be appropriate, set out, except for item 4, in chronological order; each such item (other than an item relating only to time spent in travelling or waiting) may include an allowance for general care and conduct having regard to such of the circumstances referred to in paragraph (2) above as may be relevant to that item.

Part II, which was referred to in para 1(3) above, specifies five items. These are all items of profit cost for the solicitor namely: (1) interlocutory attendances; (2) conferences with counsel; (3) attendance at trial or hearing; (4) preparation; and (5) taxation. Item (4) is in fact the main item, it covers everything the solicitor does except things covered by (1), (2), (3) or (5). The sum claimed for each item is subdivided into an A, B, C, format.

The A figure is intended to represent the average solicitor's average costs of providing fee-earning services (*Johnson v Reed Corrugated Cases Ltd* [1992] 1 All ER 169). It is calculated as a multiple of the time spent at a rate per hour sufficient to cover the earnings of such a person plus an appropriate share of the general office overheads. (If too high a grade of solicitor was used, or too high an hourly rate, the costs claimed would be unreasonable and therefore would be reduced.)

The B figure (also called the 'mark-up' or 'uplift') is intended to represent, primarily, a profit element but also an allowance in respect of matters which cannot be calculated on an hourly basis such as the other factors listed in para 1(2) above and also the expense of time spent supervising junior staff. It is calculated as a percentage of the A figure. In an averagely difficult case handled averagely well, 35 per cent will usually be awarded on items (1), (2) and (3) and 50 per cent on item (4) and (5) (see generally on this and on a rich variety of other important details *Brush v Bower Cotton & Bower* [1993] 1 WLR 1328).

If a case was handled inexpertly (eg too much reliance on counsel) a lower percentage might be appropriate. On the other hand, if a case was more difficult than the usual, or was handled very efficiently, a higher percentage may be allowed. Allowing a B figure of, or near, 100 per cent is justifiable only in cases which are truly exceptional (*Johnson* and *Brush* above).

The C figure covers time spent travelling and waiting on the client's business. This is, of course, an element in direct cost but it is shown separately from the A figure because, as para 1(3) above makes clear, there is no 'mark-up' on this element.

A policy implicit in Appendix 2 is to distinguish between expenditure on work requiring the time and skill of a professional person and expenditure on work which should be regarded as part of the overheads of the normal solicitor's office. The former covers work done by 'fee-earners' such as trainee solicitors, legal executives, assistant solicitors and partners, and attracts costs based upon the time spent by the fee-earner. The latter covers work done by typists, messengers and other

Fig 35: Questions on taxation

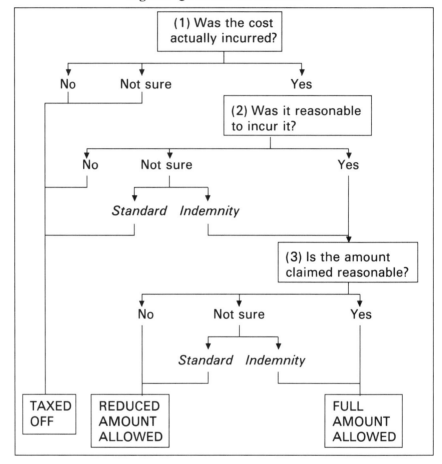

junior staff, for which no additional costs are allowed. The actualisation of this policy is achieved by a lengthy *Practice Direction* (*White Book* 62/C/1). We list here only some of the important points it makes.

(1) Telephone calls and outgoing letters may be charged as units of six minutes each (ie ten per hour). The time allowance includes time taken to peruse incoming letters and so no additional charge can be made for them.

(2) No charge can be made for the cost of postage, telephone calls, telex messages etc, or local travelling expenses. In London 'local' means within a radius of ten miles of the Royal Courts of Justice.

(3) No charge can be made for providing copy documents.

The *Practice Direction* makes clear that additional sums may be allowed for each of the above items in exceptional circumstances, eg unusually lengthy telephone calls or letters, unusually heavy telephone costs or unusually heavy copying costs.

In the county court

The factors relevant to question (3) (is the sum claimed reasonable in amount?) are exactly the same in High Court cases and in county court cases where an order for costs is made on scale 2, the top scale under which High Court practice is adopted (CCR Ord 38, r 3(3C)). On county court scale 1, some items are subject to scale maxima (see p 529). Questions as to amount are quite different in the case of costs on the lower scale because in that instance they will be assessed rather than taxed (see further p 565).

Interest on costs

An order for costs automatically entitles the receiving party to interest at the judgment debt rate (see p 18) if the order was made by the High Court (Judgments Act 1838) or, in the case of a county court order, if it has been transferred to the High Court for enforcement (see p 382) or if it is or forms part of (see below) an order for the payment of a sum of money of not less than £5,000 (CCA 1984, s 74 and the County Courts (Interest on Judgment Debts) Order 1991).

For the purposes of claiming interest thereon orders for costs are in some cases deemed to be made; eg on discontinuance without leave (see p 359) and on acceptance of a payment into court (see p 338). The deeming provision is set out in RSC Ord 62, r 5 which also applies in county court cases (CCR Ord 38, r 1). If the taxed costs are not paid within four days after taxation the receiving party can sign judgment for them (RSC Ord 45, r 15).

In the county court, the relevant rules do not expressly state whether or not, for the purposes of claiming interest, costs should be treated separately from any other money judgment obtained against the same party, eg debt or damages and interest under CCA 1984, s 69. In our view a successful litigant is entitled to aggregate costs, debts or damages and interest under s 69 even if none of them separately amounts to £5,000. Our view is based upon the form in which costs are ordered (see County Court Forms N25 and N34). The certificate given after taxation of costs (Form N255) is not in the form of a judgment.

In both courts the interest on costs runs from the date upon which the order was made, not from the date of taxation, which is usually many weeks later (*Hunt v RM Douglas (Roofing) Ltd* [1990] 1 AC 398; County Courts (Interest on Judgment Debts) Order 1991, art 2(2)). Thus, in respect of the costs awarded, the first calculation of judgment interest is almost invariably made retrospectively. Although it is payable from judgment, one lacks the arithmetic with which to calculate it until taxation unless the costs are assessed or agreed. A contrary rule as to period payable applies to judgments for damages (*Thomas v Bunn* [1991] 1 AC 362).

Where an appeal court reverses an order for costs it has power to backdate all or part of its order to, eg, the date of proceedings in a lower court (*Kuwait Airways Corporation v Iraqi Airways Co (No 2)* [1994] 1 WLR 985 and *Associated Newspapers Ltd v Wilson* [1995] 2 WLR 354, HL).

Like the costs themselves, the interest on costs belongs to the receiving party, not his solicitor. A solicitor who has not made suitable arrangements with his client may suffer significant loss and his client may be unjustly enriched. If no agreement is made as to interest, and no sums are paid on account, the winning client may receive interest calculated from the date of judgment on sums which he has not paid. Therefore, the topic of interest on costs should be discussed and agreed with the client at first interview (see p 584).

Penalty orders for costs

Delaying the taxation

The penalties for delaying taxation are set out in RSC Ord 62, r 28, a rule which also applies in the county court (CCR Ord 38, r 19A). If the party receiving costs takes more than the three months (or other period) allowed to commence taxation proceedings a taxing master or district judge has full discretion to disallow all or any part of the costs of taxation. In *Re K (a minor)* (1988) *The Times*, 21 July (affirmed by the Court of Appeal, *White Book* 62/28/3) it was said that this penalty should be readily imposed in order to discourage delay generally.

As to the costs of the action itself, a taxing master or district judge also has power to disallow or reduce these. However, as regards this penalty, RSC Ord 62, r 28 has been amended so as to provide a different practice. Before disallowing or reducing the costs of the action (as opposed to the costs of taxation) the taxing master or district judge must take into account 'all the circumstances (including any prejudice suffered by any other party as a result of such ... delay and any additional interest payable ... because of the ... delay)'.

In practical terms, the amended rule quoted above negatives the effect of *Re K* so far as concerns the main costs being claimed. Delay does not normally cause any prejudice to the paying party other than to increase the amount of any interest on costs payable. (Prejudice as to interest arises if the rate payable (ie the judgment debt rate) exceeds the commercial rate the paying party could have earned during the period of delay; *Royal Bank of Scotland v Allianz International Insurance Co* (1994) (unreported); as to calculation, see the example below.) It follows that, in most cases, no penalty should be imposed except as to the costs of taxation and except as to a sum in respect of increased interest. For example, if the receiving party delays taxation by six months the taxing master or district judge may:

(1) strike out the taxation item; and

(2) order that there be deducted from the taxed costs a sum equal to the amount (if any) by which six months' interest on the taxed bill at the judgment debt rate exceeds six months' interest at a commercial rate.

If the taxing master or district judge considers whether to impose some greater penalty (eg disallowing the taxing fee or disallowing all interest) it is appropriate first to calculate the taxed costs so as to be able to calculate the correct amount of penalty to impose (see *Pauls Agriculture Ltd v Smith* [1993] 3 All ER 122).

Commencing in the wrong court

Section 51(8) of the SCA 1981, as amended by the CLSA 1990, provides a costs sanction intended to discourage litigants from commencing in the High Court proceedings which 'should, in the opinion of the court, have been commenced in a county court'. The court whose opinion is relevant is the court at trial or on transfer. That court does not in fact impose any penalty. If it makes a ruling under s 51(8) and if some costs are later awarded to the plaintiff, the taxing officer must have regard to the ruling under s 51(8) and may reduce the costs awarded to the plaintiff by up to 25 per cent.

Orders under s 51(8) are not frequently made. Penalties are always construed narrowly. The wording 'proceedings should ... have been commenced in a county court' should be construed as meaning 'proceedings were required to ... have been commenced in a county court'. At present, the only proceedings which are in fact required to be commenced in the county court are personal injury actions unless the plaintiff reasonably expects to recover £50,000 or more and certain proceedings as to which the county court has exclusive jurisdiction (eg Sex Discrimination Act 1975, s 66).

Consider, for example, a nuisance action in which a claim for damages estimated at £10,000 is made. Such an action is not at present required to be commenced in the county court even if it is suitable for trial there (see p 375). Of course, such a case is likely to be transferred to the county court and the plaintiff may be ordered to pay the costs of transfer. However, in such a case, it seems that no certificate or ruling under s 51(8) would be appropriate.

Wasted costs orders against solicitors and other legal representatives

Section 51(6) of the SCA 1981 gives the High Court and county court power, at any stage of proceedings, to 'disallow or (as the case may be) order the legal or other representative concerned to meet, the whole [or part] of any wasted costs'. Subsection (7) defines 'wasted costs' as meaning:

> any costs incurred by a party—
> (a) as a result of any improper, unreasonable or negligent act or omission on the part of any legal or other representative or any employee of such a

representative; or
(b) which in the light of any such act or omission occurring after they were incurred, the court considers it is unreasonable to expect that party to pay.

Before making a wasted costs order the court must, usually, allow the legal or other representative an opportunity to be heard (RSC Ord 62, r 11 which also applies in the county courts; CCR Ord 38, r 1(3)).

The purpose of s 51(6) is not to punish the solicitor or other legal representative for his wrongdoing but to protect his client from the costs consequences of it *and* similarly to protect the other parties to the action. The jurisdiction is easy to apply if the applicant is the lawyer's dissatisfied client. If however the application is made by another party to the action, there are several dangers and cross-currents to be aware of. Is the applicant simply attempting to circumvent an inability to obtain effective costs orders against a legally-aided opponent? Is the lawyer attacked able to present a full defence bearing in mind the legal professional privilege which his client may insist upon, to the disadvantage of the lawyer? Is the application under s 51(6) itself an abuse of the system, seeking to intimidate or harass the opposing lawyers, or seeking to undermine their ability to give their clients objective advice and assistance?

Full, clear and explicit guidance upon all of these problems is set out in the Court of Appeal decision in *Ridehalgh v Horsefield* [1994] Ch 205. There is space here to summarise the main points only.

(1) To obtain an order for costs against a solicitor (or other legal representative) the applicant must show three things:
 (a) Conduct which is 'improper, unreasonable and/or negligent'. These terms are to be given common-sense definitions and include (respectively) conduct which is disgraceful whether or not it amounts to professional misconduct, conduct which is vexatious, ie designed to harass the opponents rather than advance the resolution of the issues, and conduct which is negligent as normally understood whether or not there exists a duty of care between the persons involved.
 (b) That such conduct caused the applicant to incur or suffer costs unnecessarily.
 (c) That, in all the circumstances, it is just to order the legal representative to compensate the applicant for the whole or part of the relevant costs. As to this the court should consider the dangers and cross-currents listed above.
(2) Applications under s 51(6) are best left until after the end of the trial.
(3) The court itself should not normally initiate the inquiry and should make full allowance for the possibility that, because of the client's privilege, the legal representative may be unable to tell the whole story.

(4) Wasted costs orders can be made against advocates even in respect of work falling within the advocate's immunity from liability to pay damages for negligence. However, it must be borne in mind that it is often reasonable for an advocate to represent unreasonable clients, ie to present hopeless cases. The court must also make full allowance for the fact that advocates often have to make decisions quickly, in the heat of battle.

Examples of wasted costs under s 51(7)(a) include acts or omissions which would otherwise result in penalty orders made against the client (see above and RSC Ord 62, r 28(6) and SCA 1981, s 51(9)(b)), failure to obey local practice directions which are designed to save time and costs (*Langley v North West Water Authority* [1991] 1 WLR 697) and acts or omissions causing last minute adjournments (*Sinclair-Jones v Kay* [1989] 1 WLR 114; *Fowkes v Duthie* [1991] 1 All ER 337 and see p 513 as to the court's power to fine parties and solicitors etc for failing to warn the court that a hearing will not be attended).

A typical example of a wasted costs order under s 51(7)(b) would be an action which is dismissed for want of prosecution because of the fault of the plaintiff's solicitor. The whole costs of the action may be disallowed as between solicitor and own client (in legal aid cases see also Civil Legal Aid (General) Regulations 1989, reg 109).

Seeking penalty orders at a taxation hearing

Penalty orders in respect of misconduct or neglect can be made against parties or their representatives at any stage of the proceedings (see p 523). In most cases, mistakes made at or before trial will be punished (or forgiven) by the trial court. However, especially with regard to matters which were not apparent to the injured party at the time of trial, penalty orders can also be sought at the taxation stage. In the High Court, a party intending to apply for such an order must take out a summons in the Supreme Court Taxing Office or in the district registry in which the taxation is proceeding (see *White Book* 62/A5/1 direction 3). The hearing will then be listed for hearing before a taxing master or district judge (a principal or senior executive officer has no jurisdiction to impose penalty orders; see RSC Ord 62, rr 11(9) and 28(7); and see RSC Ord 62, r 19(5)). An appeal from an order imposing (or refusing) a penalty in costs lies directly to a High Court judge; the normal two-stage review procedure does not apply (RSC Ord 62, r 28(5); *semble* this provision also applies in the county court so that appeals concerning penalties go direct to the circuit judge; CCR Ord 38, r 19A and Ord 1, r 6).

Drawing bills of costs

A properly drawn bill will provide the taxing officer with factual details of the work undertaken, information concerning the factors to be taken into account in deciding the amounts to allow and the solicitor's quantification of the amount of each item. The bill should commence with a brief narrative about the case indicating the issues and relevant circumstances. It should then set out, in chronological order with dates, all the relevant events whether or not any such event constitutes a disbursement or chargeable item. Next comes the main item, a description of all the work undertaken for the client (other than the few chargeable items which will have already been claimed, ie conferences with counsel and hearings in court). Last comes the costs incurred in the taxation proceedings themselves. In respect of every item for which a mark-up is claimed, the bill should identify any factors relied on as justifying an above-average mark-up (see p 533).

The drawing of a bill of costs for taxation was traditionally regarded as a specialist task. Today every solicitor should understand the principles involved and be able to draw a bill even if he chooses not to do so. Solicitors often employ an outside agency to draw all their bills (the fees or commission payable being part of the office overheads). Larger firms of solicitors often employ a full-time costs draftsman on the staff to avoid having to send the work out. However, the fee-earner concerned must still supply full information as to any item which might be challenged as doubtful (see p 527) and as to any factors relevant justifying an above average mark-up (see above).

There are two types of bill. Six-column bills, which are characteristic of cases in which the receiving party was legally aided in the proceedings, and two-column bills, which are used by non-legally-aided parties (and legal aid 'losers' bills, see p 575). A county court six-column bill is illustrated in fig 36. The six columns referred to are to the right hand side of the narrative column (which is headed 'Date and Item'). They are divided into two groups (headed 'Legal Aid Only' and 'Inter Partes') each group being subdivided into three (VAT, Disbursements and Profit Costs). Further columns (headed 'Taxed Off' and subdivided into Legal Aid and Inter Partes) are located to the left of the narrative column. Thus, a six-column bill comprises nine columns altogether, or seventeen if you note the further subdivisions each time between pounds and pence. Arithmetic about costs is often difficult to understand.

Two-column bills are much more frequently encountered. With these, the two columns referred to are the Disbursements and Profit Costs columns on the far right hand side. There is also a VAT column, then the narrative column and finally a Taxed Off column on the far left hand side. Bills with just five columns (or nine if you note the further subdivisions between pounds and pence) have always been known as two-column bills; there is little to be gained by asking why.

In an effort to reduce bulk, the first part of the bill illustrated is not set out on bill paper. This is a sensible practice which is becoming fairly common. The parts on bill paper are subdivided into 'Part One—Pre Legal Aid' and 'Part Two—Legal Aid'. Bills also have to be split into two parts on other occasions, eg where a legal aid certificate is granted after a case has begun or where there is a change in the rate of VAT.

In the High Court the bill lodged for taxation must be indorsed with the name, or firm name and business address of the solicitor whose bill it is and must be signed by that solicitor or by a partner in the firm (RSC Ord 62, r 29). The purpose of this is to reaffirm the personal duty a solicitor has to ensure that the bill is properly drawn and is justifiable. The solicitor is also required to certify that 'the castings of this bill are correct' (see *White Book* 62/C/1 directions 1.21 and 4.3. In some legal aid cases the second signature is made on a separate document, the Legal Aid Summary, as to which, see p 575). It is convenient but, in fact, not essential, to adopt the same practice in the county court. On delivering the bill for taxation the summary should be provisionally cast, ie in pencil. The figures will be inked in at, or after, the taxation.

We now comment upon some other aspects of the bill.

Witness allowances

Allowances are payable in respect of any witness it was reasonable to have in attendance at the trial (whether or not he gave evidence). In the High Court no maximum sums are prescribed. The taxing officer will take into account the witness's earnings level, the time engaged in travelling to and from, and attending at, the trial and reasonable travelling and hotel expenses etc. An expert witness is also entitled to a 'qualifying fee', ie a sum to compensate him for time spent familiarising himself with the facts of the case so as to enable him to express an expert opinion on them.

On county court scale 1, certain maximum sums are prescribed for witnesses of fact in addition to travelling etc, expenses unless the district judge is satisfied that such sums may be inadequate in the circumstances (eg attendance at trial for more than one day was necessary); CCR Ord 38, r 13. For expert witnesses scale 1 prescribes higher maximum sums plus travelling etc, expenses plus a qualifying fee.

Witnesses will often insist upon larger fees than these. Fortunately the judge has power to give a certificate enabling higher fees to be allowed and, whether or not such a certificate is granted the points made in relation to CCR Ord 38, r 9 apply (see generally CCR Ord 38, r 14).

In practice solicitors usually defer settling with witnesses until the period *after* the taxation but *before* the certificate of taxation is issued. The witness's account of his claim must be produced at the taxation.

The party receiving costs may also claim a witness allowance if he attended the trial to give evidence but not for his attending, eg legal or medical advisers.

[*continued on p 564*]

Fig 36: Specimen bill of costs

IN THE FULCHESTER COUNTY COURT

CASE NO: FC 61234

VAT No: 123 1234 12

BETWEEN

GEORGE KINGHAM   <u>PLAINTIFF</u>

<u>AND</u>

PLANTAGENET LEISURE PARK LIMITED   <u>DEFENDANT</u>

BILL OF COSTS OF THE PLAINTIFF to be taxed on the Standard Basis inter partes and in accordance with Regulation 107A of the Civil Legal Aid (General) Regulations 1989 on the County Court Scale 2, pursuant to Order dated 6th June 1997.

CIVIL AID CERTIFICATE NO: 12/01/94/13360/A dated 25th April 1996, as amended 9th May 1996.

Instructions for Hearing of the Plaintiff's Claim for damages for personal injuries sustained on 5th October 1995.

Whilst the Plaintiff was visiting a Leisure Park owned and managed by the Defendant, and was walking along the roadway in a pedestrianised area, he was knocked down by a mechanically propelled roadsweeper, which reversed into him suddenly and without warning.

Because of the accident, the Plaintiff was rendered unconscious and suffered a laceration above the right eyebrow. He was unconscious for a period of 36 hours and was detained in Hospital for 4 weeks, initially in intensive care, as it was feared that he had suffered brain damage. On discharge from Hospital, the Plaintiff required convalescence for a further period of 6 months before being able to resume any work.

It was necessary to obtain a proof of evidence from the Plaintiff's 10 year old daughter, who was the only witness to the accident.

The Plaintiff is a self-employed Pensions Consultant and suffered a serious loss of business due to his period of incapacity.

In the absence of any proposals for settlement, proceedings were commenced on the 10th May 1996. The Defence served constituted an outright denial of liability. The Defendant contended that it was not responsible for the actions of the driver of the mechanically propelled roadsweeper, as all cleaning at the Leisure Park had been sub-contracted.

Enquiries were made of the sub-contractors, who in turn denied liability, contending that no cleaning operations involving mechanically propelled roadsweepers were in progress at the time of the accident.

Detailed investigation was required. The identity of the driver of the roadsweeper was never established, but on the balance of probabilities, the Court was subsequently satisfied that it was subject to unauthorised use by other patrons of the Leisure Park, who had taken the roadsweeper for a 'joy ride' and had accidentally reversed into the Plaintiff. The Court was satisfied that unauthorised use of the roadsweeper occurred because the Defendant had inadequately secured the keys and paid insufficient regard to the probability of it being used in an unauthorised way.

The Defendants' Leisure Park was visited and detailed photographs and drawings were taken and prepared.

Apart from allowing access to the Leisure Park, the Defendant and its Insurers failed to co-operate with the investigation throughout and took no part in the investigation carried out on behalf of the Plaintiff, and did not make any detailed investigation of its own.

Details of the Plaintiff's loss of earnings were investigated with the assistance of another self-employed Pensions Consultant.

The matter proceeded to a contested Hearing on the 6th June 1997 when Judgment was given for the Plaintiff in the total sum of £35,750 together with interest and costs.

The matter was dealt with by a Partner. Expense rate employed is £85 per hour. Letters written and untimed telephone attendances charged on a 6 minute unit basis, equivalent to £8.50 each.

Where specifically referred to, work undertaken by a Clerk charged at £50 per hour.

Page 1

Fig 36: contd

Northwest Law Services – Chester

Taxed Off		Date and Item	Value Added Tax	Legal Aid		Value Added Tax	Inter Partes	
Legal Aid	Inter Partes			Disbursements	Profit Costs		Disbursements	Profit Costs
		PART ONE – PRE LEGAL AID						
		6TH FEBRUARY 1996						
		The Plaintiff instructed Messrs. Dodson & Fogg in this matter.						
		1. Preparation for Hearing. (part)						
		PART A WORK DONE						
		PLAINTIFF						
		Attending the Plaintiff and taking instruction as to the circumstances of the accident and concerning injuries sustained. Making arrangements to put the action on foot to protect the claim and interest thereon.						
		1. Personal attendance:						
		6.Feb.96. – 45 mins.						
		5 standard letters written.						
		3 Untimed telephone attendances.						
		(£131.75)						

	274 12
	274 12

DEFENDANT

4 Standard letters written.

2 Untimed telephone attendances.

£51.00)

TOTAL OF PART A

£182.75

PART B   CARE AND CONDUCT – 50%

TOTAL OF PART B

£91.37

TOTAL PREPARATION ITEM

TOTAL TIME ENGAGED: 45 MINS

TOTAL STANDARD LETTERS WRITTEN: 9

TOTAL UNTIMED TELEPHONE ATTENDANCES: 5

Page 2

Fig 36: contd

Taxed Off		Date and Item	Value Added Tax	Legal Aid Disbursements	Legal Aid Profit Costs	Value Added Tax	Inter Partes Disbursements	Inter Partes Profit Costs
Legal Aid	Inter Partes							
		PART TWO – LEGAL AID						
		25TH APRIL 1996						
		Civil Aid Certificate issued.						
		29TH APRIL 1996						
		Instructions delivered to Counsel to advise generally in conference						
		3RD MAY 1996						
		2. Attending upon conference with Counsel. (2)						
		(Attendance by Clerk)						
		Engaged 45 mins. 37.50						
		Care and conduct–35% 13.13						
		Travel 1 hour 50.00						
		100.63						
		3. Paid Counsel's fee for advice in conference – Mr. P. Quigley.				21 88	125 00	100 63
		6TH MAY 1996						
		Instructions delivered to Counsel for written advice on liability and to settle Particulars of Claim.						

4. Counsel's fee for written advice – Mr. P. Quigley (concerning limitation on the Legal Aid Certificate)	17 50	100 00			
10TH MAY 1996					
Default Summons issued out of Fulchester County Court.					
5. Paid Court Issue Fee.				70 00	
6. Counsel's fee to settle Particulars of Claim – Mr. P. Quigley.			21 88	125 00	
13TH MAY 1996					
Summons and Particulars of Claim posted to Defendants' Solicitors.					
22ND MAY 1996					
Defence served.					
16TH SEPTEMBER 1996					
Request made to Court Office for date of Trial to be fixed.					
3RD OCTOBER 1994					
Received from Court, Notice of Date fixed for Trial. (6.Jun.97.)					
17TH OCTOBER 1996					
Instructions delivered to Counsel to advise on evidence.					
	17 50	100 00	43 76	320 00	100 63

Page 3

Fig 36: contd

Taxed Off — Legal Aid	Taxed Off — Inter Partes	Date and Item	Legal Aid — Value Added Tax	Legal Aid — Disbursements	Legal Aid — Profit Costs	Inter Partes — Value Added Tax	Inter Partes — Disbursements	Inter Partes — Profit Costs
		7. Counsel's fee for advice on evidence – Mr. P. Quigley.				30 62	175 00	
		15TH MAY 1997 Brief delivered to Counsel.						
		6TH JUNE 1997 8. Attending upon conference with Counsel. (2) Engaged 1 hour 85.00 Care and conduct – 35% 29.75 114.75						114 75
		9. Attending upon Hearing before the Judge, when Order made. Defendant to pay Plaintiff's costs on Scale 2 to be taxed in default of agreement. Legal Aid Taxation. (3) Engaged 4 hrs 45 mins. 403.75 Care and conduct – 35% 141.31 Travel and waiting – 1 hour. 85.00 630.06						630 06
		10. Paid travel – 20 miles @ 36p. per mile.				1 26	7 20	

	£	p	£	p	£	p
11. Counsel's fee for Brief and conference – Mr. P. Quigley.	210	00	1200	00		
Preparation for Hearing. (Part)						
PART A WORK DONE						
<u>PLAINTIFF</u>						
Attending the Plaintiff and taking instruction as to the circumstances of the accident, concerning injuries sustained, upon advice and draft documents settled by Counsel, and concerning medical evidence and reporting progress. Taking instructions upon the medical report. Making arrangements for further medical examinations, arrangements for Trial, Order thereon and advising as to implementation of Order.						
4 Personal attendances:						
6.May.96. – 30 mins.						
27.May.96. – 45 mins.						
21.Nov.96. – 1 hour						
1.May.97. – 45 mins.						
Personal attendances totalling 3 hours						
19 Standard letters written.						
17 Untimed telephone attendances.						
(£561.00)	241	88	1382	20	744	81

Page 4

Fig 36: contd

Taxed Off		Date and Item	Legal Aid				Inter Partes		
Legal Aid	Inter Partes		Value Added Tax	Disburse-ments	Profit Costs	Value Added Tax	Disburse-ments	Profit Costs	

DEFENDANT

Attendances upon and corresponding with the Defendants' Insurers and subsequently with Solicitors concerning liability, arrangements for inspection of premises and concerning arrangements for Trial, evidence, Order made at Trial and compliance therewith.

29 Standard letters written.

15 Untimed telephone attendances.

(£374.00)

WITNESSES

Attendances upon and corresponding with:

Mr. Flack,

Mr. Dare,

Plaintiff's daughter (with the Plaintiff himself),

Obtaining detailed statements in support of the Plaintiff's Claim.

3 Personal attendances:

17.May.96. – attending the Plaintiff's daughter – 1 hour.		
5.Jun.96. – attending Mr. Flack – 1 hour.		
20.Jun.96. – attending Mr. Dare – 1 hour.		
Personal attendances totalling 3 hours.		
travel thereon by Partner to interview Messrs. Flack and Dare – 1 hour 30 mins. carried to Part C		
5 Standard letters written.		
(£297.50)		
12. Paid travelling – 35 miles @ 36p per mile.	2 21	12 60
MEDICAL EVIDENCE		
Corresponding with Mr. S. Holmes, Consultant Orthopaedic Surgeon and Mr. J. Watson, Consultant Neurologist concerning arrangements for medical examination and reports.		
7 Standard letters written.		
(£59.50)		
13. Paid Mr. S. Holmes – fee for Medical report.		200 00
	2 21	212 60

Fig 36: contd

Taxed Off		Date and Item	Value	Legal Aid		Value	Inter Partes	
Legal Aid	Inter Partes		Added Tax	Disbursements	Profit Costs	Added Tax	Disbursements	Profit Costs
		14. Paid Mr. J. Watson – fee for Medical report.					275 00	
		SITE INSPECTION						
		Personal attendance by Clerk at the Leisure Centre, the scene of the accident.						
		17.May.96. – 45 mins.						
		travel thereon – 1 hour carried to Part C						
		(£37.50)						
		15. Paid travelling – 16 miles @ 36p. per mile.				1 01	5 76	
		SPECIAL DAMAGES						
		Attendances upon and corresponding with Miss J. Marple, Pensions Consultant, concerning evidence in support of the Plaintiff's Claim as to financial losses directly occasioned by the accident. Further attendances and correspondence concerning availability for attendance at Court to give evidence in the absence of agreement.						
		1 personal attendance:						

12.Jun.96. – 1 hour 20 mins.

10 Standard letters written.

6 Untimed telephone attendances.

(£249.33)

LEGAL AID BOARD

10 Standard letters written.

6 Untimed telephone attendances.

(£86.60 charged to Legal Aid Fund)

COURT/COUNSEL

6 Standard letters written.

5 Untimed telephone attendances.

(£93.50)

DOCUMENTS

Engaged preparing (Partner):

Attendance notes on interviews with client:

6.May.96. –	12 mins.
27.May.96. –	6 mins.
21.Nov.96. –	18 mins.
1.May.97. –	6 mins.

	280	76
	1	01

Fig 36: contd

Taxed Off		Date and Item	Value Added Tax	Legal Aid		Value Added Tax	Inter Partes	
Legal Aid	Inter Partes			Disbursements	Profit Costs		Disbursements	Profit Costs
		Statements of witnesses:						
		17.May.96. – 30 mins.						
		5.Jun.96. – 30 mins.						
		20.Jun.96. – 30 mins.						
		Instructions to Counsel to advise on evidence:						
		17.Oct.96. – 90 mins.						
		Brief to Counsel:						
		14.May.97. – 1 hour.						
		Engaged 4 hours 42 mins. (all recorded)						
		(£399.50)						
		Engaged preparing (Clerk):						
		Instructions to Counsel to advise in conference:						
		29.Apr.96. – 30 mins.						
		Attendance note of conference:						
		3.May.96. – 30 mins.						
		Instructions to Counsel for written advice:						

6.May.96. – 30 mins.*

Default Summons, Particulars of Claim and Schedule of Special Damages:

10.May.96. – 48 mins.

Attendance note of site inspection:

17.May.96. – 45 mins.

Calculations of Special Damages Claim:

29.Apr.96. – 24 mins.
13.Jun.96. – 6 mins.
14.Jun.96. – 30 mins.
1.Aug.96. – 18 mins.
14.May.97. – 45 mins.

Collating all Trial documents and documents for Counsel's brief

9.Apr.97. – 3 hours
14.May.97. – 2 hours

Engaged 10 hours 46 mins. (all recorded)

(£480.00 charged *Inter Partes* plus £32.50 charged to Legal Aid Fund)

Engaged perusing (Partner):

Pleadings:

9.May.96. – 18 mins.
22.May.96. – 30 mins.

Page 7

Fig 36: contd

Taxed Off		Date and Item	Value Added Tax	Legal Aid		Value Added Tax	Inter Partes	
Legal Aid	Inter Partes			Disburse-ments	Profit Costs		Disburse-ments	Profit Costs
		Statements:						
		4.Jun.96. – 12 mins.						
		9.Jun.96. – 18 mins.						
		27.Jun.96. – 18 mins.						
		4.Nov.96. – 36 mins.						
		Medical Evidence:						
		20.Dec.96. – 18 mins.						
		7.Jan.97. – 12 mins.						
		Engaged 2 hours 42 mins. (all recorded)						
		(£229.50)						
		Engaged perusing (Clerk):						
		Pleadings:						
		26.Jun.96. – 30 mins.						
		Evidence:						
		17.May.96. – 18 mins.						
		16.Jul.96. – 1 hour						
		Engaged 1 hour 48 mins. (all recorded)						
		(£90.00)						

TOTALS OF PREPARATION ITEM CHARGED TO LEGAL AID FUND

Letters out 10	65.00
Telephones 6	21.60
Time engaged 30 mins.	32.50
	119.10

16. TOTAL PREPARATION ITEM charged to Legal Aid Fund. — 119 10

TOTALS OF PREPARATION ITEM CHARGED INTER PARTES

Letters out 76
Telephones 43
Time engaged 29 hours 23 mins.

TOTAL OF PART A

£2,879.33

PART B CARE AND CONDUCT – 60%

(Difficult and unco-operative Defendant. Matter of considerable and exceptional importance to the Plaintiff, having a significant effect upon his livelihood as self-employed Pensions Consultant)

TOTAL OF PART B

£1,727.60

119 10

Fig 36: contd

Taxed Off (Legal Aid)	Taxed Off (Inter Partes)	Date and Item	Value Added Tax	Legal Aid (Disbursements)	Legal Aid (Profit Costs)	Value Added Tax	Inter Partes (Disbursements)	Inter Partes (Profit Costs)
		PART C – TRAVEL						
		Page 5 – 1 hour 30 mins. 127.50						
		Page 6 – 1 hour 50.00						
		TOTAL OF PART C						
		£117.50						
		17. TOTAL PREPARATION CHARGED INTER PARTES						4,784 43
		18. Taxation procedure (5a)						
		Checking Bill and collating documents for lodging approx. 1 hour 85.00						
		Anticipated attendance upon Taxation approx. 2 hours. 170.00						
		Care and conduct – 50% 127.50						
		Anticipated travel on Taxation approx. 1 hour 85.00 / 467.50						467 50
		19. Anticipated travel expenses on Taxation – 20 miles @ 36p. per mile.				1 26	7 20	

WITNESS EXPENSES

20. 6.Jun.97 – paid Miss J. Marple Pensions Consultant – fee for attendance at Court to give evidence.

	£	p		£	p
				5,251	93
	350	00		357	20
	61	25		62	51

(Signed) *H. Dodson*

Page 9

Fig 36: contd

			Legal Aid			Inter Partes		
Taxed Off (Legal Aid)	Taxed Off (Inter Partes)	SUMMARY	Value Added Tax	Disbursements	Profit Costs	Value Added Tax	Disbursements	Profit Costs
		PART ONE – PRE LEGAL AID						
		Page 2						274 12
		Less Taxed Off						274 12
								274 12
		PROFIT COSTS						
		ADD VAT THEREON						
		ADD COUNSEL'S FEES						
		ADD VAT THEREON						
		ADD OTHER DISBURSEMENTS						
		ADD VAT THEREON						
		TOTAL OF PART ONE						
		PART TWO – LEGAL AID						
		Page 3	17 50	100 00		43 76	320 00	100 63
		Page 4				241 88	1382 20	744 81
		Page 5				2 21	212 60	
		Page 6				1 01	280 76	
		Page 7						

Description	£	p	£	p	£	p	£	p	£	p	£	p
Page 8	17	50	100	00	119	10	62	51	357	20	5,251	93
Page 9					119	10	351	37	2,252	76	6,097	37
Less Taxed Off												
Less Taxed Off												
PROFIT COSTS												
ADD VAT THEREON												
ADD COUNSEL'S FEES												
ADD VAT THEREON												
ADD OTHER DISBURSEMENTS												
ADD VAT THEREON												
TOTAL OF PART TWO												
ADD TOTAL OF PART ONE												
ADD TAXING FEE ON PART ONE (PRE LEGAL AID)												
ADD TAXING FEE ON PART TWO (LEGAL AID)												
CARRIED FORWARD/......												

Fig 36: contd

Certificate for completion before the taxation

I certify that a copy of this bill has been sent to the assisted person pursuant to Reg 119 of the Civil Legal Aid (General) Regulations 1989, with an explanation of his interest in the taxation and the steps which can be taken to safeguard that interest in the taxation. He has/has not requested that the Taxing Officer be informed of his interest and has/has not requested that notice of the taxation appointment be sent to him.

Signed .... J. Dodson

Partner in the firm of .... Dodson & Fogg

Dated .... 10th July 1997

Fig 37: Legal aid schedule

IN THE FULCHESTER COUNTY COURT   **CASE NO: FC 61234**
                                                    VAT No: 123 1234 12

BETWEEN   GEORGE KINGHAM   Plaintiff
                                  –AND–
                   PLANTAGENET LEISURE PARK LIMITED   Defendant

LEGAL AID SCHEDULE OF INTER PARTES COSTS

Northwest Law Services – Chester

ITEM	NARRATIVE	VAT		DISB		PROFIT COSTS	
2	Conference Attending 45 mins 24 Travel 1 hour <u>28.75</u>					52	75
3	Counsel's fee	21	88	125	00		
5	Fee			70	00		
6	Counsel's fee	21	88	125	00		
7	Counsel's fee	30	62	175	00		
8	Conference Attending 1 hour 32.00					32	00

9	Hearing
	Attending
	    4.75 hours 152.00
	Travel & waiting
	    1 hour <u>28.75</u>
						180	75

10	Travel costs	1	26	7	20		
11	Counsel's brief	210	00	1200	00		
12	Travel costs	2	21	12	60		
13	Medical fees			200	00		
14	Medical fees			275	00		
15	Travel costs	1	01	5	76		
17	Preparation 29h 23m 1,909.92 Letters 76 494.00 Telephones 43 154.80 Travel 2h 30m <u>71.87</u>					2,630	59
18	Taxation						
19	Travel costs relating to taxation						
20	Witness expenses	61	25	350	00		

Where sums claimed are reduced

If a particular item in a bill is reduced on taxation the sum taxed off, if an item of profit costs, is entered in the column headed 'Taxed Off'; if it is a disbursement the figure inserted in the bill is deleted and the lower amount allowed is written in by hand above the deletion.

Value added tax (VAT)

The VAT on each disbursement is entered in the appropriate column: contrast VAT on profit costs which are shown only as a total, in the summary. If the party receiving costs is himself registered for VAT and the legal services supplied to him are for the purposes of his business, the tax which he pays to his solicitor will be one of his own 'inputs' and will be recovered in the usual way from his 'output' tax. Thus the bill he gives the loser would not include any element of VAT. On the other hand if the party receiving costs is not registered for VAT or if the legal services supplied were not in connection with his business, he cannot recover the tax and will therefore have to bear it personally. Thus an amount equal to the VAT should be added to the bill to be paid by the unsuccessful party. This is not a payment of VAT but is to indemnify the successful litigant for the VAT he will pay on the proportionate part of his solicitor and client costs. Unfortunately because it is not a payment of VAT by him, the party paying costs is not entitled to a VAT invoice and cannot recoup the payment even if he is registered for VAT. On a taxation the burden is on the receiving party to ensure that no claim for VAT is made in the bill if the receiving party is able to recover it as input tax (see generally *White Book* 62/C/7).

Costs of the taxation

These costs follow the main costs of the action (RSC Ord 62, r 27; CCR Ord 38, r 19A). Thus, unless the taxing officer otherwise orders, they will be ordered against the party paying the main costs of the action, and will be taxed on the standard basis. When might these costs be ordered against the party *receiving* the main costs of the action? One example might be where his opponent has made a '*Calderbank* offer' as to the taxation (see generally p 343 and *Chrulew v Borm-Reid & Co* [1992] 1 WLR 176).

How should the costs of taxation be shown in the bill? At the stage of drafting the bill, this item can be no more than guesswork. You do not know whether the bill will be agreed, determined by provisional taxation or heavily disputed. In our view you should enter figures based upon your estimate of the time likely to be spent on taxation on the assumption that the bill will be heavily disputed. If a taxation hearing is held you should, if necessary, seek to amend these figures (upwards or, more likely, downwards) just before the hearing is concluded.

Some special cases

Agreed costs

The taxation of costs is an expensive and time-consuming process. Solicitors should try to avoid it by seeking to agree costs with each other and advising their clients accordingly. There are some problems in agreeing costs in legal aid cases if the certificate was granted before 26 February 1994 (but see p 572) and sometimes (see p 577) in cases involving minors and mental patients (see generally *White Book* 62/16/2 and CCR Ord 38, r 19, and the *Green Book* commentary thereto).

Assessed costs

Instead of awarding a party taxed costs the court may instead specify a fixed sum by way of 'assessed costs' or 'gross sum costs'. These terms are interchangeable in the case of costs awarded in the High Court (RSC Ord 62, r 7) and costs awarded on county court scale 2 (CCR Ord 38, r 3(3D)). For costs awarded on the county court lower scale or scale 1 only the term 'assessed costs' is correct and the pounds and pence awarded must be as specified in CCR Appendix C (CCR Ord 38, r 19; for an exceptional case see *Brown v Sparrow* [1982] 1 WLR 1269).

Costs awarded on the county court lower scale must be assessed; costs awarded on county scale 1 must be assessed 'if the solicitor for the party to whom they are payable so desires' (CCR Ord 38, r 19(1); for litigants in person see CCR Ord 38, r 17(3)).

The amount given by way of 'assessed costs' (the sum is assessed there and then at the hearing) will often be less than that which could have been obtained on a taxation. Nevertheless, assessed costs are frequently encountered in practice. There are many cases where the solicitor does not actually expect to recover the costs from the unsuccessful party and thus, as he will have to look to his own client for payment of all the costs, he would merely be 'going through the motions' of obtaining an order for costs. This is particularly common in possession actions where the tenant has been evicted for non-payment of rent. If he has not the money to pay the rent it is highly unlikely that he will have the money to satisfy an order for costs.

Fixed costs

In some cases plaintiffs are entitled only to 'fixed costs' and not 'taxed costs'. RSC Ord 62, Appendix 3, prescribes amounts for fixed costs in certain cases, in particular the costs on recovery of a liquidated sum without a trial and the costs of enforcement proceedings (and see the writ indorsement as to 'fourteen-day costs' discussed on p 202). CCR Appendix B, prescribes fixed costs for various proceedings in the county court along broadly similar lines.

Small claims in the county court

If a claim not exceeding £3,000 (£1,000 in personal injury cases) is arbitrated rather than tried the costs recoverable are restricted (see further p 279). Conversely, if the reference to arbitration is rescinded and the small claim is later tried, the successful party can expect to receive costs on the lower scale or scale 1 as the case may be (see p 529). Where the lower scale applies the costs will be assessed rather than taxed.

What is the position if a plaintiff claims unlimited damages, goes to trial and ends up with judgment for, say £250? If the case was patently worth less than the small claims limit on commencement the plaintiff will be penalised in costs (see p 281).

Litigants in Person (Costs and Expenses) Act 1975

This Act allowed the courts to make orders for costs in favour of litigants in person. RSC Ord 62, r 18, and CCR Ord 38, r 17, state that on a taxation of the costs of a litigant in person the court can allow such costs as would have been allowed if the work and disbursements had been done by a solicitor on a litigant's behalf. However, in the case of what would have been a profit costs item for a solicitor the taxing officer cannot allow more than two thirds of the sum which he would have allowed a solicitor. If the litigant has not actually suffered any pecuniary loss in doing the work to which the costs relate he cannot be allowed more than £9.25 an hour in respect of time reasonably spent by him on the work involved. Where costs are allowed for attending court to conduct his own case he is not entitled to a witness allowance for himself in addition.

Where both claim and counterclaim tried

Where a claim and a counterclaim are both successful (or both fail) the general rule is that there should be two judgments and two orders for costs (in county court cases see Form N23). The principles upon which the taxation takes place were approved by the House of Lords in *Medway Oil and Storage Co v Continental Contractors* [1929] AC 88. The taxing officer should not apportion the costs but should:

(1) treat the claim and counterclaim as two different actions;
(2) ascertain what items relate to each 'action' (eg the fees for issue of proceedings go wholly with the costs of claim and are not apportioned); and
(3) divide into two any items incurred partly for one 'action' and partly for the other (eg counsel's brief fees, the division takes account of the sum counsel would have charged had no counterclaim been made: 'the distinction between division and apportionment may in certain circumstances be a thin one. But ... the distinction is fundamental': *Medway Oil* case, above, *per* Viscount Haldane).

Where in the county court the claim and counterclaim relate to sums of money only, CCR Ord 38, r 4(3), specifies the scale of costs applicable to each.

To the general rule stated above, there is a very important exception. The court has power to give a single judgment for the balance between claim and counterclaim and may make a special order for costs (RSC Ord 15, r 2(4); CCR Ord 21, r 4). This power should be exercised wherever the counterclaim is a set-off (see p 161) or where the issues on the claim and counterclaim 'are very much interlocked' (*Chell Engineering Ltd v Unit Tool and Engineering Co Ltd* [1950] 1 All ER 378 *per* Denning LJ, *obiter*; and see generally, *Green Book* p 1627 'Costs of Counterclaim and Set Off'). What is meant by a 'special order' as to costs? This topic is considered in the next section.

Where a party partially succeeds

What order for costs is appropriate if no party has been wholly successful? For example, where a claim and set-off are both successful (see above) or, in an employer's liability claim where the plaintiff raises issues as to the safety of the machine, the safety of the system of working and the adequacy of the training and wins only on the third issue. A simple order for costs in favour of the plaintiff will sometimes be too simplistic. This 'winner takes all' approach would entitle the plaintiff to all his costs, including his costs of unsuccessfully denying the set-off and his costs of raising issues he later lost or abandoned. Modern thinking is against such a rudimentary approach (although certain aspects of it are still to be found in the rules as to costs following the acceptance of a payment into court, see p 339).

At one time the courts sought greater refinement by awarding 'costs of issues'. However, such orders can often prove difficult, if not impossible, to carry into effect. The practice of awarding costs of issues has long been discouraged.

> It is not the usual course in exercising discretion as to costs to approach the matter as if one was scoring points in a boxing match as to how many issues there were and precisely who has won on each issue (*per* Ferris J in *Colchester Borough Council v Smith* [1991] 2 WLR 540).

The special order for costs which is being made more frequently today is an order which gives one party a fraction or percentage of his costs. Whether the fraction or percentage is large or small will obviously depend upon the number and expense of the unsuccessful issues and arguments which the party receiving costs raised. It is also possible, although less common, for the court to order each side to pay a fraction or percentage of the other side's costs. There are many examples of 'fractional orders for costs' to be found in law reports, most but not all of them being appeal cases; see for example *Rantzen v Mirror Group Newspapers (1986) Ltd* [1994] QB 670; *Welsh Development Agency v Redpath Dorman Long Ltd* [1994] 1 WLR 1409; *Beoco Ltd v Alfa Laval Co Ltd* [1995] QB 137; *Sargent v Customs and Excise Commissioners* [1995] 1 WLR 821.

Orders compelling each side to pay a fraction of the opponent's costs are rare because, as a general rule, the winner should not be ordered to pay the loser's costs, even on issues he raised or allegations he made which were unsuccessful unless his conduct as to those issues or allegations has been improper or unreasonable (*Re Elgindata Ltd (No 2)* [1992] 1 WLR 1207).

Where there has been joinder of parties

This is a huge topic as to which we shall make only four points.

(1) Except when they appear in person, co-plaintiffs must be represented by the same solicitor and counsel (unless the court otherwise orders, see p 96). A division of their costs may have to be made if, eg the defendant pays separate sums into court for each of them, and one plaintiff beats his payment but the other plaintiff does not (*Keen v Towler* (1924) 41 TLR 86 and see *White Book* 62/7/8).

(2) Although co-defendants may be represented separately the additional costs caused will be allowed only if their severance was reasonable (*Harbin v Masterman* [1896] 1 Ch 351) and only to the extent it was reasonable (see *Spalding v Gamage* [1914] 2 Ch 405: same solicitor, different counsel; and see generally *White Book* 62/10/1).

(3) Where co-defendants are sued in the alternative and the plaintiff succeeds against only some of them a *Bullock* order or a *Sanderson* order may be made (see p 97).

(4) Where third party proceedings are tried orders for costs may be made between the defendant and third party and between the plaintiff and third party (see p 324).

Costs on interlocutory applications

There are a variety of orders which can be made. We show them in tabular form, classifying them in the order of preference of the successful party at the interlocutory hearing (see table 11, pp 570 and 571).

Similar orders to those shown in table 11 may be made in the county court (CCR Ord 13, r 1) but note that if no special order is made the costs are treated as costs in the cause (*Friis v Paramount Bagwash Co Ltd (No 2)* [1940] 2 KB 654) and costs awarded against the party receiving trial costs are usually assessed without taxation (CCR Ord 38, r 19(3)).

The Court of Appeal decision in *Lockley v National Blood Transfusion Service* [1992] 1 WLR 492 provides comfort for defendants who obtain interlocutory costs orders against legally-aided plaintiffs. As a general rule legally-aided parties are shielded from liability to pay their opponent's costs (Legal Aid Act 1988, s 17; see p 55). In this case the court was prepared to pierce that shield up to the value of any damages and costs which the legally-aided plaintiff may later recover. On an application for extension of time for service of the defence, the district judge granted the application and awarded costs in favour of the defendant. (Presumably the district judge was of the opinion that the plaintiff should have consented to an extension of time.) The precise order for costs was 'the costs of and incidental to this application be the defendants, not to be enforced without the leave of the court save as to set-off as against damages and/or costs'. On appeal that order was upheld by the judge in chambers and by the Court of Appeal. The latter dismissed the appeal 'with costs, not to be enforced without the leave of the court, save as to set-off against costs of action'.

Certificates for counsel

It is counsel's job to ask for these, where these are necessary. The request is for the court to certify that the application was 'fit for counsel', ie that the attendance of counsel has been of assistance to the court, or would have been of assistance had the case been opposed, where it was reasonable to assume that it would be opposed. If no certificate is obtained, no counsel's fees for that application will be allowed on a taxation of costs between litigants.

The circumstances in which certificates are necessary are significantly different in High Court and county court cases. In the High Court, counsel should seek a certificate in all hearings before a district judge (or master) in chambers and in the case of two or more counsel acting for the same party in a hearing before a High Court judge in chambers (RSC Ord 62, Appendix 2, Part 1, para 2; certificates are also required for certain other costs, see para 4).

In the county court, certificates are required in far more cases; in all interlocutory hearings, whether before the district judge or the circuit judge and whether in open court or in chambers; certificates are also required in all cases in which more than one counsel act for the same party at a hearing, whether that hearing is interlocutory or final, and whether it is in open court or in chambers.

Legal aid costs

In this section we look at the costs position as between the legal aid fund and the solicitor acting for an assisted person. The position is governed by the Legal Aid Act 1988 and the Civil Legal Aid (General) Regulations 1989 (the latter being hereinafter called 'the regulations'). The solicitor is not allowed to seek remuneration from the assisted person for any work done in the proceedings covered by a legal aid certificate whether or not that work falls within the scope of that certificate (reg 64 and see *Littaur v Steggles Palmer* [1986] 1 WLR 287 as to the effect of

[*continued on p 573*]

Table 11: Interlocutory costs

Type of order	Effect	When appropriate	Comments
1 Costs forthwith	Loser's costs not recoverable. Winner can tax and claim these costs immediately	(a) Loser's conduct unreasonable and the court wishes to mark its disapproval thereof; and/or (b) The costs in question are unusually heavy; see *Kickers International SA v Paul Kettle Agencies Ltd* [1990] FSR 436	This order cannot be made against a legally-aided party; RSC Ord 62, r 8; CCR Ord 38, r 1
2 Costs in any event Costs thrown away Costs	Loser's costs not recoverable. Winner can claim these costs when action ends	Loser's conduct unreasonable and/or the costs relate to some collateral issue, eg, a preliminary issue, or an interlocutory appeal; see *Re Dent* [1994] 1 WLR 956.	'Unreasonable' here and elsewhere in this table means 'has attempted to argue the unarguable or defend the indefensible'
3 Named party's costs in cause	See entry 2 for the loser and entry 4 for the winner	Loser's conduct unreasonable. Named party's conduct reasonable only if he later succeeds at trial	The named party's conduct is not such as to entitle him to costs unless he wins at trial
4 Costs in cause	These costs are claimable by whichever party becomes entitled to the main costs	Costs preliminary to trial and both parties' conduct appears to be reasonable	The keystone order. Each party's attendance appears to have been a necessary step, or at least a reasonable step, on the road to getting the dispute resolved by trial

Table 11: contd

Type of order	Effect	When appropriate	Comments
5 Costs reserved	As entry 4 above unless court later decides to award these costs to the other party	It is not yet possible to make a ruling upon the reasonableness or otherwise of either party's conduct	Typical of *ex parte* applications and also discovery applications where discovery is ordered
6 No order as to costs	Neither party can claim the costs of the application whether or not he becomes entitled to the main costs	Both parties conduct unreasonable (or merits equal as to a collateral issue)	Do not confuse this order with 'costs in cause'. This order means, in effect, 'a plague on both your houses'

certificates which only cover part of the proceedings involving the assisted person).

Assessment of costs by the Area Director

In certain cases the assisted person's costs may be assessed rather than taxed; see regs 105 and 106A (or reg 106 if the certificate was first granted before 26 February 1994), the most important examples being cases where no proceedings were begun and cases in which the solicitor believes that the total amount payable to the solicitor and counsel (if any) will not exceed £1,000 (if the solicitor believes that they will not exceed £500 the solicitor *must* apply for assessment).

The assessment in these cases is made by the Area Director.

Legal aid taxations

Unless assessment of costs is possible (see above) a solicitor wishing to obtain payment out of the legal aid fund must, in most cases, obtain an order from the court for a legal aid taxation; see reg 107. This regulation (or reg 107A where applicable) specifies the basis of taxation as the standard basis. At first sight this appears to promise an agreeable amount of similarity between legal aid costs and costs between litigants. In fact the two taxations are significantly different. A legal aid taxation deals with the costs covered by the certificate in respect of which prescribed rates of remuneration may apply; a taxation of costs between litigants deals only with the costs of action but remunerates that work at normal rates. Consider first the difference between *costs of certificate* and *costs of action*. Assume for example that the assisted person has won the action with costs. The loser will not be required to pay for the following items since these are not costs of action.

(1) Work done to secure the continuation or extension of the certificate (such as writing to the client encouraging him not to default in instalments of contribution or obtaining counsel's opinion so as to enable the removal of a limitation).

(2) Work done for which the prior approval of the legal aid office was obtained but which is disallowed as being unreasonable in the taxation between litigants (eg obtaining additional expert reports which the taxing officer thinks it was unreasonable to obtain: in practice the Legal Aid Board is very unwilling to grant many prior approvals these days).

(3) Work done in respect of matters for which no award of costs was made or, indeed, matters for which costs were awarded against the assisted person.

(As to costs incurred in giving opponents notices of issue of a legal aid certificate and similar notices, these are to be treated as costs of the action: see reg 111.)

How does the difference between 'costs covered by the certificate' and 'costs of action' affect the drawing of the bill and conduct of the taxation? The answer depends upon whether or not the assisted person was awarded *inter partes* costs, ie, whether he won or lost, and the date upon which the legal aid certificate was first issued, ie whether or not it was before 26 February 1994. The practice relating to winners' and losers' bills in cases where the certificate was first issued on or after 26 February 1994 is set out in a *Practice Direction* of 1994 (*White Book* 4282 Suplement) and summarised below (as to the practice to be followed in cases in which the certificate was first issued before 26 February 1994, see earlier editions of this book).

The winner's bill

If the assisted person is awarded costs two taxations are necessary. One to determine how much the loser must pay to the assisted person's solicitor (see p 526); the other to determine how much will be paid out of the legal aid fund to the assisted person's solicitor and counsel. The same bill will be used for both taxations: it will be a six-column bill headed 'Bill of costs of the plaintiff/defendant to be taxed on the standard basis both *inter partes* and in accordance with the provisions of reg 107A of the Civil Legal Aid (General) Regulations 1989 pursuant to the judgment/order dated ...' (see fig 36 which starts on p 542). A second document must also be prepared, the legal aid schedule of *inter partes* costs (see fig 37 on p 563). It is not necessary to serve a copy of this second document on the paying party; its contents are of no relevance at all to him. The bill and the schedule enable the winner's solicitor to set forth three overlapping calculations of his costs.

Costs recoverable against the Legal Aid Board only

These are set out in the Legal Aid Only columns of the bill and will be taxed at the prescribed rates applicable, if any. In fig 36 see items 4 and 16. At present there are no prescribed rates for work done in the Court of Appeal or House of Lords or for counsel's fees in any court. In most county court cases the hourly rate for work done by solicitors or their employees is £65 plus VAT (£28.75 plus VAT for travelling and waiting; see generally *White Book* 4276). The hourly rate is the same whether the work is done by a partner or by a trainee. There is no uplift to be added to these rates. However, in exceptional cases some 'enhancement' is possible; see further p 576.

Costs recoverable inter partes

These are set out in the *Inter Partes* columns of the bill and will be taxed at normal rates. In the bill illustrated in fig 36 the time spent by the senior fee-earner (a partner) is claimed at £85 with an uplift claimed at 60 per cent on most items; that totals £136 plus VAT. See, for example, item 17 in the bill; £4,784.43.

Costs payable by the Legal Aid Board in respect of costs recoverable inter partes

These are set out in the schedule. The items numbered in the schedule are identical to the *Inter Partes* items in the bill. Thus, the schedule illustrated in fig 37 has no items 1, 4 or 16: item 1 is pre-legal aid and items 4 and 16 are claimed in the Legal Aid Only columns.

Although the items in the schedule are identical to the *Inter Partes* items in the bill, the sums claimed for them in each place are quite different. The schedule shows the relevant prescribed rates only. Compare item 17 as it appears in the bill (£4,784.43) and in the schedule (£2,630.59). From the solicitor's point of view the prescribed rates are merely the first instalment, payable by the Legal Aid Board, possibly in advance of any payment being made by the loser. For these items the assisted party's solicitor hopes to recover the balance from the full taxed costs if and when paid by the loser (see p 526).

Item 17 shows the difference between the prescribed rates and the normal rates claimed *inter partes*. Another example is provided by item 2, time spent by a solicitor's clerk attending a conference with counsel. In the bill £100.63 is claimed. In the schedule, the claim at prescribed rates is only £52.75. If the senior fee-earner rather than the clerk had attended the conference the sum claimed in the bill would have been greater (£171.06) but the prescribed rate in the schedule would remain the same (£52.75).

What happens if items are challenged inter partes

Consider items 2 and 3 in the bill. Assume that the losing party challenges the reasonableness of arranging a conference with counsel at such an early stage in the action. If this challenge is successful the taxing officer will enter the figures £100.63 (item 2) in the appropriate Taxed Off column on the left hand side of the bill and will cross out the figures £21.88 and £125 (item 3) from the VAT and Disbursements divisions in the *Inter Partes* columns.

Having done so, the taxing officer must also cross out the appropriate figures for items 2 and 3 in the schedule. The question now arises, should these items be restored to the bill as Legal Aid Only items? In other words, should the figures just crossed out of the schedule (counsel's fee and the prescribed rates for the solicitor's clerk) be written in the Legal Aid Only columns of the bill? The taxing officer would have to be persuaded that, although the conference was unreasonable so far as the paying party is concerned, it was nevertheless reasonable so far as the legal aid certificate is concerned. (*Sir, if items 2 and 3 are going to be disallowed inter partes, I would ask you to move them across to the Legal Aid Only columns. As you will have seen from the attendance note which was made at the time, Sir, the conference did cover matters relevant to item 4 in the bill. Item 4 is counsel's fee for a written advice concerning the limitation on the certificate. Item 4 is already placed in the Legal Aid Only columns, Sir.)*

Legal aid summary

At the completion of the taxation the assisted party's solicitor will have to draw up a third document specifying the sums allowed on taxation; counsel's fees, other disbursements, the sums allowed *inter partes* at normal rates, the same items but calculated at prescribed rates, the items allowed in the Legal Aid Only columns and the costs of taxation. This summary when signed by the solicitor and sealed by the court becomes the certificate of taxation (for a precedent, see *White Book* para 4282). Assume that the losing party was insured and so the *inter partes* costs taxed at normal rates are paid in full. The legal aid summary would then be used for accounting purposes as between the solicitor and the Legal Aid Board. For example, the Legal Aid Board may have made disbursements to the assisted party's solicitor before trial (see p 60) and these must now be repaid.

The loser's bill

If the assisted person is not awarded costs there still has to be a legal aid taxation. This is done in a two-column bill and is quite separate from any taxation of costs between litigants which the opponent may be entitled to seek. In all cases (including High Court cases in London) a provisional taxation will be made, ie the taxing officer notifies the solicitor of the sum he proposes to allow and requires him to so inform the court office within fourteen days if he wishes to be heard on the taxation.

In addition to the prescribed rates, there are two other ways in which legal aid costs differ from costs payable by a fee-paying client. First, being taxed on the standard basis means that, for any costs as to which there is a doubt, the legal aid fund rather than the solicitor is given the benefit of that doubt (contrast solicitor-and-own-client costs which are taxed on the indemnity basis, see p 579). Secondly, the solicitor is allowed no remuneration, either against the legal aid fund or the client in person, for any work in respect of unreasonable steps the client authorised or caused (eg visits to the solicitor's office in excess of the number of visits which it was reasonable for the client to make; a fee-paying client can be required to pay for such visits if his solicitor gave him prior warning of the consequences of such extravagance, see further p 580).

There are also certain other occasions when a two-column bill will be appropriate for a legal aid taxation (see further a *Practice Direction* of 1994, *White Book* 4282 paras 22–26 and see further Form CLA 32, also at 4282).

Enhancement

The taxing officer may allow some or all of the fees at enhanced rates if:

(1) the work was done with exceptional competence, skill or expertise;
(2) the work was done with exceptional despatch;
(3) the case involves exceptional circumstances or complexity.

The meaning of this, the so-called 'threshold test' has yet to be fully explored in reported cases. For example, what does 'exceptional' mean? Does it mean all cases which are not standard or only a tiny minority of cases? Is all work done competently by a senior partner work done with exceptional competence, skill or expertise? Is all work done concerning *Mareva* injunctions, work done with exceptional despatch, involving exceptional circumstances or complexity? Time will tell (and see the case law cited in the *White Book* 4280/1).

Once the threshold test is passed the enhancement is by a percentage uplift of the prescribed rate having regard to the degree of responsibility accepted by the solicitor, the care, speed and economy with which the case was prepared and the novelty, weight and complexity of the case. This, the *quantum* test, sounds rather like a modern re-statement of the 'seven pillars of wisdom' (see p 532). In county court cases the enhancement may not exceed 100 per cent. In very exceptional High Court cases an enhancement up to 200 per cent is possible. This again raises the question, what is meant by exceptional?

Reduction

The taxing officer may also allow costs at a lower level 'where it appears reasonable to do so having regard to the competence or despatch with which the item or class of work was done' (*White Book* 4281). This provision duplicates reg 109 concerning the disallowance or reduction of costs which have been wasted. Regulation 109 is without prejudice to any other powers the taxing officer may have to penalise the solicitor (see further p 537).

Reviews of legal aid taxations

Solicitors and counsel who are dissatisfied with the sums allowed on a legal aid taxation may seek to challenge them only if the area committee grants leave (regs 112–121). If leave is granted the costs of the reconsideration or review are payable out of the legal aid fund. If leave is refused the solicitor and counsel must, perforce, accept the taxing officer's decision (*Storer v Wright* [1981] QB 336; and see *R v Legal Aid Board, ex parte Bateman* [1992] 1 WLR 711, DC).

Payments on account of costs and disbursements

These important topics are governed by regs 100 and 101 and are considered at p 60.

Assisted person's involvement in taxation or assessment

Regulations 105A and 119 make provisions concerning assisted persons who have an interest in any assessment or taxation of costs; eg legally-aided clients who have made a contribution which may not be refunded or who have recovered or preserved any money or property which may bring the statutory charge into operation (see p 53).

If the assisted person has such a financial interest the solicitor must supply him with a copy of the bill, explain what his financial interest is, how the assessment or taxation may affect it, and how he can protect it (eg by making written representations or by attending any hearing). To ensure that proper compliance is made, all legal aid bills must be indorsed with a certificate referring to the relevant regulation (see *White Book* 62/C/1 direction 4.2).

Costs between solicitor and own client

In this section we look at the costs position as between the solicitor and a fee-paying client. In such a case the client is liable to reimburse and remunerate his solicitor by virtue of the contract that exists between them. Ultimately, the solicitor can sue his client for the 'proper costs'. However, the law puts limits on the solicitor's rights of action and gives the client the right to have taxed the amount of 'proper costs' the solicitor is entitled to charge. The solicitor cannot circumvent these limits merely by accepting a cheque from the client and suing upon the cheque if it is dishonoured (*Martin Boston & Co v Levy* [1982] 1 WLR 1434).

In practice, taxation of a solicitor-and-own-client bill is quite rare. If the topic of costs was properly explained to the client at the outset (see p 21) and the case has been properly handled and the client has been kept fully informed about all matters as it proceeded then, at the end of the day, the client usually settles the bill promptly and with good grace. Unless the court otherwise orders (see below) in an action concerning a minor's or mental patient's money claim the solicitor for the minor or mental patient must apply for a taxation of his bill. This requirement provides a means of preventing unscrupulous solicitors recommending the acceptance of a low offer of compromise on the claim where the other side were willing to pay a large amount of costs; or unscrupulous next friends allowing their solicitors to make exaggerated claims for costs in addition to the costs paid by the other party. These dangers are clearly somewhat remote. In both courts, the court may dispense with this requirement, eg where the costs between litigants are agreed *or* are to be taxed *and* the solicitor agrees to waive his right to any additional costs (see generally RSC Ord 62, r 16; CCR Ord 10, r 11 and Ord 38, r 19A).

Inevitably there will be some cases where the client objects to the amount of the bill, even where the bill is perfectly proper. What follows is a short account of the solicitor's rights and obligations in such a case.

(It should be noted that the solicitor may have contracted out of the matters mentioned below by making a written remuneration agreement with his client; this is dealt with in a separate section, see p 581.)

A distinction must be made between 'contentious business' and 'non-contentious business'. Do not assume that all the work done in a solicitor's litigation department is 'contentious business'. This expression is defined by the Solicitors Act 1974, s 87, as:

> business done, whether as solicitor or advocate, in or for the purposes of proceedings begun before a court or before an arbitrator appointed under the Arbitration Act 1950, not being business which falls within the definition of non-contentious or common form probate business.

The important word in this definition is 'begun'. Assume that a solicitor is consulted by a shopkeeper who is threatened with proceedings by a dissatisfied customer. The solicitor does all the investigation work and negotiates a settlement with the customer before any writ is issued. That is not 'contentious business' because no proceedings were 'begun'.

The first bill the solicitor gives his client is usually very short, ie a 'gross sum bill' which itemises the work done but does not give a separate figure for each item: it merely states the total sum payable. If the client is not satisfied with the bill—usually this means he thinks he is being overcharged—he may request a more detailed bill, and this must be provided (Solicitors Act 1974, s 64). Such a bill, if requested by the client, wholly supersedes the gross sum bill and may be for a higher, or lower, sum (for a recent case example see *Maduresinghe v Penguin (Electronics)* [1993] 1 WLR 989).

In 'non-contentious business' where the bill does not exceed £50,000, the solicitor must inform the client in writing of the right to require the solicitor to obtain a certificate from The Law Society. If the client exercises his right within one month of being advised of his rights The Law Society will peruse the solicitor's file and issue a certificate stating what sum, in their opinion, would be fair and reasonable (whether the sum charged or a lesser sum). The client additionally has an independent right to apply to the courts for a taxation (see below and see generally the Solicitors' Remuneration Order 1994, set out in the *White Book* 3861: in order to exercise rights under this Order clients must (usually) pay to the solicitor all the VAT and paid disbursements shown in the bill and also half of the profit costs claimed). Before suing for his costs the solicitor must also inform the client of his rights relating to taxation (contrast 'contentious business' where clients cannot require a certificate from The Law Society and where solicitors need not inform clients of their rights relating to taxation).

Subject to certain minor exceptions a solicitor cannot sue for his costs before the expiration of one calendar month from the date on which a bill of those costs was delivered (a) to the client either personally or by being left at or posted to his place of business or last known place of abode, (b) signed by the solicitor or enclosed with a letter so signed (Solicitors Act 1974, s 69). In the case of both 'contentious' and 'non-contentious' business the client can apply to the High Court for an order for the taxation of the bill (on the indemnity basis with certain modifications, see below); 1974 Act, s 70. As to the procedure to follow and the forms to adopt in High Court cases, see *White Book* 106/2/1 and 391 *et seq.* If the bill is for a sum not exceeding £5,000 and relates to 'contentious business' done in a county court the application may be made to that county court (1974 Act, s 69).

The circumstances in which a solicitor should apply for taxation of his own bill are rare indeed. Almost always the better application will be the commencement of a simple debt claim in the High Court or county court leading to a default judgment or summary judgment in the form of a *Smith v Edwardes* order (as to which see *White Book* 14/3–4/30 and *Green Book* commentary to Solicitors Act 1974, s 69). If the client seeks an order for taxation within one calendar month of the delivery of the bill the court must order a taxation. In other cases the court may order a taxation. However, if the costs have in fact been paid, no order for taxation can be made on an application which was not commenced within twelve months of payment (and see further *Harrison v Tew* [1990] 2 AC 523).

If, on a taxation, the bill is reduced by one fifth or more the solicitor must pay the costs of taxation: otherwise the client has to pay them. If the bill is reduced by more than half the taxing officer must inform The Law Society (Solicitors' Remuneration Order 1994, art 5; *White Book* 3861).

In preparing a bill in connection with contentious work concerning a High Court case the solicitor must be guided by the factors listed in RSC Ord 62, Appendix 2 Part I quoted on p 532. As to non-contentious business he must be guided by the Solicitors' Remuneration Order 1994, art 3 which is in similar terms.

As to contentious business concerning the county court the solicitor must draw his bill in accordance with the county court scale appropriate to the case in which the work was done (Solicitors Act 1974, s 72(3) and see p 529; if the case concerned a money claim, the relevant scale for a plaintiff's bill is determined by the amount claimed rather than the amount, if any, which was recovered; see CCR Ord 38, r 21(2)).

Basis of taxation

Solicitor-and-own-client costs are taxed on the indemnity basis modified by three presumptions (RSC Ord 62, r 15; CCR Ord 38, r 19A):

(1) It is presumed reasonable to incur expenditure on items the client has expressly or impliedly approved.

(2) The amounts of expenditure are presumed reasonable if the client also approved those amounts.

(3) It is presumed unreasonable to incur expenditure on items which are unusual unless the client was warned in advance that these items might not be allowed on a taxation between litigants.

It should be appreciated that, as between a solicitor and his client, it may be immaterial whether any particular item or amount was an essential expense or an absurd extravagance. The crucial questions are (1) was the expense reasonable? (2) If not, did the client, having been properly warned of the risk, actually authorise that expense? Note that, in respect of unusual costs (the most likely to be challenged) the burden of proof is upon the solicitor to show that they were reasonably incurred or that he properly warned the client of the risk involved. Here are some examples of costs which may be allowed on a solicitor-and-own-client taxation having previously been disallowed on a taxation between litigants:

(1) doubtful items;
(2) doubtful amounts;
(3) items expressly or impliedly authorised by the client;
(4) amounts expressly or impliedly authorised by the client;
(5) costs which are not costs of the action (eg costs incurred in respect of persons the client considered joining but, ultimately, did not join, in these proceedings).

Moneys on account of costs and interim bills

It has always been open to a solicitor to request money on account of costs. However, any sum so received must be paid into his client account and not office account. Obviously disbursements can be paid out of this sum so preventing the solicitor from being out of pocket, but profit costs cannot be deducted before a bill is delivered. It will be appreciated that in a complicated case the solicitor may have to wait a very long time in order to deliver his final bill. However, a solicitor can now submit interim bills to his client as the case progresses. The Solicitors Act 1974, s 65(2), enables a solicitor retained to conduct contentious business to request a client to make a payment of money being a reasonable sum on account of costs incurred in the conduct of that business. If the client refuses, or fails to pay, that is deemed to be good cause whereby the solicitor may give reasonable notice to the client and withdraw.

A 'client should, at least every six months, be told the approximate costs incurred to date and in appropriate cases an interim bill should be delivered' (*Client Care—A Guide for Solicitors* 1991, The Law Society, p 21; see also *Guide to Professional Conduct of Solicitors* 1996, pp 223 and 230). Interim bills can be of benefit to the client as well as to the solicitor. Obviously a letter enclosing an interim bill will contain an up-to-date report on the progress of the case and this, at the very least, satisfies the client that the solicitor is getting on with the case. Further, the client will no doubt feel that a solicitor who is competent in conducting his own business is more likely to be competent in handling the client's affairs. Many clients prefer regular smaller bills to one large bill at the end of the case.

Interim bills differ from final bills in that the solicitor cannot sue on them for payment and the client cannot seek taxation of them (instead he must request a final bill); see further as to the distinctions between interim bills and final bills, *White Book* 3693.

Failure to bill the client regularly may ultimately cause him to seek a solicitor-and-own-client taxation. For example, if on accepting instructions, the solicitor receives a payment on account of, say, £500 and then does not seek any further payment until the conclusion of the proceedings; the client who at that stage may be given a bill for, say, £3,000, might well complain 'You never told me you'd spent the £500 yet'. Strictly speaking such a complaint may not be logical or justifiable. But given the fact that many clients are naïve about the costs of litigation it is easy enough to sympathise with a client who makes this mistake. It is vital for the solicitor who wishes to retain the client's goodwill, not to let the client make such mistakes.

Special agreements as to solicitor-and-own-client costs

Contentious business agreements

Contentious business agreements have been in existence for many years now. In the past they were of very limited use unless, eg it was possible for the solicitor and client to agree in advance a lump sum fee. However, because of amendments made by the CLSA 1990, they have become much more widely used. This is because it is now possible to make a valid agreement which fixes the solicitor's remuneration by reference to an hourly rate. Contentious business agreements are defined by the Solicitors Act 1974, s 59, as amended, as follows:

> an agreement in writing ... in respect of any contentious business done, or to be done, ... remunerated by a gross sum, or by reference to an hourly rate, or by salary, or otherwise.

For the solicitor, the main purpose of entering into a contentious business agreement is to exclude the client's right to have the solicitor's remuneration taxed by the court. The courts tax bills, not agreements, and under a contentious business agreement the remuneration is payable by agreement, not by bill. Nevertheless, the solicitor's remuneration still remains subject to judicial supervision (see below).

If work is done under a contentious business agreement, an unpaid solicitor cannot commence simple debt proceedings against his former client. Instead, he must apply to a district judge or taxing master by originating summons (see *White Book* 106/2/1) or originating application (see CCR Ord 49, r 18) in the High Court or county court in which the contentious business was done (for contentious business concerning arbitration see 1974 Act, s 61(6)(b) and (c)). Before allowing enforcement the court will examine the agreement and consider whether it is fair and reasonable. The agreement is unfair if the client did not fully understand and appreciate its effect before making it; it is unreasonable if it constitutes excessive profiteering by the solicitor.

It is noticeable that the court is required to consider the fairness and reasonableness of the agreement made, rather than the sum payable under it. Contrast taxation which inquires into the fairness and reasonableness of the bill. Taxation is the remorseless, grinding process aimed at finding the correct charge for a particular job; it looks at each and every step, document and attendance. Conversely, when considering a contentious business agreement, the court's primary inquiry is as to the circumstances at the time of the agreement. However, if the remuneration is fixed by reference to an hourly rate, the protections afforded by the 1974 Act, s 69 will still apply (see p 579). Also, in such a case, the court has power to inquire into the number of hours worked and into whether that number of hours was excessive (1974 Act, s 61(4B)). If the solicitor's time records are not believed, or are considered excessive, the court will not allow full enforcement of the agreement (cf 1974 Act, s 61(4); as to the somewhat mystifying reference to taxation in s 61(4B), which also appears in s 57(5) and (7), see the dictum of Mustill J in *Walton v Egan* [1982] 2 QB 1232 set out in full at p 584).

In many cases a solicitor will not need to enforce his contentious business agreement; he will have received payment in advance. Section 61(5) provides that, if an agreed amount has been paid, a client wishing to challenge the agreement or calculation must apply to the court within twelve months of the date of payment or within such further time as appears to the court to be reasonable.

A contentious business agreement does not adversely effect any *inter partes* order for costs which the client may obtain. Assume that the client is the successful party in the litigation and is awarded costs. The solicitor should draw up a traditional bill of the costs of action and seek its taxation if necessary. Once taxed the client can recover costs under it so long as these costs do not exceed the sums payable under the contentious business agreement (1974 Act, s 60(2), (3), see p 525).

A special rule applies to contentious business agreements made with a client acting in the capacity of a guardian, trustee or receiver of property. In these cases the agreement must be approved by the court before any payment is made under it (1974 Act, s 62).

A contentious business agreement does not prevent the client terminating the retainer (eg sacking the solicitor) at any time. In such a case s 63 of the 1974 Act makes provision for payment. Section 63 also applies in cases of death or incapacity of the solicitor.

Non-contentious business agreements

According to s 57 of the Solicitors Act 1974 (as amended by the CLSA 1990) a solicitor and client may make an agreement in respect of non-contentious business which provides:

> for the remuneration of the solicitor by a gross sum, or by reference to an hourly rate or by a commission or percentage, or by a salary, or otherwise, and it may be made on the terms that the amount of the remuneration stipulated for shall or shall not include all or any disbursements made by the solicitor in respect of searches, plans, travelling, stamps, fees or other matters.

We must emphasise three differences between the definitions of contentious and non-contentious business agreements and then explain other differences, as to enforcement and as to drafting.

These agreements, like solicitor-and-own-client taxation, inhabit two territories which are forever separated by the highly technical definition used in the Solicitors Act 1974 for the expression 'contentious business'. As explained earlier (see p 578) this expression turns upon the word 'begun'. Business, however litigious, or argumentative, remains 'non-contentious' until proceedings are begun.

Another difference between the two forms of agreement is that, in non-contentious business agreements, remuneration can be fixed as a commission or percentage. These methods of charging are of course common in the case of probate and conveyancing matters. However, they are of little relevance to charging agreements made by litigators.

A third difference between the two definitions is more apparent than real. Section 57 expressly deals with disbursements etc; s 59 does not. However, this does not affect the drafting of the two agreements. Contentious business agreements, like non-contentious business agreements, should deal expressly with disbursements (see *Chamberlain v Boodle & King (Note)* [1982] 1 WLR 1443, still good law on this point).

Enforcement of a non-contentious business agreement

To enforce the agreement the solicitor can commence simple debt proceedings in the High Court or county court. Before doing so the solicitor must comply with s 69 of the 1974 Act (ie deliver a signed bill and wait at least one month, see p 579). A non-contentious business agreement restricts the client's right to require taxation except in two respects (1974 Act, s 57(5) and (7)).

(1) Where the agreement is shown to be unfair or unreasonable.
(2) Where the agreement fixes the remuneration by reference to an hourly rate and the client persuades the court to inquire as to the number of hours worked and as to whether that number was excessive.

The principles underlying the reference to taxation in s 57(5) (and, in our view, s 57(7) and s 61(4B) first enacted in 1990) are clearly explained in *Walton v Egan* [1982] 2 QB 1232.

Where there is a special agreement under section 57 the ... solicitor's right of action is founded on the agreement not the bill; indeed so far as section 57 is concerned there is no need for the solicitor to render a bill at all. Nor is there any room for taxation under section 70, for this is concerned with bills not agreements. It is true that section 57(5) seems to contemplate that a taxation may occur, but this is in my view a procedure initiated by the court pursuant to its own inherent powers to supervise solicitors as officers of the court; it is not a procedure exercised as a right by the client. When an action on a special agreement comes before the court [eg a solicitor's simple debt claim], the matter may be sent to the taxing master so that he can enquire into the facts and report back to the court. When doing so, he is acting as a delegate of powers exercised by the court, and he is not exercising his own originating powers of taxation (*per* Mustill J).

A non-contentious business agreement also excludes the rights which the client would otherwise have to require the solicitor to obtain a 'remuneration' certificate (see p 578 and the Solicitors' Remuneration Order 1994, art 9).

Drafting special agreements under s 57 or s 59

Before setting about this task it is as well to recall The Law Society's written professional standards concerning information on costs. These standards were revised in February 1991 and are set out in a booklet entitled *Client Care—A Guide for Solicitors* 1991, The Law Society. Compliance with these standards has not been made compulsory. They are 'best practice' recommendations. However, it would be inadvisable for any solicitor to stray from them too far or too frequently (see *Client Care,* p 27) and [1994] Gazette, 28 September, 36).

The current standards are summarised on p 21 above. A convenient way of complying with them whilst at the same time proposing a special agreement as to remuneration is simply to include a final paragraph asking the client to sign and return a copy of your letter so as to confirm his acceptance of the agreement.

The *Client Care* booklet contains several excellent precedents for such a letter, dealing with the points mentioned above and also dealing with several other points which it is useful to include: regular billing, variations of hourly rates, in-house complaints handling procedures, interest on moneys recovered and interest on late payments. In May 1997 the Law Society published a Consultation Paper entitled *Costs Information and Client Care* and stated its intention to produce a series of model terms of business and costs agreements later in 1997, see [1997] Gazette 14 May, p 26).

It is important to realise that the form of agreement should be the same whether it amounts to a contentious business agreement or a non-contentious business agreement. It is not the drafting that makes the difference (unless, eg you specify one or other section number which in our opinion would be foolish). Whether the agreement is one type or the other depends upon that key word 'begun' (see p 578). If all the work is done without any proceedings being commenced the agreement lives and dies a non-contentious business agreement. However, if, or when, proceedings are begun, the agreement will, at that stage, become a contentious business agreement. As such it will cover all relevant work including, strangely enough, all the relevant pre-commencement work.

Conditional fee agreements

This is a new type of charging agreement available in certain types of civil proceedings only (personal injury cases certain insolvency cases and human rights cases before certain European courts), see generally CLSA 1990, s 58 and statutory instruments made thereunder, *White Book* 3864 *et seq.*

Briefly, this type of agreement enables solicitors to charge fees according to results; above average fees if the case is won; no fees or below average fees if the case is lost. The extent to which the fees may be increased is limited by statutory instrument to 100 per cent of the solicitor-and-own-client bill. A client liable to pay this increase cannot recoup it from his opponent even if costs are awarded in his favour (CLSA 1990, s 58(8)). If the client has winnings (eg judgment for damages) the increase will in effect be deducted from them (cf the statutory charge in legal aid cases).

It is very important to note that the maximum percentage increase which will be allowed will be a percentage of the taxed costs only. We must therefore contrast it with the American concept of contingency fees, where the lawyer may take a percentage of the winnings. We must also contrast it with the two other types of special agreements. They are aimed at avoiding taxations. With a conditional fee agreement the taxation of costs will be vital in order to identify the increased sum payable.

In practice, most conditional fee agreements are likely to be entered into in respect of *claims* (not defences) made in *personal injury cases*. For simplicity the following notes are all in relation to such cases.

The agreement must state whether the amount payable 'is limited by reference to the amount of any damages which may be recovered on behalf of the client' (*White Book* 3865, reg 3(d)). If the client subsequently applies for taxation of the solicitor's bill this limit is one (of four) factors the taxing officer must take into account (RSC Ord 62, r 15A). As to this The Law Society recommends, but does not require, a limit of 25 per cent of the damages recovered.

The agreement must be in writing and must be signed by both client and solicitor (*White Book* 3865, reg 6). The Law Society has produced and publicised a model conditional fee agreement and also a model agreement for employment of counsel by solicitors on a conditional fee basis (to be signed by both solicitor and counsel or counsel's clerk although in fact signatures are not a formality requirement for such an agreement). The Bar Council has also produced and published model terms of engagement plus standard form letters to be signed by solicitors and counsel's clerks adopting the Bar model. There is at present some controversy as to these differing terms. There are however, a few stout-hearted pioneers in each profession who have agreed compromise terms enabling them to establish and maintain good working relations in conditional fee cases for various lay clients present and future.

There is no provision for conditional fee agreements to cover the cost of expert evidence. Such agreements would of course imperil the credibility of the expert's testimony (see p 424). Instead, The Law Society model agreement contains a 'Pay as you go' option under which clients would finance the costs of experts' reports (and other disbursements) as and when they are incurred. Ultimately, the clients may recover the expenditure from their opponents, if the clients win, or from insurance, if the clients lose (as to insurance, see further, below). To cover cash flow difficulties in the meantime it may be possible to finance some if not all disbursements out of court orders for the interim payment of damages (see p 308) a topic also covered by The Law Society model agreement.

What happens if the client loses? 'No win, no fee' does not mean 'No win, no costs', because the court is likely to order the client to pay the defendant's costs. If an unsuccessful client is reduced to homelessness and/or bankruptcy in order to pay the defendant's costs it will be of no or little consequence to him that he does not also have to pay his own lawyers. Most clients entering a conditional fee agreement are likely to want insurance covering the risk of loss. The Law Society has developed and recommends a particular insurance package ('Accident Line Protect') which buys £100,000 worth of cover for a single premium (currently £85). If the claim is lost the insurance covers the client in respect of his opponent's taxed costs and his own disbursements (other than counsel's fees). This insurance is available only to clients of solicitors who are members of The Law Society's Accident Line scheme, membership of which is restricted to solicitors who have recognised skills in personal injury work (ie who are members of The Law Society's Personal Injury Panel). Other insurers may offer competing forms of insurance, eg for clients of non-member solicitors or for non-personal injury cases.

The new law of conditional fee agreements may, or may not, mark a revolutionary change for the legal professions. If the new law is to survive and thrive a great many problems and difficulties will have to be surmounted. Space constraints in this book permit only the briefest outline of some of the main problems.

(1) Ethical problems
A conditional fee agreement is just a specialised form of contingency fee agreement. In the past, the common law has always condemned such agreements because of the abuses to which they may give rise.

To put it in a nutshell, once a lawyer has a personal interest in litigation, his or her objectivity may be affected (*per* McCowan LJ in *British Waterways Board v Norman* (1993) 26 HLR 232).

There are fears that, in weak cases, lawyers will pressure clients into accepting low offers of compromise or will corrupt and distort the evidence. In strong cases lawyers will have every incentive to make work for themselves; for example, if a success fee of 20 per cent has been agreed in addition to basic costs, the lawyer will receive six hours' pay for every five hours worked.

It remains to be seen whether the various recommendations made and limits imposed on conditional fee agreements will succeed in preventing abuse and promoting public confidence in the new law.

(2) Interrelation between conditional fee agreements and legal aid
The advantage and disadvantage of legal aid to bear in mind in this context is the costs protection it gives to the assisted party (see p 55 and the burden of paying monthly contributions it may impose (see p 50). A conditional fee agreement is (or will become) unenforceable if the client has (or later obtains) a relevant legal aid certificate.

(3) Valuing the correct success fee to agree
The variables include the degree of risk shouldered by the lawyers based on the likelihood of the claim being successful, the added risk for the solicitor if counsel is not instructed on conditional fee terms and the financial subsidy the solicitor (and counsel) are giving to the client in respect of profit costs (and counsel's fees) during the proceedings.

(4) The obligation to explain the agreements to the client
The agreement must state that, immediately before it was entered into, the client's attention was drawn to various matters including the availability of legal aid and how it might affect the client, the consequences of winning and losing and the circumstances in which the client may seek taxation. Despite the no doubt excellent help given by standard forms and leaflets, the burden on the solicitor here remains heavy.

Answers to questions posed on page 522

Is it reasonable for the barrister to expect the solicitor to pay the £10,000 brief fee?   Yes, of course. It ill-becomes the solicitor to doubt or hesitate over a fee voluntarily agreed. If it is now thought that £10,000 was too much (which it probably was) the solicitor should not have agreed it.

If so, is it reasonable for the solicitor to pass that cost on to the clients?   The answer depends. A fee of this size is, without question, unusual. Although counsel was retained on the clients' instructions, did they also expressly or impliedly authorise the retention of counsel of that eminence? Did they also expressly or impliedly authorise the agreement of that fee? In either case were they specifically warned that such an expense 'might not' (see below) be allowed on a taxation between litigants? If they were not so warned and the clients now challenge this item the solicitor would not be able to pass on such a fee.

Is it reasonable for the clients to look to the losing plaintiff in respect of such a fee?   Certainly not. In theory the sub-questions to be asked are: was it reasonable to employ counsel of this eminence; and was the agreed fee within the range of possible fees which, at that time, it was reasonable to agree? The practical points are, this case could have been adequately handled by any middle-ranking barrister and thus the plaintiff cannot be required to pay any more than it would have been reasonable to agree in respect of such a barrister (£350 to £750).

Chapter 24

Enforcement of Money Judgments

Civil judgments are never enforced by the courts automatically. It is always for the successful parties to decide when and how best to enforce them (this sometimes surprises clients). Obviously not all judgments need enforcing. If the judgment debtor is insured in respect of the claim and the defence has been conducted by his insurers they can be expected to settle up promptly with good grace. In other cases the correct time to consider enforcement with the client is not when the case is concluded, but before proceedings are even begun. Is the debtor worth suing? If he is not, litigation will just be sending good money after bad.

Given that the decision to sue has been taken, there are three questions for the judgment creditor to consider: (1) Can he find the debtor? (2) Can he find out what assets the debtor has? (3) Can he take those assets from him? The courts cannot help with the first: consider employing an inquiry agent. The courts can help on the second and third questions, though as to the second it may be preferable to use an inquiry agent instead of, or as well as, the courts (see below).

In respect of county court judgments where the amount recoverable exceeds £1,000 (see *White Book* 5522 Supplement) it will often be advantageous to transfer proceedings to the High Court for the purposes of enforcement. On transfer the judgment will attract interest under the Judgments Act 1838. This statute provides a regime for judgment interest which, from the creditor's point of view, is better than the regime applicable in the county courts in at least two respects. Under the county court regime no interest is payable on judgments for less than £5,000 (see County Courts (Interest on Judgment Debts) Order 1991, art 1(2)). Also, even when interest is payable, it ceases to be payable as soon as the judgment creditor commences any enforcement proceedings in the county court (including oral examination, garnishee proceedings or a judgment summons, see below) unless those proceedings fail to produce any payment from the debtor. Contrast interest under the High Court system; it does not cease to accrue during enforcement proceedings. In our opinion, once judgment has been transferred to the High Court, interest under the 1838 Act will continue to accrue even if, later, garnishee proceedings or equitable execution (see below) is sought in the county court (see CCA 1984, s 42(5)).

Oral examination of the judgment debtor

If, after judgment has been obtained, the debtor does not pay immediately, the creditor can apply *ex parte* for an order bringing the debtor before the court in order to examine him as to his means. If the judgment debtor is a body corporate, the order can be made against an officer of the company. The order provides for the production of all relevant books or documents (see generally RSC Ord 48, r 1; CCR Ord 25, r 3; and see *Green Book Procedural Tables No 12*). In the High Court an affidavit is required: see Practice Forms 98 (affidavit) and 99 (order); as to the county court see Forms N316 (application) and N37 (order).

The respondent may be entitled to 'conduct money', ie his reasonable travelling costs to and from the court. There is no requirement to tender this in the first instance but it is advisable to do so in High Court cases, so as to facilitate committal proceedings (*Beeston Shipping Ltd v Babanaft International SA* [1985] 1 All ER 923). In High Court cases the examination should be held at the most economical court, ie at the High Court office or county court for the district in which the debtor resides (*White Book* 750). In county court cases the examination must be conducted in the county court for the district in which the respondent resides or carries on business. If necessary the proceedings may have to be transferred to facilitate this (CCR Ord 25, rr 2, 3). In the High Court the order must be served personally. In the county court postal service may be used.

In both courts if the respondent fails to attend it is possible to obtain an order for his committal to prison. In the county court, an order for attendance at an adjourned hearing must be served personally on the debtor (see Form N39). The order must be served at least ten days in advance of the adjourned hearing. At least four days in advance of the adjourned hearing the creditor must file a certificate concerning conduct money (CCR Ord 25, r 3(5A), (5B)).

Although failures to attend an adjourned hearing are common, committals are rare. This is because the order for committal usually produces the respondent (and sometimes the money).

In the High Court and county court the examination, usually, takes place before a senior clerk of the court office. The hearing 'is not only intended to be an examination, but a cross-examination, and that of the severest kind' (*Republic of Costa Rica v Stronsberg* (1880) 16 ChD 8). The examination is not conducted by the court although it may give the debtor the opportunity to make a written statement first. Many county courts use a printed *pro forma* of questions for this purpose but this does not prevent additional relevant questions being asked. The judgment creditor's representative has to attend, prepared to probe the evidence given and ask the right follow-up questions. It often helps to obtain some information as to the debtor's means before the hearing. If for example the debtor denies that he owns a car, to be able to ask him 'In that case who owns the Alfa Romeo registration number M240 GRH or the Rover 100, P230 SAH, which are both parked in your driveway most evenings?' may produce a more helpful response. The debtor may also be asked questions about assets outside the jurisdiction (*Interpool Ltd v Galani* [1988] QB 738; query whether leave would then be necessary to use any information gained for the benefit of proceedings commenced overseas, see p 392).

The court may allow the costs of the examination (see *White Book* 48/1–3/9; CCR, Appendix A, Item No 10). At the end of the examination the respondent is asked to sign a form containing a note of the evidence which he has given (RSC Ord 48, r 3; county court practice is similar).

Oral examinations and inquiry agents are not the only means of finding out what assets the debtor has. If the circumstances so warrant, the judgment creditor might also use one or both of the law's 'nuclear weapons' the *Mareva* injunction or the *Anton Piller* order (see p 294 and p 300). As to obtaining orders under the Bankers' Books Evidence Act 1879 enabling the inspection of bank accounts in the name of the debtor or his associates, see *DB Deniz Nakliyati TAS v Yugopetrol* [1992] 1 WLR 437.

Methods of enforcement

There are several methods of enforcing money judgments. Different methods are used for different forms of wealth.

> *Example*
> Inquiries reveal that the debtor is a teacher who lives in his own house (address noted) bought on mortgage six years ago. He owns a 1996 Ford Fiesta (details noted) which is parked overnight at his house. He has accounts at the National Westminster Bank, Blanktown branch: his current account is usually overdrawn: he has about £1,200 on a deposit account there. He also has some savings (about £7,000) in a Halifax Building Society account at Blanktown. Last year he inherited a legacy of £19,000 from a deceased relative (the names and addresses of the executors have been noted) which has not yet been paid. He is unmarried and has no dependants. He says he has no other debts.

Against this debtor six methods of enforcement are available (see below). The usual practice is to appropriate assets in this order: movables, money, land, equitable interests. The process of taking the 'movables' often produces the 'money' voluntarily. Concurrent enforcement by different methods is permissible (for exceptions, see below) and thus it is possible to proceed with 'all guns blazing'. A creditor taking steps to enforce a judgment is entitled to add to the judgment debt and costs, reasonable sums in respect of costs incurred on previous attempts to enforce that judgment (CLSA 1990, s 15(3), (4); in the High Court, see *White Book* 760; in the county court, see CCA 1984, s 76).

Writ of *fieri facias* (High Court); warrant of execution (county court)

This is the form of enforcement against the debtor's goods and chattels. Article 8 of the High Court and County Courts Jurisdiction Order 1991 allocates all proceedings for enforcement against chattels to the High Court where the sum which it is sought to enforce is £5,000 or more (unless the proceedings in question arose out of an agreement regulated by the Consumer Credit Act 1974). Enforcement against chattels where the sum which it is sought to enforce is less than £1,000 (see *White Book* 5522 Supplement) can be taken in the High Court only in respect of a High Court judgment. If the sum which it is sought to enforce is £1,000 or more but less than £5,000 enforcement against chattels is available in both courts. There are said to be two powerful advantages in transferring judgments for £1,000 or more to the High Court; interest on judgment then becomes available; also, execution by sheriff's officer is often considered to be more effective than execution by a county court bailiff (see generally p 382).

The High Court form is usually referred to as a writ of *fi fa* (the Latin is pronounced to rhyme with *by bay*). It is directed to the sheriff of the county in which the debtor's goods are situate. It is issued by the appropriate court office on production of:

(1) two copies of the form duly completed;
(2) a *praecipe* with the fee imprinted thereon (Practice Form 86, *White Book* 262);
(3) the judgment or an office copy;
(4) an office copy of the taxing officer's certificate (where the enforcement relates to costs); and
(5) the order granting leave to issue (where required, see below).

One form of writ is sealed and returned to the judgment creditor who forwards it to the under-sheriff who will acknowledge receipt and send the writ to his officer for execution (see generally RSC Ord 46, r 6 and *White Book* 922 *et seq*).

If the judgment is expressed in a foreign currency the *praecipe* and the writ must state the sterling equivalent of the sum at the date of issue of the writ (*White Book* 722).

In the county court the warrant of execution (see Form N42(c)) is issued on the payment of the fee prescribed and on filing a request in Form N323. The warrant is executed by the bailiff of the court for the district in which it is to be executed (if this is a different county court, see Form N53). Where the debtor is in breach of an instalment order the warrant may be issued either for the whole of the judgment debt and costs remaining unpaid or for any part thereof. However, in the case of enforcement of part of the total sums remaining unpaid that part must not be less than £50 or one monthly instalment (or, as the case may be, four weekly instalments) whichever is the greater. Before executing the warrant the court sends a notice in Form N326 to the debtor (see generally CCR Ord 26, r 1 and *Green Book Procedural Table No 13*).

A creditor need not delay enforcement until taxation of costs. A writ or warrant may be issued before taxation and a separate writ or warrant for costs may be issued later (RSC Ord 47, r 3; CCR Ord 26, r 1(5)).

Leave to issue the writ or warrant is not usually required, but note four important exceptions:

(1) Where six or more years have elapsed since the date of the judgment (RSC Ord 46, r 2; CCR Ord 26, r 5). As to the Limitation Act 1980 see *White Book* 46/2/9, *Lowsley v Forbes* (1996) *The Times*, 5 April and *In re a Debtor (No 50A–SD–1995)* [1997] 2 WLR 57.

(2) Where any change has taken place, whether by death or otherwise, in the parties entitled or liable to execution (RSC Ord 46, r 2; CCR Ord 26, r 5).

(3) Whilst a county court attachment of earnings order is in force (Attachment of Earnings Act 1971, s 8(2)(b); see generally below).

(4) In certain actions against partners (see p 92).

In each of these cases except (4) leave can be sought *ex parte* on affidavit.

In executing the writ or warrant the sheriff or bailiff can seize such of the debtor's goods and chattels in his county or district as may be sufficient to realise the judgment debt and expenses. The items seized are then sold, usually by public auction. After deducting the expenses of execution the judgment creditor is paid off and any surplus proceeds are returned to the debtor. It is always helpful to inform the sheriff or bailiff of specific items which could be seized, eg tell him the make, type and registration number of the debtor's car, if known. In practice the debtor's goods are not usually removed immediately. The debtor and the sheriff or bailiff will enter into an agreement for 'walking possession' whereby, in consideration of the goods not being removed at once, the debtor agrees not to dispose of them nor permit them to be moved (and see further, *White Book* 1081 and County Court Form N42(c)). As to the penalties for rescuing goods seized in execution see the crime of 'pound breach' and CCA 1984, s 92. A full account of the goods and chattels which can and cannot be seized is given in the *Green Book* commentary to CCA 1984, s 89. For example, it is not possible to seize goods on hire or hire-purchase to the debtor (and see 'interpleader proceedings', p 262). Certain goods are protected from seizure: such tools, books, vehicles and other items of equipment as are necessary to the debtor for personal use by him in his employment, business or vocation; also such clothing, bedding, furniture, household equipment and provisions as are necessary for satisfying the basic domestic needs of the debtor and his family. The sheriff or bailiff must not effect forcible entry to any premises unless and until he has taken possession of any goods or chattels therein (see generally *McCleod v Butterwick* [1996] 1 WLR 995).

It is possible for a judgment creditor to seek remedies against the sheriff or bailiff for any alleged dereliction of duty (in the county court see CCA 1984, s 124).

Garnishee proceedings

If the judgment debtor is himself the creditor of another, it is possible to obtain an order that his debtor should pay the judgment creditor. This is known as a garnishee order and is obtained in two stages. In the High Court one needs an affidavit in Practice Form 100 (*White Book* 271; compare the county court affidavit illustrated in fig 38) and having paid the prescribed fee the judgment creditor (the 'garnishor') will obtain 'an order to show cause' in Form 72 (*White Book* 69; sometimes called a 'garnishee order *nisi*'). This order attaches the debt 'due or accruing due' to the judgment debtor and commands the garnishee to attend at the time and place specified and show cause why he should not pay his debt directly to the judgment creditor. Copies of the order must be served, personally on the garnishee, and then, later, and by ordinary service on the judgment debtor (ie on the garnishee at least fifteen days before the return day and on the judgment debtor at least seven days thereafter and at least seven days before the return day). The order binds the garnishee as soon as it is served upon him. This is why the judgment creditor is required to serve upon the garnishee at least seven days before service on the judgment debtor.

If at the hearing the garnishee disputes his liability the district judge may summarily determine the issue or give directions for it to be tried. If the garnishee does not attend or dispute the debt the district judge will usually make the order absolute, whereupon if the attached debt is not paid to the judgment creditor execution will issue against the garnishee (see generally RSC Ord 49). This form of enforcement is discretionary. The district judge may refuse to make the order absolute if, eg the debtor is insolvent and, bankruptcy or similar proceedings being imminent, the effect of the order would merely be giving the garnishor priority over the other unsecured creditors: see *Roberts Petroleum Ltd v Bernard Kenny Ltd* [1983] 2 AC 192 (concerning a charging order to which similar principles apply). For the procedure where the debt to be attached, or the judgment being enforced, is payable in a foreign currency see *White Book* 49/1/20 and 49/2/2. Garnishee proceedings cannot be taken on a judgment for a sum less than £50 or its foreign equivalent.

County court practice is similar: see CCR Ord 30, *Green Book Procedural Table No 18*, and the affidavit illustrated in fig 38. Proceedings are taken in the county court which made the judgment but, if appropriate, a garnishee who is disputing liability may apply *ex parte* in writing for a transfer to his local court (cf p 381). The order to show

[*continued on p 596*]

Fig 38: Affidavit in support of application for garnishee order absolute

Affidavit in support of Application for
Garnishee Order Absolute

Plaintiff

Defendant

Garnishee

In the

County Court

Case No. *Always quote this*

Plaintiff's Ref.

Seal

(1) insert full name address and occupation of deponent

I, (1)

(Solicitor for) the above-named plaintiff, make oath and say:

1. That I (or   )
   on the   day   19   , obtained a judgment (or an order) in this court
   against the above-named defendant for payment of the sum of £   for
   debt (or damages) and costs

(2) where judgment entered for more than £5000 on or after 1 July 1991

2. That £   , including any interest to date (2), is still due and unpaid under the
   judgment (order).

3. That to the best of my information or belief the garnishee,
   of

(3) add if known

(4) state your grounds

   is indebted to the defendant (in the sum of £   )(3)
   The reasons for my information or belief are:(4)

4. That the garnishee is a deposit-taking institution having more than one place of business (and the
   name and address of the branch at which the defendant's account is believed to be held is:

   and the number of the account is believed to be   ) (I do not know at

(5) delete as appropriate

   which branch the defendant's account is held, or what the number of the account is) (5)

5. That the last known address of the defendant is:

Sworn at   in the

county of   this

          day of   19

          Before me

This affidavit is filed on behalf of the plaintiff

Officer of a court, appointed by
the Circuit Judge to take affidavits

The court office at

is open between 10 am and 4 pm Monday to Friday. When corresponding with the court, please address forms and letters to the Chief Clerk and quote the case number.

N349 Affidavit in support of application for garnishee order (Order 30, rule 2)   Printed in the UK by HMSO   Dd 8252126 C300 1477/1 5/91 3208644 19542 cause (Form N84) is served on the garnishee in the same manner as a fixed date summons and on the judgment debtor by ordinary service. As in the High Court the order must be served, first, on the garnishee at least fifteen days before the return day, and then on the judgment debtor at least seven days after a copy had been served on the garnishee and at least seven days before the return day. The number of days mentioned is the same as in the High Court but the computation of them will differ (see pp 9, 13 and 594). The minimum judgment sum for garnishee proceedings in the county court is £50.

A bank account is an obvious target for garnishee proceedings. However, the order made will only bite upon the credit balance in the account (if any) at the time of service of the order; a further order is needed to attach money paid in subsequently (see *White Book* 49/1/16). Also, a joint bank account is not attachable in respect of a debt owed by one of two account holders even if either of them has authority to draw on the account (*Hirschhorn v Evans* [1938] 2 KB 801).

There are several special points to bear in mind if garnishee proceedings are taken against a 'deposit-taking institution' (which is defined to include *inter alia* banks, building societies; as to the National Savings Bank and the Post Office see RSC Ord 77, r 16 and CCR Ord 42, r 14; for a full definition of the institutions included see *White Book* 49/1/10).

(1) The affidavit in support must state whether the deponent knows the name and address of the branch at which the account is held and the account number and must state such information thereto as he has.

(2) The order must be served on the registered or head office and it is also desirable to serve a copy on the branch office concerned.

(3) In making an order any conditions applicable to the account in question purporting to restrict withdrawals are to be disregarded (eg conditions requiring an account holder to give notice, or to produce a deposit book or share-account book; SCA 1981, s 40, CCA 1984, s 108, as to building society deferred shares (which are not attachable) see *White Book* 49/1/30).

(4) An order against a building society or credit union cannot require a payment which would reduce the account to a sum less than £1.

(5) Deposit-taking institutions do not usually attend to 'show cause'. Instead they merely write to the court agreeing to comply with any order made. Alternatively, in the county court only, they may give notice to the court that they do not hold any money to the credit of the judgment debtor whereupon the garnishee proceedings against them are automatically stayed unless the judgment creditor disputes the notice.

(6) Before paying the judgment creditor, the deposit-taking institution is entitled to deduct a prescribed sum (currently £30) in respect of administrative and clerical expenses (see further *White Book* 49/10/2; SCA 1981, s 40A; CCA 1984, s 109).

Judgment debtors who are self-employed often have trade debts due to them. It is possible to find out on oral examination what these debts are and then take garnishee proceedings accordingly. It is not uncommon for solicitors to be served with a garnishee order, as solicitors of course often hold money on behalf of clients.

Attachment of earnings

This is governed by the Attachment of Earnings Act 1971 and CCR Ord 27 (and see *Green Book Procedural Table No 16*). In a sense the Act provides a form of garnishee proceedings to attach 'future debts' payable by an employer. An order is made compelling an employer to make regular deductions from the debtor's earnings and pay them into court. 'Earnings' is defined to include sums payable by way of wages or salary (including, eg overtime pay) and by way of pension (but not state pensions and other state benefits). The Act does not apply to pay or allowances payable to a debtor as a member of Her Majesty's forces (but see analogous remedies under the Armed Forces Act 1971).

To obtain an attachment of earnings order the judgment creditor must complete Form N337 (illustrated in fig 39) and send it to the county court for the district in which the debtor resides. Where the judgment was obtained in a different county court the proceedings must be transferred. Except in certain Family Division cases the High Court has no power to make an attachment of earnings order. A High Court judgment creditor has to apply to the appropriate county court and file an office copy of his judgment and an affidavit in Form N321.

A notice of application for an attachment of earnings order (in Form N55) is served on the debtor (usually by the court) together with Form N56, a questionnaire which the debtor must complete so providing a statement of means. At any stage of the proceedings the court may also require information as to earnings from any person appearing to have the debtor in his employment (see Forms N338 and N61A).

If the debtor completes and returns Form N56 (the statement of means) the court staff may make an attachment of earnings order and send copies of it to the parties and to the debtor's employer. No hearing is convened unless the court staff consider that they lack sufficient information to make an order or unless either party objects to an order made.

If the debtor does not send the court a statement of means within the time allowed the court staff will automatically issue an order compelling him to do so. The order will be in Form N61, indorsed with a penal notice, to be served on the debtor personally by the county court bailiff. Continued disobedience leads, via further notices, to hearings and adjourned hearings, and ultimately to arrest and imprisonment (see Forms N63, N112, N112A).

All hearings and adjourned hearings usually take place before a district judge, who will seek the information relevant to the making of an

[*continued on p 599*]

Fig 39: Request for attachment of earnings order

Request for Attachment of Earnings Order

to be completed and signed by the plaintiff or his solicitor and sent to the court with the appropriate fee

1 Plaintiff's name and address

In the

County Court

Case Number

2 Name and address for service and payment
(if different from above)

Ref/Tel No.

For court use only

A / E application no.

Issue date:

Hearing date:

on

at   o'clock

at (address)

3 Defendant's name and\ address

4 Judgment details

Court where judgment/order made if not court of issue

I apply for an attachment of earnings order

5 Outstanding debt

Balance due at date of request*
(excluding issue fee but including unsatisfied warrant costs)

*you may also be entitled to interest to date of request where judgment is for over £5000 and is entered on or after 1 July 1991

Issue fee

AMOUNT NOW DUE

I certify that the whole or part of any instalments due under the judgment or order have not been paid and the balance now due is as shown

Signed

Plaintiff (Plaintiff's solicitor)

Dated

6 Employment Details *(please give as much information as you can - it will help the court to make an order more quickly)*

Employer's name and address

Defendant's place of work
(if different from employer's address)

7 Other details
(Give any other details about the defendant's circumstances which may be relevant to the application)

IMPORTANT
You must inform the court immediately of any payments you receive after you have sent this request to the court

The defendant is employed as

Works No / Pay Ref

N337 Request for attachment of earnings order (Order 27, rule 4(1)) (5.95)

Printed by Satellite Press Limited

attachment of earnings order. Such an order will be made only if the district judge is satisfied that the debtor has sufficient means.

An attachment of earnings order, whether made by the court staff or by the district judge, will specify the 'normal deduction rate' and the 'protected earnings rate', the latter being the amount which the court decides the debtor must be allowed to retain out of his earnings in any event. It will normally be a sum equal to the sum the debtor would receive for himself and his family if he were on income support.

Example

If the protected earnings rate is £110 per week and the normal deduction rate is £15 per week, then, in any week in which the debtor earns a net £125 or more the creditor will receive the full £15. If in one week the debtor earns a sum between £110 and £125 the creditor will receive the excess over £110. If in one week the debtor earns £110 or less then for that week the creditor receives nothing. If in one week the debtor receives advance pay (eg holiday pay) the normal deduction rate will apply to each pay period covered by the payment. Thus from a payment comprising £125 per week or more for a three-week period a sum of £45 would be deducted.

The costs of the application (as to which, see CCR Ord 27, r 9) may be fixed and allowed without taxation. The order is served on the debtor and on the employer by ordinary first-class post. The employer is usually given an explanatory booklet giving details as to how an attachment of earnings order operates. In respect of each deduction he has to make he is entitled to deduct an additional sum (at present £1) in respect of his clerical and administrative expenses (see Attachment of Earnings Act 1971, s 7 and the *Green Book* commentary thereto). The smallest sum for which an attachment of earnings order can be made is £50 or the amount remaining payable under a judgment for not less than £50.

It is the duty of both the debtor and the employer to notify the court of any cessation of the debtor's employment. Similarly, if the debtor obtains another job he must inform the court and the order can then be redirected to the new employer. The court can convene further hearings during the currency of an order, eg to compel the debtor to give information as to any change in employment.

In theory, an attachment of earnings order secures the whole amount of the judgment debt outstanding. Thus, once it has been made, the judgment creditor cannot use any other method of enforcement without first drawing the attachment of earnings order to the court's attention. For this reason judgment creditors often turn to attachment of earnings orders as a method of final resort, rather than first resort (see further p 591). An attachment of earnings order also affects any entitlement to interest under the County Courts (Interest on Judgment Debts) Order

1991 (see art 4(3)); no such interest accrues whilst an attachment of earnings order is in force.

Charging order on land

This method of enforcement provides the judgment creditor with the equivalent of a mortgage over land specified in the order. Thus, subject to any prior mortgages and charges affecting that land, the judgment creditor becomes a secured creditor. The charging order does not affect the accrual of any judgment interest payable on High Court judgments (see p 589 and *White Book* 50/1–9/23) or on county court judgments for sums of not less than £5,000 (see p 589 and County Courts (Interest on Judgment Debts) Order 1991, art 4(2)). Subsequently, if the judgment debt remains unpaid, the judgment creditor can apply for an order for the sale of the land charged so that the judgment may be satisfied out of the proceeds of sale remaining after discharge of any prior mortgage or charge. The charging order secures all judgment interest due and accruing due, including interest accruing more than six years before the eventual sale of the property (*Ezekiel v Orakpo* [1997] 1 WLR 340).

Jurisdiction of the High Court
The High Court has jurisdiction to make a charging order over land only if the judgment in question is a High Court maintenance order, or is a judgment for a sum exceeding £5,000 and which either was made by the High Court or has been transferred to the High Court under CCA 1984, s 42 (see subs (5) and see generally Charging Orders Act 1979, s 1; jurisdiction under this statute was not altered by the CLSA 1990).

Jurisdiction of the county court
The jurisdiction of the county court to make a charging order over land is unlimited. If the judgment in question is a High Court judgment, proceedings should be taken in the county court local to the debtor (CCR Ord 31, r 1(1)(c)). If the judgment in question is a county court judgment, proceedings should be taken in the county court presently seised of the action (CCR Ord 31, r 1(1)(b)).

The procedure for obtaining a charging order is similar to the garnishee procedure (see generally RSC Ord 50; CCR Ord 31 and *Green Book Procedural Table No 19*). It is necessary to apply *ex parte* for an order to show cause (in the High Court, see Form No 75; in the county court see Form N86). An affidavit in support of the application is necessary. The order to show cause should be registered against the land and the order and copies of the affidavit must of course be served. If at the hearing (before the district judge) an order absolute is made, that too should be registered. If it should be necessary to enforce the charge this is done by commencing a fresh action by originating summons in the Chancery Division (see RSC Ord 50, rr 9A and 88) or, in the county court, by originating application in the court for the district in which the land is situate. The county court has jurisdiction to order sale only if the judgment debt remaining unpaid does not exceed £30,000 (see CCA 1984, s 23(c) and the *Green Book* commentary thereto; as to the order for sale see Form N436).

A charging order can be made in respect of land the debtor owns jointly with another person (eg a spouse, see *National Westminster Bank Ltd v Stockman* [1981] 1 WLR 67). However, the order ranks as a charge upon the debtor's beneficial interest rather than upon the land itself. Thus it will not inhibit a sale by two trustees or a trust corporation (see *Perry v Phoenix Assurance plc* [1988] 1 WLR 940). To obtain an order for sale proceedings would have to be taken under the Law of Property Act 1925, s 30 (as to which the county court has unlimited jurisdiction; see the High Court and County Courts Jurisdiction Order 1991, art 2(1)(a) and see *Midland Bank plc v Pike* [1988] 2 All ER 434). As a general rule on any contest between a judgment creditor and a joint proprietor of the property or any adult or child resident therein, the interests of the judgment creditor will, sooner or later, prevail (see *Harman v Glencross* [1986] Fam 81, *Austin-Fell v Austin-Fell* [1990] Fam 172, *Re Citro (a Bankrupt)* [1991] Ch 142 and *Lloyds Bank plc v Byrne* (1991) *The Independent*, 3 June, all noted in the *Green Book* commentary to the Charging Orders Act 1979).

In exercising its discretion whether to grant a charging order the court will take into account the position of other creditors of the judgment debtor and also any trustee or person beneficially entitled to the land in question. To facilitate this the affidavit in support should state whether the applicant knows of any such persons, giving the names and addresses known. (These details should be given in the affidavit itself, not just in an exhibit thereto.) The court may then require that notice of the application should be given to these persons. In the *ex parte* proceedings the creditor has a duty to make full and frank disclosure of all the relevant circumstances of which he is aware.

Charging order on securities

By similar procedures a judgment creditor can also obtain a charging order on a judgment debtor's beneficial interest in securities of any of the following kind (1979 Act, s 2(2)):

(1) government stock;
(2) stock of any body (other than a building society) incorporated within England and Wales;
(3) stock of any body incorporated outside England and Wales or of any state or territory outside the UK, being stock registered in a register kept at any place within England and Wales;
(4) units of any unit trust in respect of which a register of the unit trust holders is kept at any place within England and Wales.

Section 2 further states that the order may provide for the charge to extend to any interest or dividend payable in respect of the asset (thus removing the need to appoint a receiver). A copy of the order obtained must be served on the Bank of England or the company concerned. Pending sale the creditor's interest may be protected by an ancillary injunction (which, in the High Court, a district judge has jurisdiction to grant: RSC Ord 50, r 9). Such an injunction can also be granted in aid of a charging order on land.

Equitable execution: appointment of a receiver

This is a long-stop method of enforcement which reaches property other methods cannot reach, such as a legacy, income under a trust fund, or income from a business the debtor owns in partnership with others (see generally *White Book* 51/1–3/11 *et seq*).

The application is made to a district judge and, save in very urgent cases, by summons (High Court, see generally RSC Ord 51) or on notice (county court, see generally CCR Ord 32). In both courts if there is a danger that the property may be disposed of before the hearing the district judge may grant an ancillary injunction.

Receivership is often cumbersome and expensive. It should not be sought if there are no impediments to legal execution.

Miscellaneous methods

In this section we outline some miscellaneous methods of enforcement which are used only rarely in practice but which every litigation solicitor needs to be aware of.

Charging order over debtor's interest in partnership property

An application can be made by summons, or, in the county court, on notice, to the district judge for an order charging the judgment debtor's interest in any partnership of which he is a member. The summons or notice must be served on the debtor and on the other partners in England and Wales. They are then at liberty to redeem the interest charged or can purchase it if a sale is ordered (see generally RSC Ord 81, r 10 and the *Green Book* commentary to CCR Ord 31, r 1; as to enforcement of a judgment obtained against a firm, see p 92).

Sequestration

This is a form of contempt proceedings which is available in both the High Court and the county court. Sequestration can be used only in respect of orders in the nature of an injunction and therefore only rarely concerns money judgments (but consider a specific performance action brought by a vendor). In the High Court, application is made to a judge by motion for leave to issue a writ of sequestration, ie a writ appointing four sequestrators and directing them to take possession of all the real and personal property of the contemnor and to keep the same until the contempt is cleared (see generally RSC Ord 46, r 5). The court may apply the property for the benefit of the judgment creditor; for a recent example see *Mir v Mir* [1992] Fam 79 wardship proceedings in which an order was made for the sale of land previously sequestrated in order to finance further litigation overseas.

In the county court, the jurisdiction to order sequestration falls within the ancillary jurisdiction of the court (see CCA 1984, s 38). As to procedure, in the absence of any specific provisions dealing with sequestration the court should adopt the general principles of practice in the High Court (CCA 1984, s 76 and see *Rose v Laskington* [1990] 1 QB 562).

Judgment summons

This method of enforcement is available only in the case of the High Court or county court maintenance orders and judgments or orders of any court for payment of certain taxes or other sums or contributions due to the state. It is a means of obtaining an order for imprisonment which is suspended so long as stated instalments are paid. In order to obtain such an order the applicant (ie a person awarded maintenance, or the state) must show that the debtor has the means to pay but has failed to pay (see generally CCR Ord 28 and the *Green Book* commentary thereto).

Bankruptcy and winding up of companies

These are not strictly methods of enforcement (*In re a Debtor (No 50A–SD–1995)* [1997] 2 WLR 57). They are considered separately in Chapter 26.

Enforcement of foreign judgments

There are a variety of provisions under which the English courts will recognise and enforce foreign judgments. Note in particular:

At common law, an action upon the judgment can be brought, ie simple debt proceedings; there are however many defences which can be raised in such an action.

Under AJA 1920 and the Foreign Judgments (Reciprocal Enforcement) Act 1933, money judgments obtained in certain countries (see *White Book* 71/1/3 *et seq*) may be registered here. Broadly speaking registration makes the judgment enforceable as if it were an English judgment. Costs of and incidental to the application (including costs of translations etc) may be awarded and, unless the registration is set aside, added to the judgment as registered. Under these statutes there are several grounds upon which registration may be refused (see generally RSC Ord 71, Pt I and the *White Book* commentary thereto).

Under CJJA 1982 many judgments, whether for the payment of money or otherwise, are registrable in the English High Court if they were obtained in another EU member state or elsewhere in the UK. Under the CJJA 1982 the grounds upon which registration may be refused are severely limited (see generally RSC Ord 71, Pt III). It is important to note that, under this part of the CJJA 1982, it is immaterial whether the defendant to the proceedings is or was domiciled inside or outside the EU. Indeed (subject to the 1968 European Judgments Convention, Article 59, see below) as against a non-EU defendant, the judgment sought to be registered may have been obtained by reliance upon the 'exorbitant jurisdiction' of the judgment court.

Example

A Frenchman will be entitled to register in England a French judgment he obtained against an American defendant who has assets here, the French court having assumed jurisdiction because of the French nationality of the plaintiff.

Article 59 of the European Judgments Convention enables each member state to enter judgment conventions with non-EU states agreeing not to recognise judgments based upon the exorbitant jurisdictions so far as concerns defendants domiciled in their states. Australia, Canada and the USA have indicated interest in agreeing such conventions with the UK but as yet no such conventions have been concluded. The procedure by which to register a judgment under the CJJA 1982 is, in outline, as follows.

(1) *Ex parte* application to a district judge.
(2) An order giving leave to register will state a time limit for appeal (see below) and will stay execution of the judgment until that time limit expires. (In the meantime the applicant should consider whether to seek, eg a *Mareva* injunction; see p 294.)
(3) Notice of registration must be served on the respondent informing him of his right to appeal and specifying the time limit imposed.
(4) A challenge to registration must be made in the form of an appeal by summons to a High Court judge in chambers.
(5) No orders for security of costs may be made solely upon the ground that the party applying for registration is not domiciled or resident within England and Wales. (Security for costs may, of course, be ordered on other grounds; and see p 314.)

In the case of a non-money judgment made elsewhere in the UK the procedure outlined above applies save that the challenge to registration must be made by an application to set aside the order, and so is made to a district judge not a High Court judge.

In the case of a money judgment made elsewhere in the UK, a much simpler procedure is laid down; lodging at the High Court a certificate of judgment issued by the original court not more than six months previously. The judgment creditor must also produce a certified copy of the certificate which the court clerk will seal and return to him. No application to a district judge is required.

The effect of registration under CJJA 1982 is that the judgment can now be enforced as if it were a judgment of the High Court (CJJA 1982, s 4(2); Sched 6, para 6; Sched 7, para 6). The reasonable costs and expenses of and incidental to obtaining the certificate or certified copy of the judgment and registration are recoverable. Interest on the original judgment runs in accordance with the registered details. Interest on the costs and expenses of and incidental to obtaining the certificate and registration accrues as if they were the subject of an order for costs and expenses made by the High Court on the date of registration of the certificate (CJJA 1982, s 7; Sched 6, para 8; Sched 7, para 7).

The court has a discretion to stay proceedings for enforcement if satisfied that a valid challenge to the original judgment has been or will be commenced in the court in which the judgment was originally made (CJJA 1982, Sched 1, para 38; Sched 6, para 9; Sched 7, para 8; and see further *Petereit v Babcock International Holdings Ltd* [1990] 1 WLR 350). Application for a stay can sometimes take the proceedings into a serpentine maze of hearings before the English court, the judgment court and the Court of Justice of the European Communities (see further, an article by Jonathan Goodliffe, solicitor in New Law Journal, 17 May 1996, p 717).

Under CJJA 1991 a regime equivalent to that which applies for judgments made in the courts of EU member states has been introduced for judgments made in the courts of EFTA states who have ratified the Lugano Convention; for a list of EFTA states, see *Green Book* commentary to CCR Ord 8, r 2.

Enforcement outside England and Wales

If a debtor has assets outside the jurisdiction of the High Court, the first point to consider is whether the proceedings themselves could be commenced outside the jurisdiction. If proceedings are taken in England the next point to consider is whether the courts for the country in which it is intended to enforce any English judgment will recognise that judgment. Also, what attitude might they take to a default judgment or any judgment made in proceedings in which the defendant took no part?

The statutes, conventions and treaties under which the English High Court registers foreign judgments are, of course, reciprocal. Before approaching the foreign court it will usually be necessary to obtain a certificate of the English judgment from the High Court or county court which awarded it (see generally RSC Ord 71, rr 13, 36, 37, 38; CCR Ord 35, rr 2, 3). Once registered the judgment can be enforced as if it were a judgment of the registering court.

If there is no reciprocal enforcement procedure in the country concerned then to enforce an English judgment in such a country fresh proceedings on the judgment would have to be taken there.

Advising the judgment debtor

Solicitors are not often called upon to advise a judgment debtor. However it would be wrong to think that nothing can be done for such a client. Usually the most sensible and practical course to take is to negotiate with the judgment creditor for payment of the debt by instalments of a realistic amount. Often the judgment creditor will insist on taking some steps to protect his interest; for example, he may insist upon obtaining and registering a charging order absolute, but will then agree that no steps be taken to enforce the order so long as the debt is paid by specified monthly instalments. It is not uncommon for an attachment of earnings order to be obtained by consent, the creditor agreeing not to register the order with the debtor's employer (thus avoiding possible embarrassment) so long as the debtor voluntarily pays the instalments regularly (and see the *Green Book* commentary to CCR Ord 27, r 7 and Form N64). In addition to negotiating along these lines the following points can also be considered:

(1) Whether there are any grounds for setting the judgment aside: see p 219.

(2) In the county court, by CCR Ord 22, r 10, a judgment debtor who is unable to pay the judgment debt forthwith may apply for an instalment order. Alternatively, if the order is already for payment by instalments, he or she may ask the court staff to reduce the instalments. After notifying the creditor, the court staff may make such an order. Either party may then apply for a reconsideration by the district judge. In the High Court the equivalent application is to apply for a stay of execution on terms (see p 520).

(3) Where two or more attachment of earnings are in force the judgment debtor can apply for a consolidated order and thereafter the sums deducted from his earnings will be apportioned between the creditors entitled thereto. Consolidated attachment of earnings orders may also be made on the application of a creditor, or the employer or indeed without any application, the court staff simply making the arrangements after giving all persons affected an opportunity of submitting written submissions (see generally CCR Ord 27, rr 18–22).

(4) A person against whom a judgment has been obtained in the High Court or county court, may apply to the county court for an administration order. A schedule of creditors is prepared detailing the amounts owing to each. The debtor is ordered to pay the total amount due by instalments. The amount received by the court is then apportioned between the creditors in proportion to the amounts due and from time to

time the creditor will receive an appropriate remittance. When an administration order has been made it is not possible for any creditor involved to issue enforcement proceedings—the duty to do this now rests on the chief clerk of the court making the administration order (see generally CCR Ord 39). Whilst an administration order is in force no interest will accrue on county court judgments under the County Courts (Interest on Judgments Debts) Order 1991 (see art 4(3)).

Administration orders are at present limited to cases where the total indebtedness does not exceed £5,000. However, the jurisdiction will become unlimited when certain amendments to CCA 1984, s 112 are brought into force. On the same day new ss 112A and 112B are likely to come into force enabling the county court to make further orders restricting creditors from pursuing remedies against debtors and preventing creditors who supply gas, electricity or water from cutting off such supply (s 112A) and enabling the court to make administration orders subject to a composition provision reducing the debtor's total indebtedness. All the new amendments and provisions are set out in the *Green Book* text on CCA 1984, s 112.

(5) For a client to petition for his own bankruptcy is a drastic step but on a rare occasion it may be appropriate. However, before taking such a drastic step, it is now always appropriate to first consider whether the debtor should try to put together some voluntary arrangement compounding his debts which is acceptable to the majority of his creditors. To give him time to do so without further threat of proceedings he may seek a moratorium against enforcement of debts (see p 613). These matters are better dealt with by an 'insolvency practitioner': indeed a report by an insolvency practitioner is essential in the case of a voluntary arrangement (as to the definition of 'insolvency practitioner', see Insolvency Act 1986, ss 390–398).

Chapter 25

Enforcement of Other Judgments

Recovery of land

Judgments for the recovery of land are enforced in the High Court by a writ of possession and in the county court by a warrant of possession.

Procedure in the High Court is to prepare a *praecipe* for a writ of possession and the writ itself in Form 66, or Form 66A if the action was brought under the RSC Ord 113 procedure (see p 264). Except in the case of a 'mortgage action' (see RSC Ord 88) or a case under RSC Ord 113 the writ can only be issued with the leave of the district judge, which can be sought *ex parte*. Leave will not be granted unless every person in possession of the whole or any part of the land has been given notice sufficient to enable him to apply for any relief to which he is entitled (see generally RSC Ord 45, r 3). The writ will be executed by the sheriff's officer, using force if necessary. In practice, it is essential for a representative of the plaintiff to be on hand to receive possession from the sheriff's officer, and it is a sensible precaution to seal up the premises and change the locks immediately thereafter.

The same writ may also direct the sheriff to levy execution on the judgment debtor's goods in respect of any money judgment given in the same action, eg for mesne profits and costs.

In the county court the plaintiff must complete a request for a warrant of possession of land certifying that the land has not been vacated in accordance with the judgment obtained (Form N325). No leave is necessary (see generally CCR Ord 26, r 17). The warrant is then executed by the court bailiff and, as in the High Court, someone should be present to receive possession of the property. The warrant (in Form N49 or Form N52 for CCR Ord 24 cases: see p 265) may also direct the bailiff to levy execution in respect of any money judgment obtained.

Recovery of goods

Judgments for the recovery of goods are enforced in the High Court by a writ of delivery and in the county court by a warrant of delivery. The form of enforcement has to comply with the form of judgment. Sometimes the judgment debtor is ordered to return specific goods.

Sometimes he is given the option of either returning the goods or paying their value. In either case he usually has to pay damages and costs (and see p 213).

The High Court and county court rules are similar (see generally RSC Ord 45, r 4; CCR Ord 26, r 16). Where the judgment is for the delivery of goods without the option of paying their value a writ or warrant directing specific delivery may be issued without leave. This form directs the sheriff or bailiff to cause the goods to be delivered to the plaintiff. Alternatively the plaintiff may enforce the judgment by committal or, in the High Court only, by writ of sequestration.

Where the judgment does give the defendant the option of paying the value of the goods the plaintiff may obtain:

(1) without leave, an ordinary writ or warrant of delivery: this directs the sheriff or bailiff to cause the goods to be delivered to the plaintiff, or, if he cannot obtain possession of them, to levy execution for their assessed value; or

(2) if the court so orders (on an application by summons or on notice) a writ or warrant directing specific delivery.

Any writ or warrant may include a clause directing execution of any money judgment the plaintiff obtained.

Injunctions

Injunctions, both mandatory and prohibitory, can be enforced by committal proceedings (see generally RSC Ord 52; CCR Ord 29), and by sequestration (in the High Court a writ, in the county court an order; see p 602). A mandatory injunction, eg to take down a wall, may also be enforced by the court directing the plaintiff to do the act required to be done, and allowing him a money judgment in respect of his expenses so incurred (RSC Ord 45, r 8; CCA 1984, s 38).

As noted in connection with interlocutory injunctions, the order must be drawn up, indorsed with a penal notice and personally served on the defendant. A prohibitory injunction may sometimes bind the defendant before service (see generally p 294). Service is compulsory in the case of a mandatory injunction unless an order dispensing with service is made. However in *Davy International Ltd v Tazzyman* (1997) *The Times*, 9 May, where a mandatory order not indorsed with a penal notice was served, the court later made an order 'dispensing with service' so enabling the plaintiff to proceed with committal proceedings: this order was upheld by the Court of Appeal.

If the injunction is not obeyed the plaintiff can apply for the defendant's committal to prison: in the High Court by motion to a High Court judge sitting in open court: in the county court by an application to a circuit judge on notice in Form N78 which requires the defendant to attend at the hearing in person. The notice of motion, or notice in Form N78, must be personally served on the respondent. However, in a very exceptional case, service may be dispensed with (*Wright v Jess* [1987] 1 WLR 1076). The standard of proof applied in committal proceedings is proof beyond all reasonable doubt (see *White Book* 52/4/4).

The defendant should attend at the hearing of the motion or application in person (see *Irtelli v Squatriti* [1992] 3 WLR 218). If he does so, the court's primary desire is to encourage obedience, not merely punish disobedience. At the first hearing the defendant is usually given a stern warning only. He will be sent to prison only if further hearings become necessary. Imprisonment for contempt of court must be for a fixed term (without prejudice to the power of the court to order earlier release). Subject to any specific statutory provision (eg Attachment of Earnings Act 1971, s 23; CCA 1984, ss 110 and 118) the maximum period is two years (Contempt of Court Act 1981, s 14; County Courts (Penalties for Contempt) Act 1983, s 1). In *Enfield LBC v Mahoney* [1983] 1 WLR 749 the Court of Appeal considered what should be done in the case of a contemnor who proves to be unshakable in his determination to flout the court's order. Once such a contemnor has been sufficiently punished he should be released if it is clear that further imprisonment will have no coercive effect.

An undertaking given to the court in lieu of an injunction is enforceable in the same way as an injunction (see *White Book* 45/5/3; CCR Ord 29, r 3).

District judges have no jurisdiction in contempt proceedings in the High Court (see RSC Ord 32, r 11). Their jurisdiction in the county court is restricted to committals in respect of assaults on staff and contempts in the face of the court (CCA 1984, ss 14 and 118) and to any application for the discharge of a committal order, unless the order in question specifically reserves such applications to a circuit judge (CCR Ord 29, r 3).

Specific performance

An order for specific performance can be enforced in the same manner as a mandatory injunction. Alternatively, in the case of a defendant who refuses to execute a conveyance or other document the court can appoint some other person to execute it. A conveyance or document so executed is treated for all purposes as if it had been executed by the defendant (SCA 1981, s 39; CCA 1984, s 38). Application is usually made by summons or on notice. It is usual for the district judge to appoint himself to execute the document.

Chapter 26

Insolvency

Every textbook on civil litigation is required to cover at least some aspects of insolvency law. However, these topics never sit easily in such a book. There is too much conflict between the aims of the law of insolvency (which are noble) and the objectives of most creditors (which seem selfish). The law of insolvency deals with and settles problems concerning individuals and companies whose debts cannot be paid as and when they fall due. Its aims are to avoid insolvencies occurring where possible; otherwise to achieve an orderly realisation and distribution of assets for the benefit of all the creditors, to investigate financial delinquencies and frauds in order to remedy them or impose penalties in respect of them as appropriate, and, in the case of individuals only, to provide for the insolvent's rehabilitation in the future (contrast corporate insolvents: they will be dissolved).

None of the aims just listed may seem important to persons who are unlucky enough to have lent money to or otherwise given credit to an individual or company which is now insolvent. A creditor's primary objective is to get his money back, or his invoices paid, as soon as possible and preferably in advance of anyone else who might make similar claims upon the insolvent. It will often be in the creditor's best interest to defeat any 'orderly realisation and distribution of assets' by executing a 'me first' policy instead.

However, insolvency law does offer one big attraction to creditors. To help them achieve their just ends, payment, it provides them with a sometimes powerful means; the ability to threaten the debtor with social disgrace, the loss of financial reputation and, in the case of companies only, dissolution. The threat of insolvency proceedings will often induce a debtor to pay up, even if he has to borrow from someone else in order to do so. The use of insolvency law as a threat appears to be an exception to a general rule of civil litigation that you should never make empty threats. A creditor who does threaten to commence insolvency proceedings can in truth add to his threat the following words: 'Don't make me do this. It will probably be bad for both of us if I do.'

Our aims in this chapter are twofold. We want to provide a short account of the whole of the law of insolvency from start to finish. Whilst so doing we want to describe in greater detail three important procedural matters; the use and service of statutory demands; the procedures by which to challenge statutory demands; and the presentation of petitions. At the end of this chapter (at p 643) we list a variety of specialist topics in the law and practice of insolvency proceedings all of which lie beyond the scope of this book. The main purpose of this list is to encourage the beginner to appreciate the complexity of insolvency law.

References to IA 1986 and IR 1986 are respectively references to the Insolvency Act 1986 and the Insolvency Rules 1986. The Act and rules are all conveniently set out and fully commented upon in *Annotated Guide to the Insolvency Legislation* by Sealy and Milman, 4th ed (CCH Editions Ltd, 1994). We gratefully acknowledge the help which this book has given us. An excellent commentary on the statutes and rules relating to personal insolvency, ie bankruptcy, is also to be found in the *Green Book*.

What is insolvency?

The terminology and consequences differ as between individuals and companies. An individual is insolvent as a matter of law when a *bankruptcy order* is made against him by a court of competent authority. The order brings about a variety of divestings, disabilities and disqualifications unless and until it is rescinded or discharged. An undischarged bankrupt is divested of ownership of assets which belonged to him beneficially before bankruptcy, is disabled from the management of any company (unless leave of the court is obtained) and is disqualified from holding certain positions of trust such as being a practising solicitor, member of Parliament, local councillor or magistrate.

A company is insolvent as a matter of law when a *winding-up order* is made in respect of it by a court of competent authority. The winding-up order, unless later declared void (see Companies Act 1985, s 651) will lead ultimately to the termination of the company's legal personality and, therefore, existence.

In proceedings commenced by a creditor the court will not make a bankruptcy order or a winding-up order as the case may be unless there is proof in one form or another that the debtor in question is insolvent; ie evidence proving or, more usually, giving rise to a presumption that, the debtor is unable to pay his debts, either presently, as they fall due (practical insolvency or negative cash flow) or potentially, taking into account all future and contingent liabilities (balance sheet insolvency).

Although, before making any order, the court looks at facts, the legal concept of insolvency remains separate and independent from the factual concept of insolvency. There are many people who are insolvent in fact but who have never been adjudged to be insolvent; for example people with debts but no assets at all. Also, because the court will sometimes presume factual insolvency from, eg failure to pay in compliance with a statutory demand, a person who has assets greatly exceeding his debts could be adjudged insolvent; for example a wealthy person who wilfully refuses to pay a debt. The fact that the legal concept of insolvency and the factual concept of insolvency may be inconsistent helps explain the relevance of insolvency law to a creditor seeking payment. If the debtor is factually solvent, a creditor who has the means of establishing legal grounds for insolvency proceedings may well threaten the debtor that he will do so unless payment is made. Contrast the case where the debtor is factually insolvent. Here, the creditor will often rush to complete his debt proceedings before any other creditor brings insolvency proceedings. If the debtor is factually insolvent the prospect of somebody else commencing insolvency proceedings threatens debtor and creditor alike.

Insolvency law as an aid to debtors

An individual or company oppressed by debts may seek help from the law of insolvency in one of two ways. First, the debtor himself may commence the relevant insolvency proceedings so relieving him of the need to continue responding to any debt proceedings already commenced against him. In the case of an individual the making of a bankruptcy order will start the slow process towards rehabilitation. In the case of a company a winding-up order in proceedings commenced by the company is a form of suicide.

The second way in which insolvency law can help debtors is aimed in the opposite direction. The law may give the debtor a moratorium on the enforcement of debts; a breathing space in which to put together some voluntary arrangement acceptable to the majority of the creditors. In the case of individuals see administration orders (p 628) and interim orders (see Sealy and Milman, 4th edn, pp 314 *et seq*). In the case of companies see administration orders (Sealy and Milman, 4th ed, pp 40 *et seq*) and the wide discretion given to the court on hearing a winding-up petition (IA 1986, s 125 and see p 642).

Statutory demands

Serving a statutory demand is now the primary method by which a creditor threatens a debtor with bankruptcy or winding-up proceedings as the case may be. The prescribed form of demand gives details of the debt in question and contains a demand that the recipient should 'pay the above debt or secure or compound for it to the Creditor's satisfaction'. Notes to the form give a warning to the recipient that the demand must be 'dealt with' (see below) within twenty-one days after service or insolvency proceedings may follow. In the case of a demand served upon an individual, the debt in question must equal or exceed £750 (IA 1986, s 267(4), noted in the *Green Book*). In the case of a demand served upon a company the debt in question must exceed £750 (IA 1986, s 123). In

[*continued on p 617*]

Fig 40: Statutory demand (debtor an individual)

Form 6.1

Statutory Demand
under section 268(1)(a)
of the Insolvency
Act 1986.
Debt for Liquidated
Sum Payable
Immediately
(Rule 6.1)

WARNING

- This is an **important** document. You should refer to the notes entitled "How to comply with a Statutory Demand or have it set aside".
- If you wish to have this Demand set aside you must make application to do so **within 18 days** from its service on you.
- If you do not apply to set aside **within 18 days** or otherwise deal with this Demand as set out in the notes **within 21 days** after its service on you, you could be made bankrupt and your property and goods taken away from you.
- Please read the Demand and notes carefully. If you are in any doubt about your position you should seek advice **immediately** from a solicitor or your nearest Citizens Advice Bureau.

NOTES FOR CREDITOR
- If the Creditor is entitled to the debt by way of assignment, details of the original Creditor and any intermediary assignees should be given in part C on page 3.
- If the amount of debt includes interest not previously notified to the Debtor as included in the Debtor's liability, details should be given, including the grounds upon which interest is charged. The amount of interest must be shown separately.
- Any other charge accruing due from time to time may be claimed. The amount or rate of the charge must be identified and the grounds on which it is claimed must be stated.
- In either case the amount claimed must be limited to that which has accrued due at the date of the Demand.
- If the Creditor holds any security the amount of debt should be the sum the Creditor is prepared to regard as unsecured for the purposes of this Demand. Brief details of the total debt should be included and the nature of the security and the value put upon it by the Creditor, as at the date of the Demand, must be specified.
- If signatory of the Demand is a solicitor or other agent of the Creditor, the name of his/her firm should be given.

* Delete if signed by the Creditor himself.

DEMAND

To

Address

This Demand is served on you by the Creditor:

Name

Address

The Creditor claims that you owe the sum of £
full particulars of which are set out on page 2, and that it is payable immediately and, to the extent of the sum demanded, is unsecured.

The Creditor demands that you pay the above debt or secure or compound for it to the Creditor's satisfaction.

[The Creditor making this Demand is a Minister of the Crown or a Government Department, and it is intended to present a Bankruptcy Petition in the High Court in London.] [Delete if inappropriate].

Signature of individual

Name
(BLOCK LETTERS)

Date   day of   19   .

*Position with or relationship to Creditor:
*I am authorised to make this Demand on the Creditor's behalf.

Address

Tel. No.   Ref. No.

N.B. The person making this Demand must complete the whole of pages 1, 2 and parts A, B and C (as applicable) on page 3.

(P T.O

1

Fig 40: contd

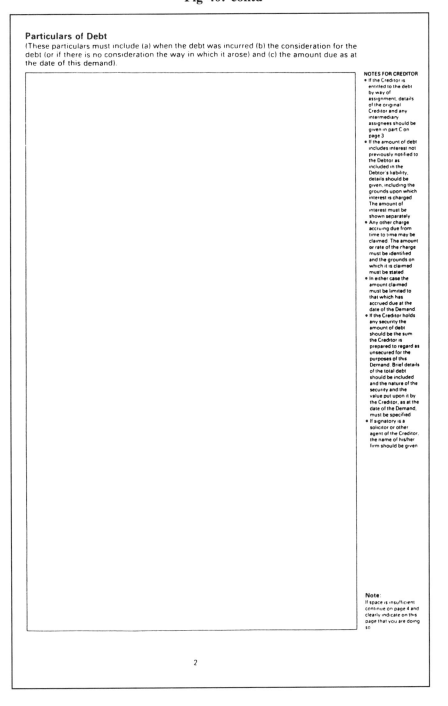

Particulars of Debt

(These particulars must include (a) when the debt was incurred (b) the consideration for the debt (or if there is no consideration the way in which it arose) and (c) the amount due as at the date of this demand).

NOTES FOR CREDITOR

- If the Creditor is entitled to the debt by way of assignment, details of the original Creditor and any intermediary assignees should be given in part C on page 3
- If the amount of debt includes interest not previously notified to the Debtor as included in the Debtor's liability, details should be given, including the grounds upon which interest is charged The amount of interest must be shown separately
- Any other charge accruing due from time to time may be claimed. The amount or rate of the charge must be identified and the grounds on which it is claimed must be stated
- In either case the amount claimed must be limited to that which has accrued due at the date of the Demand
- If the Creditor holds any security the amount of debt should be the sum the Creditor is prepared to regard as unsecured for the purposes of this Demand. Brief details of the total debt should be included and the nature of the security and the value put upon it by the Creditor, as at the date of the Demand, must be specified
- If signatory is a solicitor or other agent of the Creditor, the name of his/her firm should be given

Note:
If space is insufficient continue on page 4 and clearly indicate on this page that you are doing so

2

Fig 40: contd

Part A
Appropriate Court for Setting Aside Demand

Rule 6.4(2) of the Insolvency Rules 1986 states that the appropriate Court is the Court to which you would have to present your own Bankruptcy Petition in accordance with Rule 6.40(1) and 6.40(2). In accordance with those rules on present information the appropriate Court is [the High Court of Justice] [County Court] (address)

Any application by you to set aside this Demand should be made to that Court.

Part B
The individual or individuals to whom any communication regarding this Demand may be addressed is/are:
Name
(BLOCK LETTERS)

Address

Telephone Number

Reference

Part C
For completion if the Creditor is entitled to the debt by way of assignment.

	Name	Date(s) of Assignment
Original Creditor		
Assignees		

How to comply with a Statutory Demand or have it set aside (ACT WITHIN 18 DAYS)

If you wish to avoid a Bankruptcy Petition being presented against you, you must pay the debt shown on page 1, particulars of which are set out on page 2 of this notice, within the period of **21 days** after its service upon you. Alternatively, you can attempt to come to a settlement with the Creditor. To do this you should:

• inform the individual (or one of the individuals) named in Part B above immediately that you are willing and able to offer security for the debt to the Creditor's satisfaction; *or*

• inform the individual (or one of the individuals) named in Part B above immediately that you are willing and able to compound for the debt to the Creditor's satisfaction.

If you dispute the Demand in whole or in part you should:
• contact the individual (or one of the individuals) named in Part B immediately.

If you consider that you have grounds to have this Demand set aside or if you do not quickly receive a satisfactory written reply from the individual named in Part B whom you have contacted you should **apply within 18 days** from the date of service of this Demand on you to the appropriate Court shown in Part A above to have the Demand set aside.

Any application to set aside the Demand (Form 6.4 in Schedule 4 of the Insolvency Rules 1986) should be made within 18 days from the date of service upon you and be supported by an Affidavit (Form 6.5 in Schedule 4 to those Rules) stating the grounds on which the Demand should be set aside. The forms may be obtained from the appropriate Court when you attend to make the application.

> **Remember:** From the date of service on you of this document:
> (a) you have only **18 days** to apply to the Court to have the Demand set aside, and
> (b) you have only **21 days** before the Creditor may present a Bankruptcy Petition.

3

Reproduced by kind permission of the Solicitors' Law Stationery Society Ltd.

either case the debt in question must be just that, a debt, not damages. However, the debt in question need not be a judgment debt. So far as bankruptcy law is concerned this is a departure from the pre-1986 law which some older lawyers are still reluctant to accept. Whether one should sue first or threaten bankruptcy (or winding up) first is considered further on p 628.

In the case of a statutory demand served on a company, the debt in question must be immediately payable (IA 1986, s 123 'indebted in a sum exceeding £750 then due'): in the case of a company, only one form of statutory demand is prescribed (see fig 41 overleaf).

In the case of a statutory demand served on an individual, the debt in question must be unsecured; if some security is held the debt in question is that sum which the creditor is prepared to regard as unsecured and full details must be given of the value which the creditor puts on the security and of the total debt which is alleged by the creditor (IR 1986, r 6.1(5)). In the case of an individual, the debt in question may be a future debt which the debtor appears to have no reasonable prospect of being able to pay. In the case of an individual there are three prescribed forms of statutory demand. Figure 40 illustrates the form appropriate for a non-judgment debt which is immediately payable; the other two pre-scribed forms are for judgment debts and for future debts. However, a failure to use the correct form will not necessarily invalidate the demand (*Re a Debtor (No 1 of 1987)* [1989] 1 WLR 271 noted on p 626).

When completing a statutory demand it is important to check, amongst other things, that it is dated and signed by an individual whose name and (if appropriate) position with or relationship to the creditor is stated. The form must also specify the name and address of at least one individual to whom the recipient of the demand may direct any communications concerning it.

Statutory demands are not issued or sealed by a court. It is for the creditor or his advisers to obtain and complete the form and then effect service.

Service and proof of service

In the case of a statutory demand to be served on an individual, personal service (see p 130) should be effected if practicable. If it is not practicable, careful study must be made of the *Practice Notes* of 1986 ([1987] 1 WLR 82 and 85 and see the *Green Book* commentary to IR 1986, r 6.11 and the prescribed Form 6.12). The *Practice Notes* give guidance as to possible alternative methods of service which may be used. If a bankruptcy petition is later issued, proof of service of the statutory demand will be made by an affidavit of service sworn by the person who effected service. This affidavit must exhibit a copy of the statutory demand and must be filed in court when the bankruptcy petition is issued (IR 1986, r 6.11).

[*continued on p 621*]

Fig 41: Statutory demand (debtor a company)

Statutory Demand under section 123(1)(a) or 222(1)(a) of the Insolvency Act 1986 No. 4.1* (Rule 4.5)

WARNING

• This is an **important** document. This demand must be dealt with **within 21 days** after its service upon the company or a winding-up order could be made in respect of the company.

• Please read the demand and notes carefully.

DEMAND

To

Address

This demand is served on you by the Creditor:

Name

Address

The Creditor claims that the Company owes the sum of £   , full particulars of which are set out on page 2.

The Creditor demands that the Company do pay the above debt or secure or compound for it to the Creditor's satisfaction.

Signature of individual

Name
(BLOCK LETTERS)

Dated   19   .

*Position with or relationship to Creditor

*I am authorised to make this demand on the Creditor's behalf.
Address

Tel. No.   Ref No.

NOTES FOR CREDITOR

1. If the Creditor is entitled to the debt by way of assignment, details of the original Creditor and any intermediary assignees should be given in part B on page 3.

2. If the amount of debt includes interest not previously notified to the Company as included in its liability, details should be given, including the grounds upon which interest is charged. The amount of interest must be shown separately.

3. Any other charge accruing due from time to time may be claimed. The amount or rate of the charge must be identified and the grounds on which it is claimed must be stated.

4. In either case the amount claimed must be limited to that which has accrued due at the date of the demand.

5. If signatory of the demand is a solicitor or other agent of the Creditor, the name of his/her firm should be given.

* Delete if signed by the Creditor himself

N.B. The person making this Demand must complete the whole of this page, page 2 and parts A and B (as applicable) on page 3.

1

[P.T.O

Fig 41: contd

Particulars of Debt (These particulars must include (a) when the debt was incurred, (b) the consideration for the debt (or if there is no consideration the way in which it arose) and (c) the amount due as at the date of this demand).

NOTES FOR CREDITOR

1. If the Creditor is entitled to the debt by way of assignment details of the original Creditor and any intermediary assignees should be given in part B on page 3

2. If the amount of debt includes interest not previously notified to the Company as included in its liability details should be given, including the grounds upon which interest is charged. The amount of interest must be shown separately

3. Any other charge accruing due from time to time may be claimed. The amount or rate of the charge must be identified and the grounds on which it is claimed must be stated

4. In either case the amount claimed must be limited to that which has accrued due at the date of the demand

5. If signatory of the demand is a solicitor or other agent of the Creditor, the name of his/her firm should be given

NOTE

If space is insufficient continue on reverse of page 3 and clearly indicate on this page that you are doing so

2

Fig 41: contd

Part A

The individual or individuals to whom any communication regarding this demand may be addressed is/are:

Name
(BLOCK LETTERS)

Address

Postcode

Telephone Number

Reference

Part B

For completion if the Creditor is entitled to the debt by way of assignment.

	Name	Date(s) of Assignment
Original Creditor		
Assignees		

How to comply with a Statutory Demand

If the Company wishes to avoid a winding-up Petition being presented it must pay the debt shown on page 1, particulars of which are set out on page 2 of this notice, within the period of **21 days** after its service upon the Company. Alternatively, the Company can attempt to come to a settlement with the Creditor. To do this the Company should:

• Inform the individual (or one of the individuals) named in Part A immediately that it is willing and able to offer security for the debt to the Creditor's satisfaction; *or*

• inform the individual (or one of the individuals) named in Part A immediately that it is willing and able to compound for the debt to the Creditor's satisfaction.

If the Company disputes the demand in whole or in part it should:

• contact the individual (or one of the individuals) named in Part A above immediately.

Remember! The Company has only 21 days after the date of service on it of this document before the Creditor may present a winding-up Petition.

3

Reproduced by kind permission of the Solicitors' Law Stationery Society Ltd.

Service of a statutory demand on a company is effected 'by leaving it at the company's registered office' (IA 1986, s 123(1)(a)). The statute makes no reference to service by post but it is possible that this method of 'leaving' a document at a particular address will be effective (*Re a Company No 008790 of 1990* [1992] BCC 11, not following a decision reported in 1985). In practice until the case law becomes more clearly settled, it is safer to ensure that service is effected by a process server. The facts of service will be set out in the winding-up petition and will be proved by a standard form affidavit verifying the petition (see IR 1986, r 4.12).

Responses to a statutory demand

On receiving a statutory demand the alleged debtor may make one of two responses, ie may challenge it or attempt to comply with it. Alternatively, the debtor may make no response, ie may attempt to ignore it. The correct method of challenging a statutory demand depends upon whether the recipient of the demand is an individual or a company.

Challenge made by an individual

In the case of a statutory demand served upon an individual the method of challenge is simple and clear cut; an application in prescribed form (see fig 42) plus affidavit in support (see fig 43) made in the appropriate bankruptcy court (as to which see p 629 and IR 1986, rr 6.4 and 6.40). The application must be made within eighteen days of service of the demand. Unless the court immediately dismisses the application (see IR 1986, r 6.5) it will fix a time and place for a hearing and give notice thereof to the applicant, to the creditor and to the person named as contact in the statutory demand (see above). At that hearing the application may be determined summarily or, if appropriate, it may be adjourned to a later date for which directions may be given.

IR 1986, r 6.5(4) sets out four grounds upon which the statutory demand may be set aside:

    (a) the debtor appears to have a counterclaim, set-off or cross demand which equals or exceeds the amount of the debt or debts specified in the statutory demand; or

    (b) the debt is disputed on grounds which appear to the court to be substantial; or

    (c) it appears that the creditor holds some security in respect of the debt claimed by the demand, and either Rule 6.1(5) [see p 617] is not complied with in respect of it, or the court is satisfied that the value of the security equals or exceeds the full amount of the debt; or

    (d) the court is satisfied, on other grounds, that the demand ought to be set aside.

Grounds (a) and (b) are the grounds most frequently relied on. To obtain a setting aside the applicant need not show more than a genuine triable issue (*Practice Note* [1987] 1 WLR 119). The applicant may be

[*continued on p 623*]

Fig 42: Application to set aside a statutory demand

Form 6.4
Application to Set Aside a Statutory Demand (Rule 6.4)

*Enter High Court of Justice or ————— County Court as the case may be

IN THE*

In Bankruptcy

Re

No.   of 19   .

(1) Insert name and address of person to attend hearing

Let (¹)

†Delete as applicable

attend before the †[Registrar] [District Judge] as follows: —

Date: the   day of   19   .

Time: hours

Place:

(2) Insert name of Debtor.

On the hearing of an application by (²)
the Applicant for an Order that the Statutory Demand
dated   19   , be set aside.

(3) Insert date

The grounds on which the Applicant claims to be entitled to the Order are set out in the Affidavit of the Applicant sworn on (³)   19   ,
a copy of which Affidavit accompanies this Application.

(4) State the names and addresses of the persons to be served

The names and addresses of the persons upon whom this Application should be served are: — (⁴)

(5) State the Applicant's address for service

The Applicant's address for service is: — (⁵)

Dated   the   day of   19   .
Signed

(†)[SOLICITOR FOR THE] APPLICANT

If you do not attend, the Court may make such Order as it thinks fit.

OYEZ   The Solicitors' Law Stationery Society Ltd, Oyez House, 7 Spa Road, London SE16 3QQ

1991 Edition
11.93 F26128

Insolvency-Bankruptcy 6.4

5090311

Reproduced by kind permission of the Solicitors' Law Stationery Society Ltd.

entitled to a setting aside even if he does not have a case strong enough to oppose an application for summary judgment. This is because the making of a bankruptcy order is a draconian step. Creditors are not encouraged to abandon the summary judgment procedure in favour of the statutory demand procedure (cf *Re a Company (No 0012209 of 1991)* [1992] 1 WLR 351 noted below under *'Challenge made by a company'*). In *Re a Debtor (No 490–SD–1991)* [1992] 1 WLR 507 Knox J held that there is no 'grey area' in statutory demand cases such as exists in summary judgment cases in relation to 'shadowy defences' (as to which see p 228 and see further Muir Hunter on Personal Insolvency 7–075/1.

Where the statutory demand is made in respect of a judgment debt ground (a) but not ground (b) is available even in respect of matters which could have been raised in the action in which that judgment was obtained; see *Practice Note* [1987] 1 WLR 119 which states:

> 3. Where a statutory demand is based on a judgment or order, the court will not at this stage go beyond the judgment or order and enquire into the validity of the debt [save in respect of counterclaims etc see para 4] nor, as a general rule will it adjourn the application to await the result of an application to set aside the judgment or order.

An exception to this is made in some county court cases where the same district judge can be asked to set aside both the statutory demand and the default judgment upon which it is based. In such a case the court may adjourn the application if it is satisfied that an application to set aside the judgment will in fact be made. Indeed, often, the two applications can be determined at the same subsequent hearing (and see further, the *Green Book* commentary to IR 1986, r 6.5). If an adjournment of the setting aside application is refused the applicant should immediately apply for a stay of execution of the money judgment pending a setting aside application. A stay of execution of the money judgment will prevent the presentation of a bankruptcy petition (see *White Book* 47/1/4: *warning* it is not enough merely to stay the issue of a writ of *fi fa*).

To establish ground (b) the applicant must show a dispute which extends to the full amount of the debt. If he disputes only part of the debt there can be no setting aside unless he first pays the other part, ie the undisputed part of the debt (*Re a Debtor (No 490-SD-1991)* [1992] 1 WLR 507).

As to ground (c) 'security' refers to rights over property rather than rights over other persons, such as a guarantor (*Re a Debtor (No 310 of 1988)* [1989] 1 WLR 452). If the court is satisfied that the security is under valued in the statutory demand but its true value is still less than the full amount of the debt, see IR 1986, r 6.5(5).

As to ground (d) it will not suffice for the applicant to show merely technical defects in the statutory demand, such as the misstatement of the true debt or the use of an incorrect form, even where such defects are perplexing. A defective statutory demand will be set aside only if the

[*continued on p 626*]

Fig 43: Affidavit supporting an application to set aside a statutory demand

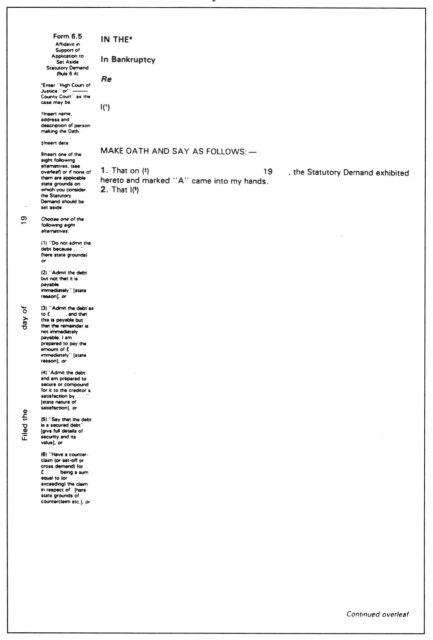

Warning: Note (4) on the statutory form is wrong and should not be relied upon as a ground for setting aside a statutory demand: it is a means of complying with the demand: see further *In re a Debtor* (*No 415–SD–1993*) [1994] 1 WLR 917.

Fig 43: contd

(7) ''Say that execution on the Judgment of the Court has been stayed'' [give details].
or

(8) ''Say that the Demand does not comply with the Insolvency Rules in that ....''
[state reason]

*State full address

SWORN at*

the   day of   19

Before me

Solicitor/A Commissioner for Oaths

· 1987 OYEZ The Solicitors Law Stationery Society Ltd. Oyez House 7 Spa Road London SE16 3QQ   1987 Edition 4 94 F27005
Insolvency-Bankruptcy 6.5   5090329
                                                                                 · · ·

mistakes made have caused or will cause prejudice to the applicant (*Re a Debtor (No 1 of 1987)* [1989] 1 WLR 271).

A solicitor may serve a statutory demand on a former client for unpaid fees, even within one month of delivering the bill (*Re a Debtor (No 88 of 1991)* [1993] Ch 286). However, it will usually be unwise to do so. The demand will be set aside if there is a genuine dispute as to quantum or if there is a genuine allegation of negligence unless, eg, a sum of costs exceeding £750 is undisputed (*Re a Debtor (Nos 49 and 50 of 1992)* [1994] 3 WLR 847).

Do not serve a statutory demand in respect of a judgment debt which is over six years old; consider instead resurrecting enforcement proceedings in the original action (see *Re a Debtor (No 50A–SD–1995)* [1997] 2 WLR 57 and see p 593 above).

An application for setting aside which is made within the eighteen-day time limit will prevent the creditor from presenting a bankruptcy petition in respect of that statutory demand unless and until the application is dismissed (IR 1986, r 6.4(3) and r 6.5(6)). If the eighteen-day deadline has expired the recipient of the statutory demand can apply for an extension of time together with (if necessary) an injunction restraining the presentation of a bankruptcy petition (see further *Practice Note* [1987] 1 WLR 119).

If an order setting aside a statutory demand is made penalty orders for costs may be made against the creditor or his advisers (cf *Re a Company (No 0012209 of 1991)* [1992] 1 WLR 351, noted below). As to consent orders granting, dismissing, or withdrawing applications, see *Practice Note* [1992] 1 WLR 379.

An order refusing to set aside a statutory demand does not prevent the debtor re-arguing the same issues later if in fact a petition is later presented (*Eberhardt & Co Ltd v Mair* [1995] 1 WLR 1180).

Challenge made by a company

In the case of a statutory demand served upon a company the method of challenge which the company may adopt is to apply for an injunction restraining the presentation of a petition, or, if already presented, restraining the advertisement of that petition. In the High Court the application should be made by originating motion (see *Practice Direction* [1988] 1 WLR 988 and *Re a Company (No 0012209 of 1991)* [1992] 1 WLR 351). Application for such relief in the county court would be appropriate in an exceptional case only (see p 640). The injunction will be granted if it appears that (1) the company has some prospect of defeating the claim made against it, and (2) the company is solvent. If both of these matters are proved the creditor may be ordered to pay costs on an indemnity basis (see p 527). The reason for awarding costs on this exceptional basis is explained in two recent cases *Re a Company (No 00122209 of 1991)* [1992] 1 WLR 351 and *Re a Company (No 006798 of*

1995) [1996] 1 WLR 491. In the latter case a *wasted costs order* (see p 537) was also made against the petitioner's solicitor.

> It seems to me that a tendency has developed ... to present petitions against solvent companies as a way of putting pressure on them to make payments of money which is bona fide disputed rather than to invoke the procedures which the rules provide for summary judgment ... [If a solvent company has no grounds at all for refusing to pay a debt or] if the court comes to the conclusion that a solvent company is not putting forward any defence in good faith and is merely seeking to take for itself credit which it is not allowed under the contract, then the court would not be inclined to restrain presentation of the petition. But if, as in this case, it appears that the defence has a prospect of success and the company is solvent, then I think that the court should give the company the benefit of the doubt and not do anything which would encourage the use of the Companies Court as an alternative to the RSC Ord 14 procedure.
>
> For these reasons the injunction will go. The basis upon which the injunction is granted is that presentation of the petition is an abuse of the process of the court. I think that it should be made clear that abuse of the petition procedure in these circumstances is a high risk strategy, and consequently I think the appropriate order is that [the party who threatened to present a petition] should pay the company's costs on an indemnity basis (*Re a Company (No 0012209 of 1991)* [1992] 1 WLR 351 *per* Hoffman J).
>
> If the company allows the petition to be advertised then there is a serious danger that the damage that will be done to the company by the advertisement [*as to which, see p 642, below*] will far outweigh any commercial advantage in disputing a genuinely disputed debt. Those facts lead to the opportunity for abuse. The presentation of the petition, or the threat to present the petition, imposes on the company a commercial pressure which is different in kind from the issue of a writ. It is of course that opportunity to exert commercial pressure which leads to the creditor's decision to present a petition rather than to take proceedings in the official referees' corridor (*Re a Company (No 006789 of 1995)* [1996] 1 WLR 491 *per* Chadwick J).

An injunction will not be granted if the genuine dispute relates only to part of the debt alleged, unless the company pays off the undisputed part (*Re Trinity Assurance Ltd* [1990] BCC 235).

Will inaccuracies in a statutory demand served upon a company invalidate that demand? As yet there is no English case law on the point. There is some slight cause for thinking that a stricter attitude will be taken in respect of mistakes made in statutory demands served upon companies than is taken in the case of statutory demands served upon individuals (as to which see p 623; and see further Sealy and Milman, 4th ed, p 162).

Complying with a statutory demand

If the recipient of the statutory demand (whether an individual or a company) pays up within the three weeks specified then, presumably, the matter is at an end as between the parties involved. The statutory demand also invites the recipient to 'secure or compound for the debt to the Creditor's satisfaction' and it also identifies an individual to whom any communication regarding the demand may be sent. A creditor who rejects a reasonable offer to secure or compound the debt will not be able to prove his grounds for insolvency proceedings (IA 1986, s 271(3) and s 125 as to which see p 643). A debtor seeking to compound his debt with one creditor may also seek to make a voluntary arrangement (see p 613) with all his creditors; as to making an offer to compound which is also a proposal to enter a voluntary arrangement, see *Re a Debtor (No 2389 of 1989)* [1991] Ch 326. In considering whether an offer is reasonable the creditor, and later perhaps the court, should take into account the amounts promised, the prospects of that promise being kept and the history of any previous promises made (and see further Muir Hunter on Personal Insolvency 3-095/1).

If in compliance with the demand the debtor makes payments reducing his debt to £750 or below (if a company) or below £750 (if an individual) the creditor will not be entitled to bring or pursue insolvency proceedings based on that statutory demand (*Re Patel* [1986] 1 WLR 221).

No response to a statutory demand

If the recipient of the statutory demand fails to make any response at all the creditor may, after expiry of twenty-one days, commence bankruptcy proceedings or winding-up proceedings as the case may be. However, if he does so, the alleged debtor has full right to defend those proceedings on the basis that he does not owe any money to the creditor. A failure to respond to the statutory demand does not give rise to any implied admission of indebtedness.

A failure to respond to the statutory demand does however have some adverse consequences for a debtor who is an individual. He cannot defeat the petition merely by quibbling about the amount of his indebtedness. A bankruptcy petition cannot be dismissed solely upon the ground that the debt was over-stated in the demand unless, within twenty-one days of service of the demand the debtor 'gave notice' to the creditor disputing the validity of the demand on that ground [or] 'paid the correct amount' (IR 1986, r 6.25(3)).

Demand first or sue to judgment first?

How should you advise a client wishing to commence proceedings in respect of a debt? Is it best for that client to threaten insolvency proceedings first? The threat alone often produces payment. But what dangers are there in making this threat? If it does not produce payment, should you carry out the threat?

Alternatively, is it best to commence debt proceedings? The letter before action may produce payment. If it does not, any debt proceedings commenced will probably end in a default judgment and the services of sheriff's officers or bailiffs can be employed. What are the dangers in suing to judgment first?

In the further alternative, is it safe to serve either a statutory demand or a letter before action? In some cases the use of either procedure may lead to the immediate disposal and/or concealment of known assets. In this sort of case the creditor should consider applying *ex parte* for a *Mareva* injunction (see further p 294).

There are no easy answers to the questions we have posed. There are many factors to be taken into account and their relative importance in any particular case may be difficult or even impossible to gauge. The tables shown on pp 630 to 632 indicate our opinions on three matters:

(1) The advantages and disadvantages of adopting the insolvency route or the debt route.
(2) Factors to take instructions upon before advising the client.
(3) A list of cases in which we say that the insolvency route must not be used.

Some of the points made are matters of opinion and some people may not share the opinions which we express. Also, the text set out in the tables is not exhaustive of all the matters which may have to be taken into account in any particular case; it is provided by way of introduction to a complex topic.

Personal insolvency: bankruptcy

Grounds for a creditor's petition

A creditor to whom the debtor owes £750 or more is entitled to present a bankruptcy petition in three circumstances. If the debtor has failed to comply with a statutory demand and the time allowed for doing so has now expired (IA 1986, s 268). If the debt is payable under a judgment and execution or other process has been issued to enforce that judgment, but has been returned unsatisfied (also IA 1986, s 268). Or, where a voluntary arrangement has been made which binds the creditor, if the debtor has, amongst other things, failed to comply with his obligations under that arrangement or has given false or misleading information (IA 1986, s 276).

Presentation of bankruptcy petition

The appropriate court in which to commence proceedings is defined in IR 1986, r 6.9. Usually it will be the court for the district in which the debtor has resided or carried on business for the longest period during the previous six months. In the London insolvency district the appropriate court will be the High Court and the proceedings will be issued out of the Bankruptcy Registry which forms part of the Chancery Division. Outside London it will be a county court. However, not all county courts have jurisdiction. It is necessary to consult the directory included in the *Green Book*. Special provision is made for proceedings brought against

[continued on p 632]

Table 12: Threatening and/or suing: advantages and disadvantages

Route taken	Advantages	Disadvantages
Insolvency ie statutory demand to be followed by petition in the case of non-payment	1 Imposes the maximum threat pressure upon most debtors 2 Only minimal costs are incurred if the statutory demand produces payment 3 The creditor can change to the debt route (see below) if the statutory demand does not produce payment 4 Enables the trustee or liquidator to reopen fraudulent or other transactions previously made and to commence various types of misfeasance proceedings against the debtor, directors agents etc	1 May cause the hard pressed debtor to commence insolvency proceedings himself and/or seek a moratorium 2 Heavy costs penalty if recipient successfully challenges the demand or gets a subsequent petition dismissed 3 Presenting a petition usually kills any chance of the debtor arranging a loan to pay off this creditor 4 Insolvency proceedings are expensive and in practice the costs may not be fully recoverable by the petitioner 5 The existence of secured creditors, and creditors with priority debts may leave little for distribution to the unsecured creditors 6 The equality of treatment accorded to all unsecured creditors (whether petitioners or not) may reduce the amount recoverable by the petitioner
Debt ie letter before action to be followed if necessary by a writ or summons, entry of judgment, and execution thereof	1 A letter before action carries some threat pressure 2 If the debtor is factually insolvent, proceedings in debt may bring the plaintiff full repayment in advance of (and possibly at the expense of) other creditors 3 This is the safest route where the creditor suspects that the debtor will dispute any proceedings taken against him	1 Low threat pressure makes it more likely that litigation will have to be commenced 2 This route may become slow and expensive if the debtor vigorously defends and/or seeks to set aside any default judgment or unopposed summary judgment obtained 3 Litigation costs incurred may be wasted because of conflicting proceedings, eg execution of judgments obtained by other creditors, insolvency proceedings and/or a moratorium

Table 13: Threatening and/or suing:
factors upon which instructions are needed

1	What assets does the debtor have?	If none, neither route is worthwhile except perhaps the making of a threat if it causes the debtor to borrow
2	What other creditors are there?	Information is needed on the number of creditors, the size of their debts, and the likelihood of them bringing conflicting proceedings, and their position in the pecking order relative to your client (ie whether their debts are secured or rank in priority). If your client's chances are likely to be postponed or swamped, are there any particular assets (see above) which you can identify and attack via the debt route? Speed is essential: you may get only one chance
3	What information is there as to fraudulent and other trans- actions which may be reopened?	Usually such proceedings are not practicable unless and until insolvency proceedings have been commenced and appropriate orders made therein
4	Is it appropriate to seek a *Mareva* injunction?	Can the creditor (*a*) show a good arguable case, (*b*) sufficiently identify assets belonging to the debtor and (*c*) show that there is a real risk that the debtor will try to arrange the dissipation or secretion of assets so as to frustrate any litigious remedies the creditor may obtain?
5	Are there any alternative remedies available?	Eg under *Romalpa* clauses in the case of sale of goods, or remedies of forfeiture or distress in the case of non-payment of rent

Table 14: When not to use insolvency proceedings

Don't use a statutory demand if:
1 The claim is not liquidated (eg it is a claim for damages) 2 The debtor has a triable defence to the claim 3 You do not know or are not sure whether the debtor has a triable defence to the claim 4 The undisputed debt is £750 or less (companies) or less than £750 (individuals) 5 Immediate protection in the form of a *Mareva* injunction is appropriate
Don't present a petition if:
1 The debtor is making a genuine attempt to borrow to repay this debt 2 Someone else has already commenced proceedings (see below and p 640) 3 Your purpose in doing so is merely to increase the threat pressure. The remedy claimed in a bankruptcy petition or winding-up order is in effect a class remedy for the benefit of all creditors. Therefore the proceedings may continue even after your debt is paid. Indeed a main purpose of the subsequent proceedings may be to reclaim that payment. A petitioner needs leave to withdraw a petition. Instead of granting leave the court may make a substitution order putting some other creditor into the petitioner's place. If subsequently the petition is successful the payment to the first petitioner may then be avoided.

non-resident or untraced debtors (London) petitions issued by a minister of the Crown or a government department (also London) and petitions issued whilst a voluntary arrangement is in force (see IR 1986, r 6.9(4A)).

Before issuing a petition it is advisable and normally essential to commission a Land Charges Search against the name of the debtor and also to inquire of the relevant court whether any interim order has been made or whether any application to set aside a relevant statutory demand has been made.

To what extent, if at all, will a bankruptcy petition based upon a judgment debt be affected by any stay of execution in the action in which that judgment was given? If there is a general stay of execution, eg pending an appeal, the judgment debt is not 'payable' and so a bankruptcy petition should not be issued in respect of it. However, if, as is more usual, there is a stay of execution only under RSC Ord 47, r 1 (ie stay of execution by writ of *fi fa*) a bankruptcy petition can be issued but is likely to be adjourned so long as the stay persists (see generally *White Book* 47/1/4).

There are four prescribed forms of bankruptcy petition. We illustrate in fig 44 the form for use in the case of non-compliance with a statutory demand concerning a debt immediately payable (see p 617). The other forms are for use in cases of non-compliance with a statutory demand concerning a future debt, or an unsatisfied judgment, or default concerning an approved voluntary arrangement. Useful guidance on drafting petitions is given in *Practice Notes* of 1986 and 1987 ([1987] 1 WLR 81 and 1424). You should prepare at least four forms of petition; one for the court, one for service, one to be exhibited to an affidavit of service and the fourth for your own file.

The following documentation must be lodged at court on presentation (ie issue).

(1) Three forms of petition: the court keeps one and seals the other two.
(2) An extra form of petition if it is based upon default concerning an approved voluntary arrangement; this is for service on the supervisor of the arrangement and will be sealed by the court.
(3) If the petition is based upon non-compliance with a statutory demand, a prescribed form of affidavit of service of the demand exhibiting a copy of it.
(4) An affidavit in prescribed form verifying the petition; as to who should be the deponent see IR 1986, r 6.12.
(5) The court fee.
(6) The deposit payable in respect of the Official Receiver's fee (currently £300; Insolvency Fees Order 1986, art 9, noted in the *Green Book*).
(7) If service is to be effected by county court bailiff (see p 133) the service fee payable.

On issue the court office will insert the time, date and place of the hearing, register a pending action against the name of the respondent, 'the debtor', in the Land Charges Department and transmit the deposit paid in respect of the Official Receiver's fee.

IR 1986, r 6.14 requires personal service upon the debtor (whether by the court, the petitioning creditor or his agent) and, as to (2) above postal service on the supervisor (by the petitioning creditor or his agent). If necessary an order for substituted service (see further p 133) can be obtained. Service must be effected (usually) at least fourteen days before the hearing date and an affidavit of service exhibiting a sealed copy of the petition must be filed in court immediately after service (forms are prescribed).

If the petition is not served an application for an extension of time for service must be made prior to the hearing date, and you should at the same time get a new hearing date. If, unluckily for you, you make your application on the original hearing date you will pay a £30 fee not a £20 fee and you will get no costs of the hearing.

The debtor's responses

The debtor's response, or lack of response, to the service of petition will affect any subsequent hearing of the petition. The debtor may:

(1) *Pay off the debt.* If despite payment the petition goes to a hearing (see IR 1986, r 6.32 and see below as to consent orders) the petition will be dismissed unless another creditor properly applies to be substituted as petitioner (see IR 1986, rr 6.30 and 6.31).

(2) *Offer to compound the debt.* Any such offer must be carefully considered. If it is refused the petitioner's solicitor should seek to gather evidence demonstrating that such refusal is reasonable (see further p 628). The court may dismiss the petition if offers are unreasonably refused. If the offer is accepted see the *Practice Note* of 1992 ([1992] 1 WLR 379) as to obtaining consent orders.

(3) *Apply for an interim order.* This would give the debtor a moratorium, a breathing space in which to put together some voluntary arrangement acceptable to the majority of creditors. An interim order will stay the bankruptcy proceedings, and other proceedings (IA 1986, s 252). Even an application for an interim order may lead to a stay (IA 1986, s 254).

(4) *File notice of intention to oppose the petition.* A form of notice is prescribed. It should be filed at least seven days before the hearing and a copy must be served upon the petitioner or his solicitor (IR 1986, r 6.21). For example, if the petition is based upon non-compliance with a statutory demand the debtor may wish to raise a triable defence to the allegation of debt. He is not precluded from doing so merely because he did not apply to set aside the statutory demand. Even if he did so apply, but was unsuccessful he can still re-argue the same issues again (*Eberhardt & Co Ltd v Mair* [1995] 1 WLR 1180).

(5) *Make no response.* This does not in fact preclude him from raising any objection at the hearing.

Hearing of bankruptcy petition

The petition is heard by a bankruptcy registrar (High Court, London) or a district judge (county court). Usually only the petitioner or his solicitor will attend although, of course, the debtor may, as may any creditor who has given prior notice to the petitioner or to whom the court grants leave. Bankruptcy petitions are not advertised (contrast winding-up petitions) and therefore creditors who do not make credit searches (contrast banks and other credit agencies) will not normally know of the petition unless, eg they have been contacted by the debtor in an attempt to put together some voluntary arrangement.

As to evidence, the petition and service thereof are proved by affidavits already filed. In order to prove that the debt is still outstanding the court will normally accept a certificate signed by the person representing the petitioner. The text of the certificate is set out in a *Practice Note* [1987] 1 WLR 120. In London the certificate is printed on the attendance slips

[*continued on p 638*]

Fig 44: Bankruptcy petition

Form 6.7
Creditor's
Bankruptcy
Petition on
Failure to Comply
with a Statutory
Demand for a
Liquidated Sum
Payable Immediately
(Rule 6.6)

No.   of 19   .

IN THE†

In Bankruptcy

†Enter "High Court of
Justice" or "———
County Court" as
the case may be.

Re‡

‡Insert full name of
Debtor (if known)

(1) Insert full name(s)
and address(es) of
Petitioner(s).

I/We (¹)

(2) Insert full name,
place of residence and
occupation (if any) of
Debtor.

Petition the Court that a Bankruptcy Order may be made against
(²)

(3) Insert in full any
other name(s) by
which the Debtor is or
has been known.

[also known as (³)

(4) Insert trading name
(adding "with another
or others", if this is
so), business address
and nature of business.

[and carrying on business as (⁴)

at

as

(5) Insert any other
address or addresses
at which the Debtor
has resided at or after
the time the Petition
debt was incurred.

[and lately residing at (⁵)

(6) Give the same
details as specified in
note (4) above for any
other businesses
which have been
carried on at or after
the time the Petition
debt was incurred.

[and lately carrying on business as (⁶)

at

as

and say as follows:—

1. The Debtor has for the greater part of six months immediately preceding the
presentation of this Petition (⁷) [resided at] [carried on business at] (⁸)

(7) Delete as
applicable.

(8) Insert address.

(9) Or as the case may
be following the terms
of Rule 6.9.

within the District of this Court (⁹)

(10) Please give the
amount of debt(s),
what they relate to
and when they were
incurred. Please show
separately the amount
or rate of any interest
or other charge not
previously notified to
the Debtor and the
reasons why you are
claiming it.

2. The Debtor is justly and truly indebted to me[us] in the aggregate sum of
£ (¹⁰)

Fig 44: contd

(11) Insert date and time (before/after 1600 hours Monday – Friday, before/after 1200 hours Saturday) of (personal) service of a Statutory Demand (or date alleged on affidavit of subservice).

3. The above-mentioned debt is for a liquidated sum payable immediately and the Debtor appears to be unable to pay it.

4. On (11) the   day of   19   , a Statutory Demand was served upon the Debtor by (12) [personal service before [after] hours [post] [advertisement] [insertion through letter box] in respect of the above-mentioned debt. To the best of my knowledge and belief, the Demand has neither been complied with nor set aside in accordance with the Rules and no application to set it aside is outstanding.

(12) State manner of service of Demand [delete as appropriate or as the case may be].

(13) If 3 weeks have not elapsed since service of Statutory Demand, give reasons for earlier presentation of Petition, (see section 270).

(13)

5. I/We do not, nor does any person on my/our behalf, hold any security on the Debtor's estate, or any part thereof, for the payment of the above-mentioned sum.

OR

(14) Delete as applicable.

I/We hold security for the payment of (14) [part of] the above-mentioned sum. I/We will give up such security for the benefit of all the creditors in the event of a Bankruptcy Order being made.

OR

I/We hold security for the payment of part of the above-mentioned sum and I/we estimate the value of such security to be £   . This Petition is not made in respect of the secured part of my/our debt.

Presented and Filed the   day of   19   ,
at   hours   and allotted to

(14) Delete as applicable.

(14) [Mr. Registrar] [District Judge]

_____

See Endorsement

Fig 44: contd

ENDORSEMENT

This Petition having been presented to the Court on
IT IS ORDERED that the Petition shall be heard as follows:—

Date: day of   19   .

Time: hours

Place:

(15) Insert name of Debtor.

and you, the above-named ([15])   , are
to take notice that if you intend to oppose the Petition you must not later than 7 days
before the day fixed for the hearing:—

(i) file in Court a notice (in Form 6.19) specifying the grounds on which you object
to the making of a Bankruptcy Order; and

(ii) send a copy of the Notice to the Petitioner or his Solicitor.

(16) Only to be completed where the Petitioning Creditor is represented by a solicitor.

The Solicitor to the Petitioning Creditor is:—([16])

Name

Address

Telephone Number

Reference

Delete if not required by the court where petition is filed.

We certify that there are no prior Petitions against the within-named Debtor within
the last three years *or*
We certify that all prior Petitions against the within-named Debtor have been
dismissed.
The last Petition was dismissed on the   day of   19   .
We certify that we are unable to certify the full christian names of the debtor.

Solicitors for the Petitioning Creditor.

This is the Petition marked "A" referred to in the Affidavit
of
SWORN before me this
day of   19   .

Solicitor/A Commissioner for Oaths

Reproduced by kind permission of the Solicitors' Law Stationery Society Ltd.

and must be filed after the hearing. A fresh certificate is required at every adjourned hearing. The petitioner may also adduce evidence in relation to any issues raised by the debtor (see responses (2), (4) and (5) above).

At the hearing the petition may be dismissed or adjourned. Alternatively, a bankruptcy order may be made. The order requires the debtor to attend before the Official Receiver. In practice, the court will also contact the Official Receiver's office by telephone. That office will then register the bankruptcy order in the Land Charges Department and will advertise the order in the *London Gazette* and in a newspaper. As to the possibility of postponing publicity, eg pending an appeal, see IR 1986, r 6.34.

Effect of bankruptcy on enforcement procedures in other actions

The commencement of bankruptcy proceedings gives a power to stay any pending actions against the debtor: the power is exercisable by the bankruptcy court or by the court in which the action is pending (if different). After the making of a bankruptcy order any person claiming that the bankrupt owes them any debt or liability must, instead of commencing or pursuing litigation, prove in the bankruptcy unless given leave to the contrary (see generally IA 1986, s 285). A plaintiff who does not learn of the bankruptcy order until after he has commenced his action may be given retrospective leave to commence proceedings (*In re Saunders (A Bankrupt)* [1996] 3 WLR 473; this case is subject to an appeal).

Contrast the position of a litigant who had already obtained judgment against the debtor. He is entitled to keep the benefits of any enforcement procedures taken so long as the enforcement in question was 'completed' before the date of the bankruptcy order (see generally IA 1986, ss 278 and 346). Execution against goods is completed by seizure and sale and (usually) the expiry of a further fourteen days unless, before that deadline, the sheriff or bailiff is given notice of a bankruptcy *petition* already presented. Execution against land is completed by seizure or by the appointment of a receiver or the making of a charging order. However, as to charging orders, note that, in the case of an order *nisi* the enforcement court may later refuse to make the order absolute. Attachment of a debt is completed by receipt of the debt.

Procedure following the bankruptcy order

On the making of a bankruptcy order the bankrupt is deprived of the power to deal with any property beneficially belonging to him. The Official Receiver is constituted trustee of the bankrupt's estate until such time as another trustee in bankruptcy is appointed. The Official Receiver's function is to protect the estate and commence investigations into the conduct and affairs of the bankrupt. He must also summon a creditor's meeting for the purpose of appointing a trustee (unless the value of the estate is too small to justify such a step). The bankrupt must collaborate fully with the Official Receiver, must deliver up all property including books, papers and records and must complete a Statement of Affairs in the prescribed forms supplied by the Official Receiver.

Ultimately all the bankrupt's estate will be collected in, sold and the proceeds distributed. This includes the bankrupt's home if it belongs to him or belongs to him jointly with another person, eg his spouse. Unless the circumstances are exceptional the maximum period of delay before sale will be one year from the date of the bankruptcy order.

Certain chattels such as tools, clothing, bedding etc are exempt from the estate vesting in the trustee (the list is the same as that given on p 593 concerning execution against goods). The bankrupt is also entitled to keep any income received after bankruptcy subject, however, to the effect of any 'income payments order' which may be made by the court on the application of the trustee. As to after-acquired property, such as a legacy, the trustee has forty-two days in which to claim it after receiving notice of it from the bankrupt. The claim is made by notice under IA 1986, s 307 the service of which automatically vests the property in the trustee.

In the case of most bankrupts, unless they commit some breach or default in the obligations imposed upon them to assist the Official Receiver and trustee, the bankruptcy order will be discharged three years (sometimes two years) after the date upon which it was made. Usually the discharge is automatic, ie no court order is necessary. To obtain formal evidence of discharge in such a case the court will if requested issue a certificate of discharge. Also the discharged bankrupt may, at his own expense, require the Official Receiver to advertise the discharge in the *London Gazette* and in a newspaper. Discharge releases the former bankrupt from liability in respect of most bankruptcy debts and may bring to an end the disqualifications and disabilities previously imposed (see p 612). However, it has no effect on the functions of the trustee or upon the bankrupt's obligation to assist the trustee. More time may be needed before a final distribution can be made to the creditors who have proved in the bankruptcy.

Corporate insolvency: winding up

Grounds for a creditor's petition

There are seven grounds upon which a company may be wound up (IA 1986, s 122). The ground most important to most creditors is ground (f) 'the company is unable to pay its debts'. This ground is defined in IA 1986, s 123. Leaving aside references to steps taken in Scotland or Northern Ireland, this section indicates four ways in which ground (f) may be established.

    (1) Non-compliance with a statutory demand served by the petitioner (see p 613).

(2) Unsatisfied judgment debt upon which the petitioner has sought enforcement.

(3) Other evidence of inability to pay debts as they fall due (ie practical insolvency or negative cash flow).

(4) Evidence that the company's assets are less than its liabilities, present, contingent and prospective (ie balance sheet insolvency).

Presentation of winding-up petition

Most winding-up petitions are issued out of the High Court, Chancery Division, (the so-called 'Companies Court') either in London or in one of the eight Chancery District Registries. The jurisdiction of the High Court at any of these offices is unlimited in all respects, value and territorial. A relatively small number of petitions are issued out of county courts. Not all of them have jurisdiction; none of the London county courts have. Even if the county court has jurisdiction, that jurisdiction is limited in value (share capital paid up or credited as paid up not exceeding £120,000) and is limited territorially (the registered office of the company must be situated in the district of the court; see generally IA 1986, s 117).

Before issuing a petition it is vital to effect a search of the Central Index of Petitions which is maintained by the Companies Court in London. It may be that a petition has already been issued by another person.

The prescribed form of winding-up petition is very brief. We illustrate in fig 45 a semi-completed form based upon non-compliance with a statutory demand. You should prepare at least four forms of petition; one for the court, one for service, one to be exhibited to an affidavit of service and one for your own file. The following documentation should be lodged at court on presentation (ie issue).

(1) Three forms of petition: the court keeps one and seals and returns the other two.

(2) Additional copies of the petition for service upon any administrator, administrative receiver or superviser of a voluntary arrangement, who has been appointed or any liquidator appointed if the company is already in voluntary liquidation (and see further examples concerning companies authorised within the meaning of the Banking Act 1987: IR 1986, r 4.7). These copies also are sealed and returned to the petitioner.

(3) A prescribed form of affidavit verifying the petition (as to who should be the deponent see IR 1986, r 4.12).

(4) The court fee.

(5) The deposit payable in respect of the Official Receiver's fee (currently £300, see p 633).

On issue the court will allocate a hearing date, usually about six weeks ahead so as to allow time for the petitioner to effect service and advertisement.

[continued on p 642]

Fig 45: Winding-up petition based upon non-compliance with a statutory demand

---

IN THE HIGH COURT OF JUSTICE   No   of 1997
CHANCERY DIVISION
COMPANIES COURT

IN THE MATTER OF [*full name of company*]
AND IN THE MATTER OF THE INSOLVENCY ACT 1986

To Her Majesty's High Court of Justice

The Petition of [*name of petitioner*] of [or whose registered office is at] [*address of petitioner*]

1.   [*Full name of company*] (hereinafter called 'the company') was incorporated on [*date of incorporation*] under the Companies Act 19 .

2.   The registered office of the company is at [*address*]

3.   The nominal capital of the company is £   divided into shares of £   each. The amount of the capital paid up as credited as paid up is £   .

4.   The principal objects for which the company was established are as follows:

      and other objects stated in the memorandum of association of the company.

5.   [*Set out the grounds on which a winding-up order is sought eg* The company is indebted to the petitioner in the sum of £25,000 being the price of goods sold and delivered by the petitioner to the company on 26th February 1997. On 17th July 1997 the petitioner's solicitor Mary Smith, a partner in Smith and Jones, Solicitors of [*address*] served on the company a written demand pursuant to section 123(1)(a) of the Insolvency Act 1986. The debt remains wholly unpaid and unsatisfied. The petitioner therefore believes that the company is insolvent and unable to pay its debts.]

6.   In the circumstances it is just and equitable that the company should be wound up.

The petitioner therefore prays as follows:

(1)   that [*full name of the company*] may be wound up by the court under the provisions of the Insolvency Act 1986
or
(2)   that such other order may be made as the court thinks fit.

NOTE: It is intended to serve this petition on the company [and]

Endorsement

This petition having been presented to the court on [*date*] will be heard at Royal Courts of Justice, Strand, London WC2A 2LL on:

Date

Time   (or so soon thereafter as the petition can be heard)

The solicitors to the petitioner are Smith and Jones, Solicitors of [*address*]

Telephone No

Reference

The petitioner must arrange service of the petition; ideally, personal service at the registered office of the company, on a director or other officer or employee (and see further IR 1986, r 4.8). An affidavit of service in prescribed form must be filed immediately after service and any additional copies of the petition required (see (2) above) must be sent to the office holder in question on the next business day following the day on which the petition was served on the company.

In order to notify any other creditors of the date fixed for the hearing of the petition, the petitioner must arrange an advertisement in prescribed form in (usually) the *London Gazette*. The effect of such publicity may be devastating to the financial reputation of the company and any related companies and also the company's bank is likely to freeze its accounts with the company. Because this is so there are fixed time limits within which the advertisement must be made; not less than seven business days after service on the company and not more than seven business days before the hearing (as to the meaning of business day in this context see pp 9 and 13 and IR 1986, r 4.11 and r 13.13). On being served with a petition, or indeed with a statutory demand, the company may seek an injunction restraining the advertisement if it considers that the presentation of the petition is/would be an abuse of the process of the court (see further p 627).

Certificate of compliance

At least five days before the hearing the petitioner's solicitor must file in court a prescribed form certifying that the rules relating to service and advertisement have been complied with. At about the same time the solicitor should consider preparing and getting instructions upon a list of the names and addresses of persons who have given notice of their intention to appear at the hearing. The prescribed form of list also shows which creditors in the list will support the petition and which will oppose it. The list should be filed with the court office on the Friday before the hearing. We recommend getting instructions as to it some days earlier because it is possible that some creditors will have given notice to the petitioner directly rather than to the solicitor.

Hearing of winding-up petition

In the High Court, the hearing will take place in open court before the registrar (London) or district judge unless it is opposed in which case it will be listed as adjourned for hearing before a High Court judge. If the company intends to oppose the petition it should file its affidavit in opposition and send a copy to the petitioner, not less than seven days before the hearing. Any hearing which is not ready for determination may be adjourned but the court is reluctant to allow many or substantial adjournments because of the deleterious effect which the proceedings usually have on the company's ability to trade. Adjournments do not involve further advertisement unless the court so orders.

IA 1986, s 125 gives the court a wide discretion to dismiss, adjourn, grant interim relief or make any other order it thinks fit. The petition may be dismissed if substantial errors in procedure have been made, or if no grounds can be established or if the majority of the creditors oppose the petition. Also in an appropriate case the court may order that another creditor be substituted as petitioner if, eg the petitioner fails to appear or no longer seeks a winding up.

If a winding-up order is made the court forthwith gives notice to the Official Receiver who must, amongst other things, notify the registrar of companies and arrange for the order to be advertised in the *London Gazette* and in a newspaper.

Effect of a winding-up order

The winding up of a company is deemed to commence, ie the operation of a winding-up order is backdated to, the time of presentation of the petition, or, if the company was then already in voluntary liquidation, to the time when the resolution for winding up was passed (see generally IA 1986, s 129). This doctrine of relating back explains why the petition has to be advertised, and why the petition may have such a devastating effect on the company's business. It upsets any contracts entered into, any dispositions of assets made or any enforcement proceedings 'completed' (see p 638) since the earlier date.

After the making of a winding-up order no action against the company can be commenced or continued unless the court grants leave (IA 1986, s 130).

The procedures following the order (investigations, realisation of assets and distribution amongst creditors) are largely the same as the procedures following the making of a bankruptcy order. There are however three major differences. The person appointed by the creditors to conduct the winding up is called the liquidator (the Official Receiver is the liquidator until such appointment). The liquidator acts as agent of the company with, eg a power of sale; legal title to company assets is not usually transferred to him. Thirdly, the final stages of winding up are not discharge (rehabilitation of a defaulter), but dissolution (death of the company).

Specialist topics in insolvency law and practice

Personal insolvency: bankruptcy

Secured debts
Future debts
Cases with a foreign element

Summary administration of small bankruptcies
Death or disability of the debtor
Death or removal of the trustee
Powers and duties of the trustees
Remuneration and costs
Preferential and deferred debts and claims
Proof of debts
Disclaimers etc
Setting aside or adjusting prior transactions including fraudulent transactions and voidable preferences
Interim receivership
Insolvent partnerships
Second bankruptcy
Criminal bankruptcy
Discharge of orders
Annulment or rescission of orders

Corporate insolvency: winding-up proceedings

Administration
Administrative receivership
Winding up foreign companies
Death, release, removal etc of liquidator
Powers and duties of liquidators
Remuneration and costs
Proof of debts
Preferential and deferred debts and claims
Provisional liquidators
Special managers
Secured creditors' rights
Disclaimers etc
Malpractice before and during liquidation
Setting aside or adjusting prior transactions including fraudulent transactions and voidable preferences
Company Directors Disqualification Act 1986
Compulsory winding up after commencement of voluntary winding up
Rescission of winding-up orders
Dissolution of company
Restoration to the register

Chapter 27

Appeals

Orders made by district judges

In the High Court

In the High Court there is a right of appeal (ie without leave) from every decision made by a district judge or master. In most cases the appeal lies to the High Court judge in chambers (for the exceptions see RSC Ord 58, r 2, noted below). In cases proceeding in London a notice of appeal must be issued within five days of the master's decision and must be served not more than five days after issue nor less than two clear days before the day fixed for hearing the appeal (RSC Ord 58, r 1). In cases proceeding outside London the notice must be issued within seven days of the district judge's decision and must be served not more than five days after issue nor less than three days before the day fixed for hearing the appeal (RSC Ord 58, r 3). Bear in mind that in reckoning periods of time of 'seven days or less' Saturdays, Sundays and certain other days are excluded (RSC Ord 3, r 2(5); see p 10) and that the court has power to extend any time period fixed by the rules (RSC Ord 3, r 5; see p 10).

At the hearing of the appeal the appellant has the right and obligation to speak first. Subject to that possible difference the judge will consider the matter afresh. The parties are not limited to the evidence they previously relied on, and the judge is not bound by the previous exercise of discretion by the master or district judge appealed from (*Evans v Bartlam* [1937] AC 473). As to the listing arrangements, place of hearing and documentation see the *Practice Directions* of 1976 and 1996, *White Book* 58/1/6, 58/1/7 and 752. These state, amongst other things, that in cases of complexity, a skeleton argument (see p 663) or a chronology (see p 495) should be prepared and filed.

In the following cases an appeal from a district judge or master lies direct to the Court of Appeal (RSC Ord 58, rr 2 and 3):

(1) decisions in any proceedings tried by the district judge or master (see p 230);

(2) decisions made on an assessment of damages under RSC Ord 37 by the district judge or master (see p 213).

In order to bring these appeals it is necessary to obtain the leave of a district judge or master or the leave of the Court of Appeal (RSC Ord 58, r 2).

In the county court

In the county court, on any order made by the district judge an appeal lies as of right to the circuit judge. Appeals from interlocutory orders must be made on notice filed and served on the opposite party within five days; as in the High Court, the judge hearing the appeal will consider the matter afresh (CCR Ord 13, r 1 and see the *Green Book* commentary thereto). Appeals from any trial or assessment by the district judge must be made on notice served within fourteen days and are dealt with in the same way as an appeal to the Court of Appeal would be (ie limited as to the evidence relied on and as to the exercise of discretion; see further, p 655) rather than by way of a fresh hearing (CCR Ord 37, r 6). There are no prescribed or practice forms of notice of appeal. Form N244 can be used (see p 14).

Where cases are referred for arbitration rather than trial (see p 279) there is no appeal from this award as such. However, a dissatisfied party can apply to the circuit judge for the award to be set aside on certain limited grounds *viz*, where the arbitrator (ie the district judge, in many cases) had no jurisdiction, where the arbitrator was guilty of misconduct and where the award contains a material error of law. Notice of the application stating the grounds relied on must be served within fourteen days after the day on which the award was entered as a judgment of the court. Such an application could also be made to the arbitrator if the award was given in the absence of one party (see generally CCR Ord 19, r 8 and *Green Book* p 2063).

Appeals as to taxations of costs are outlined on p 531.

Orders made by a High Court judge

In most cases an appeal lies to the Court of Appeal. The order appealed from may have been made in respect of some interlocutory matter (in which case it may have reached the judge by way of appeal from the district judge) or in respect of the decision made at the end of a trial. In a very exceptional case the order may have been made during the course of the trial and heard by the Court of Appeal as a matter of extreme urgency, the hearing of the trial being adjourned pending the outcome. Such appeals are undesirable for several reasons and are to be avoided wherever possible (see further *White Book* 20/5–8/12).

In some cases the right of appeal from a High Court judge is fettered; the leave of the High Court or the leave of the Court of Appeal, must be obtained before the appeal is made. The grant or refusal of leave cannot be decided by any court other than the court or courts authorised to give such leave. The imposition of such a leave requirement is intended as a check to unnecessary or frivolous appeals (*Lane v Esdaile* [1891] AC 210 *per* Lord Halsbury LC). The decision of the specified court or courts is final. It cannot be reviewed by any higher court. This leave requirement must be distinguished carefully from the grant or refusal of an extension of time for appealing, which, confusingly, is often referred to as 'leave to appeal out of time'. The question whether leave to appeal is necessary goes to the jurisdiction of the Court of Appeal; assuming such leave is necessary, the appellant's failure to obtain it is a defect whether or not the respondent takes the point (*White v Brunton* [1984] QB 570). The question whether an extension of time should be given does not affect the jurisdiction of higher courts, and can be reviewed by them.

> In my judgment what *Lane v Esdaile* decided, and all that it decided, was that where it is provided that an appeal shall lie *by leave* of a particular court or courts, neither the grant nor refusal of leave is an appealable decision ... The grant or refusal of an application for leave to appeal is one thing. The grant or refusal of an application to extend the time limited for taking a step in proceedings, including but not limited to giving notice of appeal, is quite another ... whilst it is true that a right of appeal may be barred either by a refusal of an extension of time, or by a refusal of leave, the routes by which this result is achieved and the underlying concepts are essentially different (*Rickards v Rickards* [1990] Fam 194 *per* Lord Donaldson MR).

In which cases is leave to appeal necessary? In those cases, whose leave is it necessary to obtain? The answers are to be found in SCA 1981, s 18 as amended. A distinction has to be drawn between 'final orders' and 'interlocutory orders'.

Final orders. No leave is necessary *except*, eg in the case of an appeal relating to an order made by consent or relating solely as to costs or orders resolving disputes about boundaries or easements. In these cases, leave can be given either by a judge or by the Court of Appeal (RSC Ord 59, r 1B).

Interlocutory orders. The leave of the judge or the Court of Appeal is necessary *except*, eg in the case of an order affecting the liberty of the subject. In the excepted cases there is a right of appeal without leave. Where leave to appeal an interlocutory order is required an application should be made, at first, to the court which made the decision under appeal, either at the time of decision or by subsequent application (in the latter case, the application does not have to be made to the particular judge who made the decision under appeal; *Warren v T Kilroe & Sons Ltd* [1988] 1 WLR 516). There is no appeal from that court's refusal, but the prospective appellant can then make a fresh application to the Court of Appeal (see generally RSC Ord 59, r 14, described on p 657).

Which orders are final and which orders are interlocutory can be determined by reference to RSC Ord 59, r 1A. Some orders must be treated as final; eg an order for discovery of documents made in an action for discovery only (see p 409) and an order of committal (see p 609).

Some orders must be treated as interlocutory; eg any judgment in default (see pp 212 and 247) and any 'unless' order (see p 123). For cases not otherwise listed a general test is provided which looks at the effect of the order rather than the nature of the application (as to issues relating to limitation, including applications to disapply the limitation period, see *Dale v British Coal Corporation* [1992] 1 WLR 964).

In *The Iran Nabuvat* [1990] 1 WLR 115 Lord Donaldson explained the justification for imposing the leave requirement which now affects most appeals.

> [T]he justification [is] that it is unfair to the respondent that he should be required to defend the decision below, unfair to other litigants because the time of the Court of Appeal is being spent listening to an appeal which should not be before it and thereby causing delay to other litigants, and unfair to the appellant himself who needs to be saved from his own folly in seeking to appeal the unappealable (*per* Lord Donaldson MR).

From statistics published in 1992 it appears that, of all appeals heard in the Court of Appeal, Civil Division only 27.9 per cent are successful (see further *The Times*, 23 December 1992).

Time for appealing

In all cases the time for appealing is four weeks from the date the judgment or order was signed, entered or otherwise perfected. However if leave to appeal is necessary and is granted, eg on the last day of the four-week period the time for appealing (ie serving notice of appeal) is extended to seven days after the date when leave is granted (RSC Ord 59, r 4).

Some special cases

By AJA 1969, ss 12 and 13, a 'leapfrog appeal' from a High Court judge direct to the House of Lords may be made if:

(1) all parties consent; and
(2) the judge grants a certificate: this he will do only if the case involves a point of law of general public importance concerning either:
  (a) the construction of a statute or statutory instrument (see, eg, *Daymond v Plymouth City Council* [1976] AC 609); or
  (b) a matter already fully considered by the Court of Appeal or House of Lords (see, eg, *Thomas v Bunn* [1991] 1 AC 362); and
(3) the House of Lords grants leave.

As to orders made by an official referee, see RSC Ord 58, r 4 noted on p 273.

As to appeals cases transferred to or from the High Court or county court, the fact of transfer does not affect the rights of appeal (CCA 1984, s 40(5) and (7) and s 42(4) and (6)).

Orders made by a circuit judge

As to appeals from a circuit judge, all the points made above in relation to appeals from a High Court judge apply (including in particular the need for leave, where required, in the case of interlocutory appeals (SCA 1981, s 18) and the time for appealing (as to which see RSC Ord 59, r 19(3)), but with the following exceptions:

(1) There is no provision for leapfrog appeals direct to the House of Lords.

(2) Leave to appeal a final order is required (from the county court or from the Court of Appeal) in the case of a county court judgment for debts or damages not exceeding £5,000. As to equity cases, cases in which a counterclaim is made, cases in which remedies other than debts and damages are sought and cases in which claims for debts or damages are dismissed, see *White Book* 59/1/34.

(3) Leave to appeal a final order is also required as above if the order sought to be appealed from was made by the judge acting in an appellate capacity (for example, under CCR Ord 37, r 6, see above).

On all these matters see CCA 1984, s 77, the County Court Appeals Order 1991, and the *Green Book* commentary to s 77.

At one time there was a rule that an appellant could not argue any point of law which had not been raised before the county court. No such rule now exists (*Pittalis v Grant* [1989] QB 605). The principles governing appeals based on new points of law are the same in county court cases as they are in High Court cases (see further p 666).

Orders from which no appeal lies

Some examples are listed below.

In the High Court

(1) An order granting or refusing a certificate enabling a leapfrog appeal (AJA 1969, s 12(5)).

(2) An order refusing leave for the institution of legal proceedings by a person declared a vexatious litigant (see p 94).

In the county court

(1) On questions of fact, orders for possession where, by virtue of the Rent Act 1977 and various similar security of tenure statutes the court can grant possession only on being satisfied that it is reasonable to do so (CCA 1984, s 77(6)).

(2) Consent orders made on a trial or assessment by a district judge in the county court (as to which, see further, p 653).

In both courts

(1) Where there is an agreement not to appeal. In High Court cases the agreement must be embodied or recorded in an order of the court (*Re Hall & County Bank* (1880) 13 ChD 261, and see p 456). In county court cases it is sufficient to record the agreement in writing, signed by the parties or their solicitors or agents (CCA 1984, s 79).

(2) An order made by a judge of the High Court or county court allowing an extension of time for appealing.

(3) Cases concerning merely academic points or hypothetical questions of law when there is no dispute to be resolved (*White Book* 59/1/25; cf cases on the courts' refusal to grant declarations as to academic or hypothetical questions, *White Book* 15/16/2).

In the Court of Appeal

Where leave to appeal is sought from the Court of Appeal, the court's decision thereon is final (*Lane v Esdaile* [1891] AC 219, refusal of leave; *Geogas SA v Trammo Gas Ltd* [1991] 1 WLR 776, HL, grant of leave; *John Redman Ltd v Filecroft Ltd* [1991] 1 WLR 692, grant of leave subject to a condition; and see further *Daisystar Ltd v Town and Country Building Society* [1992] 1 WLR 390).

Applications to set aside or vary orders

We are not concerned in this section with the power of a higher court to set aside or vary the judgment or order of a lower court. Here we consider in what circumstances can a party affected by an order apply or reapply to the court which made it, asking that court to set aside or vary it.

Orders made in the absence of one party

Applications to the court to set aside its own previous order are frequently made in the following cases:

(1) default judgments (see pp 219 and 250);

(2) orders made where the party applying had notice of a hearing but failed to attend, eg on a summary judgment application (RSC Ord 14, r 11) or failure to attend the trial (see p 513); and

(3) *ex parte* orders such as the grant of leave to serve outside the jurisdiction (see p 143) or the grant of leave as to joinder of parties (see p 96 and generally RSC Ord 32, r 6; *White Book* 32/1–6/14). *Ex parte* orders are essentially provisional orders only, the court not having heard evidence from the other party.

In (1) and (2) the setting aside may be on terms and the court may also make orders for the costs thrown away.

As to (3) the proper method of challenging an *ex parte* order made by the Court of Appeal is usually an application to a first instance judge (ie

High Court judge or circuit judge, but not usually a district judge); see *Paragon Group Ltd v Burnell* [1991] 2 WLR 854; and *Ocean Software Ltd v Kay* [1992] 2 WLR 633. The facts of *Paragon Group Ltd* illustrate this point clearly and also illustrate how fast and furious civil litigation can sometimes be and how quickly the courts and the Court of Appeal can respond when necessary.

> In order to comply with a contractual limitation period the plaintiff had to issue and serve a writ by 31 January 1989 at the latest.
>
> On 17 January 1989 Linklaters & Paines, the solicitors for the plaintiff, wrote to Travers Smith Braithwaite asking if they were instructed to accept service. On Friday, 27 January, Travers Smith Braithwaite replied by facsimile that they had no such instructions. The writ was issued at 4.20 p.m. on Monday 30 January. Process servers were standing by, but they were unable to effect personal service on any of the three defendants in the case on 31 January. Accordingly at 7.15 p.m. that day the plaintiff made an application *ex parte* by telephone for an order for substituted service. The application was refused by Leggatt J. The application was renewed [ie appealed] by telephone at 8.30 p.m. Lord Donaldson of Lymington MR having consulted Parker and Glidewell LJJ on the telephone, made the order with liberty to apply to discharge (*Paragon Group Ltd v Burnell* [1991] 2 WLR 854 *per* Lloyd LJ).
>
> The Court of Appeal have directed that, that order having been made by them *ex parte*, the application to discharge it should be made to a *puisne* judge who should approach it simply on the basis not that he is bound by any decision of the Court of Appeal on any point of law or principle, but as if he were considering an ordinary exercise of a discretion *ex parte* under Ord 65, r 4 upon an *inter partes* application to have the order set aside (*Paragon Group Ltd v Burnell per* Harman J).

Orders working out, supplementing or enforcing orders previously made

The making of an order, even a final order, does not thereby terminate the jurisdiction of the court which made that order. Either party may apply to the court to determine any subsidiary or consequential issues which may then arise between them, for example issues relating to the costs payable (see p 530), the methods of enforcement available (see p 590), the amount of judgment interest payable (*Electricity Supply Nominees Ltd v Farrell* [1997] 2 All ER 498). The principles here are sometimes summarised by saying that all orders carry with them an implied 'liberty to apply'. In the case of interlocutory orders the words 'liberty to apply' are often expressly included in the order so as to remove or minimise doubts thereto. The liberty to apply, whether express or implied, can be invoked for all purposes necessary to give effect to the court's order. However, it does not by itself confer a right to ask the court to derogate from its previous order (see further *White Book* 4605, *Supreme Court Practice News* Issue 5/96).

Orders varying or departing from orders previously made

Orders in respect of certain preparatory or collateral matters can never be regarded as final. Further applications on the same matter may be made if there has been a material change in circumstances: for example, a renewed application for an interim payment (see p 313) or a renewed application for transfer to another court (see p 373) or an application to vary or revoke previous orders for security of costs (see p 317). In some cases the power to vary or revoke is expressly provided for in the rules of court; for example rules permitting the variation or revocation of orders for an interim payment (see p 314) or for discovery of documents (see p 420).

Some orders expressly indicate that the court making them has power to later reconsider and if appropriate vary or discharge them: for example the usual form of interlocutory injunction which is granted 'until judgment or further order'. In such a case, if he is to obtain a 'further order' the applicant must show good grounds such as a significant change in circumstances or the discovery of new facts which could not reasonably have been discovered before the earlier hearing.

> As a matter of judicial discretion, a first instance judge will not set aside or vary an *inter partes* interlocutory order made by a brother first instance judge unless the application to set aside or vary is made on the basis of fresh material not before the court when the original interlocutory order was made. If no new material is relied on, or if the only new material is material that the applicant could and ought to have placed before the court on the original application — the applicant to set aside or vary being the respondent to the original application — then the original order can only be disturbed on appeal (*Columbia Picture Industries Inc v Robinson* [1987] Ch 38 *per* Scott J).

Even in interlocutory matters a party cannot fight over again a battle which has already been fought unless there are good grounds (*Chanel Ltd v FW Woolworth & Co Ltd* [1981] 1 WLR 485; *Lonrho plc v Fayed (No 4)* [1994] 2 WLR 209; as to appeals a different rule applies as to new evidence unless there has been a 'trial or hearing on the merits'; see further p 662).

No 'good grounds' need to be shown in order to obtain a rehearing if the previous hearing was adjourned, whether generally or *sine die*, on agreed terms; in the case of an adjourned application the first battle is not yet over (see generally *Butt v Butt* [1987] 1 WLR 1351).

No 'good grounds' need be shown in order to obtain a rehearing if the order previously made contained an express 'liberty to apply to vary or discharge the order'; for example an *Anton Piller* order (see p 300) (which is also an *ex parte* order, as to which see above). The words 'liberty to apply' by themselves are not enough for this purpose (see p 651). However, in a particular case, it may be possible to persuade the court that it previously intended to grant the wider 'liberty to apply to vary or discharge' and that it should now grant it under the slip rule (see p 519 and consider the facts of *Butt v Butt* [1987] 1 WLR 1351).

Orders made by consent

Consent orders are perhaps best thought of as being unappealable although, strictly speaking this is only true of consent orders made on a trial or assessment of damages by a district judge in a county court (CCR Ord 37, r 6; in other cases an appeal lies, without leave in the case of an internal appeal in the High Court or county court, but subject to leave of the court in the case of an appeal from the county court or High Court to the Court of Appeal; *White Book* 4606). The accepted means of challenging a consent order is an application to set aside or vary it. Such an application can be made by a separate action or, if the order itself or the rules of court so provide, by further application in the same action (see above).

Where a consent order evidences or embodies a genuine contract between the parties resolving their dispute, the court will interfere only on the same grounds as it might interfere with any other contract, eg cases of fraud or mistake; 'it is not less a contract and subject to the incidents of a contract because there is superadded the command of a Judge' (*White Book* 4608). However, the terms of that contract, properly construed, may not prevent the court exercising any usual discretion it has as to the operation of the order. In *Chanel Ltd v FW Woolworth & Co Ltd* [1981] 1 WLR 485 the Court of Appeal held that an interlocutory injunction in the usual form could be varied or discharged on 'further order' even though the original order had been made by consent if there were 'good grounds justifying a further order' (see opposite). In *Siebe Gorman Ltd v Pneupac Ltd* [1982] 1 WLR 185 where on an application for discovery an order similar to an 'unless order' had been made by consent, it was held that, in the absence of a clear agreement to the contrary, applications could still be made under RSC Ord 3, r 5 to extend the period of time specified in the order. In these cases the court's reconsideration of the previous order was in conformity with, and not in opposition to, any contractual rights which had been created (see also *Cropper v Chief Constable of South Yorkshire Police* [1989] 1 WLR 333, varying a consent order as to mode of trial).

Where a consent order is executory, ie requires one party to take certain steps, the court may, in cases of hardship or injustice refuse the other party any assistance in enforcing the order; this is akin to refusing a degree of specific performance of a contract (*Thwaite v Thwaite* [1982] Fam 1).

The main ground of the decision in *Siebe Gorman Ltd v Pneupac Ltd* (above) was that a distinction should be made between consent orders entered in pursuance of a real contract between the parties and orders where the words 'by consent' merely mean 'the parties hereto not objecting'. In the latter category it is the consent, not the command of the court, which is to be regarded as superadded and thus the court is free to make any variation of its command as it could normally make had the order not been consensual. This is similar to the principle which applies to consent orders in matrimonial proceedings (see *Thwaite v Thwaite*). In such a case a party who later wishes to challenge the order may also do so by appeal, even in the case of a consent order made by a district judge in the county court (*Director General of Fair Trading v Stuart* [1990] 1 WLR 1500).

Trial court's power to order a rehearing

In the county court, unless there has been a trial by jury (which is exceptionally rare) the trial court has power to order a rehearing of the whole or any part of the proceedings (see generally CCR Ord 37, r 1). The power is confined to cases in which no error by the trial court is alleged. The rule is intended as a convenient and economic procedure for correcting technical or procedural slips made by the parties: the proper forum in which to allege errors made by the trial court itself is the Court of Appeal. Any rehearing permitted will not be a fresh trial: the judge who is conducting the rehearing will merely review the evidence previously given and any further evidence which (on well-settled principles, *see Ladd v Marshall* [1954] 1 WLR 1489, noted on p 662) it is permissible to adduce.

An application for a rehearing should be made on notice served on the opposite party not more than fourteen days after the day of the trial and not less than seven days before the day fixed for the hearing of the application (as to the court's power to extend any time period fixed by the rules, see p 10). Once a hearing date is fixed the court will usually retain any money in court until the application has been heard. As far as practicable an application for a rehearing should be made to the same judge who heard the trial.

The High Court has no power to order a rehearing (except in cases under special procedural codes such as the Matrimonial Causes Rules 1977) and thus an application must be made to the Court of Appeal (RSC Ord 59, r 2). Although SCA 1981, s 17 enables the making of rules similar to the county court rule no such rules have been made. On the contrary the nearest equivalent High Court rules were revoked in 1988 (see the former RSC Ord 58, r 6).

Amending orders under the slip rule

The slip rule (described on p 519) is included here only to distinguish it. Under this rule the court merely alters the wording of its previous order; it does not alter any rights the parties were intended to have under that order.

The Court of Appeal Civil Division

The Court of Appeal Civil Division is composed of the Master of the Rolls, Lords Justice of Appeal and certain other senior judges by virtue of the office they hold. Much of the administration of the business of the court is the responsibility of the registrar of civil appeals. Practitioners have been invited and encouraged to seek guidance from the registrar or his staff on any points of difficulty which may arise in the bringing of an appeal. Requests for guidance should be directed to the Civil Appeals General Office, Royal Courts of Justice, room E330; the telephone numbers are given in *White Book* 59/1/8.

Jurisdiction of the registrar

The registrar of civil appeals has jurisdiction to deal with the majority of applications which are incidental to an appeal and do not involve its determination, ie all applications concerning the fixing of hearing dates, the documents to be used and their amendment, applications for the extension or abridgment of time periods fixed by the rules (even if such an application, in effect, determines an appeal, see SCA 1981, s 58(3)) and most of the general powers of the court as to matters such as orders as to security for costs or as to change of parties, etc (for the exceptions, see below). Application made to the registrar, whether *ex parte* or by summons must be heard in chambers. An appeal lies as of right from his decision to a single judge of the Court of Appeal by way of fresh application within ten days and thereafter, from the judge to the full Court of Appeal, if the full court grants leave.

Jurisdiction of a single judge of the Court of Appeal

If appropriate, any application incidental to an appeal may be made direct to a single judge, or may be referred to him by the registrar. Unlike the registrar, a single judge also has jurisdiction in relation to the grant, variation, discharge or enforcement of injunctions (or undertakings in lieu of injunctions, see p 610) and the grant or lifting of stays of execution or stays of proceedings. A single judge also has jurisdiction to grant leave to appeal (see further overleaf). Applications to a single judge are made by summons and, unless otherwise directed, are to be heard in chambers. A judge's grant or refusal of leave to appeal, if made in open court, is final. On all other decisions (eg a refusal of leave which is made upon an application in writing or an open court decision on an ancillary matter) an appeal lies to the full Court of Appeal by way of fresh application. No leave is required unless the decision was made by way of appeal from the registrar (see above). On an appeal from a discretionary order made by a judge, the full court will not seek to exercise its own discretion unless it can be shown that the judge erred in principle (see case law cited in the

White Book 59/14/14; contrast an appeal from the registrar to the single judge, compare an appeal from a High Court or county court judge to the Court of Appeal, p 666).

Applications to the Court of Appeal

If appropriate any application incidental to an appeal may be made direct to the full court (for a list of examples see *White Book* 59/14/1 para 12), or may be referred to it by a single judge, or sometimes may be taken there by way of appeal from a single judge. However, the main business of the full court is to determine the appeal itself. The court has jurisdiction to hear appeals from both the High Court and the county court. As a general rule the court hearing the appeal must consist of an uneven number of judges not less than three (SCA 1981, s 54: note Parliament's wise avoidance of the expression 'odd number of judges'). However, two-judge courts are empowered to hear certain types of appeal including the following:

(1) All county court appeals.
(2) Interlocutory appeals from the High Court, including appeals from proceedings under RSC Ords 14 and 86 (see p 230).
(3) Appeals from district judges which lie direct to the Court of Appeal (see p 645).
(4) Appeals from a single judge of the Court of Appeal.

Unless a specific application is made, these appeals will be automatically listed for a two-judge court. For the full list of appeals which may be determined by a court of two judges see SCA 1981, s 54(4), the Court of Appeal (Civil Division) Order 1982 and *White Book* 5247 *et seq*. Is the authority of a two-judge court convened under these rules the same as that of a three-judge court? The better view appears to be that the number of judges involved does not affect the doctrine of *stare decisis* (*Langley v North West Water Authority* [1991] 1 WLR 697) and see further *White Book* 4629; for authority to the contrary (see *Welsh Development Agency v Redpath Dorman Long Ltd* [1994] 1 WLR 1409).

The SCA 1981, s 54(5) provides a tie-breaker in the event of an appeal being heard by an even number of judges who, in the result, are equally divided as to what the decision should be; the case must, if any party so applies, be re-argued before and determined by an uneven number of judges not less than three, before any appeal is made to the House of Lords.

Some cases are not suitable for determination by a two-judge court; eg because they raise issues of real difficulty or of general importance, or because they are urgent and so the danger of a possible disagreement is too great (*Cambridge Nutrition Ltd v British Broadcasting Corp* [1990] 3 All ER 523). In such cases either party can apply to the registrar for a direction that the hearing should take place before a three-judge court. In practice such applications are not made as often as they might be (see

Wandsworth LBC v Winder [1985] AC 461 *per* Ackner LJ in the Court of Appeal; *National Westminster Bank plc v Morgan* [1985] AC 686 *per* Lord Scarman; *Coldunell Ltd v Gallon* [1986] 2 WLR 466 *per* Oliver and Purchas LJJ; and *Cambridge Nutrition Ltd per* Kerr LJ). There can never be any harm in acknowledging the urgency or true importance of a case. However, perhaps understandably, comparatively few advocates are prepared to acknowledge that their case is difficult. Ultimately a solution may have to be found in a redefinition of those cases automatically listed for a two-judge court (see *Coldunell per* Purchas LJ).

Procedure on appeals

Application for leave to appeal

Where leave to appeal is required (see p 647) the application should be made initially to the court which made the order appealed from. If that court refuses leave a fresh application can be made *ex parte* in writing to a single judge of the Court of Appeal. The application impliedly includes an application for leave to extend the time for appealing where this is necessary. The judge who deals with the application may grant leave, refuse leave or, alternatively, may direct that the application should be renewed in open court either *ex parte* or *inter partes*.

If leave is granted, notice of that order will be served on the parties affected by it who will then have seven days to apply to have the grant of leave reconsidered *inter partes* in open court and before a different judge; in order to succeed at that hearing they will have to show the substantive appeal will inevitably fail (*The Iran Nabuvat* [1990] 1 WLR 1115; further guidance is given in *Smith v Cosworth Casting Process Ltd* (1997) *The Times*, 26 February). As to the documentation (including skeleton arguments), the costs of copy documentation and the time allowed for oral argument, see a *Practice Direction* of 1995 (*White Book* 59/9/17 para 9; because of the time limits on oral argument, usually a maximum of 20 minutes *per* advocate, this division of the court has come to be known as the 'blitz court').

If leave is refused, notice of that refusal will be given to the applicant who then has seven days to renew his application, *ex parte* again, but this time in open court and before two judges. An applicant who is legally aided must also notify the relevant legal aid office (*Practice Direction* of 1995 above, para 6). As to the factors to be taken into account in deciding whether to grant leave, see *White Book* 59/14/7.

Where leave to appeal is required, a valid notice of appeal (see overleaf) cannot be served unless and until leave has been granted. Accordingly, it is not possible to raise the application for leave to appeal in the notice of appeal itself. The process of applying, first to the court which made the decision under appeal, and then, if necessary, to the Court of Appeal, may well take longer than the four-week time limit for appealing which is allowed. It is therefore important to note that every application for leave which is made to the Court of Appeal automatically includes an application for an extension of time for appealing (see above) and that, on every application for leave which is made to the Court of Appeal *within the four-week period*, any order granting leave automatically extends that period for seven days from the date of the order (see RSC Ord 59, r 4 and p 647, above).

Applications for extension of time for appealing

If the four-week period has not yet expired, an application for an extension of time can be made either to the court which made the decision under appeal ('the lower court') or to the Court of Appeal (RSC Ord 59, r 15). If leave to appeal is also required both applications should be made to the lower court before resorting if necessary to the Court of Appeal.

If the four-week period has already expired the application for an extension of time can be made only to the Court of Appeal. The application should be made to the registrar, or, if leave to appeal is also required, to the single judge as described above. Where leave to appeal is also required it is considered impracticable to apply to the lower court first as this would entail the making of two separate applications. An application for extension of time is impliedly included in an application to the single judge for leave to appeal (see generally *White Book* 59/14/7).

As to the factors to be taken into account in deciding whether to grant an extension of time for appealing, see *White Book* 59/4/4. The decision of the registrar (or indeed of the single judge) is not final: a further appeal can be made (see *Rickards v Rickards* [1990] Fam 194).

Notice of appeal

An appeal is brought by a notice specifying the grounds of appeal and the precise form of the order the appellant proposes to ask the court to make and specifying the list of appeals to which he proposes that the appeal should be assigned (for a precedent see *White Book* 59/3/9 and, as to the lists of appeals which are kept, see *White Book* 59/3/7). The notice must be served on the respondent on or before the last day of the period allowed for appealing: ordinary service is sufficient. On an appeal from the county court the notice of appeal must contain or be accompanied by a statement as to value (RSC Ord 59, r 3A) and a copy of the notice must also be served on the district judge of that county court. A notice of appeal does not have to be 'sealed' or 'issued' by the Court of Appeal prior to service; valuable time may be lost if the intending appellant wrongly sends it to the court for this purpose.

At the hearing the appellant will have no right to rely on any ground or to apply for any relief not specified in the notice of appeal. However, amendments may be made without leave by the service of a 'supplementary notice' at any time before the date on which the appeal first appears in the List of Forthcoming Appeals (see overleaf). Thereafter the leave of the registrar (or higher authority) is necessary (RSC Ord 59, r 7).

Setting down

Within seven days after the service of the notice of appeal (or within seven days after the entry of judgment, if later) the appellant must set down the appeal which he does by lodging in court the prescribed fee, a copy of the order appealed from and two copies of the notice of appeal. Before accepting them, the counter staff at the Civil Appeals Office will make a preliminary check of the papers and, if they appear to be in order, will send them for a further check by legal staff at the Office. Papers which appear not to be in order will be returned to the appellant who, if aggrieved, must now make application to the registrar. If the papers lodged do appear to be in order the appeal will then be entered in the records of the court and the appellant will be informed by letter that the appeal has been set down. Within four days of receipt of that letter the appellant must give notice of it to the respondent (see generally RSC Ord 59, r 5). Setting down an appeal is a step taken by the appellant not the court. This step is not a true equivalent of the setting down of a High Court action for trial (see p 482). Rather, it amounts to commencement of the appeal as far as the Court of Appeal is concerned; it does not mean that the appeal is ready for hearing. Even so the subsequent time limits (see below) are so short as to make it unwise to postpone the preparation of documents until after setting down. However, neither can one safely delay the setting down itself. The preliminary check and legal scrutiny will by themselves take some time and if mistakes are made in preparing the papers they may be returned; the process of setting down may therefore take several days to complete. After the r 5 time limit has expired an application for extension of time must be made (to the registrar); as to whether an extension will be granted see *White Book* 59/4/4.

Respondent's notice

This notice is furnished by a respondent who desires:

(a) to contend on the appeal that the decision of the court below should be varied, either in any event or in the event of the appeal being allowed in whole or in part, or
(b) to contend that the decision of the court below should be affirmed on grounds other than those relied upon by that court, or
(c) to contend by way of cross-appeal that the decision of the court below was wrong in whole or in part (RSC Ord 59, r 6).

The notice must specify the grounds of his contention and, if (a) or (c) applies, the precise form of order he proposes to ask the court to make. It must be served within twenty-one days of service of the notice of appeal and the respondent must within four days after service (or within four days after being notified that the appeal has been set down, if later) deliver two copies of the notice to the court (RSC Ord 59, r 6). As with a notice of appeal a supplementary notice may be served without leave before the date on which the appeal first appears in the List of Forthcoming Appeals.

As to the strict enforcement of the twenty-one-day time limit, particularly in cases where (a) or (c) above apply (which are in reality cross-appeals) see *VCS Ltd v Magmasters Ltd* [1984] 1 WLR 1208.

List of Forthcoming Appeals

The letter sent by the court when acknowledging the setting down, not only informs the appellant of the number allocated to the appeal and the list to which it is assigned, but also specifies the date upon which it is intended to include the appeal in the List of Forthcoming Appeals (*White Book* 59/9/2). This date marks the start of the fourteen-day time period allowed for the lodgment of further documents (see below).

Save in cases of urgency the appeal may be heard at any time after fourteen days from the date the case first appeared in the List. In practice, the exact date cannot normally be calculated until after the further documents are lodged and a fixture is made, see below; save for urgent cases, the normal time lag between setting down and hearing is indicated by a table showing the 'hear-by' dates covering different types of case (see *White Book* 59/1/13 and *Practice Direction (Court of Appeal: Revised Procedure)* [1997] 1 WLR 1031).

Lodgment of bundles and advocate's time estimates

After the time for service of the notice of appeal and any respondent's notice the court will have already received a copy of the order of the court which made the decision under appeal and two copies of the notice of appeal and two copies of the respondent's notice (see above).

Not more than fourteen days after the appeal first appears in the List of Forthcoming Appeals the appellant must deliver to the court the further papers necessary for the hearing, ie three bundles of documents (two bundles if the appeal is to be heard by two judges) each including copies of:

(1) the notice of appeal plus any statement of value required (see p 658);

(2) any respondent's notice;

(3) the order of the court below;

(4) the pleadings (if any);

(5) transcripts of the shorthand note or recording of the evidence and the judgment or, if none, the written judgment or the judge's note of the evidence and his reasons for giving the judgment (for High Court cases see RSC Ord 68, r 1, for county court cases see CCR Ord 50, r 9B; and see also *White Book* 59/9/5 *et seq*).

The full texts of the relevant rule (RSC Ord 59, r 9) and of the current *Practice Directions* are important and should be consulted (see also RSC

Ord 59, r 12A as to non-disclosure of a payment into court and p 344). They indicate that it is essential for the appellant to start preparing the documents as soon as it has been decided to appeal. Recent innovations are the requirement to supply opponents with copy bundles (not just the indices thereto) and increased emphasis on the need for core bundles (documents essential to assisted pre-reading and those likely to be referred to in oral argument) and the responsibility of the solicitor having the conduct of the case to check personally that the documentation is in order before it is delivered to the court. Practice as to core bundle was further revised in the 1997 *Practice Direction* (see above) in a further attempt to eliminate unecessary documentation.

Where there are good reasons why the bundles cannot be lodged within the fourteen-day period the appellant should apply for an extension of time. Non-compliance with r 9 may result in the appeal being listed to show cause why it should not be dismissed. The reason why Court of Appeal timetables are to be strictly complied with was explained in *A Co v K Ltd* [1987] 1 WLR 1655.

> The duty of the Court of Appeal is in a sense a supervisory duty. It has to ensure that the trials are conducted correctly and that the result is in accordance with law. But it is a jurisdiction which has to be exercised with the maximum possible expedition as otherwise successful parties, like the [respondents] in this case might well be deprived of the fruits of their judgments. Therefore this court has always taken the line that there must be strict compliance with timetables laid down, in stark contrast to the attitude taken by the trial courts. Again in deciding whether to strike out appeals on account of delay this court has not had regard to whether the respondent has been prejudiced. It has simply said that the timetables laid down are to be strictly complied with in the interests of all who resort to the Court of Appeal (*per* Sir John Donaldson MR).

A second obligation to lodge documents with the court in the fourteen-day period after the appeal first appears in the List of Forthcoming Appeals affects all parties who will be represented by an advocate (whether a solicitor with a Higher Courts Advocacy Qualification or a barrister) at the hearing. The court will supply the appellant's solicitor with a form which is to be signed by the appellant's advocate stating his or her estimate of the length of time the hearing of the appeal will take. The advocate is duty-bound to ensure that this form, duly completed, is returned to the court, and that a photocopy of the form is forwarded to the respondent's advocate (if any). The respondent's advocate must consider the appellant's advocate's estimate immediately on receipt and, if his or her own estimate is different, must so indicate on the photocopy and must then immediately lodge the photocopy with the court. If the respondent's advocate does not lodge such a document he or she is deemed to accept the accuracy of the appellant's advocate's estimate (see generally *Practice Direction* of 1995, *White Book* 59/9/17B paras 14–19).

Obtaining realistic and up-to-date time estimates vitally affects the efficient listing of appeals. The *Practice Direction* of 1995 (see above) requires that a copy of the estimate must be placed and kept with each advocate's papers. Thereafter, the advocates should reconsider the estimate on every subsequent occasion on which they are instructed in that appeal.

The registrar's directions

At any time after the appeal has been set down, the registrar must give such directions in relation to the documents to be produced at the appeal, and the manner in which they are to be presented, and as to other matters incidental to the conduct of the appeal, as appear best adapted to secure the just, expeditious and economical disposal of the appeal. The directions are given without a hearing unless the registrar issues a summons for requiring the parties to attend before him or the parties themselves apply for an appointment. As to the forms of summonses and applications, and as to the fees payable see *White Book* 59/14/2, 59/14/16 *et seq.*

There are many matters upon which the parties may apply for directions; for example—

(1) As to security for costs (see p 317); the application should be made at an early stage. Time 'is of the essence in the Court of Appeal in all respects, whether we are talking about applications by appellants or respondents' (*A Co v K Ltd* [1987] 1 WLR 1655 *per* Sir John Donaldson MR).

(2) Directions varying the requirement to lodge certain documents or extending the time for doing so. In many cases delay occurs because the parties fail to deal promptly enough with the need to obtain a note of the judgment and submit it to the judge for his comments (*White Book* 59/9/6). Such delays may lead to penalty orders for costs (see p 523).

(3) Directions as to the listing of appeals for hearing, such as listing important interlocutory appeals for hearing before a three-judge court (see p 656).

(4) Directions concerning the reception of further evidence at the hearing of the appeal. There is a restriction on such evidence in any case in which there has been a 'trial or hearing on the merits' (RSC Ord 59, r 10(2)). Except in the case of evidence of matters which have occurred since the hearing the appellant must show that the further evidence (*a*) could not have been discovered with reasonable diligence before the trial; (*b*) would have an important influence on the case; and (*c*) is apparently credible (*Ladd v Marshall* [1954] 1 WLR 1489; this restriction does not apply to interlocutory appeals unless they involve a 'hearing on the merits', for the meaning of which, see *White Book* 59/10/8). There is nonetheless a clear duty on parties to present their full case at first instance; it is very undesirable if interlocutory disputes are argued out afresh on appeal on different materials never put before the judge whose

primary decision it is (see *per* Bingham LJ in *Thune v London Properties Ltd* [1990] 1 WLR 562).

(5) Dismissals by consent: a notice of appeal once served cannot normally be withdrawn. If, after service, the appellant decides to abandon the appeal or if the parties agree to compromise their dispute, the appeal can be dismissed by consent on filing the necessary form (see generally *White Book* 59/1/15 *et seq*). The dismissal by consent may make provision for the costs of appeal. However, any other agreed terms, eg as to compensation payable or as to the costs in the court below, must be dealt with, if at all, by way of a separate contract of compromise. The court will not normally make an order in *'Tomlin'* form (as to which, see p 371). Nor will it normally permit an appeal to be allowed by consent. A dismissal by consent will not affect any cross-appeal unless the form used expressly so states and is duly completed by the respondent.

(6) Orders striking out the appeal may be made, eg for failure to set down the appeal, for failure to lodge the appeal bundles, for failure to lodge skeleton arguments (see below), or if it is clear and obvious that the appeal is hopeless or that a statement of value given is grossly inaccurate (RSC Ord 59, r 19(5A)). If, after setting down, the appellant fails to lodge the appeal bundles, time estimate or skeleton arguments and fails to apply for an extension of the time in which to do so, the appeal will be listed for a hearing for the appellant to show cause why it should not be dismissed *White Book* 59/9/13.

Delivery of skeleton arguments

The delivery of skeleton arguments is now compulsory in all applications listed for hearing before the full court and in all appeals save those heard as a matter of great urgency and those in which the court expressly orders them to be dispensed with. At least fourteen days before any date fixed for the hearing of the appeal, each party must deliver to his opponent one copy and to the court four copies of a concise statement of the submissions that party intends to make at the hearing. Skeleton arguments are not intended to diminish the importance of oral arguments. Their purpose is to identify points, not to argue them. They should not normally exceed ten pages in the case of an appeal on law and fifteen pages in the case of an appeal on fact. Points of law should be stated succinctly and any authorities relied on should be cited with references to the particular pages upon which reliance is placed (the official law reports are preferred; if specialist reports are relied on photocopies must be supplied to the court and, if the case also appears in the official law reports, an explanation given as to why the specialist report is being relied on instead). Questions of fact being raised should be identified, a statement given of the basis which, it is contended, justifies any interference with the judge's findings of fact and cross references made to any relevant passages in the transcripts or notes of evidence.

The appellant's skeleton argument should be accompanied by a separate chronology of events relevant to the appeal. A respondent's skeleton argument should refer to any authority or point of evidence the respondent will rely on which is not dealt with in the judgment of the court below. However, if the respondent's case is simply that the judgment is correct for the reasons it gives, the respondent can deliver a letter to that effect in lieu of a skeleton argument.

When first introduced, skeleton arguments were voluntary and were delivered, if at all, immediately before the hearing. Nowadays they are compulsory in virtually all cases and must be delivered at an early stage of the appeal. The change in practice was made in order to secure the following advantages. They enable the court to undertake effective pre-reading (see below) and to adjust if necessary the time estimates and listing arrangements. They bring forward the point of time at which the parties, especially the appellant, must decide whether to press on or settle: early settlements maximise the saving of costs to the parties and minimise the wastage of court time caused by doorstep settlements. Skeleton arguments save time spent at the hearing of the appeal; oral argument can at that stage be devoted to making the relevant points, not working up to making them.

Exact details as to the timetable and documentation required for skeleton arguments are given in the *Practice Direction* of 1995 *White Book* 59/9/17, paras 36–50). Before the relevant deadline arrives each advocate must prepare his skeleton argument and send one copy to his opponent and lodge four copies with the court.

The time limit will be strictly enforced (see p 661). If the deadline would otherwise expire on a day on which the Civil Appeals Office is closed, the skeleton arguments must be lodged *before* that day. If skeleton arguments are not lodged in time, the appeal will automatically be listed in a 'dismissal list'. Applications for an extension of time must be made (if possible by letter or fax) by the advocate, not by the advocate's clerk or instructing solicitor.

Arranging hearing dates

For most cases a date for the hearing of the appeal will be fixed. This is done as soon as possible after the court has received and checked the appeal bundles and time estimates, and is often done after discussions with counsel's clerks. The appeal will then come on for hearing on the date fixed or on the following sitting day although there remains a possibility that, because of other changes to the listing arrangements, the date of hearing may later have to be rearranged. A major cause of rearrangement is the need to accommodate subsequent appeals which are more urgent: as to current practice on these, ie expedited appeals, see *Unilever plc v Chefaro Proprietaries Ltd (Practice Note)* [1995] 1 WLR 242.

Every effort is made to achieve greater certainty in relation to hearing dates. This is one reason why applications to delay the hearing of an appeal will not be readily granted even if made by consent of all parties unless some good reason is shown (see *Unilever Computer Services Ltd v Tiger Leasing SA* [1983] 1 WLR 856). However, the court has now established two ways of minimising the waste of court time which can be caused by changes in the fixtures list; second fixtures for some cases and the Short Warned List.

Second fixtures are dates given to some cases which already have one fixed date. The second fixture is an earlier date upon which the appeal may be heard if other hearings listed for that day are later cancelled. This form of double booking works very well so long as information about the cancellation of earlier cases is received sufficiently far in advance to enable adequate notice to be given to the parties given the second fixture.

In some cases, instead of being given a fixed date, an appeal will be assigned to the Short Warned List. This comprises cases selected by the court as being relatively short appeals which can reasonably be prepared by substitute advocates at short notice should the parties' chosen advocates be unavailable when the appeal is called on. Normally notice of assignment to the Short Warned List will be given at least three weeks before the date from which the case will be 'on call'.

Lodging lists of authorities

Advocates must ensure that lists of authorities including textbooks are lodged with the Head Usher's office not later than 5.30 pm on the working day before the day when the hearing is to commence (and see further, *Practice Direction* of 1995, *White Book* 59/1/12, p 928). It is also customary for advocates to notify each other of the authorities they will rely on if such authorities are not already disclosed in their skeleton arguments.

Hearing of the appeal

An appeal to the Court of Appeal is 'by way of rehearing' (RSC Ord 59, r 3). Generally it is a rehearing on documents only, the appellant having the right to begin, but the words quoted indicate that:
   (1) the appellant is not limited to complaining of irregularities in the hearing of the trial: he can simply ask the Court of Appeal to review the decision of the court below;
   (2) the court (unlike the parties) is not confined to the points raised in the notice of appeal, etc;
   (3) the court is not confined to making an order which should have been made by the court below but may consider what facts have occurred since the trial (see *White Book* 59/10/10) and what relevant change has been made in the law (eg retrospective legislation or a new ruling in another case, see *McCauley v Cammell Laird Shipbuilders Ltd* [1990] 1 WLR 963).

Although appeals to it are said to be 'by way of rehearing' the Court of
Appeal never embarks upon a retrial since to do so would authorise and
compel the parties to refight their battle all over again. If the Court of
Appeal is satisfied that a retrial is appropriate it has power to remit the
case to the lower court for that purpose. Indeed parties have a right to a
retrial if, in the opinion of the Court of Appeal, some substantial wrong or
miscarriage has been occasioned (RSC Ord 59, r 11). In less extreme
cases the Court of Appeal may instead simply substitute its own decision
for that of the lower court (whether judge or jury, see RSC Ord 59, r 11;
for a recent example see *John v MGN Ltd* [1996] 3 WLR 593).

Perhaps because an appeal by way of rehearing is not a retrial, an
appeal to the Court of Appeal differs in two respects from an appeal to a
High Court judge in chambers (the nature of appeals to a county court
judge varies according to the rule governing the appeal; see CCR Ords
13, rr 1 and 37, r 6 noted in p 646). First, the High Court judge in
chambers, hearing an appeal from a district judge, always considers the
matter as if no previous ruling had been given. The Court of Appeal
considers appeals to it quite differently. It accepts the decision previously
made unless it is persuaded to do otherwise: a burden of proof is placed
upon the appellant to show, eg that the judge was wrong in his decision
on questions of fact (see *White Book* 59/1/58) or wrong as to his exercise
of a discretion (see *White Book* 59/1/59) or wrong in his decision as to
quantum of damages (see *White Book* 59/10/16). Secondly, the Court of
Appeal, unlike the High Court judge in chambers, displays an unwillingness to allow parties to raise before it new points which could have been,
but were not, raised before the lower court (see *White Book* 59/10/6) or to
adduce new evidence which could have been, but was not, adduced to the
lower court (see p 662).

The reluctance of appellate courts to interfere with the decision of
lower courts in interlocutory matters is explained in a *dictum* of Lord
Diplock concerning appeals to the House of Lords which was quoted and
applied in respect of an appeal to the Court of Appeal in *Procon (Great
Britain) Ltd v Provincial Building Co Ltd* [1984] 1 WLR 557.

> It is only very exceptionally that an appeal upon an interlocutory order is
> allowed to come before this House. These are matters best left to the decision
> of the masters and, on appeal, the judges of the High Court whose daily
> experience and concern is with the trial of civil actions. They are decisions
> which involve balancing against one another a variety of relevant consider-
> ations upon which opinions of individual judges may reasonably differ as to
> their relative weight in a particular case. That is why they are said to involve
> the exercise by the judge of his 'discretion' (*per* Lord Diplock in *Birkett v
> James* [1978] AC 297).

Thus, the preferred policy is not to interfere where the judge has not erred
in law or principle or reached a conclusion in the exercise of his
discretion which falls outside 'the generous ambit within which a
reasonable disagreement is possible' (for example, see *Oyston v Blaker*

[1996] 1 WLR 1326 at 1336). In order to defeat this policy appellants will sometimes strain to find errors of law as principle in the judge's reasoning. Consider carefully the following *dictum* of Lord Donaldson MR.

> I am bound to say that, while it is difficult to dislodge discretionary decisions by judges where they are truly discretionary, it is surprising in some fields, and particularly in the field of commercial law, how often a point of principle emerges from the woodwork when the discretion of the judge is being analysed (*per* Lord Donaldson MR in *The Iran Nabuvat* [1990] 1 WLR 1115).

Conduct of the hearing

Gone are the opening speeches, the lengthy recital of facts and the quotation *in extenso* of pages of authorities and transcripts. Whatever the estimated length of the hearing, the court will (wherever possible) form its own estimate (based on the judgment appealed from, the notice of appeal and the skeleton arguments lodged) and will limit the time for oral argument accordingly (*Practice Direction* of 1995; *White Book* 59/9/17 para 19).

Delivery of judgments

After the hearing of the appeal the court will often adjourn for judgment to be given at a later date. The parties will be notified when the judgment is ready, but to save time, ie to save time attending merely to hear the judges read out their judgment, it is now the normal practice for a judgment to be handed down in writing on a day prior to the adjourned hearing date. The written judgment is still confidential at this stage and a 'time embargo' will be noted upon it. This enables the parties to consider whether it is necessary to make further applications to the court, eg for costs (ie the costs 'here and below'); or for leave to appeal to the House of Lords (see further *Practice Direction (Court of Appeal: Handed Down Judgments)* [1995] 1 WLR 1055).

Appeals to the House of Lords

About one tenth of the cases which go to the Court of Appeal Civil Division are taken on further appeal to the House of Lords. Under the Administration of Justice (Appeals) Act 1934 the prospective appellant must obtain leave to appeal either from the Court of Appeal or from the House of Lords itself. The criteria upon which leave is granted include: (*a*) the general public importance of the case; (*b*) the likelihood of success; and (*c*) often the most significant, the degree of dissension the case may have previously caused, ie the Court of Appeal decided by a majority and/or reversed the trial judge's decision (see generally Blom-Cooper and Drewry, *Final Appeal* (1972), pp 125, 134; *Lonrho Ltd v Shell Petroleum Co Ltd* [1980] 1 WLR 627, HL; and *Garden Cottage Foods Ltd v Milk Marketing Board* [1984] AC 130). It is quite wrong to assume that, if the House refuses leave to appeal, it thereby impliedly indicates some approval of the decision sought to be appealed, *Re Wilson* [1985] AC 750.

The procedure on appeal to the House of Lords is governed by standing orders (see *White Book* Vol 2 Pt 16). What follows is a brief introduction to two of the main forms of petition, the petition for leave to appeal (or leave to appeal out of time) and the petition of appeal or cross-appeal. Both forms of petition are prescribed. Neither of them operates as a stay of execution of any order appealed from. A party seeking a stay should apply to the court below, not to the House of Lords (*Practice Direction (House of Lords: Procedure Amendments) (No 2)* [1996] 1 WLR 1220).

The title of the proceedings will be the same as the title in the court below. Save as stated below in relation to leapfrog appeals, a copy of the petition must be served on the respondents or their agents either by delivery in person or by first-class post. They must also be given notice of the intention to present the petition on or after a specified day. The original petition must then be 'presented' (ie lodged) in the Judicial Office of the House of Lords indorsed with a certificate of service.

Respondents intending to take part in the proceedings should enter an appearance (ie give details of their names and addresses to the Judicial Office by post or in person) as soon as they have received service. Also, parties intending to take no part in the proceedings should so notify the Judicial Office. On a petition for leave to appeal no fees are payable save as to taxation of costs. On a petition of appeal, fees are payable on lodging the petition, on entering appearances and at other stages (*White Book* Vol 2 16-116). Solicitors outside London are not now required to appoint London agents. However, if they do not, and if this increases the costs incurred, the increased costs may be disallowed on taxation. London agents are intended to act as a point of liaison with the Judicial Office and it is expected that all communications are made through them (*White Book* Vol 2 16-031A).

Special provisions are made for commencement in the case of a leapfrog appeal. The petition for leave to appeal may be presented by all or any of the parties. If it is presented by some of them it need not be served on the others, although they must be given notice of the intention to present.

Next after commencement comes a short period of time in which to prepare for and complete the lodging of papers (by the appellant in the case of a petition for leave to appeal) or the lodging and exchanging of cases (by all parties in a petition of appeal or cross-appeal). Once the paperwork is complete the proceedings will move forward for determination by an Appeal Committee or an Appellate Committee, as the case may be (see further, below).

If any costs are awarded bills for taxation must be lodged with the Judicial Office within three months of the date of the relevant committee's judgment or decision. All orders of the House of Lords which reverse or vary orders of a lower court must be made orders of the High Court (see further RSC Ord 32, r 10). For the purposes of enforcement, other orders of the House of Lords (eg an order for costs) may also be made orders of the High Court.

Petition for leave to appeal

An application for leave must first be made to the Court of Appeal (unless of course it is a leapfrog appeal). The time limit for an application to the House of Lords is one month from the date of the judgment or order being appealed, or within such extended time as the House of Lords may allow. An application for leave and for an extension of time may both be included in the same petition. The time limit for leave is automatically extended in cases in which an application for legal aid has been made. However, in such a case, the application for legal aid must be reported to the Judicial Office before the one-month period expires and notification of the proposed petition must be given to the other parties. The time limit for the appellant to lodge the necessary papers is just one week after the lodgment of the petition.

A petition for leave to appeal (or leave to appeal out of time) is usually referred to an Appeal Committee consisting of three Lords of Appeal. In the case of a leapfrog appeal, the application for leave is always determined without a hearing. In many other cases also the application for leave to appeal will be determined without a hearing ie cases where the Appeal Committee reaches a unanimous decision, whether for or against the grant of leave (a unanimous decision for the grant of leave is provisional only and the respondents will be invited to lodge written objections). A hearing will be convened in cases in which the opinions of the members of the Appeal Committee are divided, or where, for some other reason, oral argument is required. The likely time delay between lodging all necessary papers and obtaining some notification thereon is eight sitting weeks. As to applications for expedited consideration see direction 4.17 (*White Book* Vol 2 16-024 supplement, [1997] 1 WLR 167). At a hearing only one agent or counsel may appear on each side and, if costs are awarded, no fees will be allowed in excess of a junior counsel's fee. As to the costs of proceedings determined without a hearing, see *White Book* Vol 2 Pt 16 direction 5.1. An Appeal Committee never gives reasons for its decisions.

Petition of appeal or cross-appeal

A party can commence an appeal or cross-appeal only if *either*:
(1) the Court of Appeal has granted leave and the petition is presented within three months of the decision appealed from (in the case of an appeal) or within six weeks of an appeal (in the case of a

cross-appeal). In the case of an appeal there is an automatic extension of time in cases in which an application for legal aid has been made but, in this instance, it is still necessary to give information about the case to the Judicial Office and to the respondents before the initial period expires; or

(2) the House of Lords (in determining an earlier petition, see above) has already granted leave to appeal and/or has already extended the time for appealing.

On commencing an appeal the appellant must give security for costs by payment of £18,000 into the House of Lords Security Fund Account. No interest is payable on security moneys. Security is not required from an appellant who has been granted legal aid, an appellant in a cross-appeal, or in any other case in which all the respondents agree to security for costs being waived (see generally *White Book* vol 2 16-038, 16-039 and 16-116).

The time limit for the appellants to prepare and lodge their 'Statement of Facts and Issues' and the 'Appendix' and to set down the appeal is six weeks from the presentation of the appeal. House of Lords cases are, *ex hypothesi*, cases of general public importance which have already resulted in several previous hearings in the lower courts. It is therefore not surprising that the amount of documentation which has to be prepared and lodged within six weeks of the presentation of the petition is, on any view, formidable.

Statement of facts and issues

This is a comparatively brief document which will be read in conjunction with the Appendix (see below). It must summarise the facts and issues involved in the appeal but need not contain any account of the proceedings below or the judgments previously given. Appellants and respondents must seek to collaborate in the preparation of the statement. However, if they cannot agree the appellants' statement the respondents may prepare their own which should then be appended to the appellants'.

Appendix

This should contain any extracts from documents used in evidence or in recording proceedings if they are clearly necessary for the support and understanding of the argument of the appeal. References to the contents of the Appendix must be entered in the outside margin of the statement of facts and issues (see above). The costs of preparing the Appendix initially falls on the appellants but its contents 'must be agreed between the parties' (*White Book* Vol 2 Pt 16 direction 13.1).

Time estimates

Within seven days of setting down (ie within seven weeks of presentation of the petition) each party must notify the Judicial Office of the amount of time in hours considered necessary to present that party's case. A hearing date will then be arranged.

Appellants' and respondents' cases

As soon as possible after setting down and in any event no later than two weeks before the proposed date of hearing the parties are required to lodge their 'cases' ie a succinct statement of the arguments to be made on their behalf (and see further direction 16.3–16.7). The lodgment of a case carries the right to be heard by two counsel one of whom may be leading counsel.

Respondents also are required to lodge a case: the time limit for them is as for appellants or within fourteen days after lodgment of the appellants' case if longer. Respondents can lodge separate cases if it can be shown that some conflict of interests arises between them (contrast appellants who must always combine together to lodge a single case and compare p 96). Respondents acting as such are not entitled to lodge a case which seeks some variation of the decision of the court below. Contentions of that nature must be made the subject of a separate petition of cross-appeal. It is very important to note that the presentation of a petition of appeal does not entitle the respondents to present a cross-appeal; they, like the appellant must first obtain leave, either from the court below or from an Appeal Committee.

Parties must exchange cases but there is no obligation to do so before lodging them. For a table showing the number of documents and copies normally required for the hearing of an appeal see *White Book* Vol 2 Pt 16 16-114.

Lists of authorities

If and when briefs to counsel are delivered the Judicial Office should be informed of the names of the advocates briefed (as to the recovery of costs of separate representation where parties have the same interest in the appeal, see *Bolton Metropolitan District Council v Secretary of State for the Environment* [1995] 1 WLR 1147). At least one week before the hearing date the agents for all parties who have lodged a case must forward to the Judicial Office a list drawn by junior counsel of the law reports, textbooks and other authorities on which they rely.

The hearing of the appeal usually takes place before an Appellate Committee consisting of five Lords of Appeal sitting in a committee room of the House of Lords. Any submissions as to costs should be made at the hearing of the appeal immediately the argument is concluded (ie not after judgment is given as is the practice in most other courts).

As to the delivery of judgment, the speeches prepared by the members of the Appellate Committee are considered in the Chamber of the House of Lords and voted on. In theory votes are cast by the House; in practice they are cast only by the members of the Appellate Committee involved. Agents are notified in advance of the date of judgment. For each party or group of parties who have lodged a case only one junior counsel is required to attend and no more than a junior counsel's fee will be allowed on taxation.

After judgment has been given, a final order will be drawn up by the Judicial Office. Any security moneys received are returned to the appellant, subject of course to any prior claim the respondents may have if costs were awarded to them. If in such a case the respondents fail to lodge bills for taxation within time, see the *Practice Direction* of 1990 ([1990] 1 WLR 1083). As to making the order of the House of Lords an order of the High Court, see p 669.

Index

673

INDEX